Mum,
ve from Lisa + Emma,
Christmas '90
x

HEDGECOE

ON VIDEO

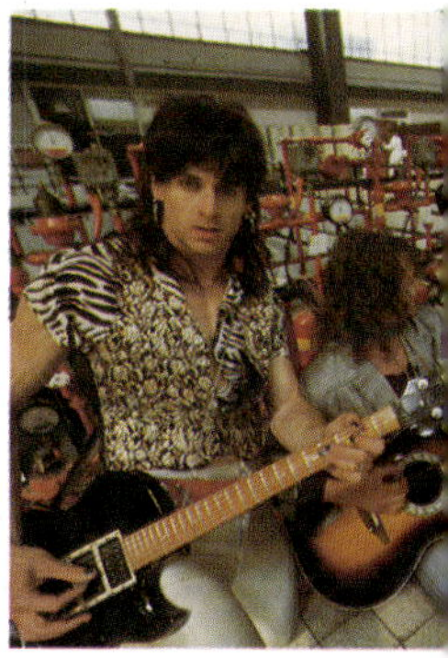

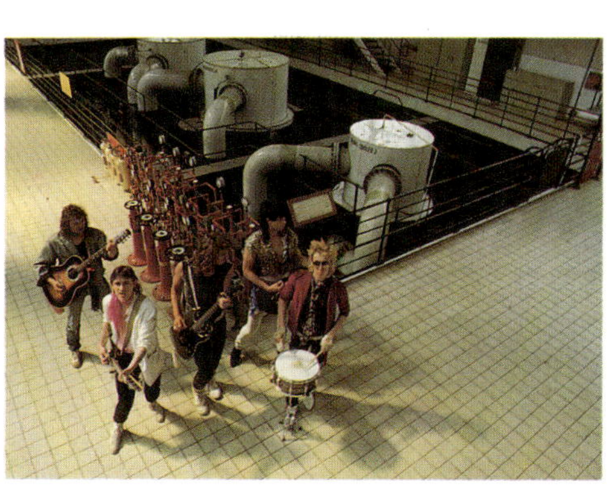

A COMPLETE
CREATIVE &
TECHNICAL
GUIDE TO
MAKING
VIDEOS

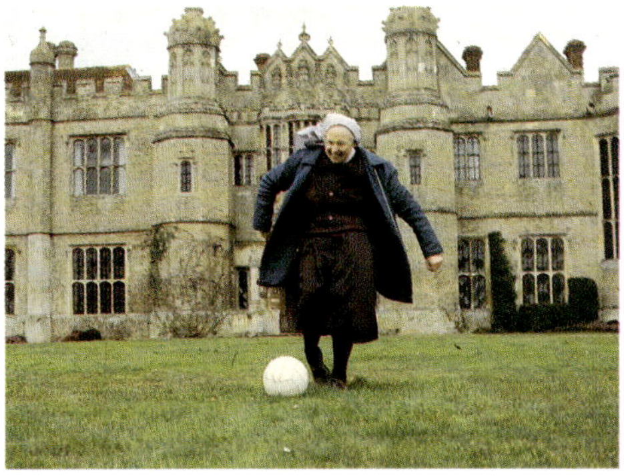

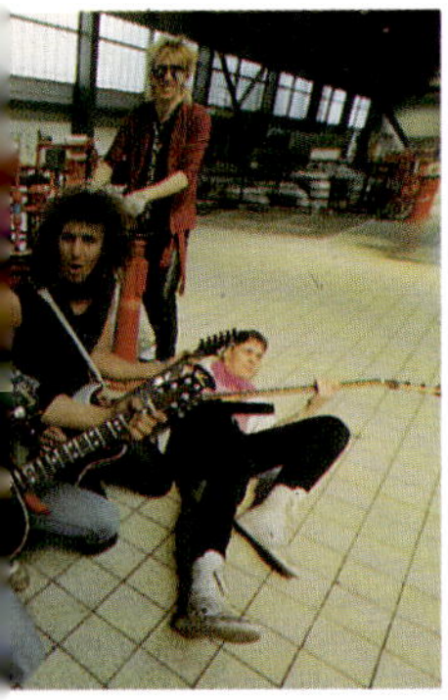

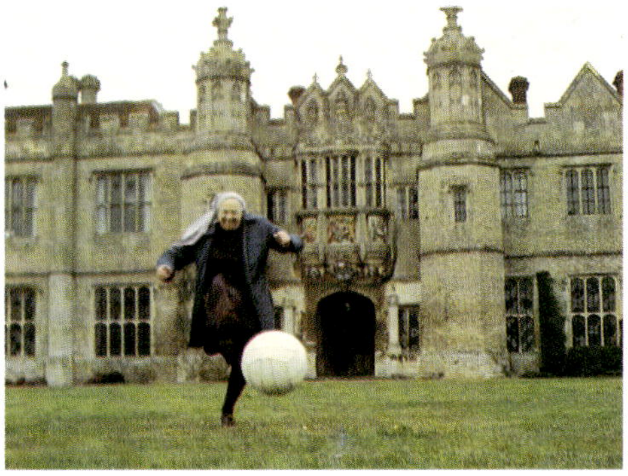

HEDGECOE ON VIDEO

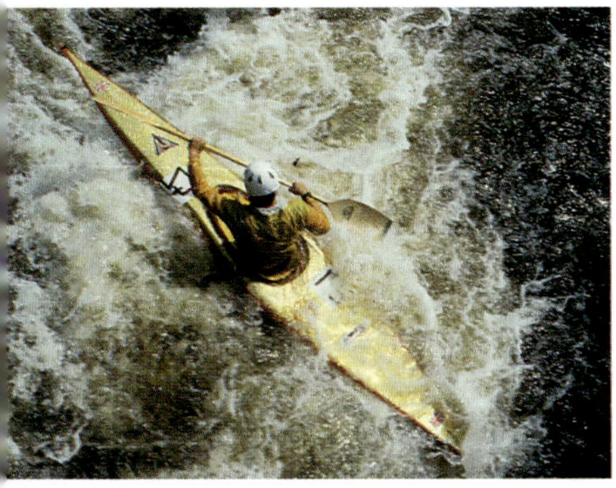

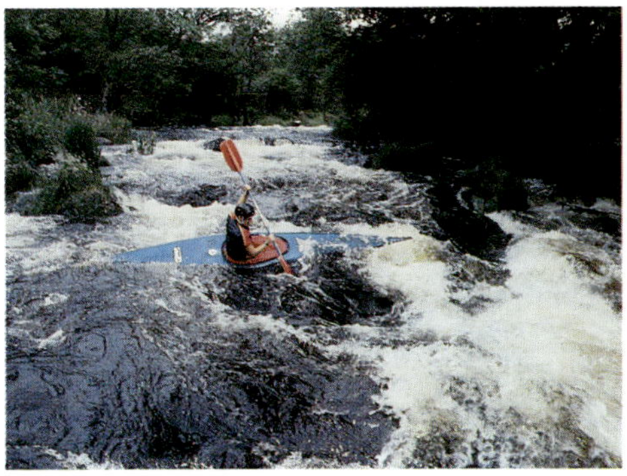

A COMPLETE CREATIVE & TECHNICAL GUIDE TO MAKING VIDEOS

PYRAMID BOOKS

HEDGECOE ON VIDEO

Additional text:
James McCarter
Philip Wilkinson

This edition first published in 1989
by Pyramid Books, an imprint of
the Octopus Publishing Group,
Michelin House,
81 Fulham Road,
London SW3 6RB

ISBN 1 871307 34 1

Printed and bound in Spain by Graficromo, S.A., Cordoba

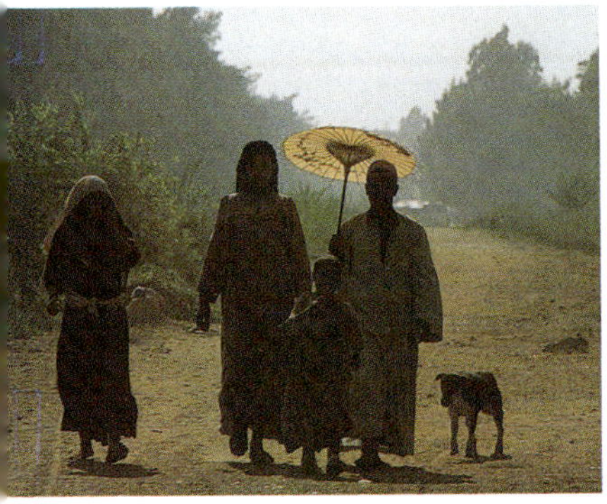

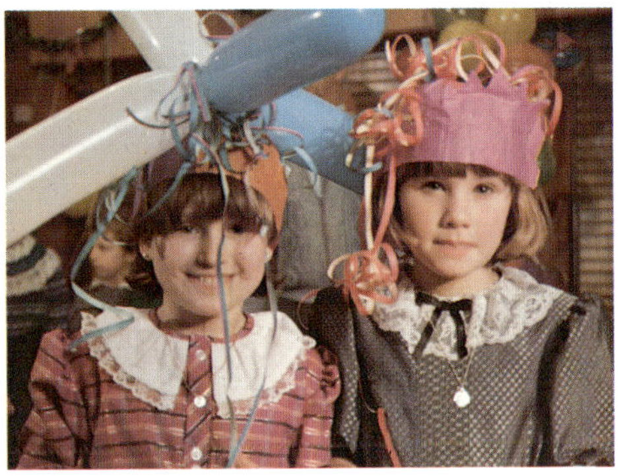

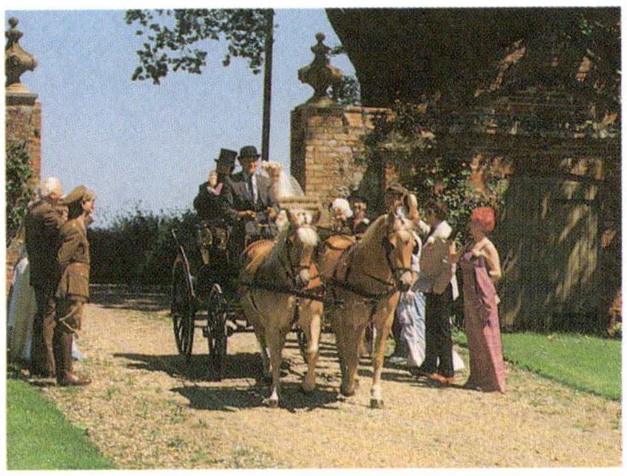

CONTENTS

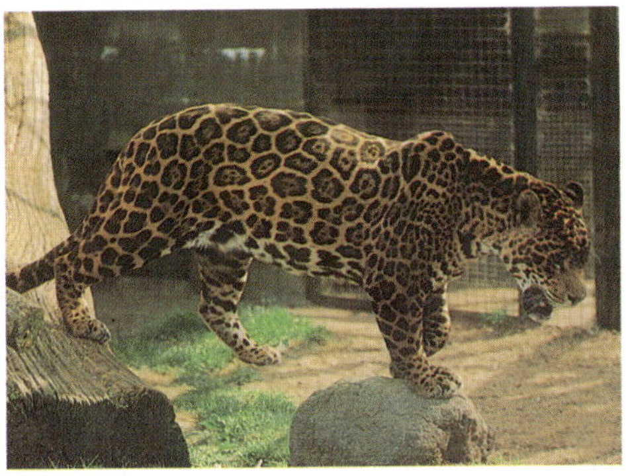

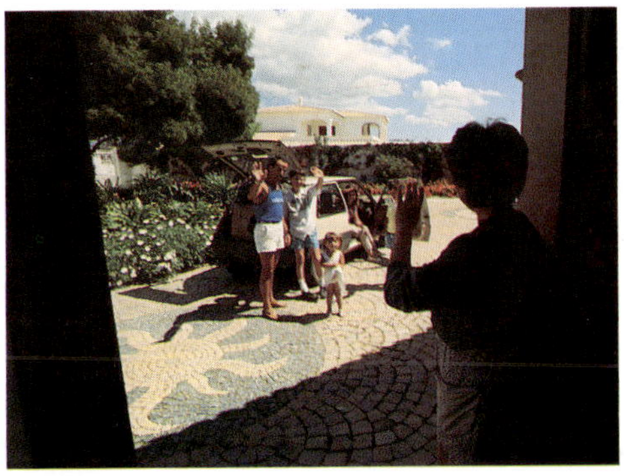

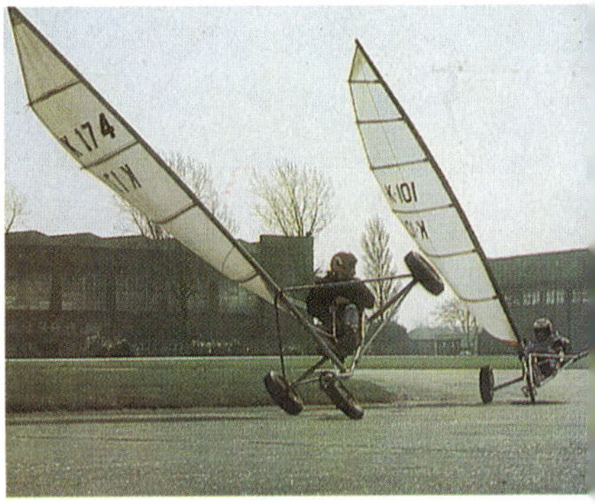

FOREWORD

I first picked up a video camera about ten years ago. Compared with the compact camcorders available today, it was a cumbersome thing, with a separate portable recorder pack that weighed heavily on the shoulder. Nevertheless, I was hooked. The instant replay of friends and family on the television screen made me realise the great flexibility offered by the medium.

The first thing that struck me was that many of the techniques I'd perfected in still photography applied to the video, but there were many others that didn't. The big difference was that you had to think of time and action as well as of the more static concepts of composition and lighting.

The technology has come a long way since then, and millions of people have discovered the creative freedom that video offers. Image quality has improved dramatically, and colour rendition is now as good as that available with film. Automatic functions make the camcorder simplicity itself to operate – in most situations you can simply switch on and shoot, not bothering about technicalities such as exposure levels and focusing requirements. Although most enthusiasts begin with tapes of their family life, there really is no limit to the material you can record. Documentary issues, sports, travelogues and dramas are all accessible.

This book is designed as a guide to acquiring those video skills which are needed in order to capture best a subject on videotape. It deals with technical points where necessary, but the emphasis is placed on an artistic, visual understanding of the discipline. More than anything else, good video is dependent on forward planning: planning both what you intend to shoot and how you want each shot to look.

One final word: videotape is cheap and reusable, so don't hesitate to experiment with your shots. If you suddenly think 'I wonder what it would look like if . . .', try it and see. There really are no rules in video, only guidelines. I hope the guidelines I've put down in this book will add to your enjoyment and understanding of an exciting and satisfying form of communcation.

JOHN HEDGECOE

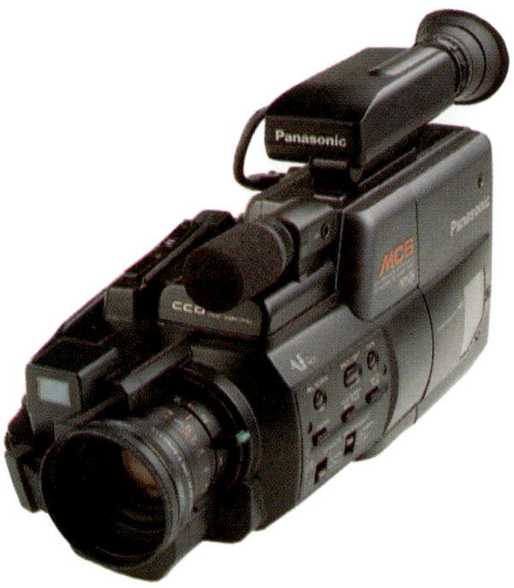

INTRODUCTION

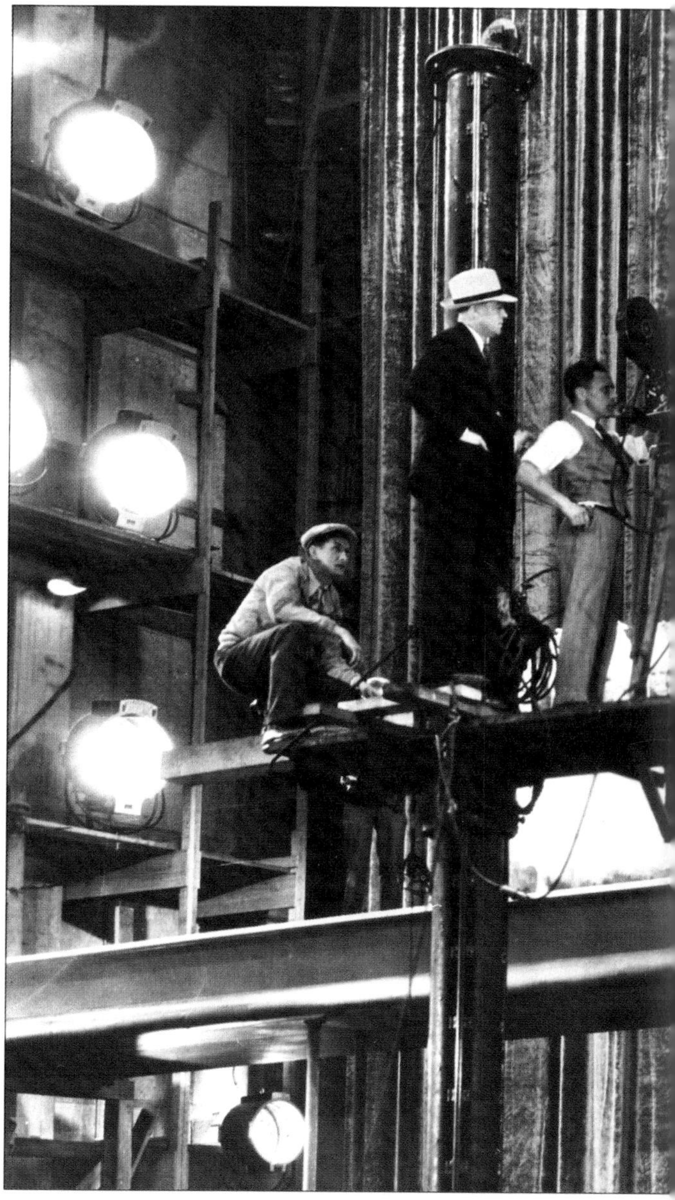

If anything characterizes the twentieth century, it is the proliferation of images. First came the silent movies, followed by 'talkies' in the late 1920s. At about the same time television was being developed. In the 1950s and 60s, television became almost universal. In the 70s and 80s came home video. Today, the average person watches as much as three to four hours of television each day — an occupation that takes up more time than anything else but sleep and work.

The result is that we have all become used to watching moving images on the screen. We have absorbed the techniques used by programme makers to such an extent that they are second nature to us. We understand about close-ups and cuts from one shot to another. We instinctively know when time is supposed to have passed.

One of the unspoken conventions is that what we see on the screen is, for want of a better word, 'reality'. In fact, of course, it is anything but that. That documentary shot of people living in a high-rise flat was only achieved by using an army of researchers and technicians. A great deal of time and effort is spent by professional programme makers in hiding this fact. Time is another quality that is frequently manipulated. A videotape which runs as long as the actual events that it depicts would appear interminable. We are used to whole days' or weeks' events being telescoped into a half-hour of screen time.

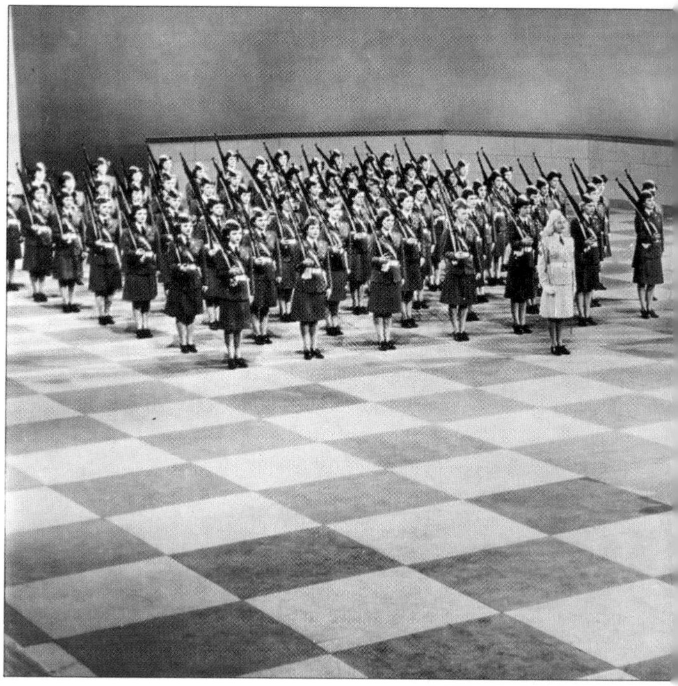

When it comes to making your own videos, you will probably feel an initial sense of disappointment in that your images don't look like those you're used to seeing each night on the television. This may be partly due to basic deficiencies of technique, such as keeping the camera steady, which can be readily overcome with perseverance. But it will also be because you haven't followed the accepted practices that the professionals use, many of which can only be achieved in the editing process.

However, it is easy to be daunted when thinking of the resources available to video and television professionals. But this would be to forget the importance of the basic techniques

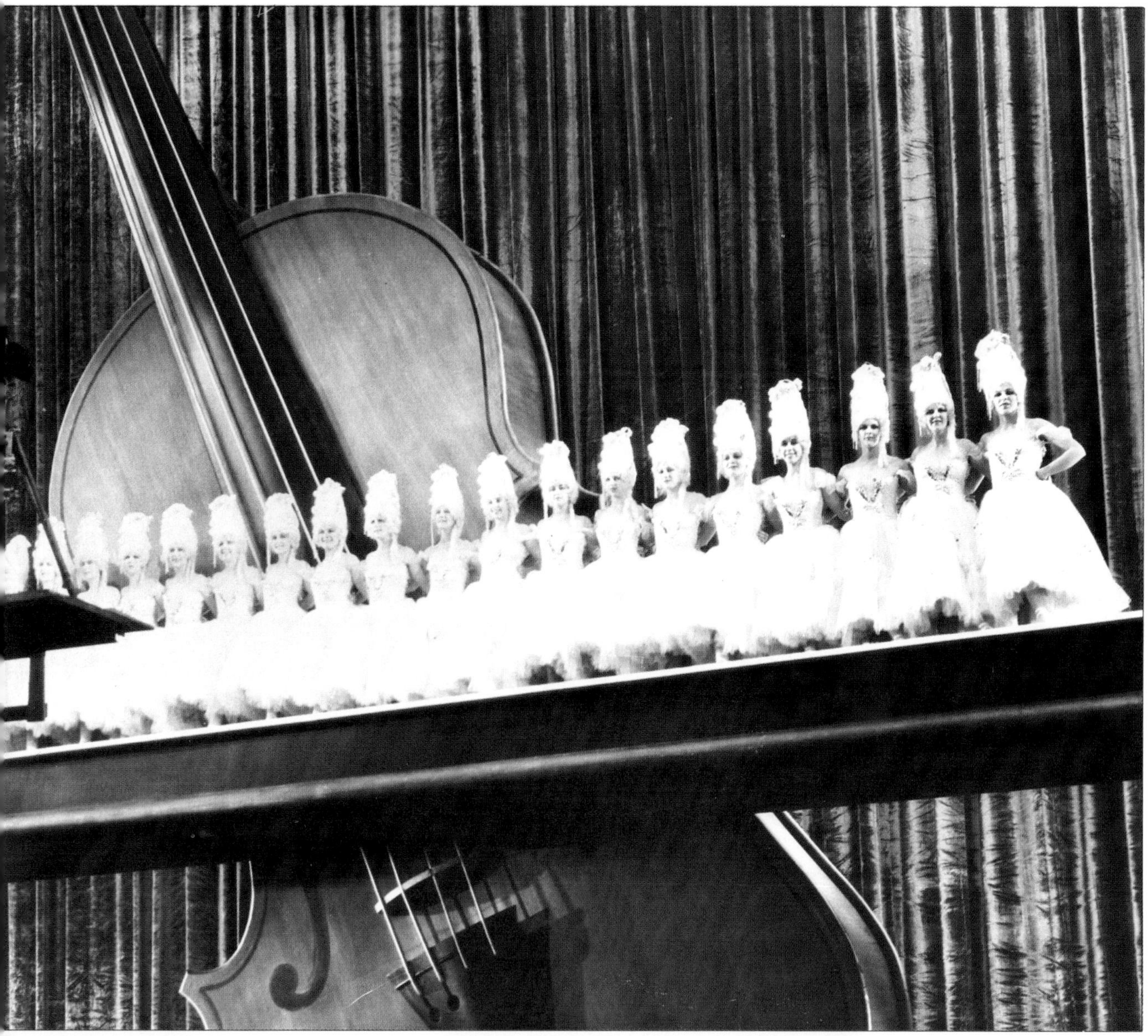

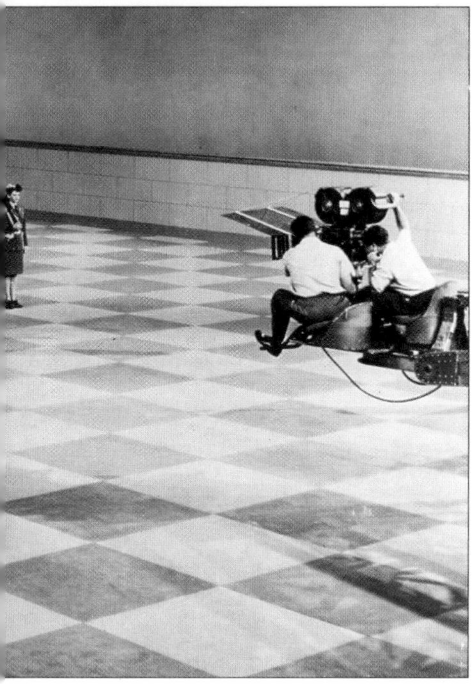

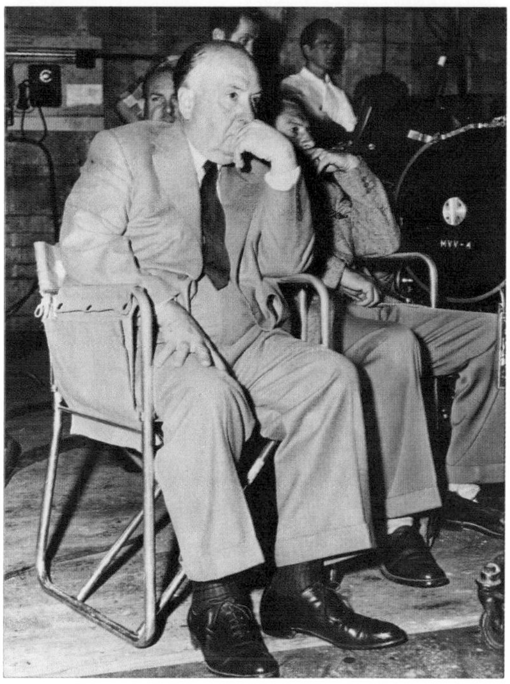

Above and left: *In the heyday of Hollywood directors created elaborate visual effects. But the early film makers' attention to detail provides a vital lesson for the modern video director.*

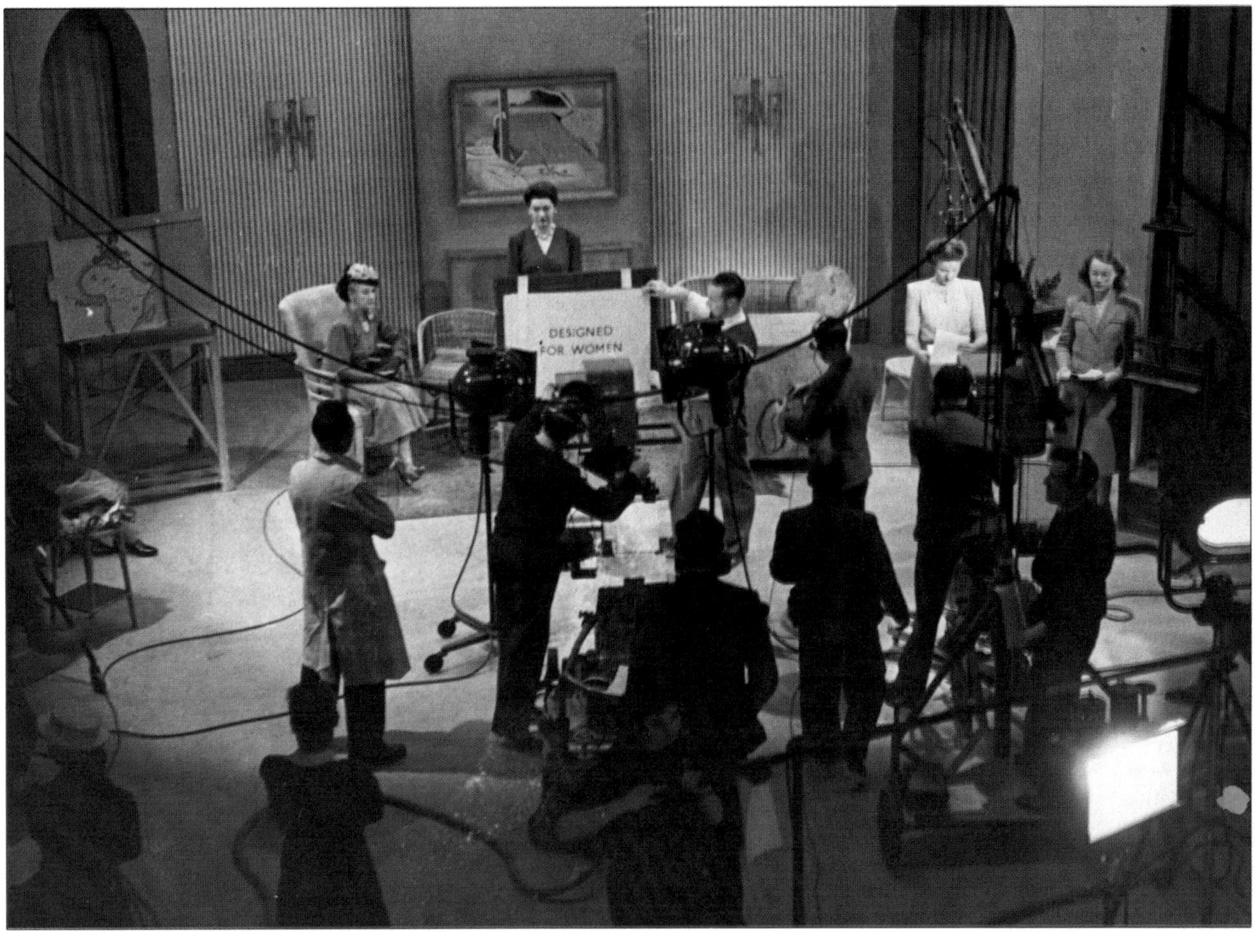

that go into programme making. First and foremost are basic research and observation. Any time spent researching a project will not be wasted. The more you know about your subject, the richer and more compelling your coverage will be. Secondly comes a strong visual sense. People who have worked in stills photography will acquire the sense of looking at the world through a viewfinder, of observing a scene selectively. The habit holds good with video, provided the need for action is remembered. Two people could shoot in the same environment, but the one with the best observational and compositional sense will produce the most interesting images.

Perhaps the third requirement is an organizational ability that would be appreciated in a company manager. You need to be able to simultaneously conceive of a project in its broad terms and remember detail. Will you be able to use lights when you intend to shoot indoors? Did you remember to pack spare batteries? Do you know exactly how long it is going to take you to get from location A to location B?

Finally, successful video is all about timing. Everything that you record is worth a certain

Above and right: *Although the equipment looks antiquated, the early television studio contained the same elements as a video studio set-up: a close-knit team responsible for camera, sound, lights, props and direction.*

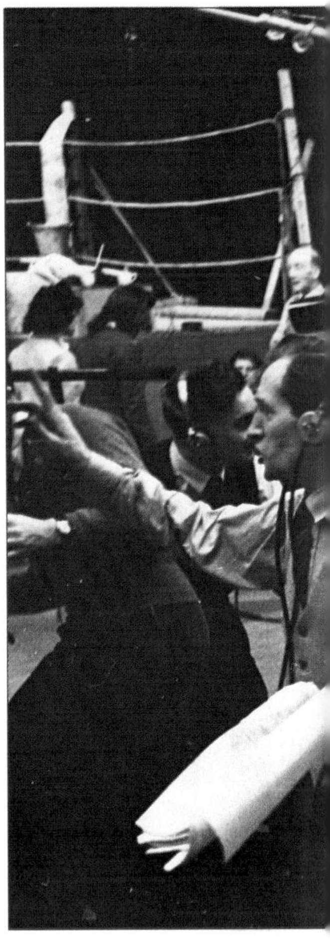

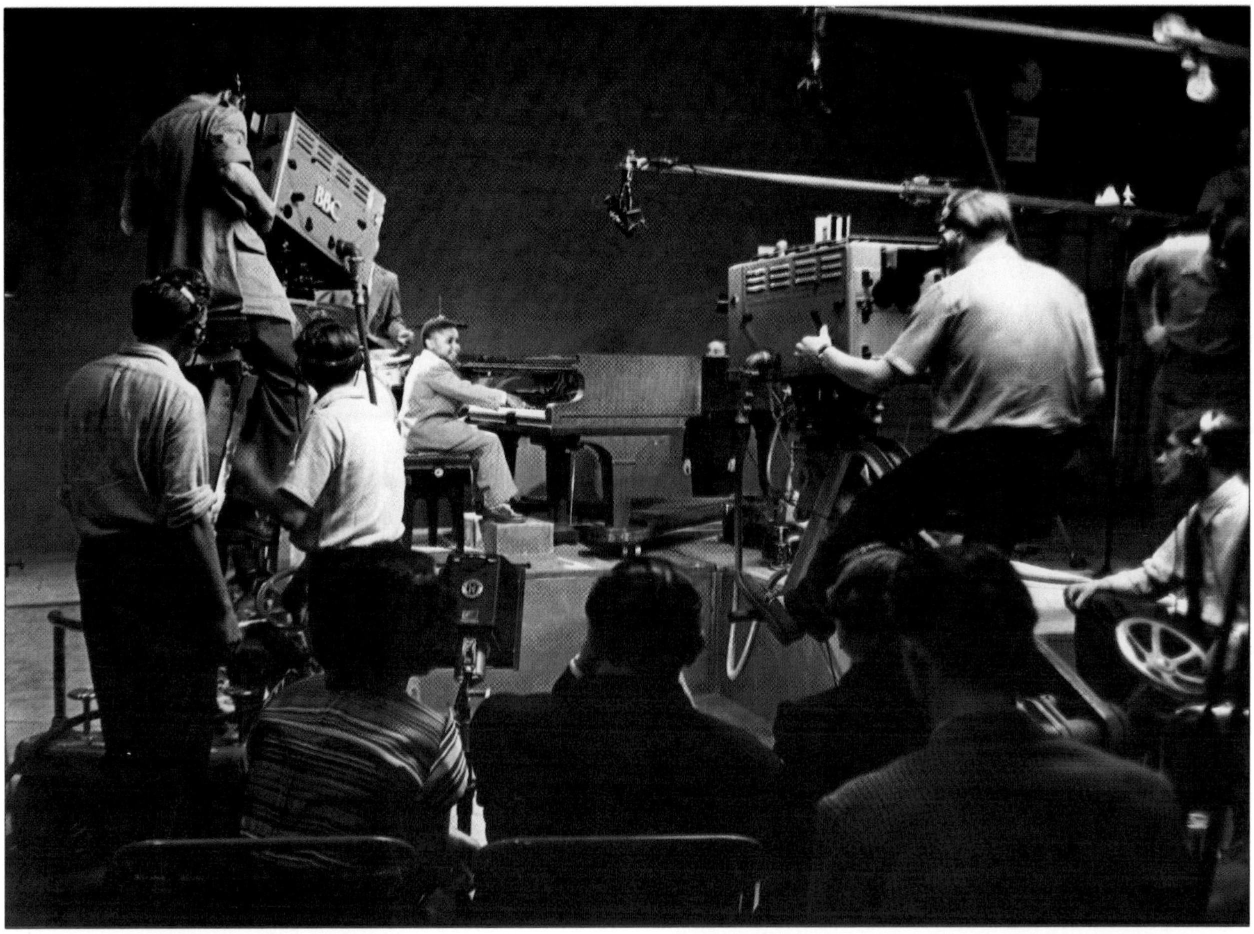
BBC

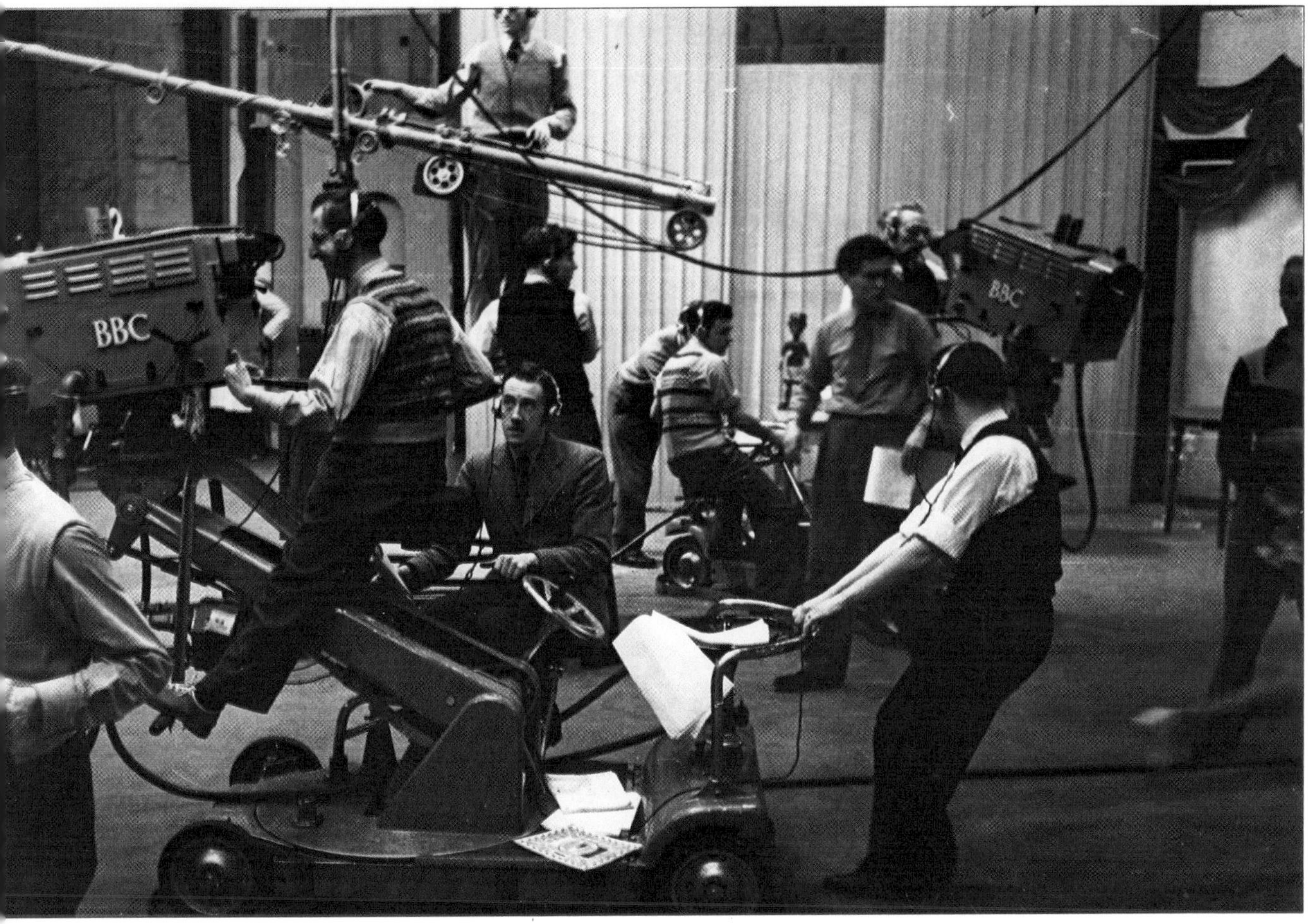
BBC
BBC

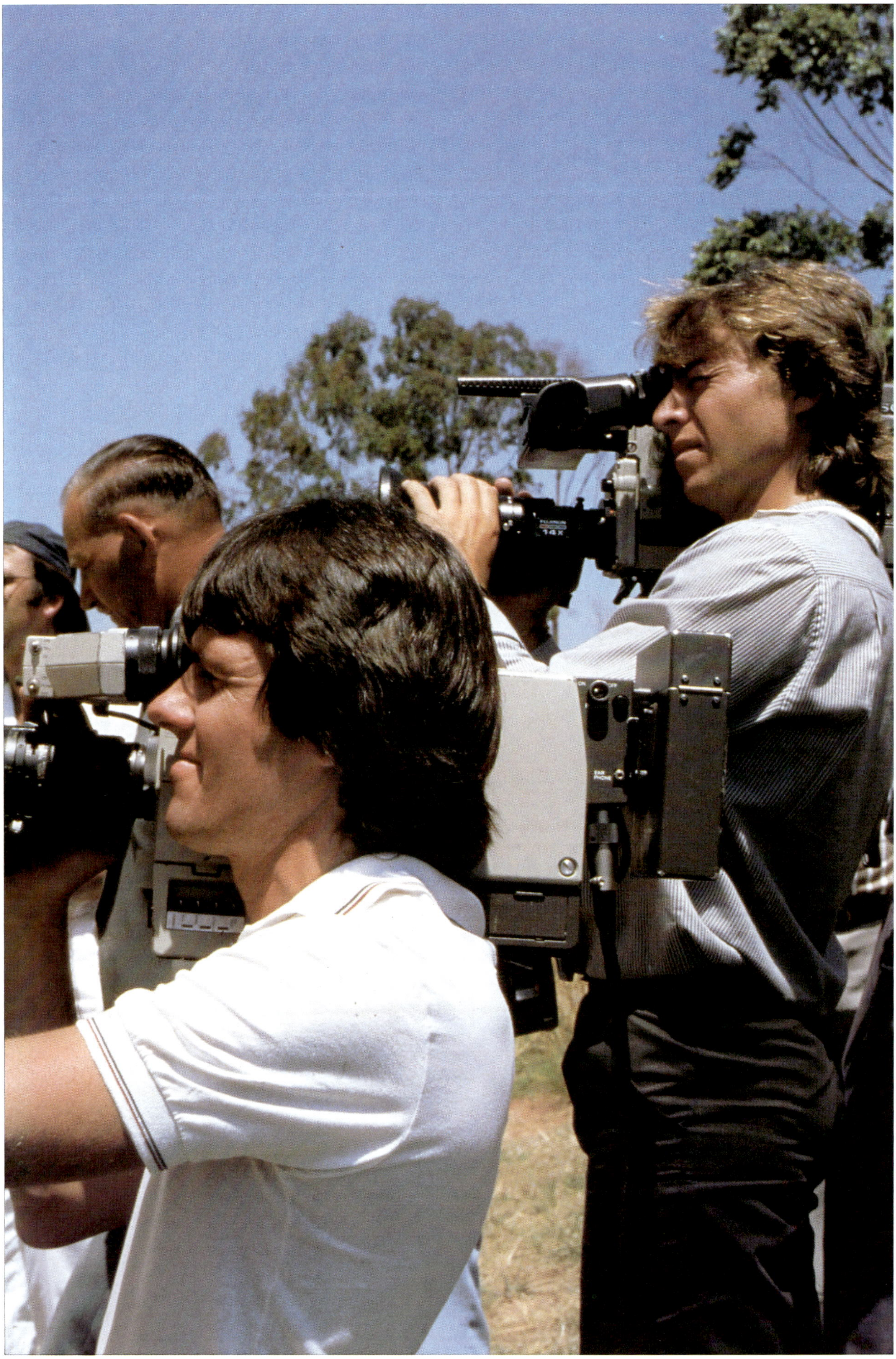

Left and right: *Whether you choose a large professional-style camcorder or one of the latest portable models, familiarity with your equipment is essential if you are to concentrate on getting the coverage you want.*

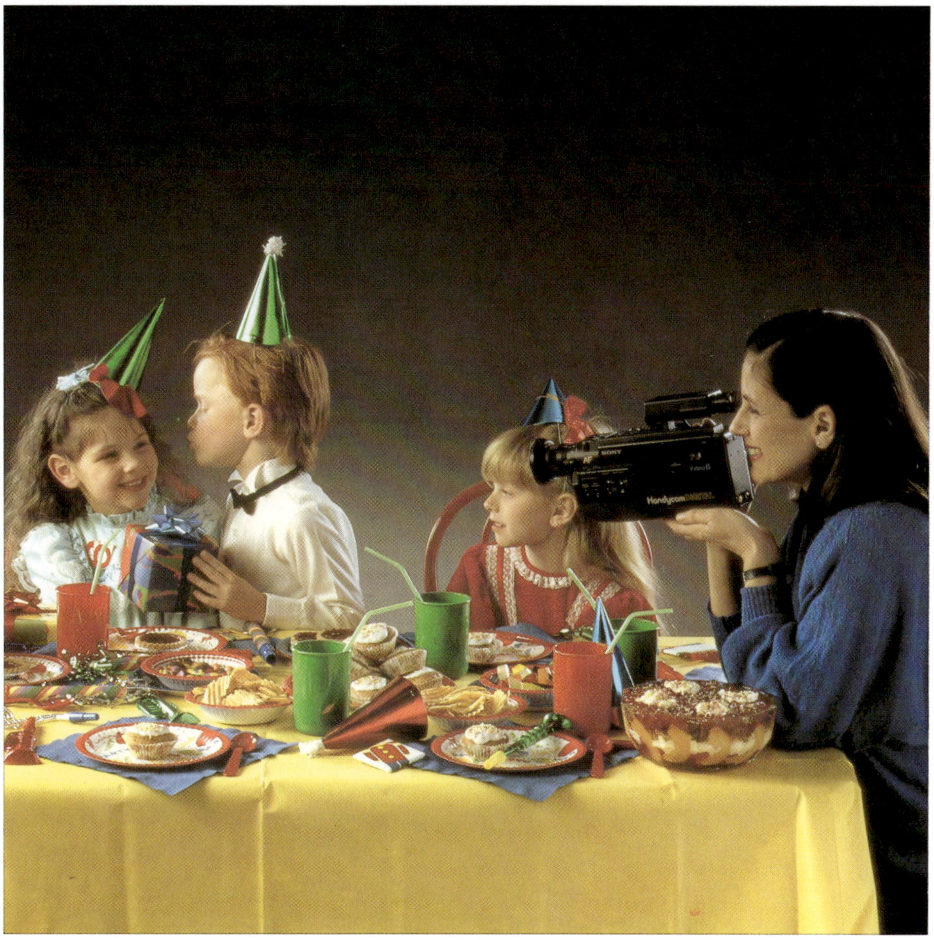

amount of time, and no more. Exactly how much time is a matter of judgement, depending both on the subject and on the intended audience. Even the most devoted grandparents may become a little restless after two hours of baby's first tottering steps have passed on the screen. In general, think of which aspects of the action you are recording and give them an according amount of screen time. Most shots will give average coverage if they last for about ten seconds. This is enough time for the audience to assimilate what is being presented them on the screen. For informal family events, a running time of about thirty minutes is usually quite long enough.

Within the main body of this book are a number of video projects of progressive complexity. After a review of equipment and basic techniques, the first project tackled is a wedding, something everyone with a video camera will be called on to record sooner or later. Next comes a chapter on recording individuals in different contexts, followed by coverage of a family holiday. A documentary feature follows, based on a day in the life of a small convent. Sports coverage comes next, then a chapter which looks at techniques for creating tension and suspense in dramas. The final chapters look at the expanded possibilities available if you can work with a larger crew and greater facilities, and at the central importance of editing, with the additional choice of incorporating basic special effects and graphics facilities offered by the latest generation of home computers.

Because the image is so important in our society — for informing, explaining, selling and a host of other functions — working with video can begin with home movies and graduate to a whole range of activities. Many amateurs move on to become semi-professionals, recording weddings, or creating promotional material for their companies. The opportunities are everywhere: the school play or sports day, local sports and social clubs — most will be more than willing to allow you to turn up and record. Since you are not going to be paid for your services, you can use these occasions to experiment. If the experiments don't work, no one loses out. With experiment comes technical competence and growing confidence. There really is no limit to what you can do once you start to master the creative techniques and begin to get access to greater facilities.

HEDGECOE

ON VIDEO

A COMPLETE CREATIVE & TECHNICAL GUIDE TO MAKING VIDEOS

VIDEO BASICS

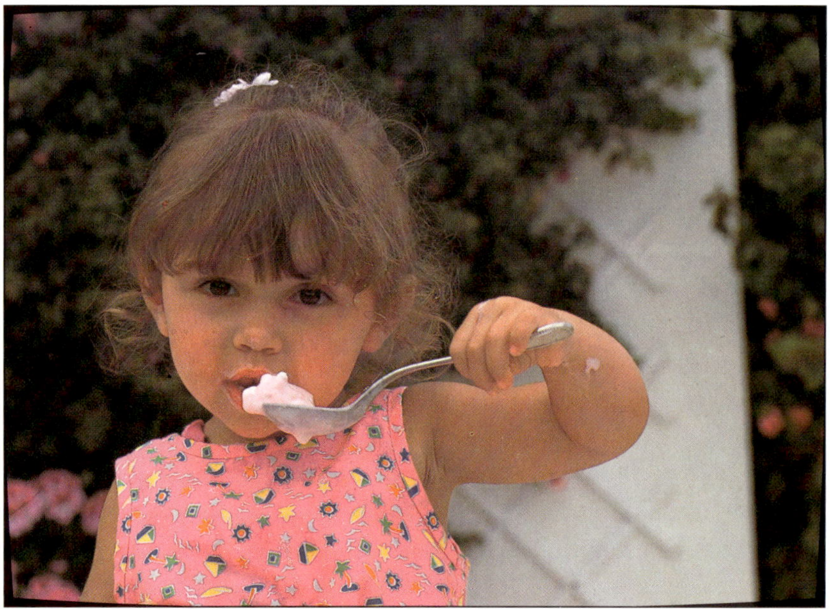

1: *To be effective, a still shot relies on the photographer capturing a particular moment which typifies the subject. The action is frozen in the frame, but the viewer can readily imagine what follows. Techniques of selecting the correct exposure and lens speed, and choosing how to frame the shot, are used by the photographer to achieve a clear image and a sense of immediacy.*

MOVING PICTURES

It is worth stressing right at the beginning that although video and still photography have certain points in common, the differences are so great that the two approaches must be regarded as separate disciplines. But while certain visual skills learned in still photography will be of great use when making a video, there will be many new techniques to master, as I quickly found out when first tackling the medium. Another important point to note is that when you look at the photographs in this book you must try to see them as instants captured from a sequence of rapidly moving pictures, for in video time is rarely frozen.

Video audiences are interested first and foremost in what is happening now, and in what will happen next. Therefore the first key lesson in mastering video techniques is appreciating that videos tell a story, even if it is merely how clouds move and change shape. You must also appreciate that when composing a video shot, you are doing so not just in terms of two-dimensional space, as in still photography, but in time and volume, using the camera to move around the subject. To an extent, the subject is therefore the action which unfolds in the space in front of your viewfinder.

In the quest to make interesting, creative and satisfying home movies, ranging from straightforward records of family events to more sophisticated mini-dramas and documentaries, you can improve your video skills considerably if you watch television critically. This doesn't mean deciding whether a programme is good or bad. It means thinking about the camera position and angle of each shot, noticing when the shot changes and how the change is accomplished. Ask yourself what a scene might look like if shot from a different angle, or what would be the effect if the main character was shown in close-up rather than from a distance?

The chapters in this book tackle eight projects designed to explain the creative and organizational techniques vital to video success. They cover everyday situations which most camcorder owners will want to tackle, from a wedding and family holiday, to more ambitious ideas, such as scripting and recording a drama, and making a pop promo video. Since first videos are often disappointing you may conclude that without the huge budgets and technical resources of the professionals you have little chance of producing a tape that can compare with the images that you see on television. But if you plan carefully and work within your limitations, you will be surprised at the polish you can attain.

The first hurdle

Although home editing facilities are improving all the time, for many people the capacity to edit their video is very restricted. This means that you may have to edit as you shoot – known as 'in-camera editing' – which will have a major bearing on the way in which you approach your subject. Home editing can be done with a minimum of equipment – and this book will show you how – but the projects have been so designed that you can use in-camera editing if preferred.

And finally, try to use your camera as much as possible. Experimentation and innovation are at the heart of this exciting and accessible new medium. The more different subjects you tackle, the more you will become proficient in the huge range of cinematic techniques.

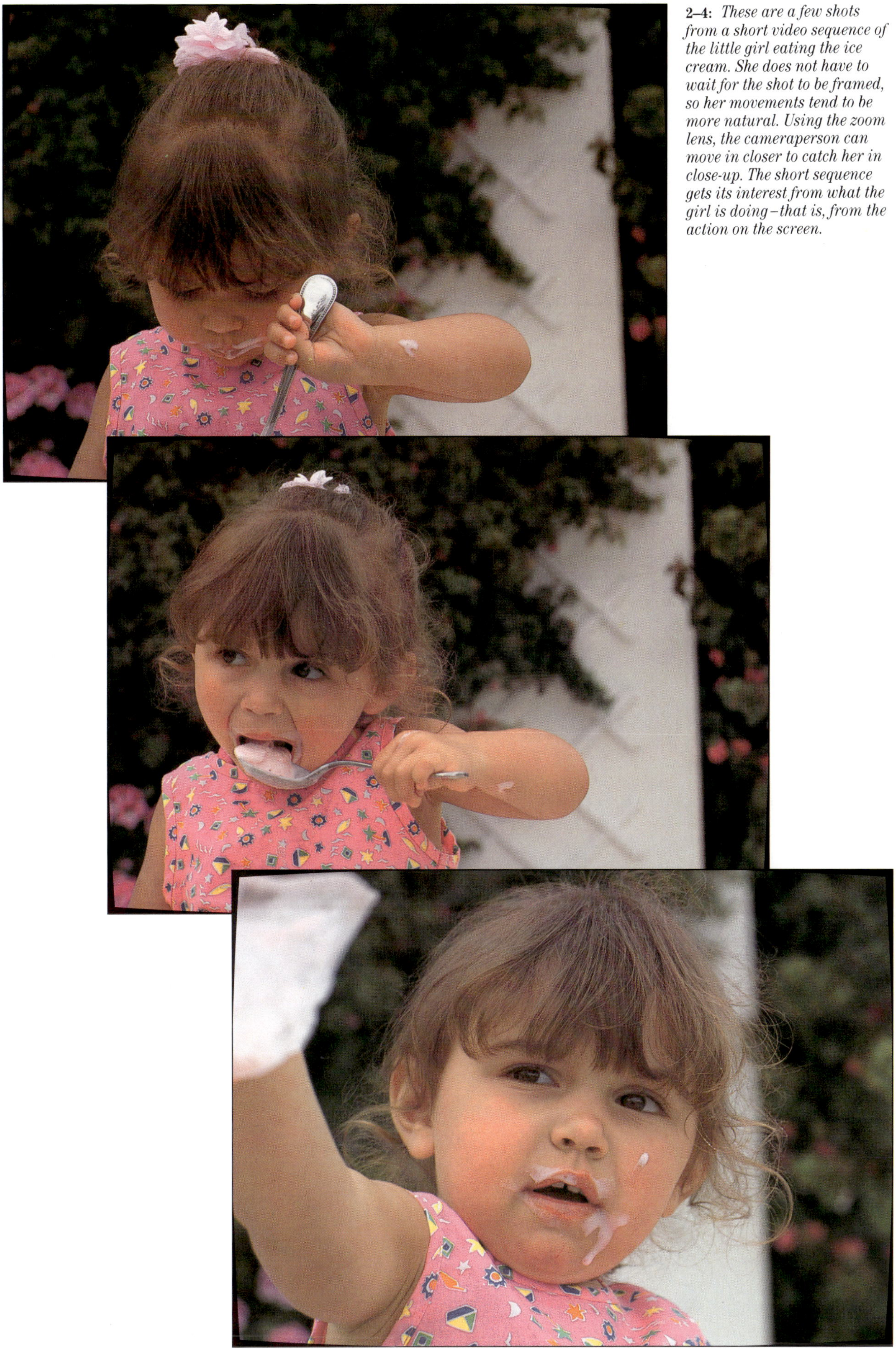

2–4: These are a few shots from a short video sequence of the little girl eating the ice cream. She does not have to wait for the shot to be framed, so her movements tend to be more natural. Using the zoom lens, the cameraperson can move in closer to catch her in close-up. The short sequence gets its interest from what the girl is doing–that is, from the action on the screen.

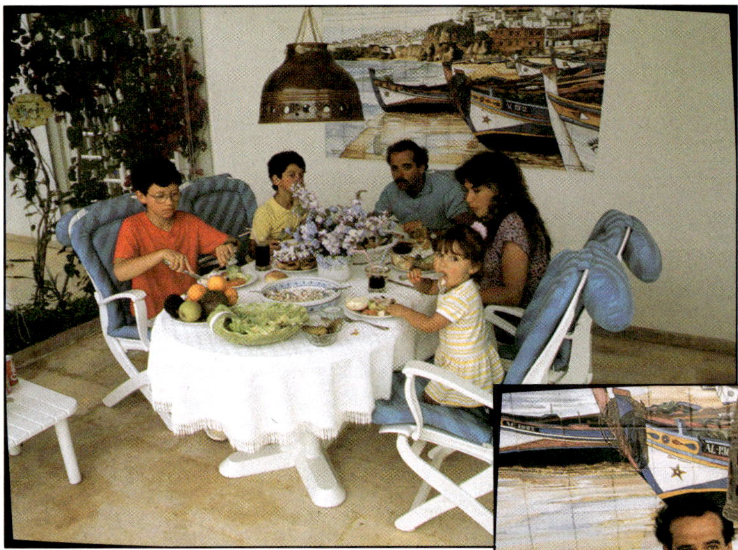

1: *This simple holiday sequence of people eating a meal shows how the family snapshot can be translated into video terms. The first shot shows them around the table. It includes some information about the room, so that we can see where they are, but there is not very much action.*

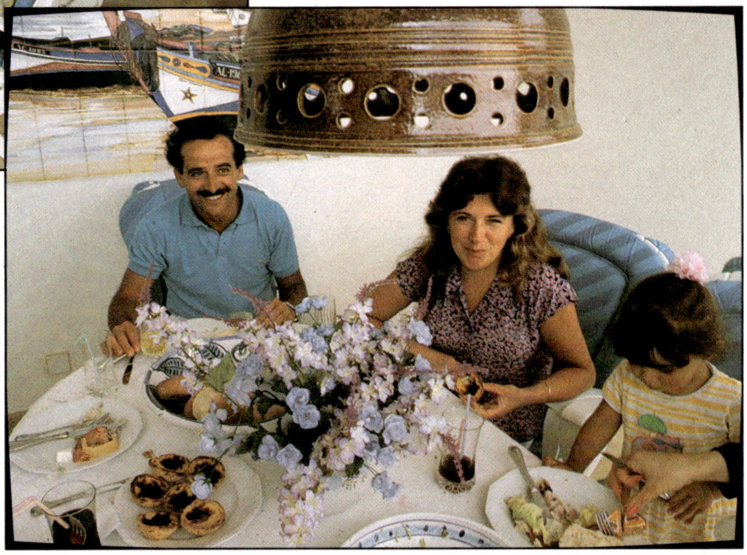

2: *Zooming in on part of the table gives the sequence more dynamism – but don't be tempted to overuse the zoom in this way.*

3: *Shots like this may seem unremarkable as stills, but the action – father helping himself while the child takes a drink – gives movement to the video.*

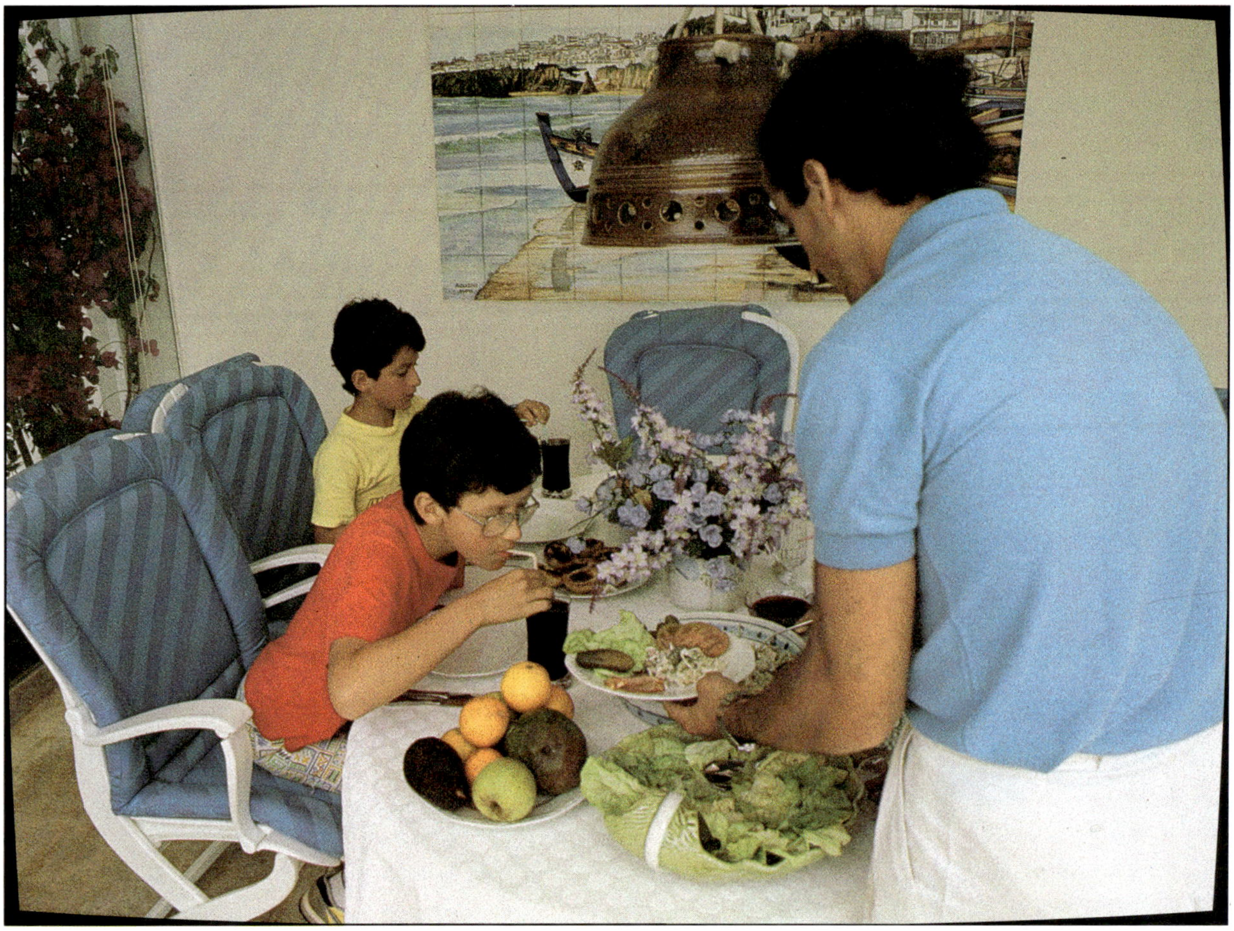

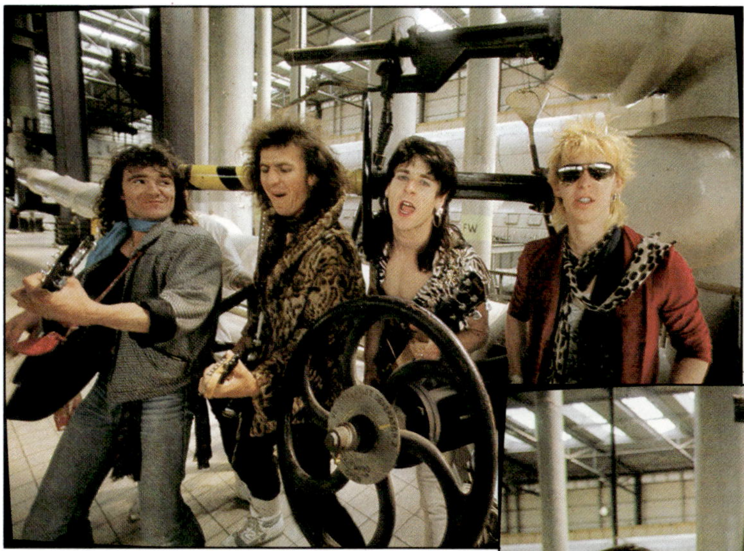

1-2: *These shots from a rock video show a different problem – the subject is moving all the time. To keep the shots simple, one particular performer (the guitarist on the left) becomes the focus.*

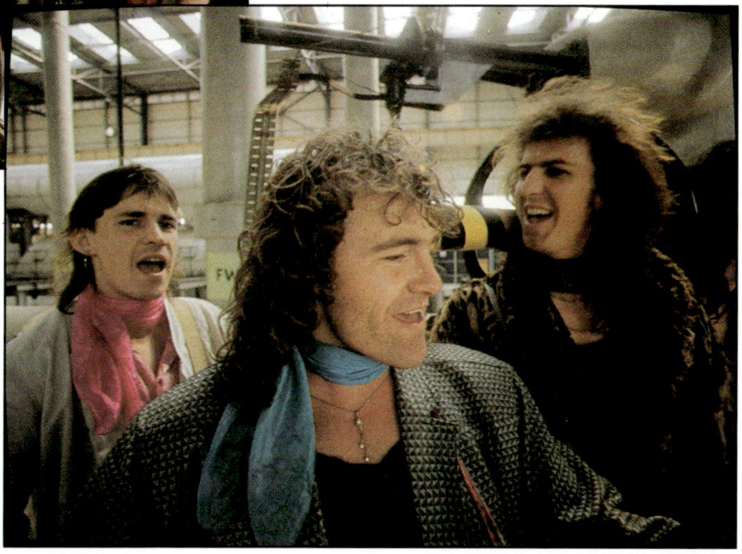

3: *The camera crabs around to give a different angle, but the guitarist is still the centre of attention. Notice how, as the camera lingers here, all the elements in the background (railings, pillars, etc) lead the eye to his face.*

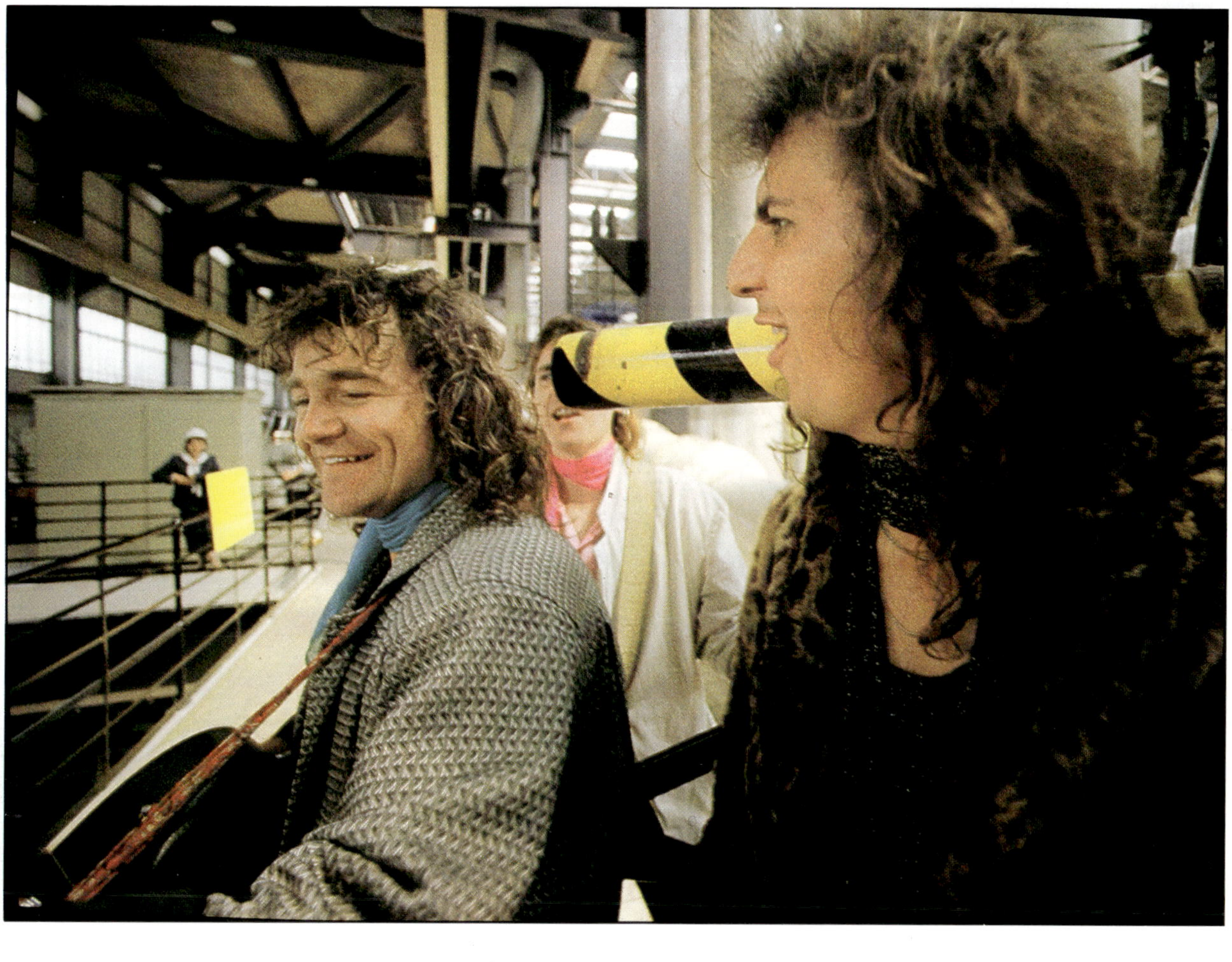

VIDEO AND FILM

Video is an electronic medium. The light passing through the lens falls on to a light-sensitive component known as a charge-coupled device (CCD) or, in older cameras, on to a pick-up tube. In either case, a small electrical current is created, its strength varying with the intensity of the light. This current travels to the recording elements of the camcorder and in turn creates a small magnetic field which is recorded on the magnetic coating of the video tape. To view the image, the process is reversed: the magnetic field on the tape creates an electric current which is used to generate the image on the television screen. A more detailed explanation of this process would be very complex, and is unnecessary for the video-maker. Just one principle needs to be remembered – light to electric current to magnetic tape.

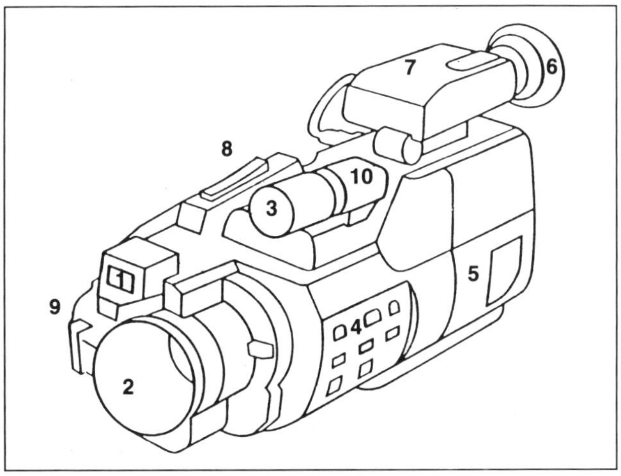

Camcorder features

1 Light sensor
2 Zoom lens
3 Built-in microphone
4 Camcorder controls
5 Tape compartment
6 Eyepiece
7 Viewfinder unit
8 Zoom motor control
9 Handgrip
10 Microphone socket

Video advantages

The great advantage of video tape over film is that you are dealing with an instant process, and the image you see in the electronic viewfinder is the one you will record except that the viewfinder image is usually in black and white. You don't have to wait two weeks for the film to come back from the processing laboratory to discover that you've over-exposed. Another advantage is that video cameras will record in very low levels of light (since the weak electric current generated can be electronically boosted by circuits coupled to the automatic gain control, or AGC) and that many of the difficulties over lighting experienced with conventional film (both still and movie) do not apply to video. Most camcorders will record a candlelit meal quite readily. In documentaries, where the quality of the picture is less important than the subject matter, this can heighten the sense of drama.

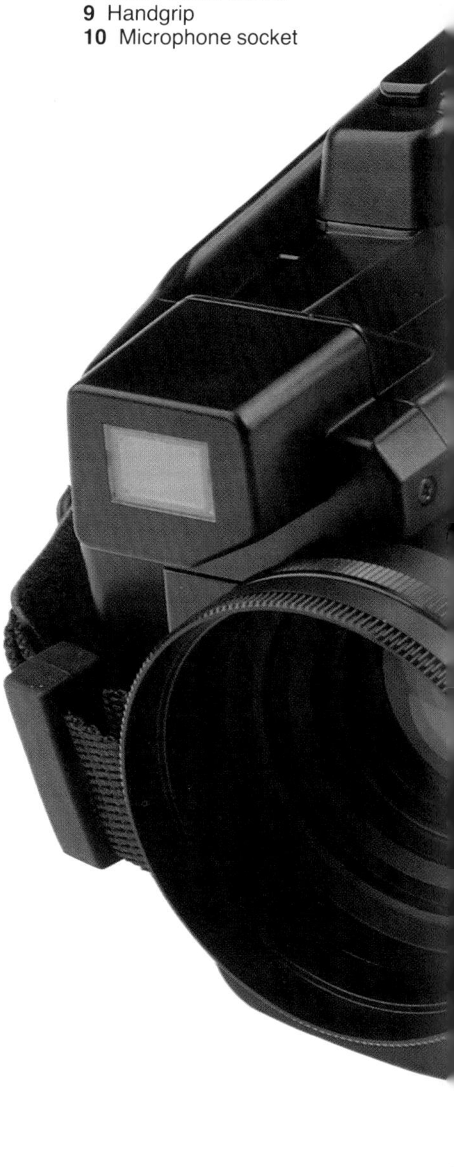

Electronic editing

Editing is another area in which the electronic nature of video is crucially significant. Editing film is a straightforward mechanical process: you cut out the frames you don't want and join up the ends of film to either side of the deletion. However, there are no visible frames on video tape. The frames exist as magnetic patterns laid in diagonal strips across the tape (they are laid diagonally to pack as much information as possible on to the tape). To edit video, the images that you want must be rerecorded onto a clean master tape in the new sequence required. In principle this is relatively easy, but to get a clean 'cut' at the editing point (where the two sequences are joined) requires quite sophisticated, specialist editing equipment. All this is explained much more fully in Chapter Eight.

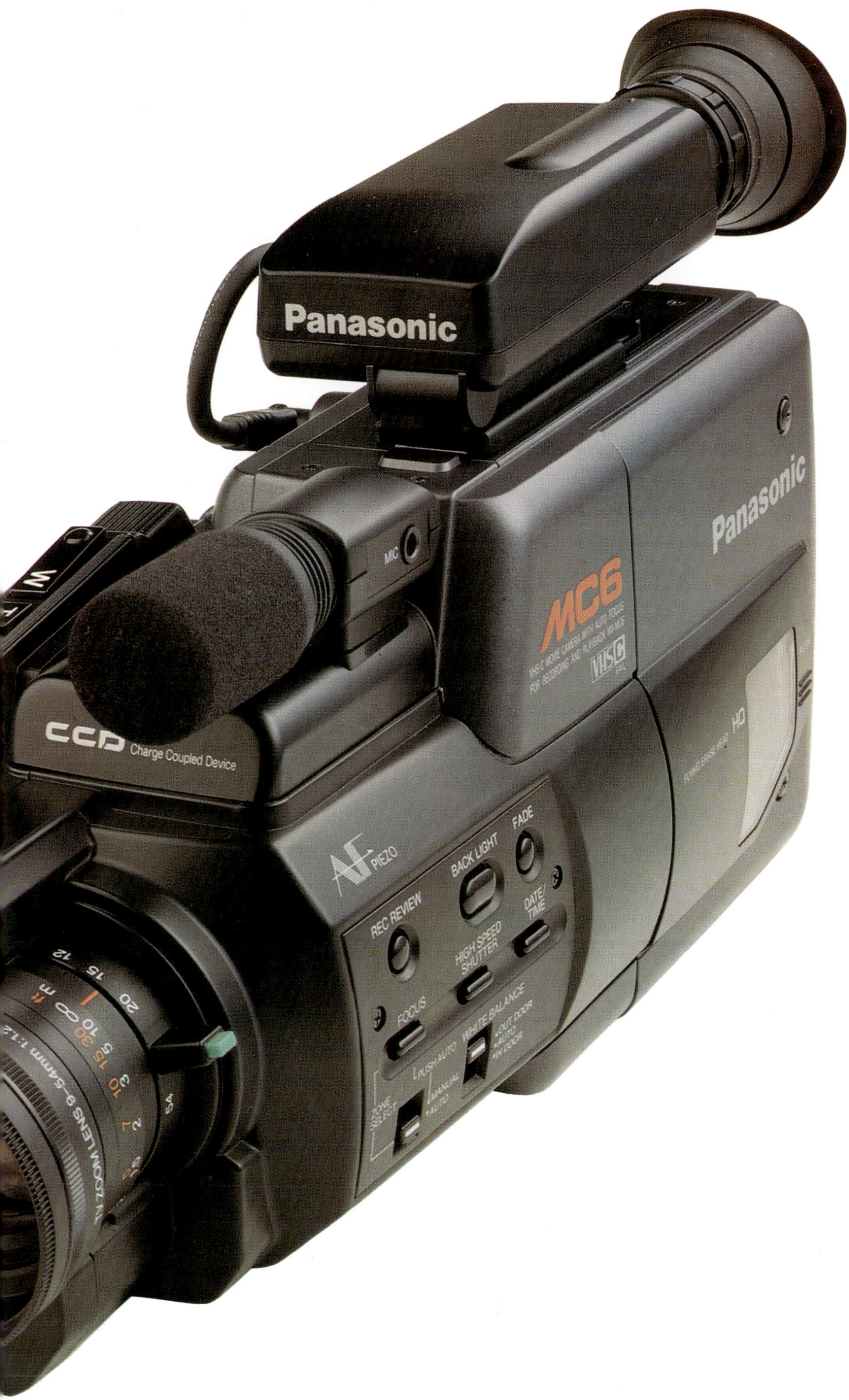
Panasonic
Panasonic
MIC
MC6
VHS-C MOVIE CAMERA WITH AUTO FOCUS
FOR RECORDING AND PLAYBACK
VHS C
PAL
CCD Charge Coupled Device
AF PIEZO
FLYING ERASE HEAD HQ
FADE
BACK LIGHT
REC REVIEW
DATE/ TIME
HIGH SPEED SHUTTER
FOCUS
WHITE BALANCE
OUT DOOR
AUTO
IN DOOR
PUSH AUTO
MANUAL
AUTO
TONE SELECT

CAMCORDER FUNCTIONS

The development of home video-making has followed three main stages. First there was the video camera and separate portable video cassette recorder (VCR). With this system, the video maker had to carry a bulky camera linked by cable to the recorder. Although the recorder was a portable unit, it too was quite bulky and had to be carried on a shoulder strap. At best, this way of working was uncomfortable; at worst, it rendered some areas of filming, such as action work, difficult or even impossible. Then the camcorder appeared, in which the video recorder's functions were incorporated into the body of the camera, making a single piece of equipment with consequent advantages in ease of use. The third phase has been the increasing miniaturization of the camcorder, so that some are now little bigger, or heavier, than a conventional quality 35mm stills camera or a Super 8 movie camera. These developments have led to a number of different video formats, each with its advantages and drawbacks. As a general rule, miniaturization makes a camcorder more portable and less obtrusive. The disadvantage is that the lighter the camera, the more difficult it is to hold it steady. While larger camcorders are usually designed to rest on the shoulder, smaller ones must be held unsupported in front of the eye. The type you will use partly depends on which kinds of subject you most want to cover.

Choosing a camcorder

If your interest is in shooting family videos, where it is vital to have the camera ready at all times to film unpredictable and spontaneous family scenes, a lightweight camcorder that you can carry around easily is probably the best option. If you are more interested in subjects like drama, where you will plan everything meticulously, make your own set-ups, and work as part of a team, then a larger model may be more suitable. But your choice will also depend on what feels best in your hands. There is no substitute for visiting a good video dealer and trying out as many as possible of the camcorders you are considering. Make a note of how accessible the controls are on each model, how comfortable they are to handle, and how easy they are to hold steady.

Major camcorder elements

The chart shows the features you can expect to find on your camcorder, although some top-of-the-range models will have additional items while older models may not be equipped with autofocus or auto-exposure. There are three basic systems: the optical elements, the electronic functions (which control the video signal), and the recorder motor and controls. Power can be supplied either by a rechargeable battery or, in most cases, from a car battery or the domestic mains.

Familiarity with equipment, to the point of being able to operate it as second nature, is the foundation of good camerawork. At first sight there appears to be a daunting number of controls on most camcorders. Usually they are placed in two groups, those that operate the recorder functions and those that control the video signal and the light entering the camera. Read the instruction manual carefully to become familiar with the function and layout of the controls on your particular model before shooting. The most important functions are listed here and will be treated more fully in later sections of the book.

Zoom lenses

Virtually all camcorders have a zoom lens, with zoom ratios (the difference in magnification of an image seen from the telephoto and wide-angle ends of the lens) ranging from 6:1 to 10:1. The angle of view at the wide-angle end of the zoom range is approximately the same as that of a 35mm still camera with standard lens. Many camcorders also provide powered zoom, but while this is valuable, a manual option is also very desirable, as is the case with all the automatic functions offered.

You will find many references to the use of the zoom control throughout this book. It can be employed in many ways but the cardinal rule is to avoid overuse of the zoom during shots. Constant zooming in and out can be wearing on the viewer's eyes. Nevertheless, the zoom is an excellent tool for framing – getting the subject exactly the size that you want, and then keeping it there.

Microphones

The built-in microphone is located above or to the side of the lens. The sound quality recorded will vary considerably, ranging from poor to good quality hi-fi sound. The sound being recorded can be monitored using headphones. Most camcorders have a facility allowing an auxiliary, external microphone to be used. This is convenient because it allows you to record only the sound that you want – on-camera microphones will often pick up all the extraneous sound you do not even notice when you are filming – the noise of the traffic in the street, for example, or of people talking out of shot. The disadvantage of using an off-camera microphone is that you usually need an assistant to hold it for you.

FUNCTIONS	USES
Auto-exposure/auto-iris The iris on a camcorder controls the amount of light passing through the lens. Under auto-exposure this is adjusted automatically to suit the prevailing light. Manual override allows the iris to be adjusted manually using the calibrated scale on the lens barrel.	You can use the auto-exposure facility in most shooting situations. Occasionally you will find that abnormal lighting (for example backlighting or very strong contrast with some bright and some dark areas in the same scene) means that you get better results using manual override.
Autofocus A system which automatically adjusts focus as you shoot. It tends to focus on the nearest object, centre-screen. Manual override allows you to adjust focus using the focus ring on the lens barrel.	Useful in most situations, although you may find with some systems that the camera focuses on the object in centre screen, or that the mechanism is fooled by reflective surfaces.
White balance White balance ensures that colours are rendered faithfully in most lighting conditions. Some camcorders do this automatically, otherwise the balance should be taken each time you begin to shoot and when you move from one lighting environment to another (from indoors to outdoors, for example).	Always set the white balance before shooting. An increasing number of camcorders perform this function automatically for you.
Daylight/tungsten filter Used in conjunction with the white balance to obtain true colour rendition.	Consult the user's manual for your camcorder to see how your system works.
Backlight For adjusting the iris to obtain correct exposure of a subject when there is a strong light source behind it.	Used to override the camcorder's auto-exposure facility, so that the backlit subject does not look too dark.
Lowlight This electronically boosts the video signal in conditions of very low light. However, since the whole signal is boosted this also means an increase in video 'noise'.	Useful in poor light when there is no chance of improving the situation by employing artificial lighting.
Fade A facility on some models which allows you to end a shot with a gradual fade to black (white, in some models) over two or three seconds.	Can give a professional feel to the ends of sequences, particularly if you do not intend to edit your tape at a later stage.
Video negative An effects option in which colours are reversed.	Effective if used sparingly.
Pause Used during shooting to give a clean transition between shots. If the pause is held too long, tape damage can occur. Consequently most camcorders automatically switch off from pause.	Limited in use, since you will often want to pause longer between shots than the system allows. Another option that is useful if you do not intend to edit.
Record-Review Replays the last few seconds of tape shot in the viewfinder.	Ideal for checking your coverage before moving on to the next shot.
Fast forward/Rewind Same as on a domestic VCR.	As on domestic VCR.

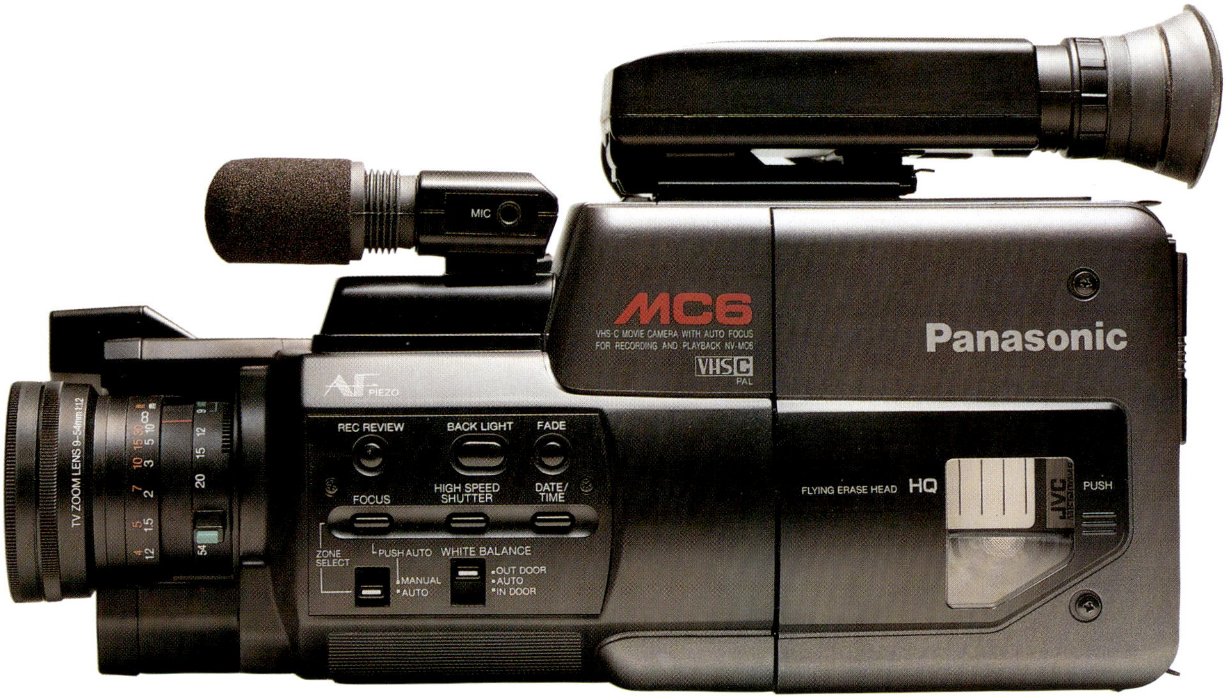

Above: *On most camcorders a number of the operating controls are placed on one side and are designed to be used with the left hand. On this model, these controls include several that you use while the camera is running. There is a focus button and a selector for manual or autofocus; a compensation control for backlit subjects; and a fade facility. The white balance control, which you set before starting to record, is also on the side panel. The built-in microphone, although lined up with the lens, will inevitably pick up sounds you do not want. The socket on the side therefore allows you to connect another microphone, which you can aim more precisely at the sound-source you want to record.*

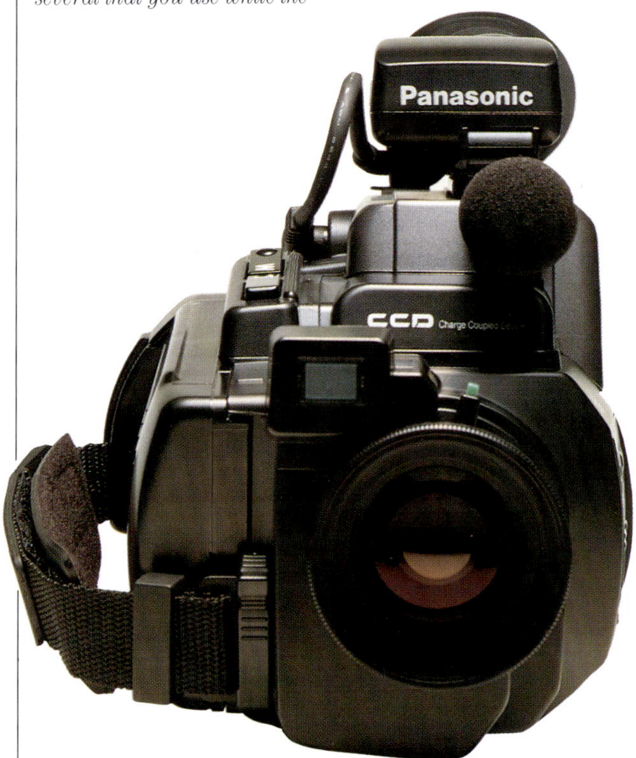

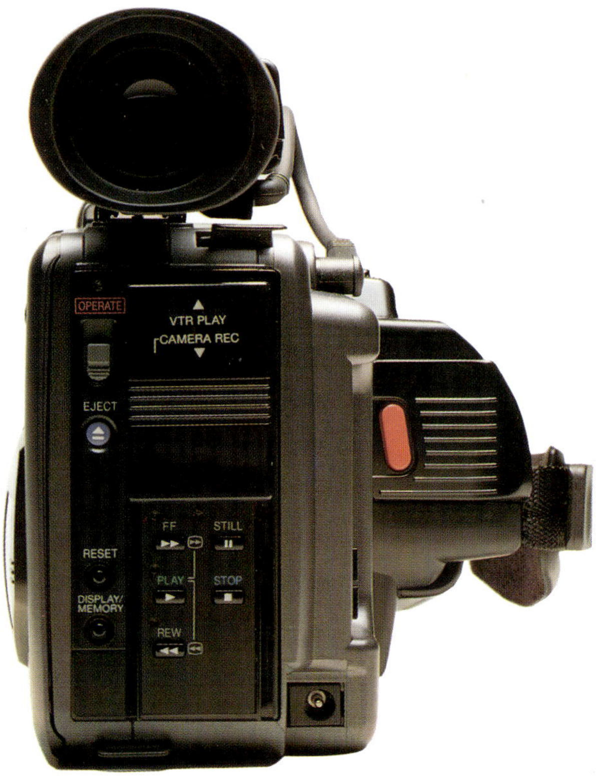

Above: *From this angle the lens and carrying handle are clearly visible. The lens gathers light which then passes on to the CCD light-sensing device inside the camera. The adjustable carrying handle is designed to allow the right hand to slip comfortably through to grasp the side of the camcorder. It is then possible to operate the control that selects the zoom's focal length with the fingers*

Above: *A sliding panel at the rear of the camcorder reveals the array of controls for playing back a tape through the camcorder – the same sort of controls that you would find on a conventional VCR, in fact. These controls are placed at the back because you do not need to operate them during recording.*

When selecting a camcorder, you have several different formats to choose from. Each format uses a different type of tape cassette and, with one exception, tapes and equipment made for one format are incompatible with those made for the others. VHS is the most popular format among home VCR users. Tapes are therefore widely available in a range of lengths from 30 to 240 minutes. The main disadvantage is that VHS cassettes are large (they use tape half an inch wide) and make for a bulky camcorder. One solution to this is to use the VHS-C system. A VHS-C camcorder accepts cassettes containing half-inch tape which are far more compact. You can play them via a regular VHS video recorder using a special adaptor. Another popular format is Video 8. This also provides compact cassettes (using 8 mm tape, they are only slightly bigger than audio cassettes) and lightweight camcorders. Playing times of up to 90 minutes are available. But if you already have a video recorder of another format, your tapes will not be compatible with it. Another drawback is that the range of equipment for this format is not so wide as that for VHS and VHS-C. On the secondhand market, you may come across the Betamax format. This was developed in the mid 1970s, proved less popular than VHS, and has been phased out, although tapes are still available.

FORMATS

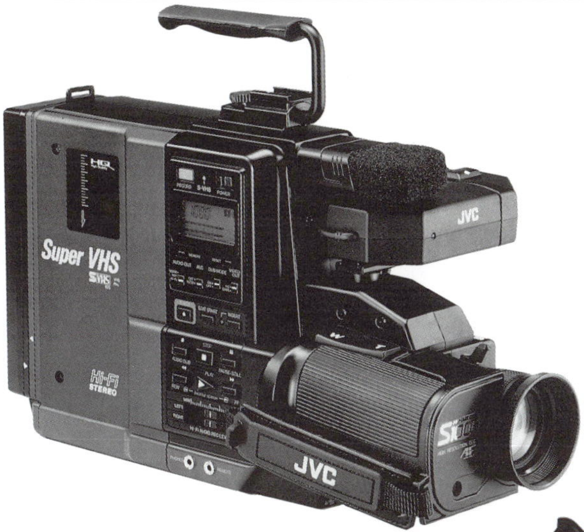

Super VHS camcorder

Video 8 camcorder

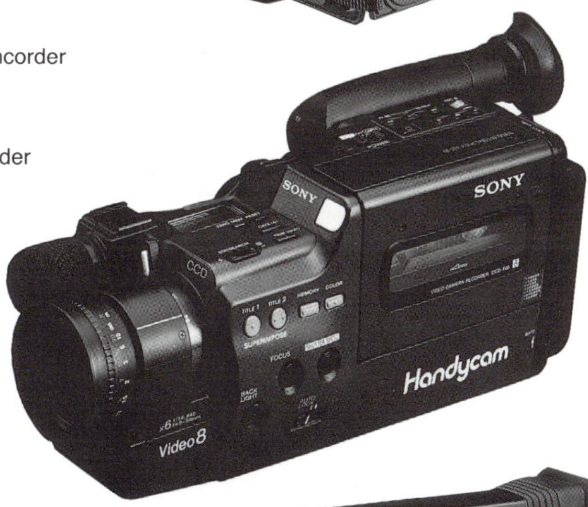

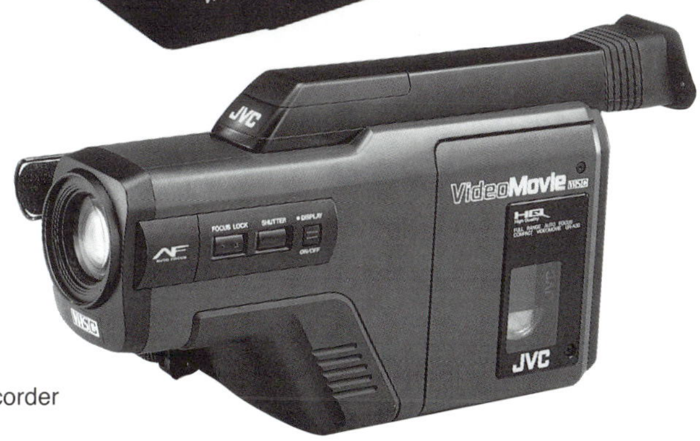

VHS-C camcorder

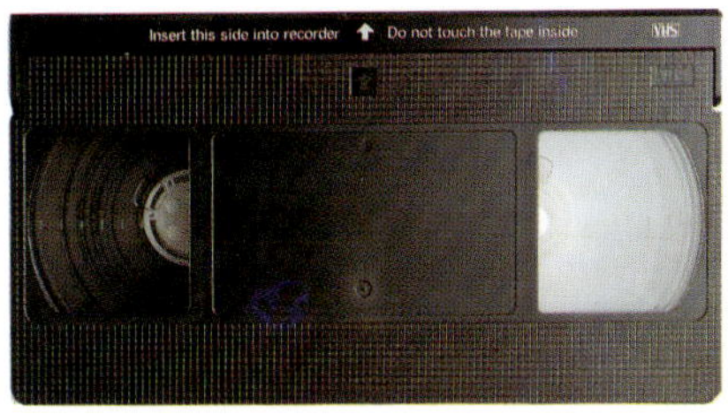

VHS tape

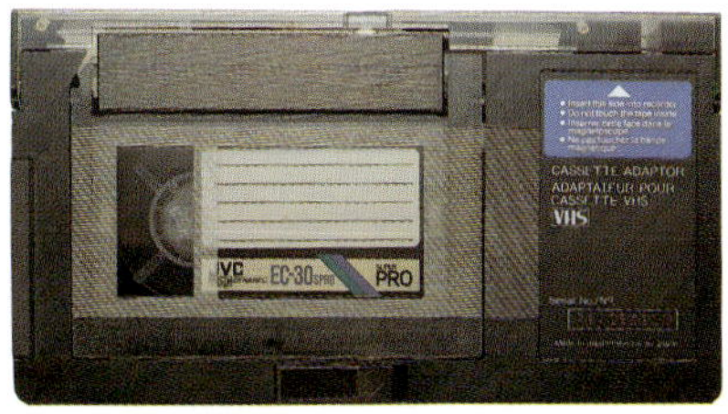

Adaptor for playing VHS-C tape
in VHS recorder

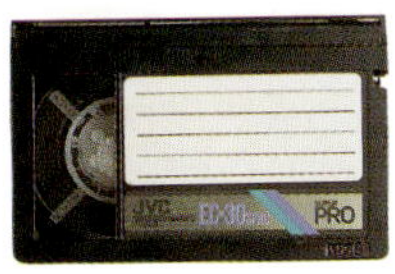

VHS-C tape

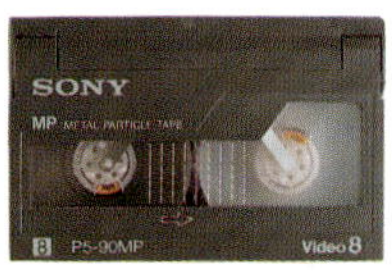

Video 8 tape

The white balance and the daylight and tungsten filters on a video camera are used to ensure the correct rendition of colour. The daylight filter is engaged when you are shooting outdoors, and the tungsten filter when shooting under artificial light. These filters are necessary because in daylight colours from the blue end of the spectrum tend to predominate, while artificial light has a reddish cast. The human brain automatically tends to compensate for this, but the video camera cannot. The daylight filter therefore removes the bluish cast of daylight, while the tungsten filter reduces the reds in artificial light. The first rule, then, is to engage the correct filter. (Unless, of course you deliberately want to create a colour imbalance – a fireside scene, for example, shot with the daylight filter will be suffused with a warm, reddish glow.)

When this has been done, the white balance must be set. This is done by pointing the camera at a white card (or often a white lens cap) and pressing the white balance button. If you are in a hurry, you can set white balance off a white wall, or someone's shirt – it doesn't matter so long as it is white and lit by the prevailing light. Remember, if your camcorder does not have an automatic white balance adjustment, you must do this each and every time you switch on the camera and whenever you move from one lighting condition to another or add supplementary lighting to the scene.

Some people find the white balance a little mysterious, perhaps because it is unique to video. In fact it serves to ensure that colours are rendered correctly, and the principle is very straightforward. The white card or lens cap serves as a standard 'pure' white for the camera – you are telling the camera that this is pure white. With this standard set, the rendition of all other colours follows automatically, since white is a mixture of all colours.

THE WHITE BALANCE

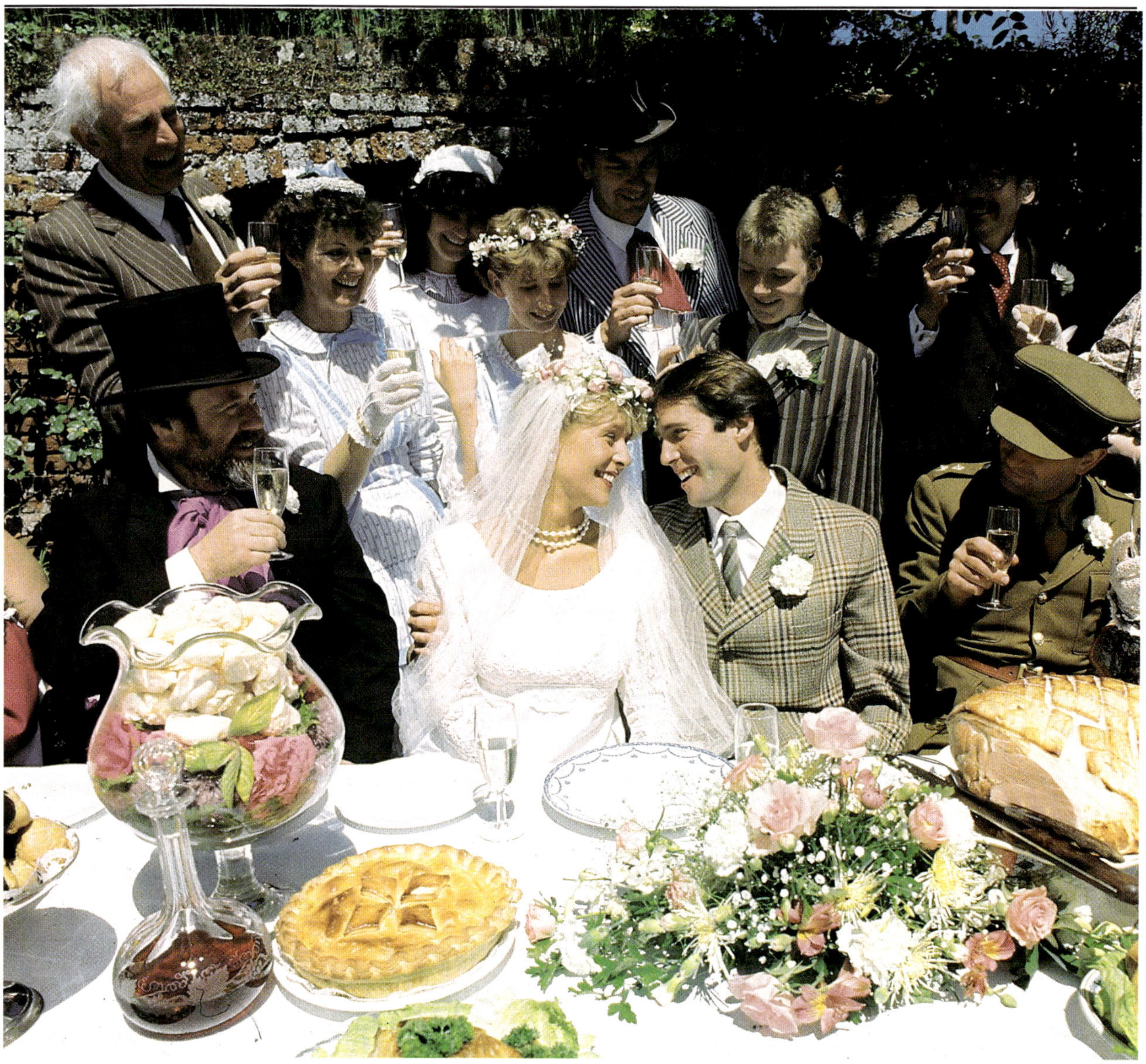

1: *With the white balance set for indoor shooting, an outdoor scene will have a reddish cast.*

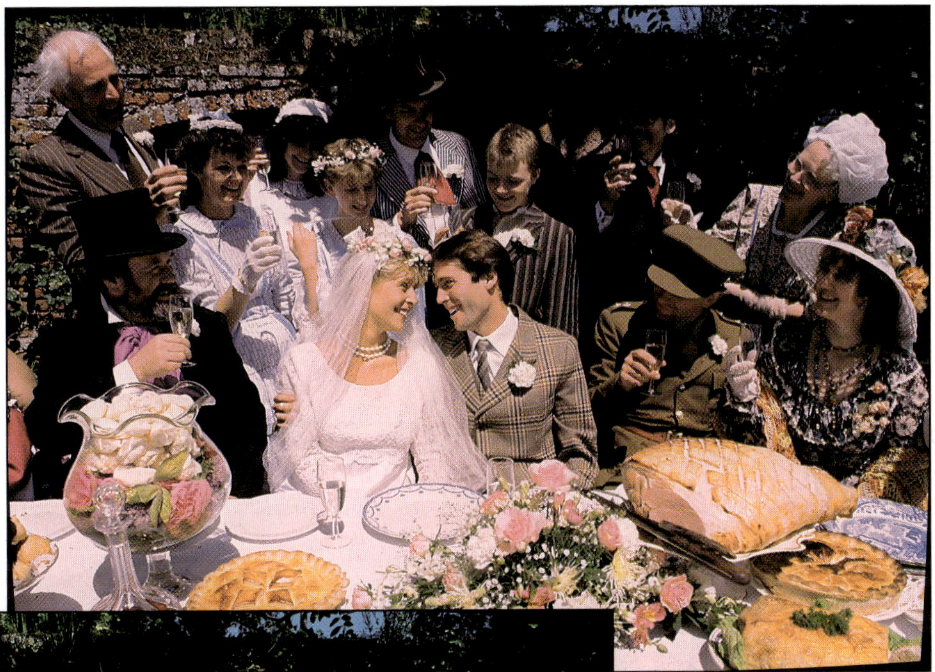

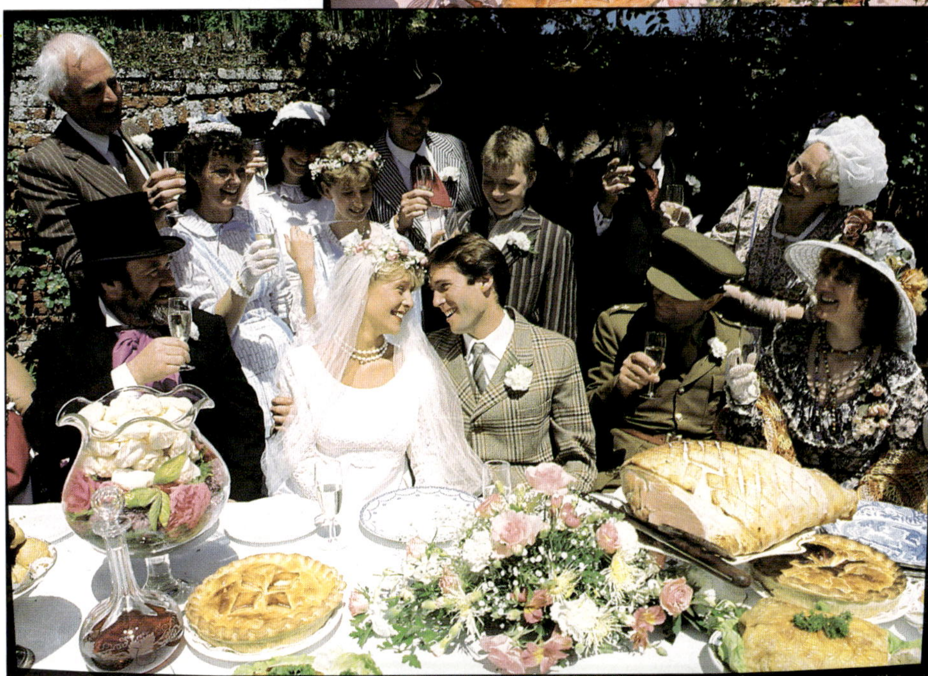

2: *The white balance is properly set and the colour rendition of the shot is correct.*

3: *A slight bluish cast indicates that the white balance is not quite right in this shot – although the effect is not as obtrusive as in shot 1.*

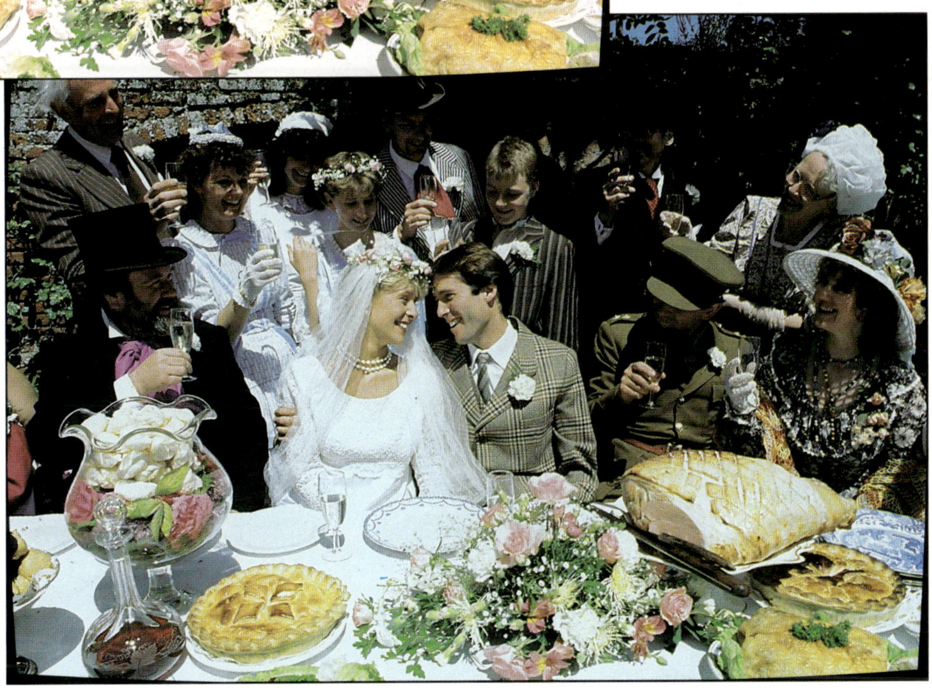

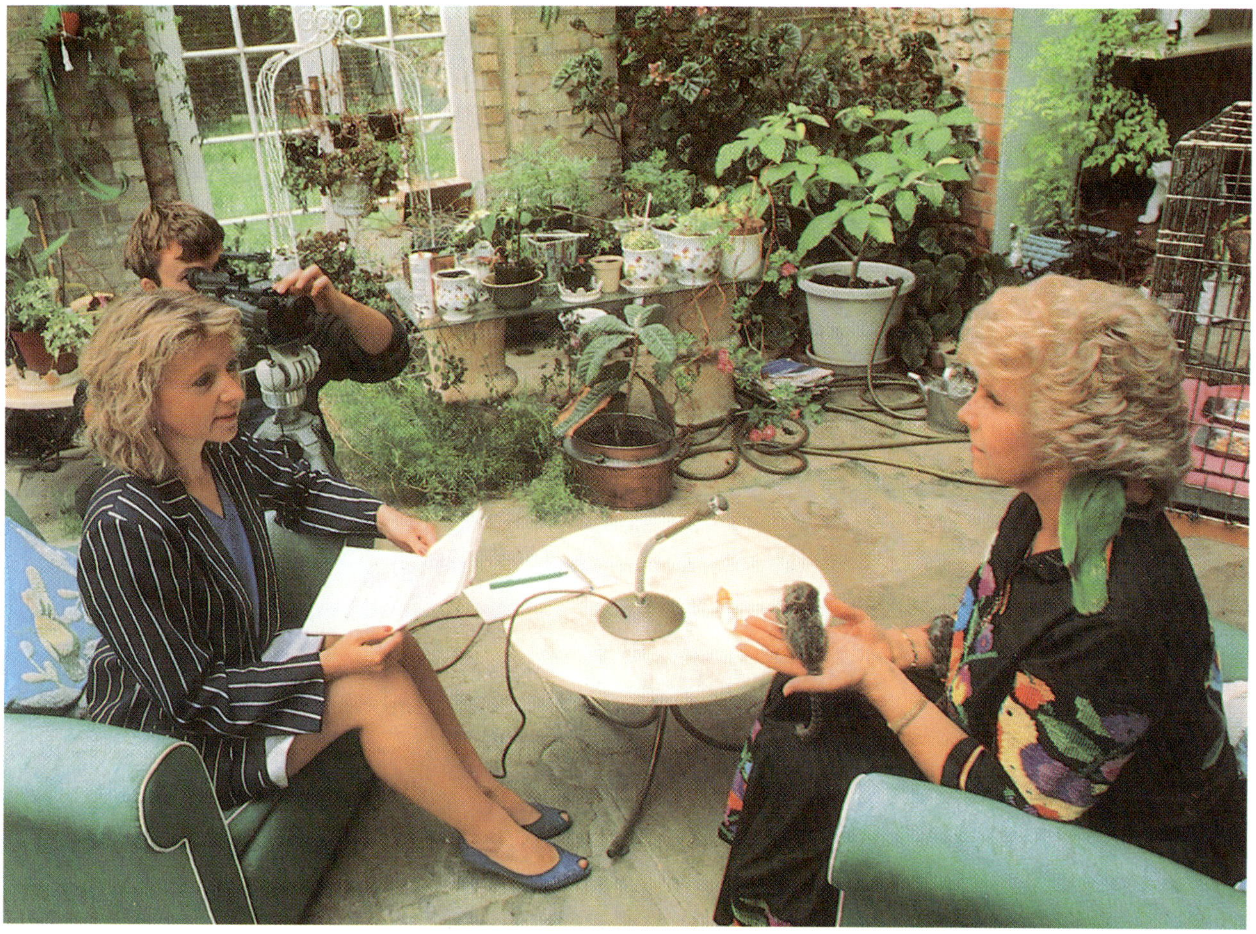

HOLDING THE CAMERA

Steadiness when hand-holding the camera should be one of the first techniques to master. Video cameras and camcorders weigh little more than a 35mm SLR. While that greatly reduces the strain of carrying them about (and for someone used to the technology of 10 years ago that's no small achievement) it does make them more difficult to hold steady. The problem is greater with those cameras which offer no shoulder support and have to be held in front of the eye. A steady grip is important and comes with practice and concentration.

First, you must adopt a comfortable stance, with your legs slightly apart and your elbows tucked into your sides to give firm support to the camera. The right hand does the steadying, leaving the left free to adjust the lens. If you must move to follow the action, turn from the waist at half-speed, making your movements rhythmical and deliberate, not jerky. Make test recordings of your friends and family – to begin with you will almost certainly see that you are still moving too quickly and abruptly.

Next, minimize your movements as much as possible. Most people are far too eager to change their position or to pan the camera round to include other elements in the action.

Adopt a camera position which allows you full coverage of the action you wish to record. The more the action develops in view of the camera, and the less obtrusive your movements, the more 'natural' will be the result. A valuable exercise is to switch on the camera, tuck it under your arm and go for a walk. The tape will show you what the camera sees without you directing it and you will be surprised at how much of interest it contains.

Any movements you do make should be slow and deliberate, almost rhythmical. For practice, use a spare videotape and record anything – your garden, shots of people walking down the street, a member of the family doing everyday tasks. Make it a continuous sequence lasting a few minutes, then play it back for close examination. Look for any instances of camera shake, or where you have moved the camera too quickly when following the action. You can carry out this exercise a number of times, rerecording on the same tape. As you follow a moving subject try to keep the main point of interest in the middle of the frame. It is not easy, but you will get better with experience. You will find that your admiration for professional camera operators at sports events like golf tournaments will increase dramatically!

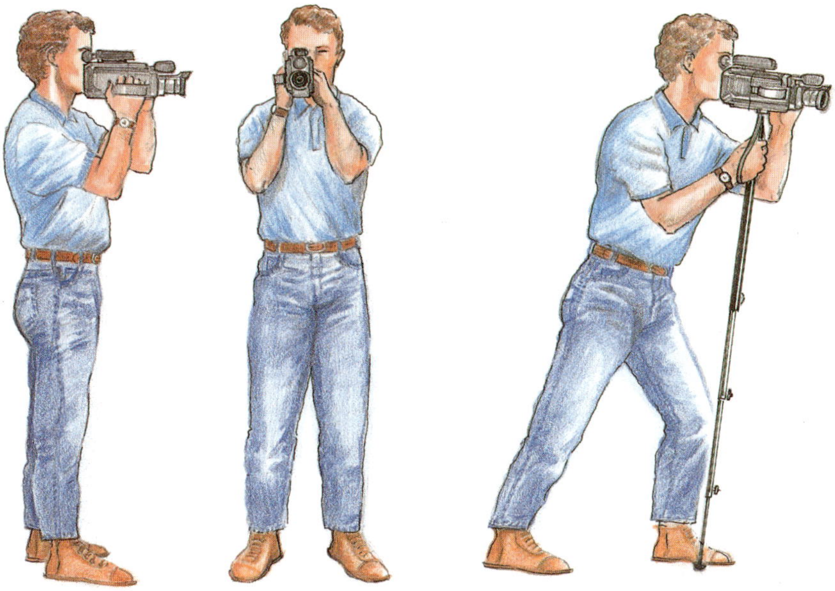

Left: *The normal way to hold a camcorder is to balance it on one shoulder. One hand can then hold the hand grip and work the zoom motor. The other hand can operate the other camcorder controls. Occasionally a monopod offers extra support.*

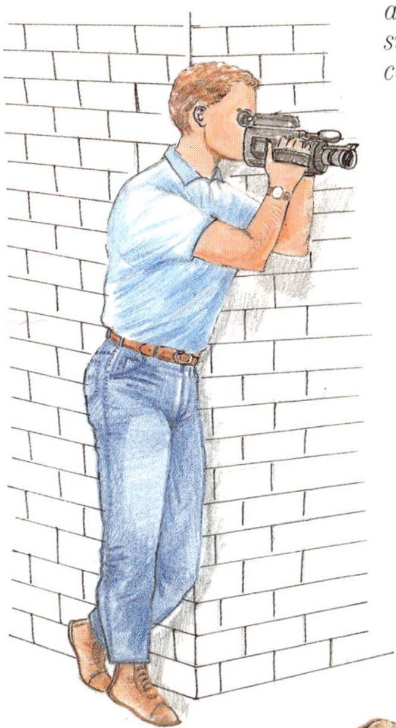

Left: *Leaning against a wall is a good way of gaining extra support for shots in which the camera is stationary.*

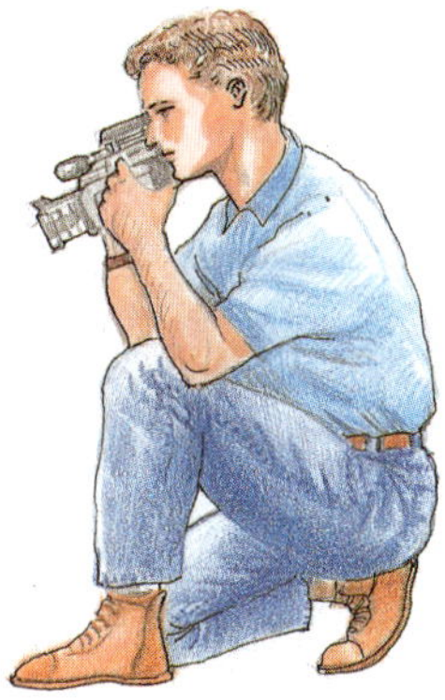

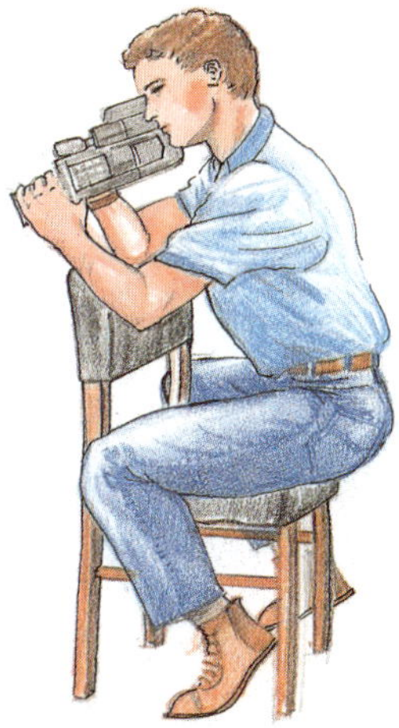

Above and left: *Brace yourself when angling the camera downwards. Use a convenient support, such as a chair, if you can. Otherwise put one knee on the ground to keep your body steady.*

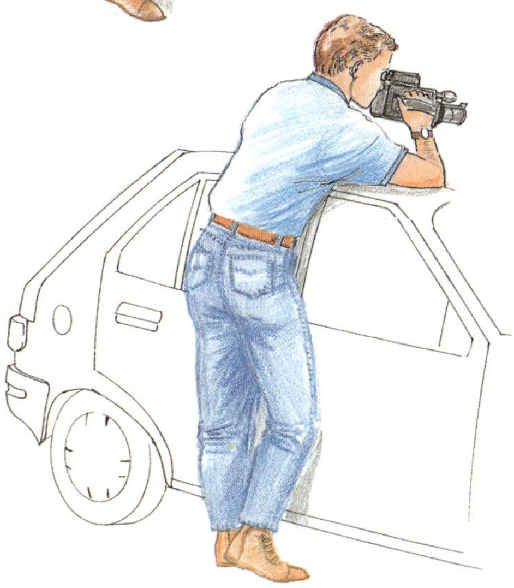

Above: *Don't neglect the car roof – it provides a stable platform.*

Right and below: *At outdoor events you usually have to improvise. For low shots, you may prefer to lie on your front, like a marksman. A sitting position will give a higher angle – use your knees for support.*

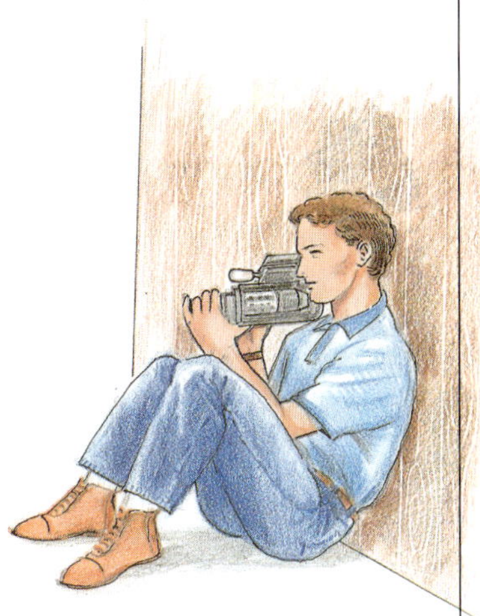

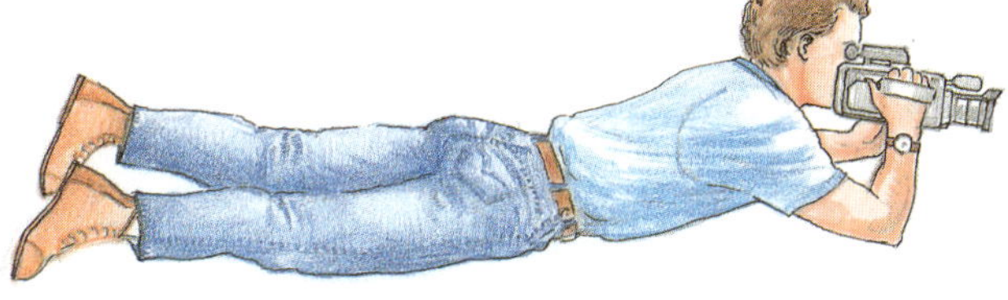

Another good technique when taking hand-held shots is to look for extra support such as a wall, a doorway, or the back of a chair. For low-angle work, kneel and rest your right elbow on your knee, or lie prone with the camera resting on a pile of books.

There will always be a degree of unsteadiness to hand-held shots, but this will be far less apparent using the wide-angle end of the lens, particularly when close in to a subject. You should therefore try to confine yourself to this type of shot when hand-holding. At the telephoto end, steadiness is virtually impossible to achieve, particularly if following a moving subject. Use a tripod for such shots, or try to move in closer to the action.

Using a tripod

No matter how proficient you become at hand-holding the camera, you will never achieve the absolute steadiness that comes with using a tripod. A good tripod is not an option, it is essential. Choose a good quality, sturdy model. Don't be persuaded that an ultra-lightweight version that you can carry effortlessly for hours is the one to buy. A good tripod should be a bit of a nuisance and have a degree of heaviness. When buying one, remember that it will seem more sturdy on the smooth floor of a showroom than it will on rough ground on location. And finally, check how far the legs will extend for low-angle tripod shots.

The tripod head allows movement from side to side (the panning action) and up and down (tilting). The simplest head is the pan and tilt head, but its operation tends to be rather jerky. A friction head gives a smoother motion, while fluid heads are perhaps most popular of all. A good friction or fluid head should operate smoothly and evenly, although there should also be some sense of weight, and some resistance to movement. Of course, with all tripod heads it is essential that the camera is locked firmly in its set position.

Use the tripod whenever the situation demands. For 'fluid' impromptu situations, the mobility and portability of a hand-held camcorder come into their own. Note that since tripod-based and hand-held shots of the same scene do not mix, planning how you intend to shoot is vital. A second drawback of such a switch is that you will almost certainly miss part of the action. Instead of transferring from the hand-held position to a tripod, use the unexpected action that may occur during shooting.

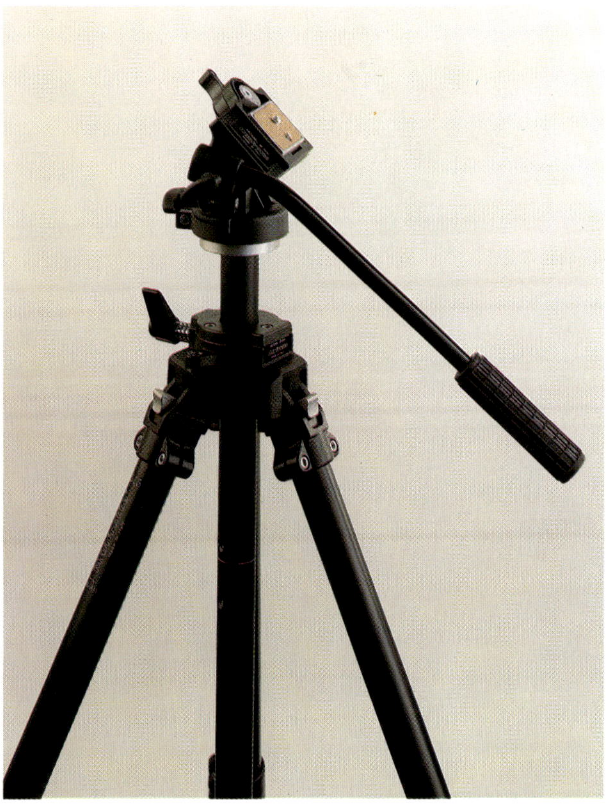

Above: *Amateur still photographers are familiar with the friction tripod head. This is a simple form of tripod head. The moving parts are made so that they fit tightly together and are held in place by bolts which you tighten when you have adjusted the tripod. This is adequate for clamping the camera in a single position, but can result in a rather jerky movement if you are using the tripod to pan or tilt the camera while it is running.*

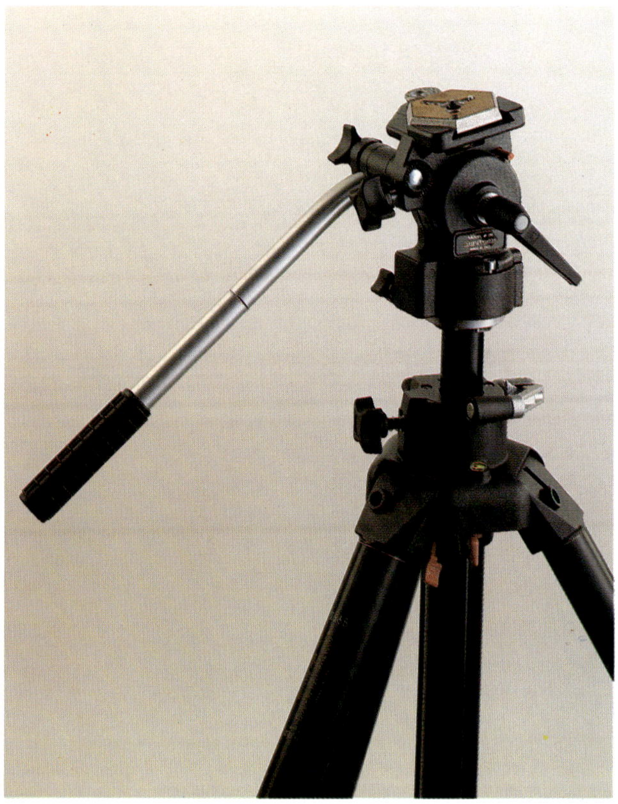

Above: *The best head for a video tripod is the fluid head. With this design the moving parts are enclosed in a casing containing fluid, rather like the hydraulic systems used on tipping trucks. The result is smooth camera movement – perhaps the feature that most often makes professional videos stand out over amateur ones. This type of tripod head is expensive, but it is invaluable if you want really high-quality results.*

Below: *One of the most important features in a tripod is versatility. For example, you may need a tripod-mounted camera for low-angle shots. In this case, a tripod that allows you to splay the legs wide so that the camera is very near the ground will be ideal.*

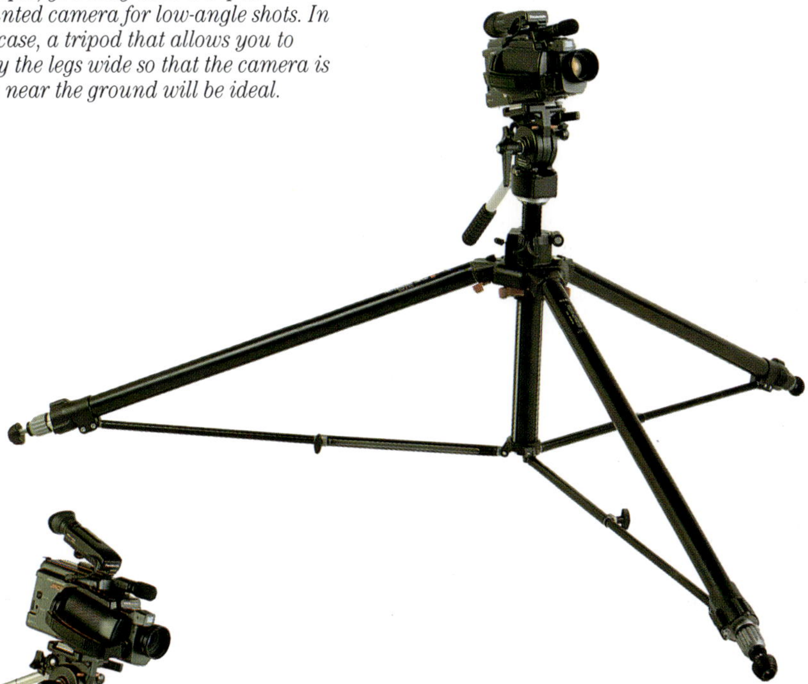

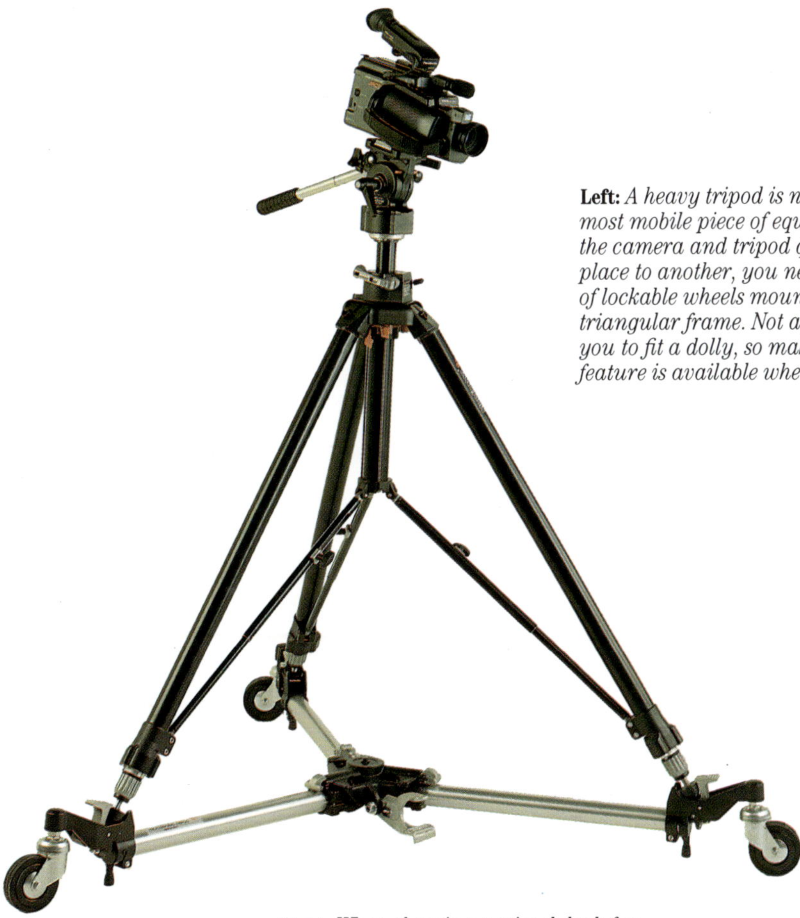

Left: *A heavy tripod is not always the most mobile piece of equipment. To push the camera and tripod quickly from one place to another, you need a dolly – a set of lockable wheels mounted on a triangular frame. Not all tripods allow you to fit a dolly, so make sure this feature is available when you buy.*

Right: *When choosing a tripod, look for stability. This will mean that the tripod is heavy and that it has braces connecting the legs with the centre column to give a sturdy support.*

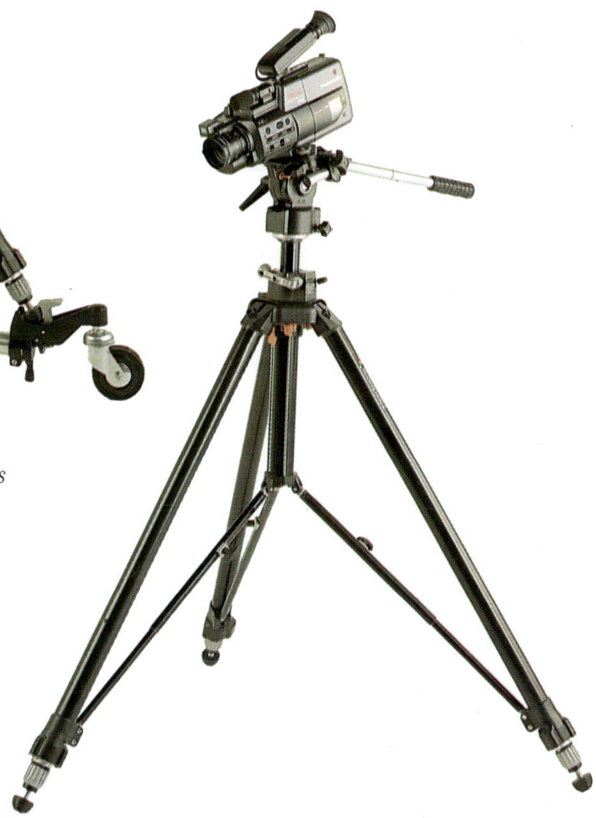

The lens on a video camera is constructed on the same optical principles as the lens on a still camera. The amount of light entering the camera is controlled by increasing or reducing the lens aperture, which is in turn controlled by an iris of overlapping metal leaves. Today, all domestic video cameras have automatic exposure, by which the camera continually adjusts the aperture according to prevailing lighting conditions.

The auto-exposure circuits set exposure for the overall brightness of a scene but in certain situations this can create problems. The first can occur when, for example, your shot moves quickly from an area of sunlight to shade – a momentary jump in the exposure may be noticeable on viewing the tape. Second, when there is a small area of shade in an otherwise bright scene it will tend to be underexposed. And third, when there is a subject with bright light behind, it too will be underexposed.

Many camcorders have a backlight switch to compensate automatically for this by opening the iris, often resulting in a background that appears overexposed and bleached.

Although auto-exposure works perfectly well in most situations, it is recommended that whenever possible you set the exposure manually. You therefore choose the exposure you want for your shot. As this book will stress time and again, thinking ahead and planning each shot in advance is vital.

To set exposure manually, remember that 'what you see is what you get'. If exposure looks right in the electronic viewfinder then it will look right on the tape. In addition, many viewfinders have exposure warning lights to indicate that there is insufficient light for the shot. Camcorders are not calibrated in *f*-stop numbers, but some have an aperature indicator, others have no such indicator at all. When setting manually, choose your exposure and rehearse the shot. If your shot contains contrasts of light and shade that are too great to be covered with a single exposure setting – a shot moving from the lawn to a shaded patio, for example – then treat the two areas as separate shots and set the appropriate exposures for each.

It's advisable to experiment with auto-exposure and practise setting exposure manually by shooting in different lighting conditions. That way you will soon be able to judge the exposure requirements of any particular lighting condition as part of your preshooting preparation routine.

EXPOSURE

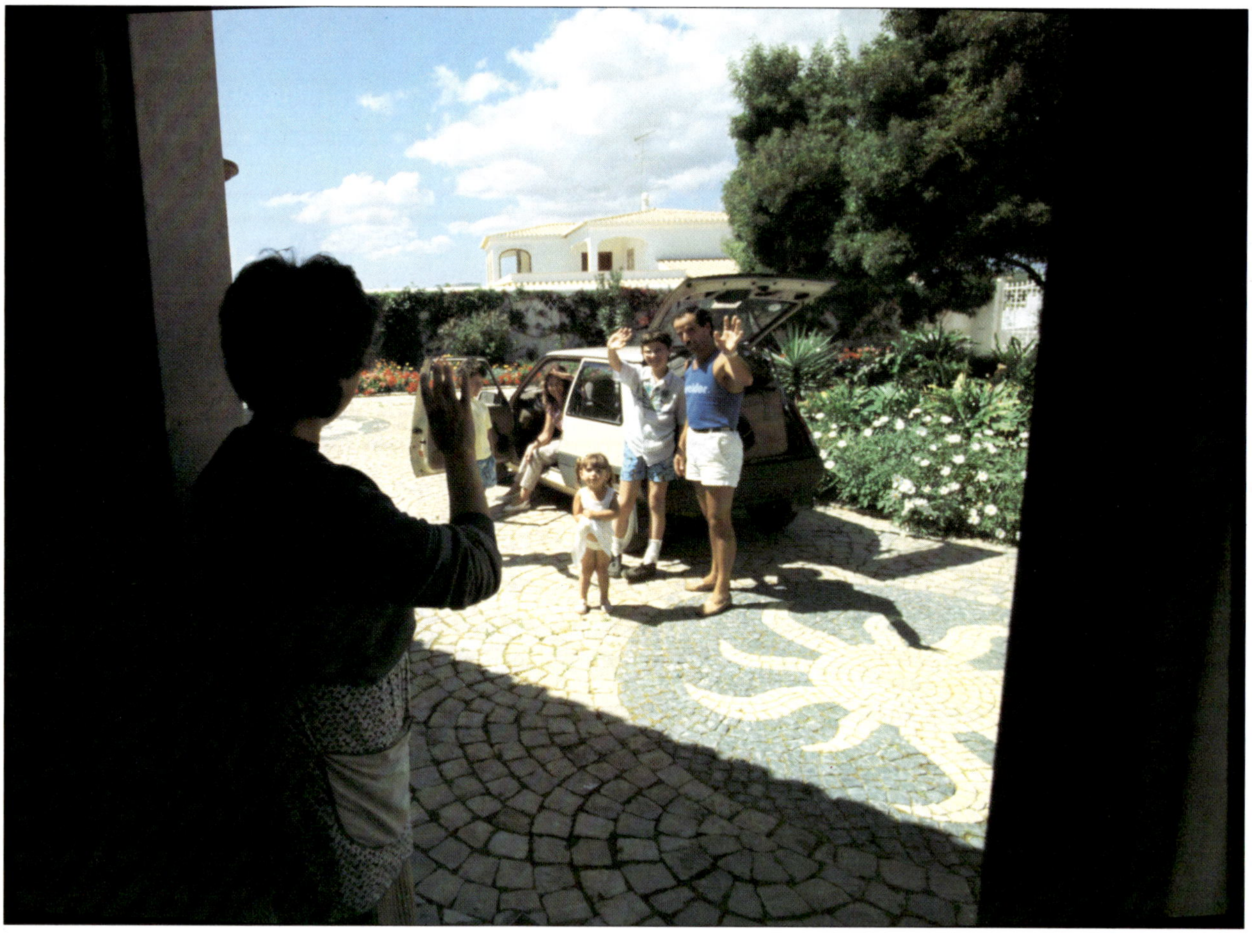

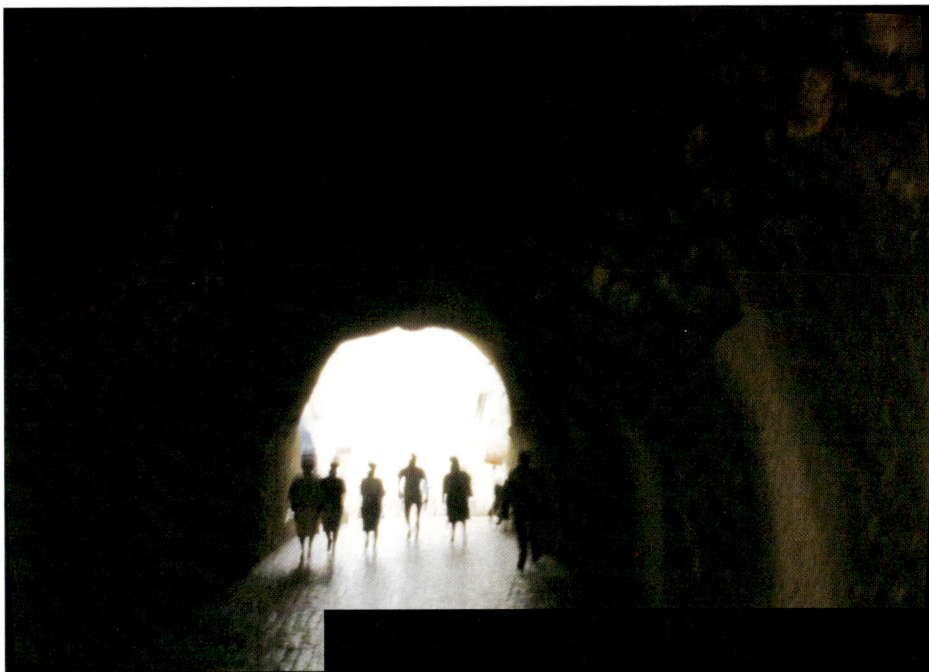

2-3: *When the subject moves from one lighting environment to another, there will be a noticeable lag in exposure at the point of transition, as the automatic exposure controls seek to determine the new exposure levels. There is little you can do to avoid this.*

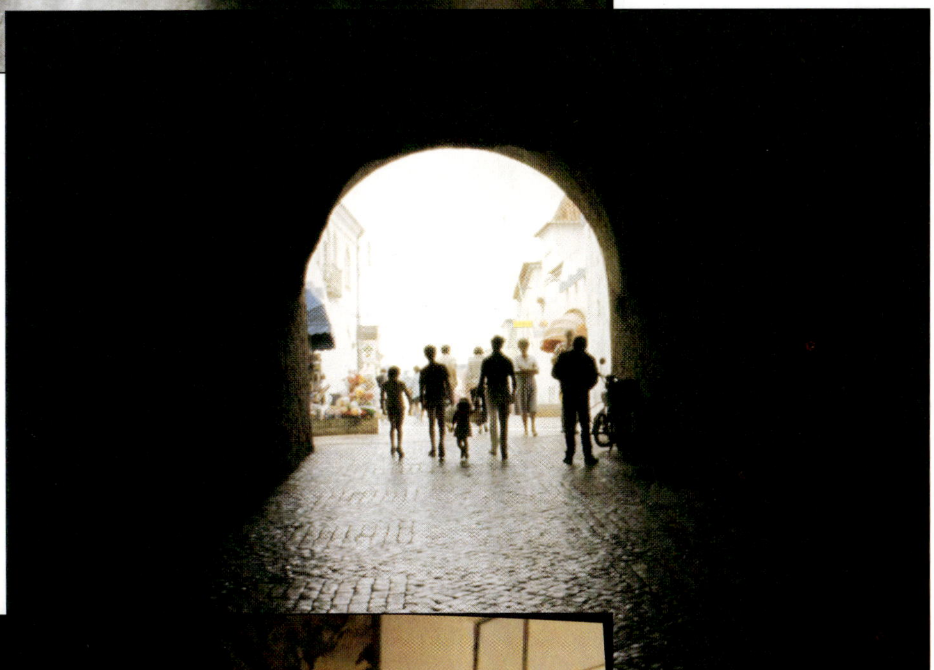

1: *Many stills cameras would have great difficulty in achieving an image in lighting conditions such as these. Video cameras have a greater light sensitivity and can operate in very dim lighting. With automatic exposure, the camera will tend to set exposure for the overall lighting, rather than for the bright area at the end of the tunnel.*

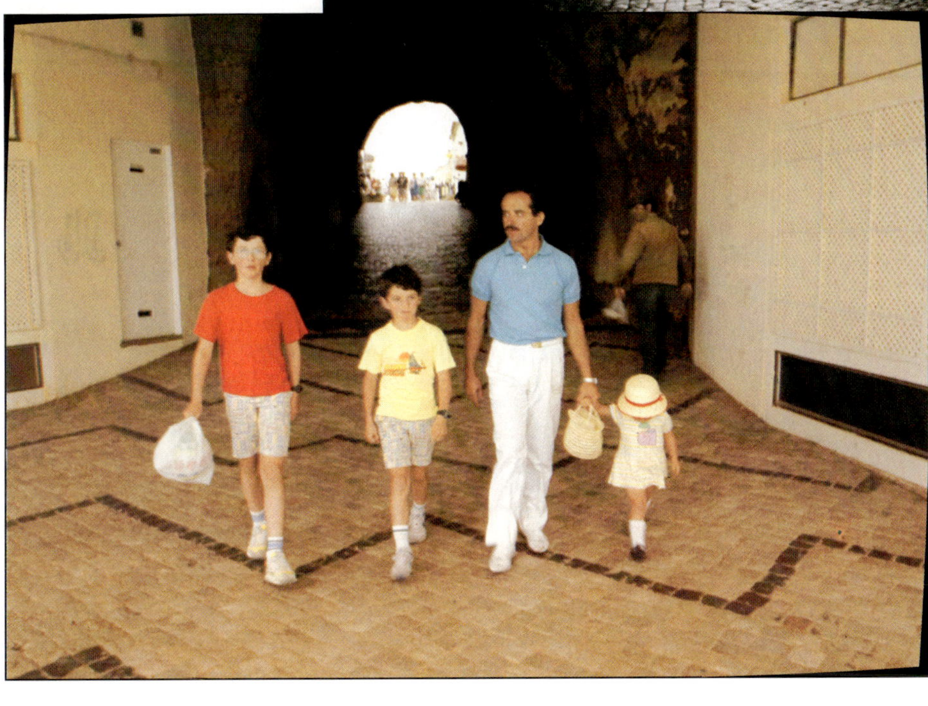

4: *Shooting from deep shadow into bright sunlight can cause problems when using autoexposure: the camera cannot decide which to use as a standard, and the exposure 'wobbles' between the two extremes. If this happens, set exposure manually.*

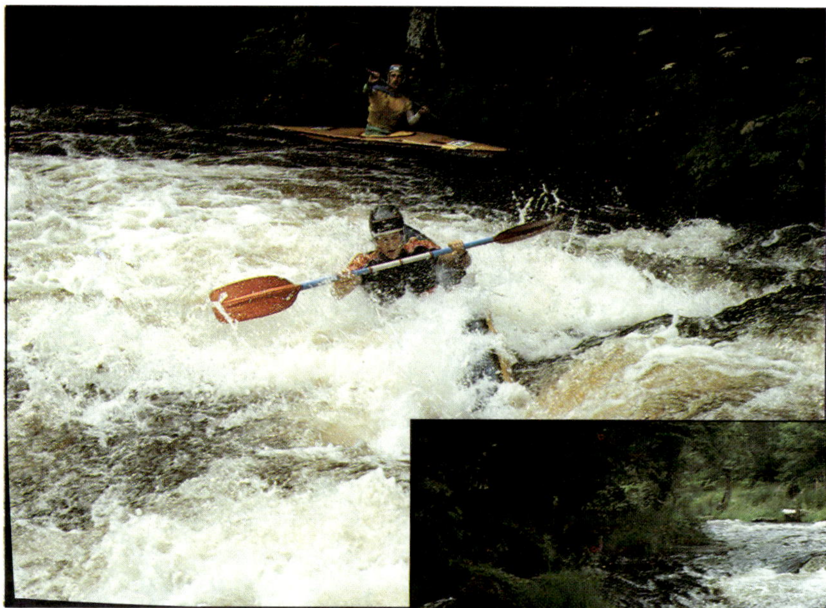

1: *For fast action sequences, the autofocus option provided in most camcorders can prove to be invaluable. In a situation like this, however, there is a danger of water spray confusing the focusing system. Do a trial run and check through the electronic viewfinder.*

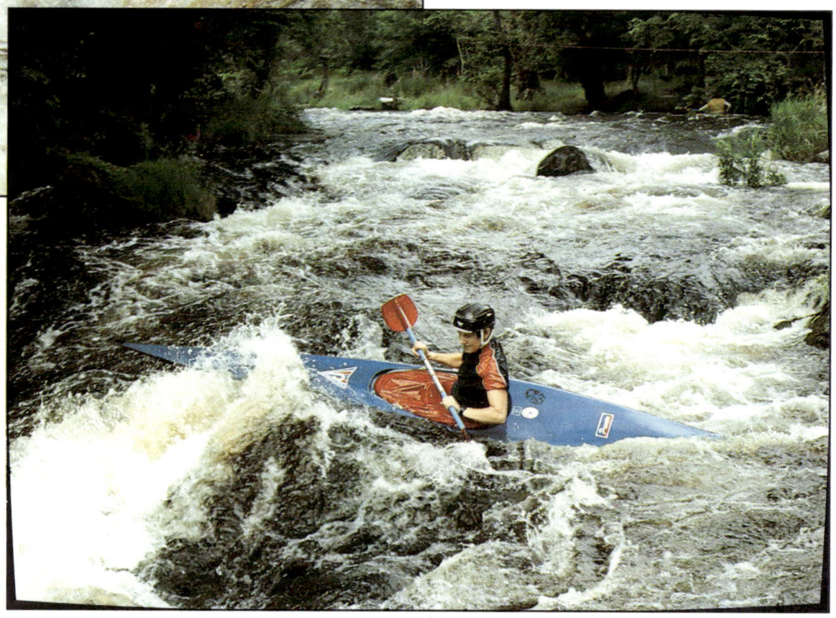

2: *The sequence was taken using the telephoto end of the zoom lens, where depth of field is least. Using autofocus, this presents no problem, but with manual focusing the lens has to be continuously adjusted as the subject approaches the camera.*

FOCUSING AND DEPTH OF FIELD

Most camcorders now have autofocus, with the option of manual override. Autofocus works when the camera picks up a reflected infra-red beam and uses it to calculate the distance of the object from the camera. There are two drawbacks though. Off-centred subjects can cause problems with autofocus. And when either the camera or the subject moves, a brief adjustment in focus may be seen on viewing the tape as the camera searches for a new focus reading. Further problems occur in shots where there is continuous perspective and no apparent 'subject' – a line of trees in a wood, for example. Rain and snow can also 'throw' autofocus systems, and subjects behind glass or netting are also problematical with some types.

Manual focusing

As with auto-exposure, autofocus comes into its own when you have no time to rehearse the shot. Otherwise, set the focus manually as you establish your angles. For a zoom-in shot, first set up the beginning of the scene and then zoom in to a close-up of the subject (with people, focus on the eyes; with buildings or landscape find significant detail such as the lettering above a shop door, or a clump of flowers in a field). Adjust the focus until it appears pin-sharp in the viewfinder (again, what you see is what you get). You can then zoom out again and begin shooting.

Focusing on moving subjects

Manual focus for moving subjects is more difficult because you will have to adjust the focus while taking the shot. Again, rehearse the shot if possible, first taking a focus for the subject at the beginning of the shot. Next, take a second focus midway through the scene when the subject is at an easily identifiable point (passing a telegraph pole, say). Finally, take a focus reading for the end of the shot. These three readings serve as a guide to the gradually changing focus as the shot progresses. At all but the telephoto end of the zoom, the depth of field is such that the subject will keep in focus.

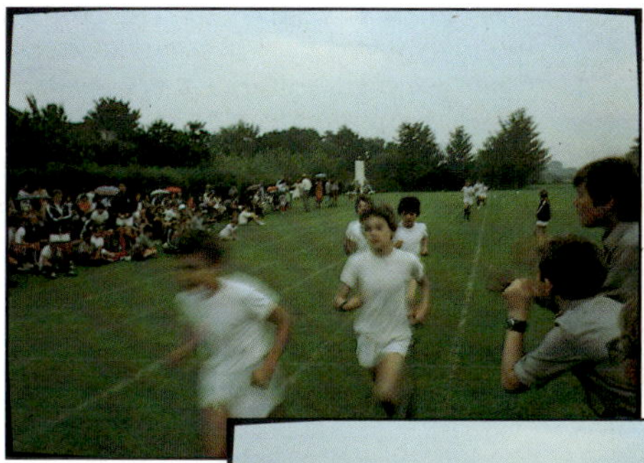

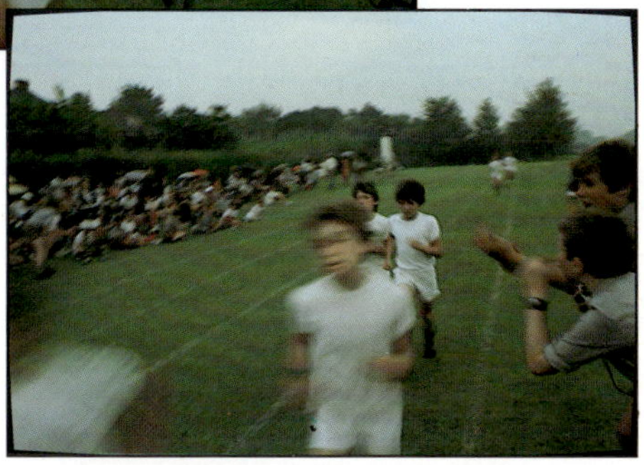

3-4: *The two shots above, taken from a video made on a school sports day, show the effect of depth of field when shooting using a fixed focal length. Notice how the runners come out of focus as they approach the camera.*

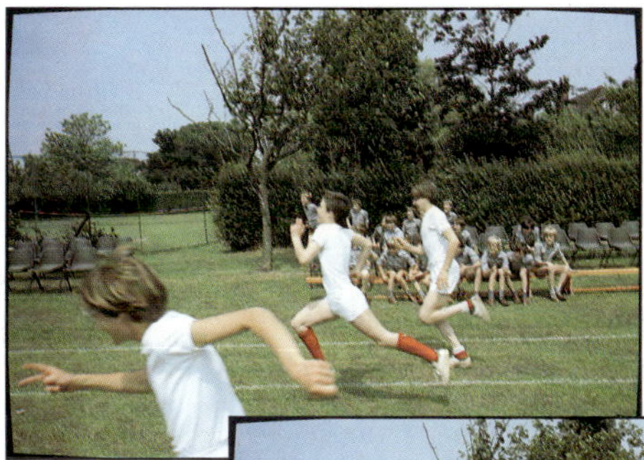

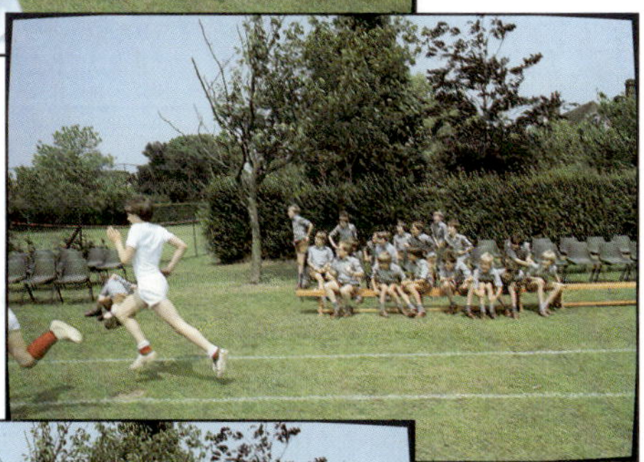

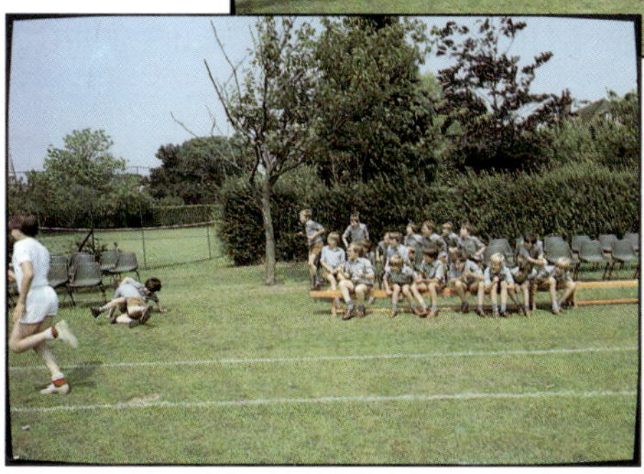

5-7: *For this sequence at the sports day, the focus was set up manually. It was important that all the runners across the track were in focus, and not just those nearest the camera. This meant a relatively large depth of field was required, so focus was set using the wide angle of the zoom lens. As with other situations, it is a good idea to rehearse the shot before actually taking it.*

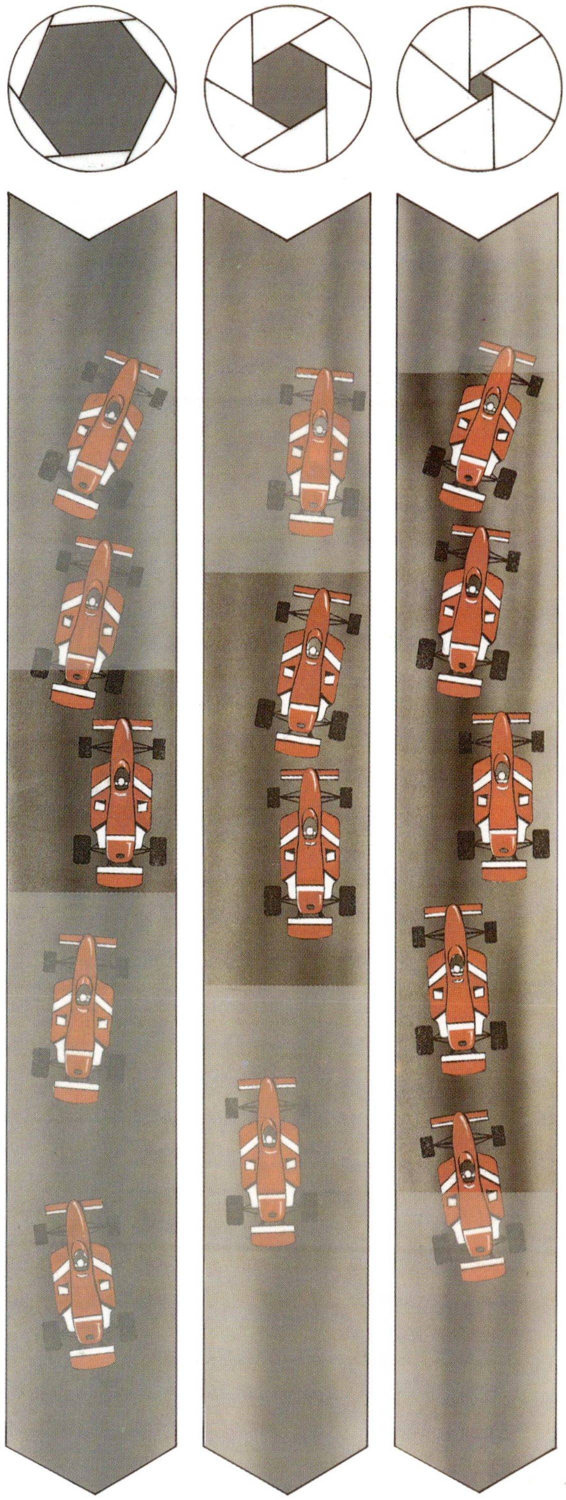

DEPTH OF FIELD

Depth of field is the distance between the nearest and farthest objects that are in focus in any given shot. Depth of field is greater at the wide-angle end of the zoom and least at the telephoto end (it also depends on the size of the lens aperture, but in video this is predetermined by exposure requirements). Depth of field extends further behind the subject than it does in front. The limited depth of field at the telephoto end of the lens can be used to isolate subjects, or to put the background out of focus. Conversely, a shot taken at the wide-angle end of the lens, focused on a distant object, will give great depth of field.

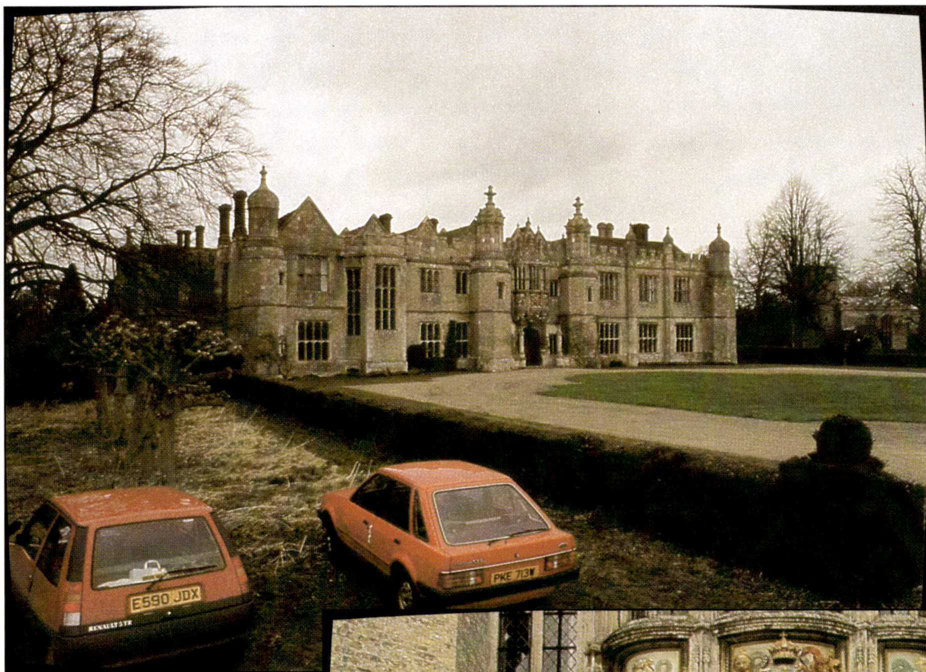

1: *This video about the life of a convent was introduced with a sequence of scene-setting shots of the building itself. This began with a very long shot of the convent, which was followed by progressively closer shots.*

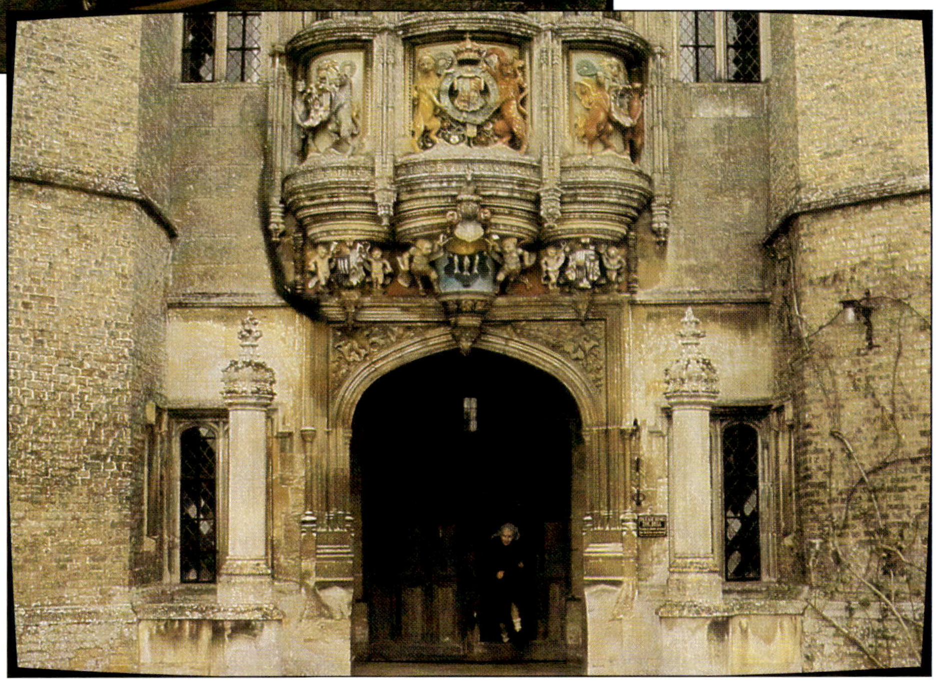

2: *After the initial shot a different camera position was adopted directly in front of the building. The lens gradually zoomed in towards the door and the first human element was introduced in the shape of the approaching figure.*

THE RANGE OF SHOTS

A shot is a section of continuous, uncut footage and is the basic unit of video work. The three basic shots are the close-up, the mid-shot and the long-shot – CU, MS and LS in the abbreviations used in the television and film industry. They are defined in terms of human subjects, although of course they apply to shots of landscapes and inanimate objects too.

A close-up is a head-and-shoulders shot of a single individual. When only the full face occupies the screen, the shot becomes a big close-up (BCU). Any closer than this (a shot of the eyes or mouth only, for instance) and you have an extreme close-up (ECU). Each gives what the audience perceives as an increasingly intimate view of the subject.

The mid-shot extends to just below the waist (notice not *to* the waist – cut-off points that correspond to human sections look odd on television). Where a shot contains two people it is a 'two-shot'. The mid-shot concentrates on the subject, but includes a sense of background.

The long-shot contains the full human figure, from head to toe. It also tells the viewer where the subject is and how he or she relates to the environment. The long shot can extend to become a very long-shot (VLS) and an extreme long-shot (ELS).

While these definitions are mainly for general guidance, helping the writer or the director tell the

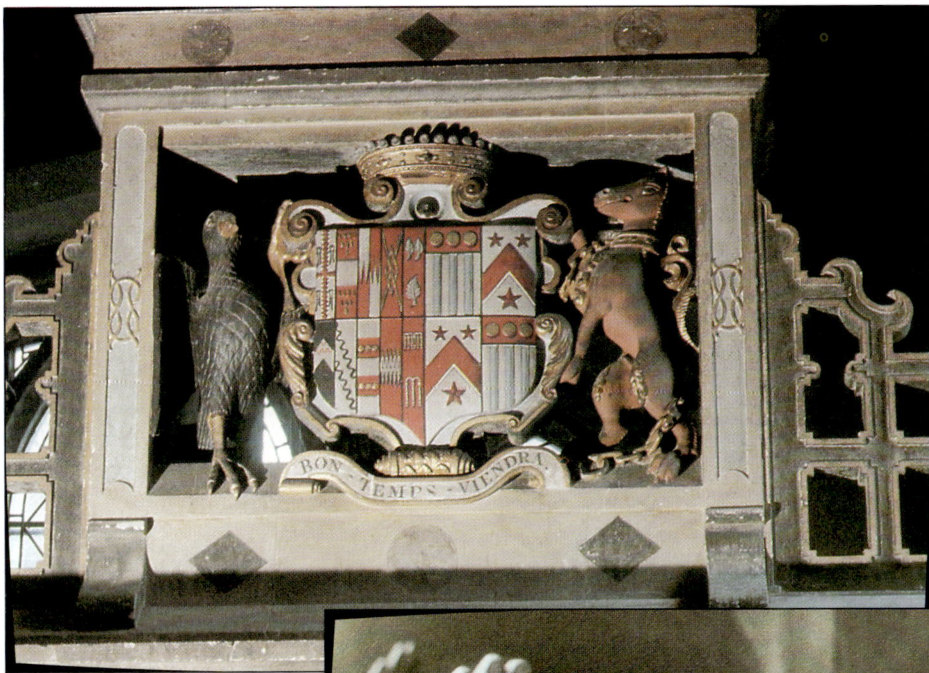

3: *Details can be very revealing. This was a building with a long history and the camera could record many close-ups that reflected this.*

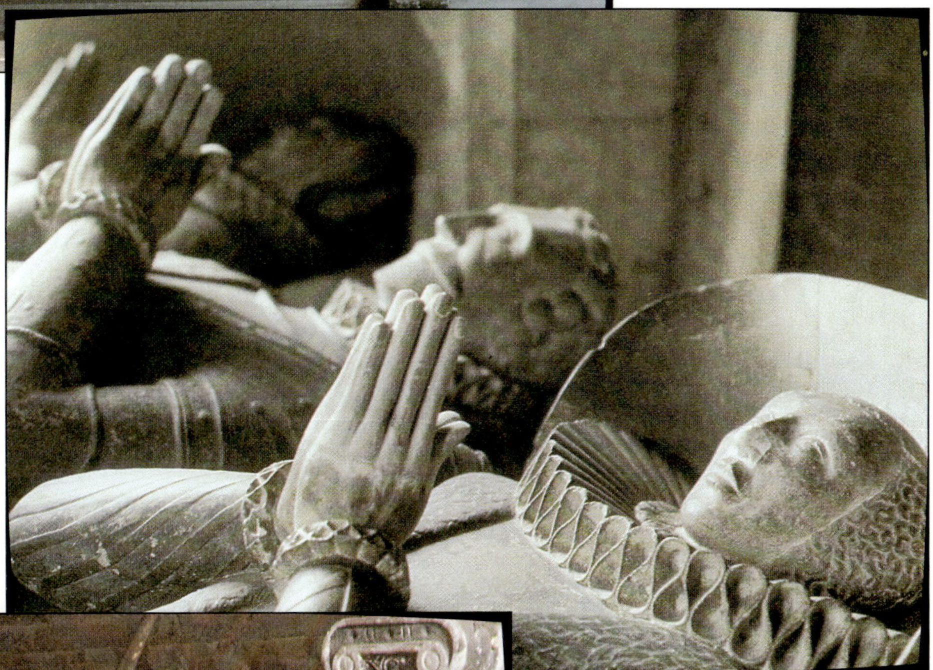

4: *The camera panned around the chapel, coming to rest on these Elizabethan tombs.*

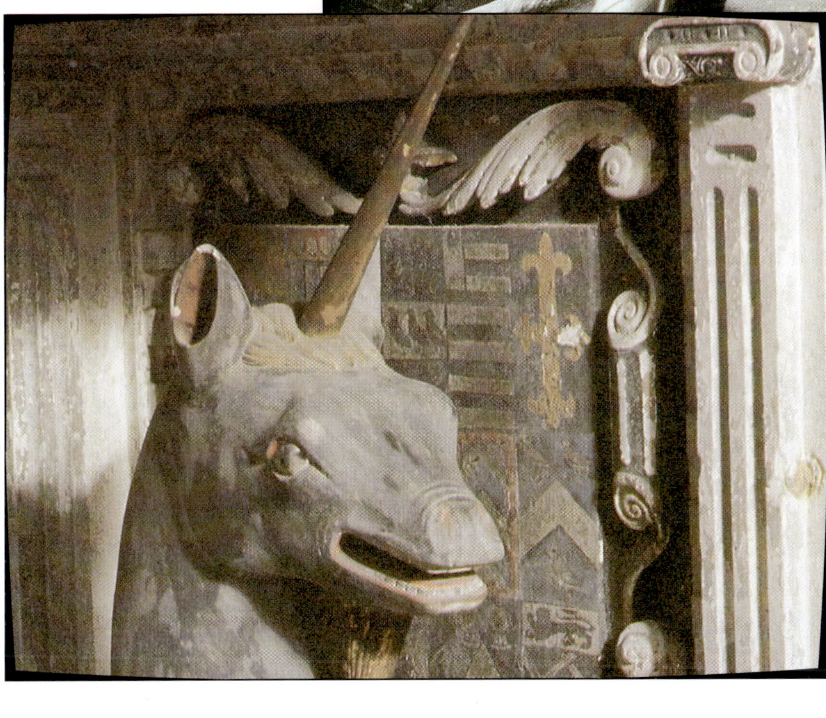

5: *Another close-up in the chapel, introducing a touch of humour to the otherwise solemn atmosphere.*

camera operator the kind of shot required, they also form a useful shorthand with which to plan your video. By writing down the different shots you hope to get you will begin to see how your video is acquiring a sense of pace and rhythm.

Motivated shots

Each basic shot has a different emotional impact upon the viewer, which should be kept in mind when shooting a subject. Notice how on television a newsreader is never shown in more detail than a close-up. The big close-up or extreme close-up implies an intimacy that would be inappropriate (such shots tend to be reserved for an emotional response and are intrusive, bringing us closer to the subject than would happen in real life). Similarly, someone talking in long-shot appears distanced and isolated. It is obvious that they are talking to the camera and not to us.

Of course, shots must not be considered in isolation but be related to the preceding and following images. In most situations these different shots should have a similar feel about them and the transitions should not be too great. A move from extreme long-shot to close-up would be obtrusive, and the progression would be better broken down working through extreme long-shot, long-shot, mid-shot and close-up. The reverse is also true: if you are about to take a second shot of the same subject from a different angle, the change is much more effectively achieved if you change shot size too. So, if the first shot was in mid-shot, begin the second in long-shot or close-up.

Make a video of an everyday subject – preferably in an outdoor location, such as a street market – and explore the effect of different shots and the way they relate to each other. In the ideal tape, each shot inevitably flows into the next, with the audience being unaware of the camerawork. A common mistake made by many beginners is in timing the duration of the shot: the camera either lingers too long on a scene in which nothing is happening, or it darts from shot to shot in an irritating, fragmented way. The first error can be avoided by common sense – if nothing is happening, why are you recording it? The second is cured by experience. Tell yourself to hold your shots that bit longer than you feel is necessary. Also ask yourself why are you moving from one shot to another? Unless there is a good reason (perhaps to take in the background or to catch an expression on a face) the shot will almost certainly fail on screen.

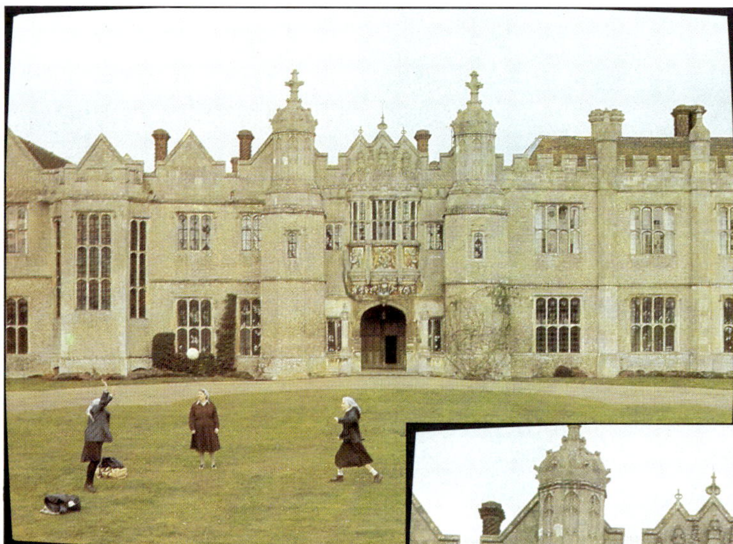

1: *An amusing moment in the life of the sisters was captured using a wide range of different shots. The sequence began with a very long establishing shot giving a broad view of the location and what was going on.*

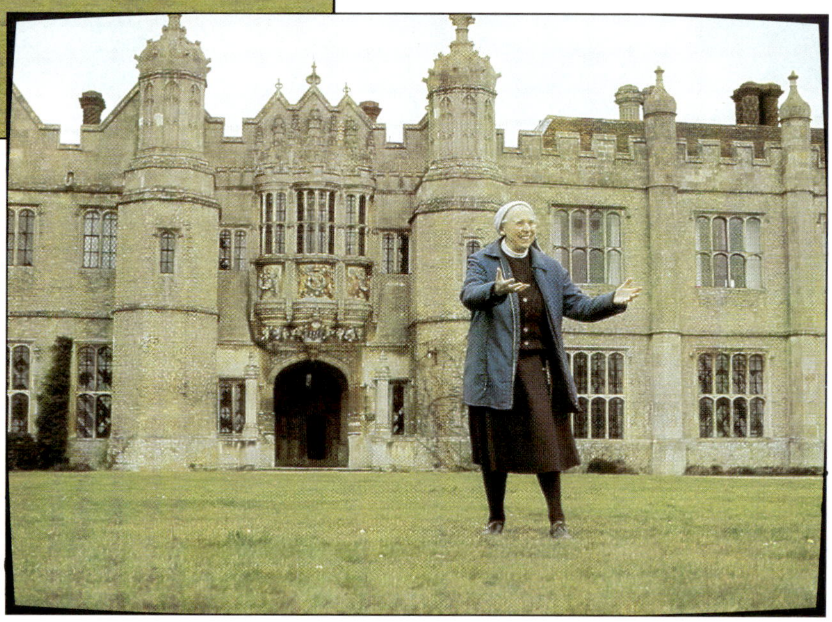

2: *Individual characters can be introduced in long-shot – an ideal way in which to show gesture and body movement.*

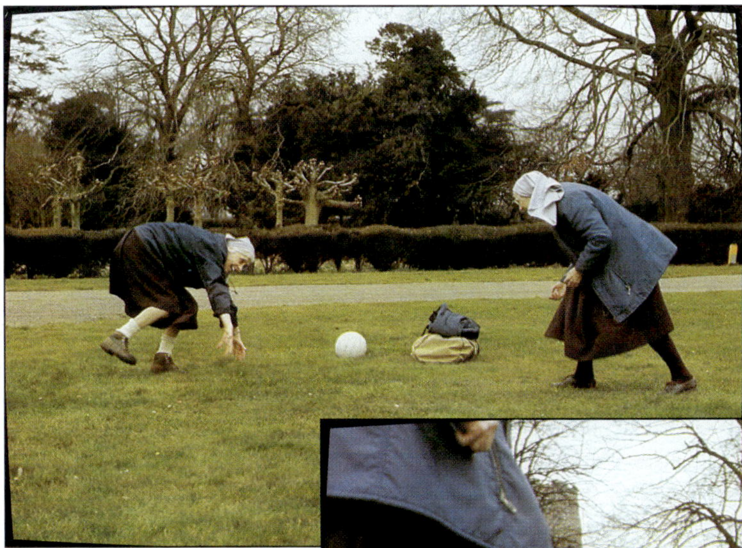

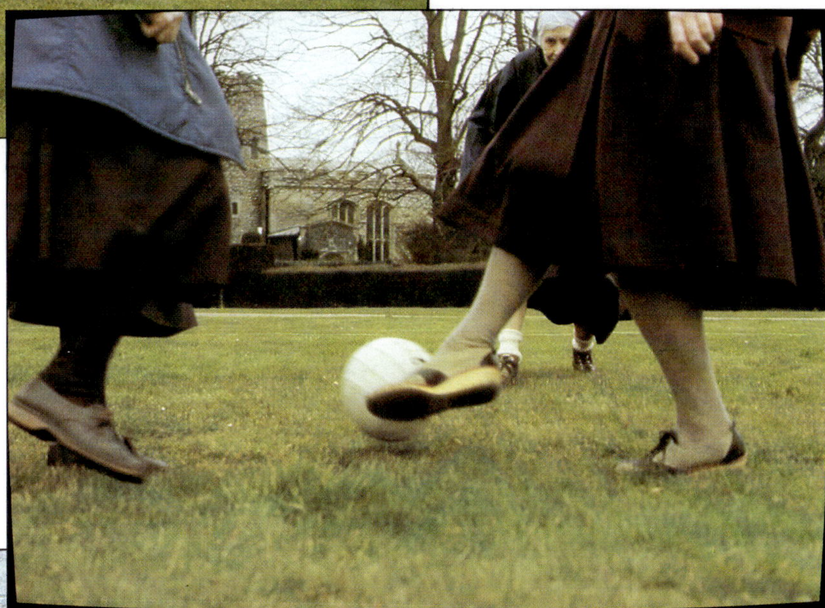

3-4: *With a subject involving action you will have to be prepared to move the camera and follow the subject – as well as occasionally zooming in for close-ups of details.*

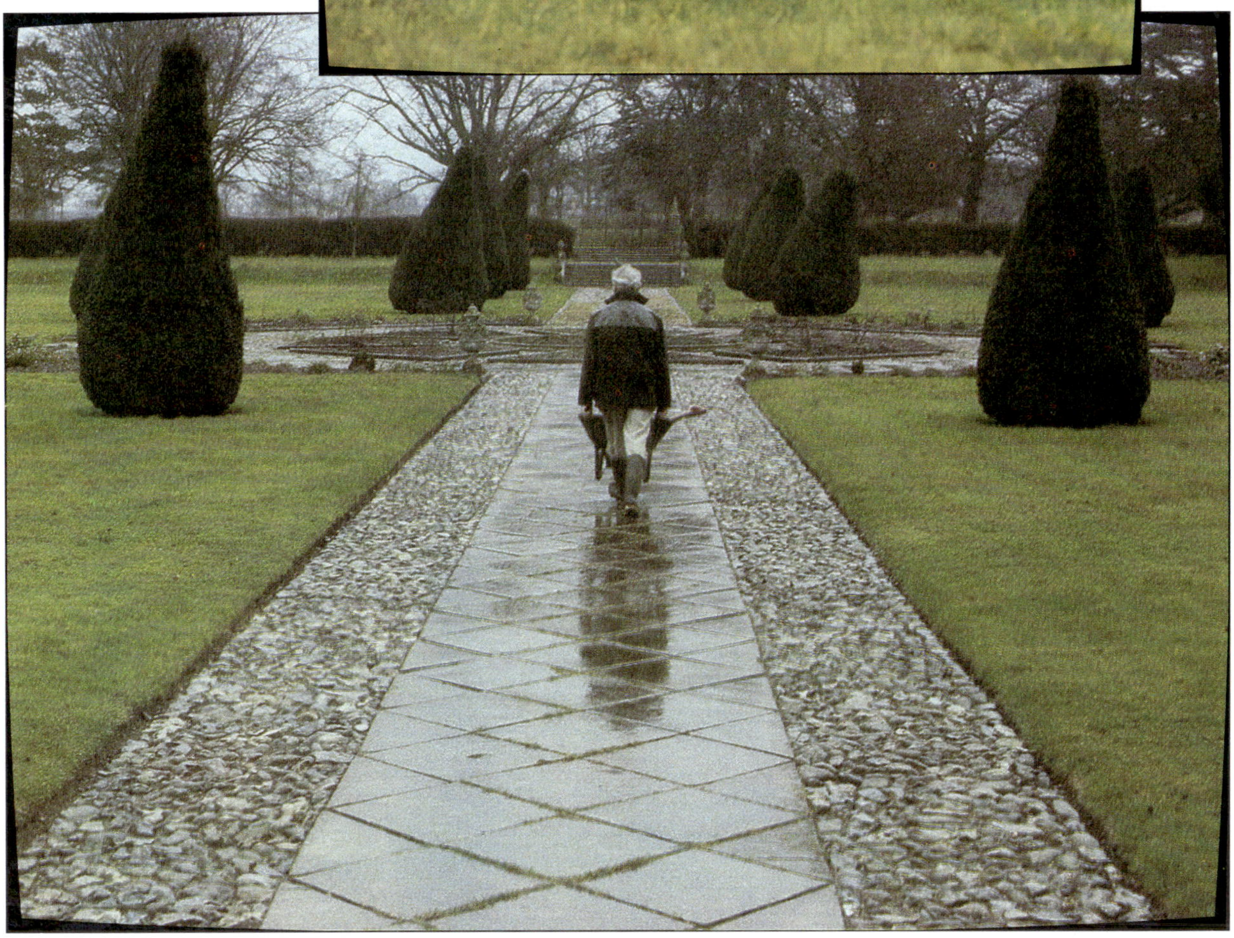

5: *From close-up to long shot: as the gardener walks into the distance the shot lengthens before your eyes. This is a type of episode that can be used to end a sequence effectively.*

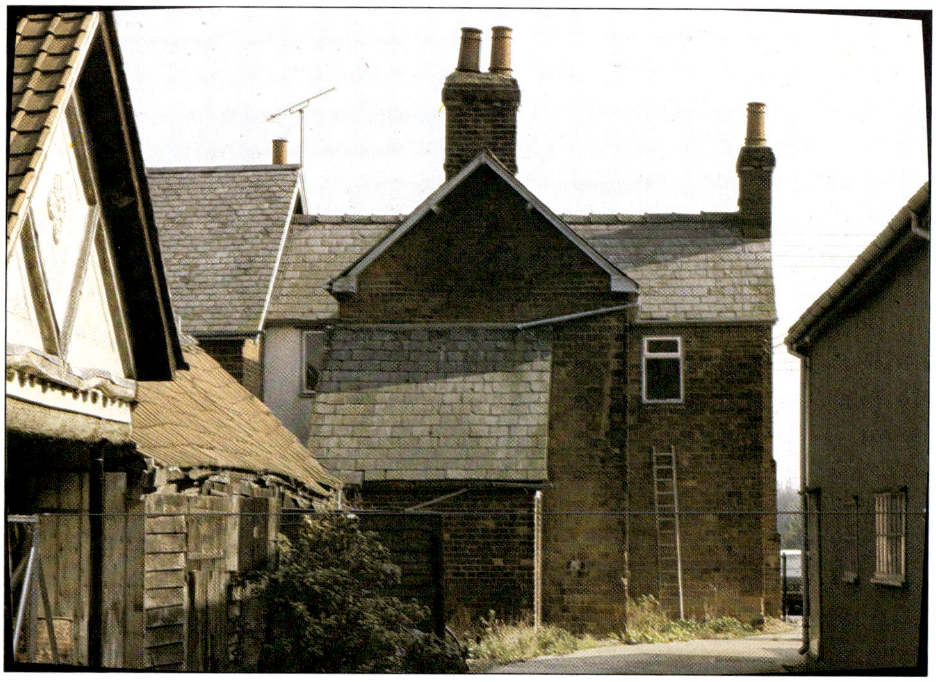

1: *The scene is set as the camera pans across this unassuming backyard and comes to rest on the rope itself. The shot is held just long enough to stimulate the viewer's curiosity about what is going to happen.*

OBTAINING COVERAGE

Before beginning any video project you should work out exactly what you want to achieve. Consider this example of a video showing a tightrope walker in action.

The first point is to show where the performance is happening. And what is that building in the background – is it a barn or a house? Is the performer approaching through empty streets to practice? Or is he passing excited children, queuing early for his performance? Filming, like writing, is a matter of providing signals, pointing your viewers in the right direction. You must also satisfy them with certain basic information. Hopefully, once hooked, they will stay to the end.

You also need to tell the viewers who your characters are. If the performer has been hired for a children's birthday party you need to make clear which child is having the birthday, and perhaps which of the adults are his parents. If a previously unseen character appears three quarters of the way through the tape, the audience will wonder who it is.

Next, consider the performance itself. Do you

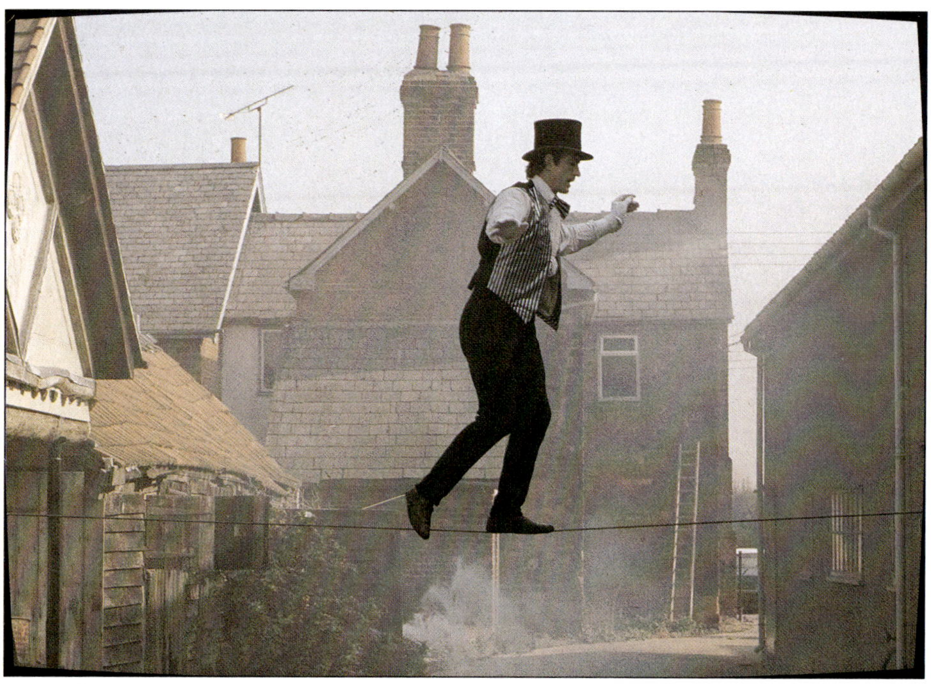

2: *The next shot reveals the tightrope walker in action. At this point there is enough interest to keep the same camera position.*

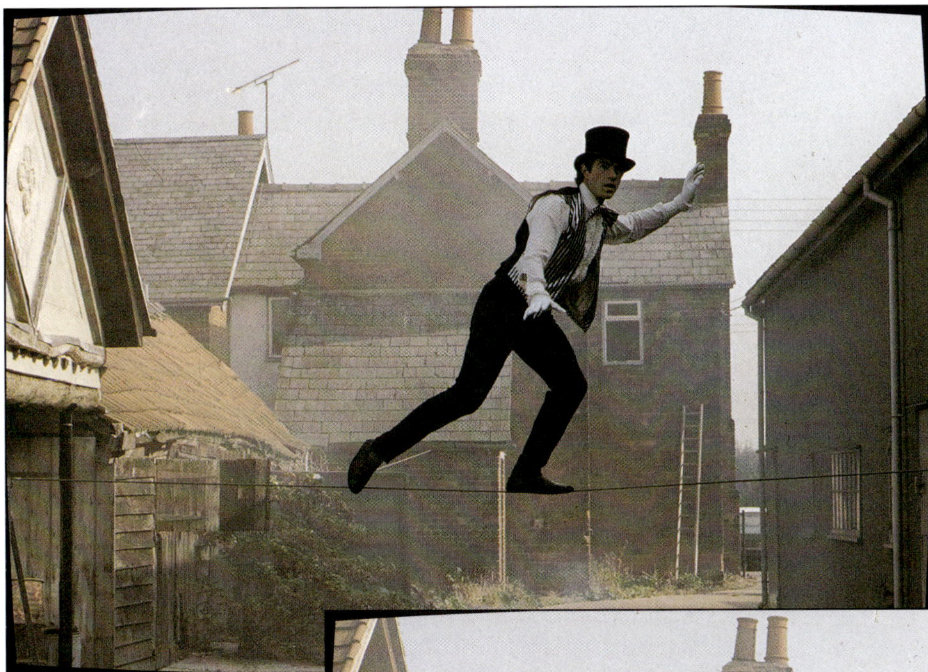

3: *The tension builds up as the performer reaches halfway – will he make it across the rope?*

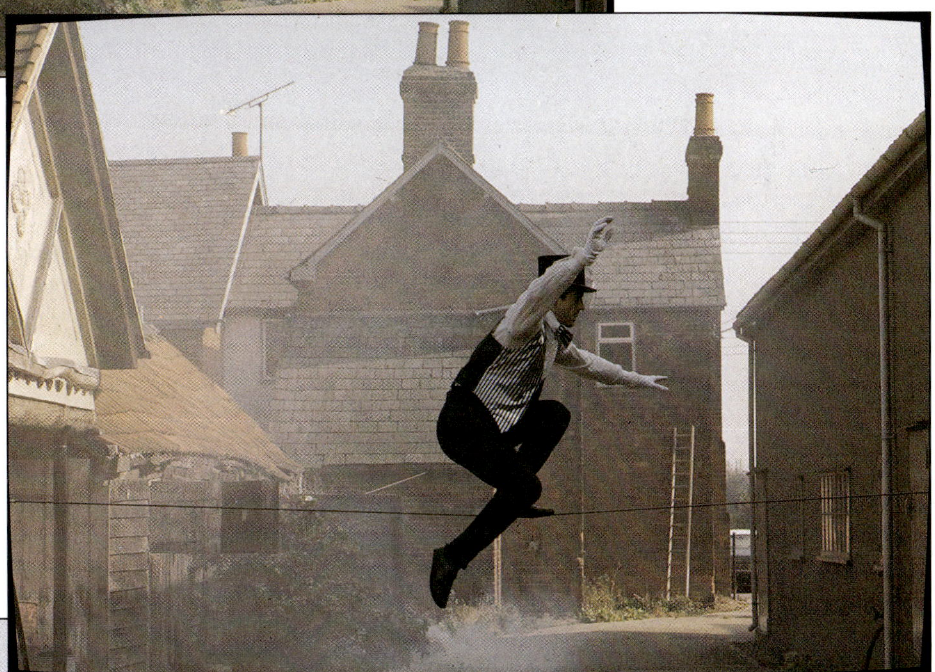

4: *There is a temptation to zoom in as the tightrope walker loses his footing – but this would be a mistake because if we could not see the space around him we would miss the sense of danger.*

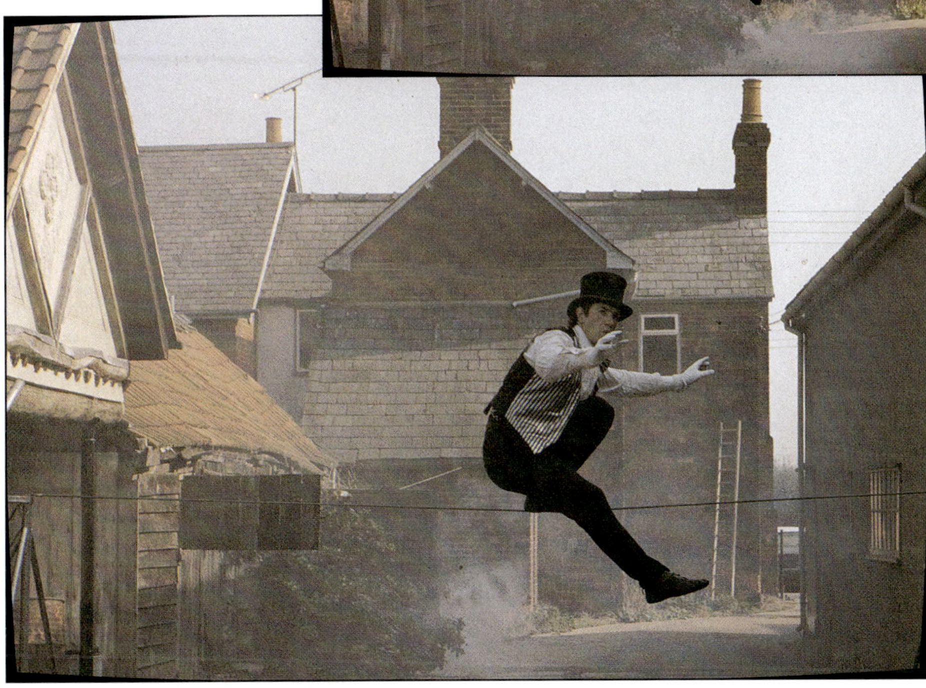

5: *The same position is held as the performer regains his balance.*

want to show the performer getting ready or do you want him to make a dramatic entrance? With a tightrope act, the excitement lies with the performer balancing on the wire. Close-up shots of his feet will convey how precarious is his position, but a VLS will also give an indication of the surroundings and how far off the ground he is positioning. At a children's party the range of reactions from delight to fear will be worth including.

By thinking critically about the narrative and asking such questions you will avoid elementary mistakes and convey the full atmosphere of the event. Make a list of scenes and decide how you will treat each one – long-shot, mid-shot or close-up? Having done that, you must then turn to practical considerations, and in particular to the question of whether you intend to edit in-camera.

As far as coverage of the tightrope walker is concerned, the ability to edit after shooting gives you the ability to cut unsuccessful parts.

In this case, a wide-angle shot of a farmyard, showing the performer setting up the wire, would establish the setting and theme of the video. A zoom-in shot (ending as an MS) of the young boy would indicate that he is also an important character in the plot. All of these shots were taken with a tripod-mounted camera.

The actual performance should also be rehearsed and shot from a tripod, although the camera would need to be repositioned. A good impression of the act calls upon a very long-shot, long-shot, mid-shot, and big close-ups of the performer's face, hands and feet. Since this is a private performance, the tightrope walker could be persuaded to repeat the act a number of times while each separate shot is set up, rehearsed and then recorded.

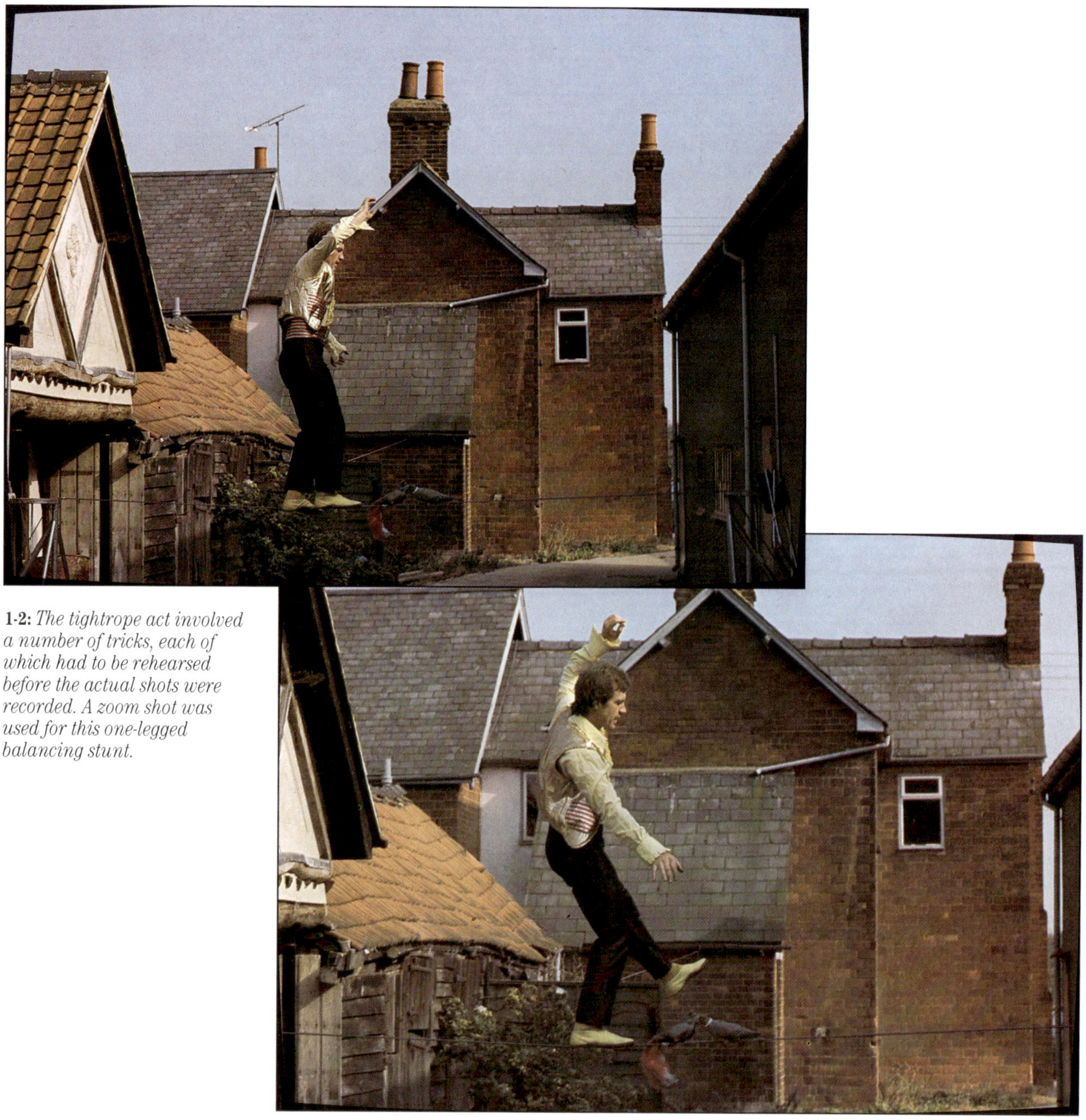

1-2: *The tightrope act involved a number of tricks, each of which had to be rehearsed before the actual shots were recorded. A zoom shot was used for this one-legged balancing stunt.*

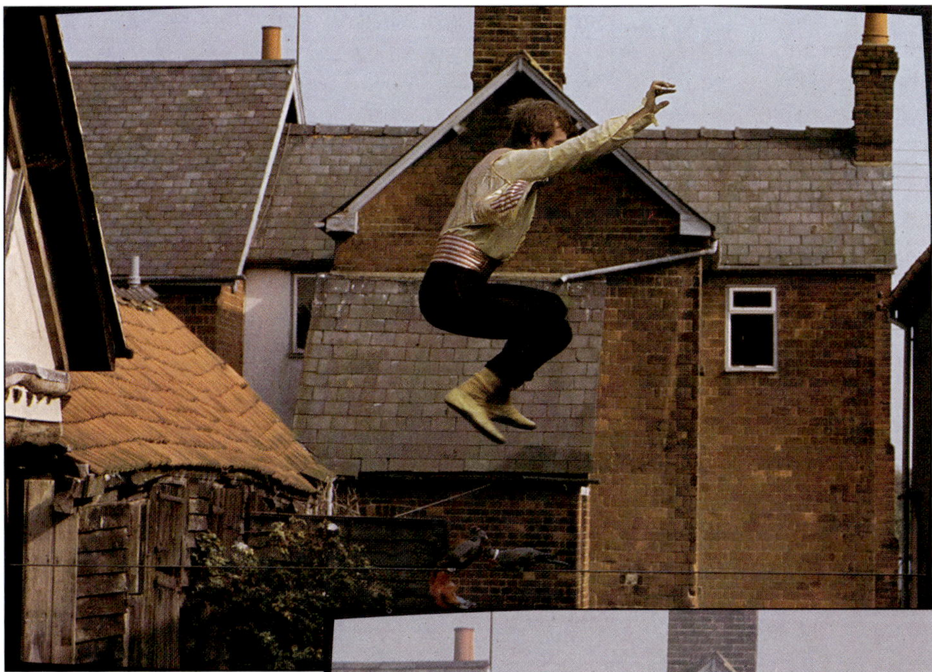

3: *The jump is the most spectacular stunt in the act. From the video point of view the challange here was to get the framing right – too close, and the performer would leave the frame, too distant, and the jump would seem insignificent.*

4: *The sequence continues with the tightrope walker repositioning himself after the jump.*

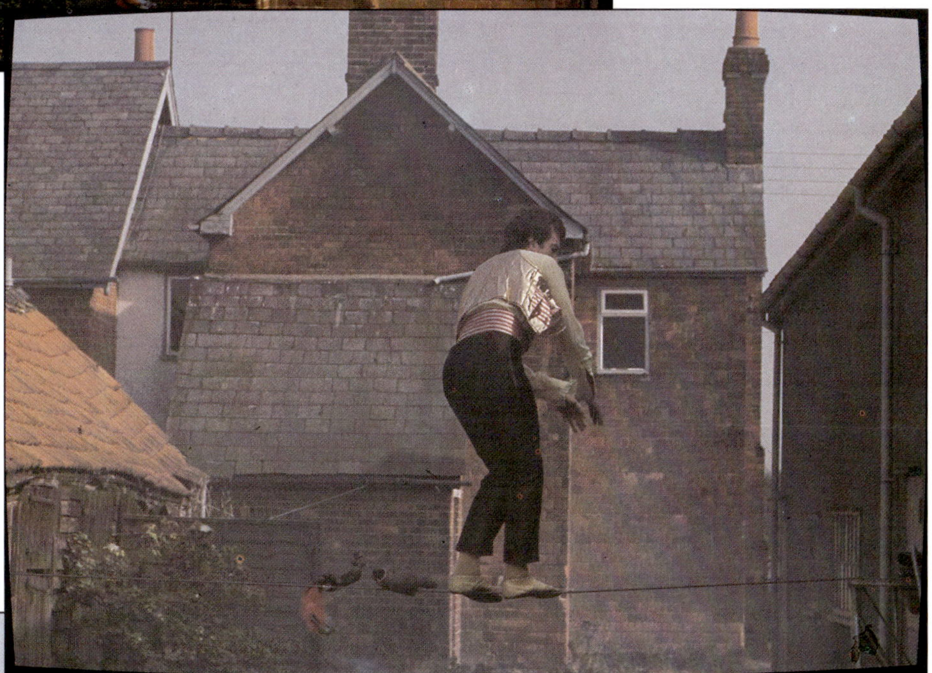

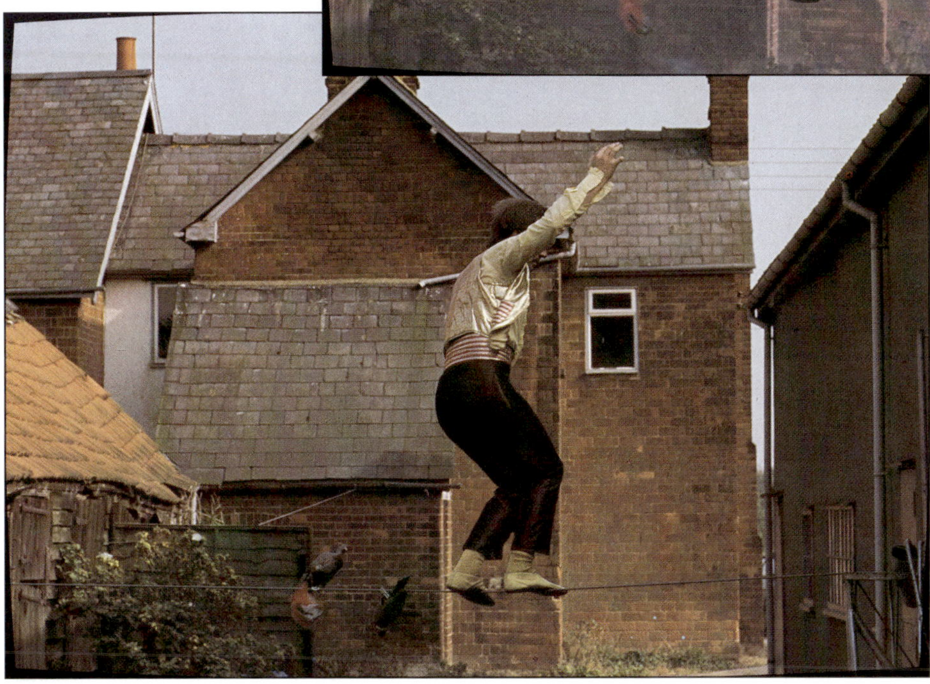

5: *In the final shot before he jumps down to take a bow, he has regained his balance and his poise once more.*

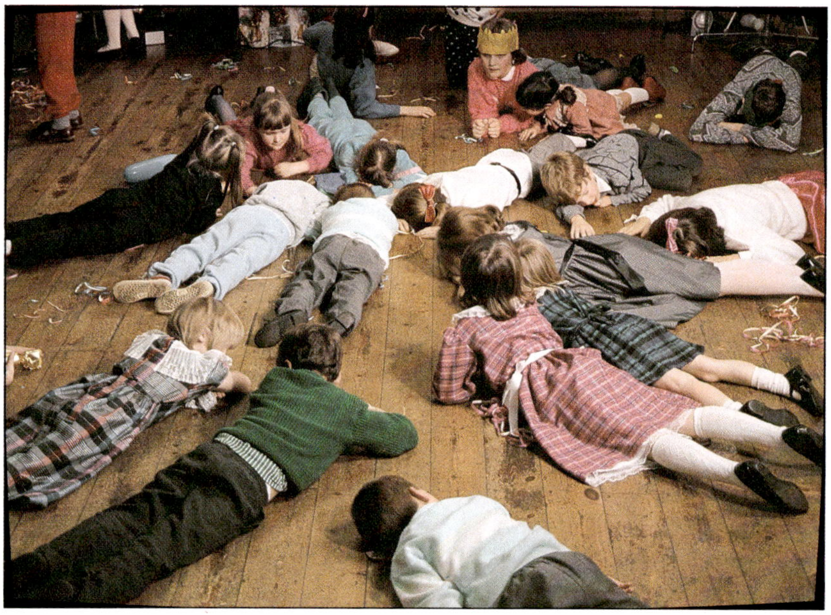

1: *A high-angle shot of this game at a children's party gives a sense of the whole scene. It could be complemented by low-angle shots giving the 'child's-eye view' of the situation.*

CAMERA ANGLES

The 'normal' position for the camera when shooting is at eye level, pointing straight ahead. Such a shot maintains the illusion that everything on screen is seen as the viewer would find it in 'real life'. But shoot from a high or low angle and a completely different effect is conveyed.

Low-angle shots have a number of uses. Most obviously they can be used to convey the point of view of one of the subjects in the video – that of a child, for example, or of someone lying in the grass. In the video of the tightrope walker, the low-angle shot exaggerates the height of the wire above ground and adds to the drama. But in other cases a low-angle shot conveys impressions of submission and authority.

The cliché 'looking up to someone' conveys a truth about the way human beings see one another. That is why executives often make sure that their chair is just a little higher than any other in the office. And it takes only a relatively small deviation from the horizontal to convey this effect of dominance in video, so check that you are not unintentionally doing so. High-angle shots have the opposite effect, placing the viewer in a position of authority, looking down on the subject.

Both high- and low-angle shots, especially when taken with the wide-angle end of the lens, can create a sense of distortion and threat. Shots with a distorted perspective, pointing up the side of a tall building from directly beneath, for example, can convey the point of view of an unseen intruder.

While these shots undoubtedly add visual variety and excitement to your videos, it is dangerous to overuse them, or to use high- and low- angle shots in an inappropriate context.

Camera moves

A pan is the sideways movement of a camera from a fixed position. It can be used to reveal more of the surroundings of a given location, or to follow the movements of a character. Like all camera movements, the pan should be executed slowly and deliberately, giving the audience time to assimilate the changing image.

A tilt is a 'pan' executed in the vertical plane, and may be used to reveal detail in locations and buildings – a tilt shot up the side of a building, for example, might be used to draw attention to a particular window, or to imply that someone who has just entered is climbing the stairs.

Both pan and tilt shots can be combined with the zoom. For example, you could have a pan shot of someone walking towards the camera at an angle, and gradually zoom in on the subject. Such a shot should be rehearsed beforehand and you should use the manual or power zoom.

The rule for both pan and tilt shots, whether combined with zoom or not, is to plan for the end of the shoot. The audience expects something to be revealed, but if the expectation is unfulfilled the shot loses its motivation.

In addition to these shots are those taken when the camera moves with the action. These are tracking, crabbing and craning shots. Tracking involves moving alongside a moving subject, with the consequent problem, for the home video-maker at least, of camera shake. Crabbing is a movement around the subject in an arc. It is an effective shot giving the viewer a three-dimensional view of the subject and his or her surroundings. Craning means moving above and over the top of the subject.

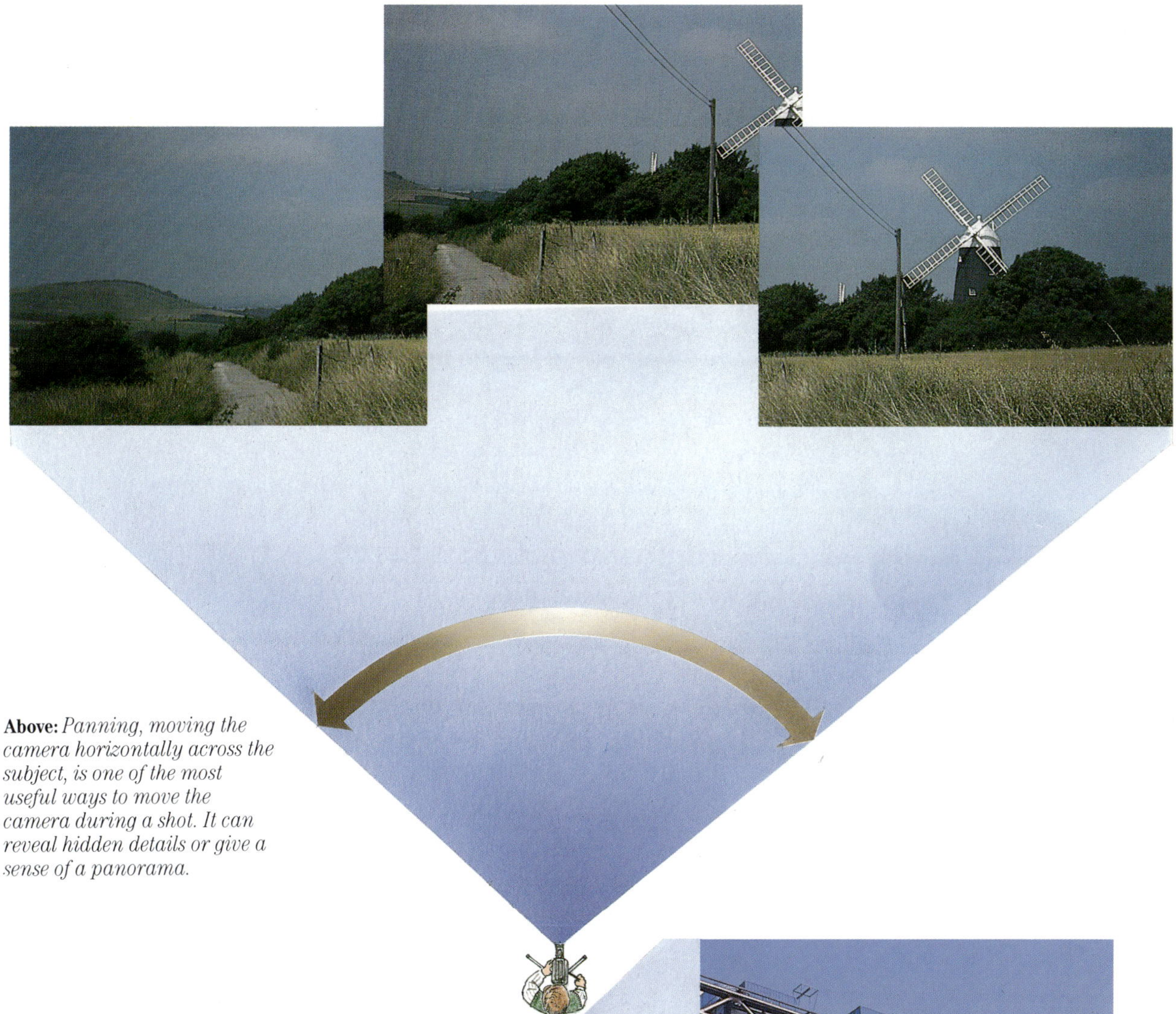

Above: *Panning, moving the camera horizontally across the subject, is one of the most useful ways to move the camera during a shot. It can reveal hidden details or give a sense of a panorama.*

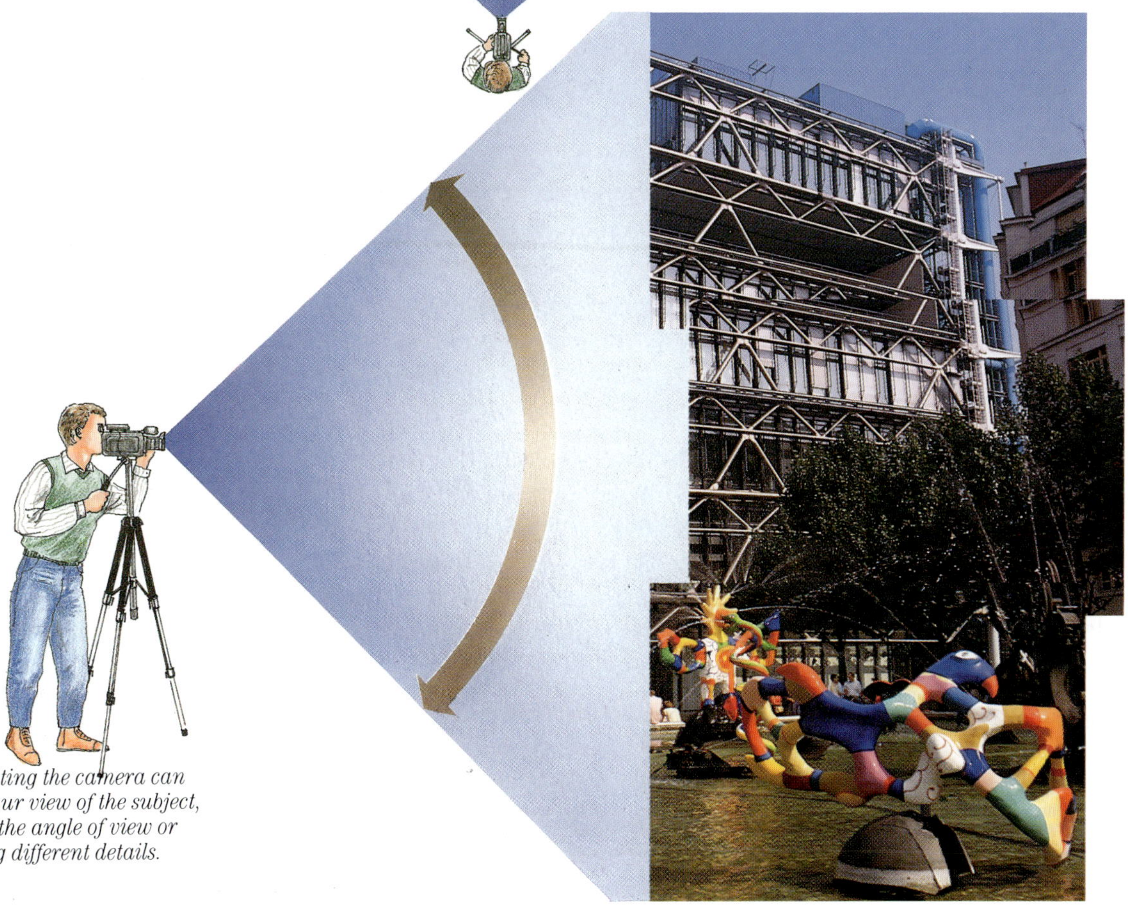

Right: *Tilting the camera can change our view of the subject, altering the angle of view or revealing different details.*

The television has made us extremely familiar with a huge variety of moving images. Scenes covering everything from famine to sporting triumphs are fed into millions of homes each day. The result is that people have high expectations about the quality of moving pictures, and these expectations are the ones by which your home video will be measured.

At the simplest level, this means your screen subject should not wobble about. It also means that everything you show must be part of the narrative – if you move a shot from a building to a person there must be a good reason for doing so. If you don't have one the viewers will supply their own, which may well result in dreadful confusions. And most importantly, the images you show should reveal a single viewpoint, be readily accessible, and enable the audience to forget that the film is an artificial construct. At least half the art in making good videos involves producing a seamless whole. The audience should be aware of the story and not your techniques. The more sophisticated your videos, the better you should be at hiding your art, no matter how sophisticated it is.

You should also remember that audiences expect events to happen in a particular order and in a certain way. This is especially likely if they are watching coverage of something with which they are familiar – like the wedding featured here. If so, you should aim for the best balance of the predictable and unusual in your coverage. In this way you will satisfy the people who want the obvious shots and sequences, while preventing the boredom of those who want something more.

AUDIENCE EXPECTATIONS

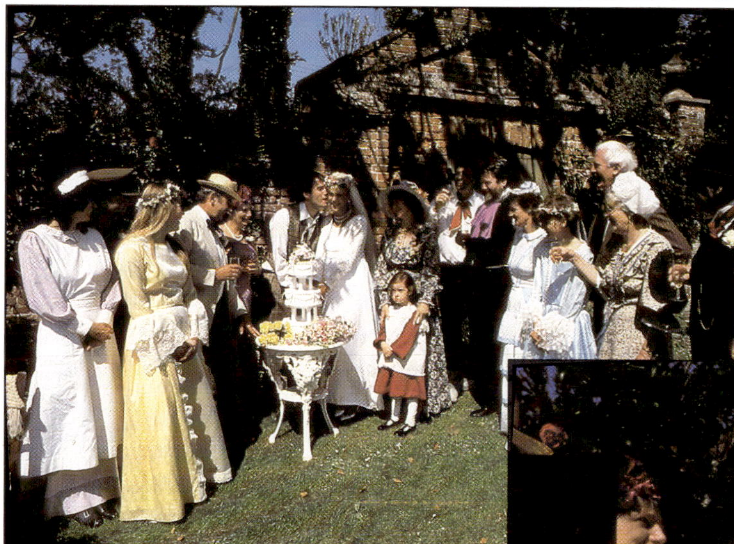

1: *A favourite scene at most weddings is the cutting of the cake. Start with a broad establishing shot of the whole gathering before moving in to record the expected close-up of the bride and groom.*

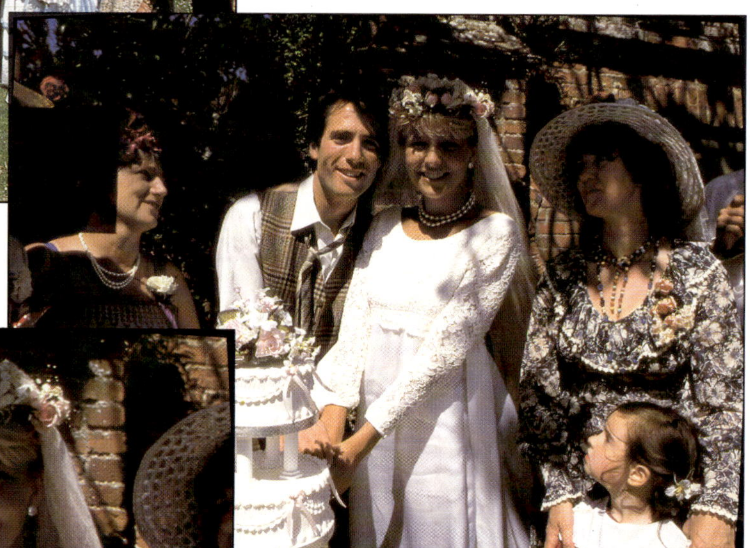

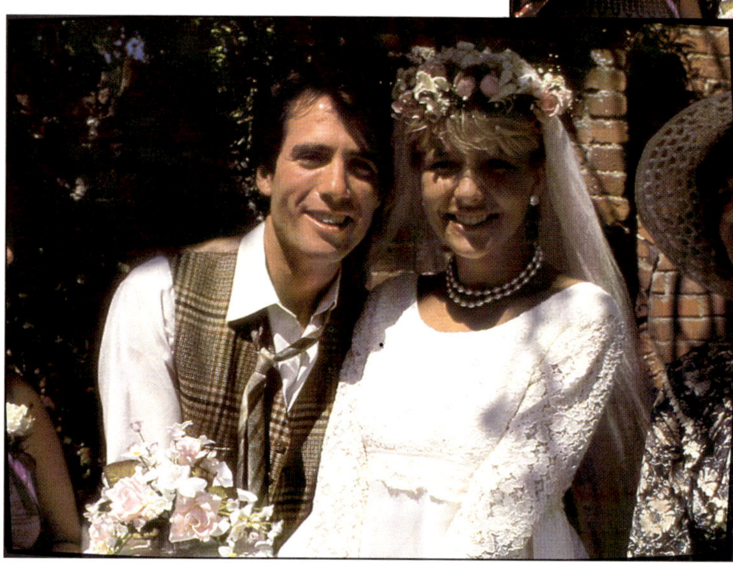

2-3: *At the beginning of the shot, some of the detail around the couple has been kept in the frame, so that we can identify the scene. The camera has then zoomed in to record the couple's smiling faces.*

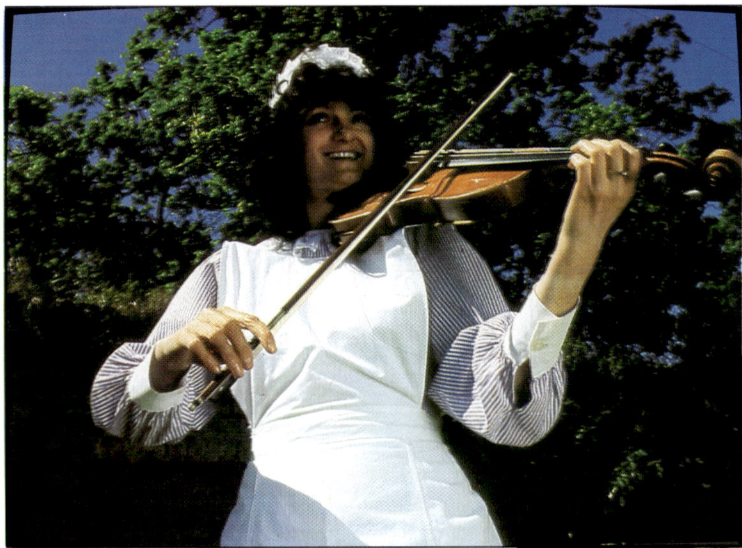

4-5: *In this sequence of merrymaking at the wedding reception, mid-shots and close-ups alternate with long-shots showing the whole scene. After seeing the girl playing the violin, the audience expects to see the people listening to her.*

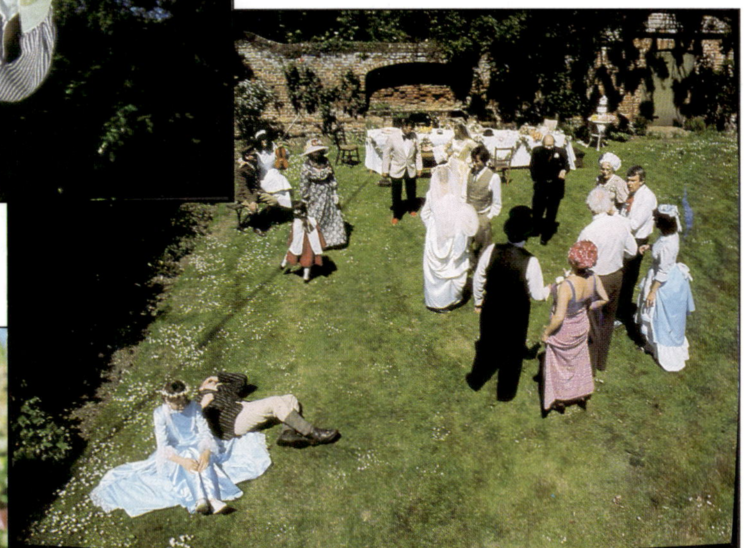

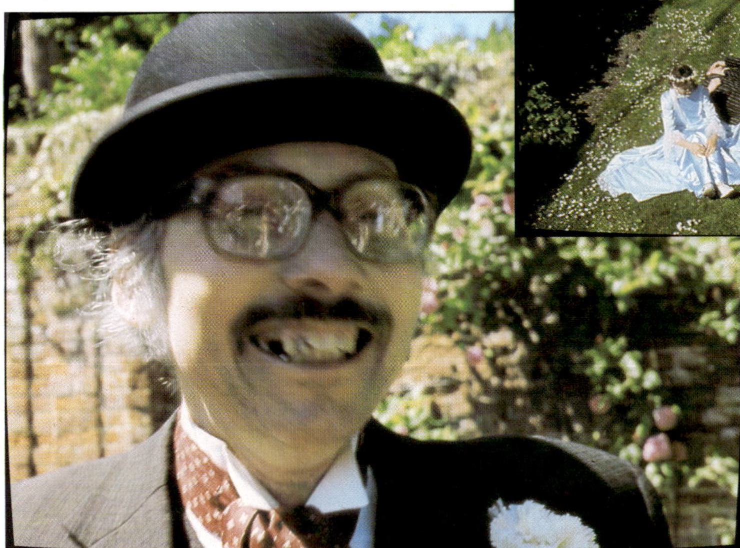

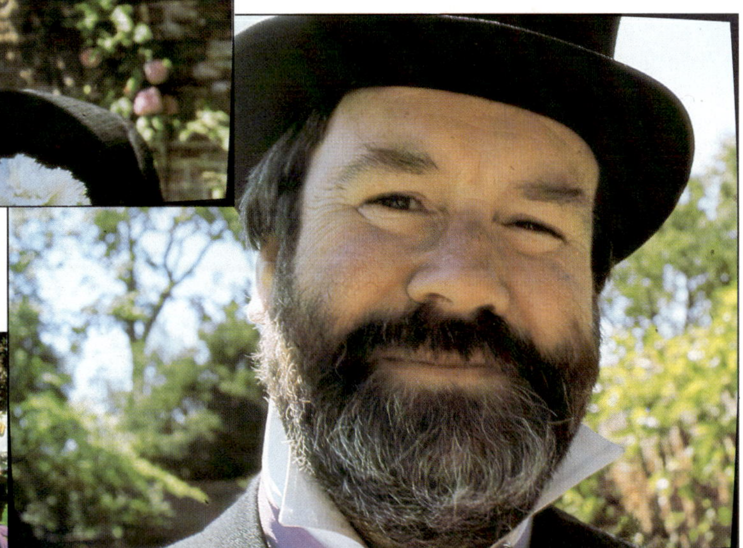

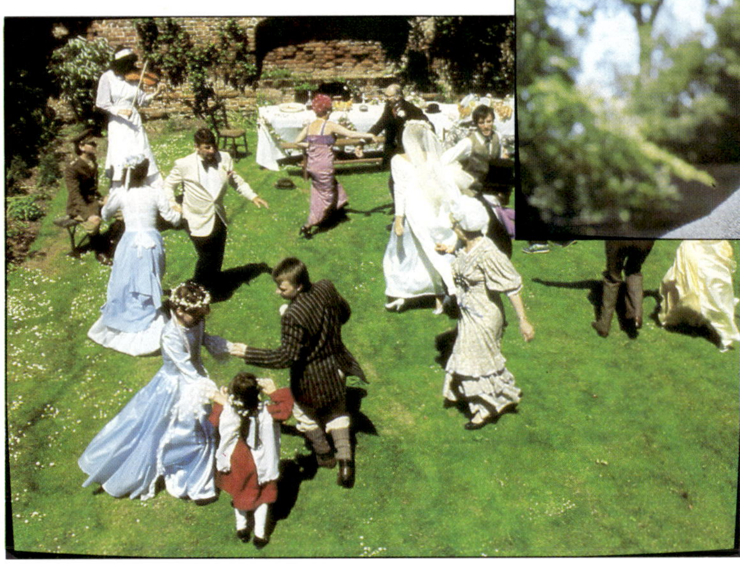

6-8: *The alternate close-ups and long-shots continue, with the general mood of merriment mirrored in the smiling faces of the guests. This type of sequence requires careful planning to allow you to get from one position to another, but it is worth the effort.*

Modern camcorders are able to produce pictures under very poor lighting conditions. Manufacturers often quote one lux as the minimum light level for many of today's models, and this is the equivalent of candlelight. This is of course a very low level of illumination indeed and while few people actually shoot video by candlelight, one would imagine that there should be no problem with filming in average domestic interiors, which are far more brightly lit – in fact probably at least ten times as bright.

Even so, compared with daylight, domestic interiors are dimly illuminated. For example, the figure on sunny days can be as high as 30,000 lux. So the video camera has to cope with a very wide range of lighting conditions. In addition to this, there are colour variations between indoor and outdoor lighting conditions. The human eye is very good at compensating for this great range of conditions; the video camera, on the other hand, can only operate well over a comparatively narrow range. True enough, you can produce pictures of a kind at 100 or even 20 lux. But for crisp, clear, watchable video, most machines need a level of at least 1,000 lux – in fact 2,000 lux is a better safe working standard.

The problem is not simply that the camera's image sensor is not so sensitive at low light levels. Where illumination is not very directional, the modelling of the subject is not likely to be very satisfactory, meaning that the different planes in the picture will seem poorly differentiated.

Artificial light

For all these reasons, professional video-makers take care to light their subjects with meticulous attention to subject modelling and overall contrast. To meet this need, a wide variety of lighting units of varying powers and beam-spreads have been de-

LIGHTING UNITS

SAFETY

Floodlights consume a great deal of electrical power – around four amps for every 1,000 watts of light. It is therefore important to check that you are limiting the lighting to your available power supply. You should spread the load over as many different circuits as possible, and do not connect two lamps to a single socket.

Keep people away from the lamp units – they get hot, especially if they have metal barn doors. Do not handle hot lamps – allow them to cool before removing them from the units.

When choosing high-intensity quartz-halogen lamp units, look for those fitted with a diffuser. This will provide some safety should a bulb explode. This is a rare event but it sometimes happens.

Keep electrical supply cables in good condition and securely connected to plugs and sockets. Do not allow them to trail over the working area and do not let them get wet.

Uncoil cables from storage drums before connecting them to the power supply.

If a fuse blows, make sure you find the cause – do not simply replace the fuse and wait for it to happen again.

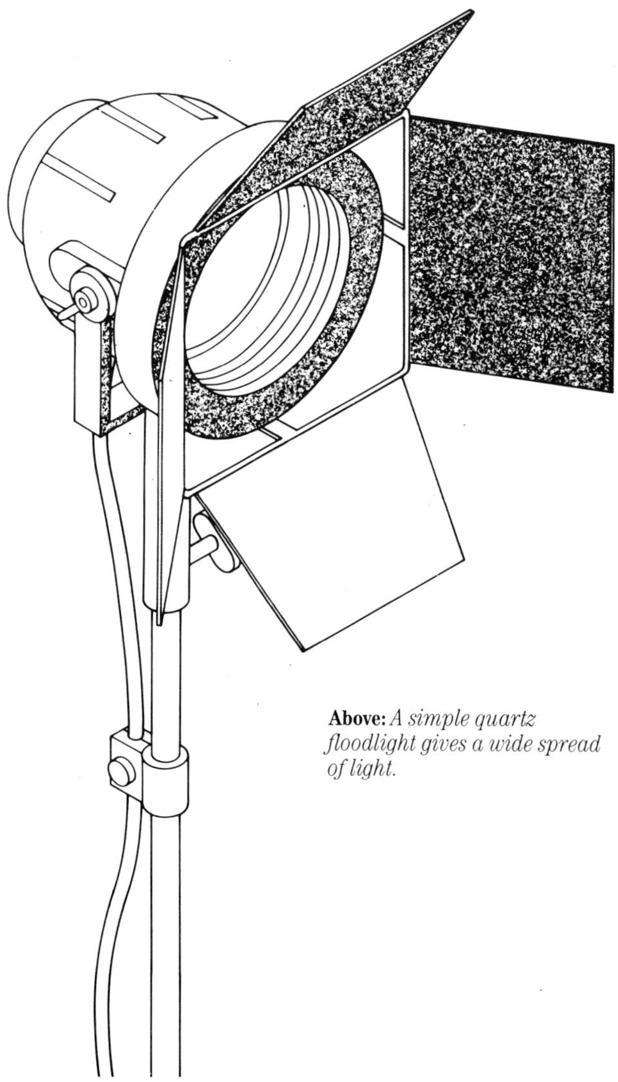

Above: *A simple quartz floodlight gives a wide spread of light.*

veloped, and cheaper versions of these costly units have also become available for amateur use.

The earliest form of high-intensity photographic lighting was provided by 'photoflood' bulbs in spun aluminium parabolic reflectors. These are essentially ordinary tungsten bulbs which are overrun and therefore have a limited life. (Typical life-spans are three hours for a 275 watt bulb and six hours for a 500 watt type.)

The more recent high-efficiency halogen quartz lamps are usually rated at 1,000 watts per lamp. They come in complete units which generally incorporate a facility for fan cooling; this means that they can be run for long periods without overheating. The lamps take the form of either bulbs or bars, and the built-in reflectors are either dish-shaped or rectangular to suit the two forms of lamp. The more expensive models include low-power switching for increased lamp life when setting up, and they also make provision for the insertion of diffusion gauges and filters of various kinds in a frame spaced away from the front of the lamp. This enables the light to be softened for fill-in and colour-corrected to match daylight. Some floodlights can be focused down to a narrow beam for use as spotlights. This is a useful extra facility, as it makes for more flexible lighting.

Lower-power portable mains-operated lighting units are also available, for mobile use. Some of the units can be hand-held; those of smaller wattage can be mounted on the top of the camcorder, connected to the accessory shoe. For complete mobility, self-contained battery-operated units can be obtained. These contain a lamp unit, rechargeable battery, and the mains charger.

Controlling the light

Reflectors also have a useful part to play in video lighting. They are particularly useful for filling in shadow areas by reflecting some of the illumination from the key light. Using a reflector in this way can be a workable substitute for a second lamp.

Another useful method of controlling light direction is to use barn doors. These are the movable flaps attached to most modern video lights.

Below: *A quartz floodlight, fitted with a diffuser. This is a fan-cooled unit that can be switched to low power for setting up.*

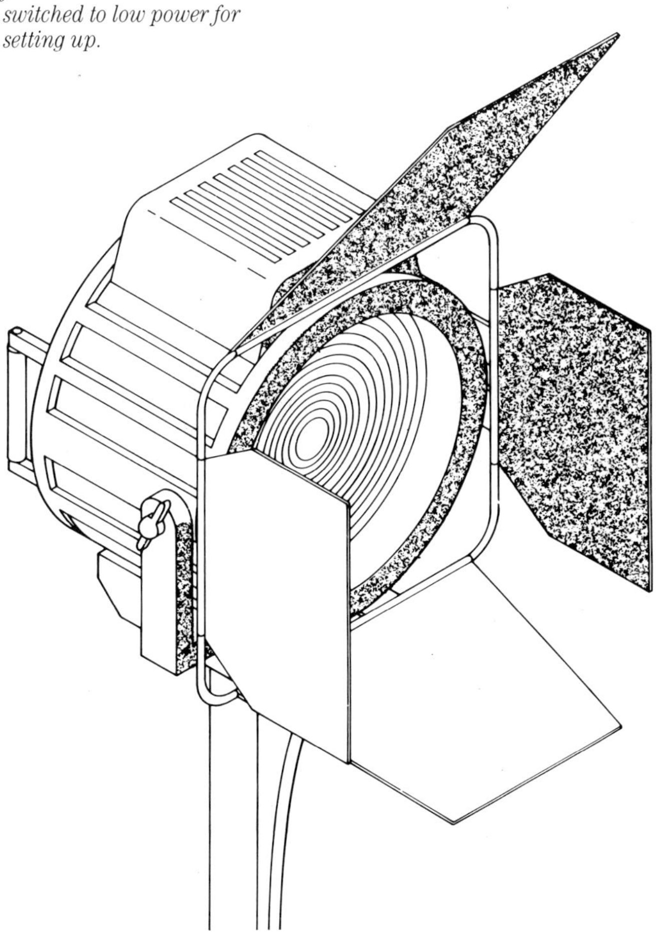

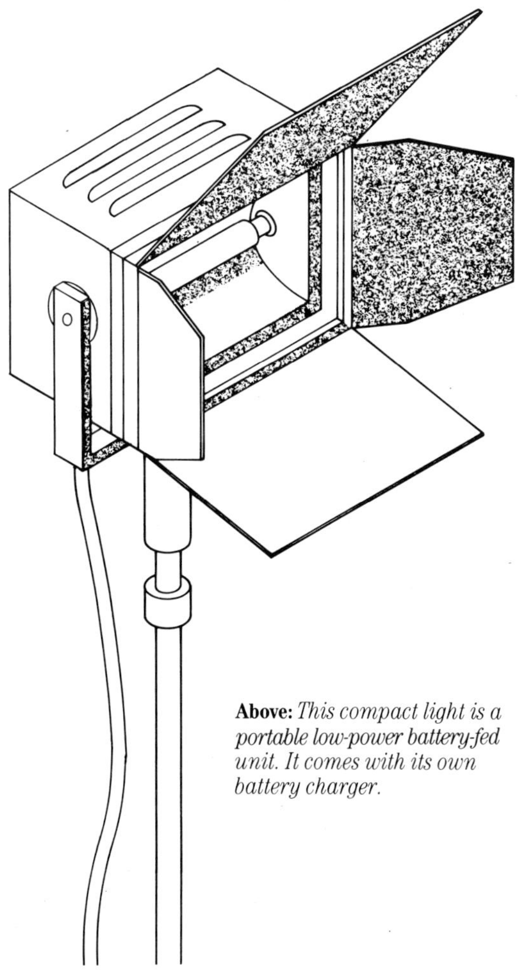

Above: *This compact light is a portable low-power battery-fed unit. It comes with its own battery charger.*

LIGHTING SET-UPS

Before you invest in a video lighting system, experiment with the lighting that exists in your home. You will find that domestic lamps, though hardly ideal, will help you to supplement available light, filling in shadows and brightening up the picture generally. Trying different lights and using them in different positions will also be a good preparation for creating your own set-ups with true video lamps.

The sun gun

The most basic of video lighting set-ups is illumination from a single lamp. Its most common application is to be found in the 'sun-gun', so-called because it is either used to boost poor daylight or employed at night to make filming possible in what are essentially 'newsreel' situations. Using a sun-gun is basically a one-man professional technique. A battery-operated lamp unit is mounted on top of the camcorder, thus providing a fully portable light which is always aimed straight at the subject. While it has its uses in amateur video, this type of single-lamp frontal lighting is not very pleasing aesthetically – it produces a harsh effect with very little modelling. But it does provide a useful last resort if you are recording material in poor light and do not have the time or the assistance to create a more elaborate set-up.

It is possible to improve the modelling, to give more of an idea of the subject's three-dimensional form, by detaching the lamp and getting an assistant to angle it towards the subject from one side. This can be a good technique for informal shots such as outdoor parties and beach scenes at night, but it is not an acceptable alternative to properly balanced lighting using a number of separate lamps positioned around the subject in a controlled set-up like a proper studio.

Multi lamp set-ups

Techniques using multi-lamp set-ups have become established over the years as a means of providing balanced lighting in a studio-type environment. These are professional techniques, but they are easily adapted to amateur use, the 'studio' being replaced by a domestic interior or some other indoor setting where electrical power is available and the conditions for the shoot have been planned ahead and are in your full control.

A typical application of multi lamp set-ups is the video interview. The scene might be a room in which two people are having a formal discussion. The interviewer is off-camera and the camcorder is being aimed at the main subject, the interviewee, who is sitting in an easy chair. The subject is lit by a main light, known to video-makers as a 'key light', which is aimed from alongside the camcorder. This light alone would produce a strong shadow down one side of the subject's face, so this effect is softened by diffused light coming from a 'fill-light', placed on the other side of the camcorder. A third lamp can be used to separate the subject from the background. This lamp is usually a spot, and should be aimed from behind the subject's head, to illuminate the hair and give a halo effect. The subject should now be well illuminated, but there may be distracting shadows in the background. A fourth lamp can be brought in to light the background and eliminate any unwanted shadows. Alternatively, if only three lights are available or time is short, the key-light and fill-light can be supplemented by a third light aimed at the background, from which some illumination may reflect back towards the subject's head in any case.

Bounced lighting

One problem with the type of multilamp set-up

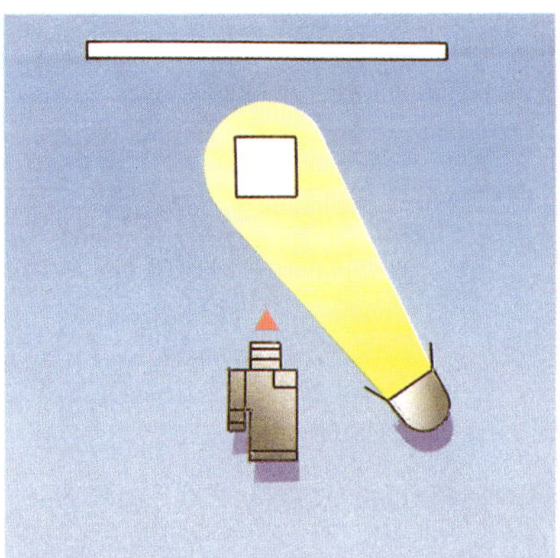

1: *First position the key-light.*

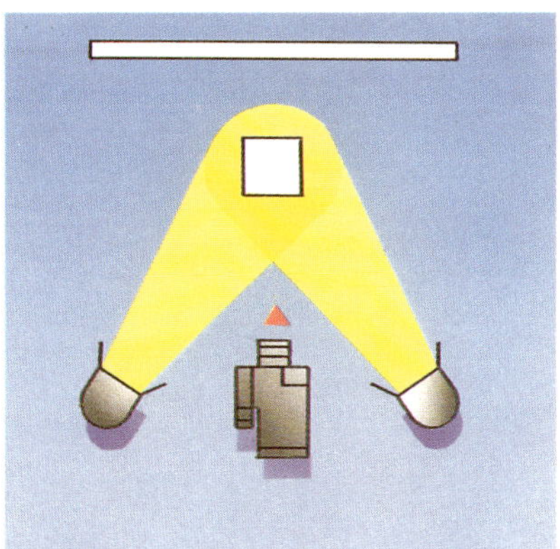

2: *Add the fill-light on the other side.*

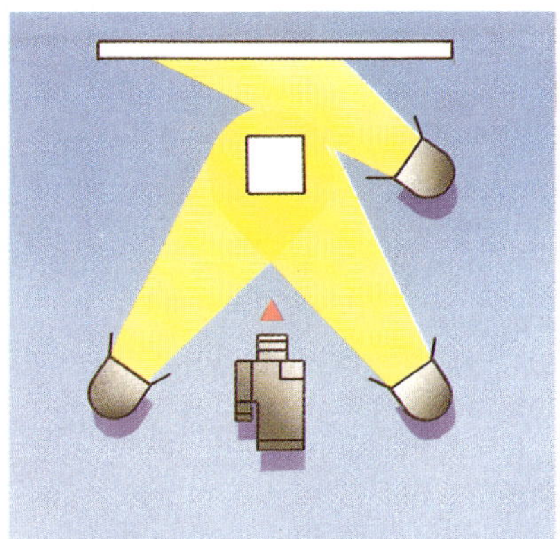

3: *Illuminate the background to cut out shadows.*

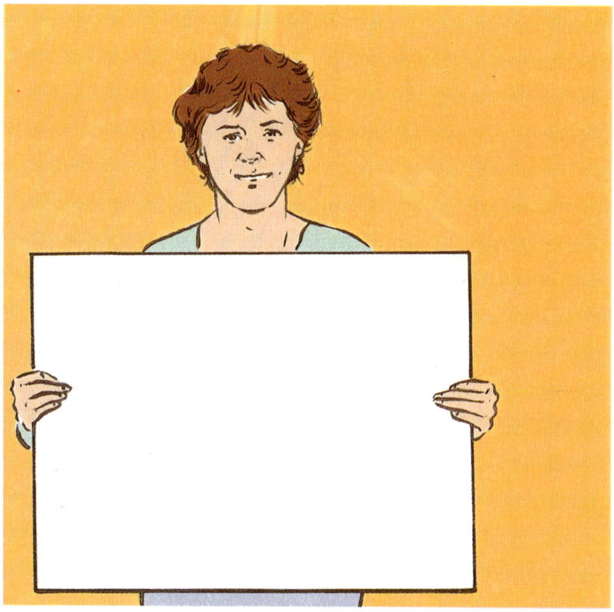

Left: *Although you can buy specially-made reflectors for video and photographic work, you will get results that are just as effective with a piece of white cardboard or hardboard, or a sheet of expanded polystyrene.*

described above is that it works only with a stationary subject – if the subject moves position, the carefully arranged lighting will be rendered useless. Another drawback is that many subjects find the glare from the floodlights unpleasant and difficult to work under. Also, unless the lights are positioned with great care, the results on screen can sometimes appear rather hard and unnatural.

An answer to these problems may be found in bounced lighting. As the name implies, the illumination comes not from a lamp aimed directly at the subject, but from light bounced on to the subject, thus softening the effect and eliminating glare. Bouncing the light also has the effect of distributing it over a wider area, thereby allowing the subject to move around without affecting the lighting balance too much. In practice, the usual technique is to aim the light upwards and to bounce it either off white ceilings and walls or off reflectors made of sheets of expanded polystyrene.

Reflectors

These provide a cheap and easy way of balancing lighting without the need to bring in extra lamps. A particularly useful application is found with a subject lit from the daylight coming through a window. The shadow side of the subject will be too dark, and artificial lighting will be difficult unless you use a lamp that is colour-corrected to match daylight. This is possible by covering the lamp with a special blue filter gel. But it is usually a much easier solution to reflect some daylight back from the window on to the subject's shadow side. Outdoors, reflectors are often used to balance strong sunlighting, or to enhance diffused daylight.

SOME LIGHTING TERMS

Background light Lamp aimed at the background to illuminate it.

Back-light Forward-facing lamp placed behind the subject to illuminate the subject's outline.

Barn-doors Adjustable flags attached to the edge of a lamp's housing to allow the direction and spread of the beam to be changed.

Diffuser Material placed in front of a lamp to soften the beam.

Fill-light Lamp introduced to eliminate unwanted shadows from the subject.

Filter Material placed in front of the lamp to change the nature of the light. The most common are coloured filters, which can be used to correct the colour balance of the lighting or provide special effects.

Flood Lamp providing broad, overall illumination.

Key light The main light in a multi-lamp set-up.

Snoot Conical attachment placed in front of a lamp to narrow the beam width.

Spot Lamp providing a narrow beam of light.

Sound is too often treated as an afterthought, a secondary consideration to getting the images right. But a poor soundtrack will irritate an audience and can easily spoil what is otherwise a successful video. Conversely, a soundtrack of good quality which has been recorded and compiled with a little thought can often help to mask any visual mistakes. Remember that sound is being recorded continuously while you are recording images and that the sound is recorded directly on to the tape alongside or beneath the video images. This means that, although it is possible to edit the sound element of your video recordings, it is far easier to get the sound right at the start, while you are actually recording. The built-in microphone on your camcorder has to be used carefully in order to achieve this. It will probably pick up not only the ambient sound, but also the camera's mechanical noises, the whirr of the zoom motor – and perhaps even the grunts and sighs of the operator as well! Although modern camcorders are better than older models in this respect, all on-board microphones suffer from some of these problems.

Another drawback can be the position of the microphone on the camcorder itself. Some models have the microphone located in the hand-grip. With this type of design it can be quite easy to place one finger on the foam covering of the microphone. This can have the effect of blocking off some of the ambient sound, while the finger's movement can itself cause unwanted noise on the sound track. Some, but not all, camcorders have an ear-piece to monitor the sound entering the camcorder's microphone and you should use this for all but the most casual video work. Better still, use a pair of headphones – and ask a friend to monitor the recorded sound for you if you can.

The problems of working with an on-board microphone can be avoided by plugging in an exterior microphone on a long lead. This has the added advantage of allowing you to get the microphone close in to the source of the sound. But it will mean that you will have to plan your shooting carefully. Although you want the microphone near to the subject, you will almost certainly want it outside the frame, and this can be a problem. Again, you may have to enlist the help of a friend who can hold the microphone above the subject and out of shot.

The quality of the sound that you record depends very much upon the environment. Before you begin recording do check that any electrical appliances are turned off. Hard, flat surfaces tend to reflect sound too strongly, resulting in reverberation – an unwelcome 'booming' quality to the sound. Muffling walls and floors with rugs and blankets can overcome this problem. Alternatively, sound reflectors can be used to direct sound to the microphone. Sheets of hardboard (smooth side facing the microphone) can lift sound when it is too muffled or low. A particular drawback with low sound, when recording with the on-camera microphone, is that some models automatically boost the signal, so that unwanted noise and recorder rumble increases. A home-made boom microphone constructed with a broom handle often enables you to get closer to the

BASIC SOUND

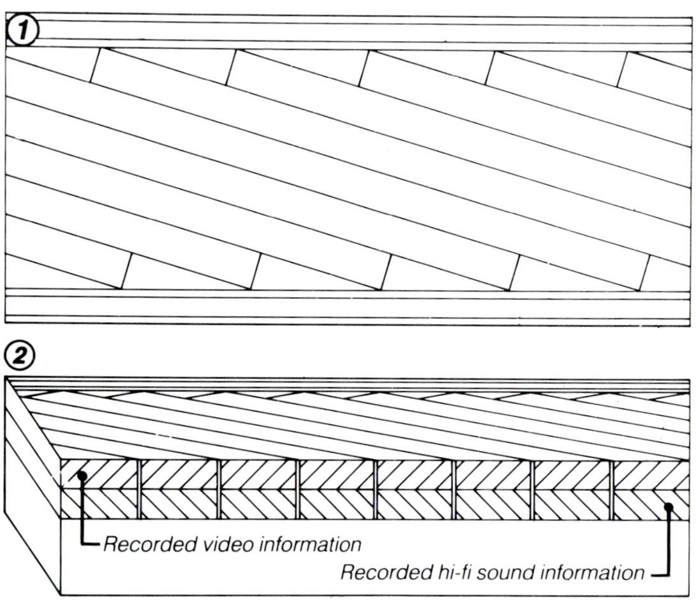

1: *Regular sound track recorded along the edge of the tape.*
2: *Hi-fi sound track recorded underneath the video signal.*

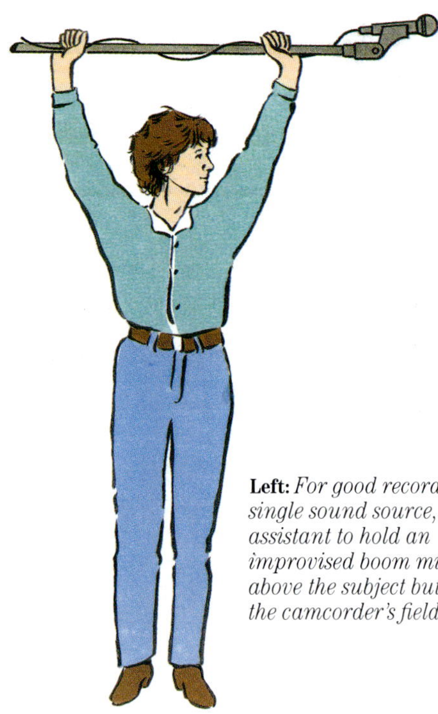

Left: *For good recording of a single sound source, ask an assistant to hold an improvised boom microphone above the subject but outside the camcorder's field of view.*

second source, and it is also worthwhile placing a cardboard cone around the microphone to cut out unwanted sounds.

On-camera and extension microphones can be either omnidirectional or unidirectional. An omnidirectional microphone picks up sounds from all around. As such, it is valuable for recording the overall sound of the scene you are filming. A unidirectional microphone picks up sound in an arc of about 180 degrees. Its advantage is that sounds behind the camera (and the sound of the camera itself) are effectively screencd off. A unidirectional microphone is particularly useful for recording informal group shots – friends at a dinner party for example. Even more directional is the rifle microphone which is superdirectional. Its pick-up cone allows you to match the sound to close-up shots and isolate individuals from groups, catching snatches of conversation, for example. As such, it is probably the most useful auxillary microphone you can buy.

With the advent of television sets that provide stereo sound, along with hi-fi video recorders, video sound tracks in stereo are becoming increasingly popular. There are a number of cameras that can record in stereo. They have two microphone sockets, one for the left channel and one for the right, and the success of the recording will depend to a large extent on where you position the microphones connected to these. Simply mounting them on the camera will only duplicate the problems associated with on-camera mono microphones. The stereo effect will also be destroyed when you pan the camera. So it is far better to mount them on separate stands which remain in the same place when you are moving the camera. Exactly where you place the stands will depend on the subject you are recording. An additional advantage of using microphone stands is that they help isolate the microphone from vibrations. If you placed a microphone directly on a table during a dinner party, for example, you would hear a great deal of distorted noise from the plates and cutlery – and very little of the conversation!

Microphone types

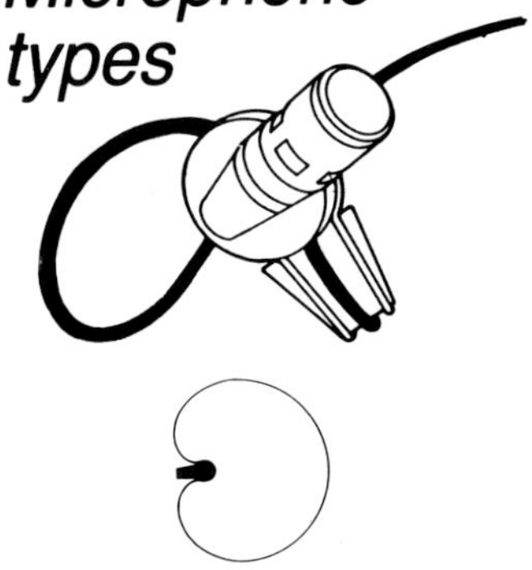

Tie-clip microphones are portable and unobtrusive. Use for interviews or when making voice-overs to camera, particularly on location.

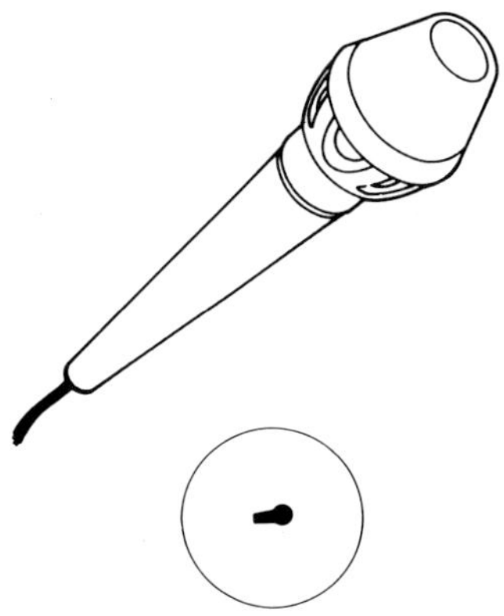

Use an omnidirectional microphone to pick up the overall sound of the environment. Note that traffic noises will dominate, unlike the sounds of nature.

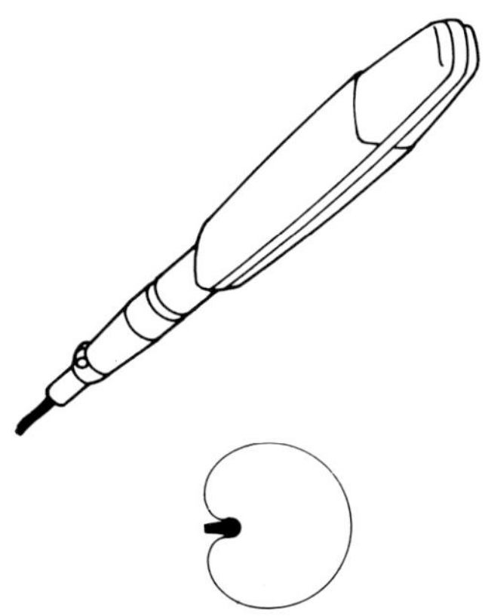

The limited pick-up zone of a unidirectional microphone helps to eliminate unwanted sound. Informal recordings of groups or group interviews are best conducted using them.

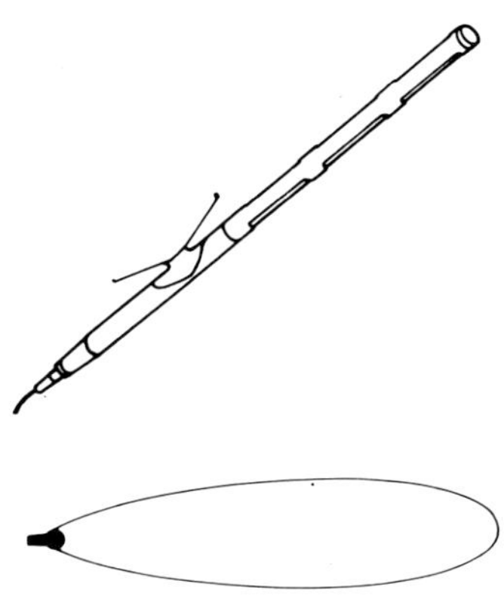

Highly directional microphones are available with various ranges. They can lift an individual from the background, or be used to record subject sound during a long shot.

BASIC VIDEO EDITING

The editing of video usually involves the rearrangement of the original shot order and sometimes the opportunity is taken to add to or otherwise to improve the recorded sound. As has already been explained, the rearrangement of the shot order has to be done, not by physically cutting the video tape but by a process of copying it on to a second tape, during which unsatisfactory shots can be dropped and the beginnings and endings of sequences can be tidied up. In the case of sound, the original synchronized sound can be totally replaced by non-sync background effects; music or commentary may also be added. The original sync sound can be combined with the additional material though this requires the use of special equipment.

Insert editing

Before we consider the practical details of all this, there is an editing technique which can be carried out directly on the original video recording – this is called 'insert editing' and it involves the use of the insert facility which is to be found on some camcorders and video recorders. With this, it is possible to replace the original video pictures with completely new material; on most machines, this is done without erasure of the accompanying sound which therefore continues to be heard over the insert.

One application of insert is the editing in of titles on to an existing video. Suppose you have recorded some children taking part in a school sports day. Provided that your recording includes relatively unimportant material here and there which can be sacrificed to make room for inserts – say, overlong shots of competitors waiting at the starting line – titles can be substituted to advantage as 'subheadings' to major sequences. This will help to reduce dead spots in your movie and give it a more professional look.

The titles – for example, 'Johnnie's Big Race' – are first prepared by producing lettering on suitable backgrounds. These can be either plain-coloured pieces of card or photo stills. The first one of these is then carefully lined up in front of the camcorder and lit with a couple of ordinary lamps. The recorded video is then played back over the camcorder until the place is reached at which the insert is to begin. Hold it on pause at this point and switch the camcorder to 'insert', then go to 'stop'. You have now edited the title into the original recording.

In a similar way, the original sound recording can be replaced wholly or in part by inserting new material via the audio-dub facility, and this is explained in more detail in the following section on sound editing. You will, of course, appreciate that care has to be taken if you are carrying out insert edits and audio dubs onto the original video tape – a mistake here could spoil the whole recording. It is safer to carry out these operations on a copy rather than the original tape, and consideration of making copy tapes brings us to the point where we can look at the whole question of true video editing.

Assemble editing

In essence, 'assemble editing' is quite simple. Basically, all you do is connect two video machines back-to-back so that the original recording – both audio and video – can be played back from the replay or service machine into a rerecord or edit machine. This is known as a 'two-machine edit' and is the basic set-up irrespective of whether the machines are simply controlled manually – as I shall describe – or whether more sophisticated automatic means of control are used. Nothing special in the way of video machines is required, provided that the edit deck has 'backspace edit' – this will be explained in more detail later. It also helps if the machine has 'flying erase' since it will produce clearer edits than with a machine without this facility.

The video interconnection is made by using 'copying leads' which are so called because they have the correct terminations to suit the video out and the video in sockets on the respective sound machines. The audio connections are described in the later section on sound editing.

In order to help you see what you are doing, you will also need to connect in a monitor screen. An ordinary portable colour TV is quite adequate and its aerial socket should be connected to the 'RF out' socket on the edit machine. You will no doubt wonder how we can get away with only one screen to show pictures from two machines. It's simple – the 'source' machine pictures are fed to the screen via the 'edit' machine and will show whenever the edit deck is on 'record' or 'stop'. Otherwise, the screen will show the copy tape pictures whenever it is on 'play'.

So far, so good. With your original recording loaded into the source machine and a fresh tape on the edit machine, you can make a start on your assemble edit. To begin, first run the original tape on the source machine to find the start of the first shot to be copied or 'assembled'. You can, if you like, use slo-mo or freeze-frame to help you find it accurately. Hold the machine on play-pause, and then set the edit machine to record-pause. Then release both machines from pause to play and record respectively. Stop both machines when you have run a few seconds beyond the end of the first section.

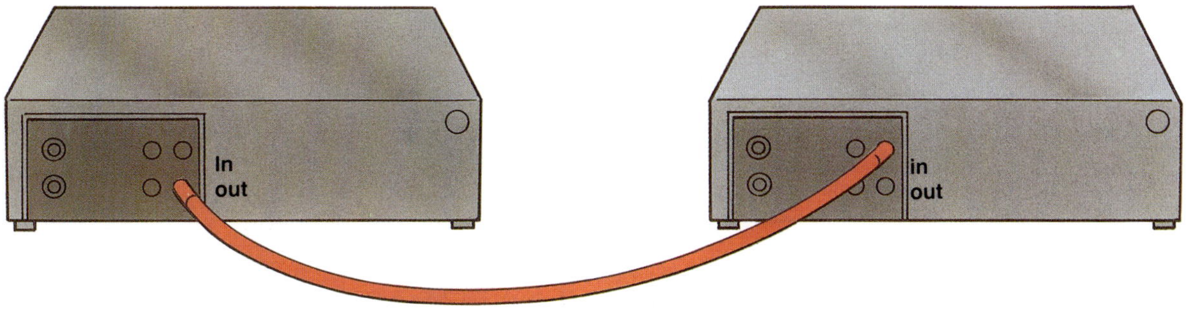

The next thing to do is to check that all is well with the copy, so rewind it and play it back, stopping on record-pause when you reach the edit point for the beginning of the next shot. Now you can run the source deck to the beginning of the next section, stopping as before on play-pause. Assemble it onto the copy as before, and continue to the end of the movie.

Although the basis of video editing is this simple, it has to be recognised that it must be done precisely under basic manual conditions for it to work well. If you are not good at pushing buttons simultaneously, you will be better off if your machines have synchro edit sockets. If they have, and you have the special lead to connect them together, you have a convenient way of releasing both machines off pause simply by pressing one button.

Locating edit points

There are also one or two other points to bear in mind. The first is that you should try to minimise the amount of time that the machines are held on pause – otherwise the tapes may begin to wear. So organise the location of the edit points on the source tape in advance – there are specimens of shot log sheets and edit planning sheets in the Technical Section (see pages 238-43). Go through the tape and note the counter readings relative to the beginning of each section so they can be located easily and quickly. Use cue-review and fast replay to speed up this operation. If the search is likely to take time, switch the edit deck to stop. When you are ready to resume the transfer, locate the edit point on the copy tape by repeating the routine already described so that the edit will be made cleanly and exactly at the correct point on the tape.

Another consideration is that you may need to make allowance for the technical feature known as 'backspace edit' on the rerecord deck. If you watch carefully, you will find that the first second or so is missing at the start of each new section on the copy. This is because the edit machine, each time it is released from record-pause, takes a little time to start actually recording since it first has to back-track to find and lock on to the video controls signals at the end of the previous section to enable it to make a clean edit without annoying picture break-ups. This can also happen when inserts are being recorded.

Quite often this loss of the beginnings of shots will not matter too much – in fact it may even be a positive advantage in helping you to trim off unwanted material. If, on the other hand, important action is being left out, it is necessary to offset the backspace time, either by setting the tape on the source machine one to one and a half seconds early relative to the true edit point, or to release it from pause later by the same amount of time relative to the edit machine. It may sound a little complicated but it becomes easier with practice!

BASIC SOUND EDITING

As we have already suggested in the section on Basic Video Editing, the original sound recording can be replaced wholly or in part by new material which is recorded on to the video tape via the feature known as 'audio-dub'. By no means all camcorders and video machines have this facility; for instance, 8mm machines with hi-fi FM audio do not enable audio to be redubbed separately from the picture, as the two signals are inextricably intertwined on the tape. It is, however, a feature which is often provided on VHS and VHS-C machines for they have lower-quality sound which is recorded as a low-speed edge track and this can be recorded independently of the video.

Audio-dub

Audio-dub is a useful creative feature, and it can often be the means of saving a recording which is otherwise spoilt by poor sound – say by wind noise on the microphone. Of course, any new sound which is dubbed in is not, unlike the original audio, perfectly synchronized with the pictures. It therefore has to be limited to general background effects to hide the fact that it is a later addition. Backgrounds suitable for dubbing in are sounds typical of the 'sea-shore', 'countryside' (birdsong etc), 'crowds' and so on. You can either prerecord your own background effects on a cassette recorder or buy one of the special effects records or tapes which are available for amateur use. There are 'mood music' tapes and discs, too.

To dub new audio, you will of course need to connect in a source record player or recorder to the audio-in socket on your camcorder or VCR. On some machines, though, you have to connect it instead to the microphone socket via a special attenuating adaptor-lead. You should also have some means of controlling the level of the new audio so that it matches that of the original recording on either side of the dub. The simplest way to do this is to feed the signal or signals via an audio mixer. You can use just one channel of this as a volume controller or take the opportunity to mix sound from two or more sources, using the video pictures themselves as cues.

The audio-dub operation (which is 'all or nothing': you erase the original sound) is quite straightforward. Having first done a dummy run to establish the sound levels via the monitor speaker, set the video machine on play-pause at the dub start-point. Presss for audio-dub, start the background source player and release the video machine from pause. Go to stop when you reach the end of the section to be audio-dubbed, so that the original sound track can continue from that point.

So far as assemble editing is concerned, the basic set-up for audio is much the same as for simple audio-dub, except that the source is the replay video machine. If no additional sound is being mixed in, the audio transfer becomes one of simple level control, assuming that the original recording requires to be adjusted in this way. Bear in mind, though, that there will be a break in the audio recording at each edit restart and the type of background used has to be chosen with this in mind. For this reason, mixing in music is not a good idea unless the lengths of the sections between breaks are long enough to make this practical.

Recording commentary

You may also wish to add commentary to your video by superimposing it over the original sync sound. As is the case with background music, this can be recorded while the video copy is being assembled, provided that the sections are long enough between breaks for recording lengths of commentary. Otherwise you will have to settle for a full length audio-dub run after the video has been assembled. In this case, you have to have background sound in place of the original sync sound unless you have special recording equipment.

For recording commentary the mixer set-up is used. A microphone is connected to one mixer channel and the background source and/or the replay video machine is connected to one or more of the other channels. The commentary is spoken while watching the source for cues – turn down the monitor speaker while this is being done to prevent 'howl round'. You will probably need an assistant to operate the equipment and adjust the mixer levels for you, with the monitoring being done via headphones. Incidentally, it is now becoming possible to carry out simple premixing while the original sound is being recorded on the camcorder by the use of one of the new 'mixer-mikes' which have inputs for connection to additional sound sources. Commentary and recorded music are discussed in more detail on pages 226-9.

Still more ambitious sound tracks can be built up if you have the facility to 'lift off' the sync sound from the assembled copy video and to transfer it onto a separate sound tape on a recorder with multitrack, sound-on-sound mixing. If the runs are short, say five minutes or so, an ordinary cassette or reel-to-reel machine will be adequate for building up a composite track and laying it back on to the video tape while still maintaining approximate sync. For longer continuous runs, speed drift becomes a problem which can only be overcome by the use of a special tape recorder which can be sync-locked to the video signals. These are available but are fairly expensive to buy.

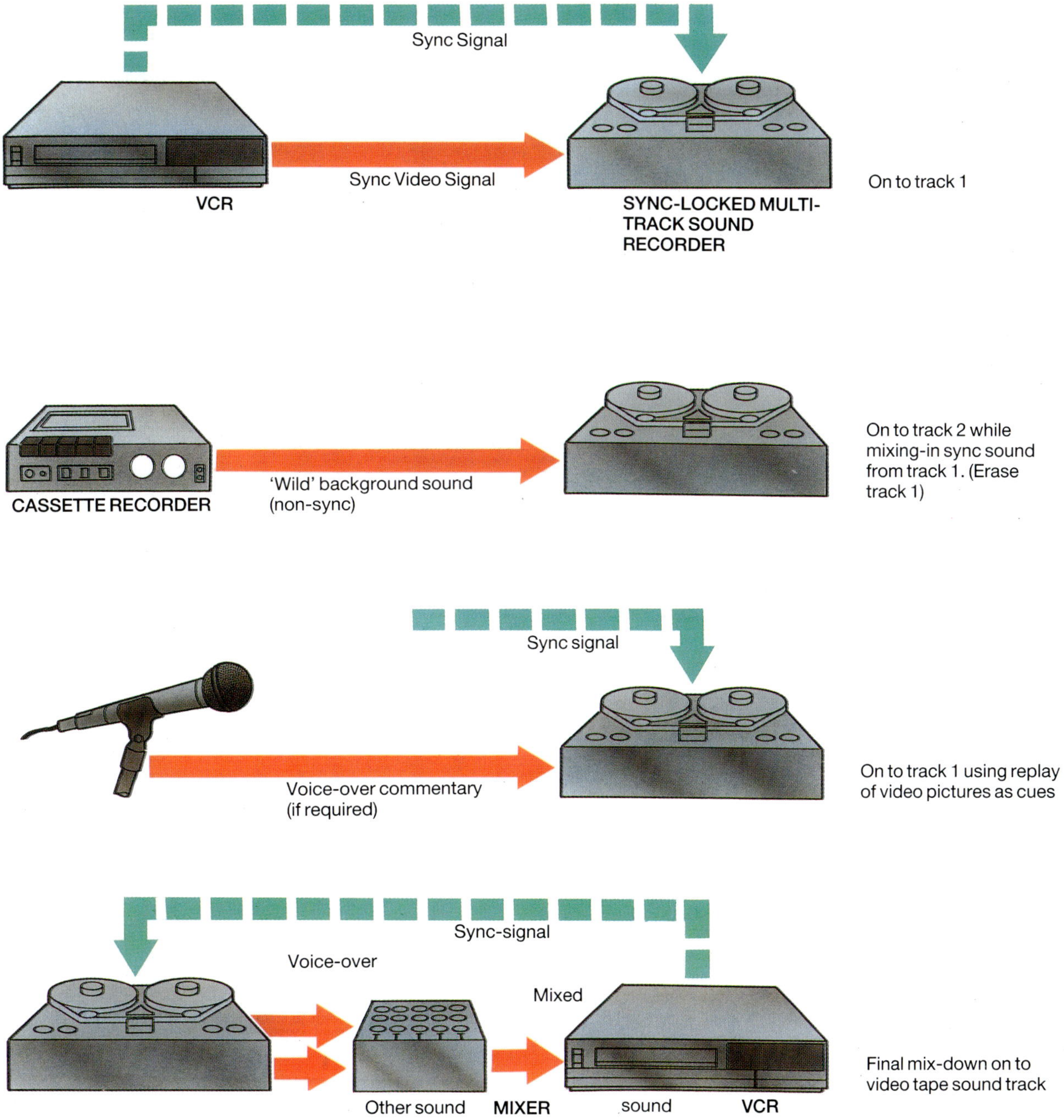

1: *The first stage in building up the composite video sound track is to record the sync sound effects on your video tape on to track 1 of a multitrack sound recorder.*

2: *Background sound recorded on location using a portable cassette recorder can next be recorded on to track 2, while mixing in the sync effects from track 1.*

3:*You can now use track 1 of the tape to record a voice-over commentary. This can be recorded in the studio using a microphone if this is required.*

4: *Finally use a mixer to combine the two sound tracks and record them back on to the video tape in the VCR. Synchronized sound and video are complete on the same tape.*

ADDITIONAL EQUIPMENT

The growing mass market in camcorders has brought into being a whole industry devoted to the production of video accessories, which range widely in both cost and usefulness. The small advertisements in the video press provide a rich source of information about this type of equipment; a few of the more useful items are described here.

There are many types of lens filters and converters. Screw-on converters can add extra wide-angle or telephoto range to your camcorder's zoom lens, and there are polarizing, neutral density, split-screen and multilens attachments, as well as numerous different coloured filters to choose from.

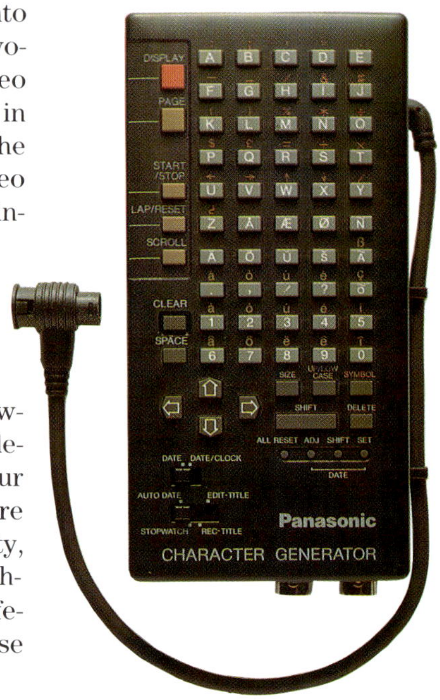

Plug-in character generator

Telecine converters allow you to transfer your old home movies on to video tape. These range from simple screw-on converters to freestanding telecine screens, on to which you can project films for transfer on to tape.

Camcorder battery power is a constant preoccupation if you shoot much video away from home, and a spare battery is almost essential. If you need still more power, there are battery belts that allow you to carry several batteries around on a shoot. Car-operated chargers and special leads that allow you to connect a camcorder to the car battery via the cigar lighter socket are also available.

Equipment for sound

Sound recording, dubbing and editing also create a need for extra items. A good set of headphones with large earpieces is vital for good location sound-monitoring. A spare single earpiece can also come in useful, as these small items can easily be lost.

There are many different tape recorders and mixers that you can use for sound editing – how far you go along this road depends on your interest and budget. A simple two-track cassette machine that can be linked to VCRs via plug-in sync units provides a basic sound-editing system. But professional multitrack audio machines with track-to-track mixing and sophisticated cueing arangements are available for the ambitious video maker.

Wireless microphones are now practical for amateur use. There are reasonably priced units available that consist of lapel microphone, transmitter, and a receiver that you can plug into the camcorder's external microphone socket. With this type of equipment, you can shoot really professional sound outdoors at a distance from the subject, without running long cables or using bulky stick microphones. Sound can also be captured from a distance by using a gun microphone, but you will need an assistant to operate it. Boom microphones (either purpose-built or improvised with a broom handle) are also useful for gathering exactly the sound you want.

Enhancing the picture

Video enhancer units are useful when editing. You connect the enhancer between two VCRs when carrying out a 'back-to-back' edit. You can then use the unit to mix the audio and also to improve and modify the picture as it is being copied. Circuits control colour saturation, picture definition and brightness level. Some models also provide direct picture comparison on a single monitor screen. Another type allows you to create 'wipes' and various different masking patterns.

While some camcorders have their own in-built character generators for superimposing titles and other information on the picture, plug-in character generators are available for many camcorders that do not. Each type is dedicated to a particular make or model of camcorder, and some units can be connected during the editing process. The problem with most character generators is that they produce crude, mechanical-looking type. It is often better to create your own titles by filming printed or hand-lettered cards.

Special effects generators produce a wide range of other changes to the video image. These enhancements start with simple dissolves and wipes that allow you to replace one picture with another, but also include advanced facilities, such as the ability to insert one picture into another. Techniques like this are increasingly common in professional video work; but are expensive for the amateur. Such facilities are a usual part of a professional studio package.

THE WEDDING VIDEO

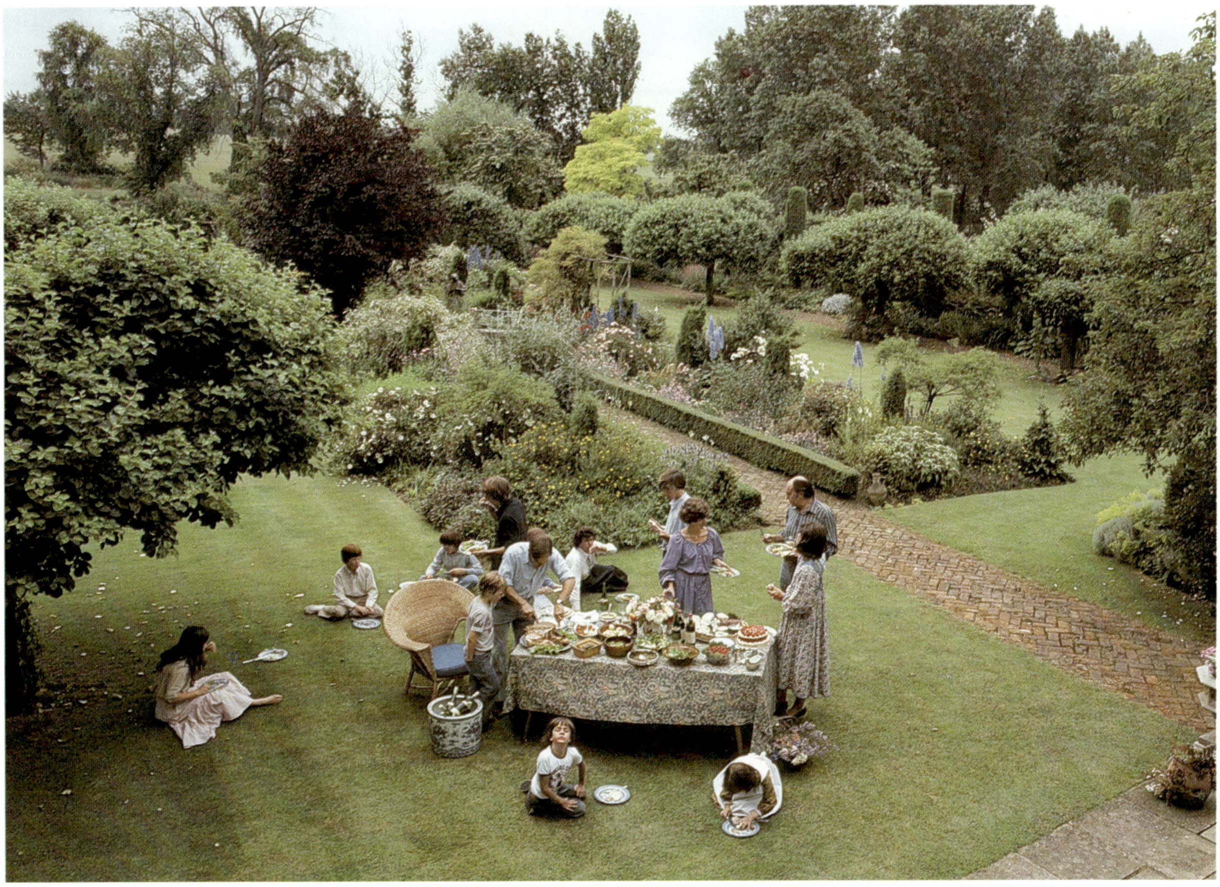

Thorough planning is the keystone of making a good video, and involves visualizing the event which you are about to cover. First, think about the nature of the location and the lighting conditions you can expect to find there, and ways of overcoming any potential problems. Then consider how the nature of the event will affect your treatment. In the wedding project covered in this chapter – something which most people with a camera are likely to be asked to cover – there is no chance for a second take. Everything must go right on the big day, for the couple and for you.

WEDDING CHECKLIST

Wedding of ....

Date ....

INITIAL COVERAGE

VENUE (EG BRIDE'S HOME) ....

TIME ALLOWED ....

COVERAGE OF CEREMONY

VENUE OF CEREMONY ....

TRANSPORT DETAILS

Distance To Venue	Time For Travel	Traffic Report

TIME GUESTS ARRIVE ....

TIME BRIDE ARRIVES ....

TIME CEREMONY BEGINS ....

IS FILMING PERMITTED DURING CEREMONY? ....

TIME CEREMONY ENDS ....

COVERAGE AFTER CEREMONY

COVERAGE OF RECEPTION

VENUE OF RECEPTION ....

TRANSPORT DETAILS

Distance To Venue | Time For Travel

TIME WEDDING PARTY/RECEPTION EXPECTED TO END ....

SPECIAL COVERAGE REQUIREMENTS

____

____

____

____

PEOPLE

BRIDE
BRIDESMAIDS

BEST MAN
BRIDE'S PARENTS

GROOM
ATTENDANTS

GROOM'S PARENTS

OTHER GUESTS

______	______	______	______
______	______	______	______
______	______	______	______
______	______	______	______
______	______	______	______
______	______	______	______
______	______	______	______
______	______	______	______

TELEPHONE NUMBERS

BRIDE'S FAMILY
CEREMONY VENUE

RECEPTION VENUE
OTHERS

EQUIPMENT REQUIREMENTS

☐ CAMCORDER AND ACCESSORIES
☐ BATTERIES

☐ TAPES
☐ OTHER EQUIPMENT

The ceremony is only one element of the wedding day, the reception and the departure of the bride and groom being further high points that you will need to cover. The latter will provide many excellent opportunities to take informal shots of family and friends to complement the set-piece sequences. You should also discuss in advance which relatives and friends the couple want you to concentrate on. It may help if together you take a look at old family albums to enable you to recognize such key characters on the day.

One important consideration at this stage in your planning is whether you are going to edit after shooting. If you are, you will have much greater flexibility in terms of coverage – poor material can therefore be cut out and interesting sequences juxtaposed with one another. If this is the case, remember to include a lead-in time of about five seconds on each shot.

However, without editing facilities, everything you shoot will appear in the same sequence on the finished tape. Therefore note how long each sequence you intend covering might last, and stick to this schedule when it comes to the actual shoot. This not only adds an element of structure to the video, but also prevents you from running out of tape at a crucial moment.

If you have a recording time of one hour available, plan for the coverage to last about 50 minutes, so that you have 10 minutes to include extra interesting footage. In general, this should be quite long enough to cover all the main elements of the event, as well as being short enough to avoid repetition and retain audience attention.

PLANNING COVERAGE

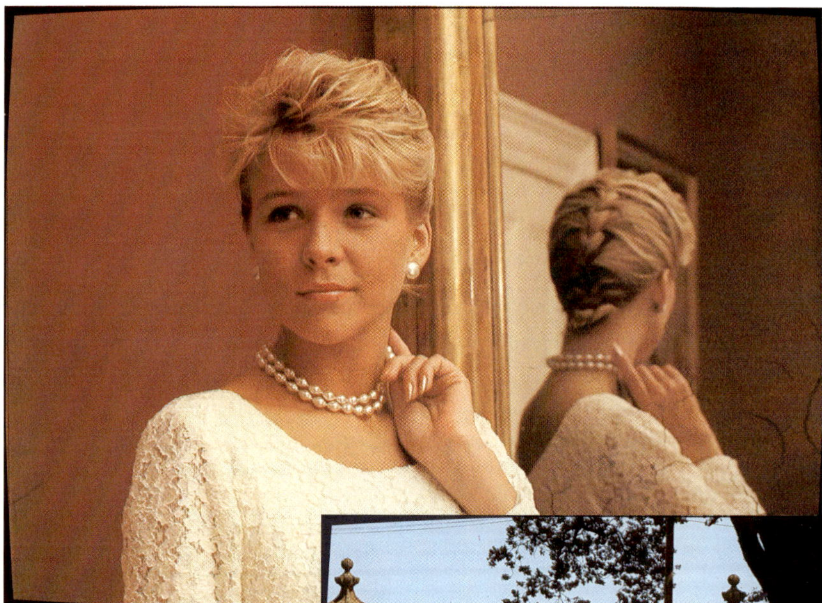

1: *Coverage of the bride's preparations for the big day makes a good introduction to the tape. Make sure, though, that she includes you in her schedule. The old adage 'something old, something new, something borrowed, something blue' could make a good theme for this part of the video.*

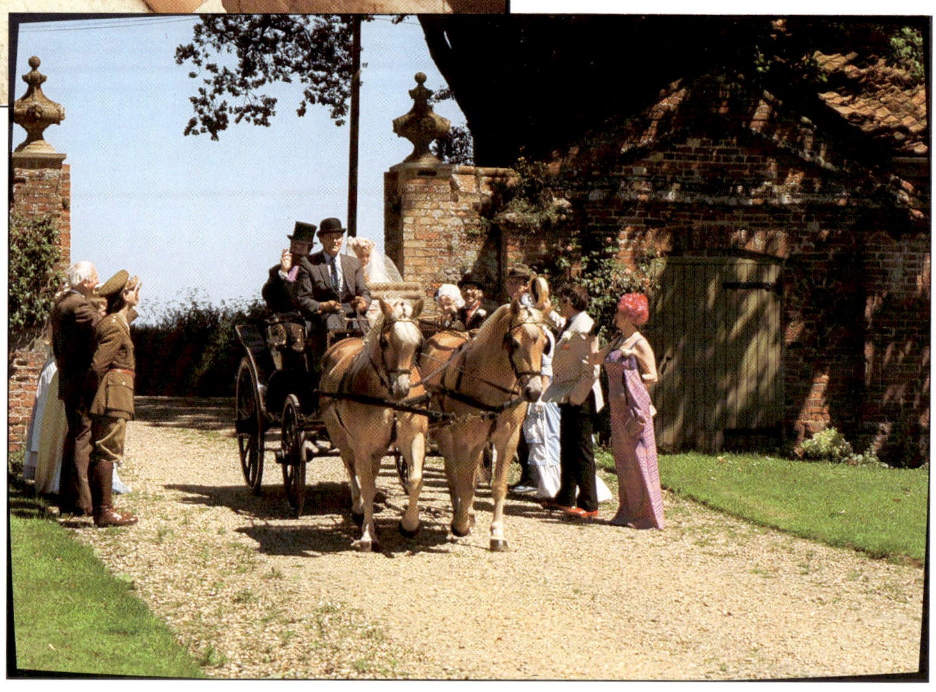

2: *When the bride and groom really go to town on their transport, it is essential to catch the pomp of their arrival. In covering such a scene, begin in long-shot and move into close-up on the bride's face – she, after all, is the star of the day. Catch the reaction of friends and family as the bride arrives.*

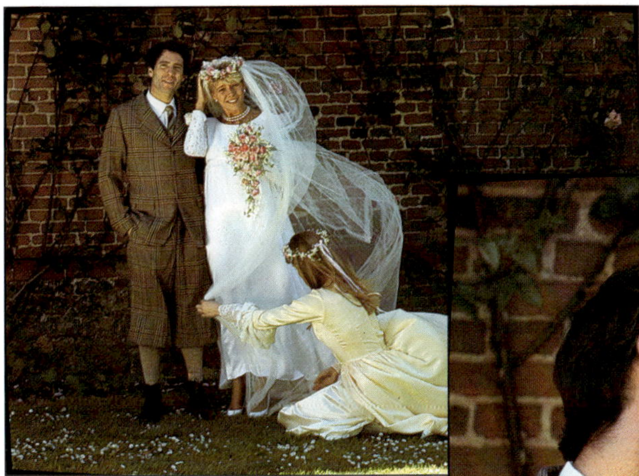

3-4: *The kiss is another high point that should be included in your coverage. Don't try competing with the official still photographer for such shots, but discuss with him at the start of the day the best means of getting the right people together.*

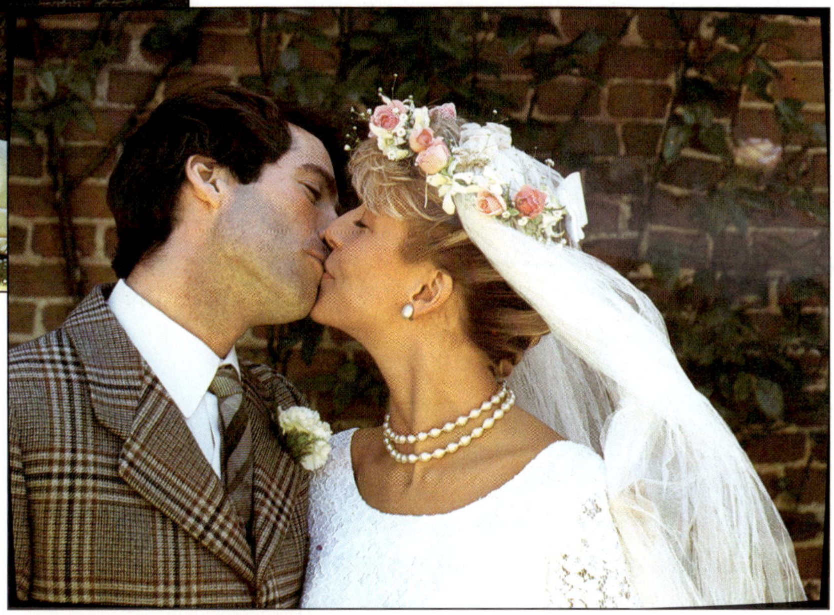

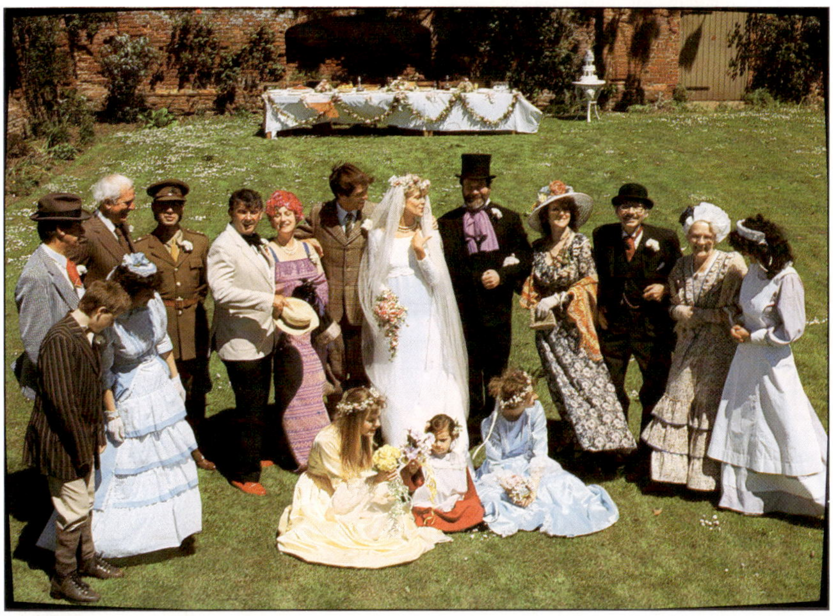

5: *Formal groups can appear static on video, so such coverage should not be extensive. This scene, taken from a slightly high angle, establishes the background and the atmosphere of the reception.*

6-7: *At the reception, it is possible to get informal shots of the guests enjoying themselves. By moving in close and seeming to become part of the celebrations, you will probably find people respond well to the camera, instead of shying away from it.*

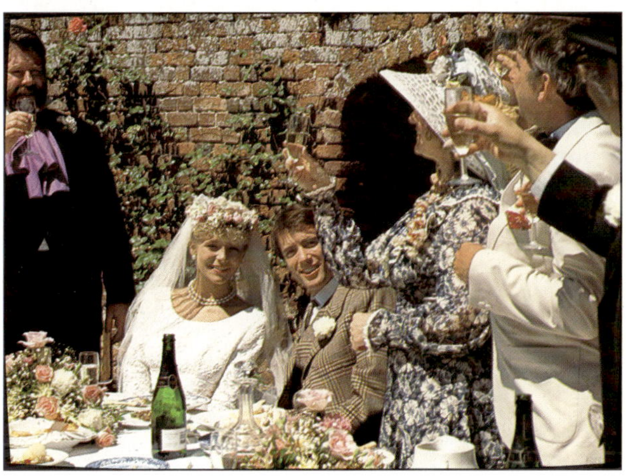

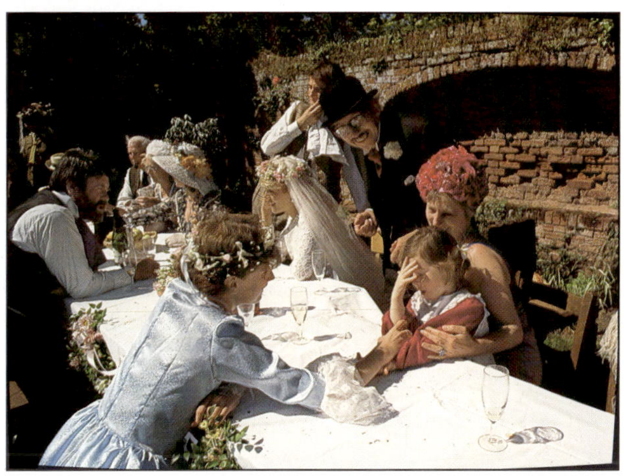

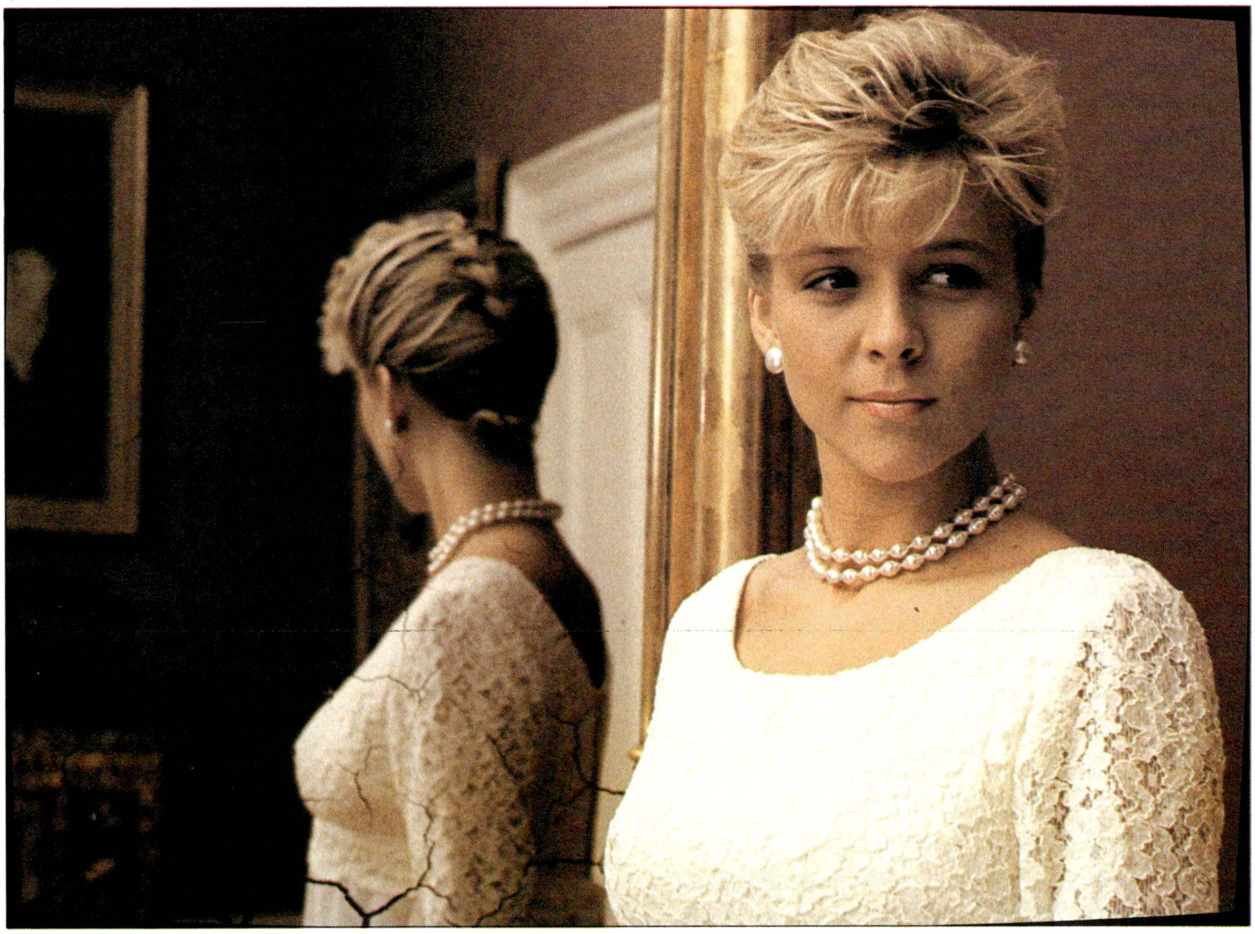

THE RIGHT START 1

Even with such an apparently relatively straightforward project as a wedding video, it is important to treat it with the same professionalism as any other project. Your first concern must be to grab your audience's attention.

An opening shot of the bride makes a fine start, and the way in which you deal with this sequence will, to an extent, set the tone and pace of the tape. For example, if you shoot the chaotic preparations in the bride's house, with all the last-minute checks and setbacks, the initial feel would be one of hurry and bustle. You could, at this stage, incorporate some amusing, candid shots such as the principal characters desperately searching for the elusive wedding ring, flowers and buttonholes! Such sequences have the added advantage of informally introducing the most important members of the two families. This part of the tape will interestingly and dramatically contrast with the formal ceremony which follows. If you choose such an opening sequence, devote about 10 minutes to it. Any more and the video audience will grow impatient for the bride's departure to the church.

An alternative would be to create a gentler, more reflective approach, emphasizing the importance of the day. An opening shot of the bride alone in her room, sadly taking a last look at the images of a life which she is about to leave behind, could be highly effective. This could be shot earlier in the week when everything is less hectic. You could develop this theme by following up with shots of the bride's parents discussing the reception plans and giving their daughter encouragement and moral support for the events of the coming big day.

In many ways the choice of treatment depends on the bride's personality. The first approach would be more appropriate to an extrovert; the latter to someone who is more introspective. In either case, discuss the options first. And finally, remember that the last thing the bride or groom wants in the nervous hours before the wedding is you interrupting proceedings by telling them what to do in order to get a particular shot.

The opening sequence should lead naturally into the material which follows. In this case, the bride's departure makes a logical point at which to bring this section to a close. You should already have made sure that you then have enough time to get to the church, set up your camera, and capture the arrival of the bride.

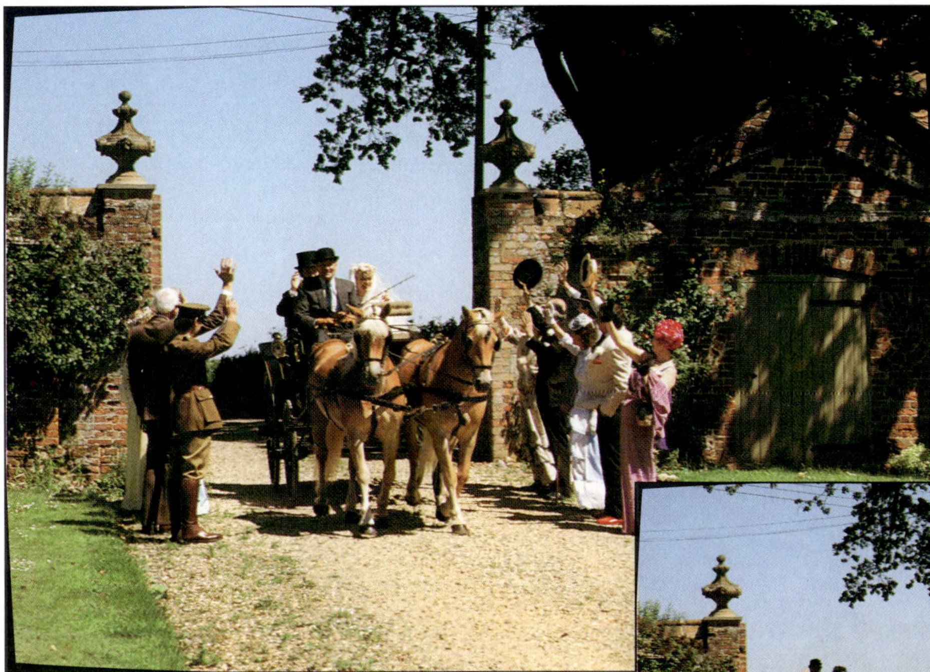

2-3: *Luckily, a fast car can beat a horse-drawn coach any day. so it was not difficult to record the bride's departure from her house and get to the church in time to set up the camera for her arrival.*

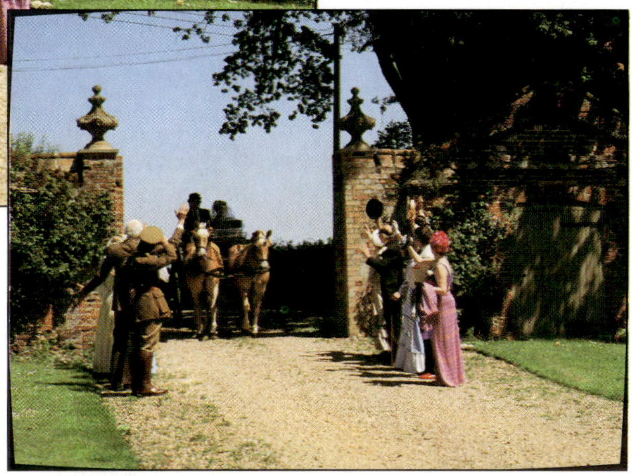

1: *An opening sequence of the bride taking a last look around her home. The framing against the mirror brings additional interest to the shot.*

4: *As an opening shot this breaks with the tradition of the groom not seeing the bride until she reaches the altar. It does, however, have the advantage of showing the two main characters at the outset.*

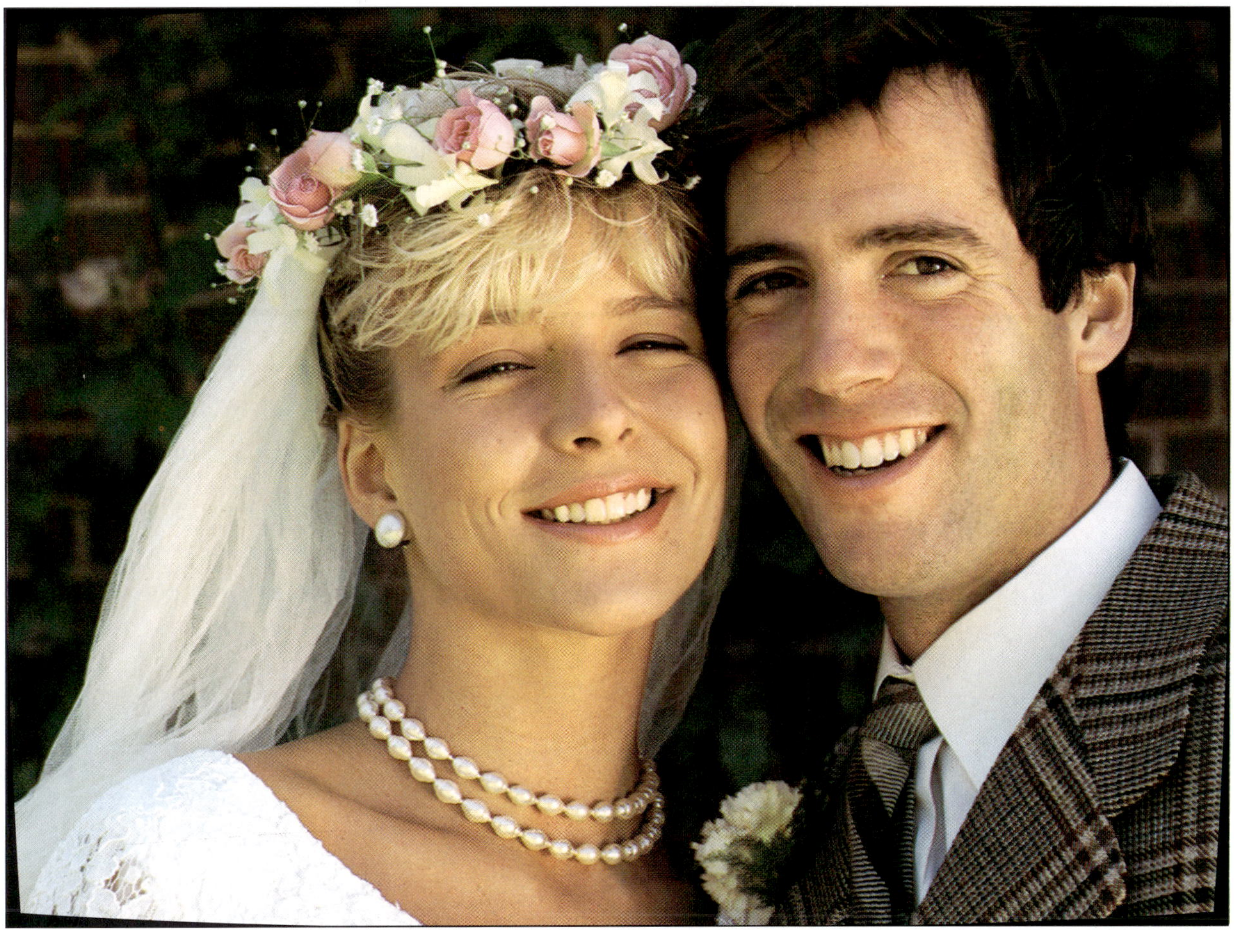

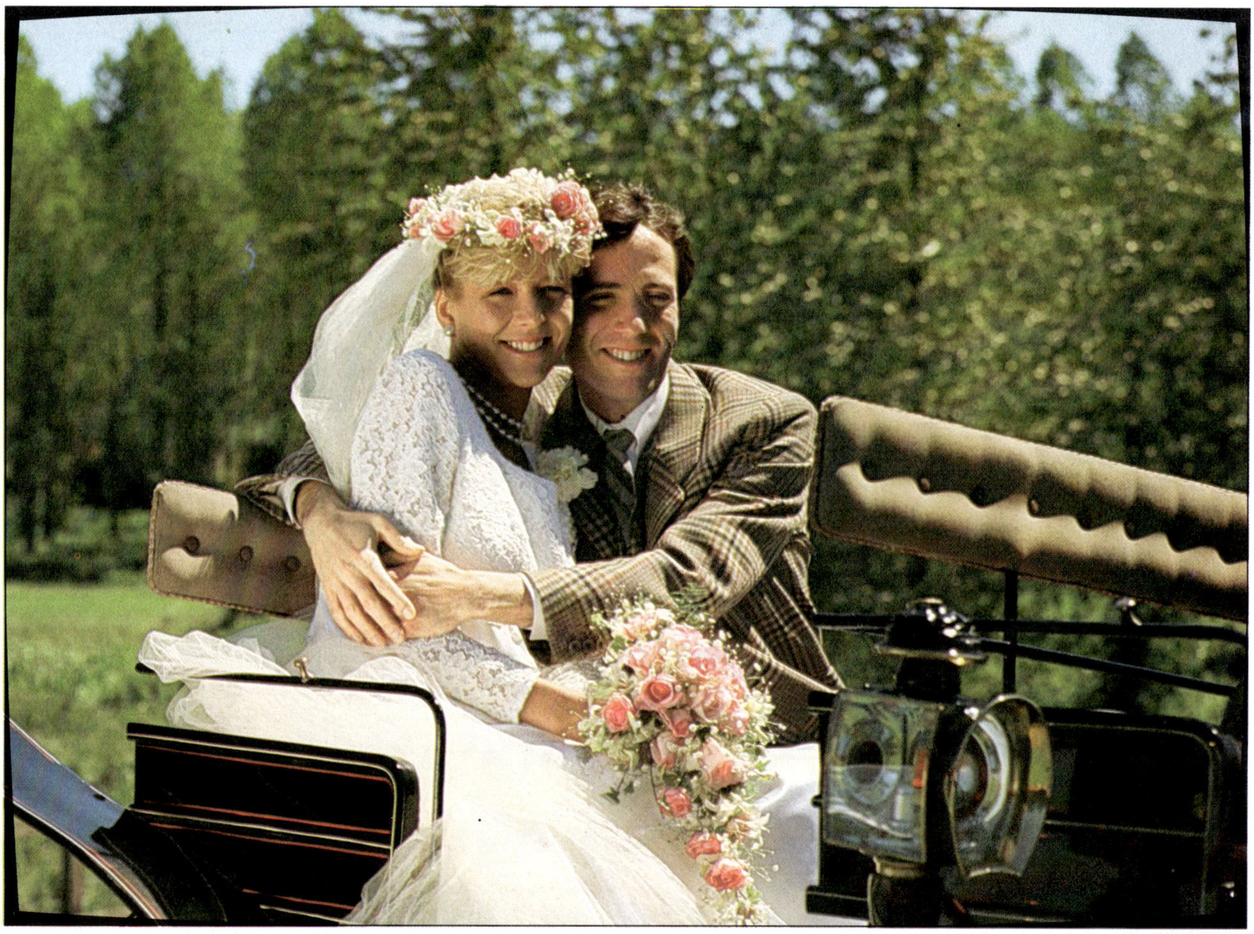

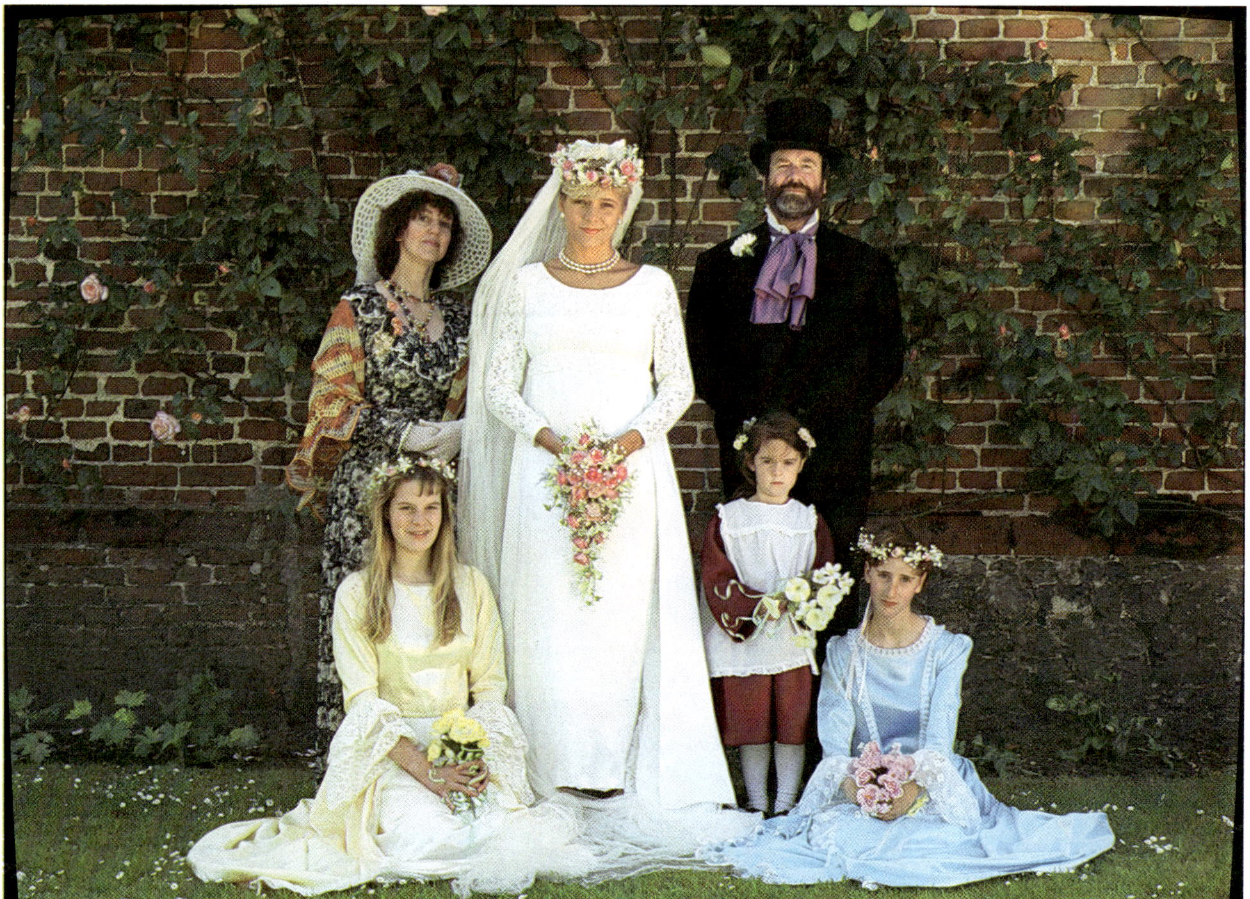

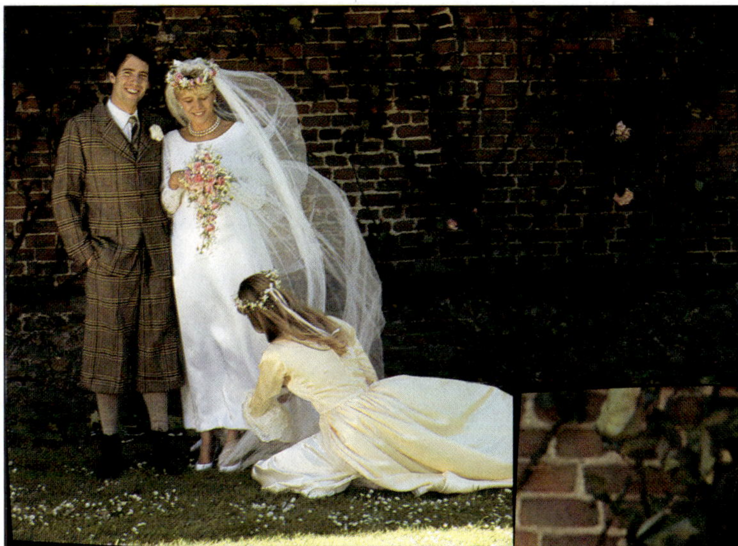

7-8: *While you should make sure that you get coverage of the guests enjoying themselves, don't neglect the bride and groom during the reception. Be on the look out for candid coverage which reveals their quieter moments together.*

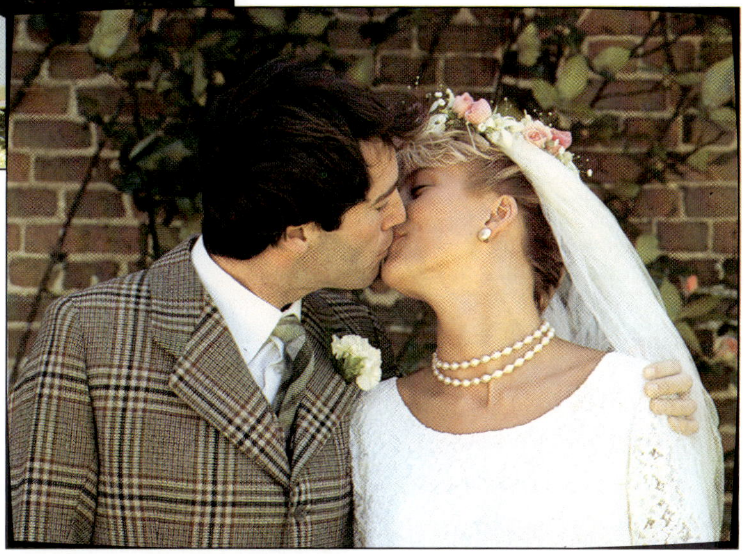

5-6: *Following the ceremony, the next part of the coverage is the wedding reception. This could be introduced by shots of the bride and groom together, emphasizing the idea of marriage. An alternative, suggested in this case by the attractive Edwardian dress of the guests, would be to arrange formal poses to introduce the members of the family present.*

9: *The high angle used to record this formal group distances the subject from the audience. The camera panned to include the reactions of other guests watching the official photography.*

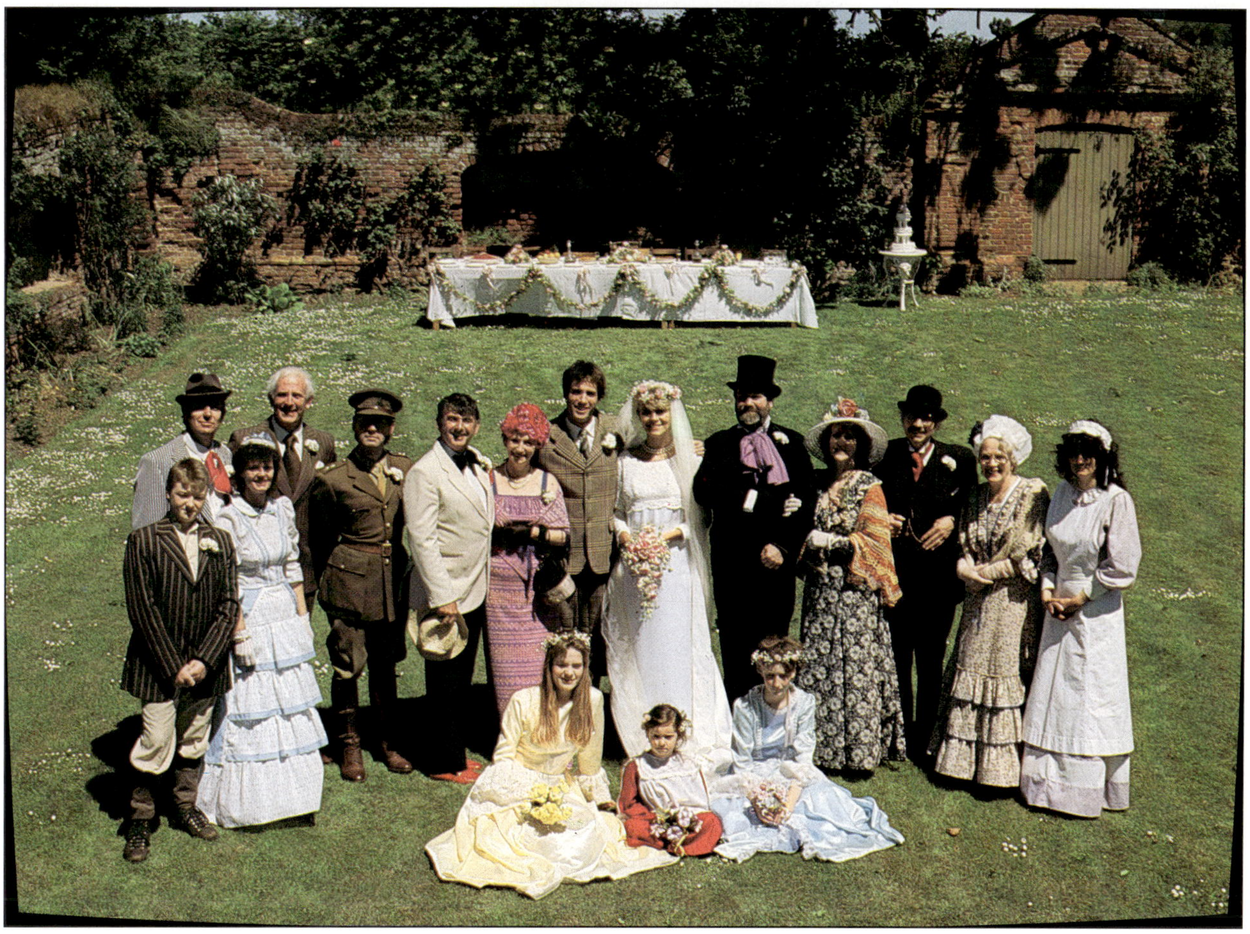

It is easy to forget the practicalities of making a video in the heat of trying to achieve your planned coverage. To begin with, it is essential that you set the white balance each time you move to a new lighting environment. Inside the church, you will probably have set exposure and focus manually – this usually produces a sharper image, and is relatively simple in a formal situation in which the subjects do not move from one position to another. (For coverage of the bride coming down the aisle, you should have rehearsed your positions and each focus on your exploratory visit to the church.) At the reception, your coverage will be more informal and it is probably best to rely on the camera's autofocus to get the shots right.

Lighting is another matter. In the project shown here, the reception took place outside on a glorious afternoon with the sun beating down. But these otherwise excellent weather conditions can cause problems of exposure (if possible, take a test recording beforehand). For example, too much glare from the white table cloth when you use auto-exposure will create problems. Also note that the auto-exposure often adjusts too much, leaving other elements in the scene bleached out as it tries to compensate for extremely bright features in the foreground. You may find that by setting the exposure manually you can get better results.

You should also beware of shooting directly into the sun, particularly if using an older tube camera, in which burn-out can occur. Again, the automatic backlight control, if used, may overcorrect the exposure in very bright conditions, so manual adjustments of exposure are advised.

PRACTICAL CONSIDERATIONS

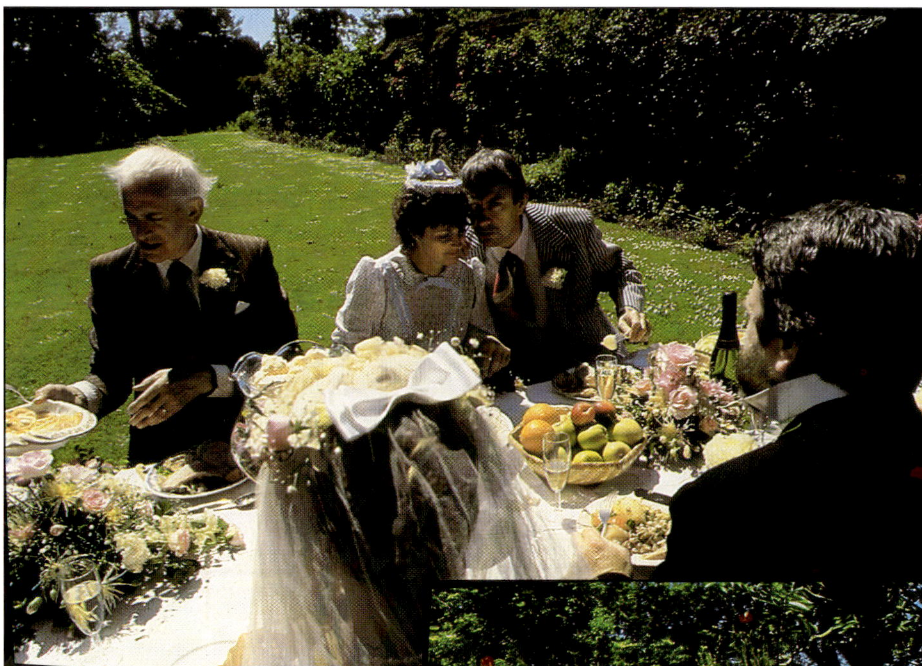

3: *Bright sunlight doesn't just cause problems for the camera operator. Everyone at the wedding party was feeling the heat, but ties remained the order of the day!*

4: *Once the white balance has been taken, and the correct exposure decided on, the colour values of the shot will remain constant unless you suddenly move from sunlight into deep shadow.*

1: *In strong sunlight, avoid shooting directly into the sun or deep shade. This shot was taken with the sun over the camera operator's left shoulder.*

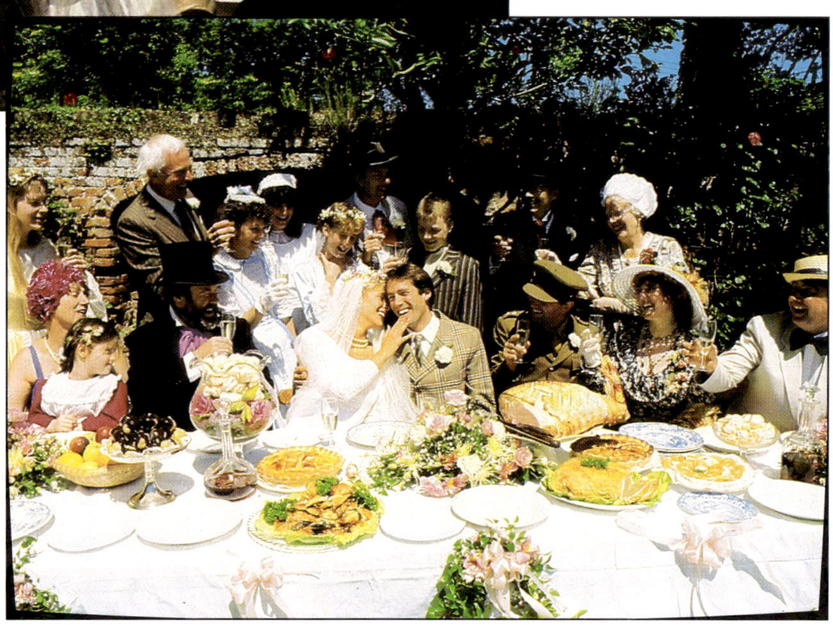

2: *Full sunlight on a brilliant white tablecloth can result in exposure problems. This shot of the wedding party was taken using manually adjusted exposure.*

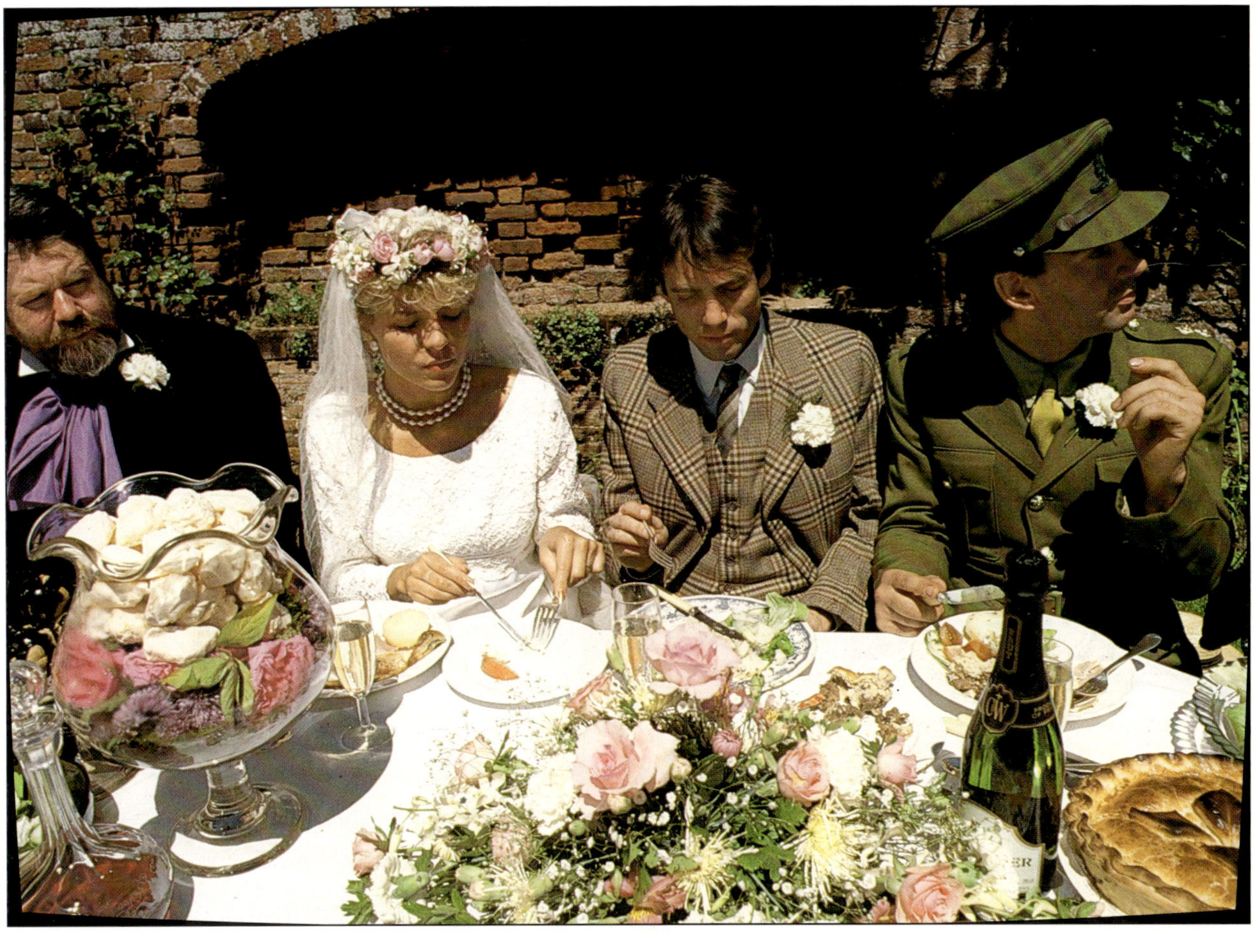

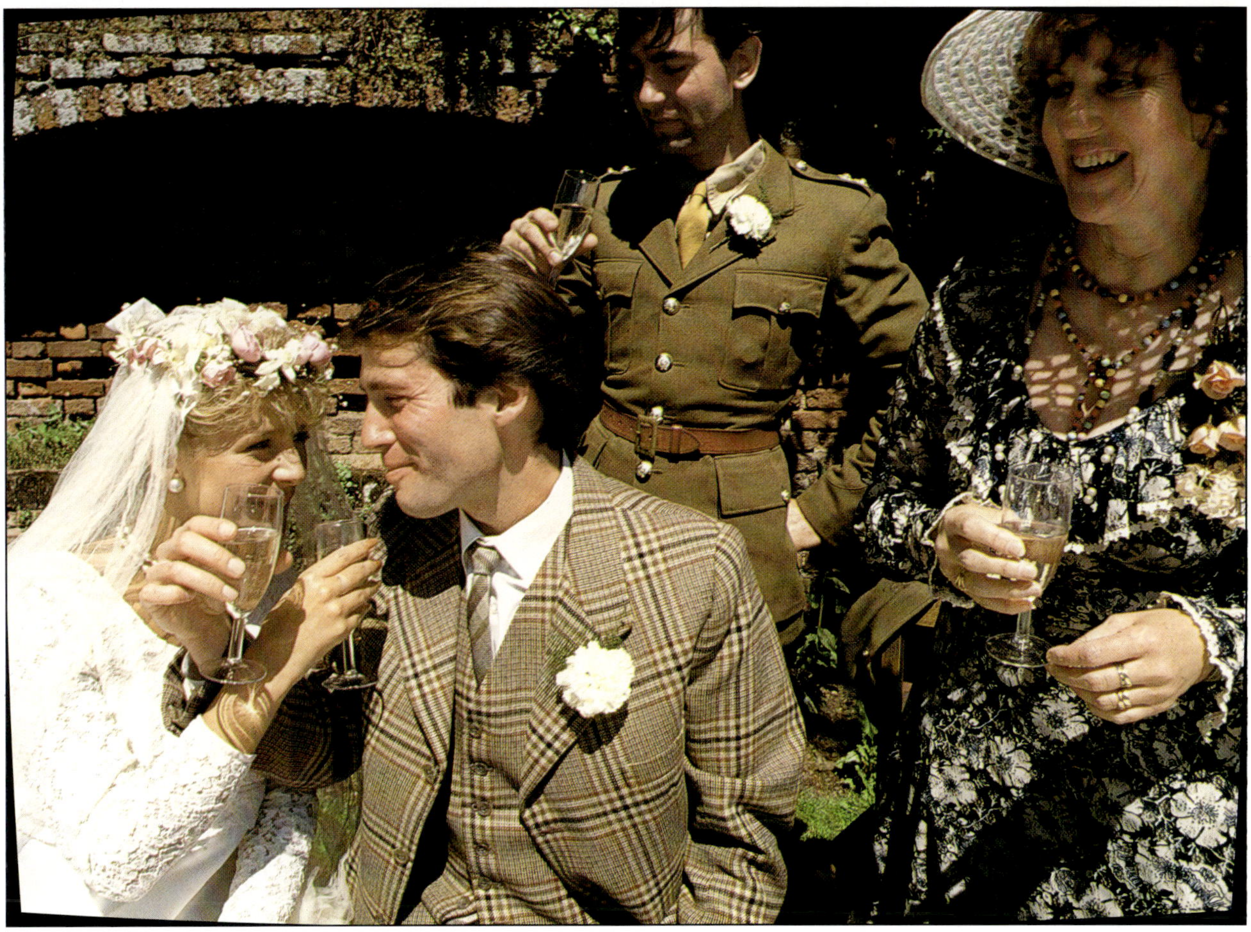

The reception or wedding party is your opportunity to talk to the guests and ask them for reminiscences of the bride and groom. Try to act as a participant yourself – you will be far more likely to get interesting comments from other guests if you approach in a friendly, conversational manner. Although the bride and groom may not want anecdotes of their childhood revealed, they are sure to be told and you could make amusing inserts of such stories.

Don't forget the older, more retiring members of the party, and remember that children will provide an interesting change of pace. When talking to them, remember to crouch down to their level, to put them more at ease and get the best camera angle.

Set pieces don't just include the main events of the day, but also smaller, equally highly prized moments, such as the reading of telegrams and letters of congratulations. Such moments are an important ritual, as is the tradition of the bride and groom cutting the cake.

The final event of the day that you must be sure to cover is the departure of the bride and groom, when the former will toss the bridal bouquet. Be sure to provide a close-up of the delighted face of whoever catches it. And make sure that the groom's best man lets you know in good time when the couple intend to slip away.

FURTHER COVERAGE

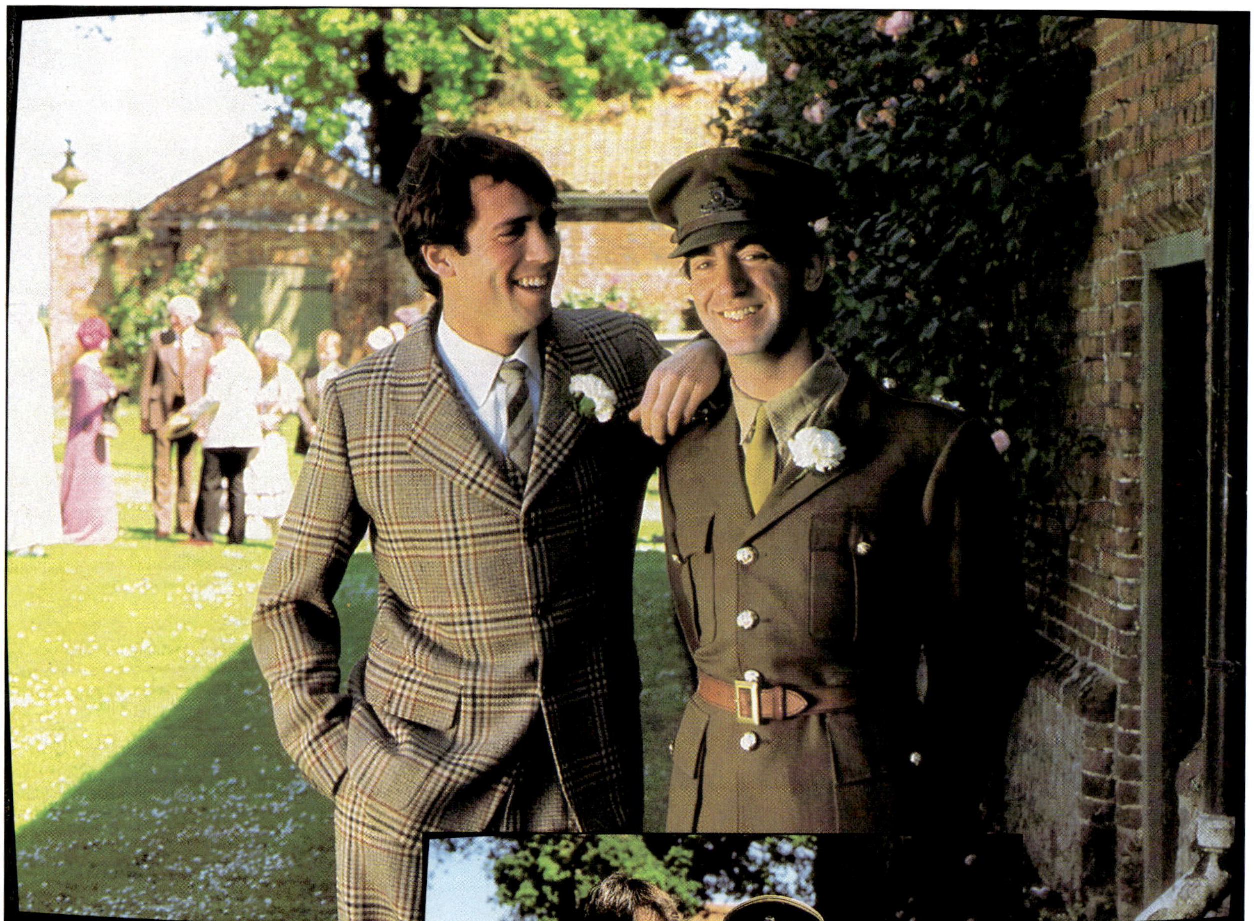

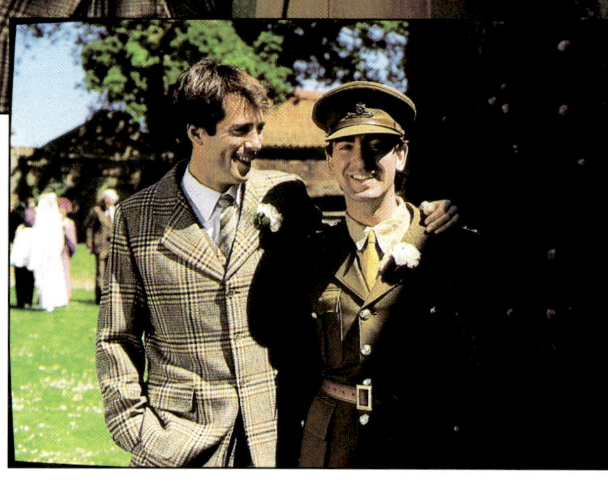

1-2: *Since the best man will be the groom's closest friend, and with a key role in the day's proceedings, it is vital that you feature him in the video, ideally with the groom. Note how in recording this sequence the extreme sunlight and shade caused exposure problems.*

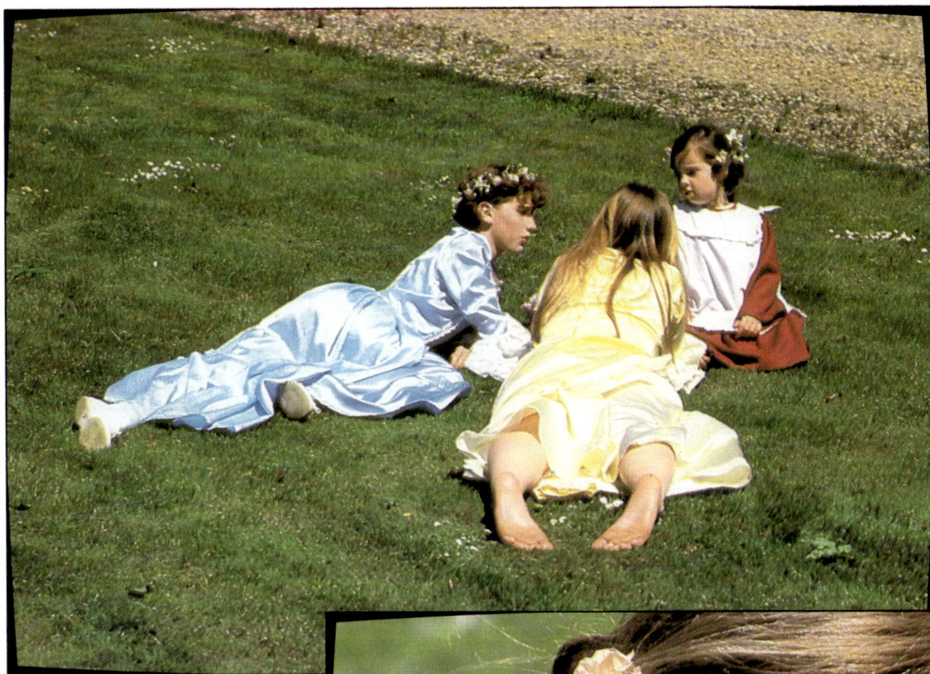

3: *Keep an eye out for for children at the reception, especially when they get away from the adults. Children can add charm and humour to your coverage of the reception. See how this group were entirely engrossed in their own conversation and completely unaware of the presence of the camera.*

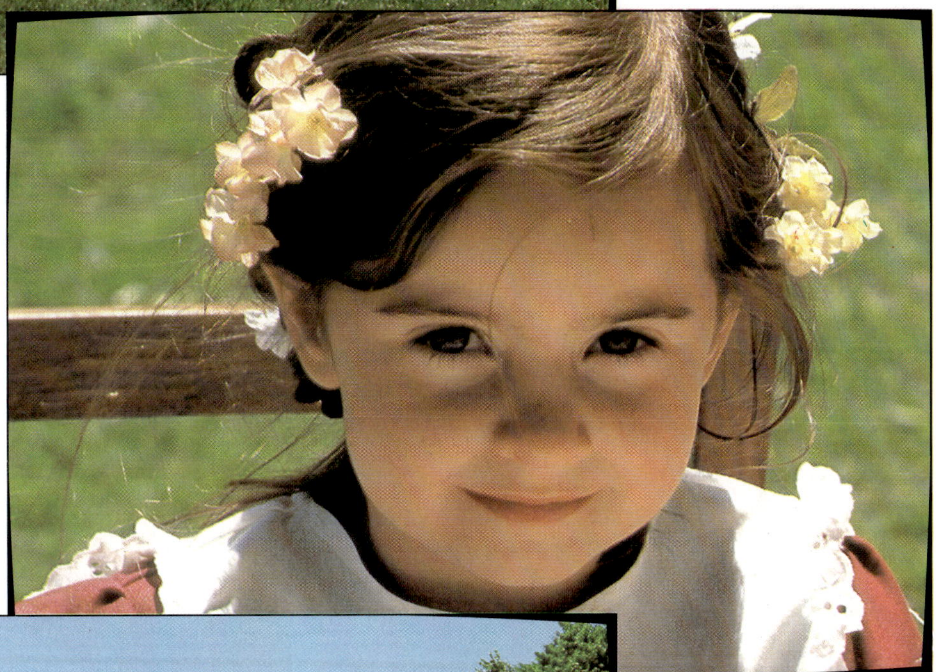

4: *Children are less intimidated by the camera when you get down to their own level. Ask them about their impressions of the day, whether or not they liked the food, or if they intend to get married, in order to draw them out and, hopefully, to get some amusing answers.*

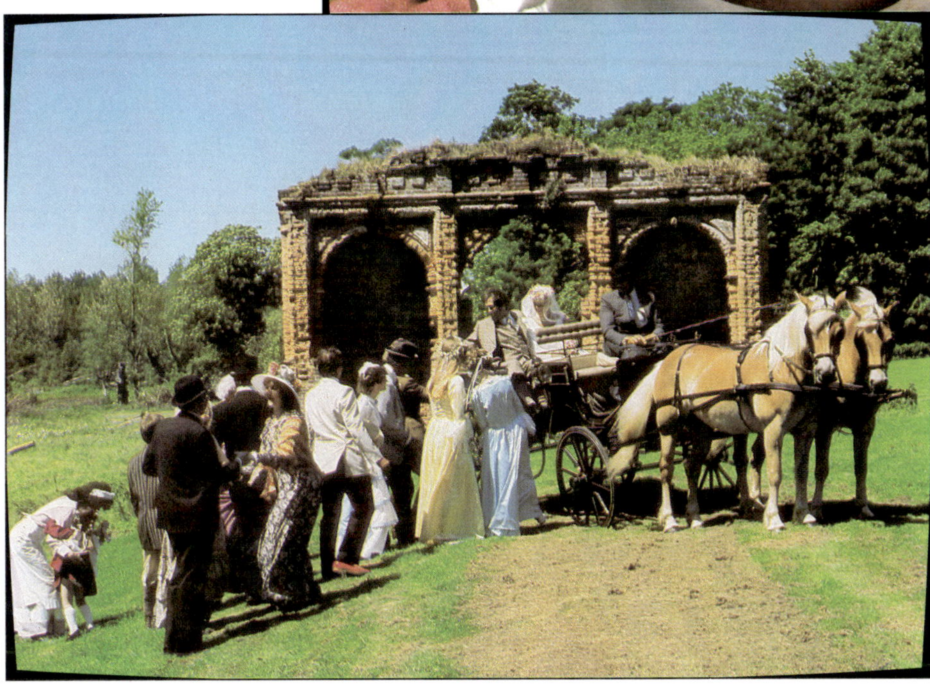

5: *The bride and groom departing by carriage. Coverage of this moment should include long shots to show the overall scene, as well as close-ups of individual guests identified earlier in the day.*

One of the difficult choices to make when covering the wedding reception is to decide how long your coverage should last. If you are unable to edit, you will probably have allocated something like 20 minutes, but the set pieces will take up most of that time. This leaves you with little space for interviews with family and friends. It is also easy to get carried away and record almost continuously, thus losing a sense of structure in the tape.

In fact, it is far better to be selective about your coverage and to limit the sequences that you record to quite short chunks. When you ask friends to say something about the bride and groom, a few short sentences are more effective than a long, meandering monologue. Similarly, coverage of people eating and drinking becomes rather tedious to watch after a while. By shooting in 20-second bursts at regular intervals, you convey more visual interest and indicate the passing of time through the course of the afternoon. This also allows you to relax and to integrate more fully into the celebrations, and that in turn will make the coverge that you get more relaxed and lively. As long as you remain alert to the major moments of the afternoon, you will be able to produce a video which accurately reflects the atmosphere of the bride and groom's big day and gives great pleasure to everyone involved.

TIMING SEQUENCES

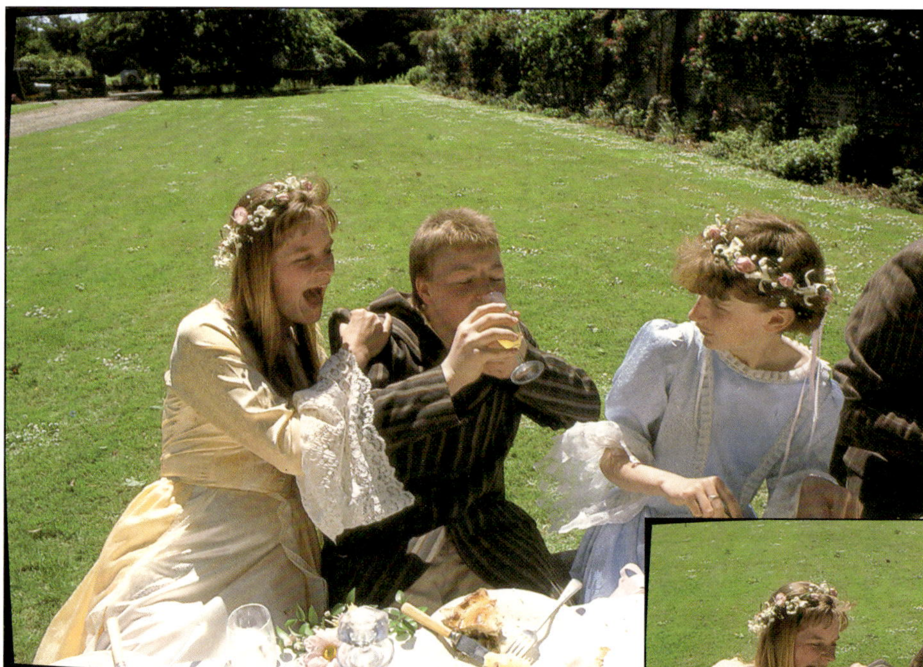

1: *This shot comes from a short section of the tape covering a group of friends at the party. Such antics can be highly entertaining, but do not dwell on them for too long.*

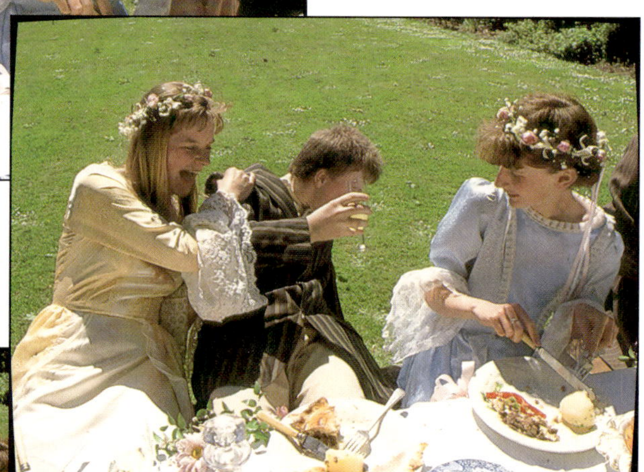

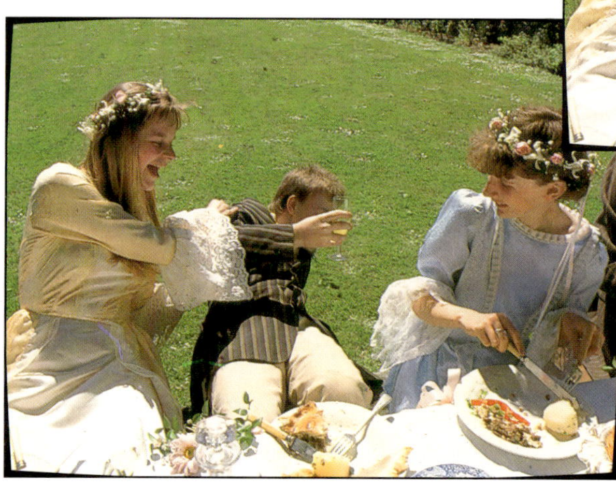

2,3: *This shot shows one of the guests tumbling unexpectedly backwards onto the grass. At such unexpected moments be sure to swivel round to catch the reaction of those standing by. Twenty seconds of this scene is quite adequate to convey the action and the atmosphere.*

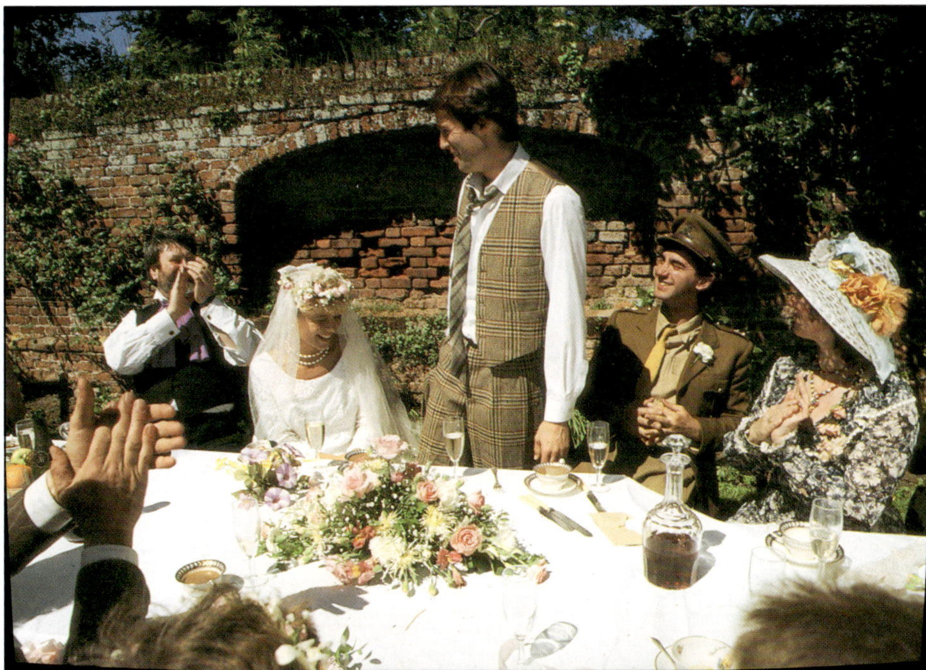

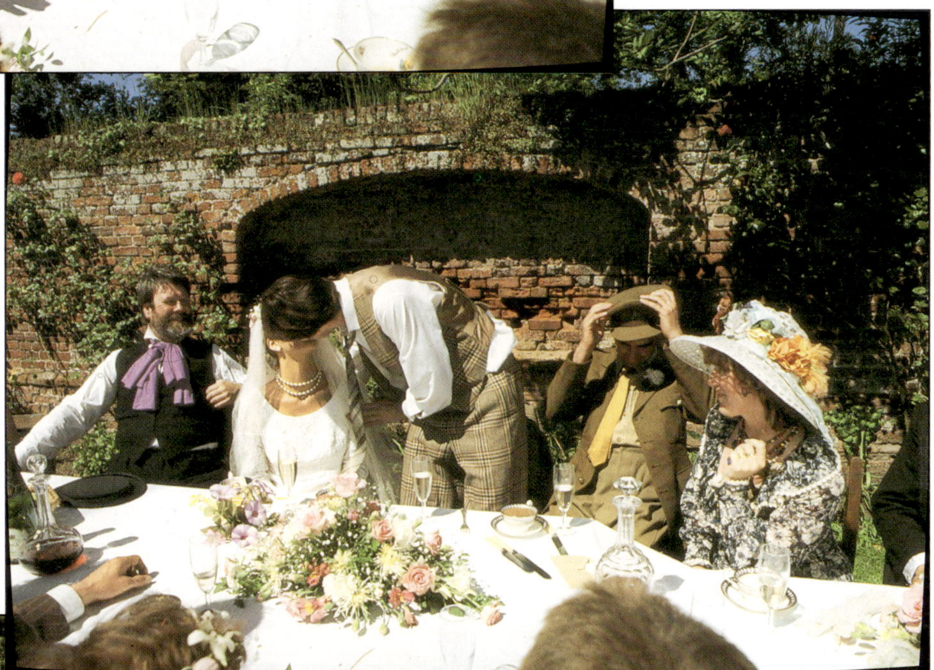

4,5: These shots are of the bridegroom responding to the telegrams and speeches. If possible, record the speeches using an external microphone placed centrally on the table (it can easily be hidden). Nearby sound, such as guests clapping, will be over-prominent using the in-camera microphone.

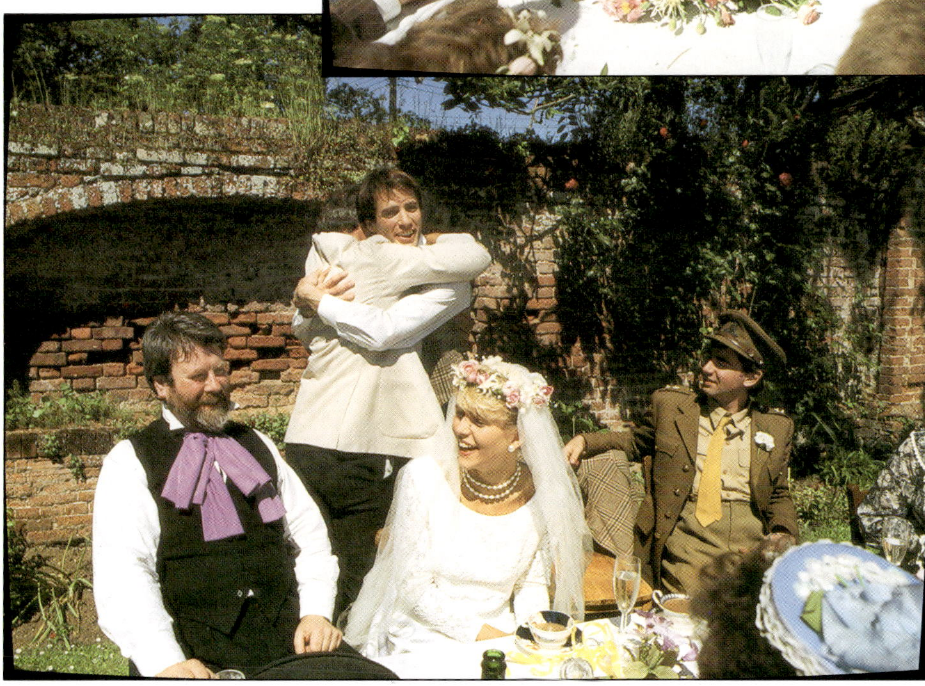

6: Your coverage should reflect the fun of the wedding party as much as it did the formality of the ceremony. The exchange of kisses after the speeches is shown here.

If you are going to edit your coverage after shooting, then you do not have to be so selective about the coverage and timing of your material. Any shots that do not work can be discarded, and over-lengthy sequences can be cut down to a more manageable size.

With editing you can also introduce cutaway shots, which are not central to the main action in the sequence, into your video. Such material, for example, could be of someone trying not to fall asleep while speeches are being made, or of a young child abandoning the banquet to prowl beneath the dining table amidst a forest of legs. Such material could, of course, be captured without editing, but necessitate rapid camera movements which look disconcerting to the viewer, and are thus best avoided. Remember that cutaways should have a five second or so lead-in time to facilitate editing.

Repeated cutaways can add a second, subsidiary storyline to the tape. For example, if the camera goes back to shots of the dining table throughout the afternoon, this acts both as a record of the guests congregating at this focal point, and also signals time passing as we see the plates gradually being emptied of food. Other cutaways can be used to keep track of interesting characters.

As a general rule try to keep them to but a few seconds. Otherwise, the effect will tend to diminish.

CUTAWAYS

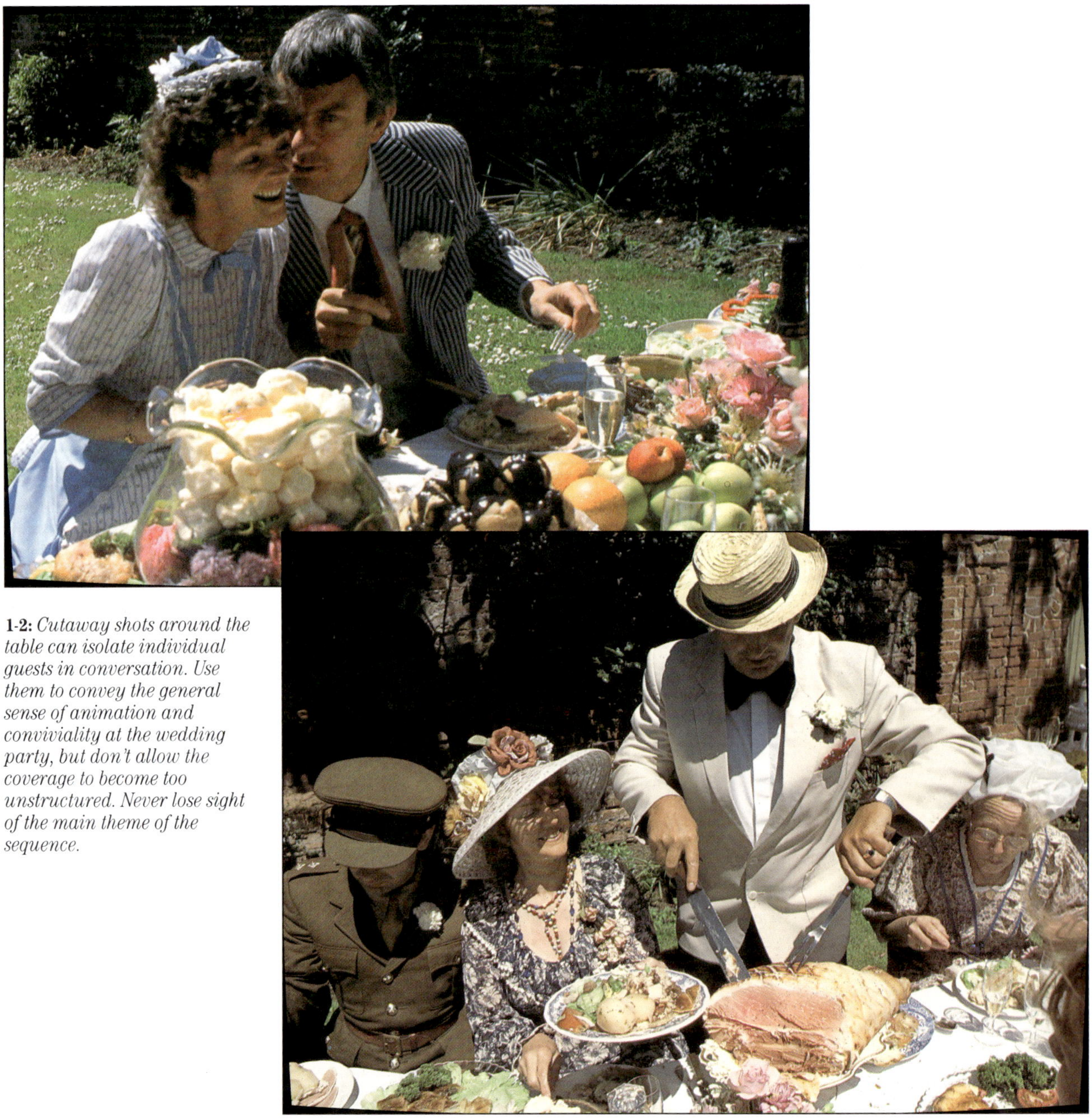

1-2: *Cutaway shots around the table can isolate individual guests in conversation. Use them to convey the general sense of animation and conviviality at the wedding party, but don't allow the coverage to become too unstructured. Never lose sight of the main theme of the sequence.*

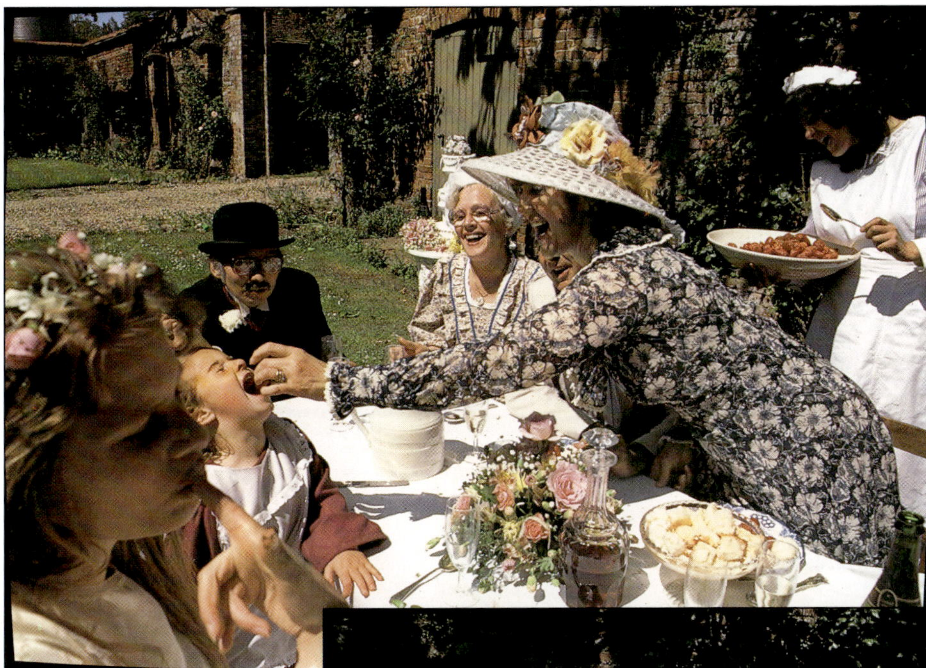

3: Frame some of the cutaway shots between other participants. This allows you to use the zoom to move in on people and catch them in a more spontaneous mood.

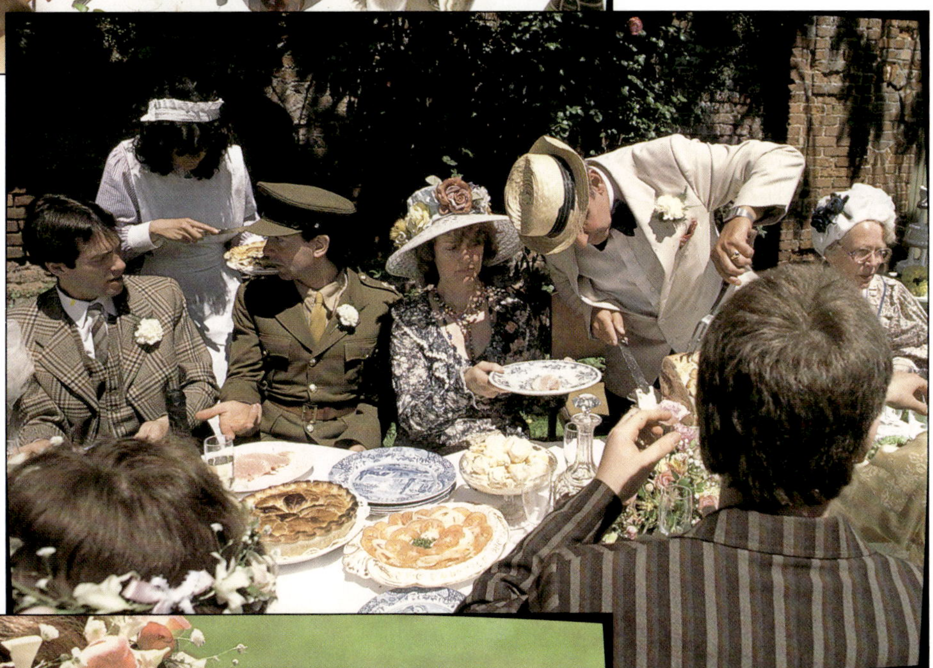

4: Cutaways do not necessarily have to be in close-up. In fact, if the main part of the sequence is filmed in close-up or mid-shot, cutaways are often more effective in long-shot.

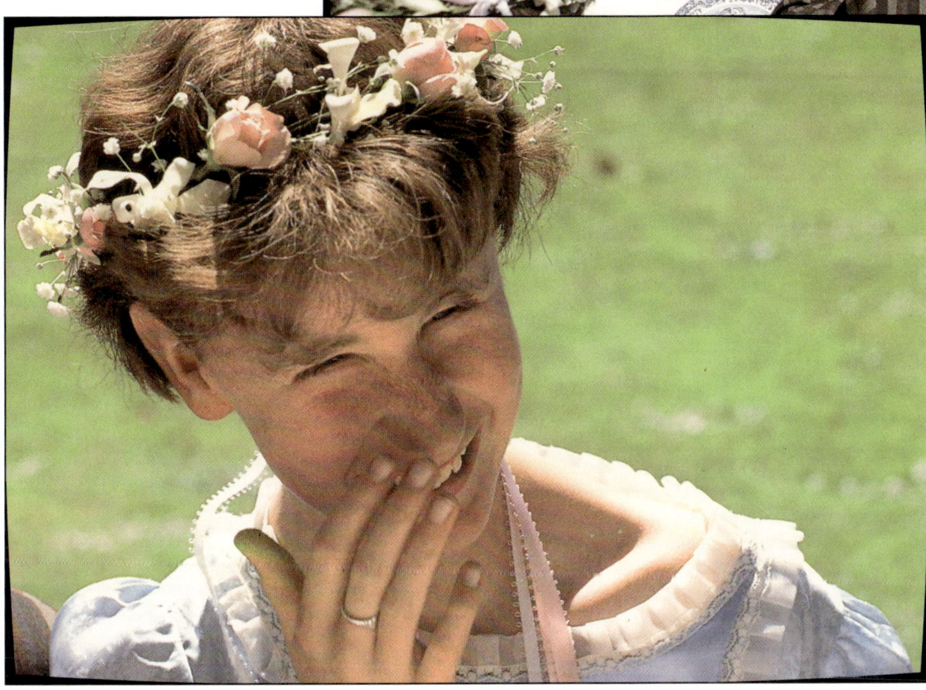

5: By their informal nature, cutaway shots should not be posed. They should give the impression that they are glances away from the main action, capturing people unaware of the presence of the camera.

The golden rule in video is to let the action happen in front of the camera, not to let the camera chase the action. However, shots of the reception in progress taken from a fixed camera position could easily seem rather static, compared with the liveliness of the event, although this can be overcome to a considerable extent by changing camera positions when new shots are required.

Despite this general rule, you could indulge in some camera movement. The most successful of these shots will be when the camera moves around and across the action it is recording – *crabbing* is the term for sideways movement, *arcing* when the camera moves round a subject. Such shots allow the viewer to observe the subject from different viewpoints and to place him or her within the broader context of the scene. The crabbing movement should be slow, and the camera should remain at a constant distance from the subject. In this sense it differs from the pan: the pan introduces new material into the frame, while the crab show shows the same material from a new angle.

The arcing shot is also useful when recording moving subjects. If someone is walking toward the camera, you can exercise a slow action around them so that the shot ends with them walking away from the camera. While the arcing shot is useful in varying your coverage, use it with moderation.

MOVING CAMERA SHOTS

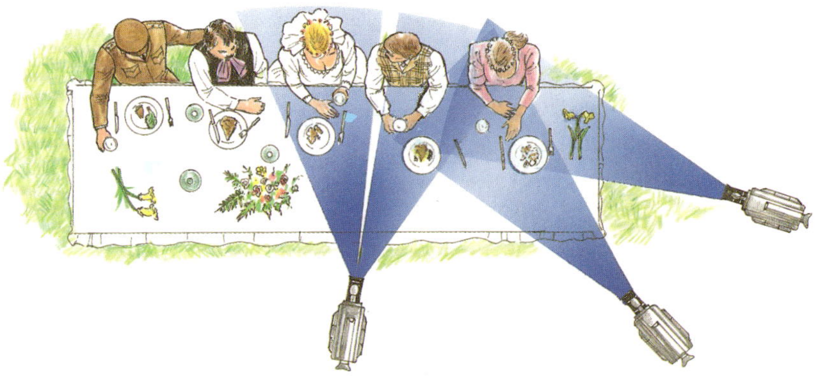

1: *The arcing action is one in which the camera makes a 180 degree sweep around the subject. It can be used on any shot – close-up, mid-shot or long-shot. Combining an arcing shot with one in which the size of the image within the frame changes simply does not work.*

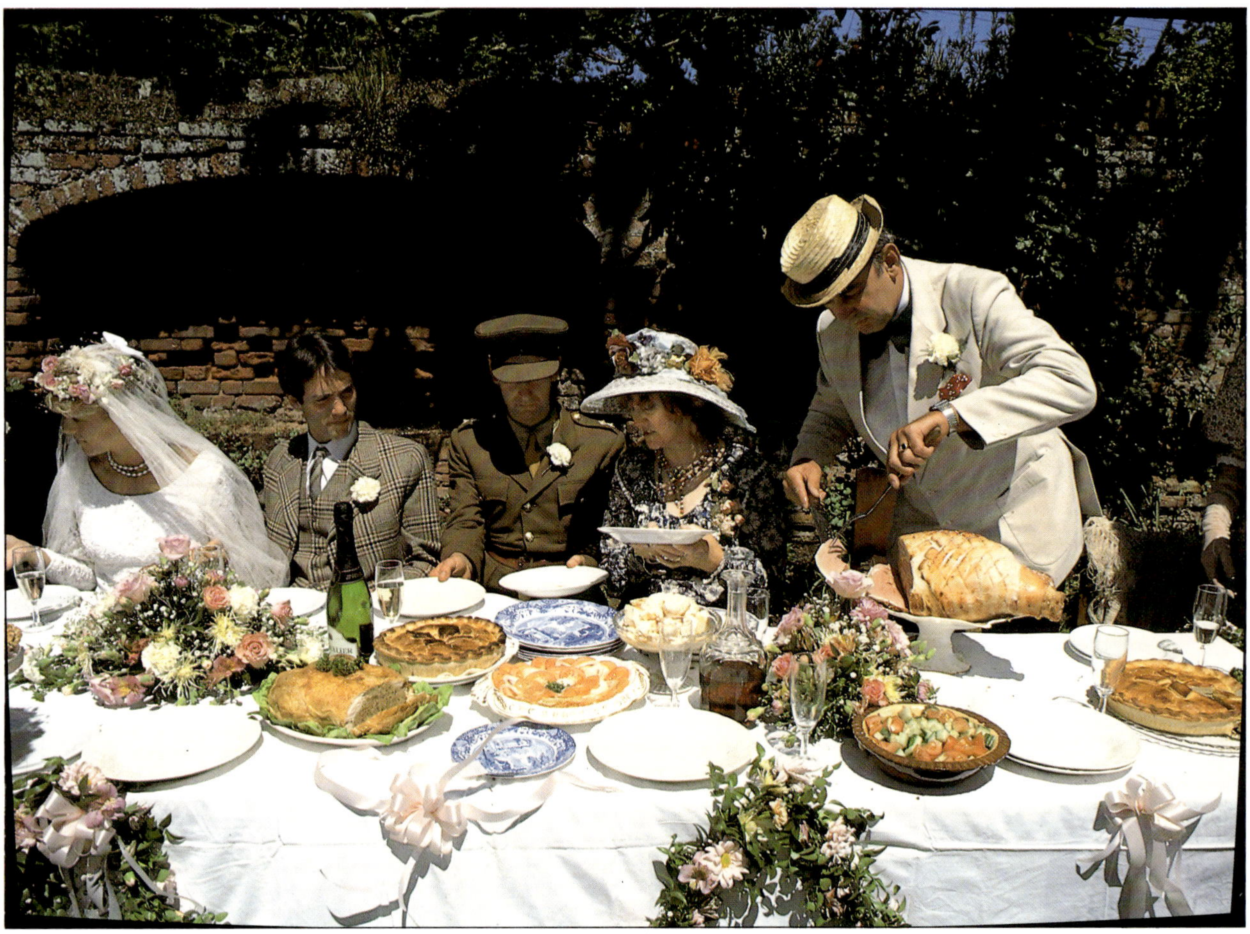

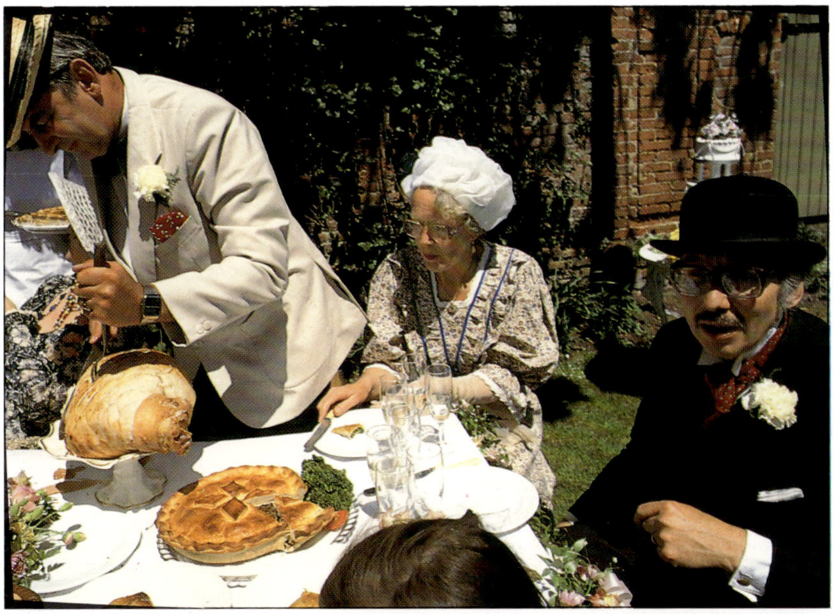

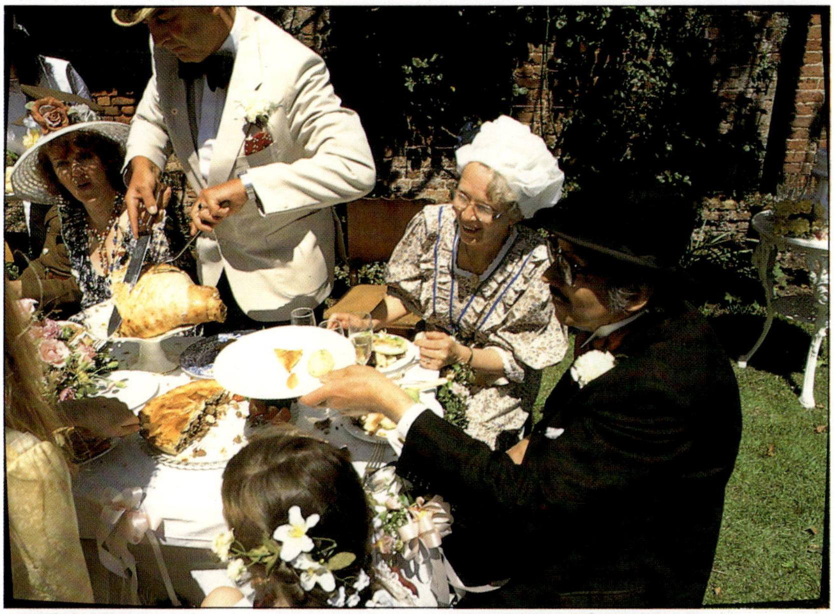

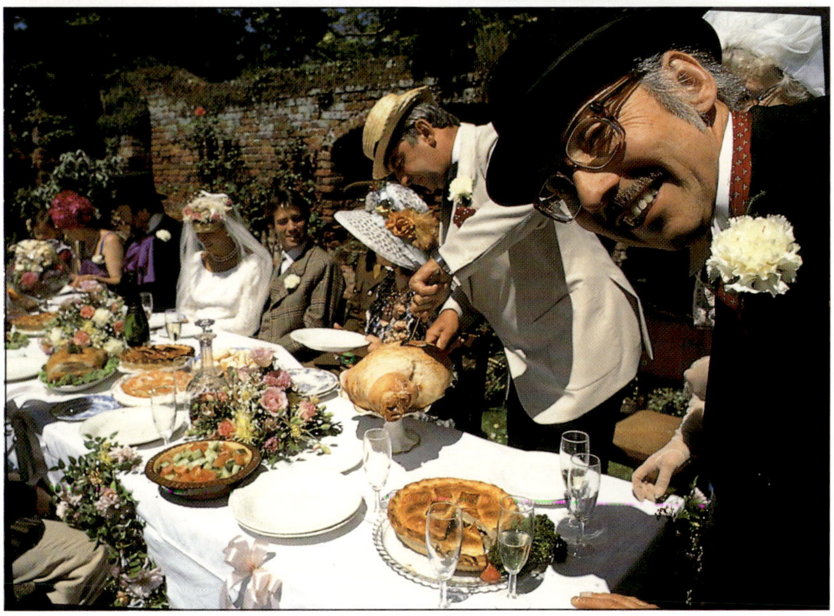

2–3: *The arcing shot around the guest wearing the bowler hat also includes the other guest carving a ham. The two subjects are placed in relationship by the moving camera.*
3–4: *As the arcing shot ends, the guest carving the ham comes into greater prominence and the camera starts to pull back from the table.*

Although you should do as much advance planning for every shoot as you possibly can, you should not approach your video-making with too many preconceptions about exactly what is going to happen. There are bound to be certain sequences that you will want to capture, and that the bride and groom will want you to record. And of course you should go all out to film these. But this should not blind you to the other opportunities for coverage that you may not be able to plan. Be alert for these at all times and you will produce a video with the right mixture of the expected and the spontaneous.

The shots on this page come from a wedding video that illustrated this blend very well. There were plenty of predictable sequences – such as shots of the bride before she left home, and coverage of the couple immediately after the ceremony. But there were also surprises – the colourful guard of honour with musical accompaniment, and the unexpected telegrams with their humorous messages. Both these scenes were gifts to the video maker, adding colour, movement, and amusement, as well as providing plenty of chances for the video to capture the surprised reactions of the guests to the various happenings. It is often these 'added extras' that make a video truly memorable.

RANGE OF COVERAGE

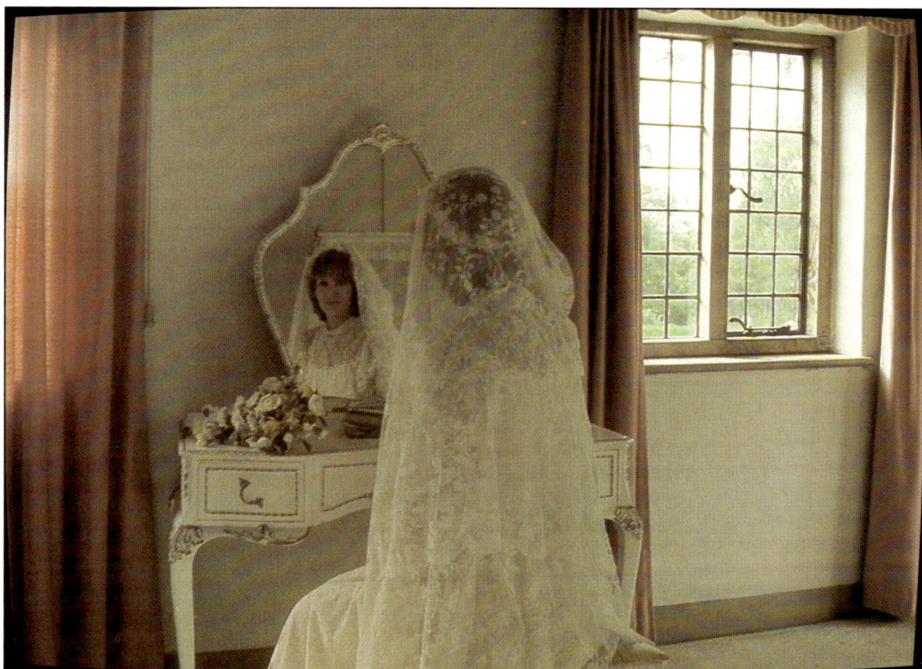

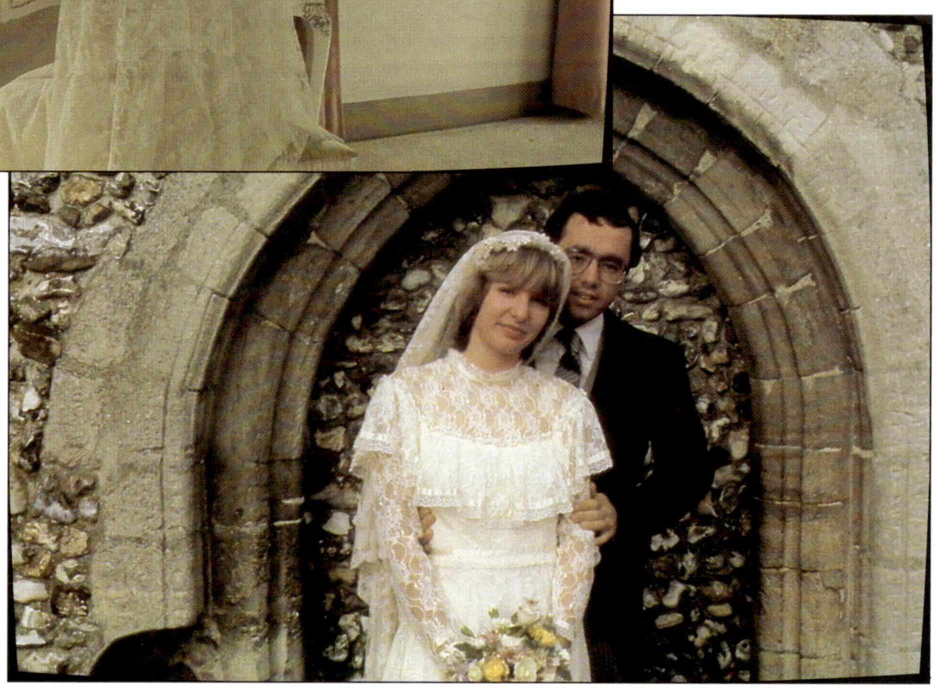

1-2: *Shots like these of the bride and the couple might seem predictable, but people will expect to see them in a wedding video.*

3-4: *The unexpected – whether ceremonial or simply humorous – will add variety and a little light relief.*

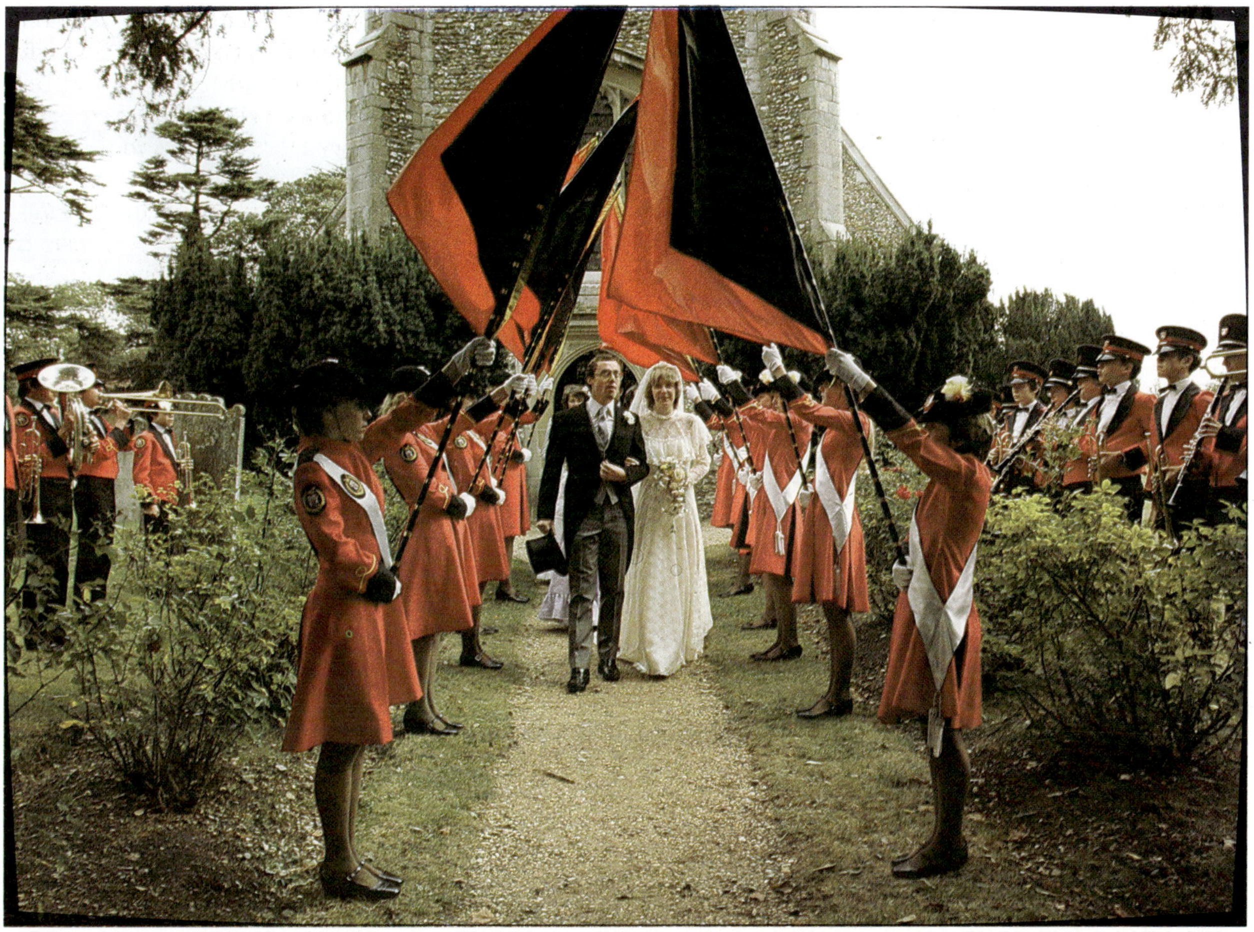

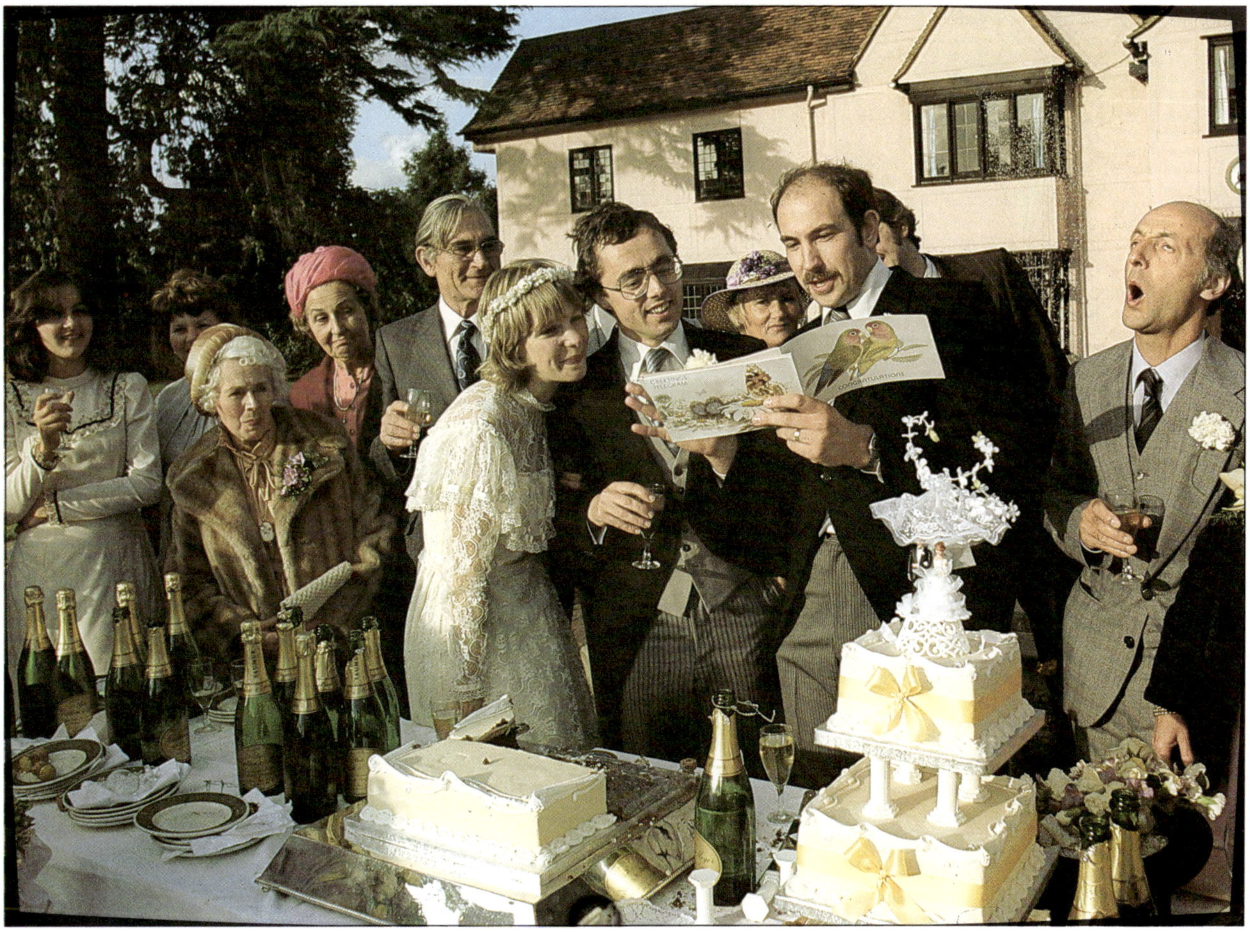

PROJECT NOTEBOOK

WEDDINGS

These project notebooks (there is one at the end of every chapter in the book) are designed to offer an informal *résumé* of some of the ideas that have been introduced and to pinpoint some of the problems that have already been encountered. Since the range of video experience is as exhaustive as the range of subjects that you may choose to cover, no book can be comprehensive. Make your own notes about techniques, situations, and problems encountered and solved as you go along. Such a record will be as invaluable as the experience you gain from tackling different projects as you explore the world of video.

■ The manual might say: Turn up, turn on, point and shoot – it's as easy as that. Experience proves, after the first few shots, that there is no substitute for planning the shoot in advance.

■ Planning that is not carried out in detail is as bad as no planning at all.

■ Video is a combination of art and practicalities: the composition of the interior shot might look great, but have you remembered to re-adjust the white balance?

■ When you've got a great exterior location for an event, it always rains – make contingency plans.

■ Think coverage first, sequences second, shots next.

■ People are not robots, they don't run to time or to orders.

■ Don't be obtrusive: mix and be friendly. Let others enjoy and enjoy yourself.

WORKING WITH PEOPLE

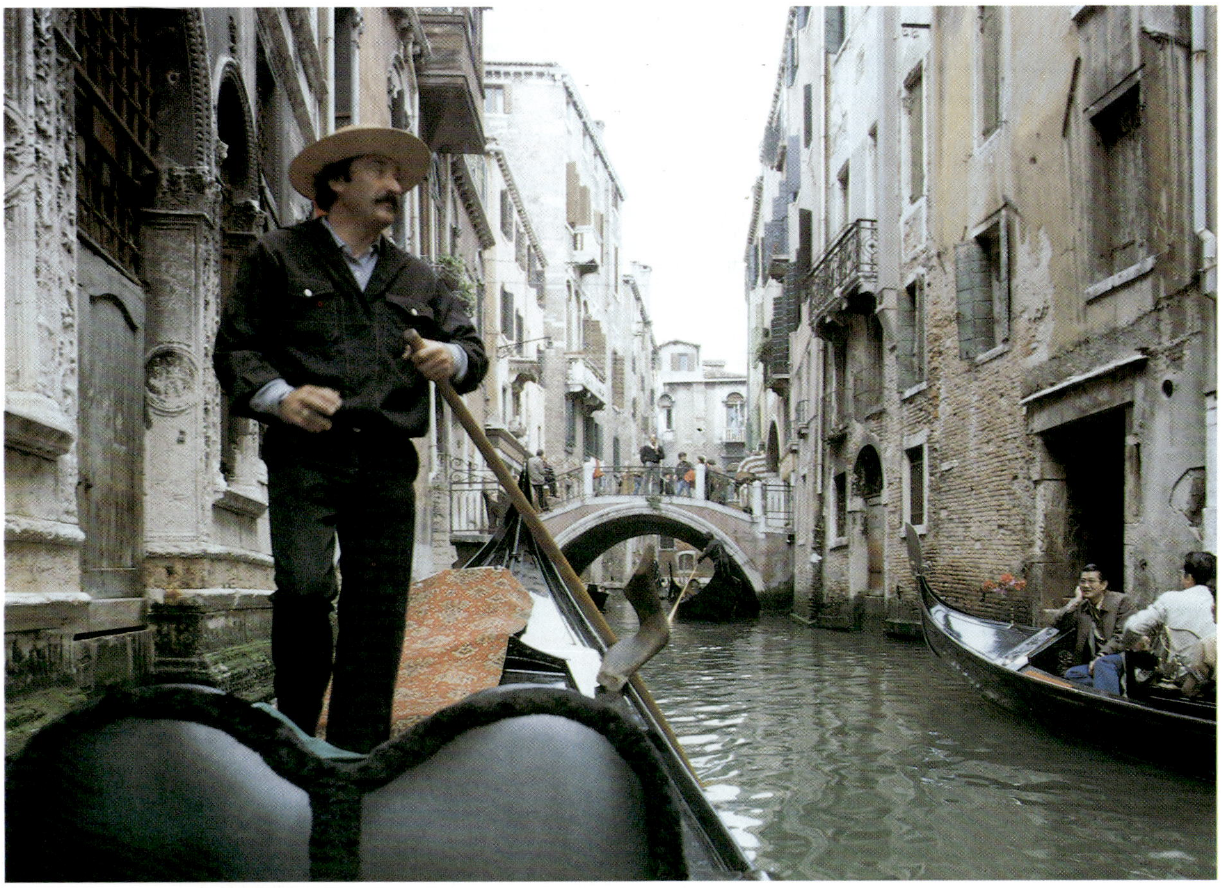

The basic unit of the language of video is the 'shot', which should contain sufficient information for the viewer to understand what is going on at any particular point in the narrative. But shots should be more than informative, they should be pleasing to look at, too.

This chapter – which concentrates on videos of people, from footage of the family to more highly structured interviews – therefore examines some of the basic rules for composing such shots. But while many of the principles are the same as in still photography, there will be additional techniques to master.

If you watch television, you'll notice that most shots of people are taken from shoulder level and frame the subject with a long-shot. Mid-shots and close-ups are used for more intimate situations, such as interviews, or shots which record the reaction of the subject to something that has happened earlier in the narrative. While the significance of these different types of shot has already been considered, note how the position of the camera also has an effect on the way the viewer 'reads' the image.

The most obvious camera angles are the low- and high-angle shots. These immediately imply a sense of either inferiority or superiority. This can be used to imply certain relationships between characters: for example if, in an interview, the subject is shown from a slightly low angle, he or she naturally assumes a greater authority on the screen. This is because the audience automatically identifies with the shot, and subconsciously agrees with its point of view. Of course, if the camera angle is too low, the shot will instead appear odd, and the psychological effect will be lost.

Camera angles also help to establish a sense of space within the screen and create a more satisfying sense of composition. A head-on shot of a character gives the viewer little sense of depth. But by placing the camera at 45 degrees to the subject, elements of the background are more fully integrated into the frame. In general, shots taken from such an angle are seen as 'neutral' – the camera is regarded as an observer of the scene, rather than an active participant, as is implied by a head-on shot.

Extreme camera angles call attention to themselves, and should only be used if your intention is to convey a sense of the extraordinary. In film and television, they tend to be used for suspense or shock effects. So, if you use a similar extreme angle for an everyday event, such as an elderly person recalling their childhood, you will inadvertantly imply that there is either something very unusual about this, or the shot will just look odd.

CAMERA ANGLES

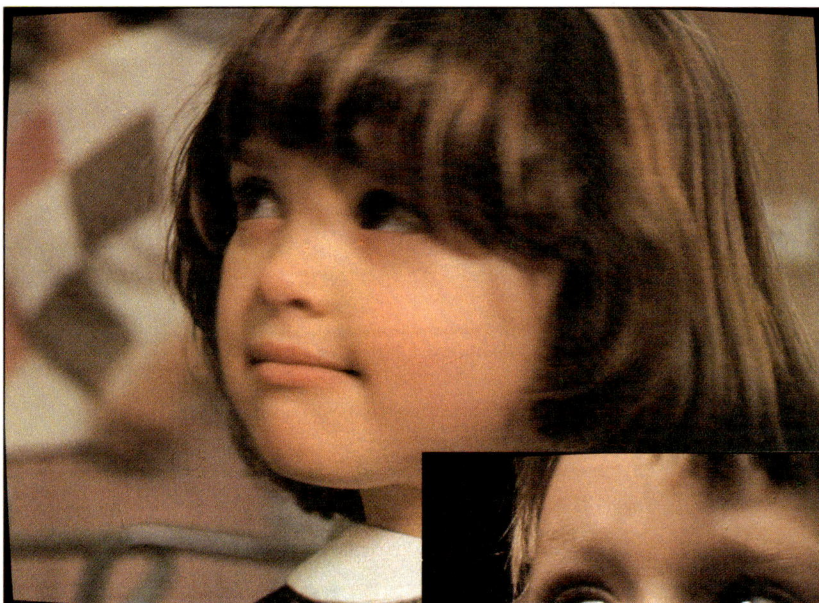

1: *Shots of children are too often taken from an 'adult' high-angle level. By bending down, and shooting from a slightly lower angle, the individuality of the child is given more emphasis.*

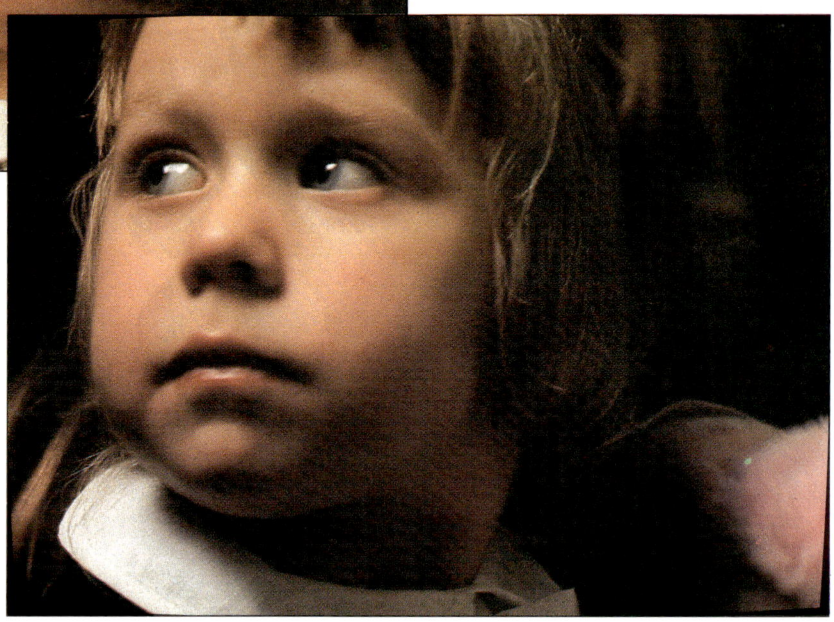

2: *The choice of camera angles should take eyeline into account. When the subject is looking away from the camera, a head-on shot effectively appears as one taken from an angle.*

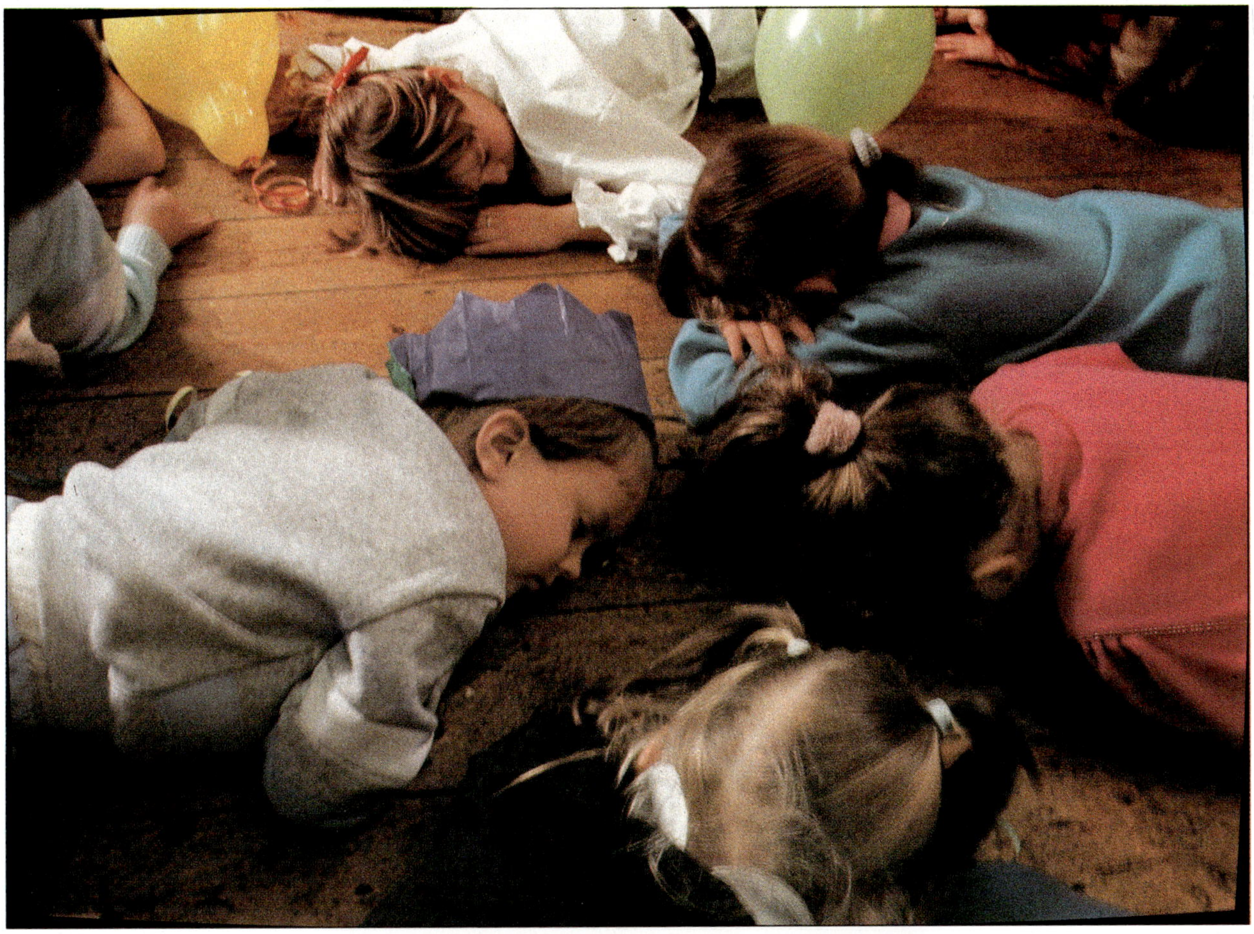

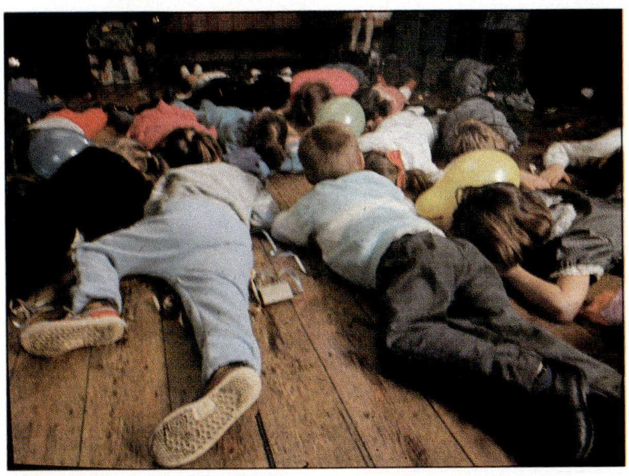

3-4: *These shots of children playing at a party gain an immediacy by the camera angle used. The viewer is quickly brought close to the action.*

5-6: *Note how by following the rules of composition this shot could have been improved. The head appearing at the bottom left-hand corner of the shot distracts the audience's attention and disrupts the composition. The solution is to move in that little bit closer and exclude it.*

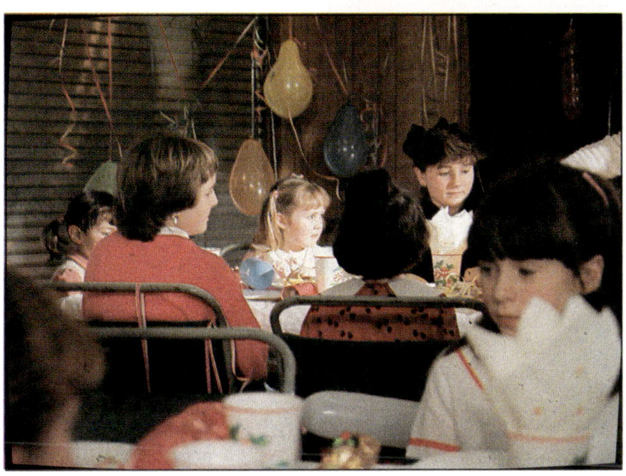

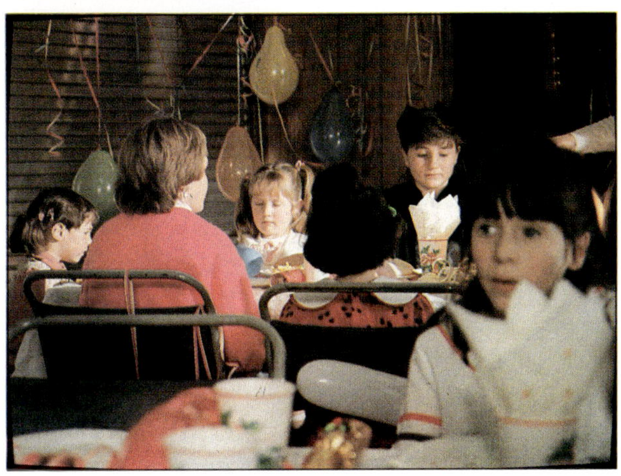

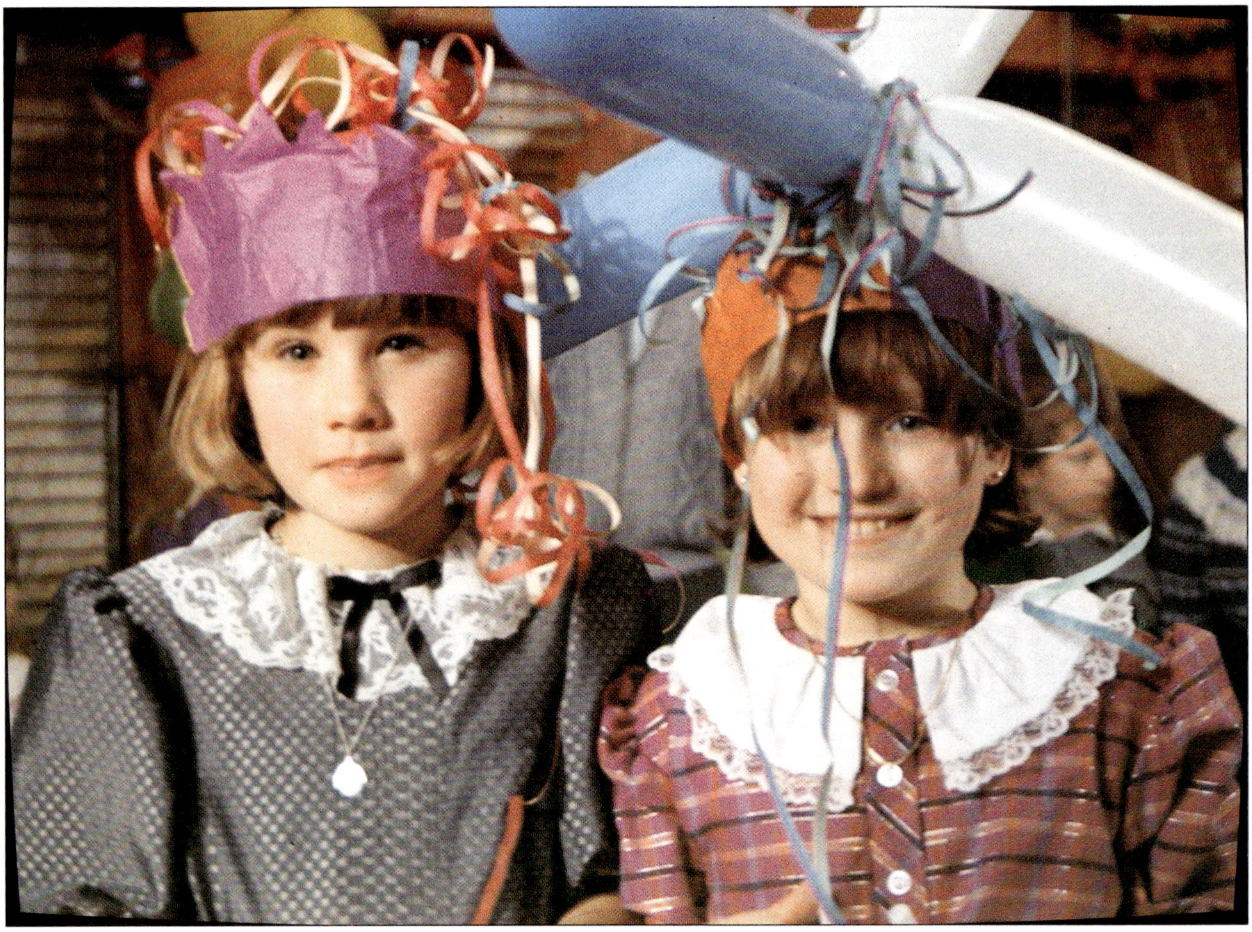

BALANCED COMPOSITION

The basic rules of composing the shot are very similar to those that govern composition in still photography. However, the frame area that you have to work with is that of the television screen, an area four units in width by three in depth. The first consideration is that the subject should be framed centrally on the screen. Yet the screen area allows little room for freedom, and its edges command little attention from the viewer. If subjects are framed too low, this will give the impression that they are 'dropping out' of the screen.

Close-up shots should be framed at a head and shoulders level, rather than head and neck. In fact, there are a number of cut-off points on the body that are best avoided – the knees in a long shot and the waist in mid-shot. For big close-ups, frame the subject from the chin upwards, allowing the top of the head to project just out of the top of the screen. When taking long shots of people, allow a certain space between the feet and the bottom of the screen. It looks very odd if the subject appears to be walking along the bottom of the frame.

The purpose behind all framing techniques is first to concentrate the viewers' attention on the main subject and, second, to achieve a visually pleasing image on the screen. The first objective is achieved by framing centrally, while the second requires a good deal of thought about the elements within the frame.

In addition to the subject, the frame will also contain elements in the foreground and background. By cleverly using foreground elements you can suggest that we are spying on the main subject. A clichéd example of this involves the camera lens peeping through foliage, which is visible round the edges of the screen. Such framing gives an interesting sense of depth to the shot. The technique can be extended by focusing first on the foreground and then using the zoom to concentrate on the subject. This gives you the best of both worlds – the context together with detailed coverage of the subject itself. But be careful not to overuse the zoom with this technique.

The background elements help the viewer to place the subject of the shot within its context. But when framing subjects in close-up be careful that you do not omit the background. It is usually better to frame the subject in mid-shot, so allowing the viewer to take in the background, and then slowly move in for a close-up.

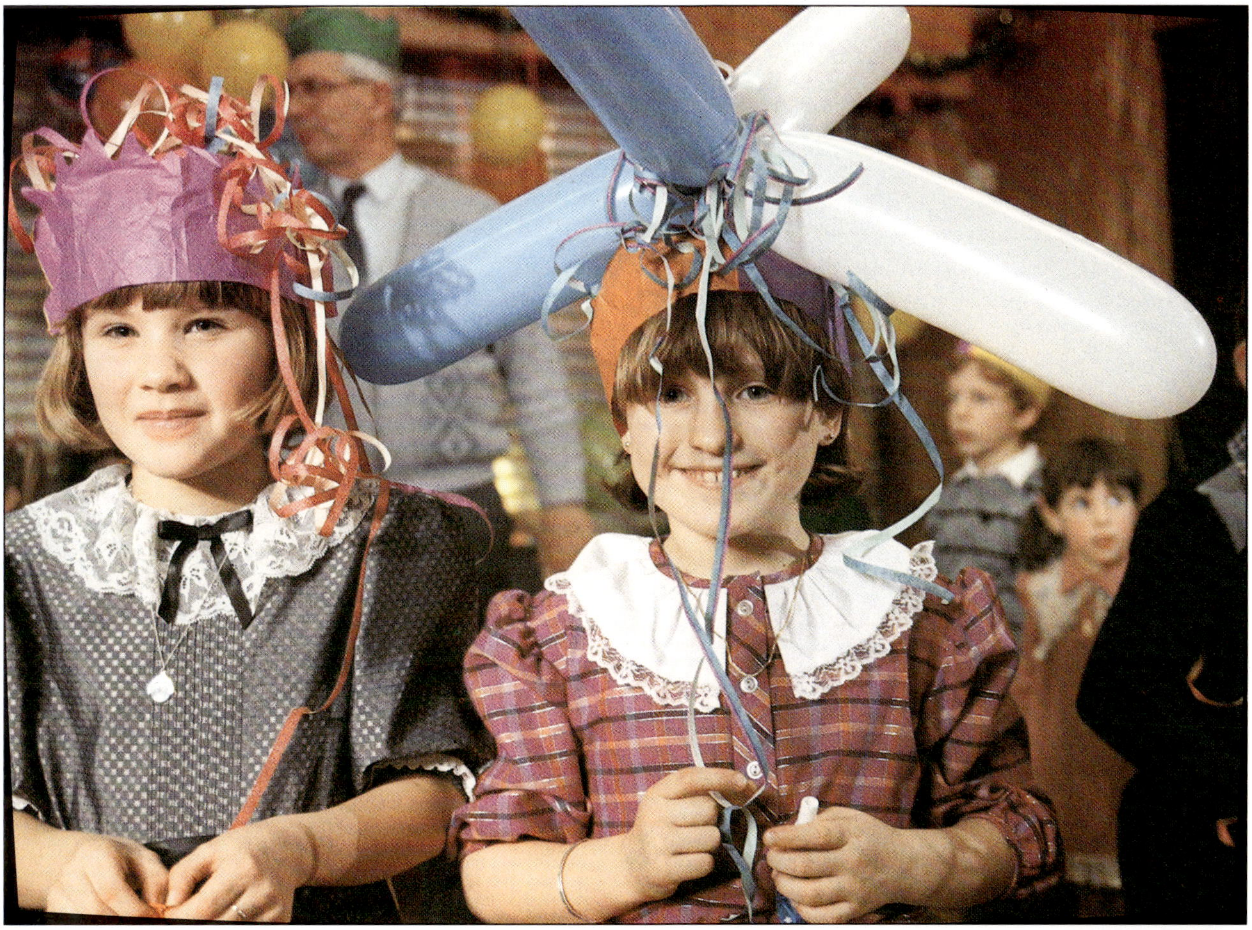

1-2: *The two shots above show how small changes in framing can have considerable effect on the image. Shot 1 fills the frame and looks balanced. Shot 2 is off centre so that the viewers' attention is drawn towards what is happening in the background.*

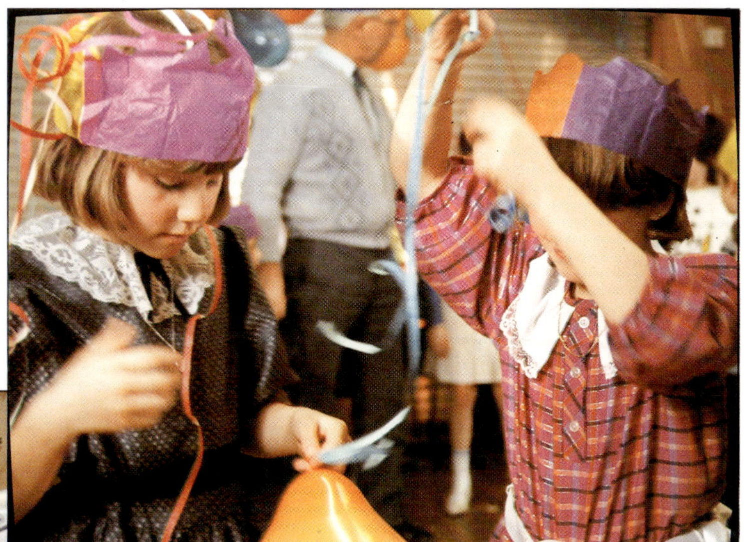

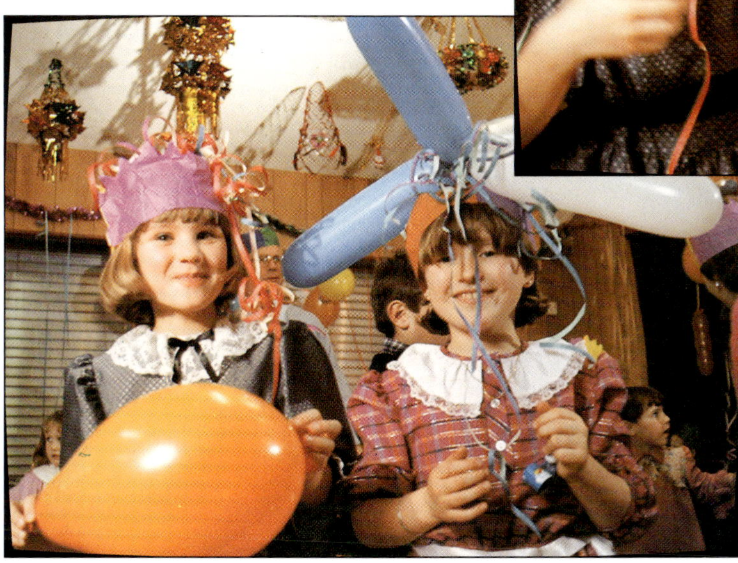

3-4: *Head-on shots are less successful in video than in still photography, partly because the subject becomes too conscious of the camera. The side-on shot of the two girls is much more relaxed and natural.*

Since video is about moving images, framing techniques must also take motion into account. Many shots will be of people or vehicles moving from one location to another. In such shots it is necessary to leave 'lead space'. This means that subjects should be placed to one side of the screen, leaving approximately two-thirds of the screen area for them to move into. Without this lead space, subjects appear to be too contained by the borders of the screen.

A further convention on framing movements is that they should occur diagonally across the screen so avoiding the head-on shot which draws too much attention to the camera. An extension of this convention applies to entering and leaving the screen area.

The diagonal rule means that subjects should not enter or exit the frame from the sides of the screen. To the viewer, this again looks as if the subject is 'falling out' of the shot. While subjects can enter the shot from any direction, they should first appear by the corners of the screen.

When framing moving subjects, there are two basic options. The camera can either follow the subject as it moves, or remain static, allowing the subject to enter and exit the frame. Following the subject implies that the shot will end at a specific destination. Such shots are best achieved by a tracking and panning action in which the camera moves around the subject, who then exits from the frame moving away from the camera.

There are occasions in which you may require the action to happen head-on. Such motion can bring with it an enormous dramatic impact, as happens in so many film car chases. The convention is also used by documentary film-makers to imply that the subject is unaware of the camera, so lending authenticity to the project.

IN AND OUT OF THE FRAME

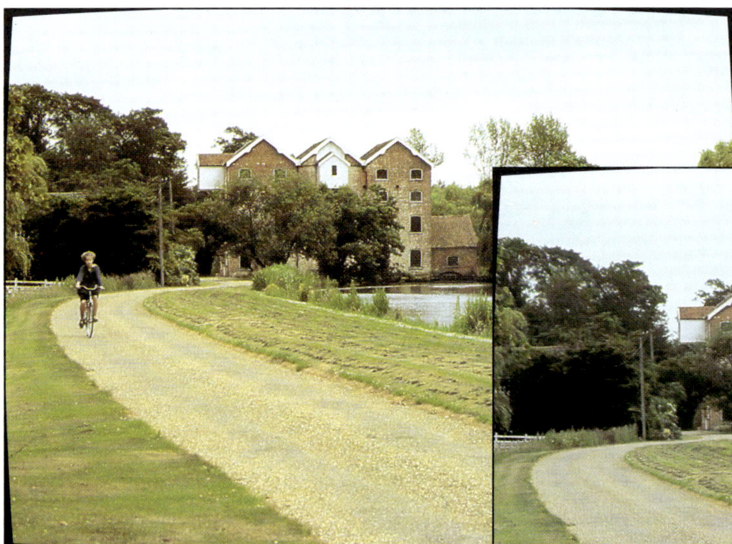

1: *The classic composition of a moving action shot. The subject in long-shot, the road leads diagonally out of the frame, providing lead space for the subject to move into.*

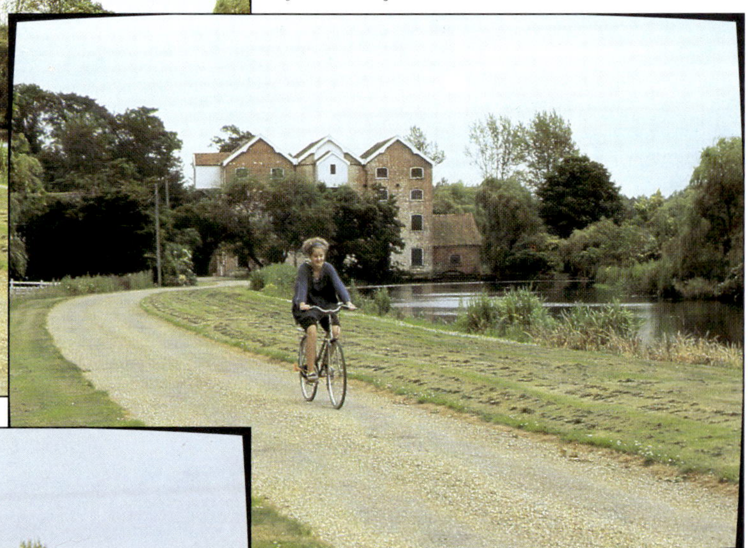

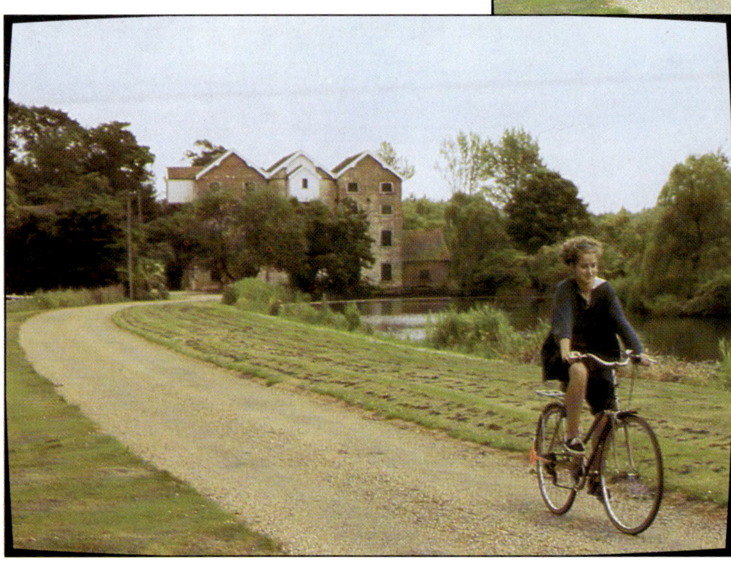

2: *From a fixed camera position, the subject moves toward the centre of the frame. Once the subject moves beyond this point, the viewer accepts that they are about to leave.*

3: *Because the action was framed diagonally, the subject exits the frame from the corner of the screen. If a pan of the action was intended, it should have begun at an earlier point when there was more lead space in the frame.*

4: *Head-on shots of moving subjects present more immediacy to the viewer. Since there is no movement relative to the frame itself, these shots should be centrally framed.*

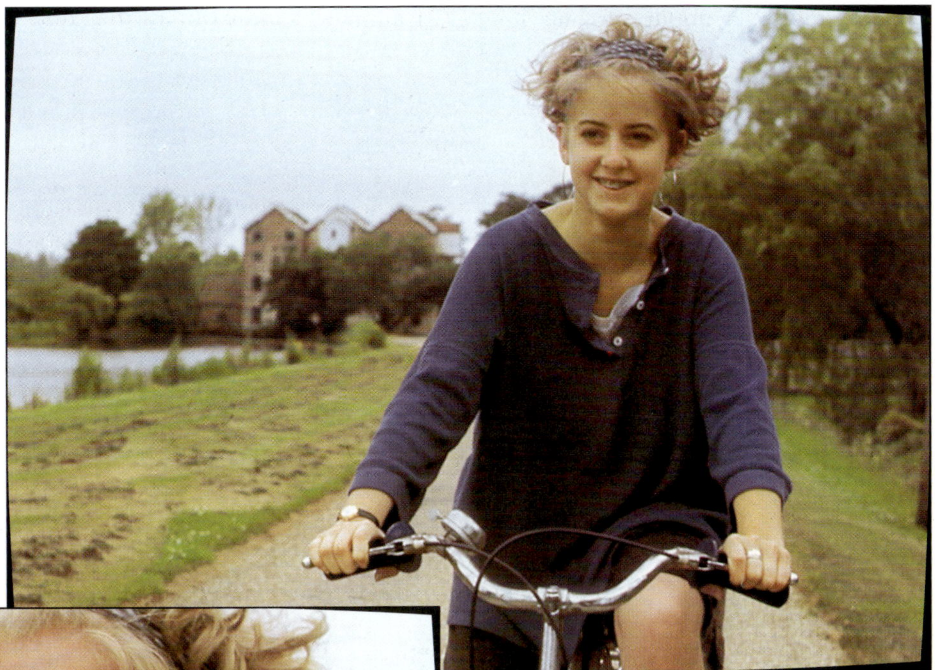

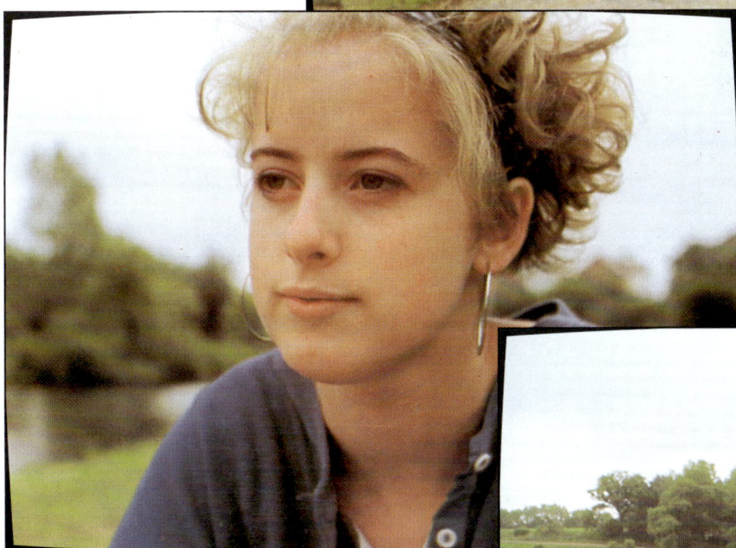

5: *As the subject comes into close-up, the diagonal rule of entering and exiting the screen applies. The diagonal line here is given by the subjects' eyeline.*

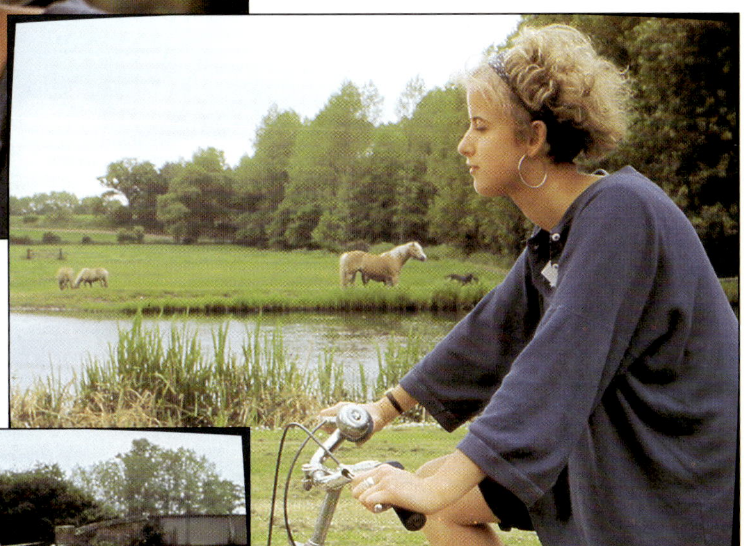

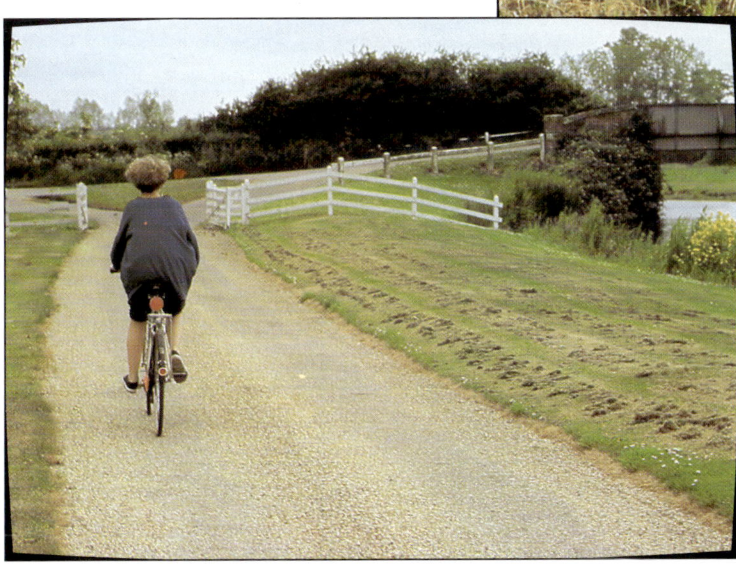

6: *A scene from a panning shot. The subject is given lead space in which to move. This space should be kept throughout the pan. If this were a static camera shot, the subject would appear to enter and exit from the sides of the screen – an obtrusive shot for audiences.*

7: *The pan ends with the camera coming to rest. The subject naturally exits from the shot in the far distance.*

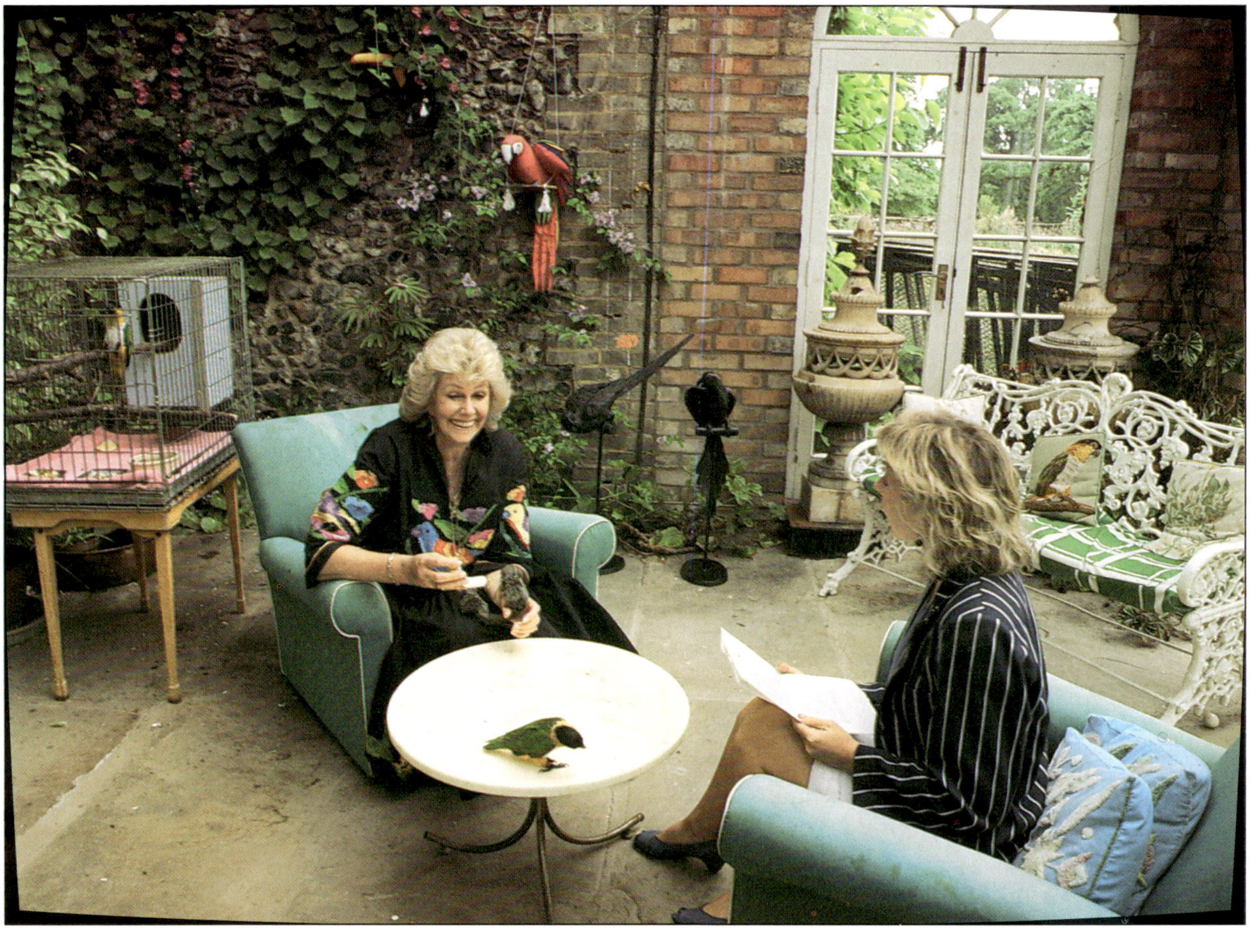

THE INTERVIEW 1

Interviews require two separate skills: those which establish the character of the interviewee and the camera skills which provide the best coverage of the interview.

Interviewing skills grow out of good research. Unless you have a detailed knowledge of your subject, it's unlikely you will ask the right questions, or give the interview any structure or purpose. Obviously, the nature of this research depends on your subject matter. Many public figures have had extensive press coverage which you can examine in libraries and newspaper files. But preparing an interview with someone who has attracted comparatively little press attention means that you will have to do your own homework. Without such research you will be in danger of asking non-questions, or of concentrating on side issues so leaving your viewers frustrated as they wait for you to tackle the main issues.

Apart from exceptional occasions your main concern will be to put your subject at ease. This means that you must be relaxed in front of the camera, otherwise your nervousness will quickly 'infect' your subject. To further relax him, you might reveal beforehand the questions you will be asking, though this approach might lead to stilted, set-piece replies. Its great advantage, however, is that your subject will have had time to consider the questions and, therefore, will be able to give fuller replies.

Also, avoid asking questions which can be answered with either a 'yes' or 'no'. Instead, introduce topics on which the interviewee can expand. And don't so concentrate on your next question that you either miss responding to what's being said, or ignore an unexpected opportunity to discuss other interesting subjects. Nor should you go to the other extreme, relentlessly interrupting. The viewer wants to hear your subject's opinions, not yours.

Camera technique will also be determined by the nature of the interview. In the project shown here, the subject kept a unique private zoo specializing in South American birds and animals, so obviously the background was very important. (In other situations, coverage would be kept very much to mid-shots and close-ups of the interviewer and the interviewee.) If you are able to edit your coverage afterwards, concentrate on filming your subject. You can shoot the interviewer putting questions and responding afterwards, and insert this footage at appropriate points in the edited tape.

The opening shots of the interview should establish the background in which it takes place. In this case, the colourful interior of the subject's house provided interesting material in its own right.

1: *The opening shots of the interview should establish the background in which it takes place. In this case, the colourful interior of the subject's house provided interesting material in its own right.*

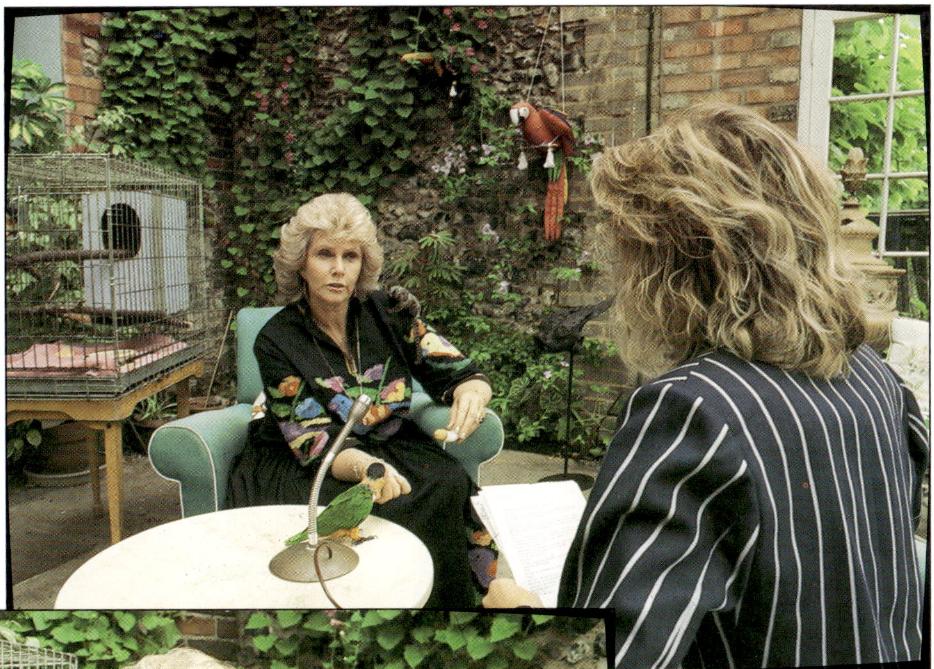

2: *The over-the-shoulder shot is useful for establishing the subject's immediate reaction to a question. However, if the shot lasts too long, the presence of the interviewer's back on screen becomes irritating and distracting.*

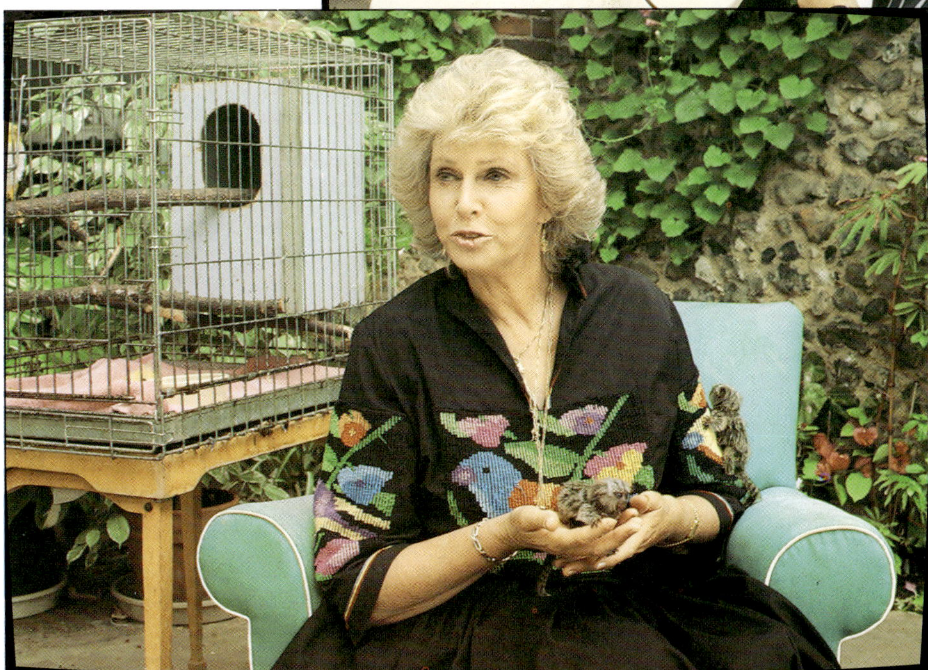

3: *In an informal interview, most shots can be framed at mid-shot. Close-ups intrude upon the subject and imply that the interview is in fact a dramatic interrogation.*

4: *Where the situation permits, allow the subject to perform or demonstrate a point. In this case, the animals from Lady Fisher's collection provide an additional source of interest and reveal the interviewee's close relationship with them. In other situations, you could show sequences of the subject at work, or demonstrating, for instance, a particular cooking point. When you are fortunate enough to have a very interesting subject, use a close-up. In an interview with a zoo owner, viewers will naturally want to see some of her animals and will rightly feel aggrieved if denied an opportunity to do so.*

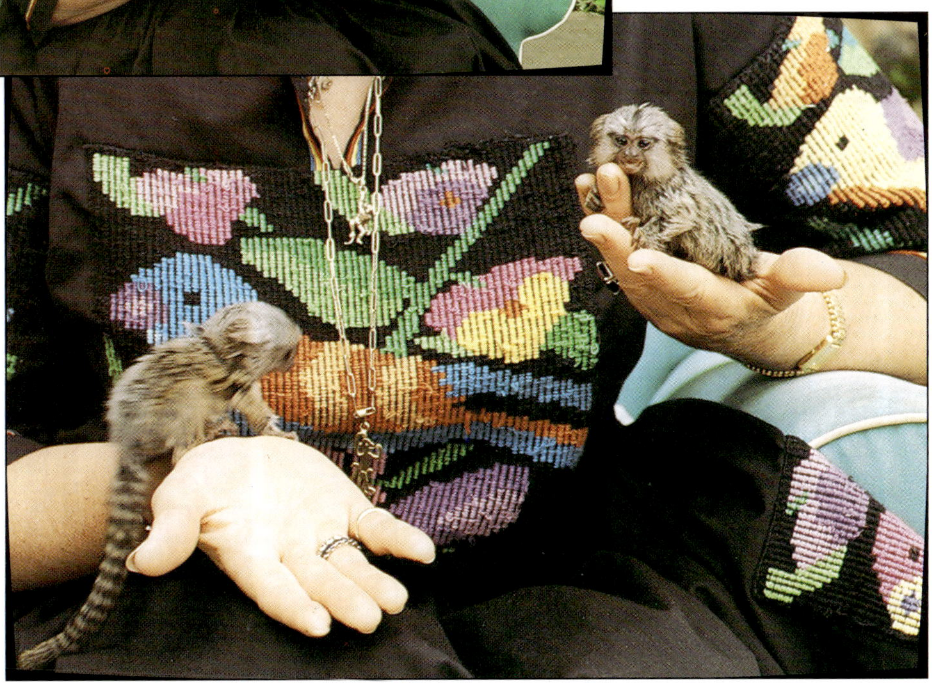

THE INTERVIEW 2

Like any other video project, interviews should have a clear, logical structure, with a beginning, middle and end. The piece can be introduced by the interviewer giving a brief outline of the ground that the discussion will cover. Alternatively, you could begin with a long shot of the interviewer and subject in conversation, gradually moving in to pick up what they are saying.

During the interview there are three basic shots to use in providing coverage. These are a big close-up framed at the chin, a close-up just below the shoulders, and a mid-shot taken at the breast. You can alternate between these shots as the interview progresses, but try to keep the frame size as constant as possible. Of course, there is no need to restrict yourself to these three shots, but they should provide you with sufficient visual variety. If there are natural pauses or breaks in the interview, they can be emphasized by recommencing with shots taken from a new camera position. The end of an interview can be indicated in two ways. The interviewer can thank his subject for having taken part in the film. And the camera can reinforce the sense of an ending either by resting on the subject or by gradually withdrawing into long-shot.

Below: *Three basic positions for recording interviews. Here (i) has two cameras recording the interviewer and interviewee respectively. With (ii), both interviewer and subject will be in each shot. The head-on shot (iii) is best used for a direct speech to camera – when the interviewer introduces the interview, for example.*

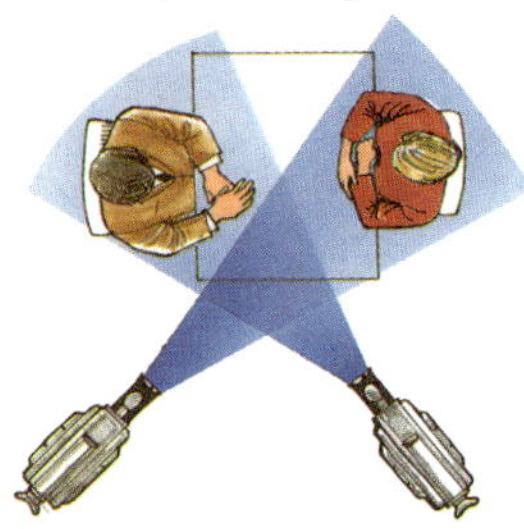

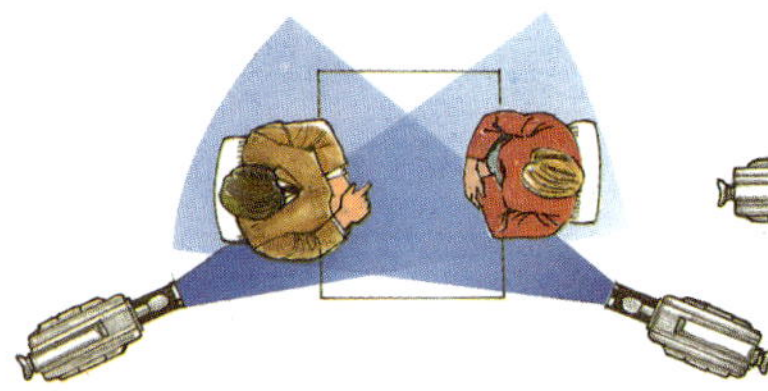

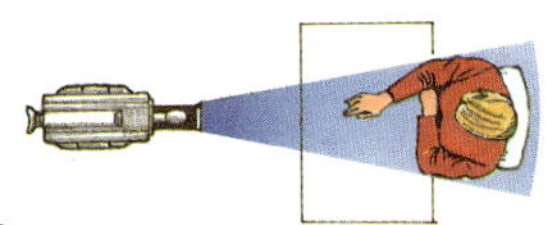

1: *To ensure that you get full coverage of the subject during the interview, you can take all your shots of the interviewer asking questions in a separate session afterwards. Match the frame size of these shots with those taken of the subject.*

2: *A good opening shot for the interview. The interviewer and subject are seen in long-shot, framed against the attractive conservatory windows. Use the zoom lens to move into mid-shot.*

3: *The interview is being recorded by a single hand-held camera. An experienced interviewer will be aware of the camera's position and make sure that he or she does not obscure the subject.*

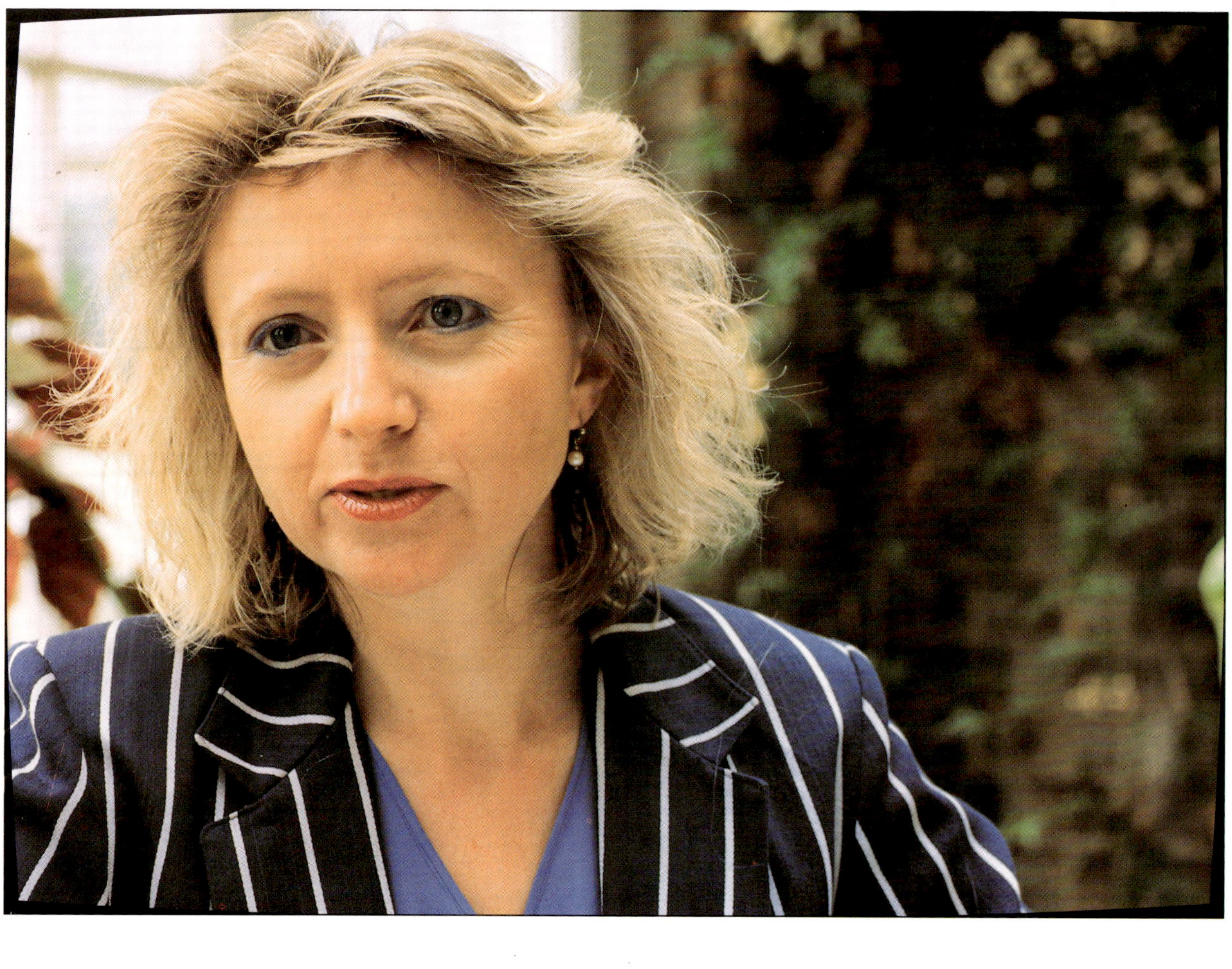

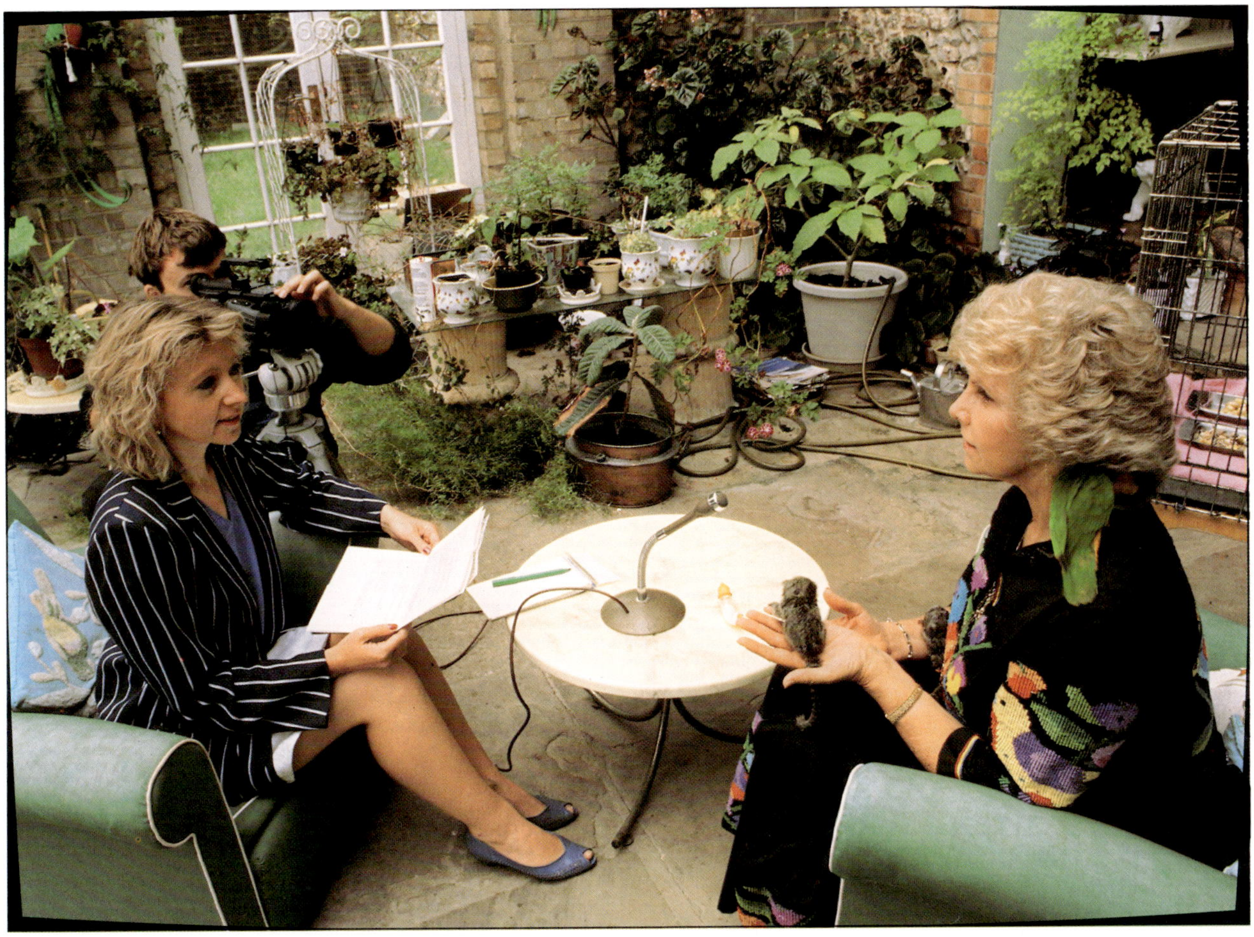

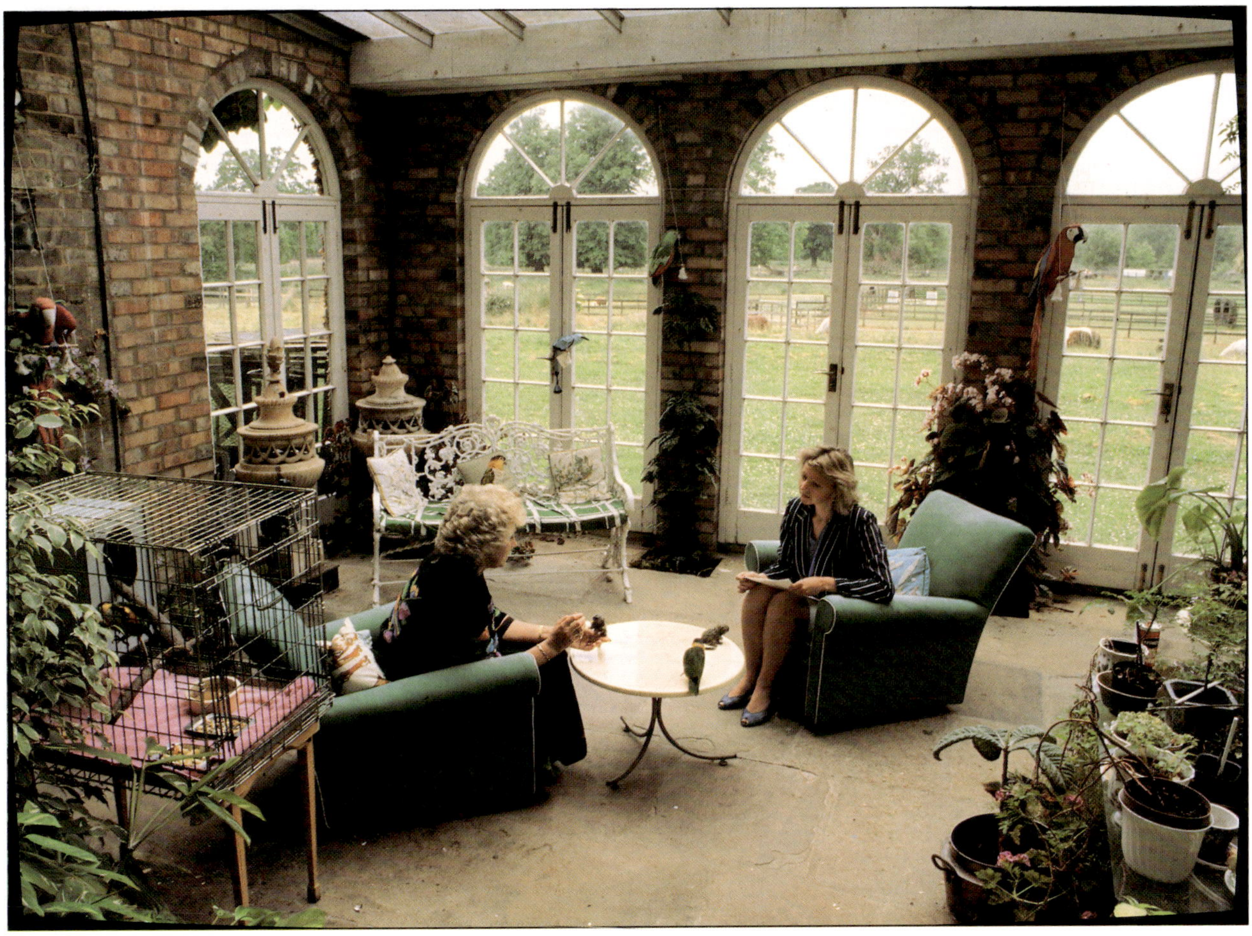

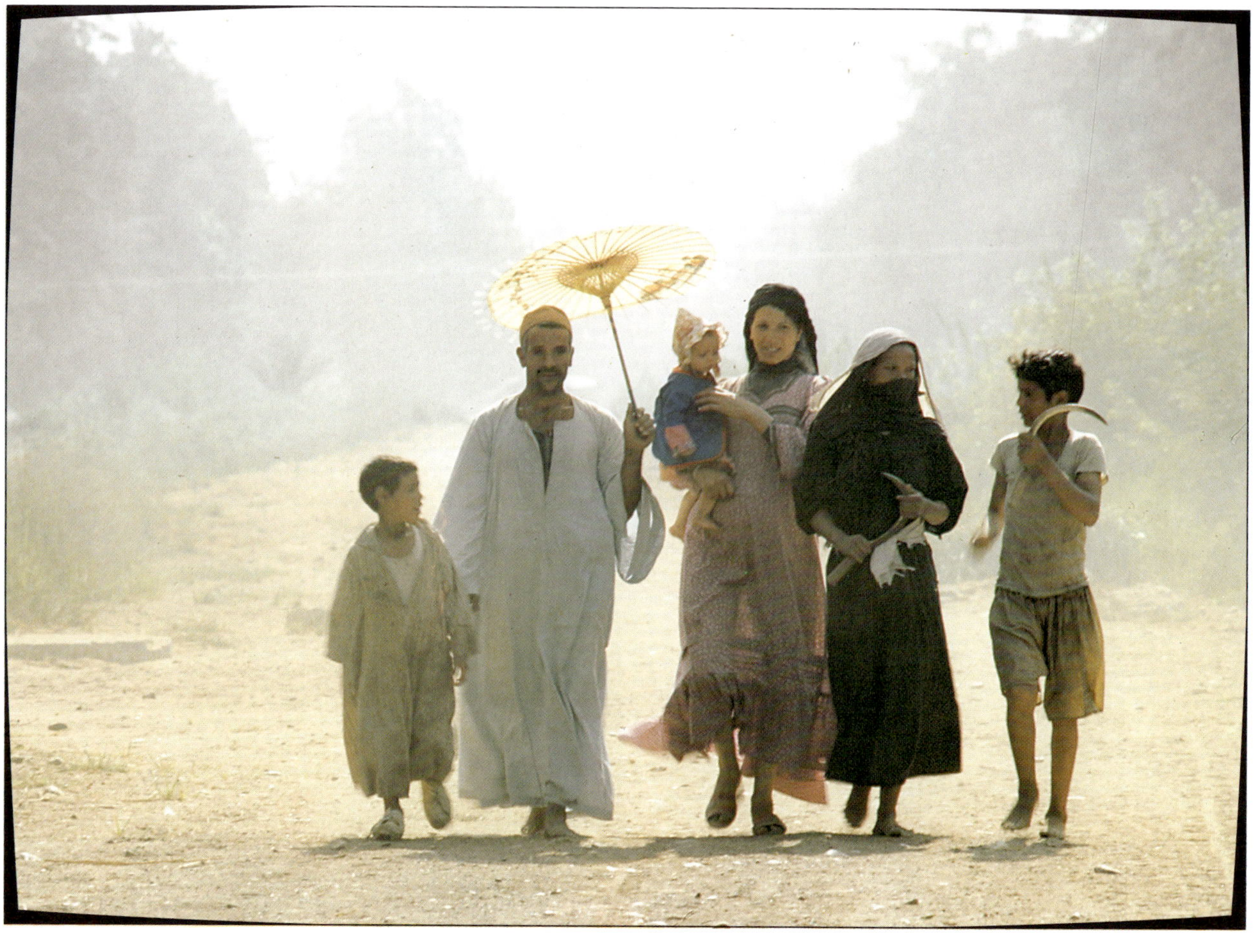

SHOOTING GROUPS

When shooting groups composition is far more difficult than when framing a single individual. Groups are by their nature rather untidy, and they also tend to suffer from a number of people competing for your camcorder's attention!

A common mistake is for the camera operator to move in too close so as to concentrate on an individual. Unfortunately the temptation is then to keep referring back to this individual, which results in confusing, jerky coverage with too many camera movements.

How you approach different situations will depend on how much control you have over your subjects. For example, a brass band playing in a local park is in a static position, so you can plan your shots from fixed camera positions. With smaller groups you may be able to ask the participants to stand within a particular area, and again you can plan your coverage beforehand, using fixed camera positions. In formal situations you can even arrange groups to fit a particular composition – smaller members of the group standing in front of larger members, with the major participants located somewhere in the centre of the shot.

Usually, a group becomes a crowd when you have little or no control over its actions. Again, the coverage will depend to an extent on the situation. Where crowds are basically static, as in the stands at a sports event, it is easy to isolate individuals. In a busy shopping centre it is far more difficult to pick people out.

In general, crowds should be covered in long-shot. This allows the viewer to place the action within its context, and means that the action can develop in front of the camera. If the situation allows, use a tripod-mounted camera, since shake is more obvious when using the telephoto lens. Use slow pans to take in more of the scene, resting on an additional point of interest.

Since the audience will concentrate its attention on the centre of the screen, frame items of particular interest centrally. If you zoom in on an individual or some other detail, it is usually best not to go in too close since extreme changes of scale tend to appear obtrusive. Such a zoom shot could therefore be followed by a pan before moving back into a long-shot of the scene. In this way your video will have more variety and the audience will not forget the context of the shot – there is an individual there, but he belongs to the crowd.

1: *This group scene was easily framed. It was taken in Egypt, with the dusty road and hazy light in the background conveying a strong sense of place. The family group is on its way to a local market.*

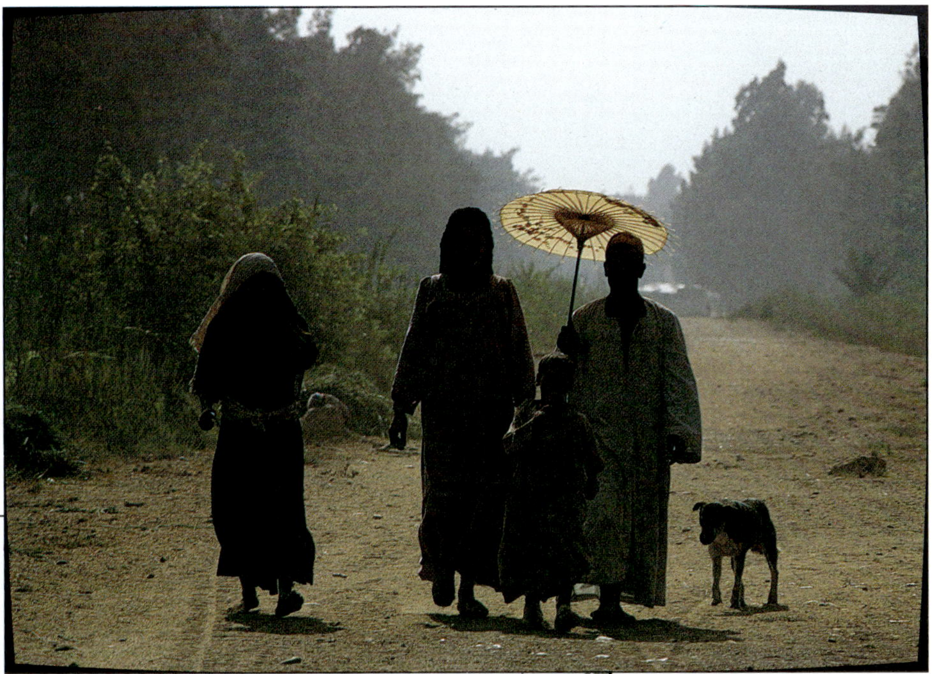

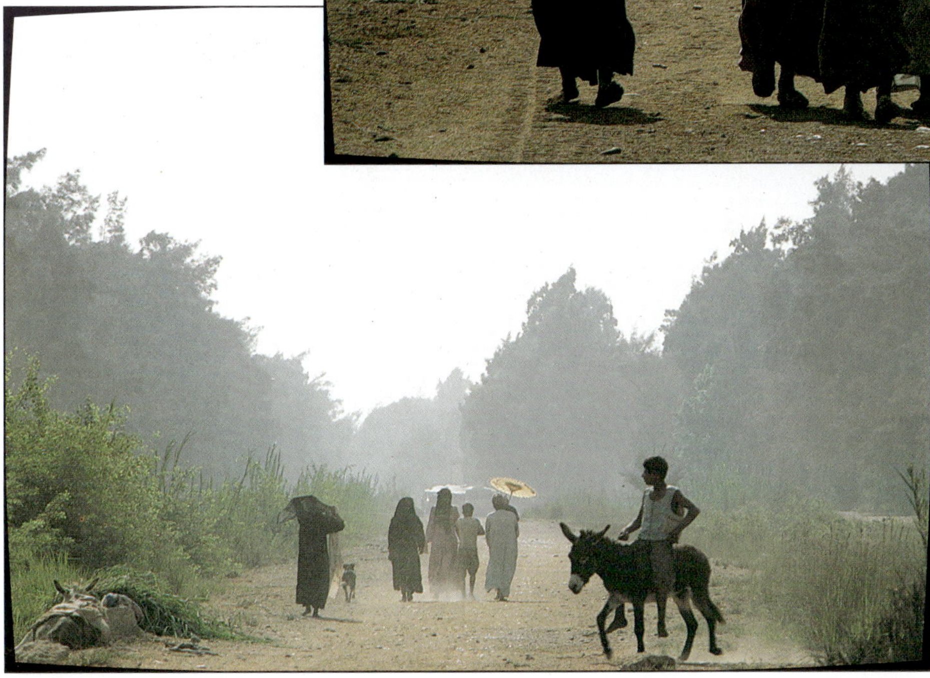

2: *Many people naturally arrange themselves to provide good shots. You will often find that a husband and wife walk together, with their children on either side, providing instant symmetry.*

3: *The conclusion of a long shot of a family group. With the camera mounted on a tripod, the subjects move into the far distance. The duration of such a scene can add to the overall atmosphere conveyed by the video.*

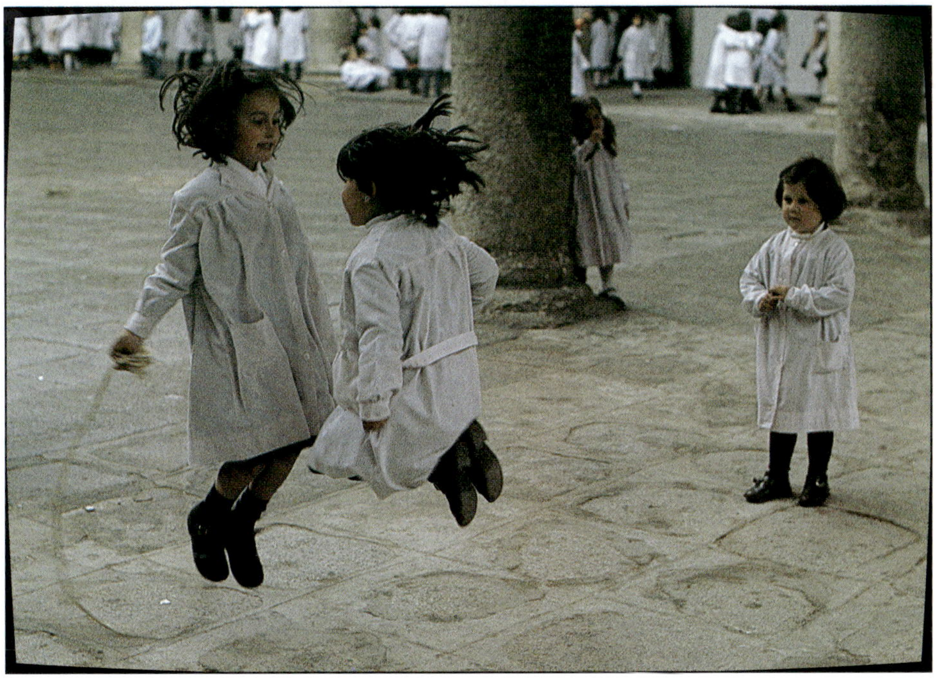

4: *Children playing in the street. The two skipping girls were framed slightly off-centre so that the other children could also be included in the sequence.*

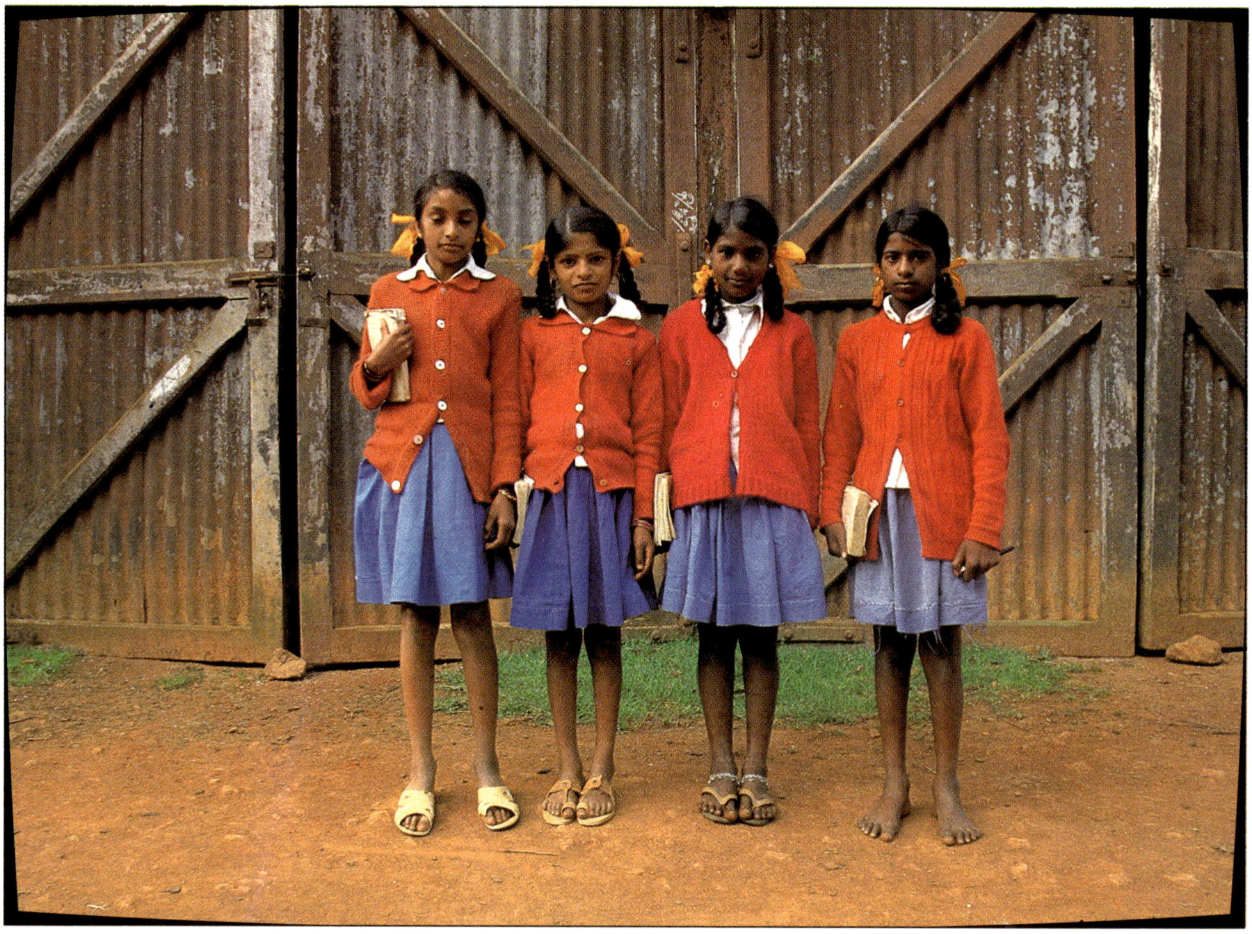

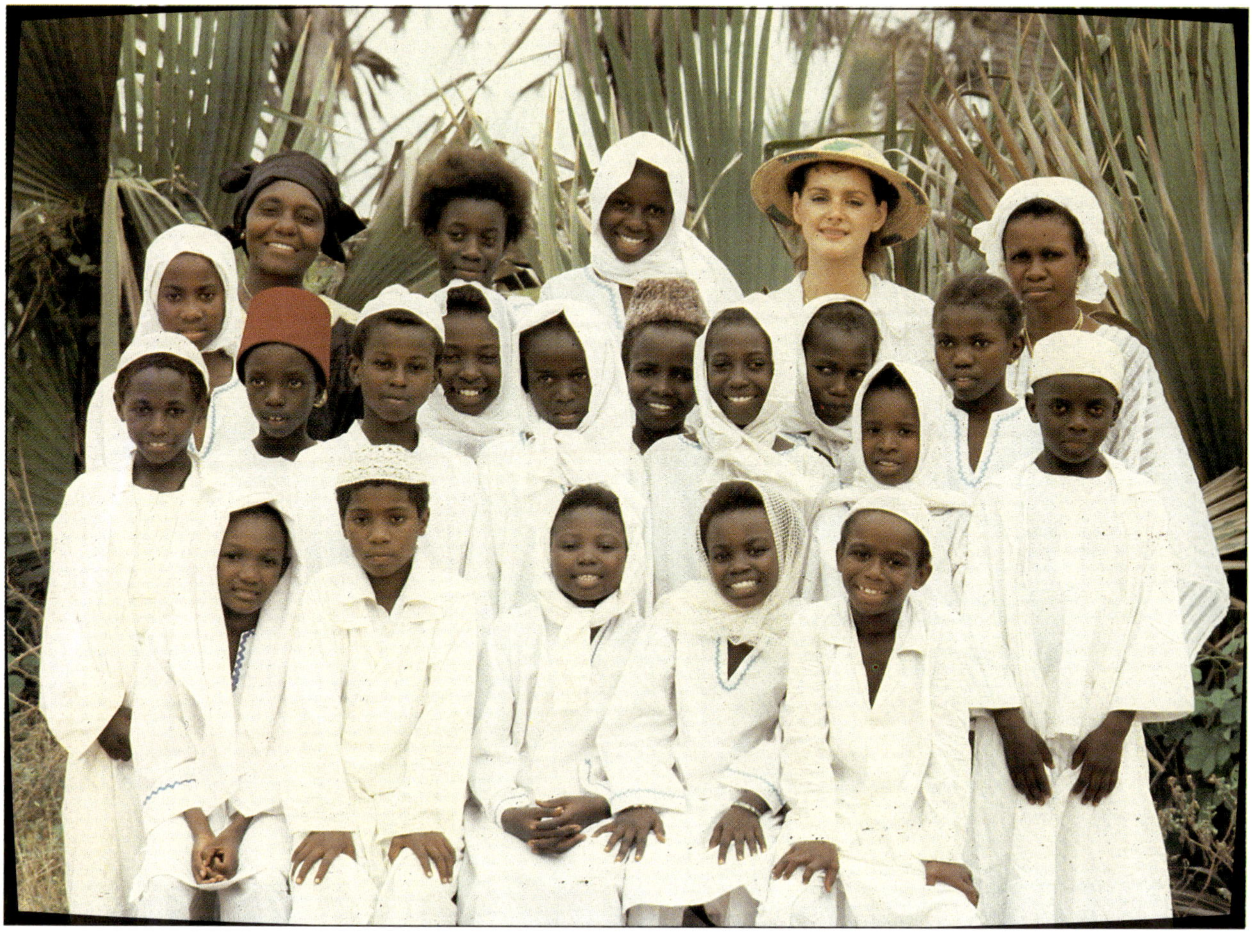

3: *The long perspective down the street draws the viewer's eyes away from the group in the foreground, sitting at the cafe tables.*

4: *The same scene from a slightly higher position. The viewer gets the impression of looking in on the group, almost of spying. Such a camera position tends to place the audience in a more objective position than one taken at eye level.*

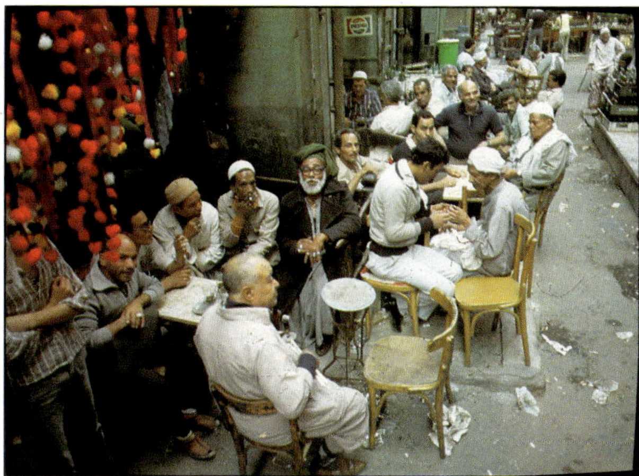

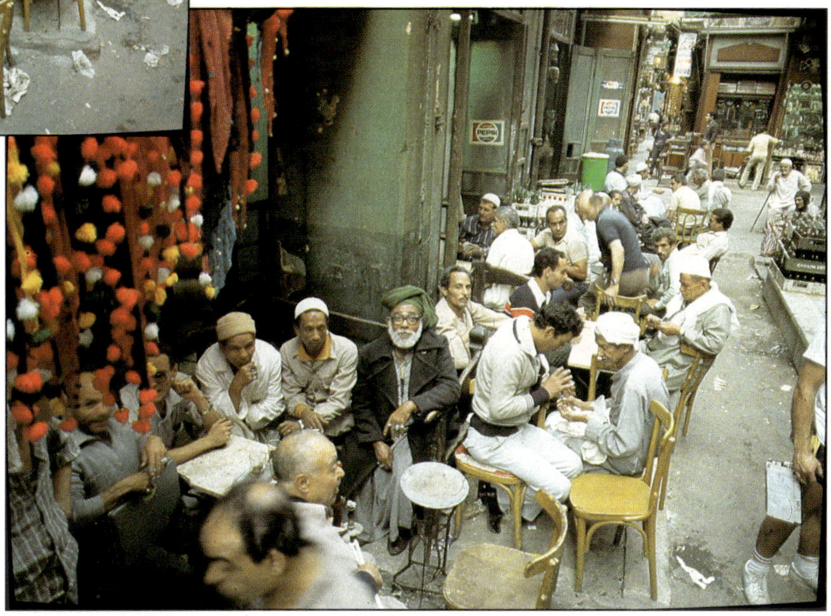

1: *This group of girls dressed in their bright school uniforms posed rather self-consciously in front of the camera. But their giggling response to a few questions saved the shot, and made it quite charming.*

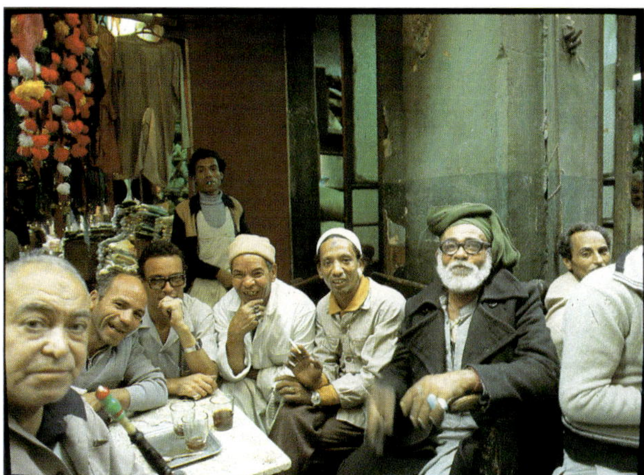

5: *Wherever you go with a camcorder you will become the centre of attention. Most people are curious and amused about being filmed, but some can be resentful. If someone requests you to stop shooting it is prudent as well as polite to comply.*

6: *You can encourage your subjects to react by moving in close and picking out individuals from amongst the crowd.*

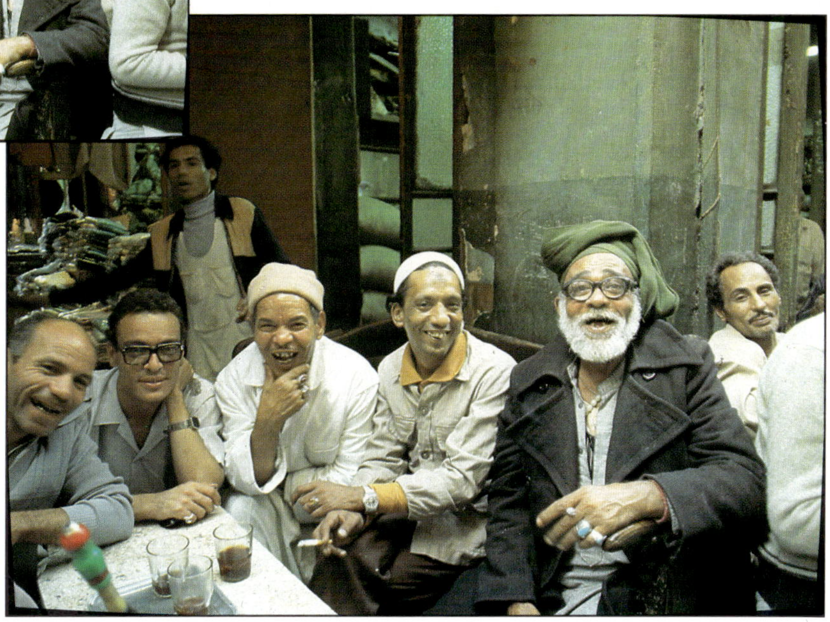

2: *Formal group compositions can work on video. While this group was being posed for a still photographer, it was clear that the event was actually a marvellous subject for a video sequence.*

The importance of aesthetically pleasing framing has already been discussed. But beyond this, creative framing can add considerably to the meaning of the shot. In fact, the choice of camera angles and the relationship of elements in the shot often amounts to a form of directorial style. It is an instructive exercise to look at film and television productions from a purely technical point of view. Try to estimate where the camera was placed for each particular shot, and notice how long individual shots are held.

Although the director usually has the last say about shots, the writer of the script will indicate how he or she has visualized the moment, often quite precisely. The final shot seen on screen will be the result of a collaborative effort of the video crew.

In still photography, framing can be used as an end in itself. In video, the progress of the narrative comes first, with framing serving to inform the audience of what is going on and then to give some insight into the characters on screen. A typical example of framing adding to the narrative is the classic 'it's behind you' shot that occurs in suspense films. The frame allows the audience to see something in the background while the main characters remain unaware of it.

Framing to imply character often uses slightly high or low-angle shots. For example, if one character in a drama is usually shown from a high angle from another character's point of view, it implies a sense of superiority. Reverse these angles at the conclusion of the drama, when the second character gains dominance, and the psychological impact will be implicitly understood by the audience.

Creative composition makes full use of objects in the foreground and background. Remember that prominent foreground objects will distract the audience from the central characters, so they should lend some significance to the narrative if they are going to be included. In drama, for example, a compromising letter may lie between the camera and a main character. In a more mundane example, you could place airline tickets in the foreground in an opening shot of a holiday video. Background objects are less prominent, and their significance can be emphasized by a slow zoom in from the main area of action if you want to make a specific point about them. A slow change of focus from foreground to background can help to make a background object more dominant.

CREATIVE FRAMING

1–3: *What works as a static image on the page may not do so as video. These shots were taken from an experimental sequence in which the camera moved in a circle in front of the stationary girl, causing her head to fall out of the bottom and sides of the screen at times. The technique could be extended to convey a sense of madness and hallucination in a dramatic thriller.*

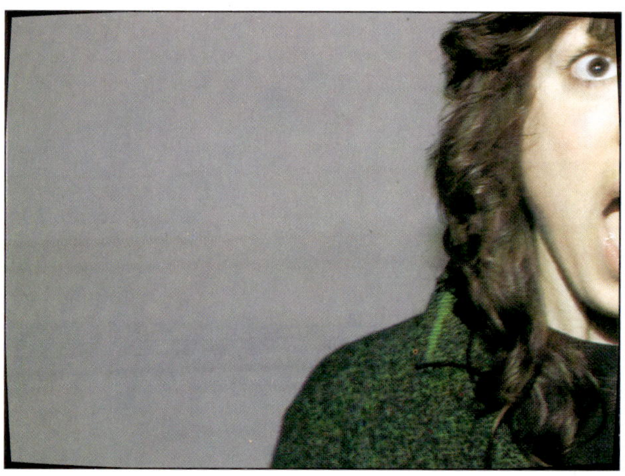

4–5: *A full profile on a television screen always looks unnaturally posed, perhaps because in real life we seldom look at people from that angle. Used in a video it gives a distancing effect. Similarly with the lower image: the man between the two women seems estranged from them, and the audience's attention will waver between him and them.*

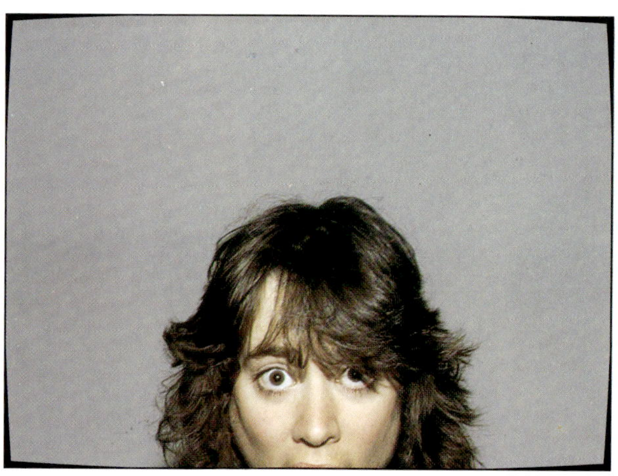

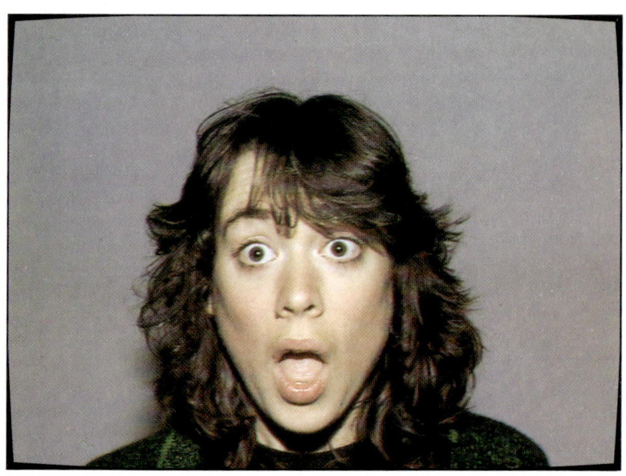

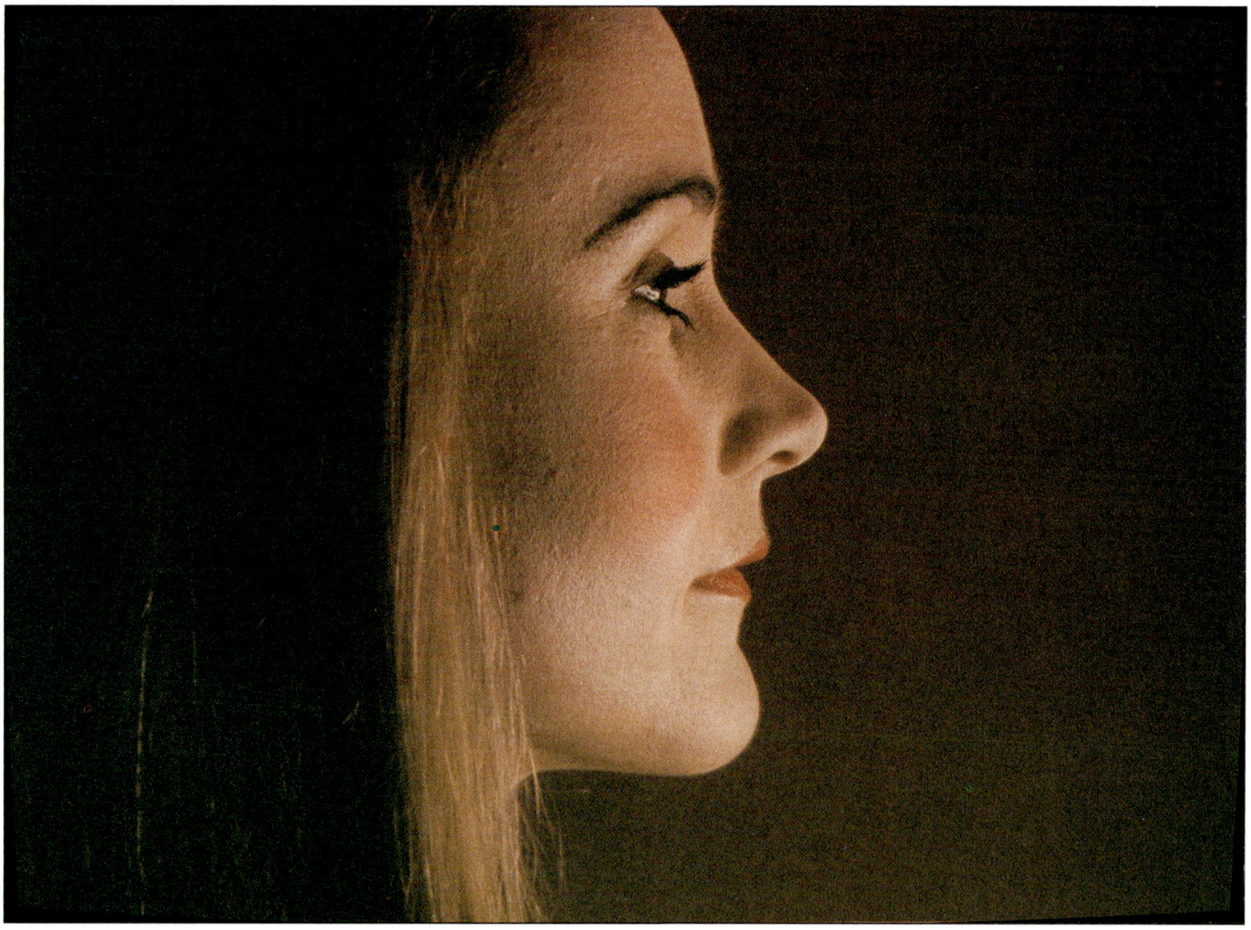

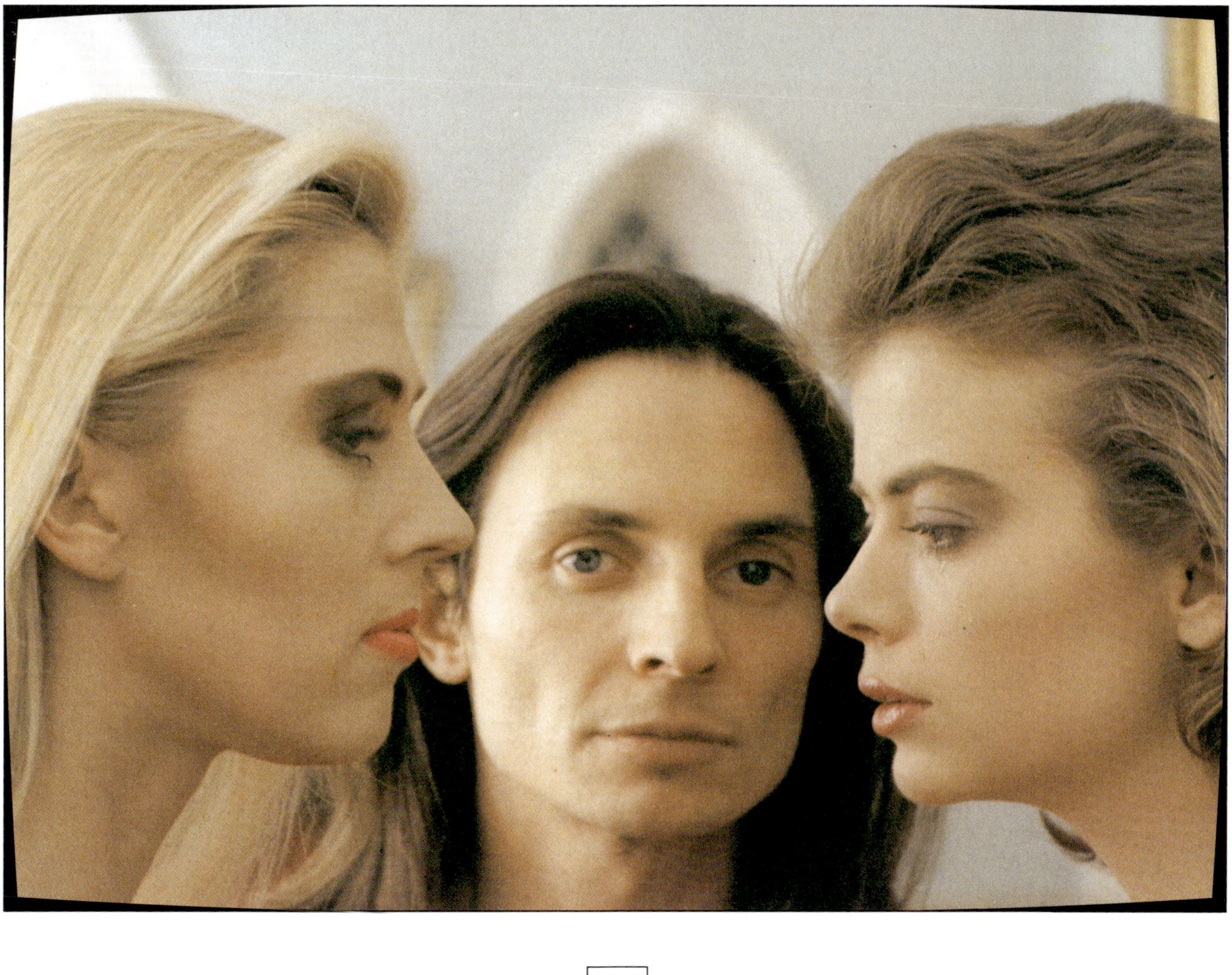

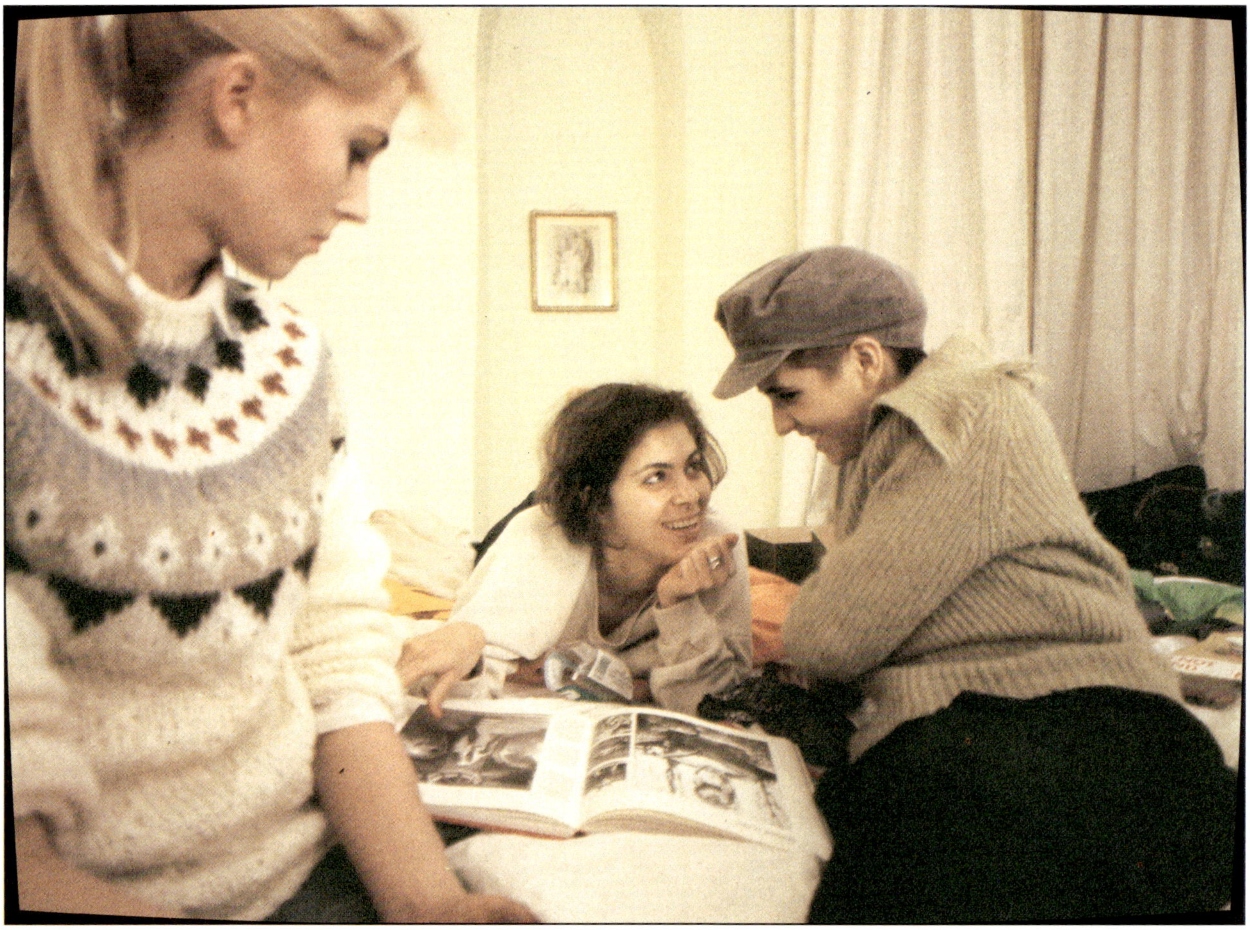

EYELINE

The direction of a subject's gaze on screen is one of the major clues that the viewer uses in order to understand what is happening in the narrative. When in one shot the subject appears to be looking toward the left, the viewer expects the next shot to reveal what the subject is looking at. In this way, eyeline establishes the direction of the action and sets up a sense of space on screen. This means that when two characters are talking on screen, they must be shown looking in opposite directions – so that they are still facing each other when shown individually in close-up.

The video camera can imitate the angle of the character's gaze as well as direction. If one person is seated, then a point-of-view shot from that position should be taken from a low angle. This effect can be a useful ally when you want the audience to identify strongly with one particular character.

Where there is little action happening on screen, eyeline can provide the missing dynamics. Viewers usually concentrate on screen characters' faces, and therefore follow the direction in which they are looking. This means that eyelines can be used as a powerful tool when planning the composition of relatively static shots.

When there are more than two characters involved in the on-screen action, the eyeline becomes more complex. In such situations, the direction of gaze can establish a number of separate eyelines, linking different characters in different relationships: the eyeline between A and B, B and C, A and C, and so on. Depending on what action unfolds, any of these established eyelines may be dominant in a scene. And as the action develops, and the characters move to different positions, so these eyelines will change.

It is possible to become over-obsessed about complex eyelines. A useful approach is to sketch out eyelines while drawing up the storyboard. This at least helps you to have a clear idea in your mind about the priorities for that particular scene, and will help you position characters correctly when it comes to arranging the shot. Remember, it is the direction of the eyeline from one shot to the next that is important in terms of how the audience interprets screen geography, and unless you think about this clearly while shooting you may run into problems at the editing stage. A sudden cut in which the direction of one character's eyeline changes radically is bound to be noticeable.

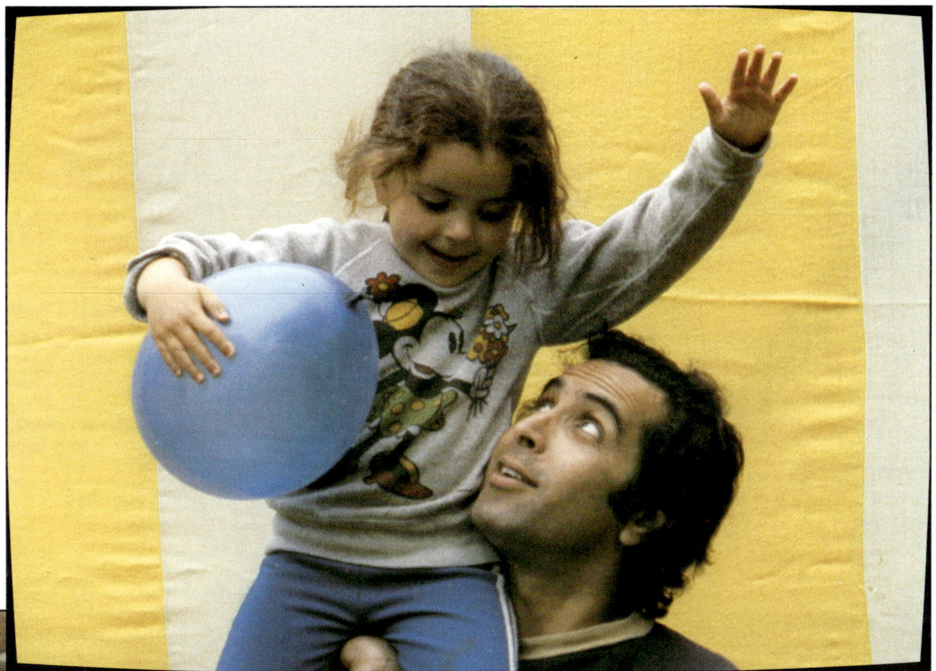

1: *The eyelines encountered in shots like this are relatively simple. If the couple are shown in close-up and turn to face the third character, this will be readily understood by the audience, but if by changing the camera position they appear to face in the opposite direction, the audience will be misled.*

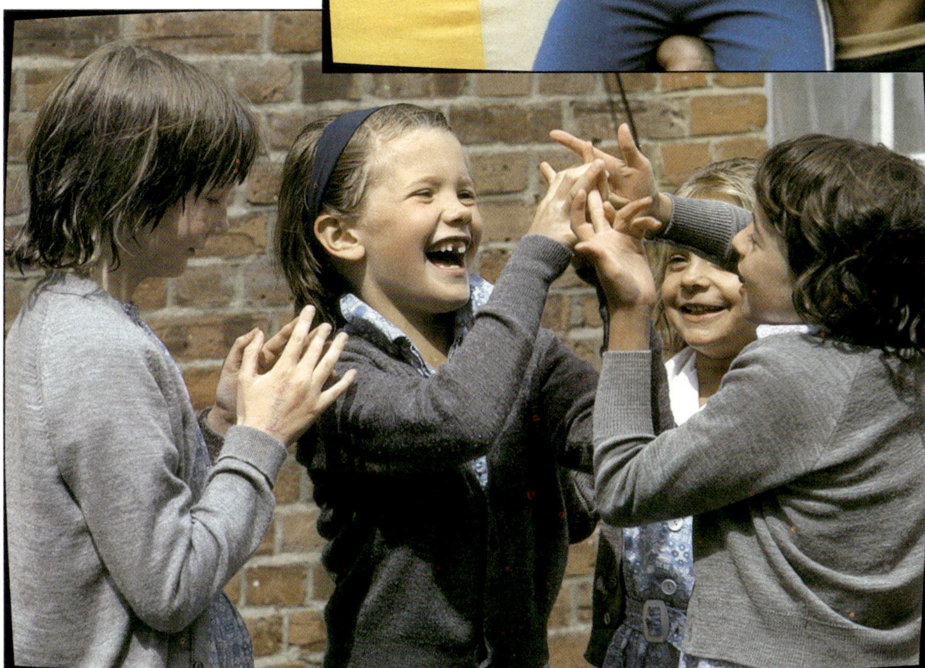

2: *No problems over eyeline with this particular shot. But if the father were to look out of the frame, the audience would follow his eyeline and expect the next shot to reveal what he is looking at.*

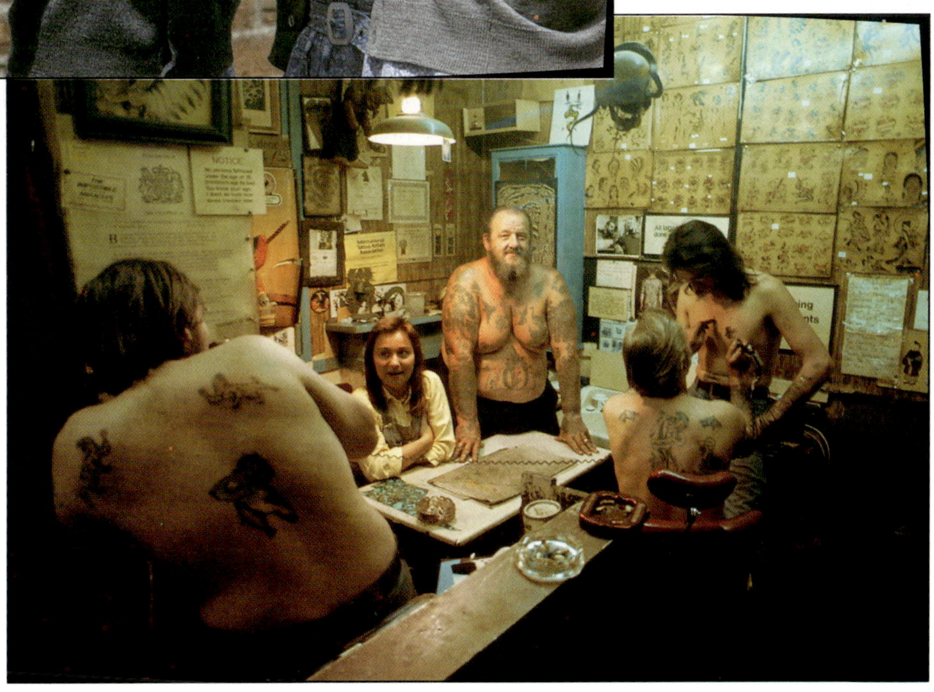

3: *Again, the eyelines here are concentrated on the centre of the action and cause no problems over screen geography for the audience. It is only when different individuals are being emphasized by different eyelines that complexity and confusion set in.*

4: *In this scene a number of eyelines have been established between characters and groups. When moving in to close-up so as to record characters' reactions, it is easy to disrupt the sense of geography if the eyelines are not thought about.*

The video image can gain extra visual interest by framing subjects within naturally occurring frames present on the screen. The most obvious example of this is the framing of subjects within doorways. The strong horizontal and vertical lines of the doorway give a powerful sense of composition to the total image. If you watch films and television dramas closely you will notice that this technique is widely used. Such shots will have a static quality to them which causes the viewer to look at them more closely, almost as if the shot were a painting.

In many cases such shots will also contain strong lighting contrasts, since the doorway will either be in shade, or backlit if the shot is taken from the interior. Such contrasts add to the atmosphere of the shot, perhaps emphasizing the isolation of a character, or perhaps suggesting mystery or suspense.

Of course, doorways are not the only internal frames available. Try composing scenes through car windows, with the outline of the window forming a second frame inside the boundaries of the television screen. This can often also serve as a point-of-view shot — the audience recognises the shot as the view seen by the car's occupant. Most scenes offer some naturally occurring frame which you can use creatively in this way suggesting that the scene is being observed from a particular point of view.

FRAMES WITHIN FRAMES

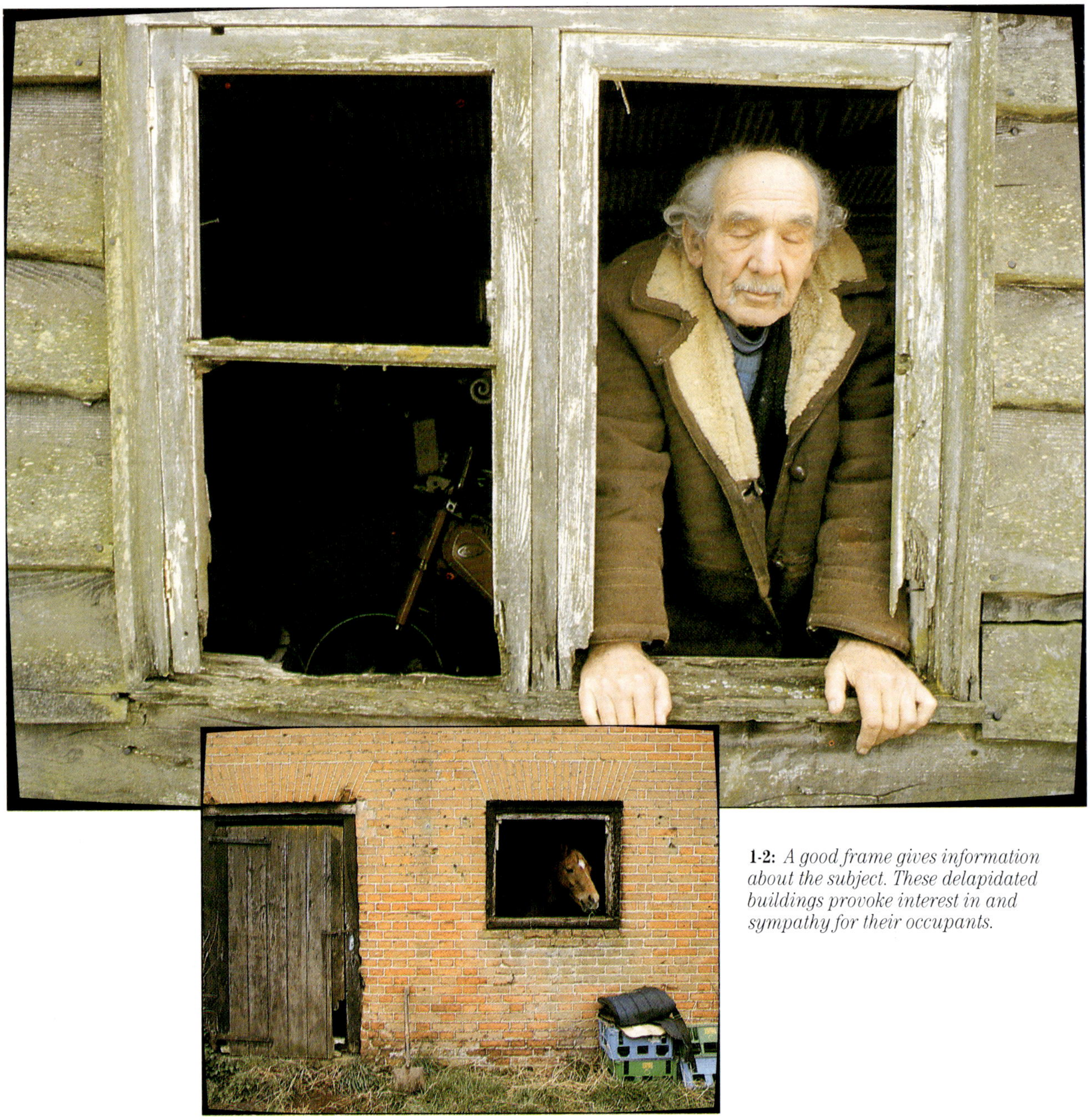

1-2: *A good frame gives information about the subject. These delapidated buildings provoke interest in and sympathy for their occupants.*

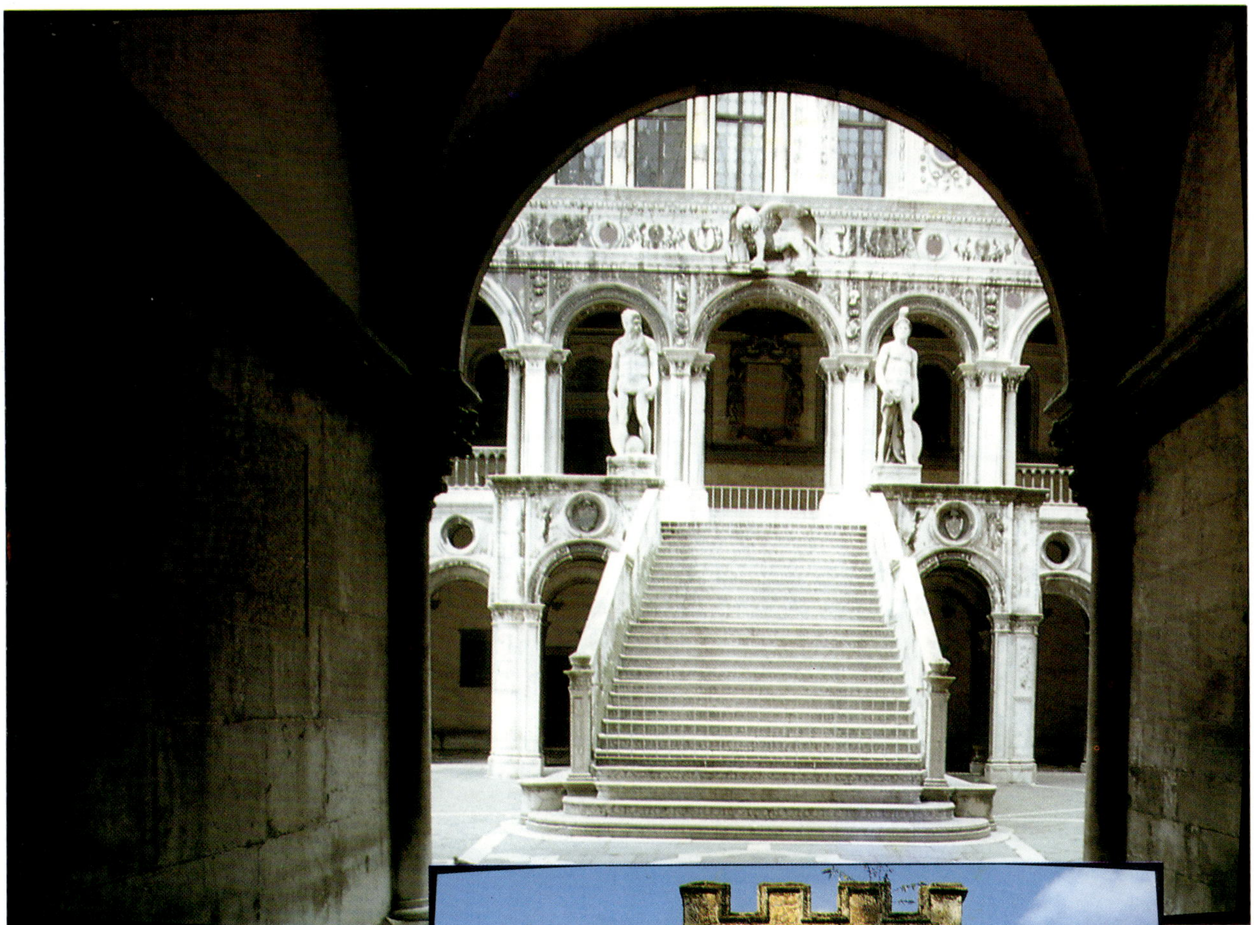

3: *This magnificent staircase is given added grandeur by being framed within the foreground archway. The strong contrast between background and foreground also directs the viewer's attention.*

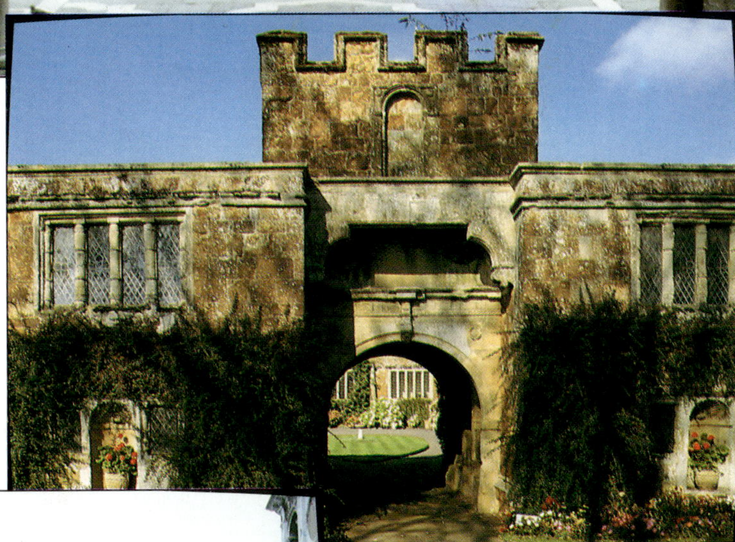

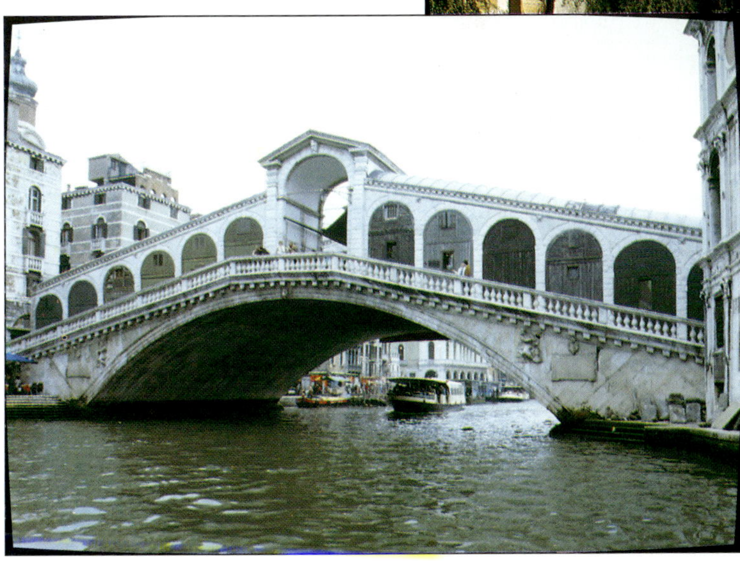

4: *A shady archway with sunlight beyond excite our expectations – what is the courtyard like and who is there?*

5: *Bridges form good frames for boats. They are also interesting subjects in their own right.*

Video is the ideal medium for recording artists and craftsmen at work, since the tape can be instantly reviewed to check that full coverage was obtained. If the subject isn't satisfied with what has been recorded, you can quickly arrange another session.

There are two basic options as far as camerawork is concerned. You may choose to mount the camera on a tripod in front of the subject, using the zoom to go in for close-ups of the subject's face, or of the hands at work. The static coverage allows the audience to concentrate on what the subject is actually doing. On the other hand, you could choose a roaming-camera, documentary-style approach. Some subjects may be put more at ease by this less formal method of working.

It is a good idea to preface the tape with some background material. This might include a short interview with the artist, in which he or she explains the intentions behind the work. A short guided tour of the studio also makes interesting coverage, and the subject can explain the functions of the different tools and materials used later in the demonstration. While the artist is actually working, encourage him to explain what is going on, going into detail over any particular problems encountered. The tape could conclude with the finished product shown in close-up from different angles.

ART ON VIDEO

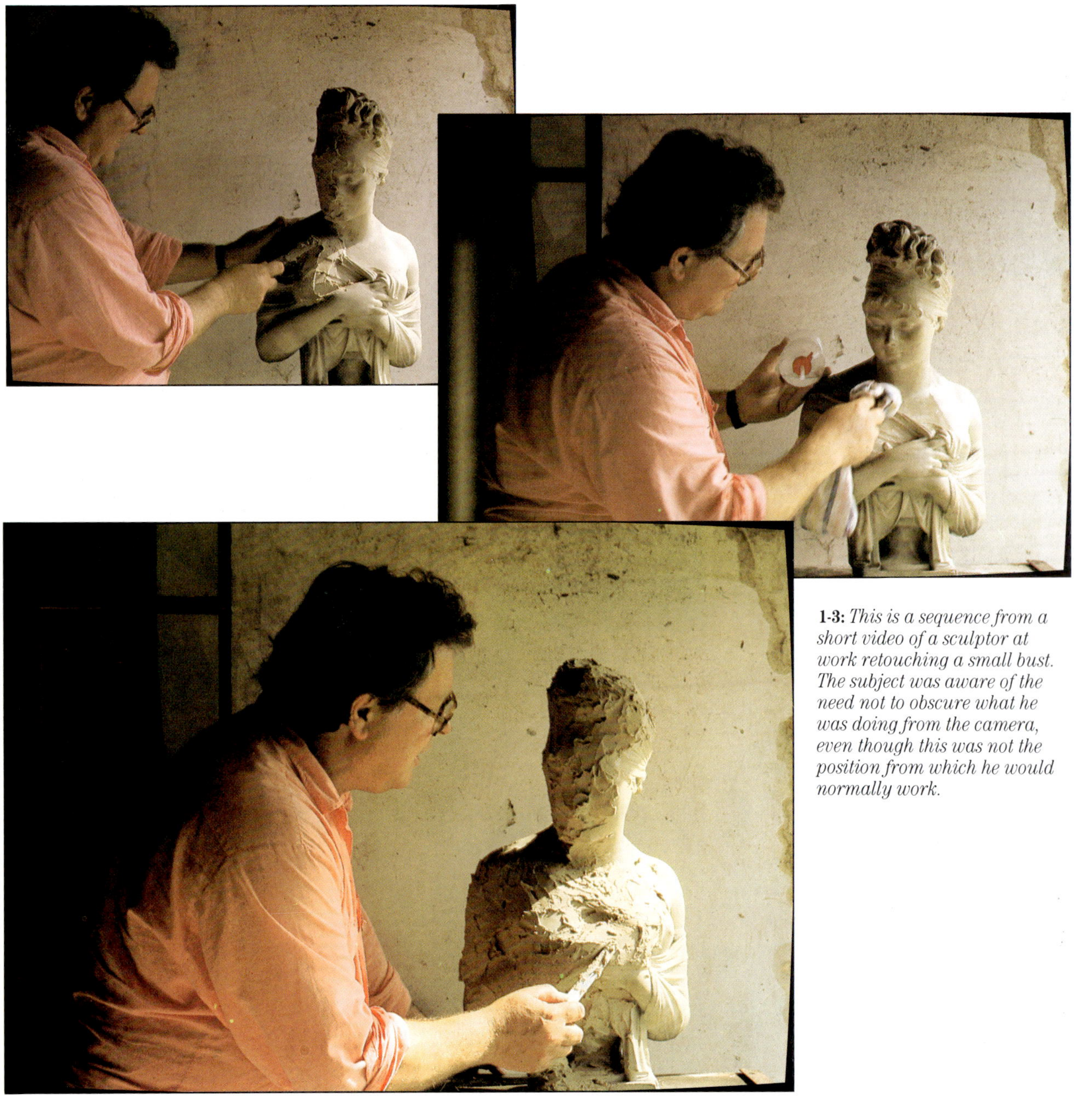

1-3: *This is a sequence from a short video of a sculptor at work retouching a small bust. The subject was aware of the need not to obscure what he was doing from the camera, even though this was not the position from which he would normally work.*

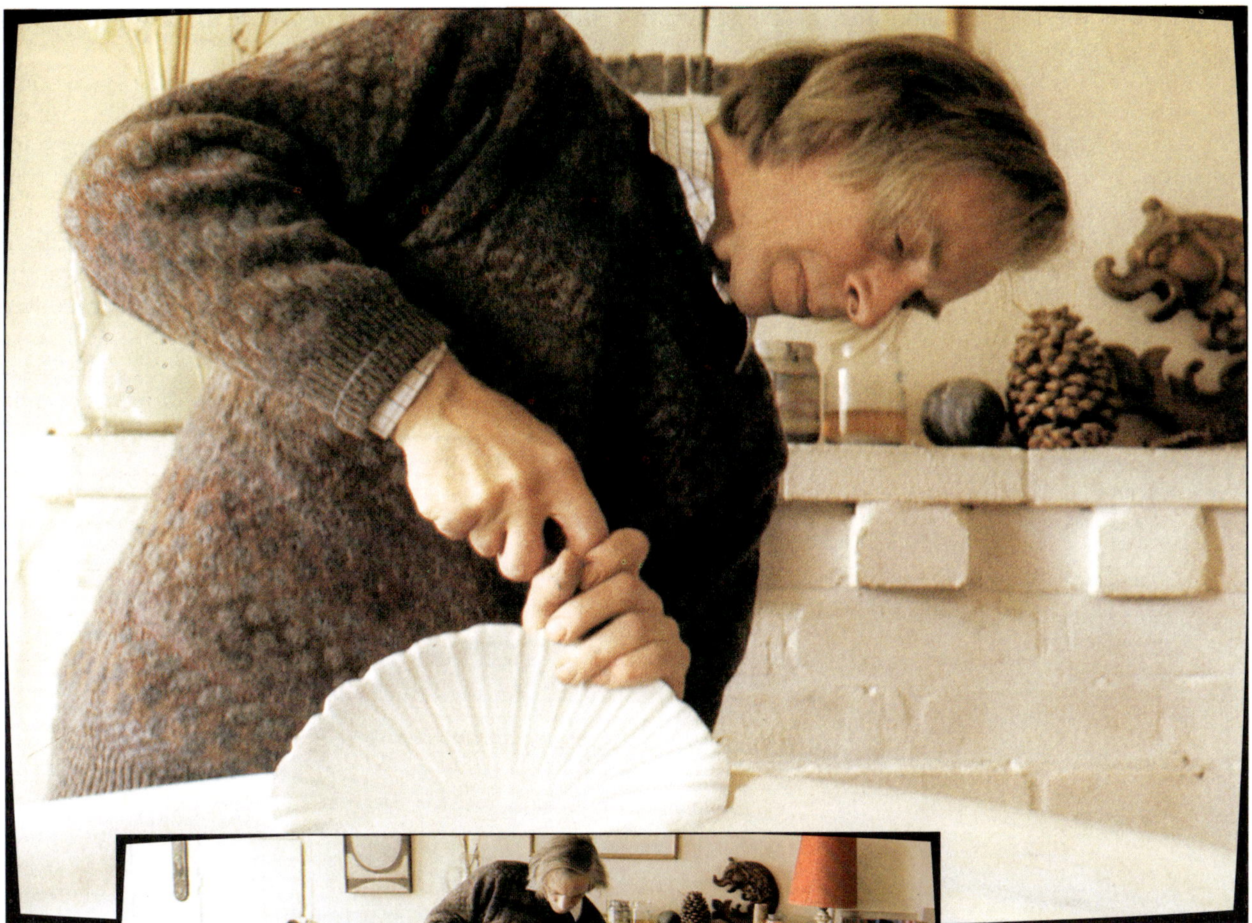

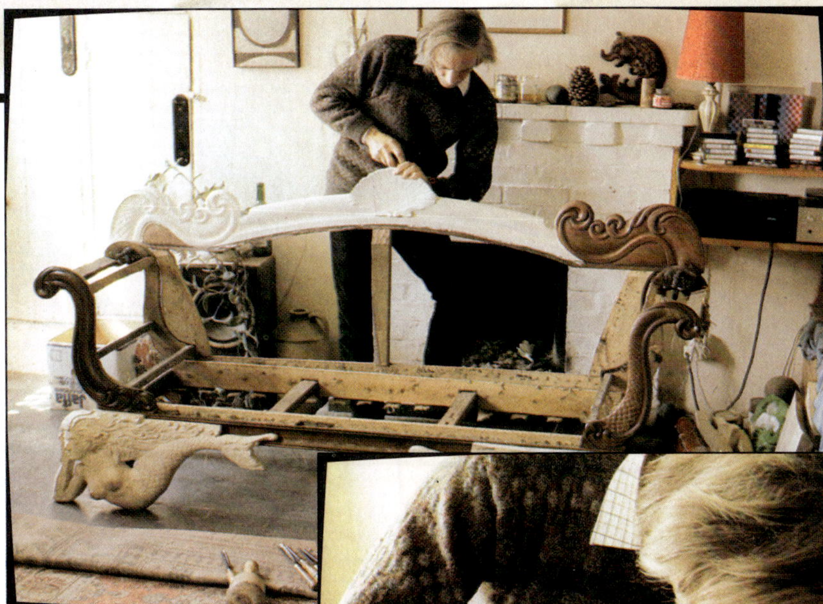

4: *Hands and faces are the most important visual elements of someone working at an art or craft. With the subject positioned away from the camera, a clear view of what was happening was obtained.*

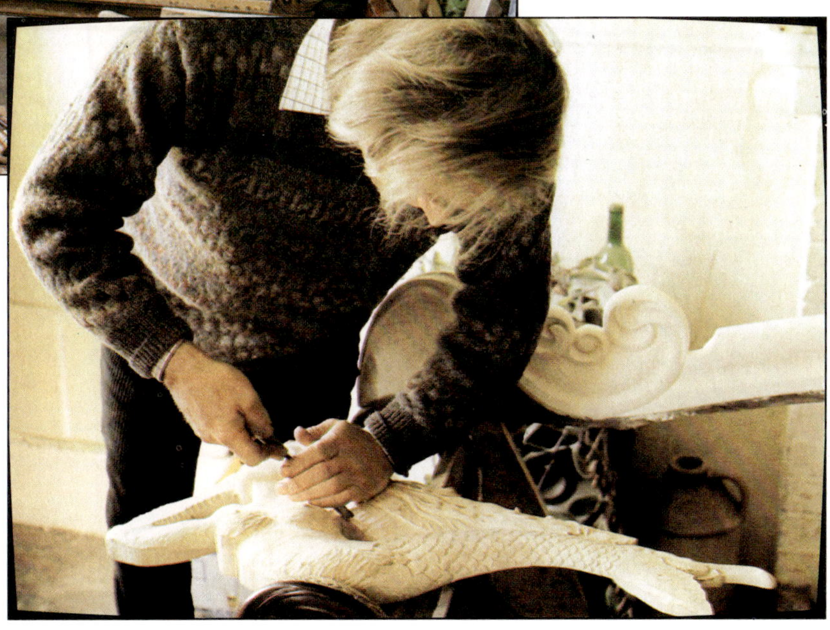

5: *A long shot reveals the environment in which the craftsman works. But it is difficult to make out exactly what he is doing, so it should not be held for too long.*

6: *This shot is well-framed, with the viewer's attention being drawn to the carving. The next shot could be a slow zoom into a close-up of the carving action.*

PROJECT NOTEBOOK

PEOPLE

Compostion of the image within the frame is the technique in which practice meets that of still photography. The important difference to remember, though, is that video images are moving images, and you must take into account the beginning *and* end of any given sequence. A pleasing, relaxed composition on screen allows the audience to concentrate on what is being shown, rather than being distracted by clumsy, or over-fussy camera techniques.

■ The viewer's attention is drawn irresistibly to the subject's eyes and automatically follows the direction of his or her gaze.

■ Keep a social distance. .Human beings don't conduct conversations at extreme distances, nor do they like their personal space invaded. Mid-shots and close-ups are safe. Extreme close-ups imply interrogation.

■ Let the action happen in front of the camera. Keep the camera in the same place unless you have a definite reason for changing the angle.

■ Horizontal and vertical movements within the frame look wrong. Think diagonals.

■ People get nervous in front of a camera. Time spent chatting to your subject, demonstrating how the camcorder works, and taking exposure checks, will help your subjects relax and help you to achieve a more naturalistic result.

■ If you don't research in depth, you won't be able to ask the right questions in an interview.

■ Wherever possible, involve subjects in the whole video project. You should also ensure that they are given the chance to view the finished tape.

SHOTS AND SEQUENCES

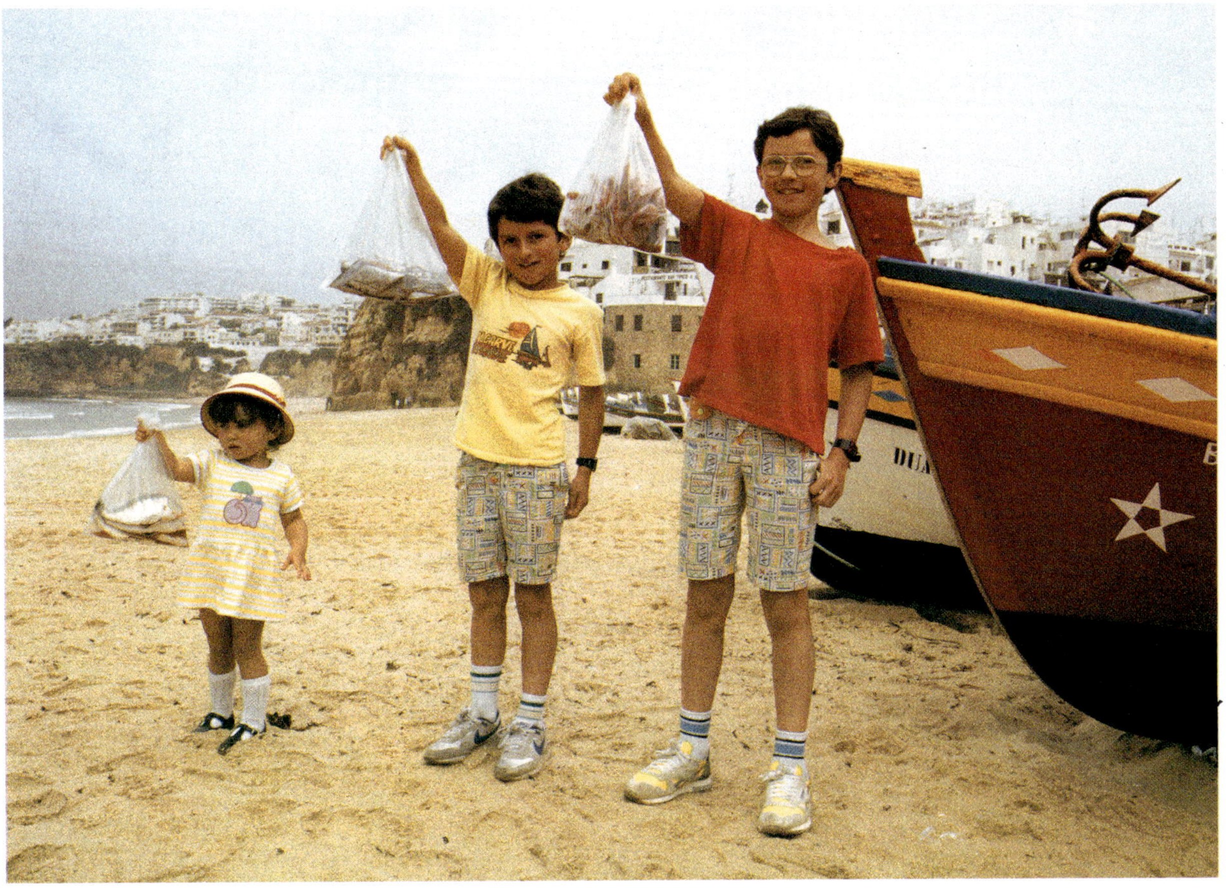

The shot may be the basic unit of the 'language' of video, but unless it is related to further images it tells the viewer very little. This chapter is therefore concerned with the techniques for turning shots into sequences.

Sequences are the vital ingredient for giving a video pace and rhythm, and also help establish the growing momentum of the story being filmed. They can be short or long, from a few seconds to a few minutes, depending on the effect you wish to create. Most of the sequences in this chapter are taken from an informal record of a summer vacation.

Vacations are not all sitting around the poolside, or on the beach. For many, they are one of the few opportunities available to try a number of interesting and exciting sports, such as windsurfing, snorkelling or hang-gliding. If these acitivities are part of the vacation, then you should include coverage of them on the video, or the record will be incomplete.

Some of these sports present difficulties. For a start, many of them take place near seawater, and seawater has a habit of getting on equipment, with the subsequent risk of corrosion. The only thing to do is to take extra care. When recording windsurfing, you will probably have to shoot at the telephoto limit of the zoom. Try a few practice shots to see how this will look in the frame. You may have to instruct the windsurfer to keep within certain limits if you wish to get close-up coverage – one windsurfer on the horizon looks much like any other and won't hold audience interest for very long.

Snorkelling is altogether more problematic, since all you can show is the snorkeller getting equipped and going out to sea. It may be possible to rent a special waterproof video camera designed for recording underwater – it could be worth asking around if snorkelling is a major activity in the area. Alternatively, use a waterproof stills camera and transfer the stills on to video later.

HOLIDAY ACTION

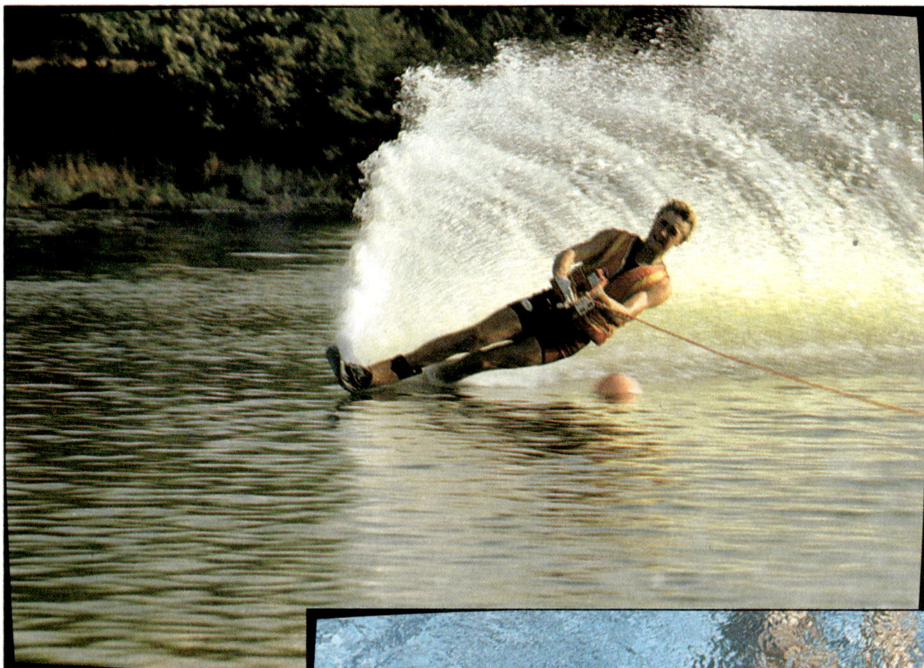

1: *Water skiing is a popular and spectacular vacation activity. It is also one for which it is relatively easy to get good coverage. Shooting from the power boat, you can get good close-up shots of the skier and the soundtrack will carry the noise of the boat. Beware of spray, though, and protect the camcorder with a plastic covering.*

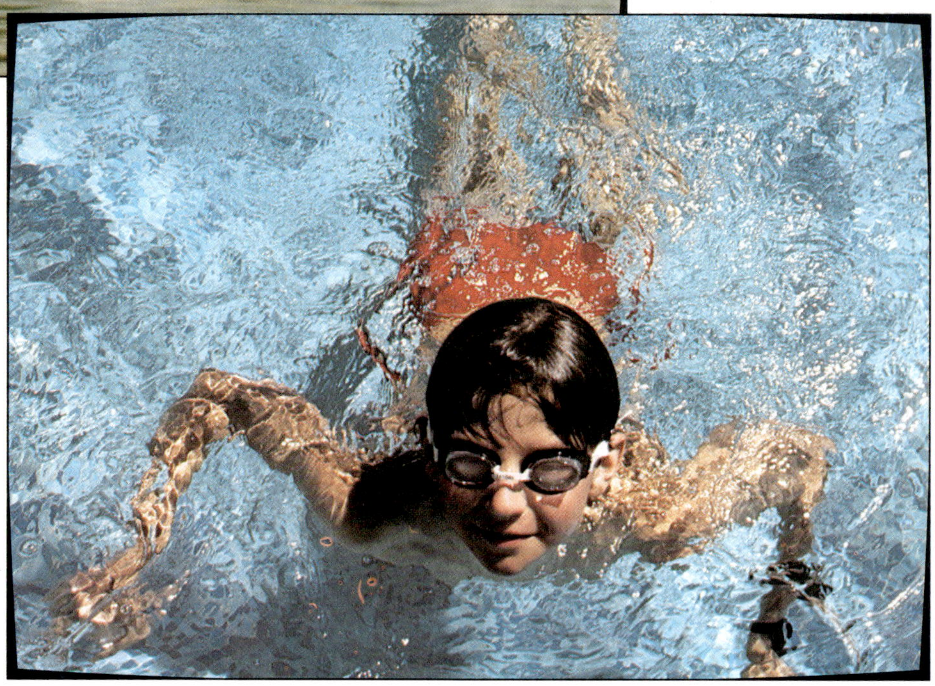

2: *Poolside shots of members of the family enjoying a swim are easiest of all to capture. Get close-ups and the overall poolside scene.*

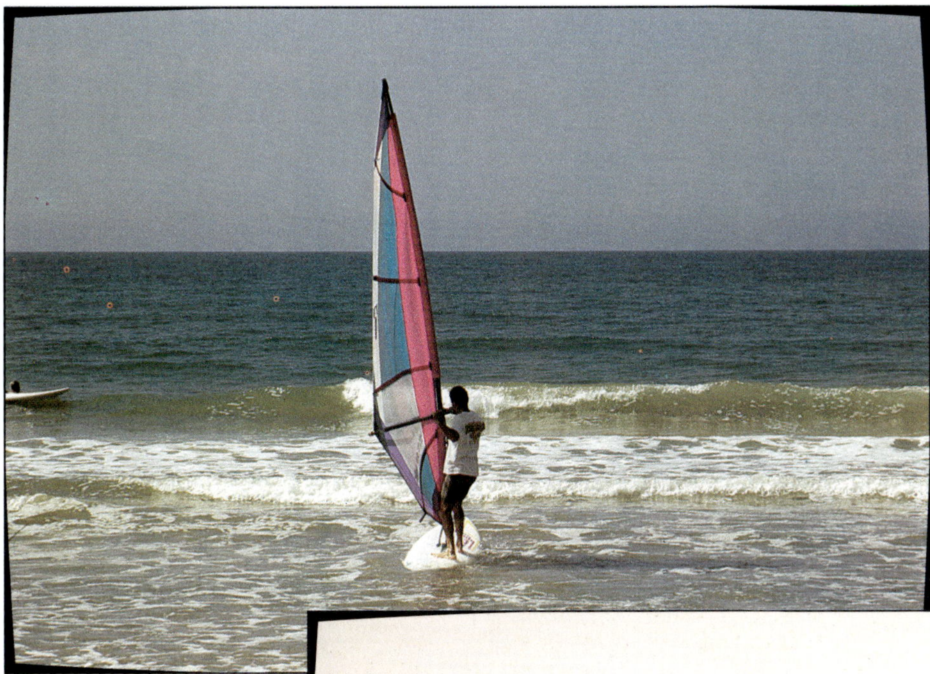

3: *Windsurfing provides dramatic and colourful shots, and is always worth including in a holiday video. This shot shows the windsurfer preparing to go for it.*

4: *A Bedouin horse race outside Marrakesh in Morrocco is an exotic enough location. Treat it as you would any other race and take up a position that gives a full view of the action.*

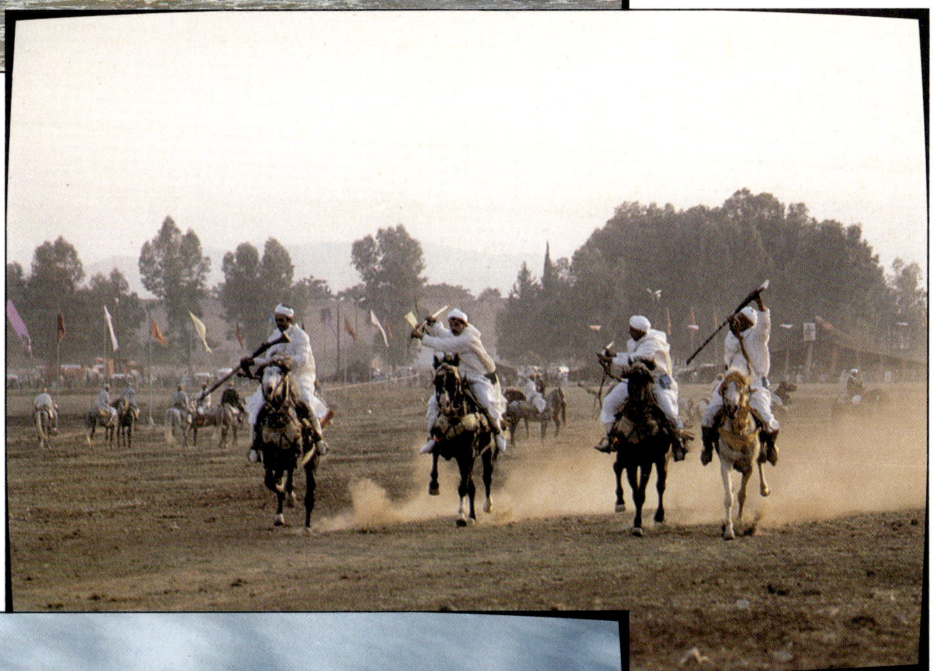

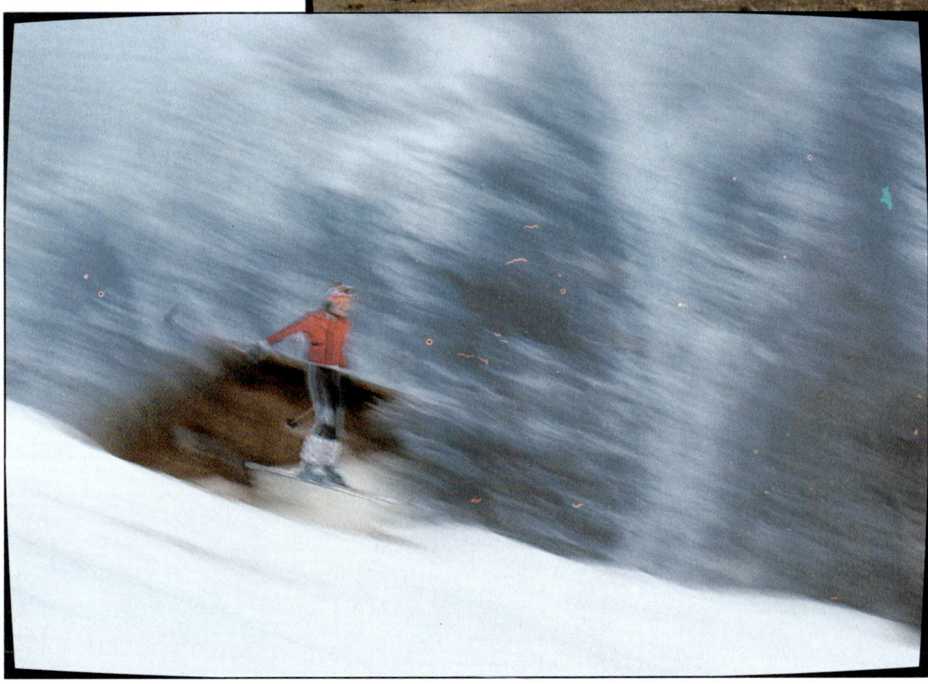

5: *Out on the ski slopes you can get some impressive material. Skiers come fast, so either take up a position and stick to it as the skiers come past, or track an individual skier.*

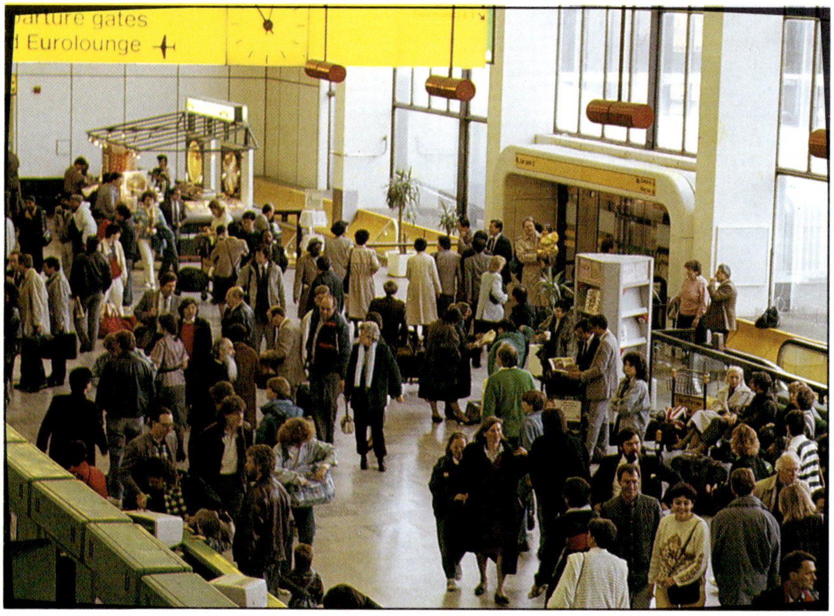

1: *A typical airport scene. While shooting at the airport makes a good beginning to the tape, the coverage should not be too extensive – two or three minutes is quite enough.*

OPENING SHOTS

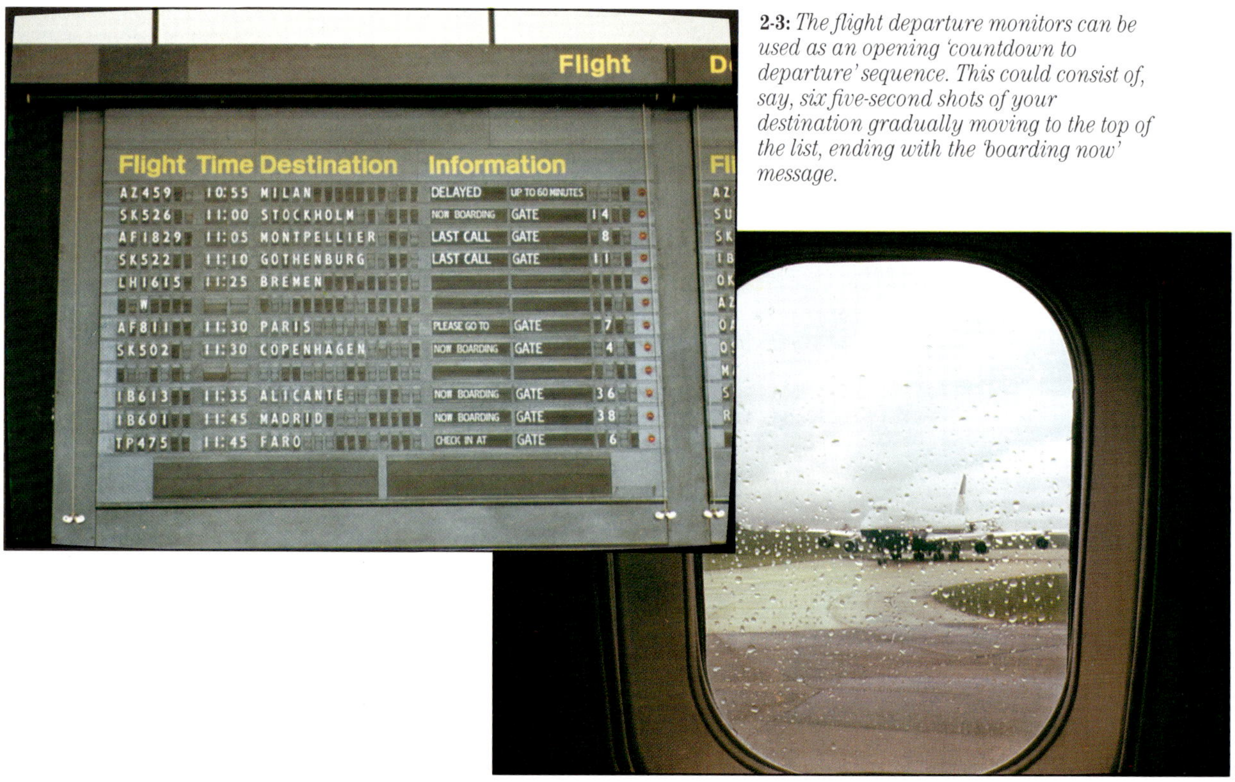

2-3: *The flight departure monitors can be used as an opening 'countdown to departure' sequence. This could consist of, say, six five-second shots of your destination gradually moving to the top of the list, ending with the 'boarding now' message.*

Journalists know that the opening sentences of an article are crucial. They must immediately catch the reader's attention, convey the story's essence, and compel him or her to read on. The principle applies equally well to making videos, for the opening shots must similarly 'hook' the viewer. But how to decide on the most effective opening sequence?

When making a holiday video, an obvious opening sequence is of the family's frantic, last-minute attempts to finish packing. This effectively conveys a sense of anticipation, of the informal nature of the holiday, and introduces the members of the family to the viewer. However, unless the scene is particularly comic it could easily flop, becoming an uninteresting low-key record of a tedious chore. Consequently something far more dramatic is required to grip the viewer and set the scene.

An airport departure lounge has the necessary visual variety to make a lively introduction if filmed

4: *Arrival at the villa. Obviously to get this shot you (or an accomplice) will have to jump out of the car before the rest of the family to take up position. Framing the shot in the doorway emphasizes the fact of arrival.*

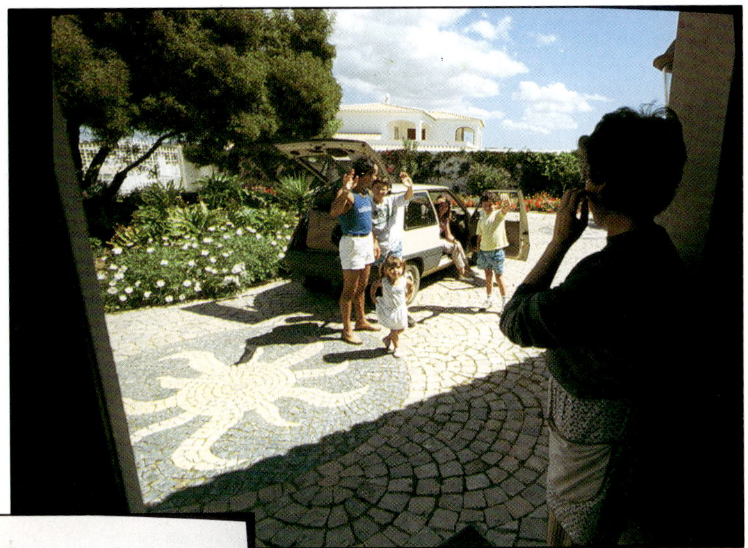

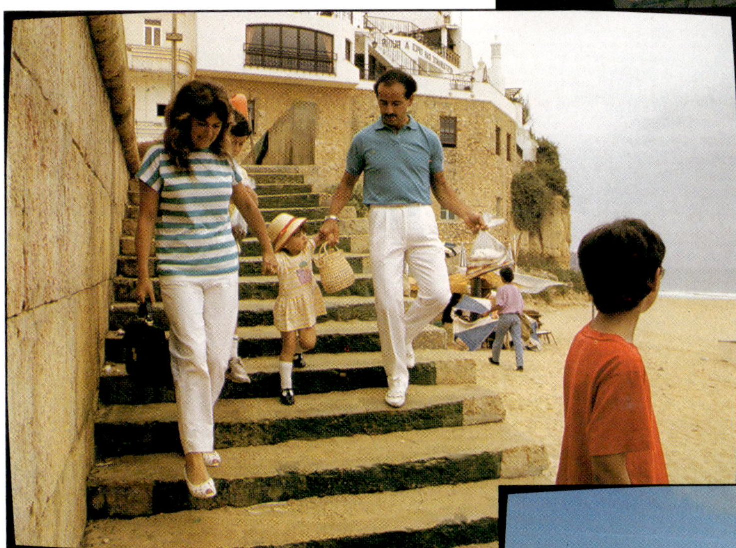

5: *A sequence on the beach the next day makes a good contrast to earlier airport scenes, indicating that you have well and truly arrived. If you choose this option, emphasize the contrast by making the sequence noisy and vibrant, shooting from close-up to capture the excitement on the children's faces.*

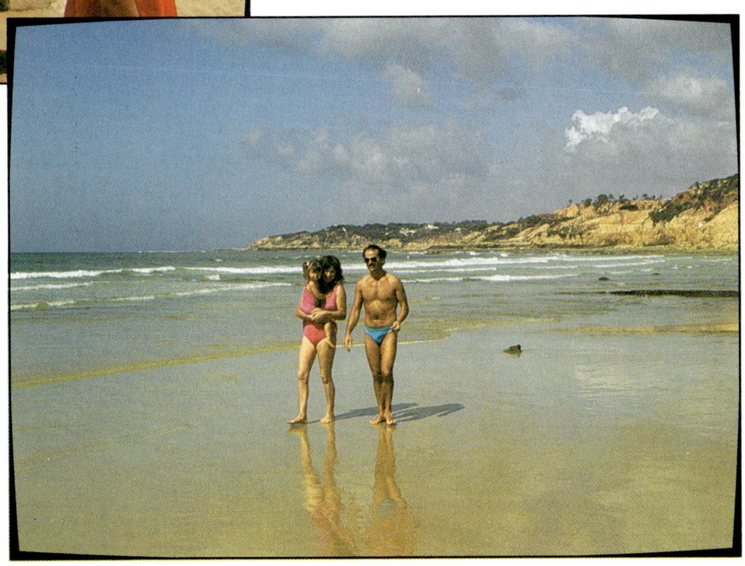

6: *If you are lucky enough to find a beach as deserted as this, make use of it. A sequence of the family walking along will convey a sense of relaxation and tranquility.*

selectively. This particular scenario begins with a departure board's list of destinations, before zooming in on the right flight. Then comes a few minutes – but no more – further coverage of the passengers assembling as they wait to board the plane.

This opening sequence could then cut to the arrival, but in so doing would miss out on interesting shots of *a* (not your!) plane's take-off, and the plane's interior. However, do check with the airline before filming because while you will be allowed to take the camcorder on board as hand luggage, few companies permit inflight filming. The camcorder's electrical signals could dangerously interfere with the plane's highly sophisticated electronics.

Once you have indicated that you're up and away, conclude this opening sequence with scenes of your arrival. These could consist of signs in a foreign language, a scene giving a visible sense of 'having made it' as you unload your cases at the hotel or, as here, a family's first moments on the beach.

1: *The sequences establishing the villa are relatively straightforward. They were taken early in the morning when there was deep shadow and little glare. The bright colour of the flowers in the foreground helps to balance the image. The shot continues with the family emerging from the villa to inspect their garden.*

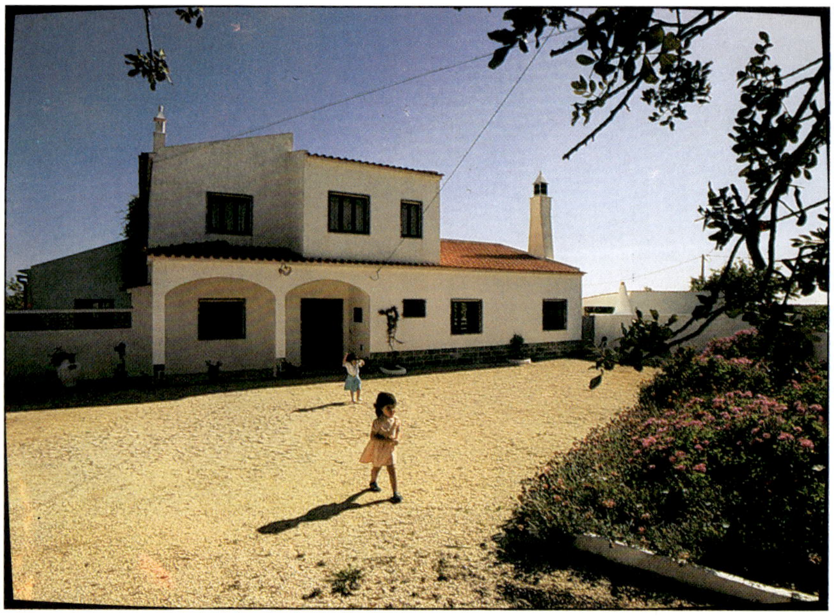

ESTABLISHERS AND LINKS

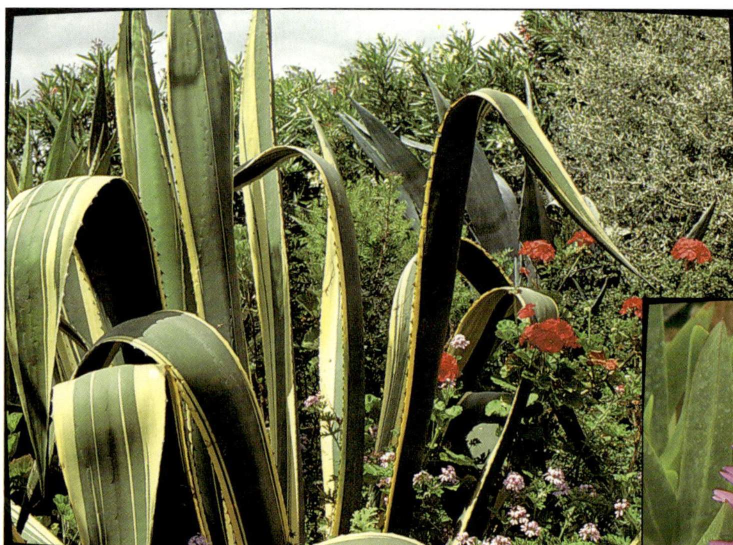

2-3: *The luxuriant vegetation around the villa made a great impression on arrival. Close-up shots of the plants, showing the rich range of green, bright red and purple flowers, are of much greater interest than simply showing the garden in long-shot. This particular shot is from a hand-held sequence which first panned the garden and then moved in for closer detail. The sequences were shot from a crouching position, which is much more effective and natural than pointing the camera downwards.*

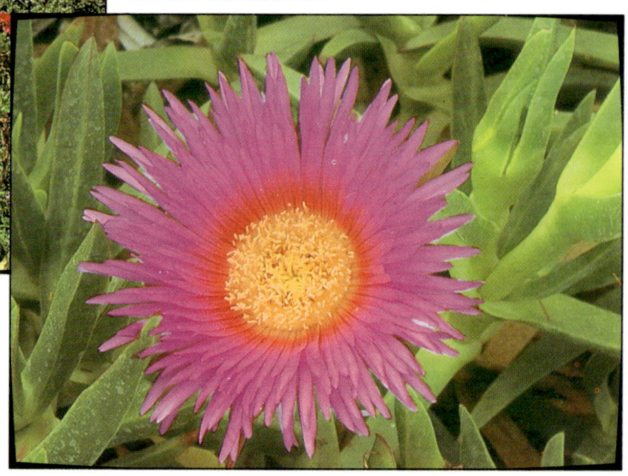

Shots of the location which show the viewer where the action is taking place are known as *establishing shots*, or establishers. They usually come at the very beginning of a sequence, although you may choose to start by homing in on a particular feature of the scene, before pulling away to reveal the context and location of the video.

The action you are recording will usually dictate the nature of the establisher. In the holiday video the family's villa was obviously an important location, being the starting point of all their excursions. Several establishers of this location were therefore shot, including the villa itself, various aspects of the garden, and the view from the garden out to sea.

Whenever possible try to include action in an establisher, even if it's only of a major character setting off on an outing. Preferably, such establishers should be in long-shot so that the figure does not dominate the scene. Hold the shot just long enough for the audience to absorb the information, but no more because, as there is no real action, they will start to lose interest.

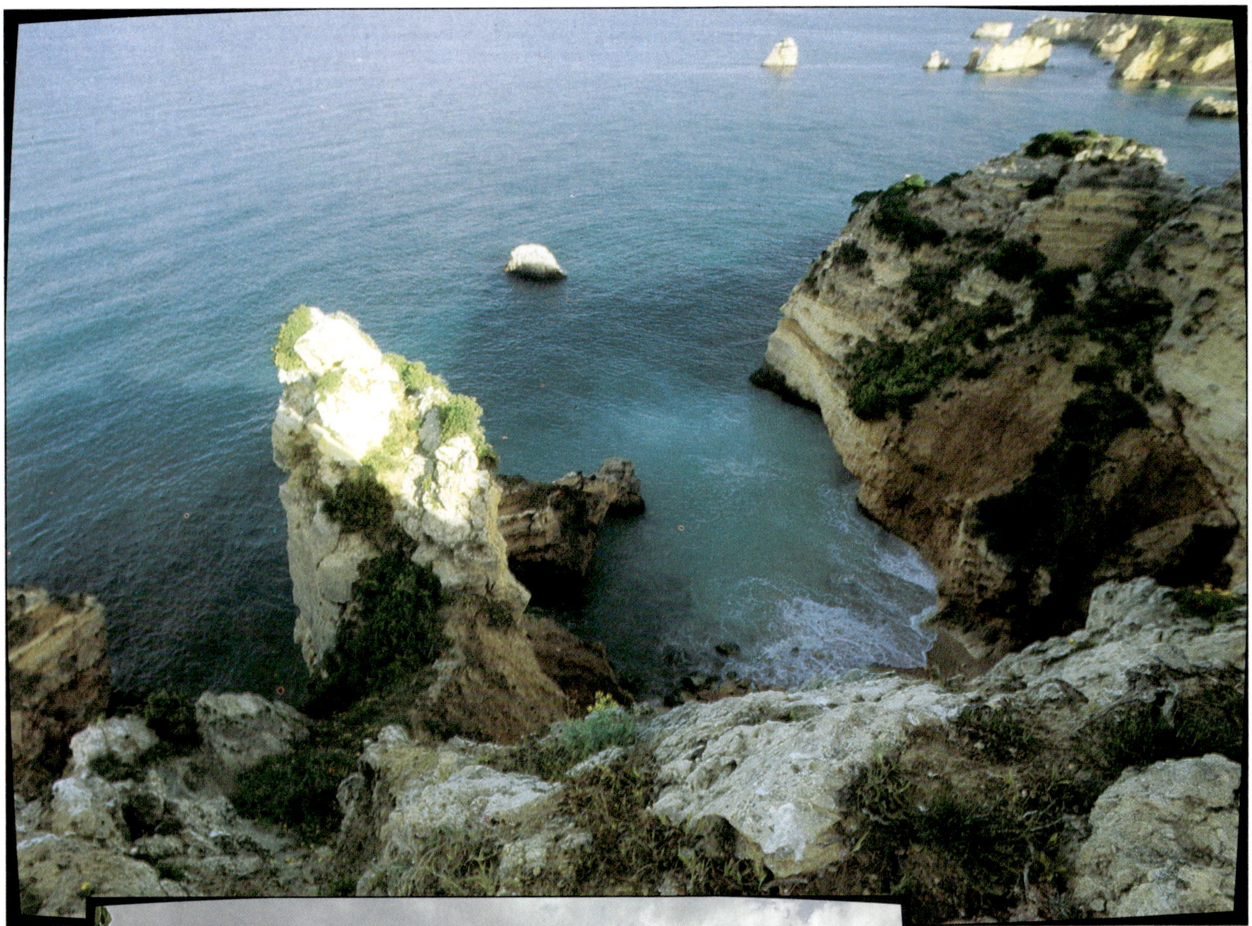

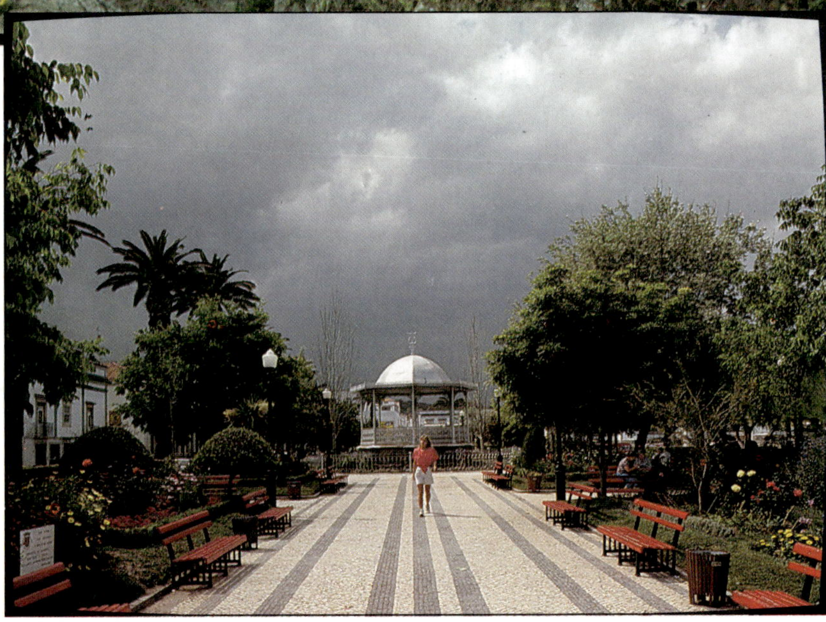

4-5: *These two shots are from a brief exploration of the surrounding area soon after the family arrived at the villa. In video terms, they are really no more than picture postcards. People are usually so impressed by their new surroundings on arriving in a new country that there is a dangerous temptation to linger for too long on such scenes.*

Linking shots

With an informal video, such as one of a vacation, you have much greater freedom to include additional material. Since you are not really concerned with telling a highly structured, formal story (beyond recording what you did and what you saw), sequences do not necessarily have to build on preceding images. So, between a sequence of, say, the villa and its surroundings, and one of a day on the beach, you can shoot short links of anything that might be of interest, such as highly attractive views, local characters, or colourful street scenes or market traders selling their wares.

When shooting other kinds of video, perhaps a drama or documentary, you will find link material equally valuable, particularly if you are going to edit your tape. In most cases, the inclusion of links between main sequences implies the passing of time. Of course, the links should have some relevance to the story being told – audiences are easily distracted and puzzled if the camera lingers on something for no purpose at all.

Pace and balance in video work are hard to define precisely. They imply a pleasing flow of images, with no sequence being unduly longer than any other. Pace and balance are also achieved by contrasting sequences – perhaps by following an introspective moment with frenetic activity – and by gradually increasing the tempo. But there are no hard and fast rules for achieving this aim. You have to develop a feeling for it, as when getting the balance 'right' in composing a single shot.

As you are filming, remember this important need for pace and balance (it helps if you look at the scene in the viewfinder as if it were unfolding on a television screen). Obviously, if you are going to edit the tape, you will be able to fine-tune the pace of your sequences at this later stage, but even if you are limited to in-camera editing you can still achieve balance by thinking about the length and content of your sequences beforehand. (A useful tip is to write down the intended duration of each sequence to be covered.)

Let's consider the example of a day's outing to a nearby town. The coverage will include scenes of the family at the local market, a sequence on the beach, the afternoon meal, and places of local interest. A shooting plan would allocate five minutes to the market, eight to the beach, and three minutes each to the meal and local scenes.

Don't forget that there must be a sense of pace and balance *within* each individual sequence, as well as *between* sequences. Also, avoid the temptation to instil pace into sequences by changes of camera angle and by moving from long-shot to close-up and vice versa, particularly if the action you are recording is relatively commonplace. As has already been stressed, too much intrusive camera action is distracting for the viewer. And finally, ensure that within sequences shots are of equal pace. So, for instance, you should never cut from a fast long-shot pan of a scene to a slow pan of an individual walking in close-up: the difference in pace will merely confuse the viewer.

PACE AND BALANCE

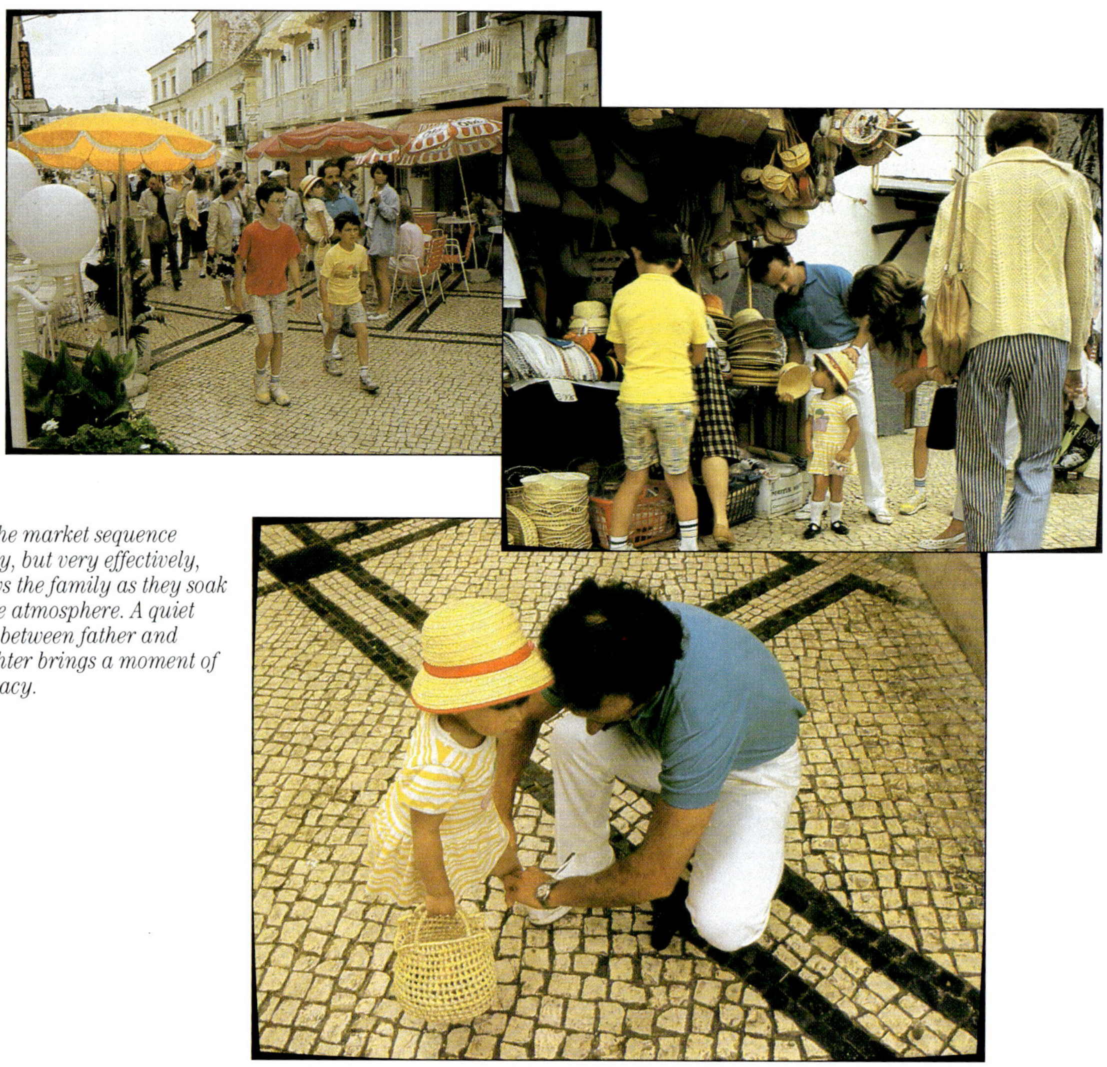

1-3: *The market sequence simply, but very effectively, follows the family as they soak up the atmosphere. A quiet word between father and daughter brings a moment of intimacy.*

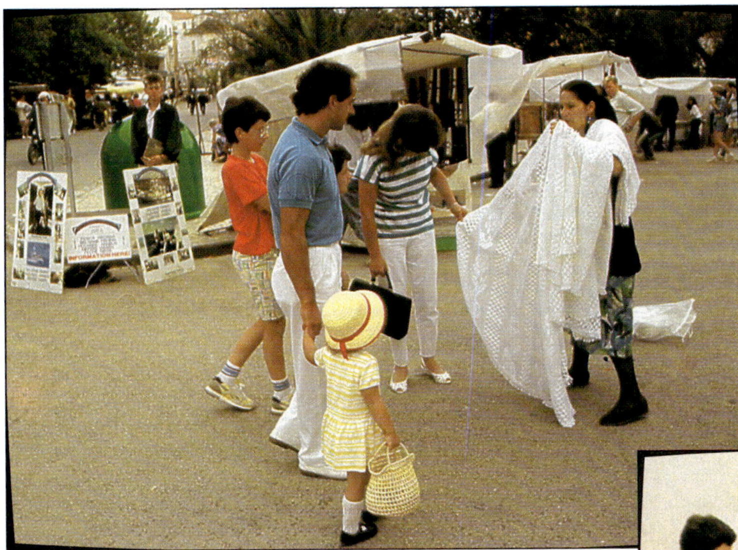

4-6: *Several close-ups of interesting displays and the family reactions to them help to create a change of pace within the sequence. So the appreciation of fine lacework contrasts with buying a beach ball or children's clothes.*

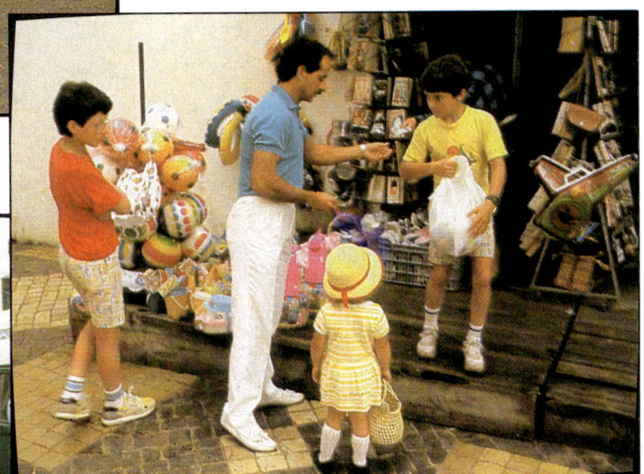

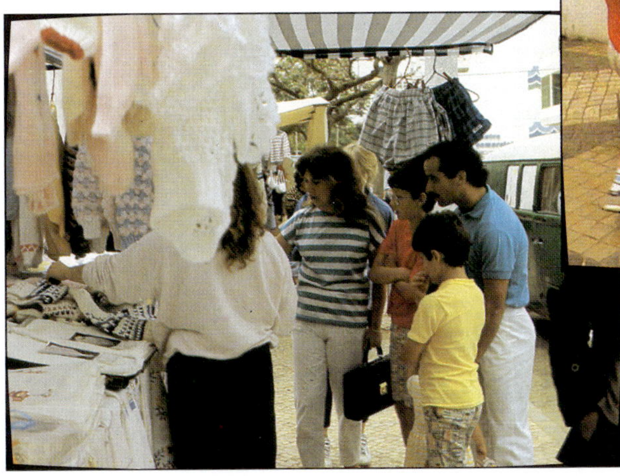

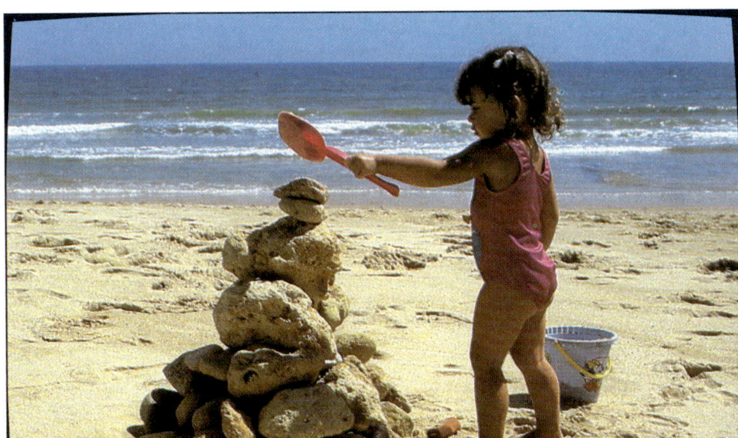

7-8: *Although the film of the family on the beach shows them highly relaxed, it doesn't mean you can stop thinking about your techniques. The shots of the young child engrossed in playing on the sand give a pleasing change of pace from the faster action of the football game. The quiet beach made filming easy.*

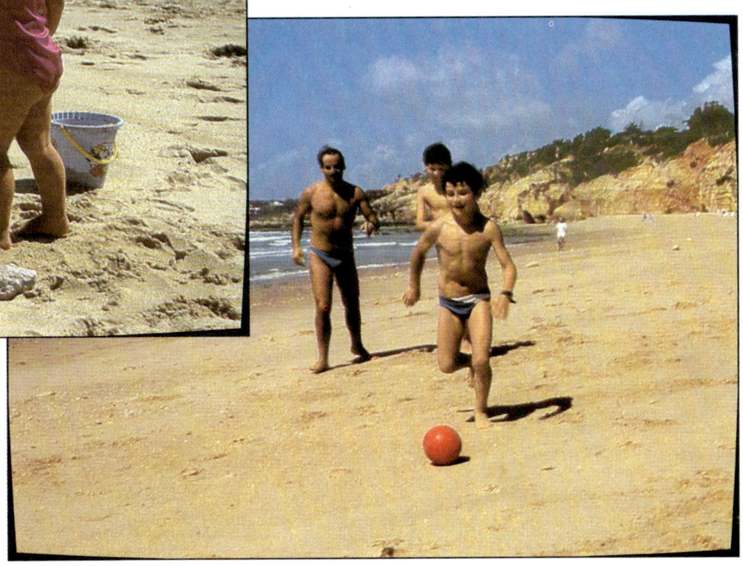

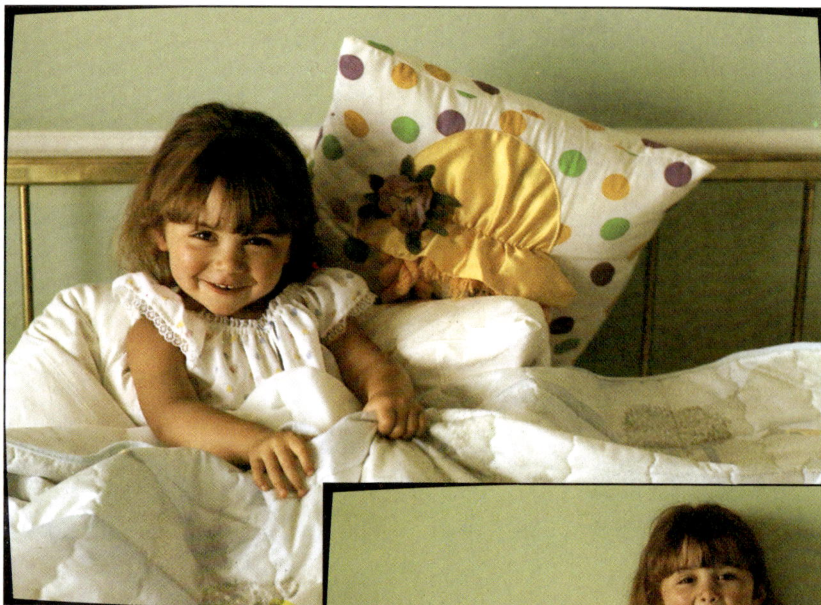

1-2: *This sequence of a child waking up has a slow, gentle pace. It will act as a useful punctuation between some of the more lively, dynamic scenes of the holiday video.*

3: *The charm of the subject and the simplicity of the setting mean that the technique has also been kept simple. A slight broadening of the shot as the child emerges from the bedclothes is all that is needed.*

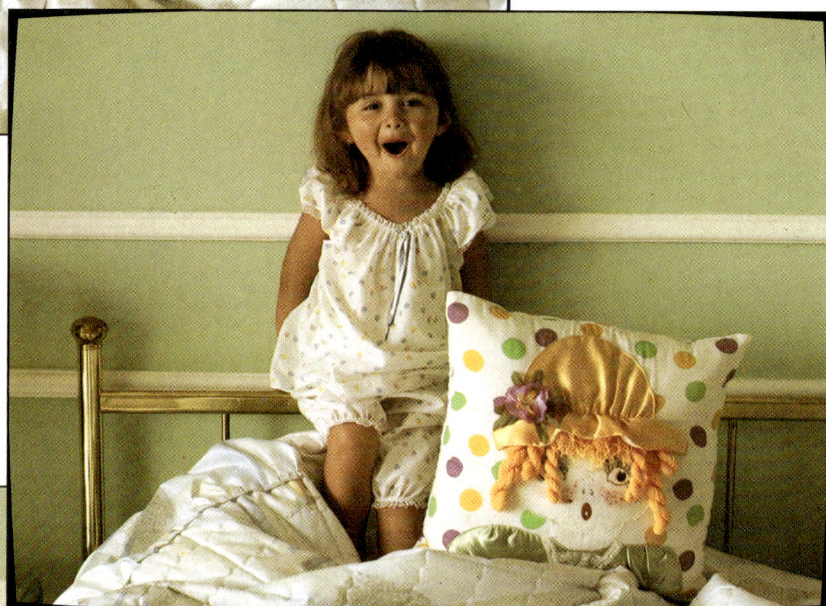

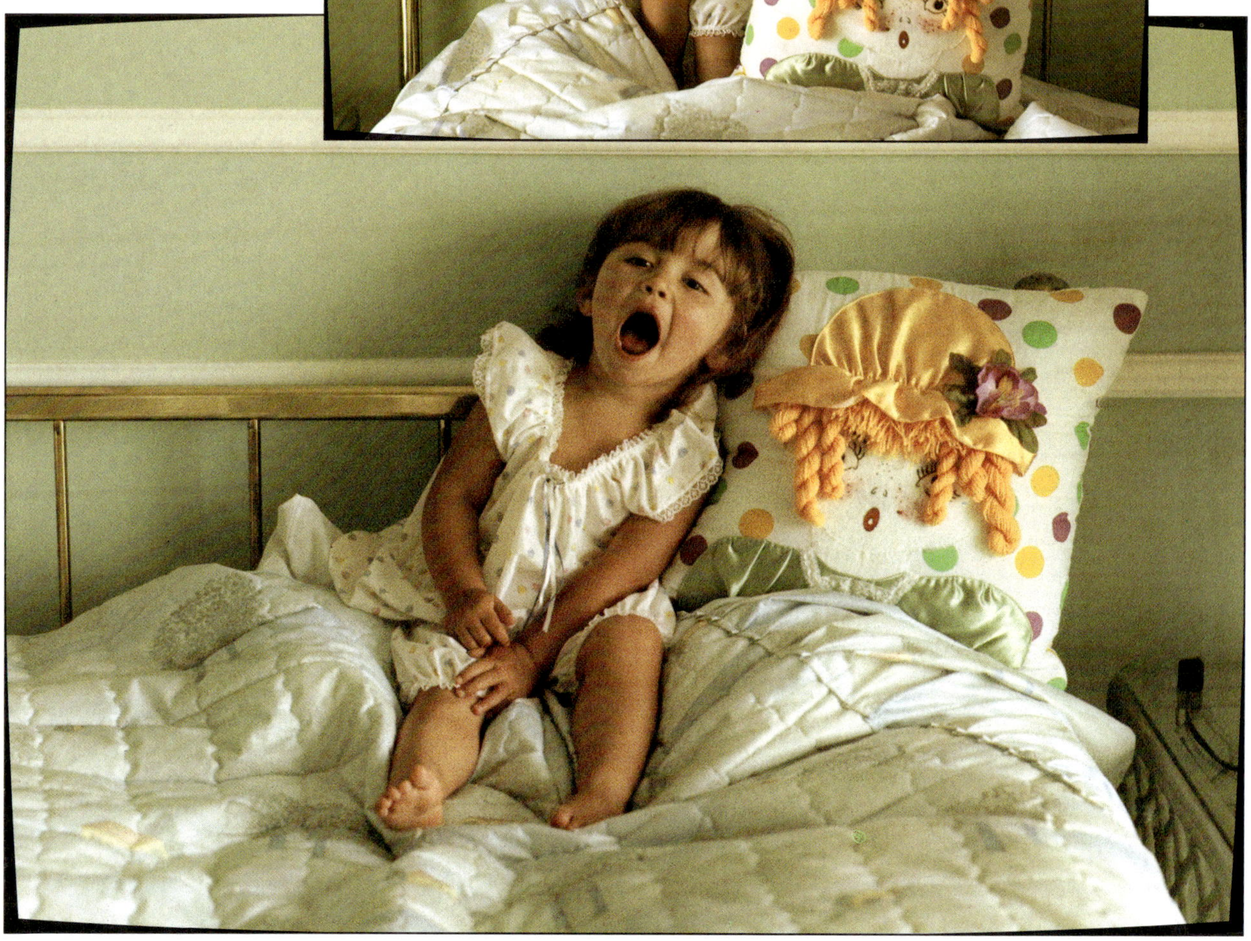

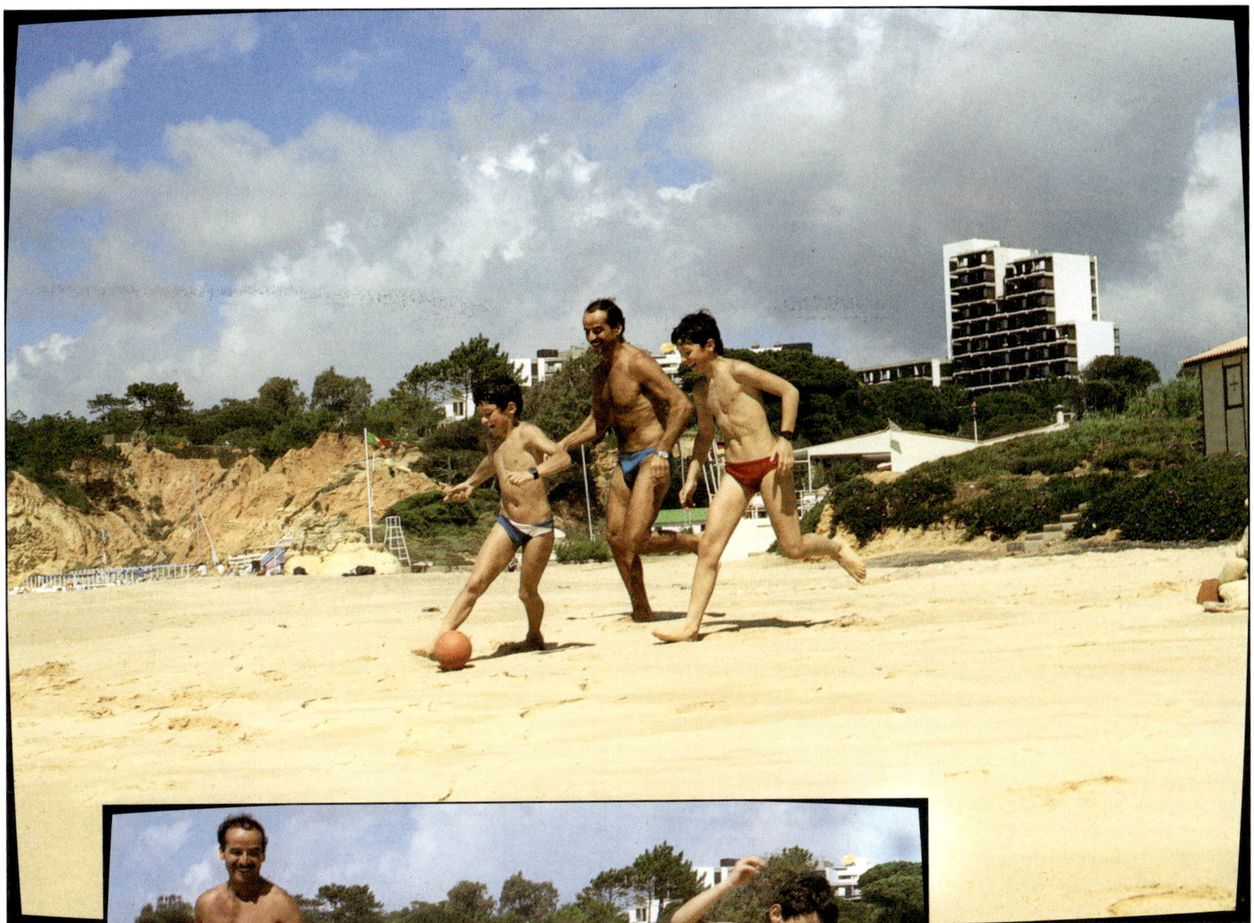

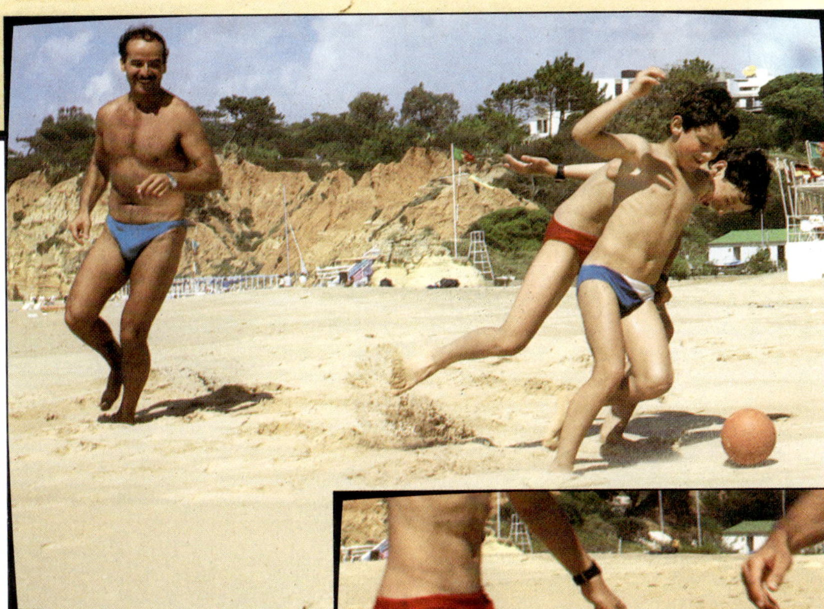

1-2: *This fast-paced sequence is typical of many holiday beach scenes. The rapid movement of the footballers was followed with a fast pan in long-shot.*

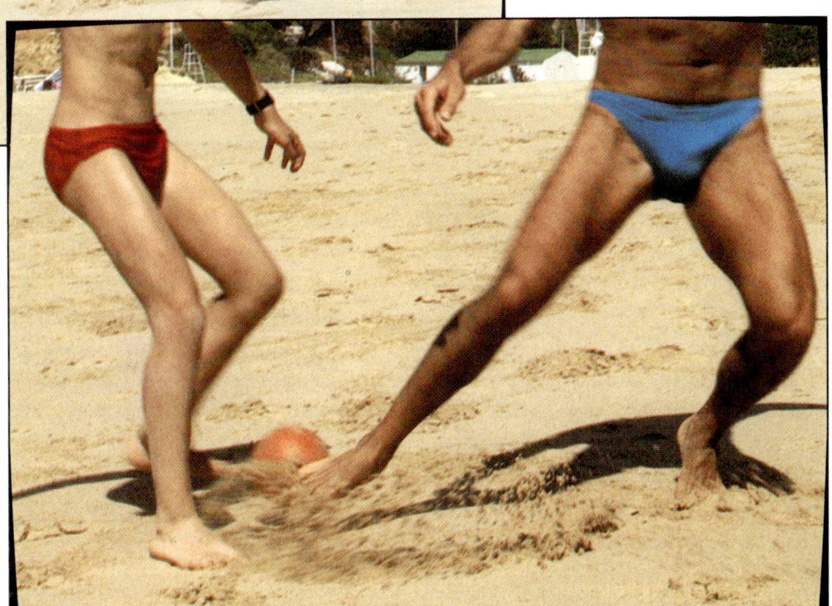

3: *A close-up like this following a fast pan will work if the subject is still moving too. It adds to the sense of action – but you will have to have good reactions to capture such a shot successfully.*

1: *The light by the sea can be quite dazzling and contrast can therefore be greater than the camcorder can cope with. The highlight on the rock background just avoids an ugly 'burn out'. The foreground is quite dark but is saved from becoming a shadowy non-event by the boats and the ripples.*

2: *This shot is more evenly lit and is less likely to cause video problems. Use a polarising filter on the camera lens to cut out all surface reflections and show the clear green depths of the water.*

3: *Strong backlighting of a subject should be avoided even if you have a backlight button to apply some correction. This shot is typical of the muddy colours and loss of detail of backlit shots.*

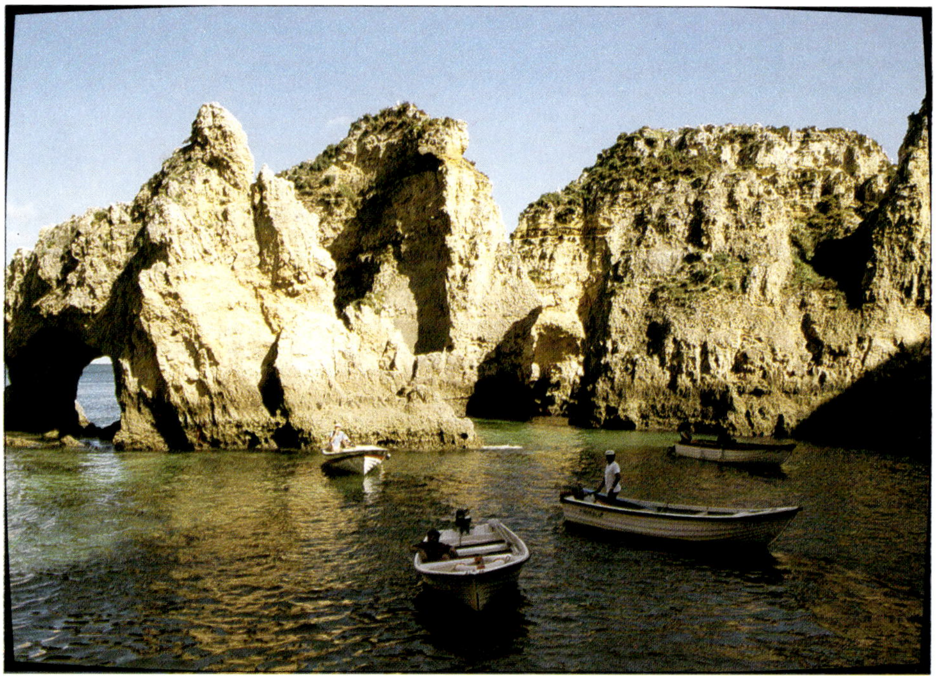

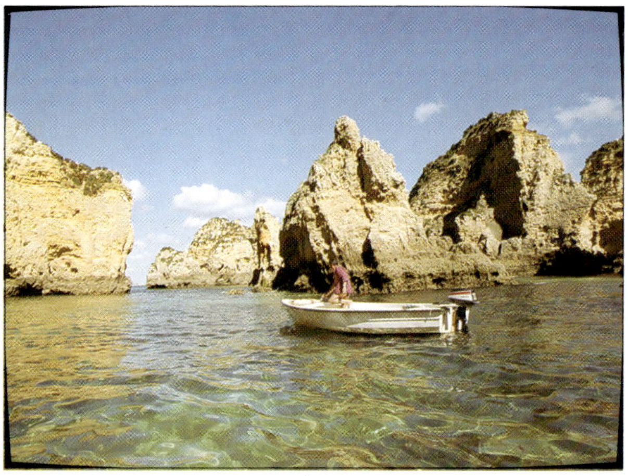

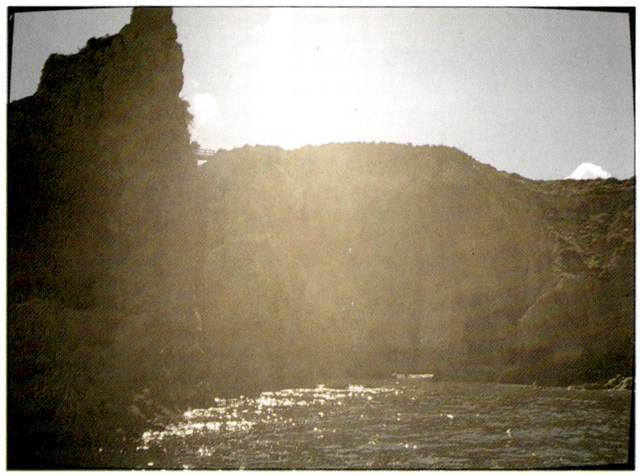

SUN, SEA AND SKY

The beach in sunny weather can be an ideal place to shoot video, but taking your camcorder on to unfamiliar ground has its potential pitfalls.

The coastal environment can be hazardous to video gear. Avoid loading your tape cassettes into the camcorder in windy conditions as gritty dust, sand and salt sea-spray can wreak havoc with the video heads. Keep the camcorder lens covered except when it is actually being used and protect it with a screw-on plain glass filter. Don't leave the camcorder lying about in the hot sun and be sure not to get it wet – so keep it clear of the sea and don't use it in the rain either. Some camcorders can be fully waterproofed for underwater use. Rain protection hoods can also provide some protection.

Power supply

Be sure you have sufficient cassettes to see you through the holiday – particularly if you are shooting on VHS-C – additional cassettes may not be readily available at the location. Another important point to remember is that you will need to be able to recharge your camcorder batteries as you go. You will therefore need the availability of a mains power supply to plug your battery charger into, unless it is the kind that can run off a car battery. When you are travelling abroad, remember that different countries use different types of mains plugs as well as varying voltages. Take the relevant adaptor. Plugging the camcorder into your car's lighter socket is a useful way of saving battery power on a trip.

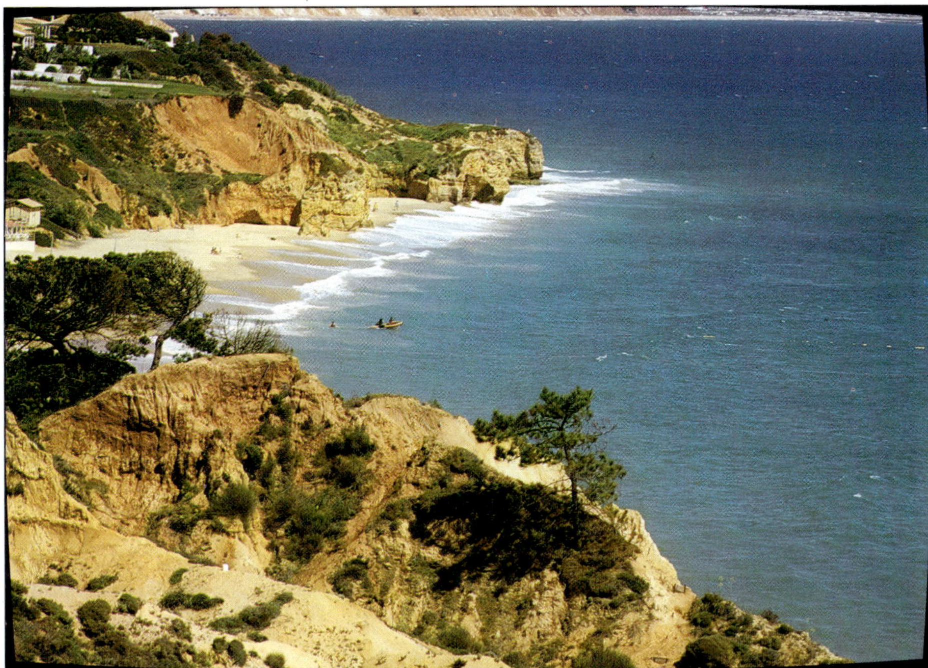

4-5: *The colour and appearance of subjects depends to a large extent on the direction and 'colour temperature' of the light.* **4** *was shot in full sun and the colours are fully saturated and vivid. The same scene was taken on a different day* **(5)**. *The sun is hazy and shining from the top right hand corner of the frame, the result being cooler, with more pastel colours and dramatic modelling of the landscape.*

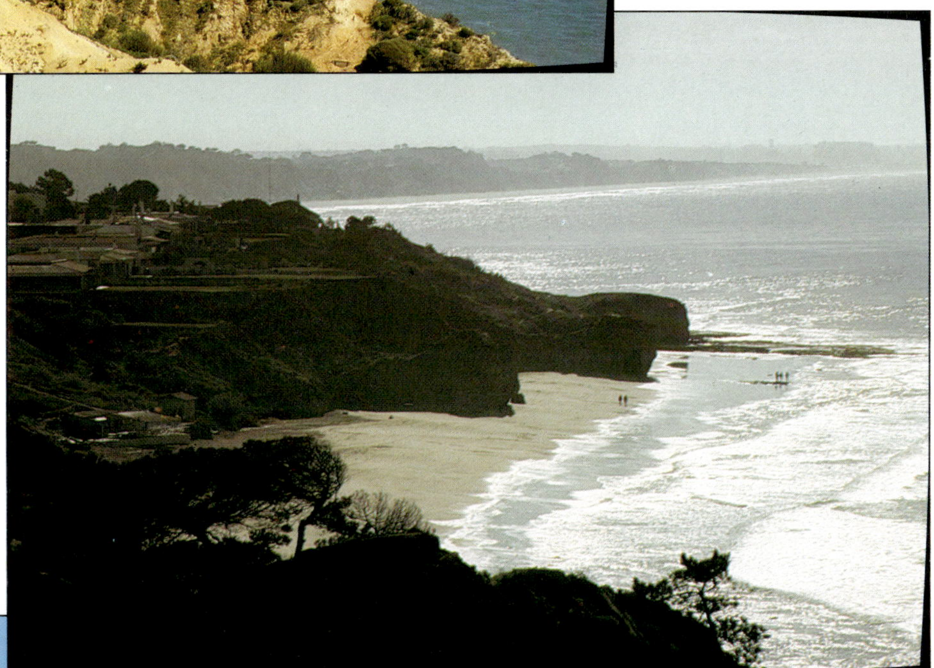

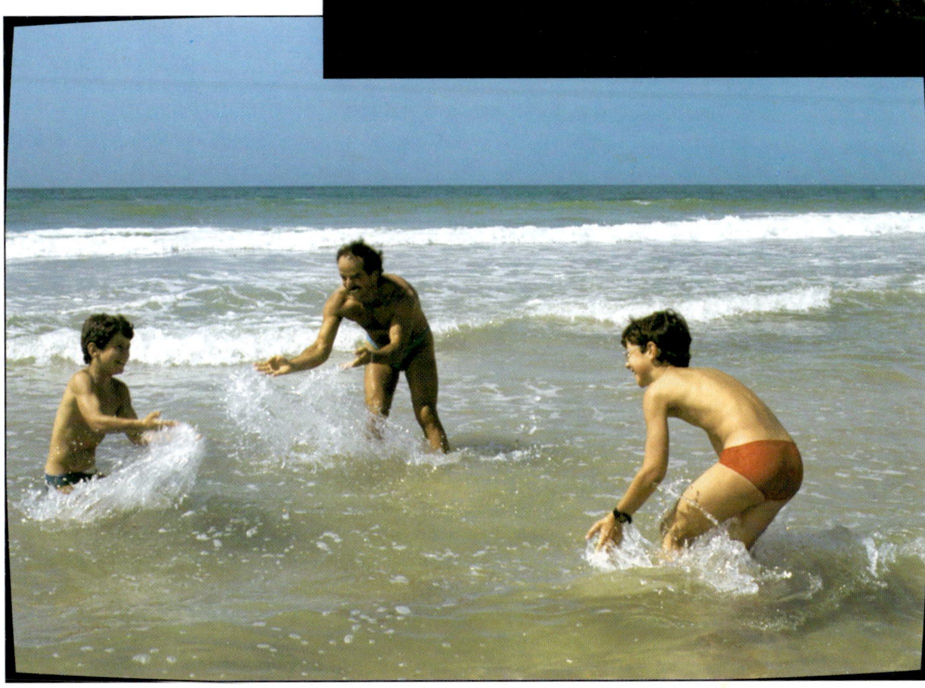

6: *A sunny action shot which is three quarters side lit to throw the subjects into relief. The only photographic hazard is the sea spray, which must not be allowed to get onto the camcorder lens!*

Natural history can become an absorbing interest, and can provide fascinating video material. To make a video recording of wildlife requires great patience. You must investigate all aspects of your subject's behaviour – how the animal feeds, where it sleeps, when it mates, and how it reacts to the presence of man. You may need to spend weeks observing the animal, noting down its every move.

Once the animal's habits are known, you will be in a position to set up a hide and begin recording. A bait of water or food can be used to persuade it to come out into the open. Count on a lengthy stay and take with you food and drink, binoculars and a sleeping bag.

Ideally, you should work with a long lens – about 800mm produces excellent magnification on an average camcorder. If this is not possible, use the telephoto end of the zoom, but the results will be less impressive. You will also need a heavy tripod, since with this range of magnification the slightest tremor can cause you to lose the image.

To record sound as well as image, you will need an extension microphone, positioned in a concealed place close to where you believe the animal will appear. A directional mike with a pick-up zone of about ninety degrees will produce the best results.

Never disturb an animal's natural habitat. This means not pulling down vegetation in order to get a clear view. This is particularly important with nesting birds – even if the bird itself is not disturbed, any change in the vegetation will give away the presence of the nest to predators.

Of course, it is not necessary to trek into the wilderness to record wildlife. The bird table in the garden is a good place to start. Safari parks and open zoos are also ideal. Here, you will have to shoot from a car – never be tempted to get out to obtain a better shot. Brace the camcorder against the window frame, perferably using a small clamp. Keep the engine running and have the car pointing toward an escape route in case large animals show signs of resenting your intrusion.

RECORDING WILDLIFE

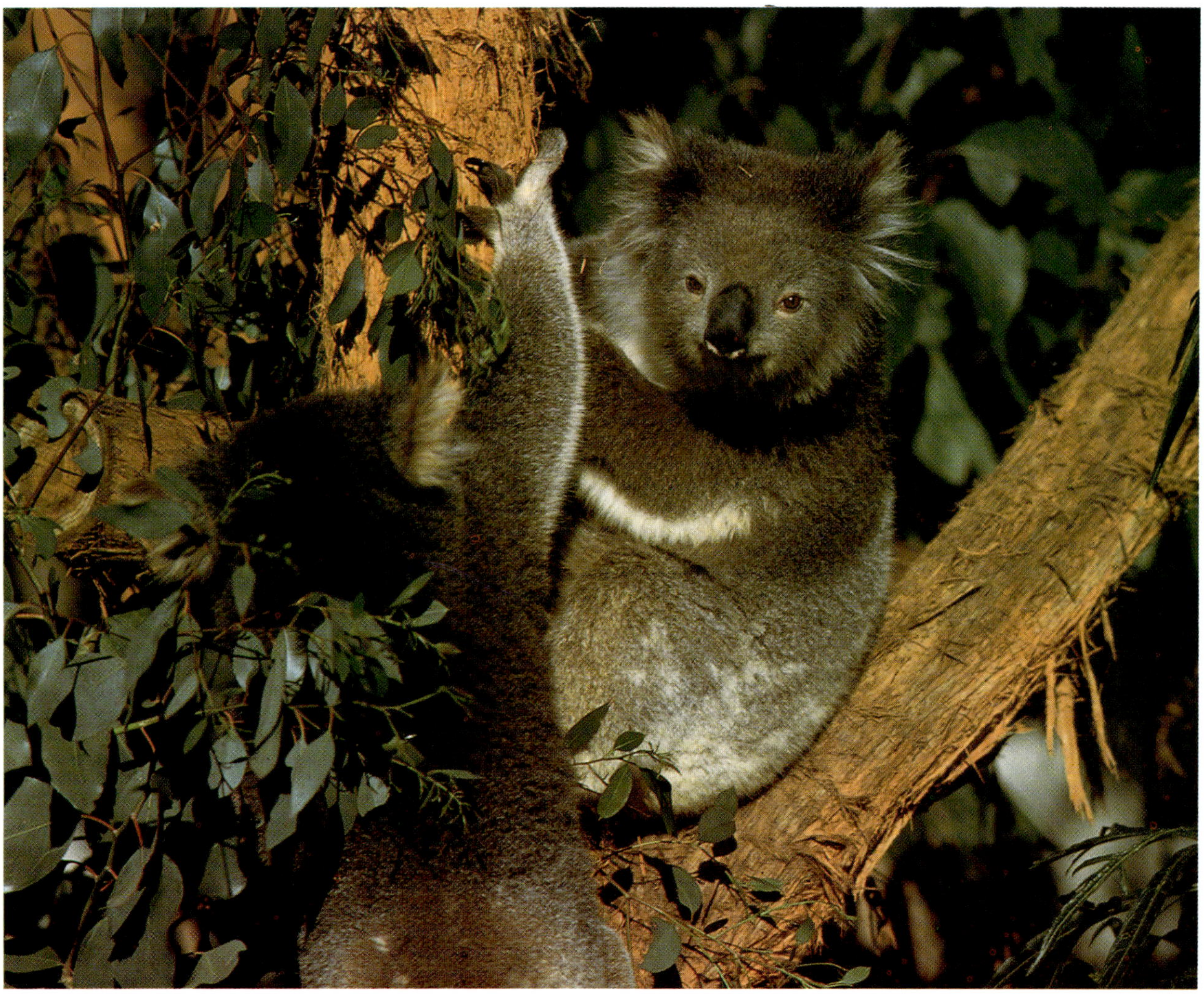

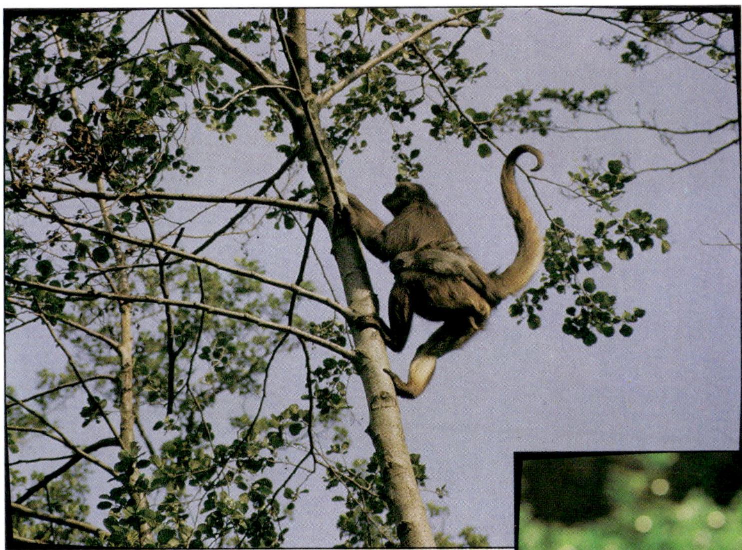

1: *This howler monkey could easily be in its natural habitat in the Amazonian rain forest. In fact it was shot in an open zoo. With a long lens, it was possible to record the monkeys' behaviour in detail, including close-ups of facial expressions and gestures between members of the group.*

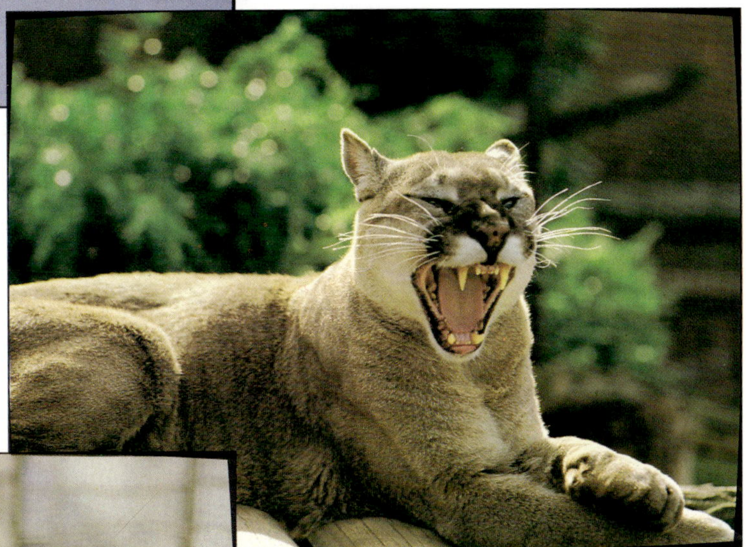

2: *The problem with animals in some zoos is that they appear inactive. In fact, many animals in the wild spend their time dozing between meals. This big cat was recorded at a zoo in which the animals were kept in large enclosures.*

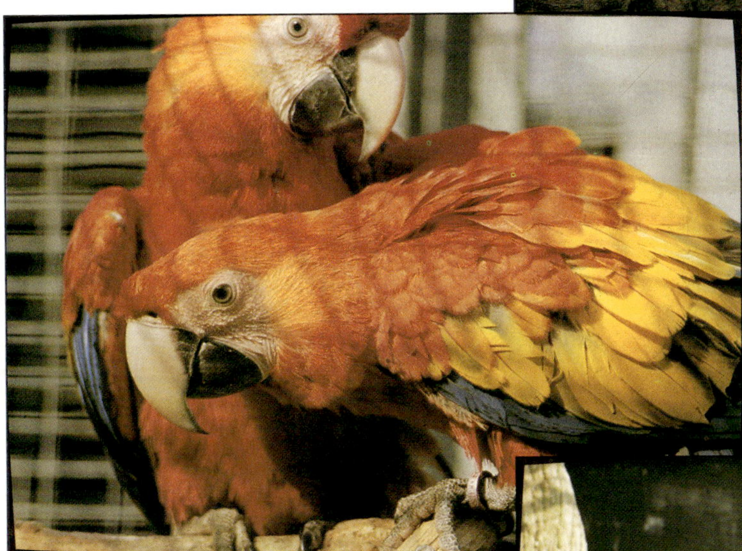

3: *Animals in cages or behind bars prove a problem. Use the limited depth of field of the telephoto lens to blur out the bars in the foreground. Remember also to use manual focusing.*

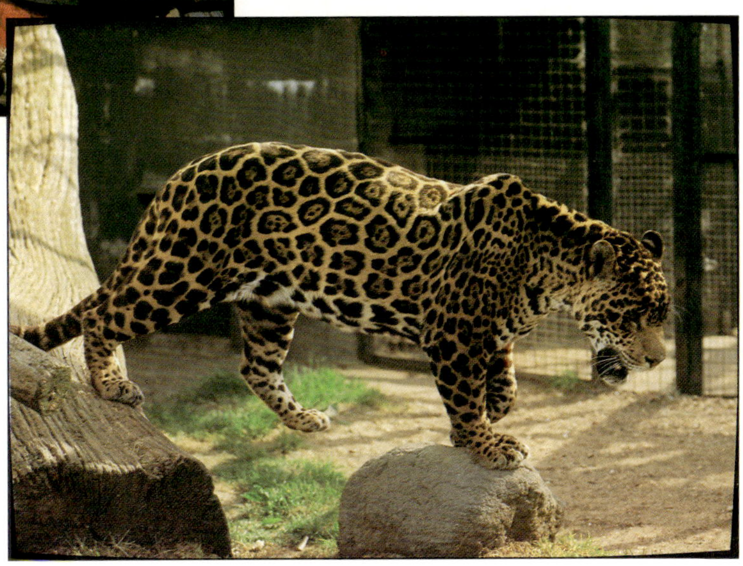

Left: *The telephoto end of the zoom's range is ideal for recording animals perching in tall trees.*

4: *A magnificent jaguar on the prowl. When recording animals in zoos, check out feeding times beforehand. Animals usually get restless as feeding time approaches and the sight of a big cat tearing into a chunk of meat provides exciting coverage.*

On many camcorders, the zoom lens also offers a macro option – a lens setting that allows you to record subjects that are very close to the lens at high magnifications. Usually, this mode is obtained by adjusting the lens to the widest setting and then either pressing the appropriate switch or pulling the zoom lever to the macro setting. The setting works by rearranging the lens elements so that those at the rear are moved forward, altering the light path to give a high degree of magnification. In effect, the lens arrangement inside the zoom becomes equivalent to that used in a microscope. Fixed focal-length macro lenses are available for some camcorders.

The most obvious use for the macro setting is for recording small subjects such as plants and insects, in close-up. At the macro setting, depth of field is very shallow, particularly when a wide lens aperture is also used. This means that you will require a high level of ambient light when recording, and supplementary lighting is usually advisable.

The shallow depth of field, and the magnification of the image obtained, means that it is best to take macro shots with a tripod-mounted camera. This places limits on field work. You will obtain better results if the environment is controlled – a short documentary sequence on insect behaviour, for example, could be made by placing the insects inside a specially-built glass-sided container.

THE MACRO LENS

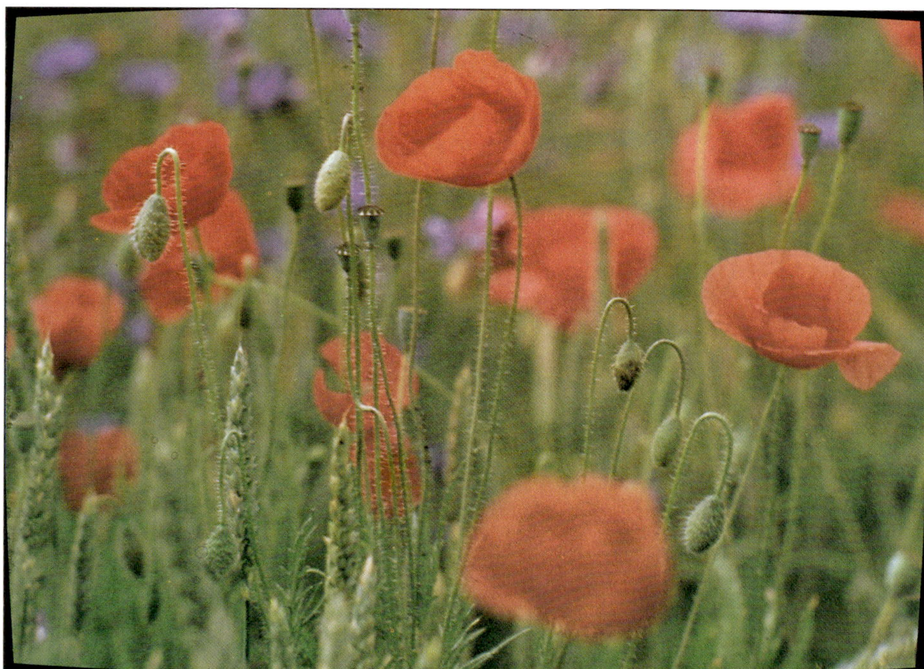

1: *Part of a sequence in an English meadow, this macro shot provides a welcome break from a succession of long-shots that included little interesting detail.*

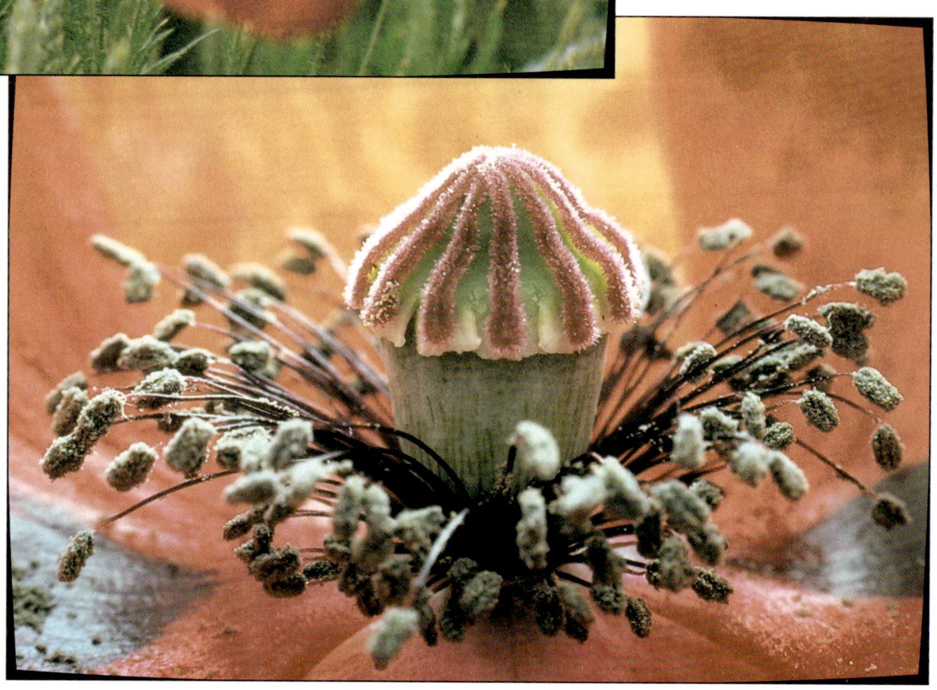

2: *This is an even closer shot of the inside of one of the flowers. The specimen had to be screened from the wind to prevent movement because of the shallow depth of field.*

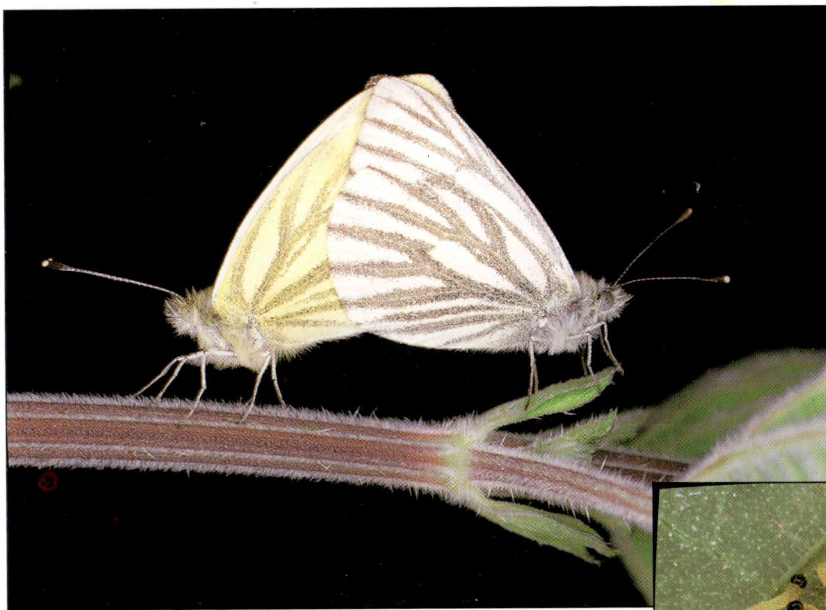

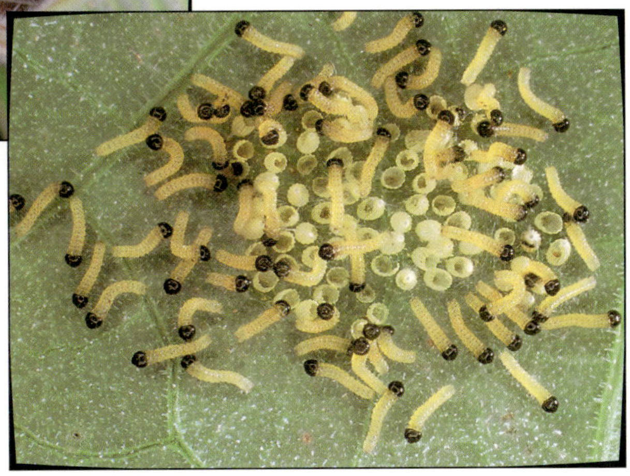

3: *A glass tank, good lighting, and a tripod-mounted camera were essential for this shot of butterflies mating. Patience is as important as the right technique when tackling this type of subject.*

4: *Caterpillars are excellent subjects – there is plenty of movement, but it is mostly in one plane, so depth of field is not a problem. A high degree of magnification on the lens is needed, however.*

5: *When recording insects, be prepared for short shots, before the subject takes flight.*

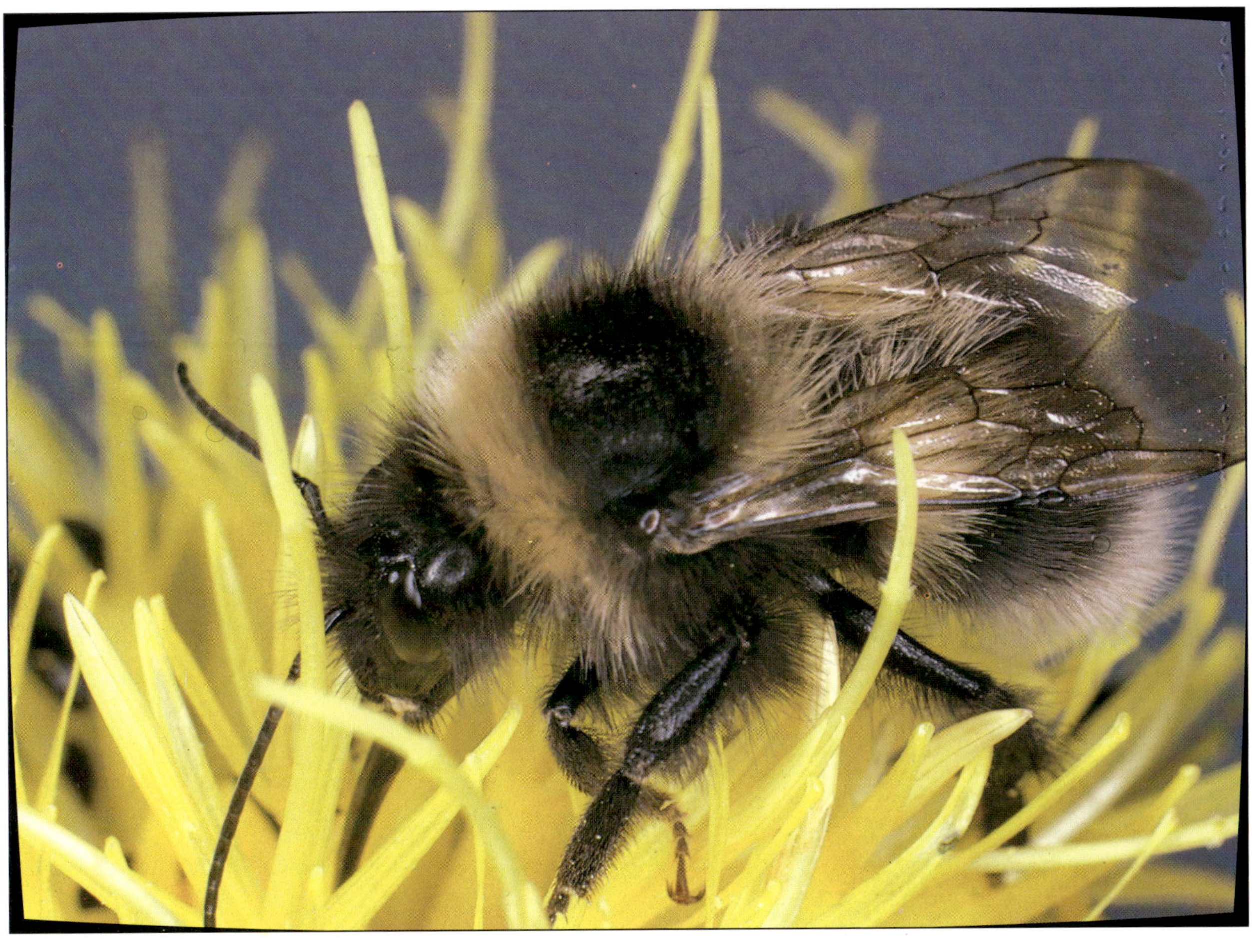

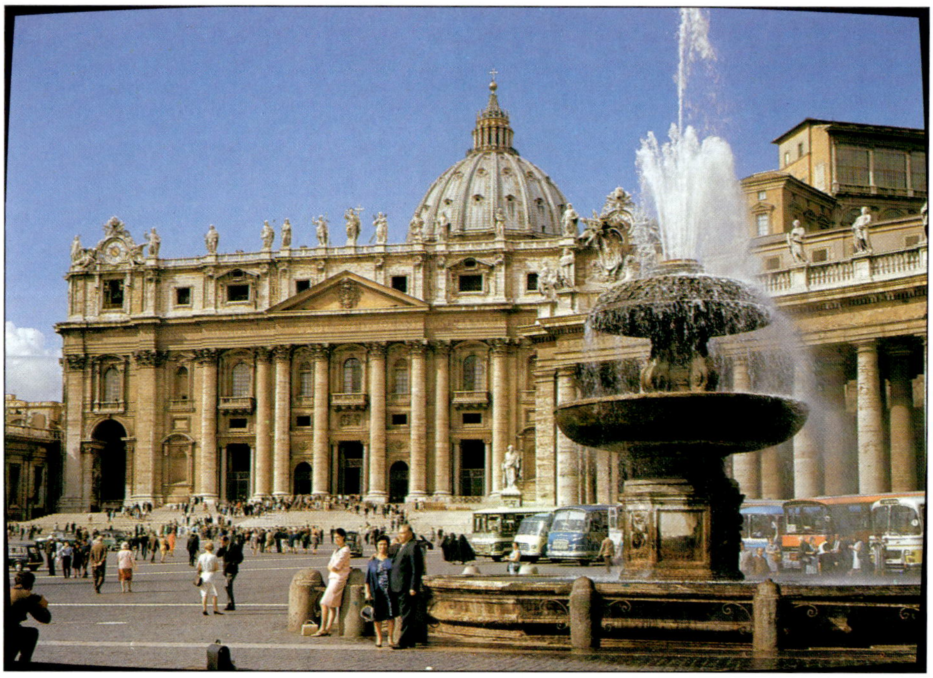

1: *The fountains and crowds outside St Peter's, Rome, give the scene a sense of movement that the building itself lacks.*

ARCHITECTURE

Buildings form one of the most common subjects that you will encounter on holiday. They are often among the most interesting features of a foreign town, and you will want to film them to give a faithful impression of your visit. But because buildings do not move they are difficult to video. It can also be hard to get far enough away from a building to include all of it in the frame. One solution is to record the life around the building – the throngs of people in an Italian square or the guards outside a royal palace. This will help convey the atmosphere of the place but will not give a sense of the architectural details that make the building what it is. To do this you will need to pan slowly across the structure, halting at the most telling details. You should also look for unusual camera positions, so that you avoid the obvious views of your subject. Another interesting possibility is to use the building as a vantage point, and film the view as well as the building itself. Church spires and domes, castle towers, and skyscrapers all lend themselves to this approach. It will not only give you a new angle on the building's setting, but may also offer a good way of recording other places you have already visited on your vacation – in fact you will be amazed at what you can see!

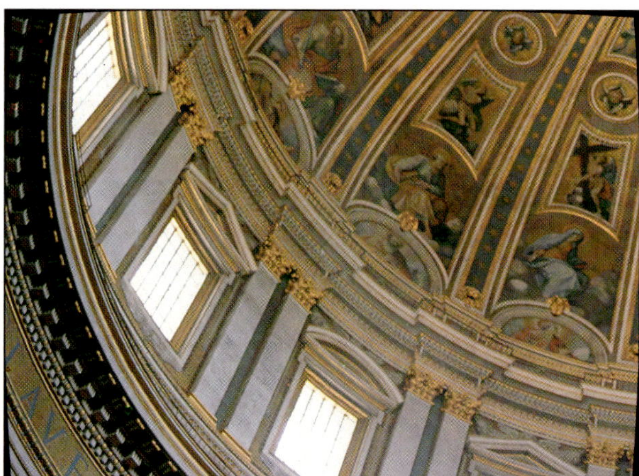

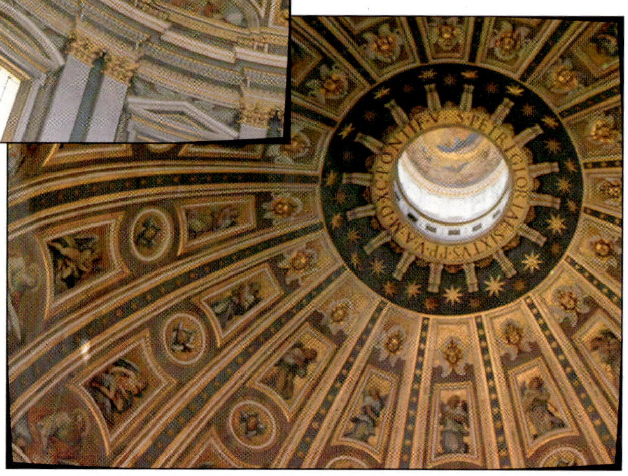

2-3: *Inside the church, the dome is the most imposing architectural feature. These shots are taken from a sequence in which the camera began by recording details.*

4: *The camera has pulled back to show the whole of the dome.*

5: *After a sequence showing the dome, a shot looking down from the gallery helps to put the dome in context. It also gives a wide enough angle of view to take in parts of the church that would otherwise be difficult to record.*

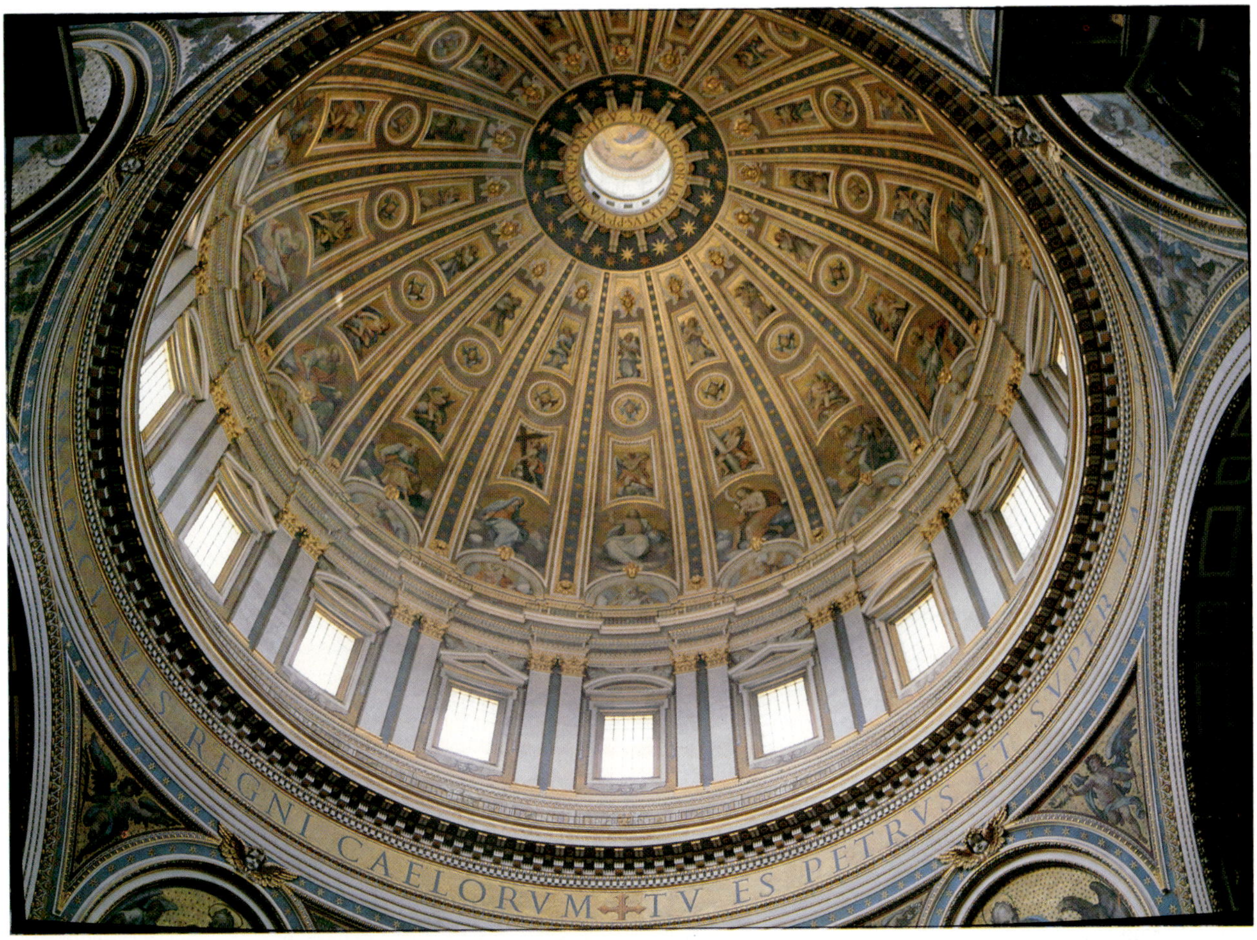
REGNI CAELORVM TV ES PETRVS ET SVPER

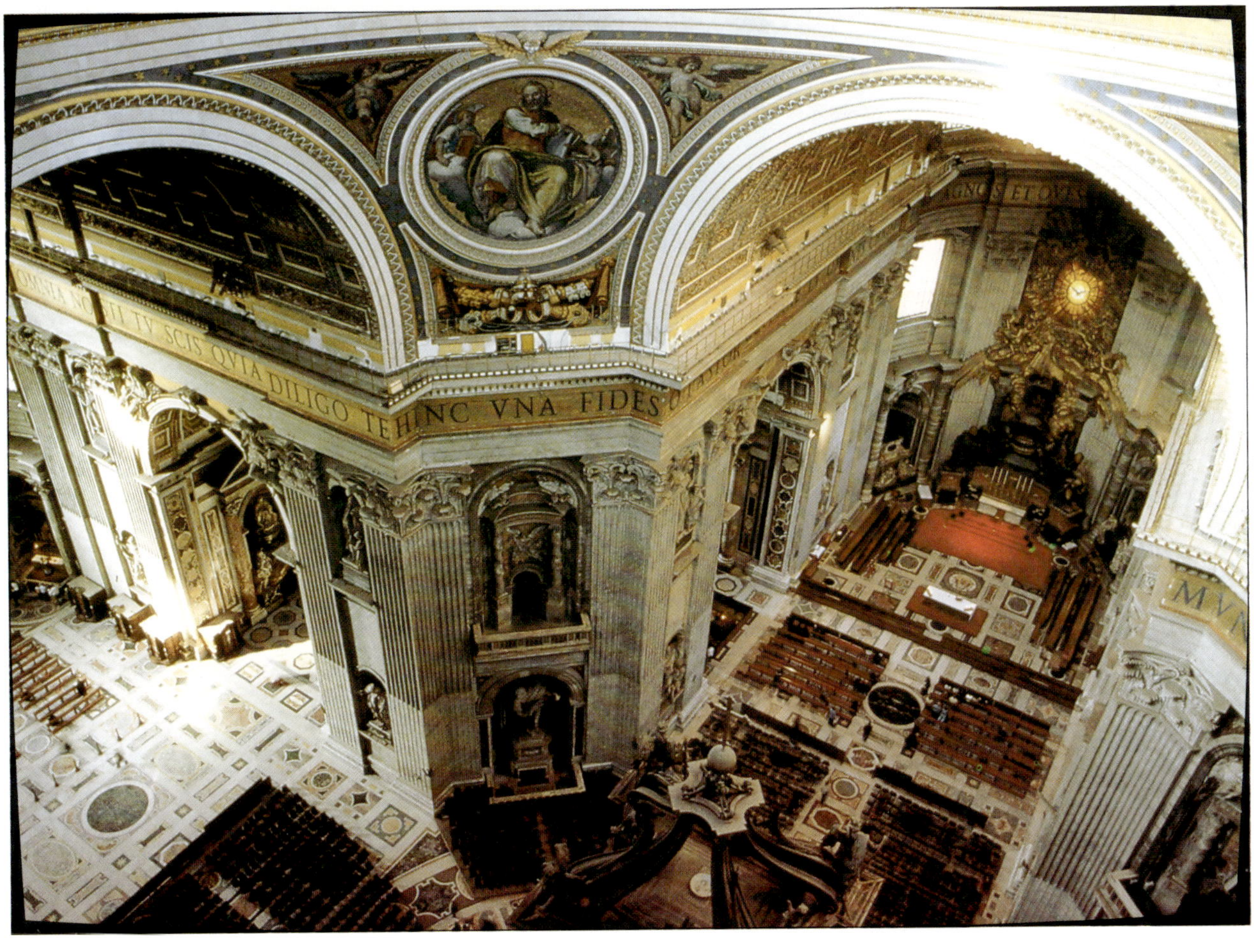
TV SCIS QVIA DILIGO TE HINC VNA FIDES

CLOSING A SEQUENCE

It is an accepted rule that before beginning a shot you should know how it is going to end. For example, if you are planning a slow pan of a beach scene you should rehearse it to ensure that the shot ends on an interesting or attractive feature. In addition, the shot which closes a sequence should be static, so preparing the audience for the change to a new image at the commencement of the next sequence. In effect, the static frame at the close acts as a visual full stop.

There are a number of accepted, if rather clichéd, devices for concluding a sequence. These can be determined either by the action, or the camera. For example, in a drama, a typical concluding shot to a sequence might well include someone walking slowly out of shot, away from the camera. Alternatively, the figure might leave a room, with the camera briefly resting on the closed door. While such shots are often highly appropriate, you may prefer to veer away from the obvious, if instantly recognizable end, to more original conclusions.

Another type of closing shot can be created in-camera, either through a concluding camera movement, or by adjusting the focus or, in certain situations, the exposure. The most obvious camera movement for closing a shot is the slow pan coming to rest on either a significant detail, or an image of the location seen in long shot. In the vacation video, a shot was taken of the harbour towards evening, panning round and then coming to rest on the deserted beach. Both camera movement and content indicate the end of the sequence.

Other camera techniques involve throwing the scene out of focus at the end of the shot. If the next sequence begins out of focus too, the audience will interpret this as indicating that time has passed. They will do so because they have been trained to interpret such conventions in this way by television and film makers. In fact, the more of these conventions you use the more sophisticated your videos will appear, and the more information you will be able to convey to viewers in a shorter time span. Another effect involves gradually closing down the aperture to darken the scene.

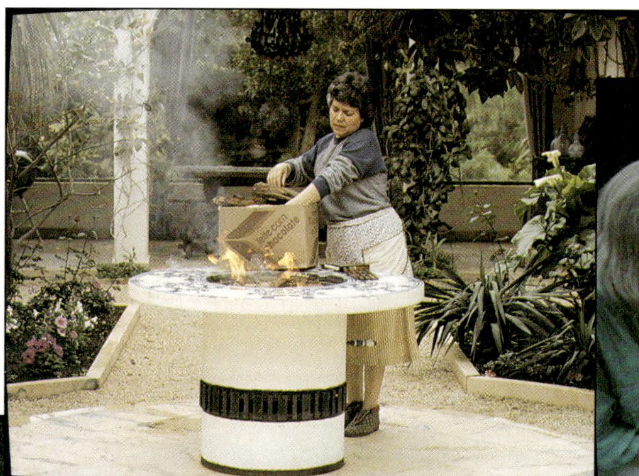

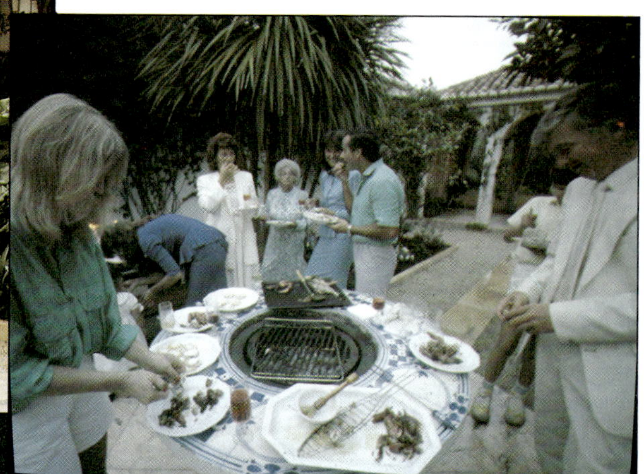

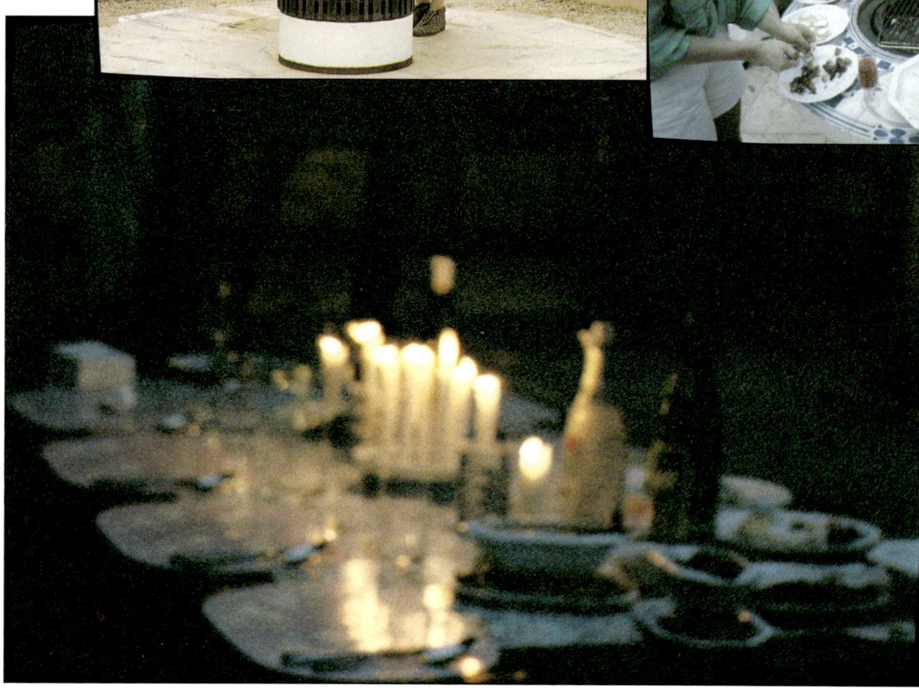

1-3: *A closing shot in which the camera slowly moves around the table, with the candle flames gradually going out of focus.*

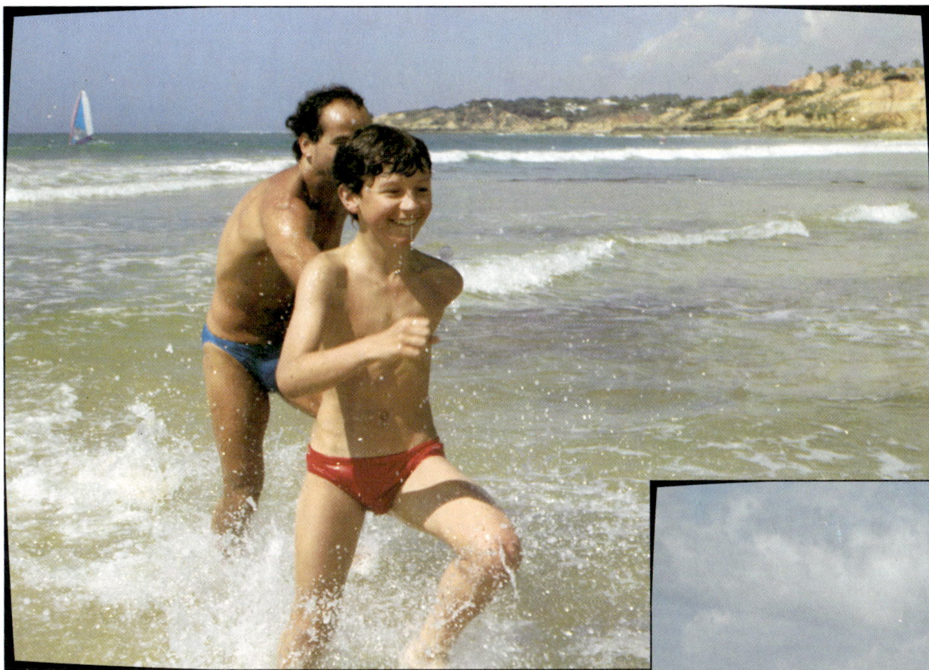

4-5: *These shots illustrate a typical end to a sequence. The bathers are running out of the sea and out of shot. Make sure that initially there is enough lead space, and that the subjects cross the screen on the diagonal. The final shot rests on the beach itself.*

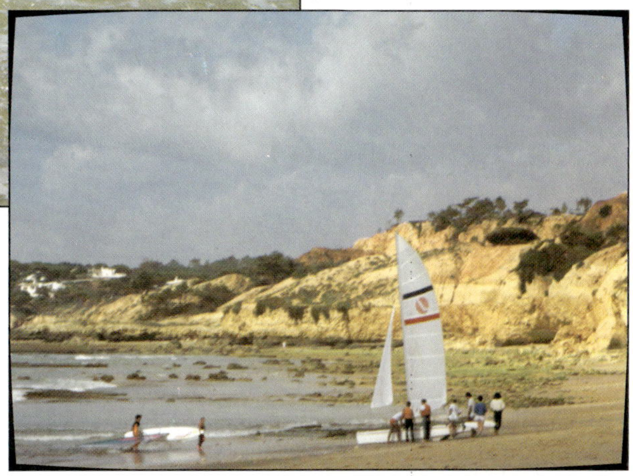

6: *This scene contains the elements required to end a particular sequence. The shot is taken from a position of deep shade into strong sunlight (exposure was determined by manual adjustment and checking through the viewfinder). The shot ends with the door closing and the screen darkening almost to black.*

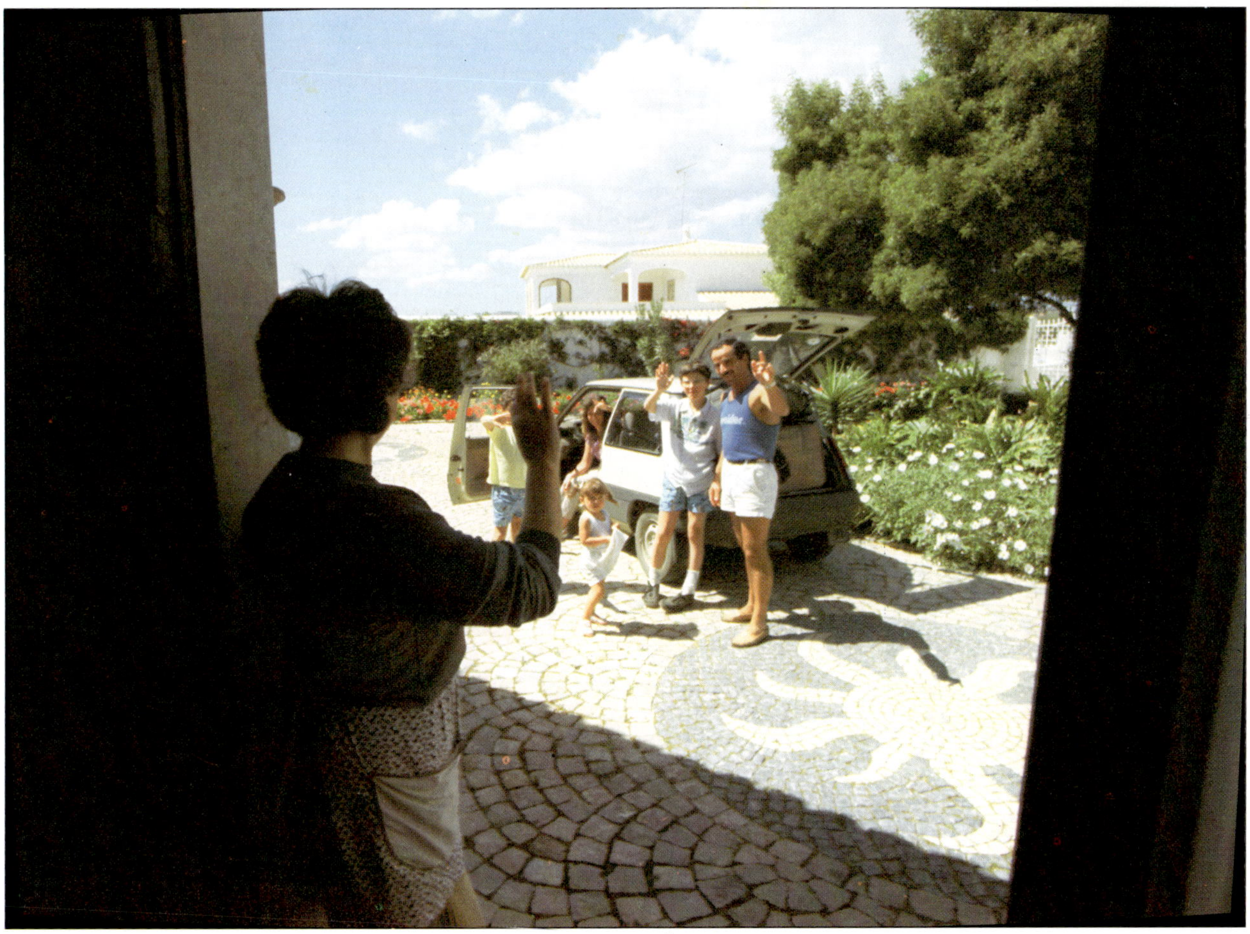

PROJECT NOTEBOOK

HOLIDAYS

A family holiday video is not going to be the next *Citizen Kane.* But it does offer an opportunity to shoot in a new, and often interesting, location, and to get shots of your family and friends having a good time. The intention should be to convey a relaxed, entertaining atmosphere, and if you adopt that approach when you shoot, then you are ten times more likely to convey that impression to the viewer. If you do, then you've made a good video.

■ Check the relevant customs regulations concerning the import and export of equipment.

■ Pack your equipment carefully. Have you got enough batteries? Do you need special filters?

■ What is the TV standard used in the country of your destination, and is it compatible with your equipment?

■ Every picture tells a story. A little forward planning should enable you to incorporate a beginning, a middle and an end to your holiday video, thus greatly increasing the audience-interest factor.

■ You can't video yourself. Obvious, yes, but this means that if you want shots of the family arriving at the hotel or villa, you'll have to get someone else to operate the camcorder, or arrive earlier yourself, and 'fake' it.

■ Don't contrive too many sequences – you're on holiday as well!

■ Remember, intense sunlight, sand and seawater are not best friends to the video camera's sensitive electronic systems.

■ In some countries, locals do not take lightly to having a camcorder pointed at them. Always be polite and ask permission before shooting.

DEVELOPING A STORY

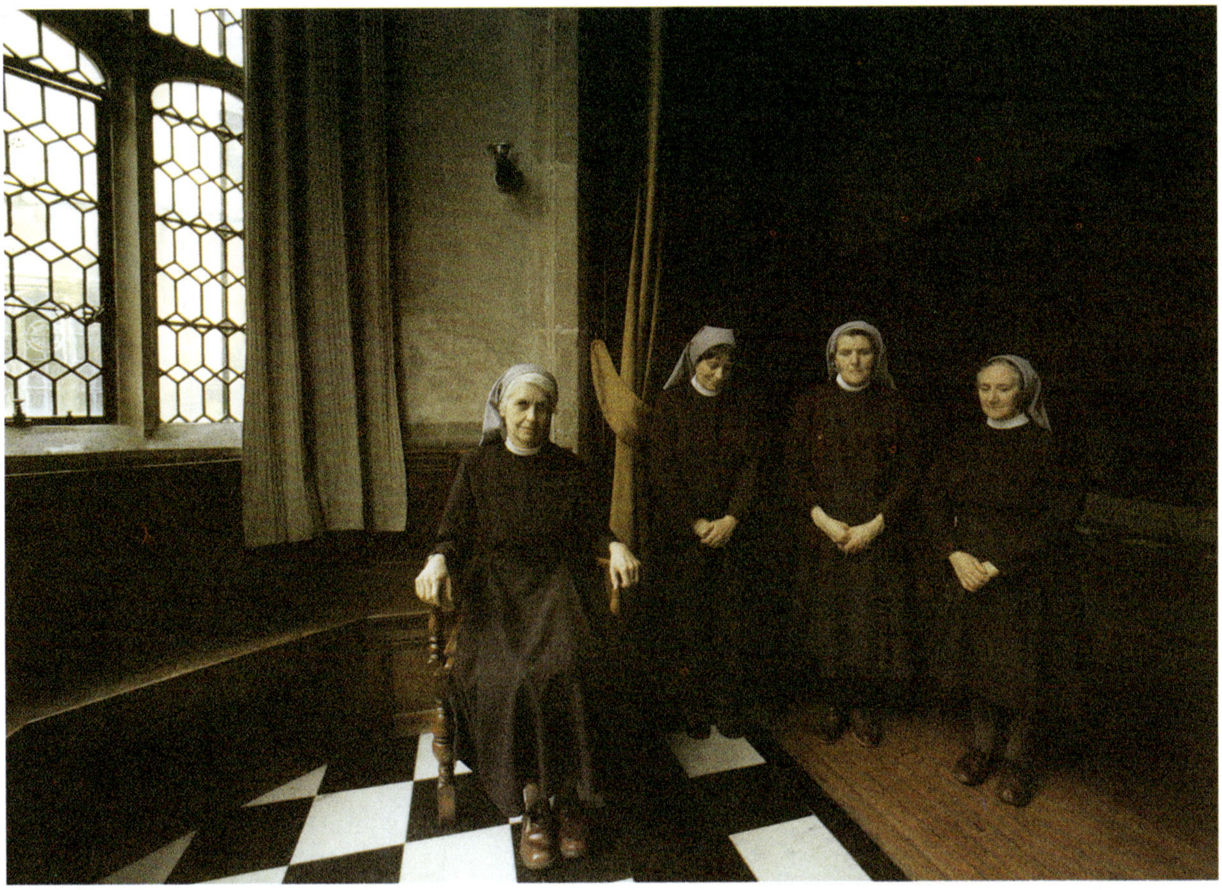

The home video-maker is immediately faced by two decisions – What's my story? and – How am I going to treat it? For instance, are you going for a relatively straightforward approach, perhaps revealing how events unfold over the course of a day, or will you opt for a more sophisticated line? This might involve creating a cast of up to five characters, revealing how their relationships develop.

Once such general considerations have been tackled, you must set about more specific problems. In the following video project we reveal how to film a community of nuns. As you'll see, such a potentially general subject throws up a huge number of possibilities, continuously forcing you to redefine your aims until you have a specific storyline and viewpoint. Without it the film will lack focus and coherence, and you will stand little chance of holding your audience's attention.

Good shots of buildings are in some ways more difficult to obtain that those of people; people, after all, are usually doing something, which in itself creates interest. With buildings, activity is implied by the camerawork alone. So the camera must explore a building as would the human eye.

The first sequence in the video establishes the location for the action. There are a number of ways of doing this. Most approaches would begin with a long shot and then move in for more detail. (Since long shots reveal camera shake such shots are best taken from a tripod.) Any detail that is to be highlighted should be significant – it could be a signboard revealing the location or the landscape if it is going to have a significant effect on the action.

7: *Shooting the scene from an unusual angle is another way of giving visual impact. By beginning the sequence with a close-up of a detail that doesn't indicate the nature of the whole, followed by a movement away from the subject which is now fully revealed, the audience will experience first puzzlement and then recognition. However, although such a technique is useful it wasn't considered for the video of the convent – it seemed ill-suited to the pace of convent life.*

FIRST APPROACHES

Such sequences are necessarily static: movement comes from changing the focal length of the lens or by panning or tilting the camera. Another option is a moving shot, taken either on foot or from a car. Although you will undoubtedly get camera shake, this will also provide additional drama. The viewer will interpret this movement as an arrival, and from then on will identify with the camera's 'eye' as it surveys the convent.

1-3: *A pan shot of the impressive exterior of the convent both establishes the location and indicates the special life lived within it. Consequently the camera position is important: you need to be far enough away to take in the whole building, but not so far that you can't zoom in effectively to the telephoto end of the lens if required.*

4-6: *The next step is to consider shots taken from a position midway along the driveway to the convent. This approach adds to the sense of arrival, but the car parked outside the convent distracts attention. If in a subsequent sequence the car has disappeared, the viewers will wonder whether this has any significance.*

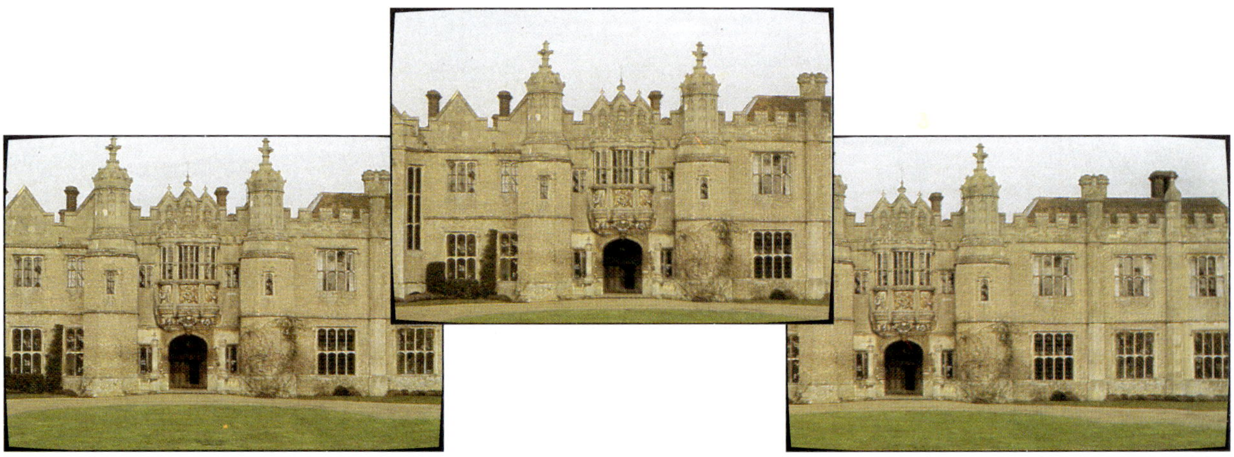

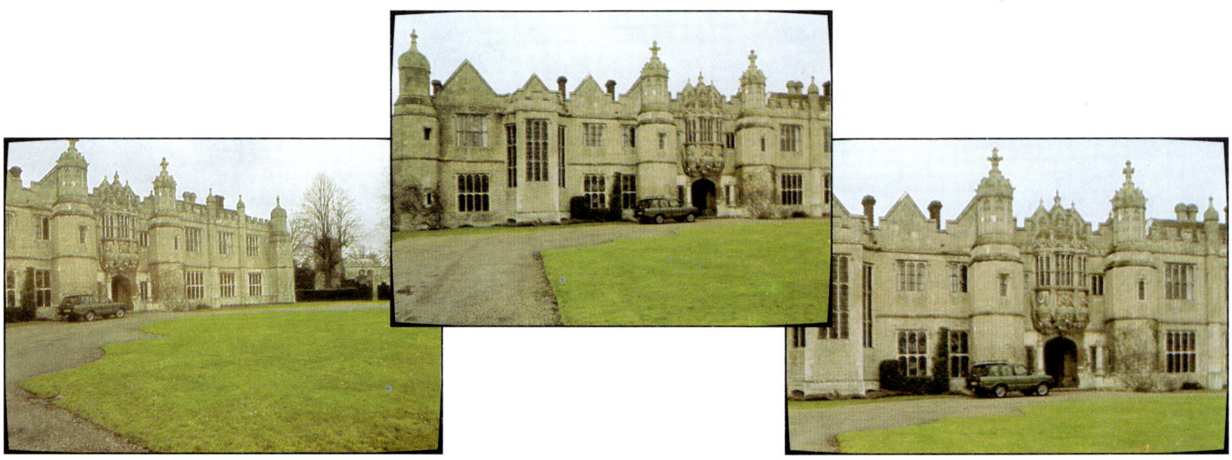

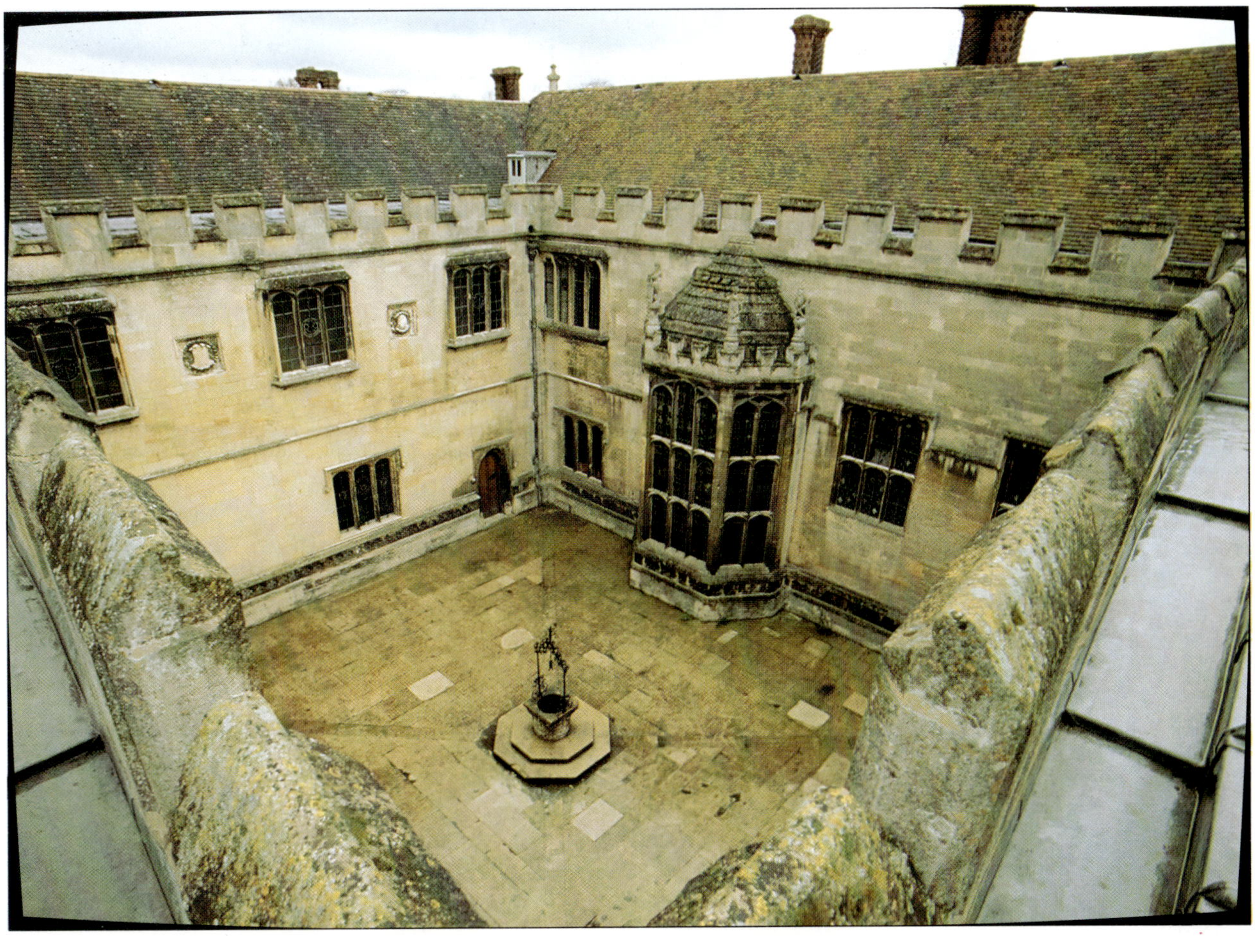

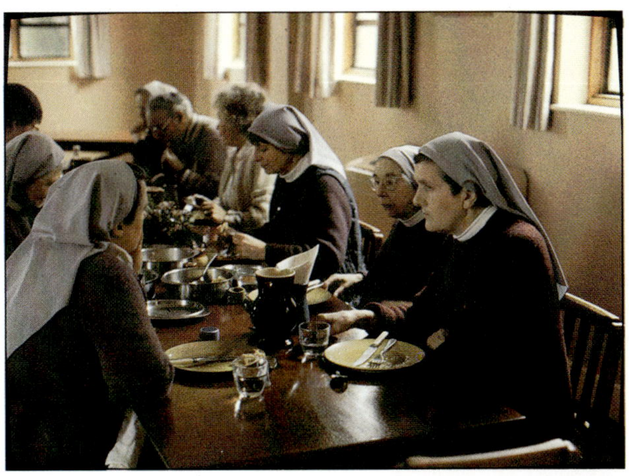

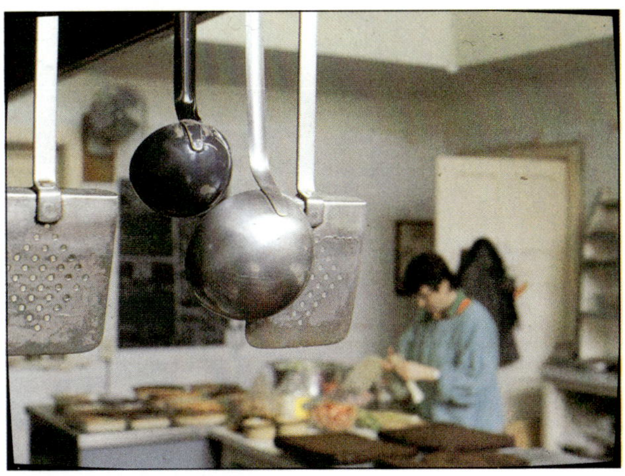

8-9: *It is also important to maintain a coherent sense of geography within the sequences so that the viewer knows where something is happening. The important locations at the convent are the chapel, the courtyard and the dining room. In general, try to keep such locations to a minimum, instead of endlessly shifting from one place to another. You don't have to show everything to convey the sense of full coverage.*

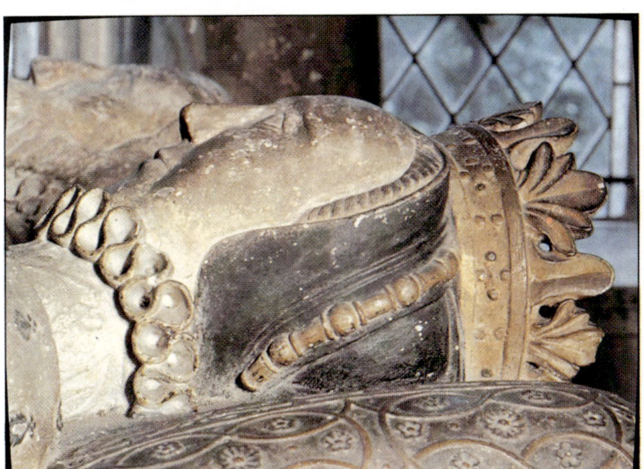

10: *Note that from the outside the convent could be mistaken for a stately home, a nursing home, or even a private school. In fact, the house became a convent only recently and the documentary tells the story of its past alongside the contemporary life of the nuns. This shot is of an effigy on a tomb in the chapel where the nuns worship several times every day and it makes a good link between the past and the present households.*

The first question is how to approach your subject. Research will have already helped you fill out your ideas, and may have suggested alternative treatments. Now, as you will see in this chapter's example of a video featuring a convent, a number of basic story lines immediately suggest themselves.

In the first, you could concentrate on the life of the whole community over a 24-hour period. It would begin with morning prayers, examine the different tasks that have to be undertaken during the day, and conclude with the sisters assembling in the evening to dine and celebrate their faith.

An alternative approach would concentrate on personalities: What is the Mother Superior's role? How is life viewed by a novice? But although the idea is valid, conversation with the sisters quickly revealed that they did not see their community in terms of a hierarchy. For them, each member had equally valued contributions to make. Consequently

PLANNING THE STRUCTURE

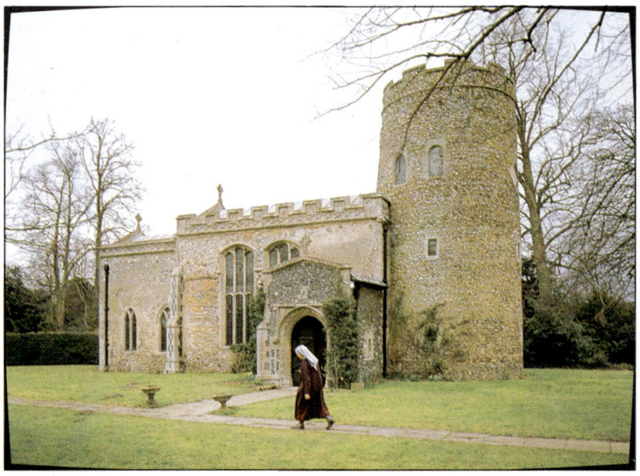

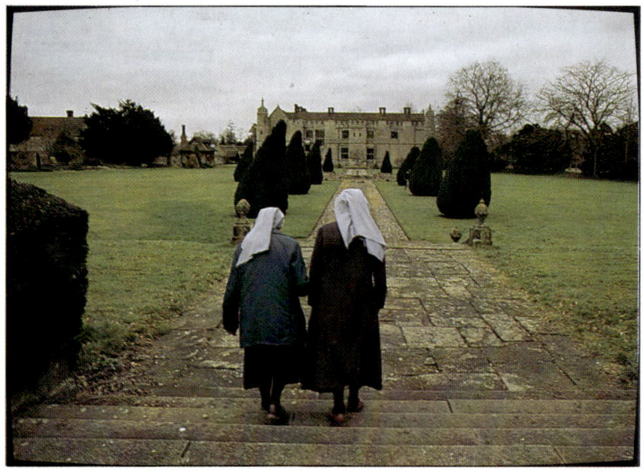

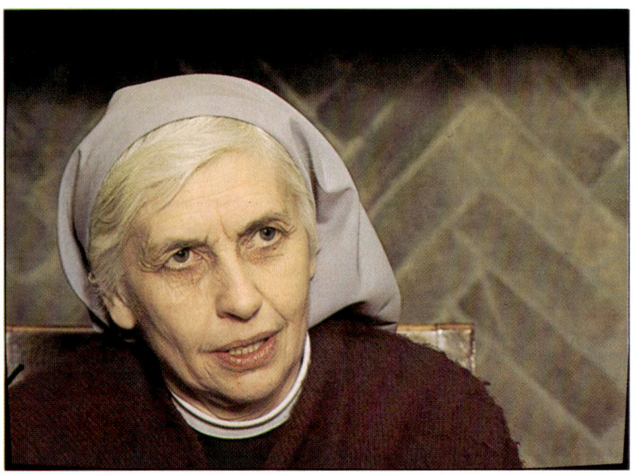

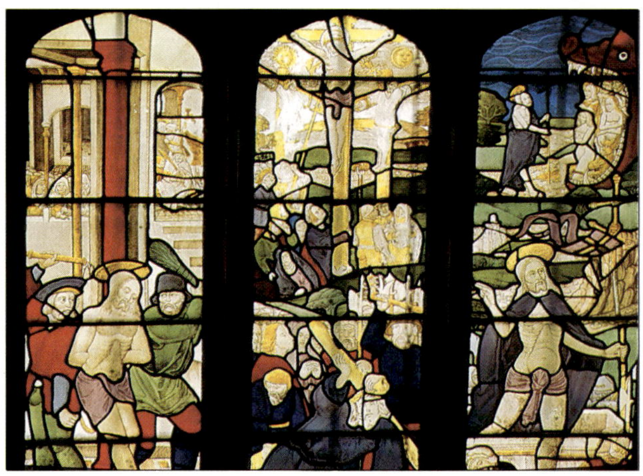

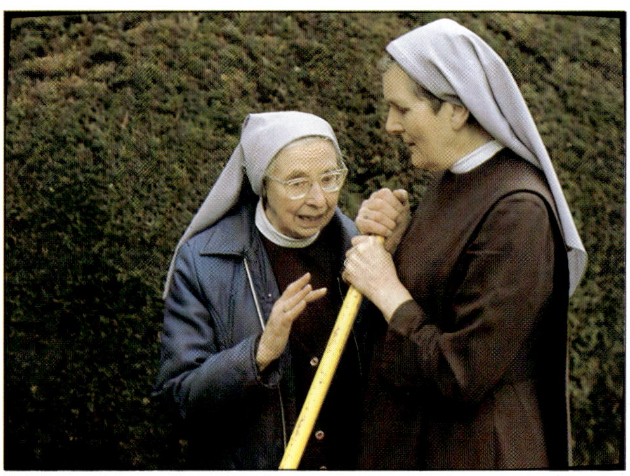

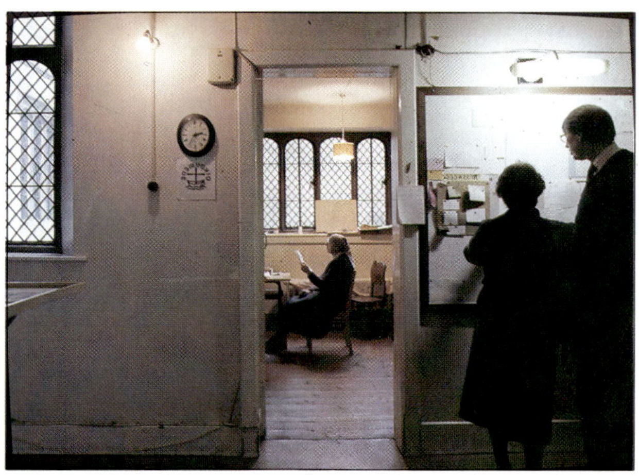

a treatment based on personalities should reflect this view that the community has of itself. Another possible approach would show the sisters engaged in vital social work, helping teenagers from deprived backgrounds to overcome their problems. Whichever approach you choose, try to keep to it consistently through the video.

By clarifying your intent in this way, you can establish the structure of the video in greater detail. And once you have established an objective you must decide how best to realize your aims. The three sequences shown below illustrate three different story ideas, revealing how each might affect the way you approach the video.

1-12: *When planning a video of this type, work out beforehand the range of different shots it could contain. They will include everything from close-ups to long shots, and from solemn scenes to witty ones.*

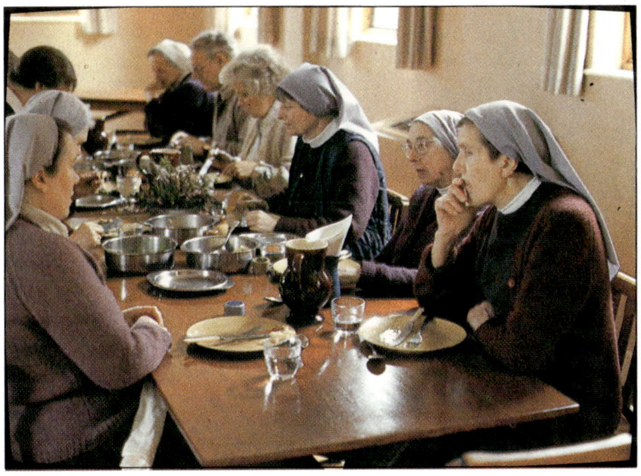

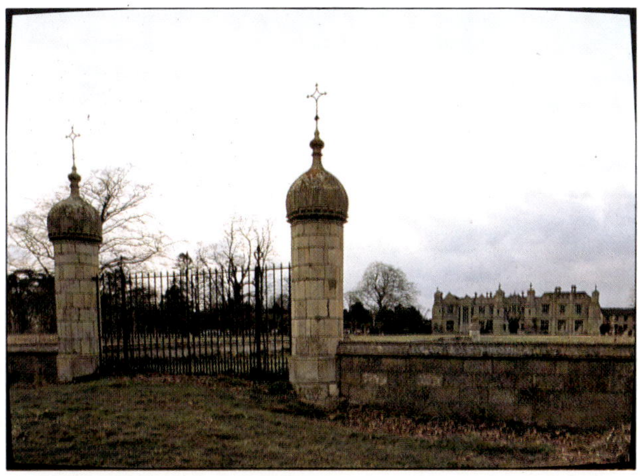

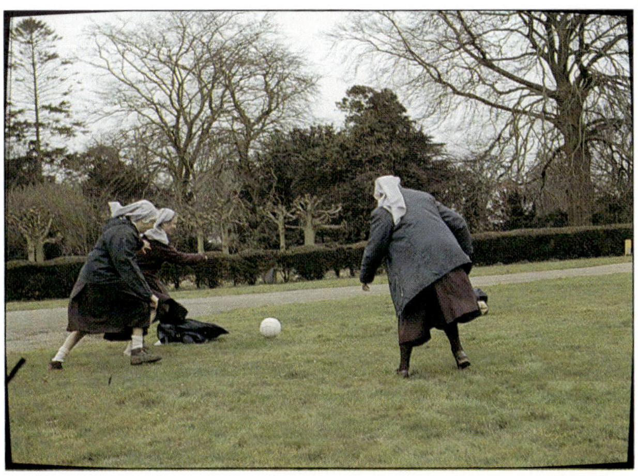

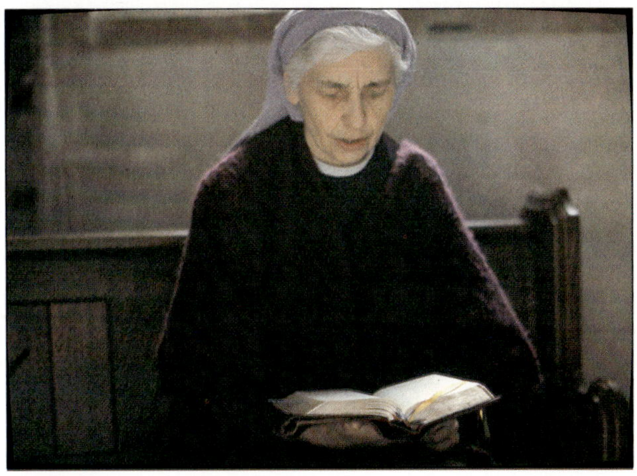

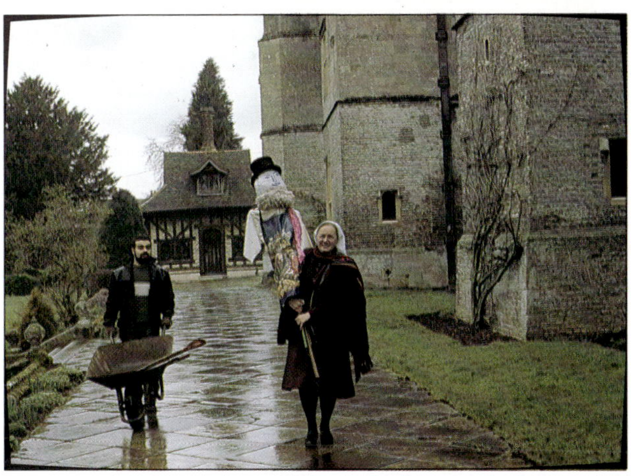

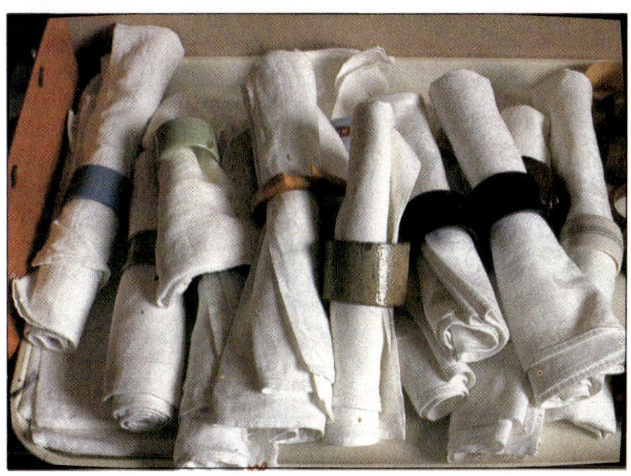

Having decided on the basic theme you want to get across, the next stage is to draw up a synopsis and then a storyboard – a detailed plan of what you intend to shoot. In professional work the storyboard is the preliminary to a shooting script, giving details of each shot, including its subject matter, the camera angle, type of shot and duration. (It is not always practical to go into this much detail when working on one's own). The sequences you include in the storyboard should have been very clearly worked out. A shortened script, in which you detail points that have occurred to you while planning the storyboard, will prove to be invaluable on the day on the shoot.

STORYBOARD AND SCRIPT

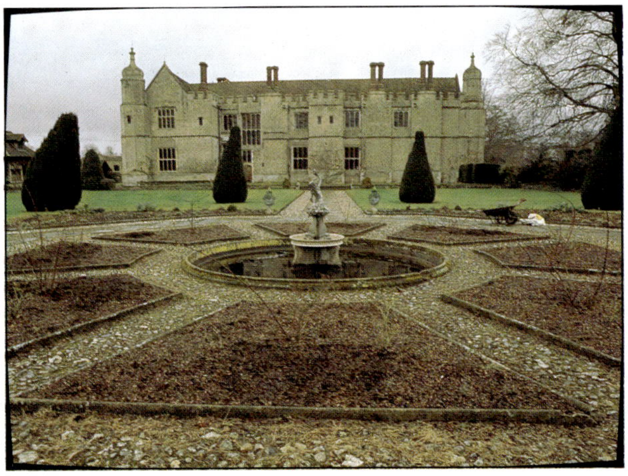

1: *A long shot of the convent opens the video and establishes where the action is taking place. The building is so impressive that it forms a major part of the story. The sequence was taken from a tripod and later contains a slow, controlled zoom-in, which was rehearsed first.*

2: *The storyboard contains 12 main areas, representing sequences that will constitute the complete video. These can be rough representations, particularly if you are going to make more detailed notes of the type of shots you hope to get in the shooting script.*

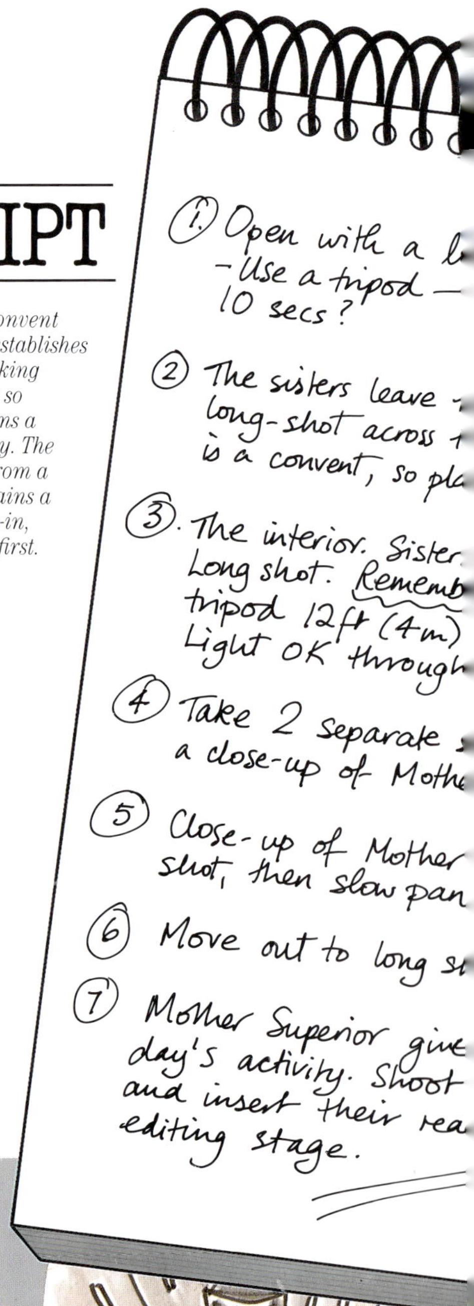

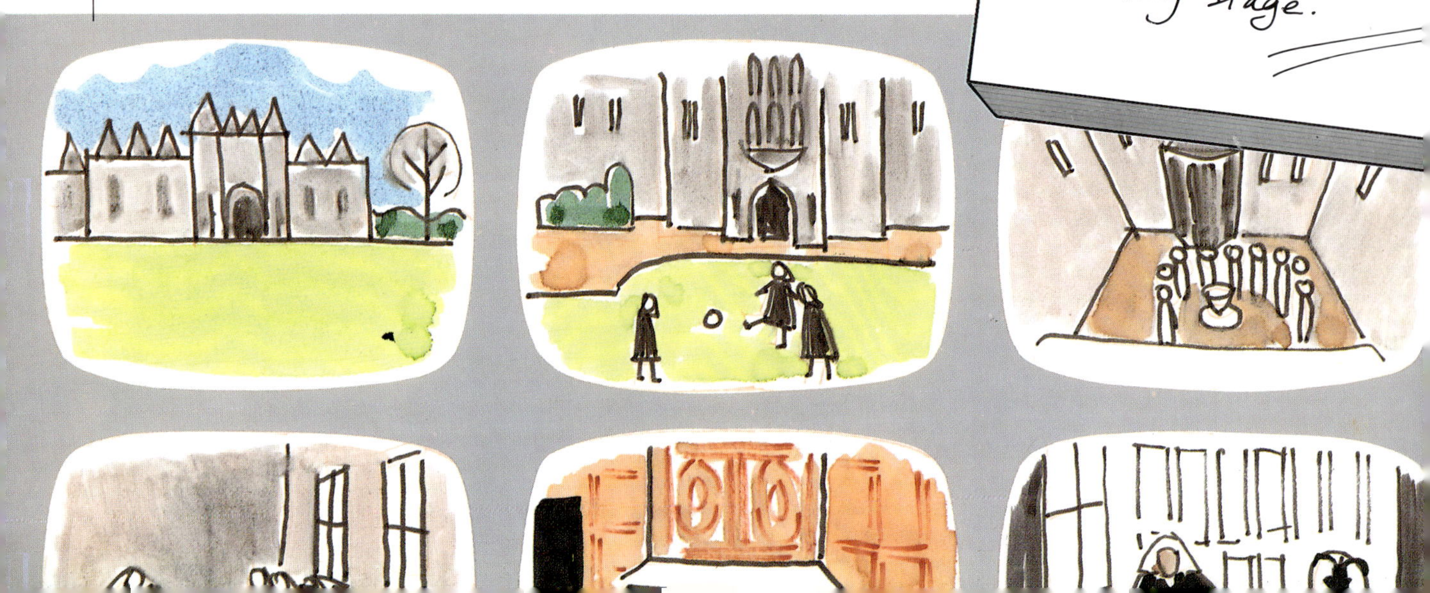

Below: *The shooting script can be as detailed as you like, but note that with documentary material you have less control over the exact type of shot you can get. Professional shooting scripts have a particular style of layout, but for amateur videos two columns will suffice. Give a brief description of the shot on the left-hand side and any special notes on the right.*

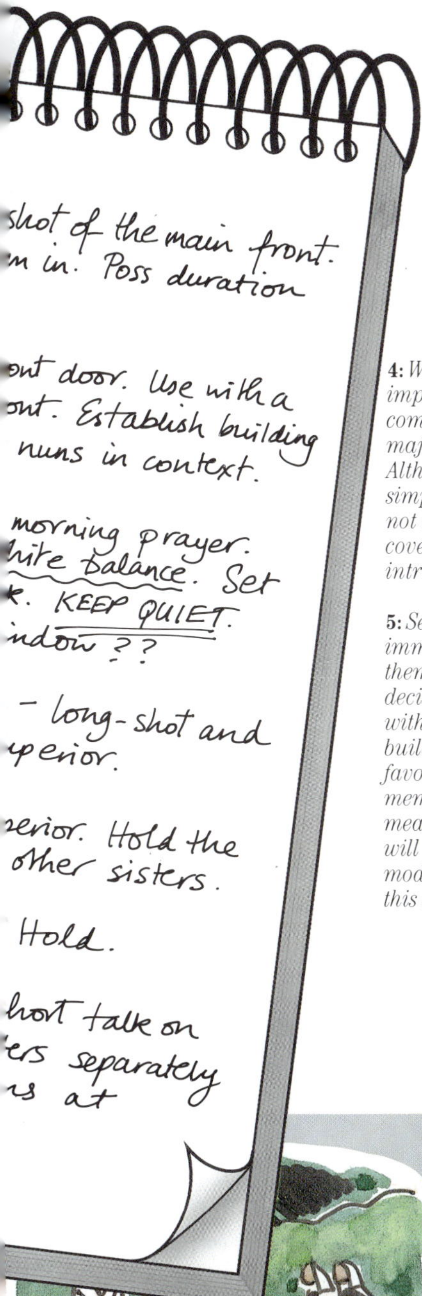

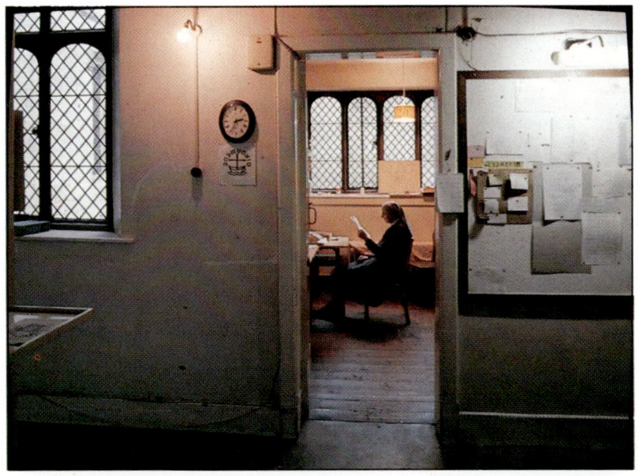

3: *Sequences showing the nuns relaxing helped pace the video between the more significant set pieces, such as prayers, worship, and meals. The sisters were consulted beforehand, so they were not startled out of their repose by the unexpected presence of a cameraman. Forewarned, they were able to appear quite 'natural'.*

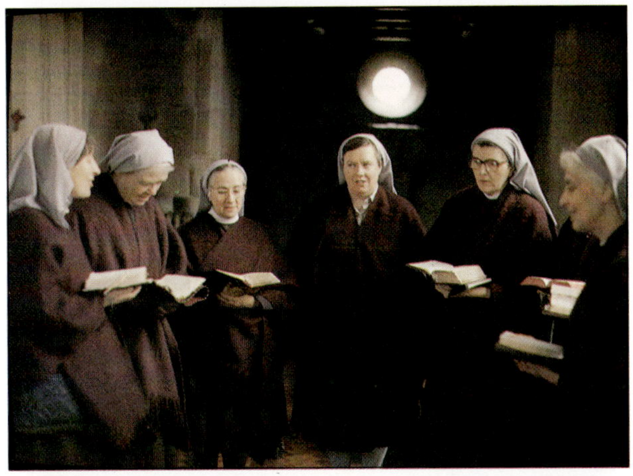

4: *Worship was a very important part of the life of the community, and became a major element in the story. Although their services were simple and intimate, it was not difficult to obtain good coverage without being too intrusive.*

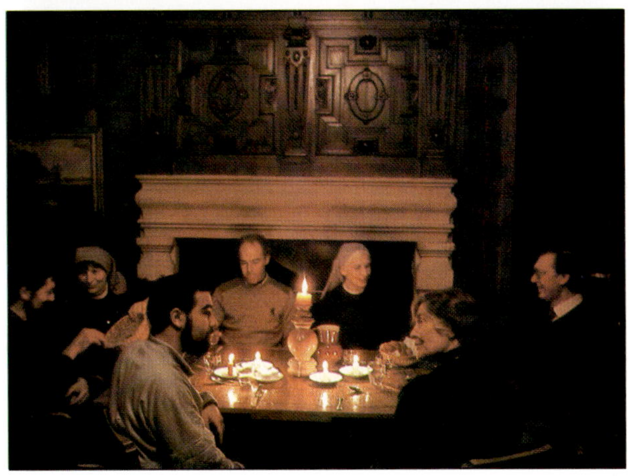

5: *Several closing sequences immediately suggested themselves. The original decision to conclude the video with a shot of the convent building was rejected in favour of the nuns and lay members at their evening meal. Since most camcorders will record well even in moderately bright candle light, this shouldn't be a problem.*

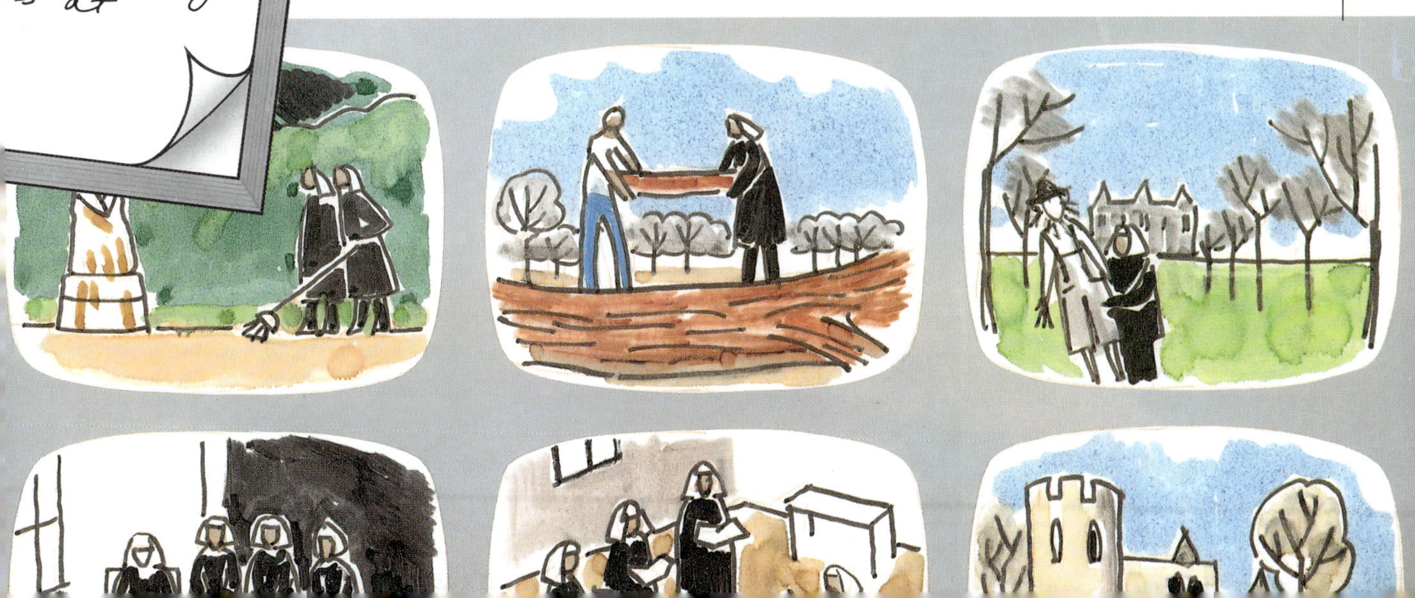

So far, the first sequence in the video has answered the question 'Where?'. The next question is 'Who?'. In other words, the video must establish the characters on whom we are going to focus. If you watch most television programmes closely, you'll notice that in both drama and documentary the number of major characters is limited to perhaps four or five. Any more and the plot could easily get out of hand, with audiences failing to identify with anyone. So while other people may appear, the story and our attention concentrates on these figures alone.

Although the community of nuns is small enough for everyone to appear, a number of individuals stand out. A sequence such as of the nuns at prayer allows the camera to rest on the faces of all those taking part, giving viewers adequate time to remember and note the full 'cast'. But because of her role at prayer, it's quite clear that the Mother Superior is a leading character. Other characters to appear are the lay members who share the sisters' everyday tasks. They are gradually introduced working in the kitchen or the garden, so ensuring that too many characters are not introduced simultaneously. Subsequent coverage of the sisters and lay members dining and talking together revealed how the community is integrated.

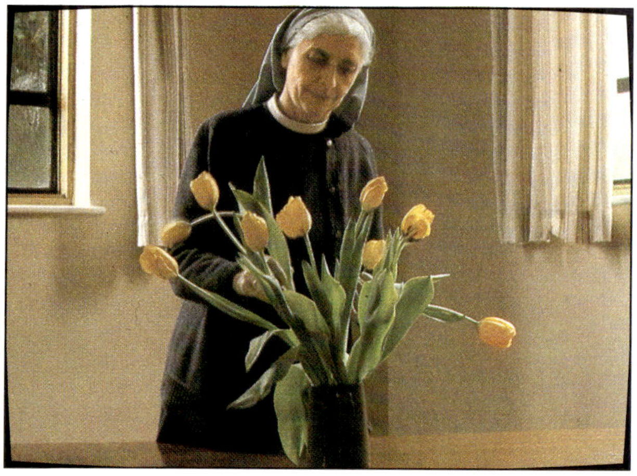

INTRODUCING THE CHARACTERS

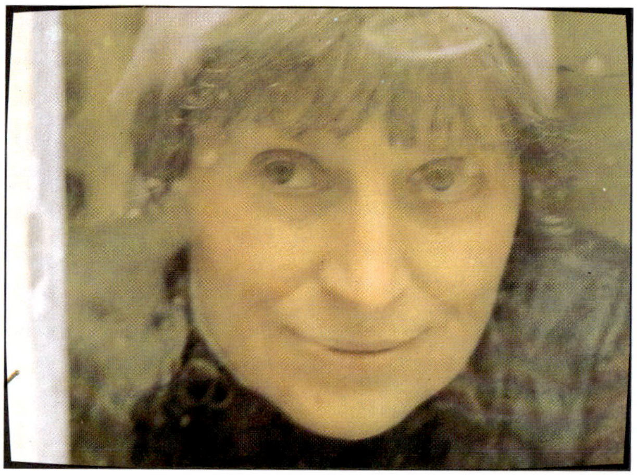

One point that applies to this project, and to video work in general, is avoiding close-ups in which the subject is looking straight at the camera (easier said than done). It's far better to film people at work or tackling a job, so conveying something about them and not about their self-consciousness in front of the camera.

Another useful tip when filming groups is to follow eyelines as the camera moves from one subject to another. It not only looks more natural, but also helps to establish a relationship between the characters.

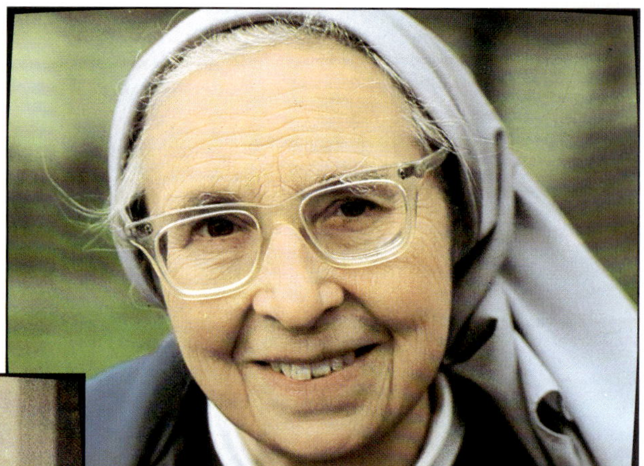

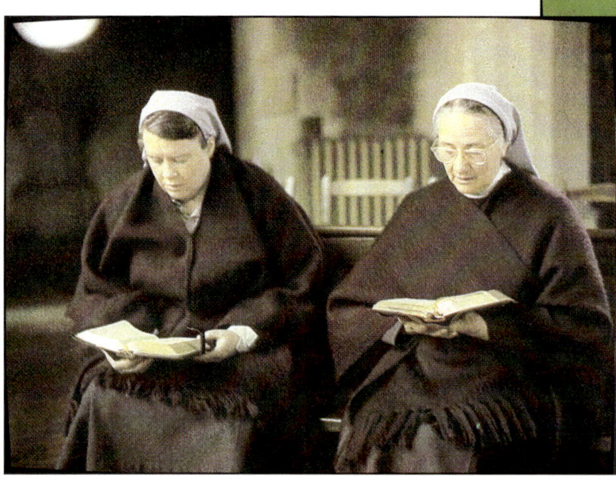

1-9: *While carrying out your research you will have decided which characters you wish to feature. Of necessity some will be more prominent, depending on their personalities and the story you have chosen. Since no video can tell the total story, this is neither wrong nor misleading. The pictures are arranged here to show who are the main characters in the convent, and their relationships with others who have been given less screen time.*

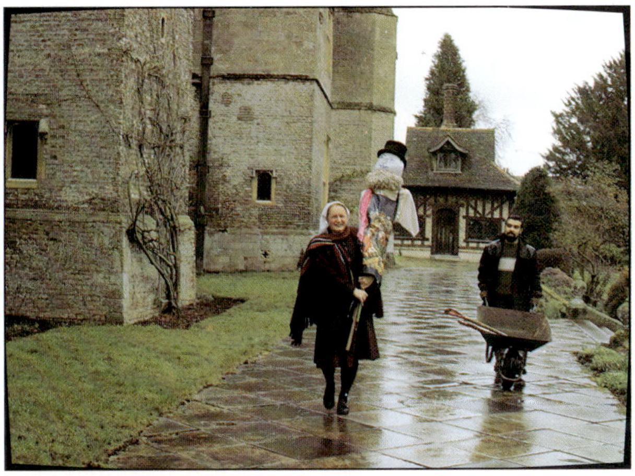

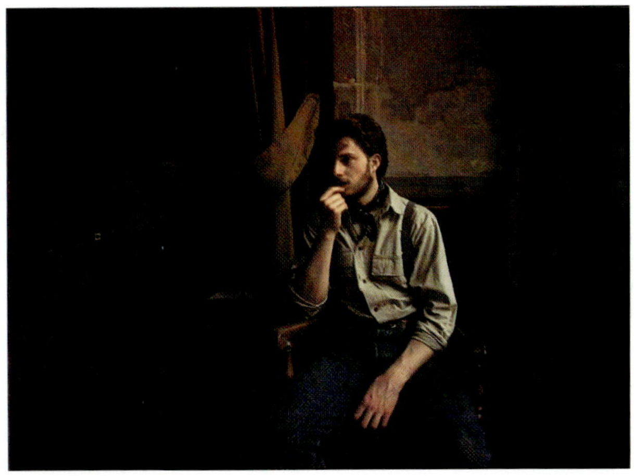

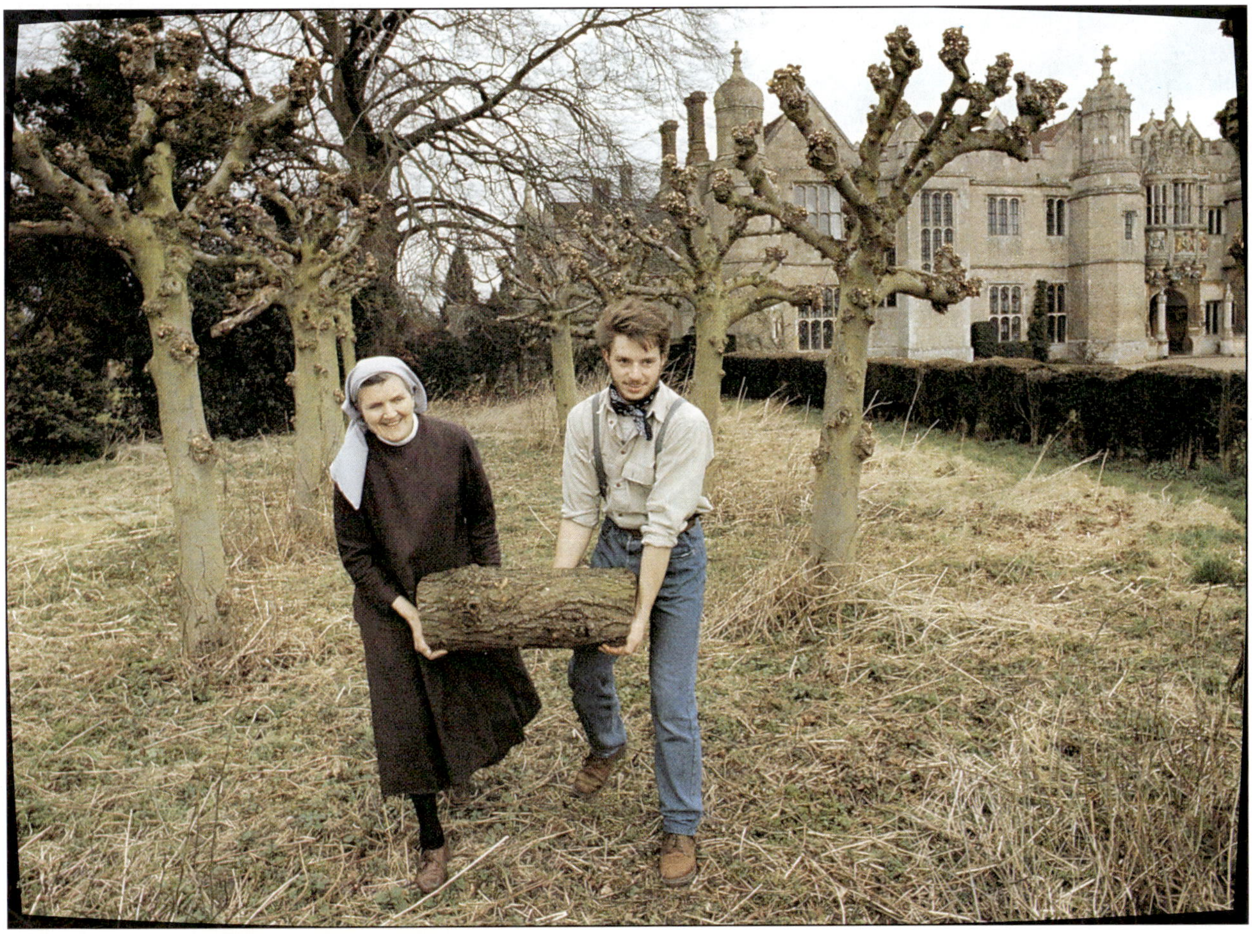

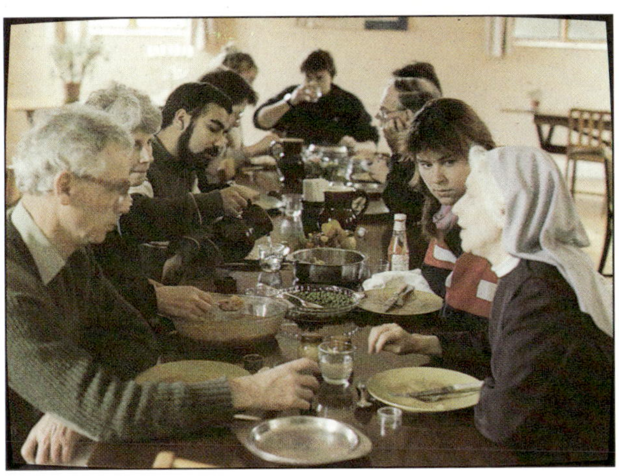

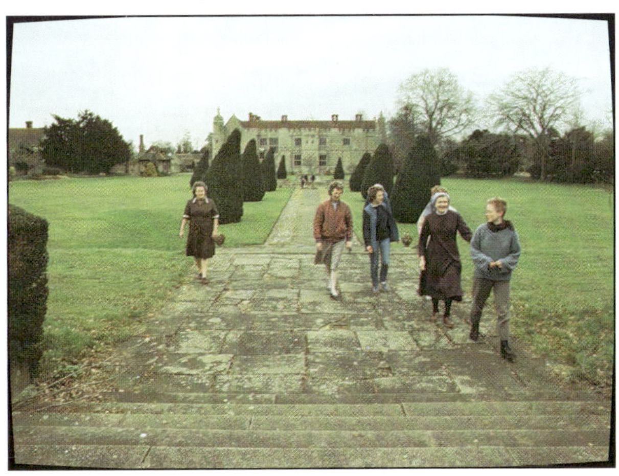

A video consists of a series of sequences which combine to tell a story. Each individual sequence should have a coherent structure with a beginning, middle and end. Without it your viewers will be quickly lost.

Sequences should begin by concentrating on the main subject of the shot. This is usually best done by having the subject in long-shot – close-ups introduce the subject too suddenly.

The sequences in the convent video mainly show the sisters at work, in discussion or with guests. While they are talking the film concentrates on and highlights their various relationships. Two-shots and slow pans from face to face, following the eyeline to record the expressions of the participants, concentrate viewers' interest on the subject. The camera moves should therefore be motivated by what is happening in the scene – unnecessary changes of angle will reveal little about the characters' personalities and irritate the audience.

When you are filming people at work, viewers will want to see exactly what is going on. When shooting in a kitchen, for instance, you should let the camera rest on the ingredients, and show the pots and pans, and cooking facilities. Film the cook at work – over the shoulder shots provide a clear view of a meal being prepared. Another interesting technique is to include the occasional close-up of the main subject's hands, showing precisely how she is tackling that recipe.

The end of a sequence should be as logical and assured as the beginning. By thinking about the close of a shot before you commence filming you can avoid poor sequences that badly fall away, so undermining what's gone before. For example, in a kitchen sequence, the shot can close with the food being imaginatively arranged on serving dishes, signalling the end of the preparation and providing a lead into the meal itself. In other instances your 'characters' can be briefed to perform a 'closing' action, such as shutting a book or leaving a room, anything that will be interpreted as an ending.

HOLDING THE VIEWER

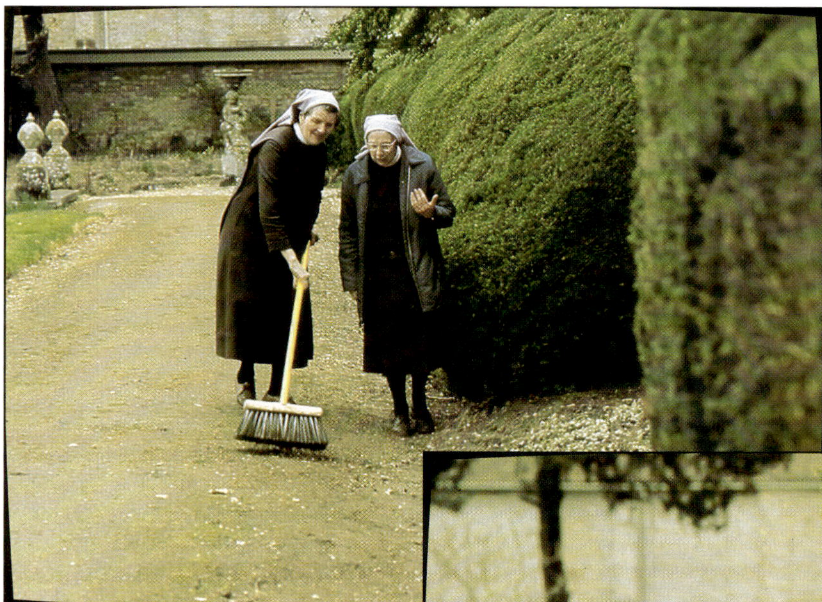

1-5: *This sequence shows an amusing conversation between two of the sisters. It begins as a long-shot showing them walking towards the camera. They stop, and the camera zooms closer. The conversation (about a problem in the kitchen earlier that day) is recorded in a mid-shot containing both participants. The zoom is used to move in slightly closer to give a sense of intimacy. Notice that the shot is framed to concentrate attention on the sister relating the story – the major character in the sequence.*

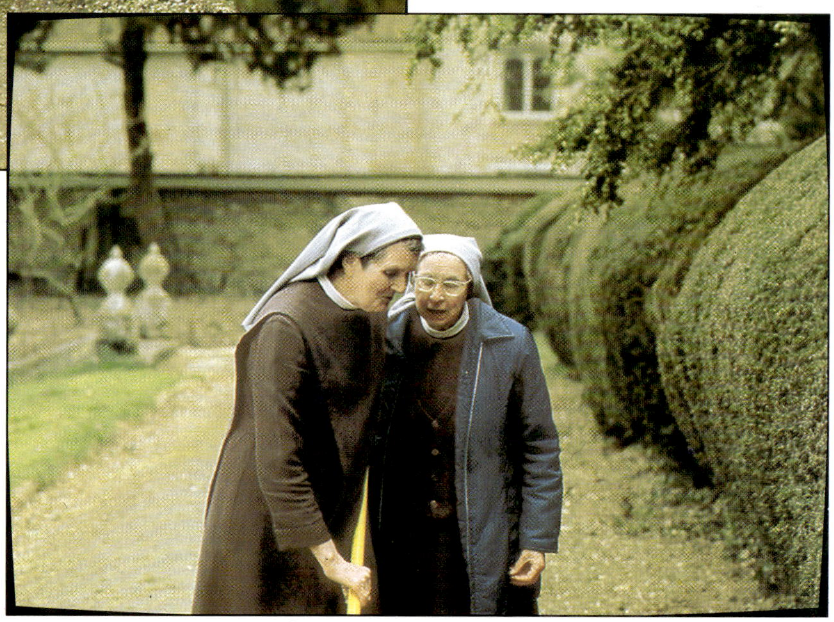

3: *When the sisters stop and engage in conversation, the camera moves from the long shot gradually into mid-shot to overhear what it is they are talking about. Notice that they were framed in such a way as to occupy the whole screen, so that the audience is not distracted by anything in the background of the shot.*

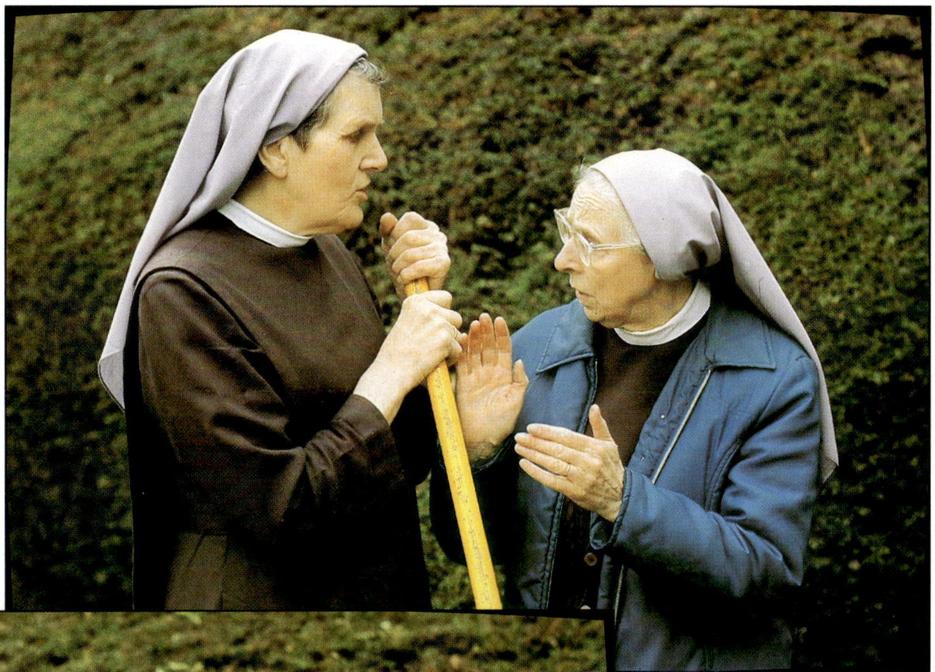

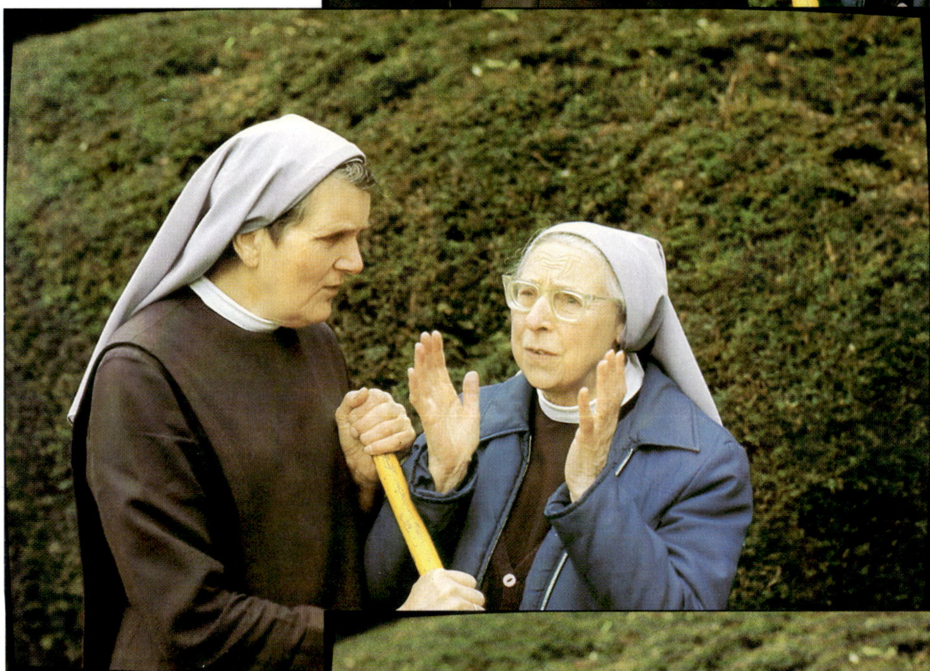

4: *The sister obviously had some important news to tell, and as she is the principal speaker, the audience's attention will be most drawn to her. The actual news was about a minor catastrophe that occured in the kitchen earlier in the day.*

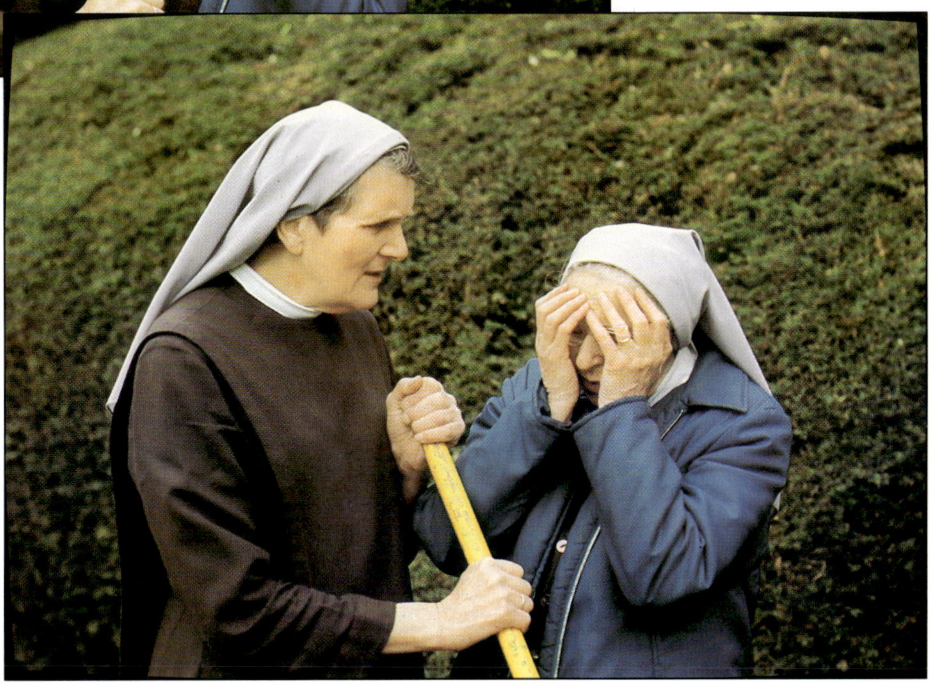

5: *In this sequence, changes in shot were kept to a minimum. The interest for the audience is in what is occuring in front of the camera. Although a close-up on the sister is tempting, it would deprive the audience of the second sister's reaction to the news.*

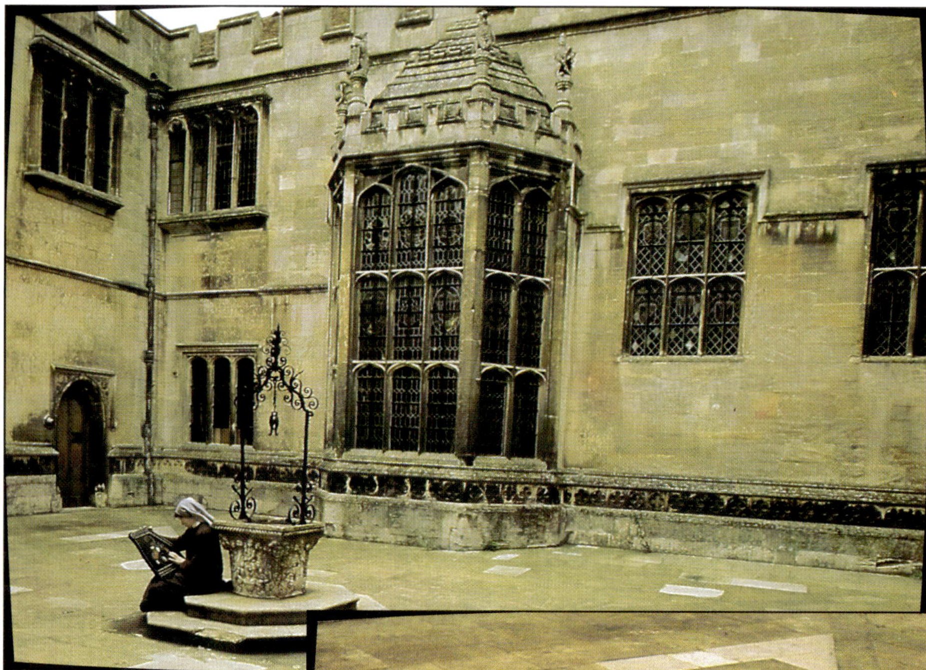

1: *Another sequence in the documentary on life in the convent concentrated on one of the sisters who was an accomplished player on the lyre. The sequence opened with the sister shown in long shot sitting in the convent courtyard, an attractive setting chosen earlier in the day.*

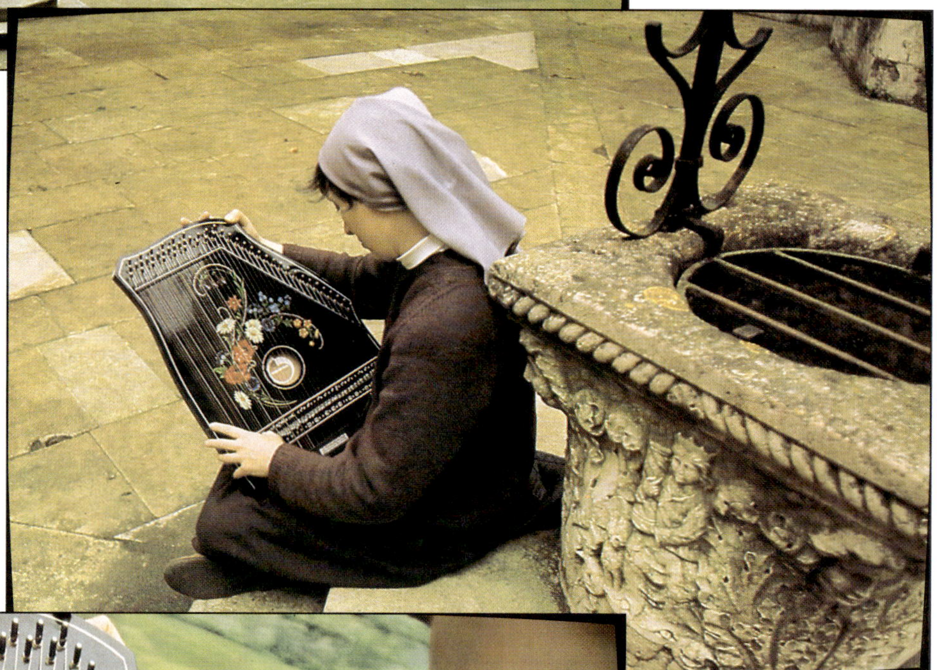

2: *To continue the sequence, the camera moved to a position slightly behind the sister's left shoulder. This avoided the subject being shown head-on, a rather unnatural looking shot if held too long. The zoom was used to move into a mid-shot of the sister as she played.*

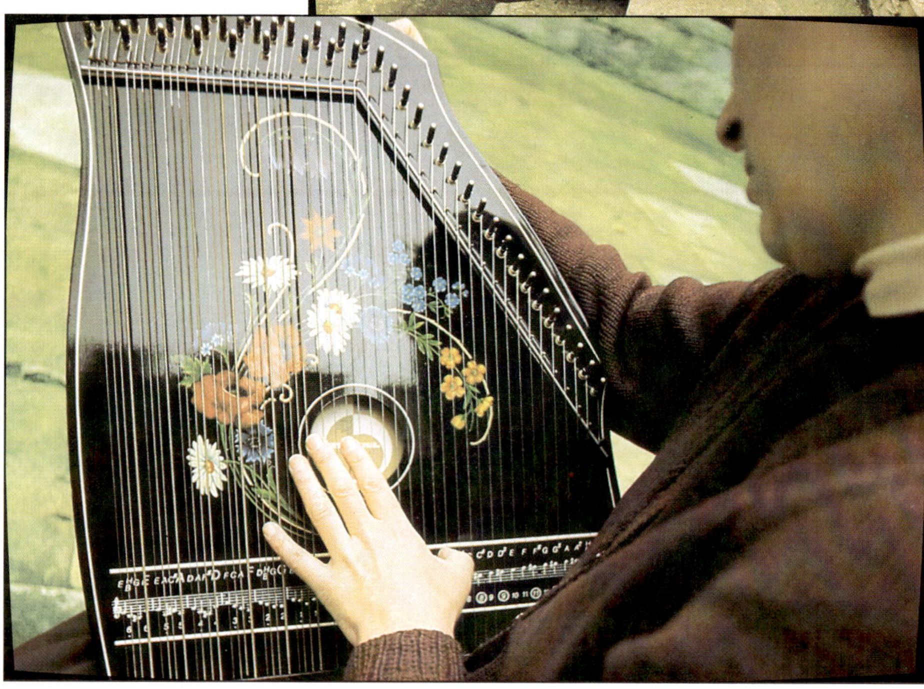

3: *Still using the zoom, the shot continued by going into a close-up of the lyre and the sister's fingers on the strings, it is this sort of detail that the audience is interested in and the shot was held for about thirty seconds, before the sequence ended by pulling out into long shot as the music came to an end.*

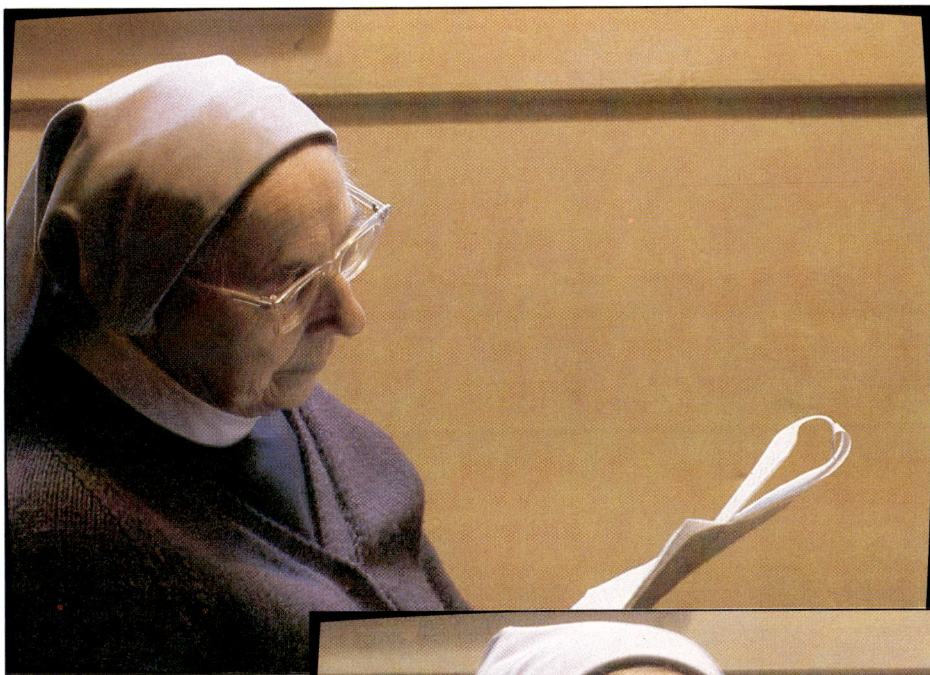

4: *Don't forget that the interference caused by the camera operator can become part of the story. This sequence is intended to capture the sister engrossed in her paperwork, but she soon finds she cannot keep up the pretence.*

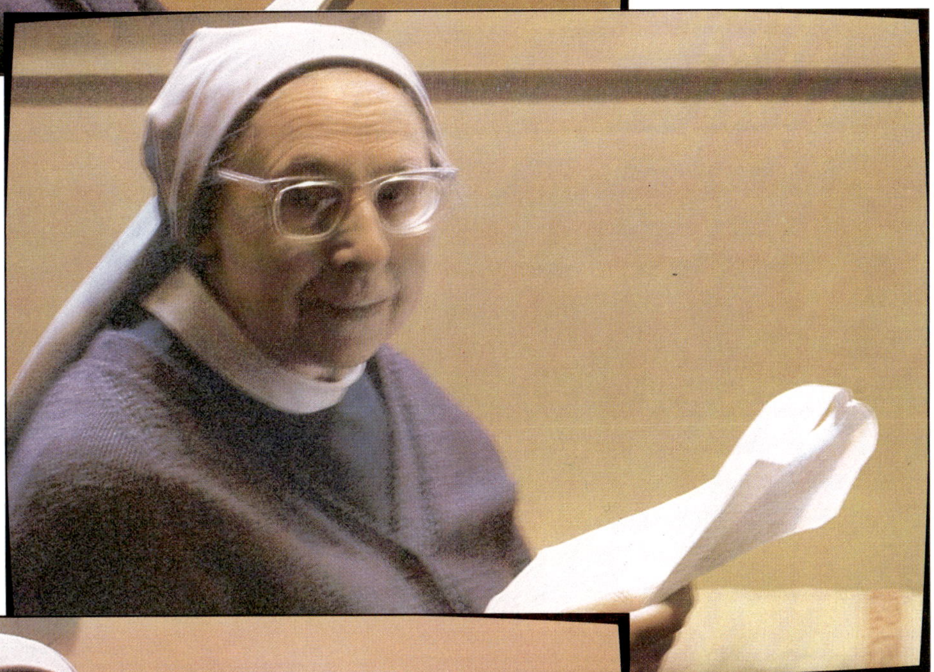

5: *One of the unspoken conventions of many television documentaries is the pretence that the camera isn't really there. In reality, most people respond to its presence and find it difficult to pretend otherwise. The sister was unable to resist glancing upwards toward the camera.*

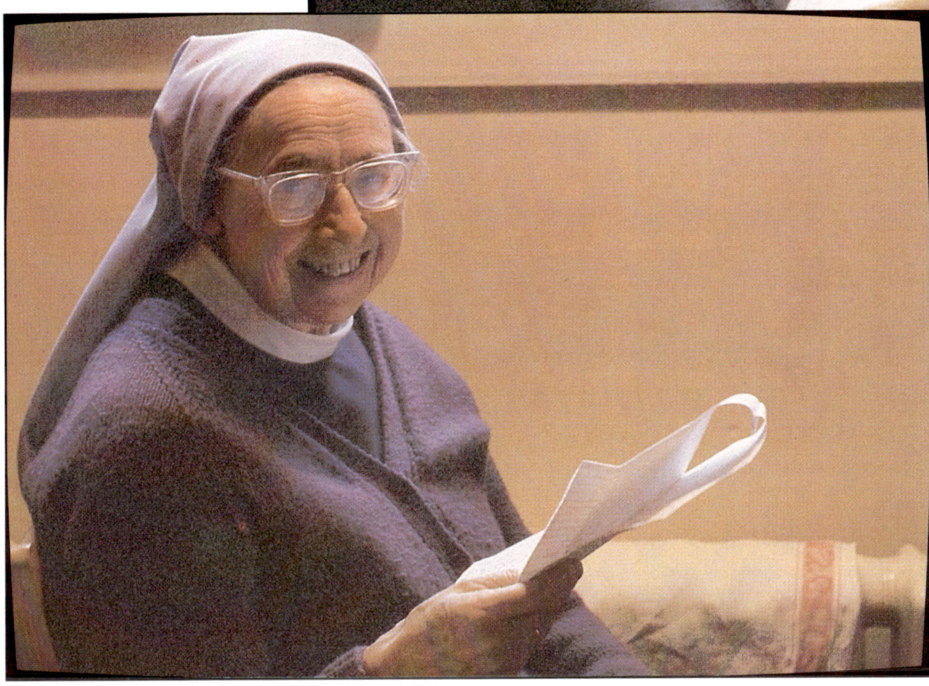

6: *The sister's reaction to the presence of the camera became itself part of the story related in the sequence. In fact, by responding to the intrusion in the way she does, she reveals her gentle sense of humour and adds great charm to this simple sequence.*

An important way to hold audience attention involves varying the pace between different sequences. Pace is partly a matter of timing the length of each sequence, and is partly conveyed by what is happening on the screen. The early sequences of the video of the community are slow and gentle, showing the convent building and introducing the nuns at prayer. The closing sequences were planned to convey a similar mood. But if the whole video was to be shot in this way, the effect would become monotonous. Consequently it was planned to increase the tempo during the middle stages, for which a relatively lively action sequence was required. It was decided that the sisters' recreation period in the late afternoon would fill this gap, while reinforcing the sense of informality in the community.

The sisters were asked if they would play a rough and ready game of football! They readily agreed, since they sometimes play with groups of youngsters who visit the convent. An informal series of shots of the sisters at play, taken with a handheld camera from both close-up and in long-shot, provides the change in pace required. That some of the shots are shaky and sometimes a little out of focus is no disadvantage and will make the sequence seem more natural.

Most video projects will contain an opportunity for similar sequences. For example, in a video portrait of a local school, the frantic activity in the playground can be contrasted with the quiet periods of study. If you were shooting life in a small town, the activity in the market could be contrasted with the peace and quiet in a local park or in the surrounding rural landscape. Try to think of as many opportunities as possible for varying pace when you plan your video. In this particular project the sequence runs as shown below.

CHANGES OF PACE

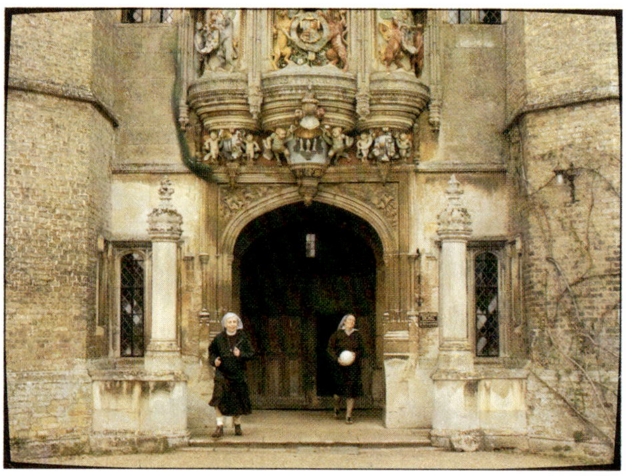

1: *Start of the game: the sisters come out to play football. The sequence requires no formal treatment, and begins with the sisters approaching the camera.*

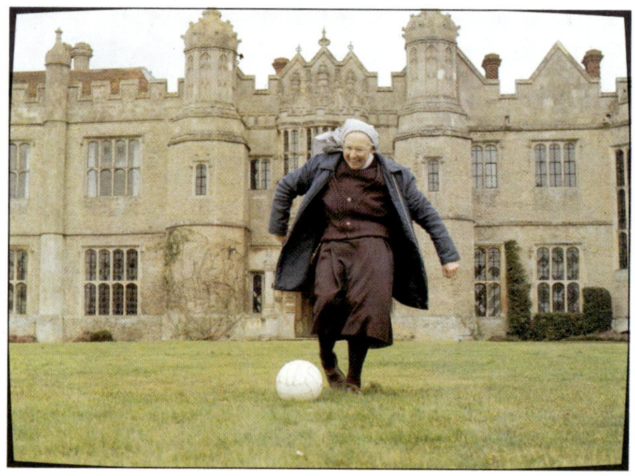

2: *By shooting with a handheld camera in amongst the nuns, a sense of excitement and involvement is immediately conveyed to the viewers.*

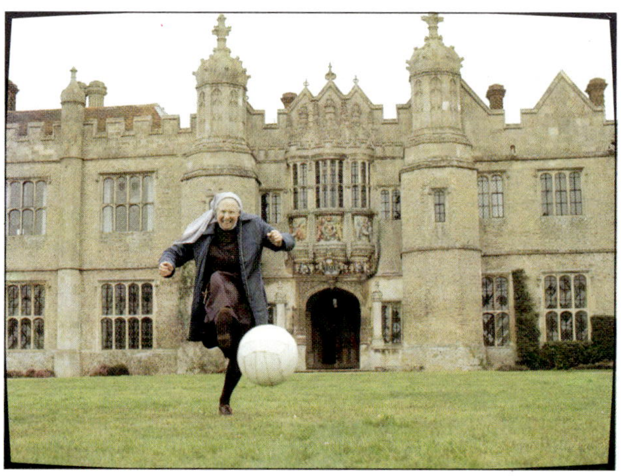

3: *The sisters soon lose their self-consciousness as the game progresses. Shots of the ball coming toward the camera are always effective in such sequences.*

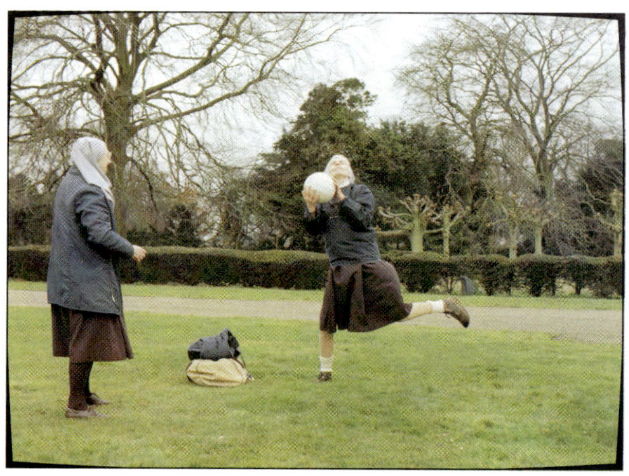

4: *In effect these shots represent the point-of-view of one of the participants. Shot from an observer's viewpoint, the sequence would have been too static for the required change of pace.*

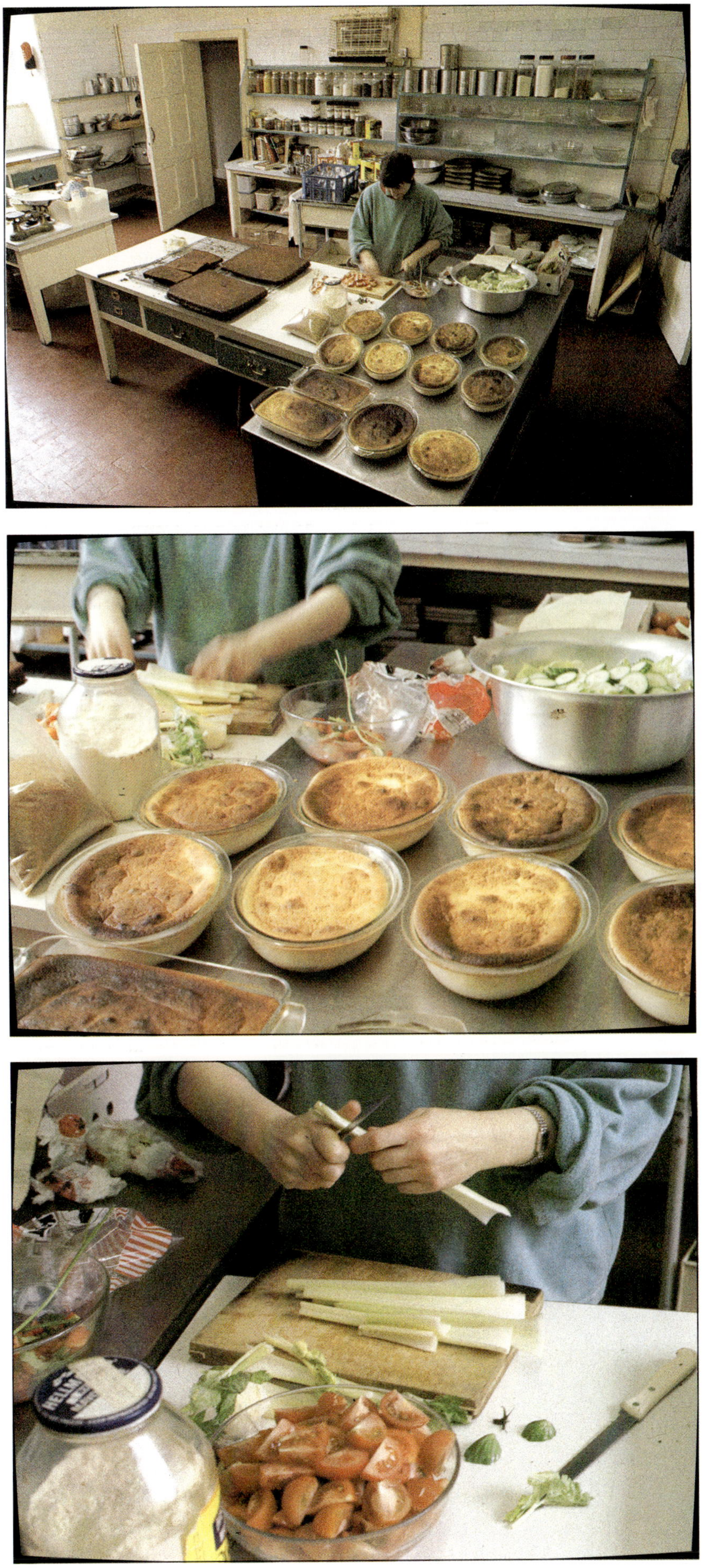

5-7: *These shots are from a sequence in the kitchen. They were shot in a more formal way, to convey a sense of people getting on with their work. From the point of view of pacing the video, their effect is to increase the tempo from an earlier, more contemplative scene.*

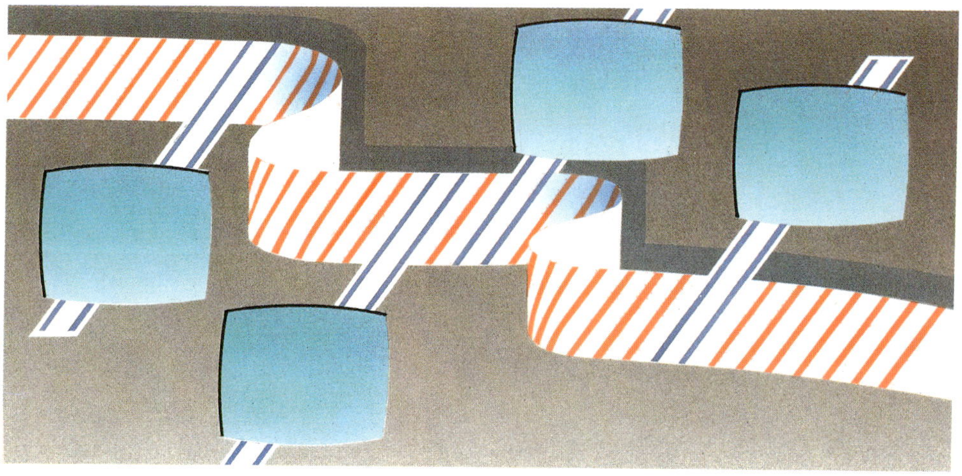

Left: *This diagram gives some idea of the pacing of the video. The main sequences are outlined in red, and the shorter 'interludes' in blue. The viewer will still follow the narrative of the tape, since the narrative sequences predominate. The interludes are discrete sequences in themselves, giving extra description, rather than adding to the story itself.*

INTERLUDES

Most projects can be conceived in terms of major sequences. They can be interspersed with shorter pieces revealing interesting details and asides, adding more visual variety. Since the viewer's interest in the story being told is satisfied by the overall structure of the tape, these 'interludes' can be of almost anything relevant to the subject. Of course, the more visually interesting these images are, the better.

The photographs on this page show some of the types of shots available. The image of the sister in the mirror, taken in the great hall, is a good example. The mirror frame itself has a rich texture, and the slight distortion adds interest. Reflection shots are available in many situations and it's worth thinking about such possibilities beforehand.

However, do always ensure that there is no chance of your reflection being caught in the mirror. On the other hand, there may be some instances where you could make a feature of this. In such instances close in on the reflection so that it is clear this is a deliberate technique.

Interesting architectural details are also well worth including. The convent has many such features, but if shown as a continuous sequence they might well fail to hold the interest of some viewers. However, if used as an interlude they will enliven the film, and become shots of special interest.

Another technique for adding interest involved a lay member of the community reading from an appropriate text in the Bible, while the camera recorded the stained glass and statuary in the chapel. This works well, providing a contrast on the soundtrack too. It also provides a good concluding point to the shot, with the reader coming to the end of the text and closing the book.

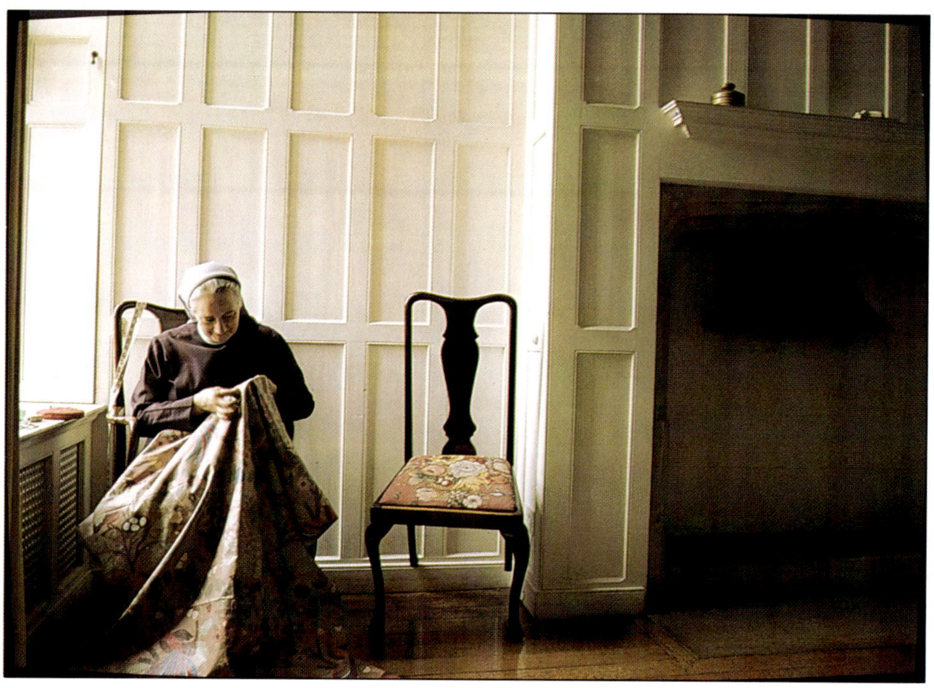

1-2: *The main point of this additional coverage is to provide visual variety, and a greater visual texture to the video. Shots of the sisters at their needlework* (**1**)*, or in the hall* (**2**)*, convey the everyday life in the community, and give a sense of time passing.*

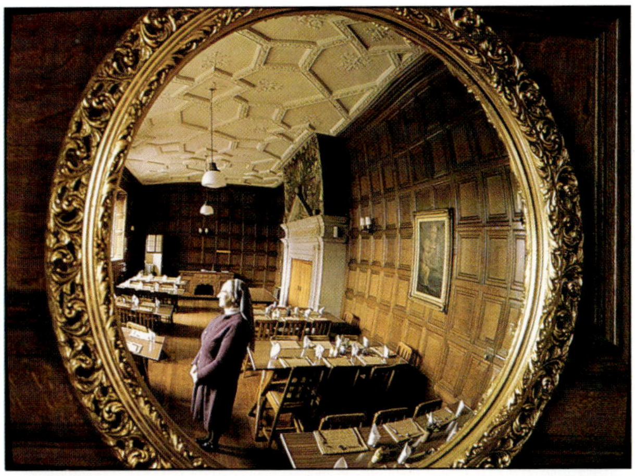

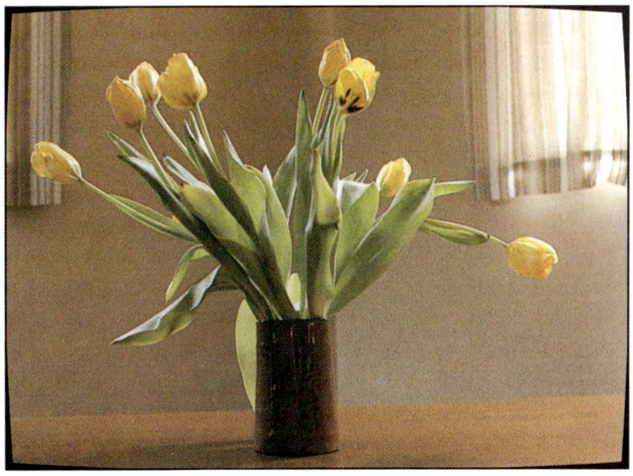

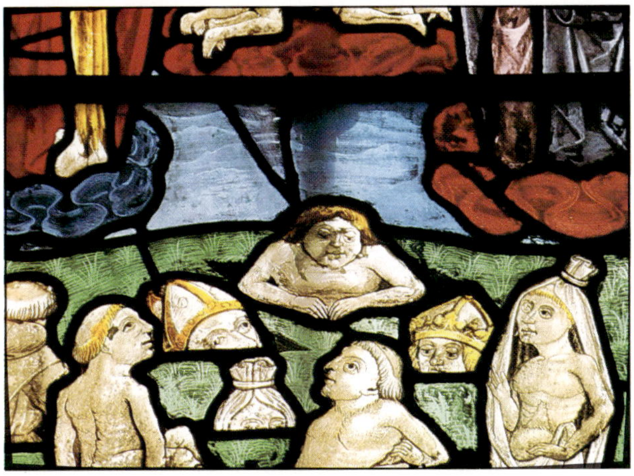

3-4: *Other shots of such details as spring flowers* (**3**) *in a vase, and a close-up of the stained glass* (**4**), *could be used as cutaways when the tape is edited. Of course, with editing in mind, it is better to shoot too much material than too little. What you don't want can always be cut from the tape.*

5: *The lay reader provides an interesting and appropriate soundtrack by reading from the Bible while the camera surveys the chapel. The shot was set up next to the carved head for added visual interest. Oddly enough, there is a distinct resemblance.*

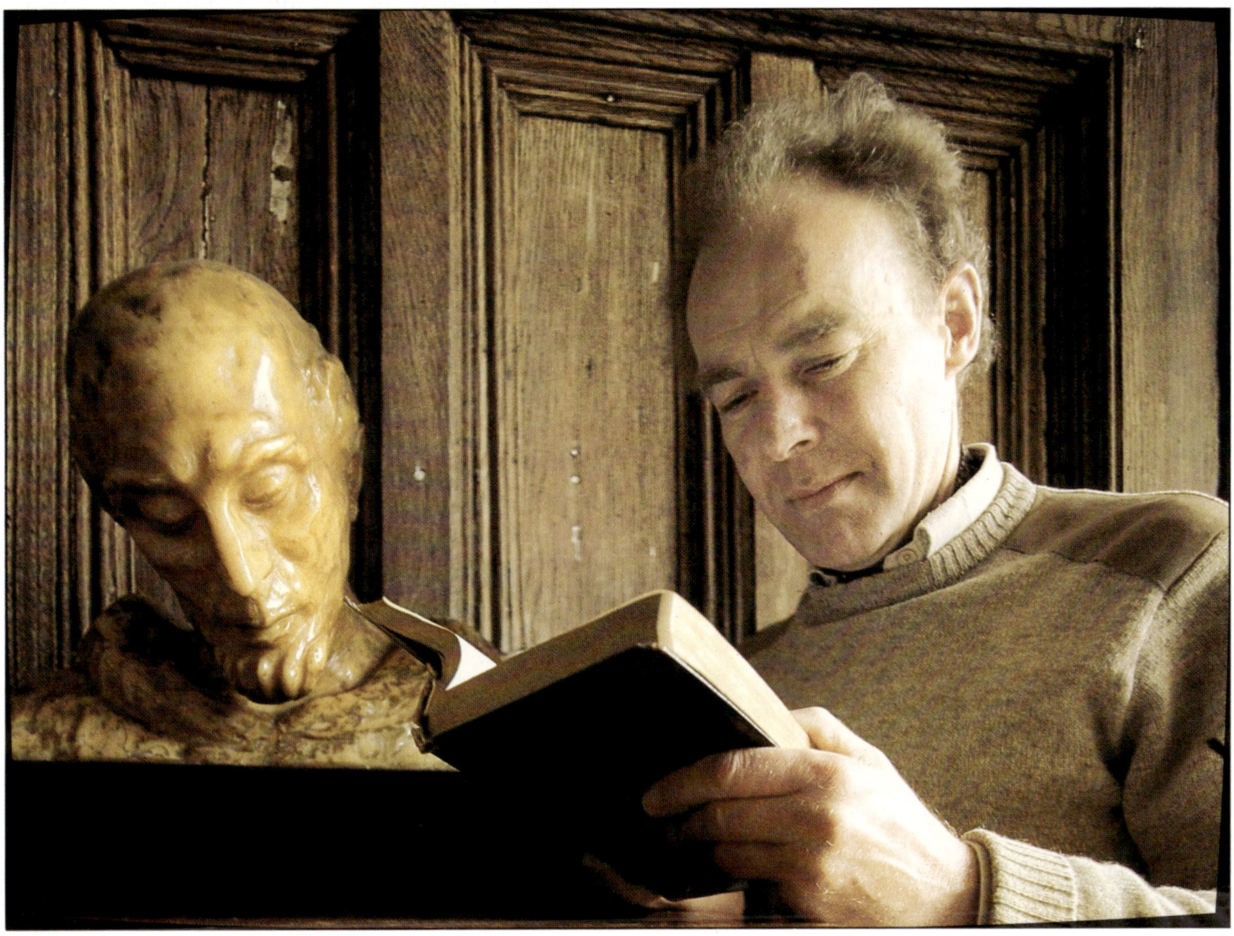

DOCUMENTARY CHECKLIST

Subject ....

VENUE RECONNAISSANCE

Place	Date	Time	Transport	Accommodation

SHOOTING PLAN

INTRODUCTION

Place	Date	Time	Details of coverage

MAIN THEMES

Place	Date	Time	Details of Coverage

CUTAWAYS

Place	Date	Time	Details of Coverage

ALTERNATIVES

Place	Date	Time	Details of Coverage

CLOSING SEQUENCES

Place	Date	Time	Details of Coverage

CONTACTS

Name	Address	Telephone Number

EQUIPMENT REQUIREMENTS

☐ CAMCORDER AND ACCESSORIES ....
☐ BATTERIES ....
☐ LIGHTING ....
☐ TAPES ....

The final sequences should bring the video to a satisfying and appropriate conclusion. In a drama, the final sequence might be designed to shock the viewer and leave a lasting impression in the mind. In a documentary exploring a controversial issue, the piece could end with a question, prompting further thought. Of course, the way you hope the viewer will answer it will entirely depend on your editorial approach. The intention of this project was to convey the sense of peace and fellowship present in the community. There were two obvious choices for ending the tape: the sisters at evening prayer, or the community gathered together for the final meal of the day.

THE FINAL SEQUENCES

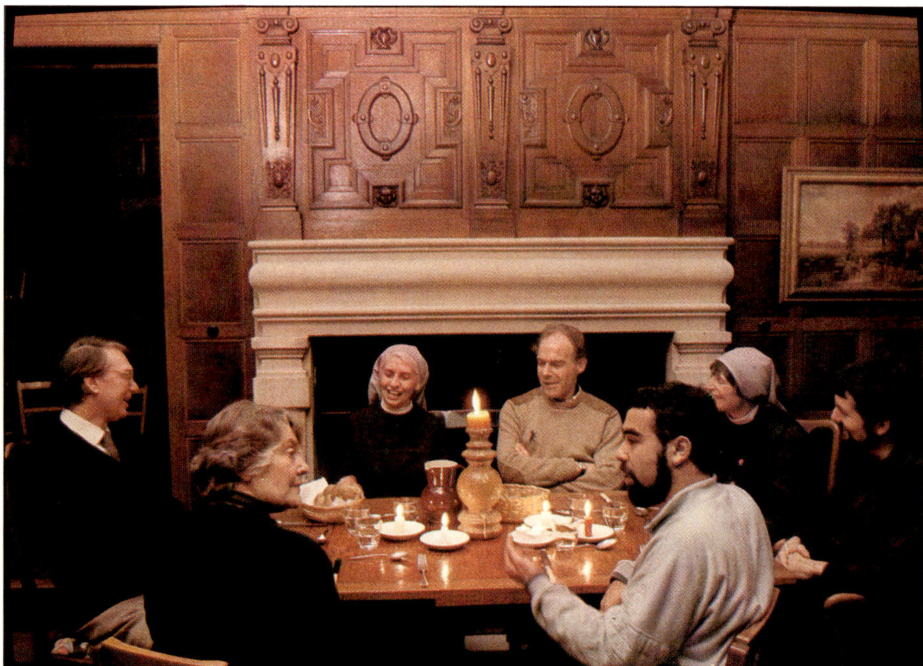

1-2: *At the evening meal the sisters and various lay members gather together. They dine by candlelight but, while there is sufficient light to film, the image is dark. The sequence begins with the blessing, whereupon additional lighting is used. Then the lighting is gradually reduced and the sequence is brought to a close by a slow fade to black. A CCD camera is used, so there is no problem with the dim light from the candle flame, as there might have been with an older tube camera.*

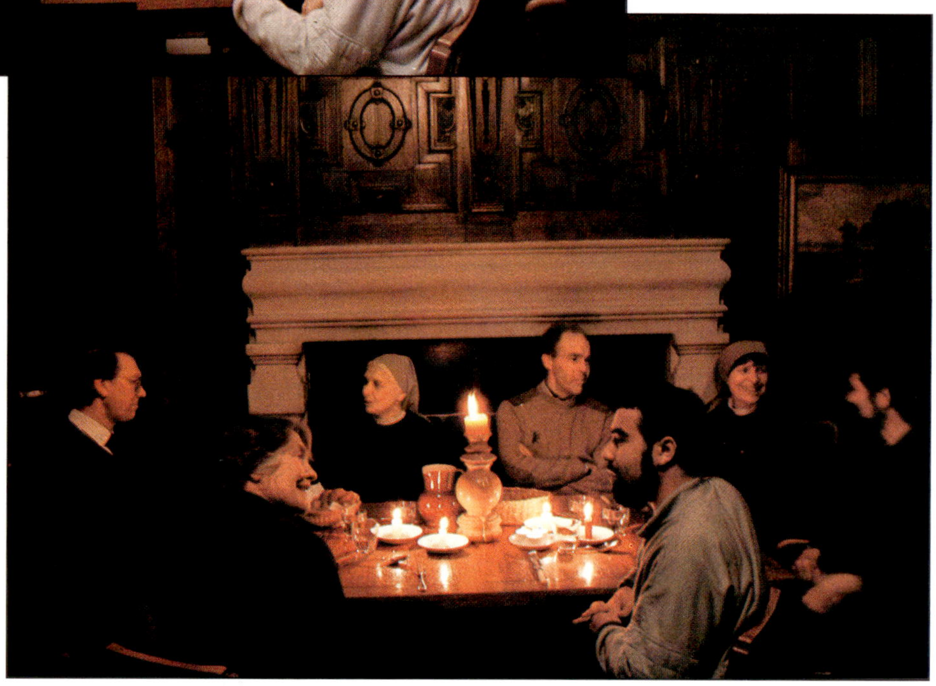

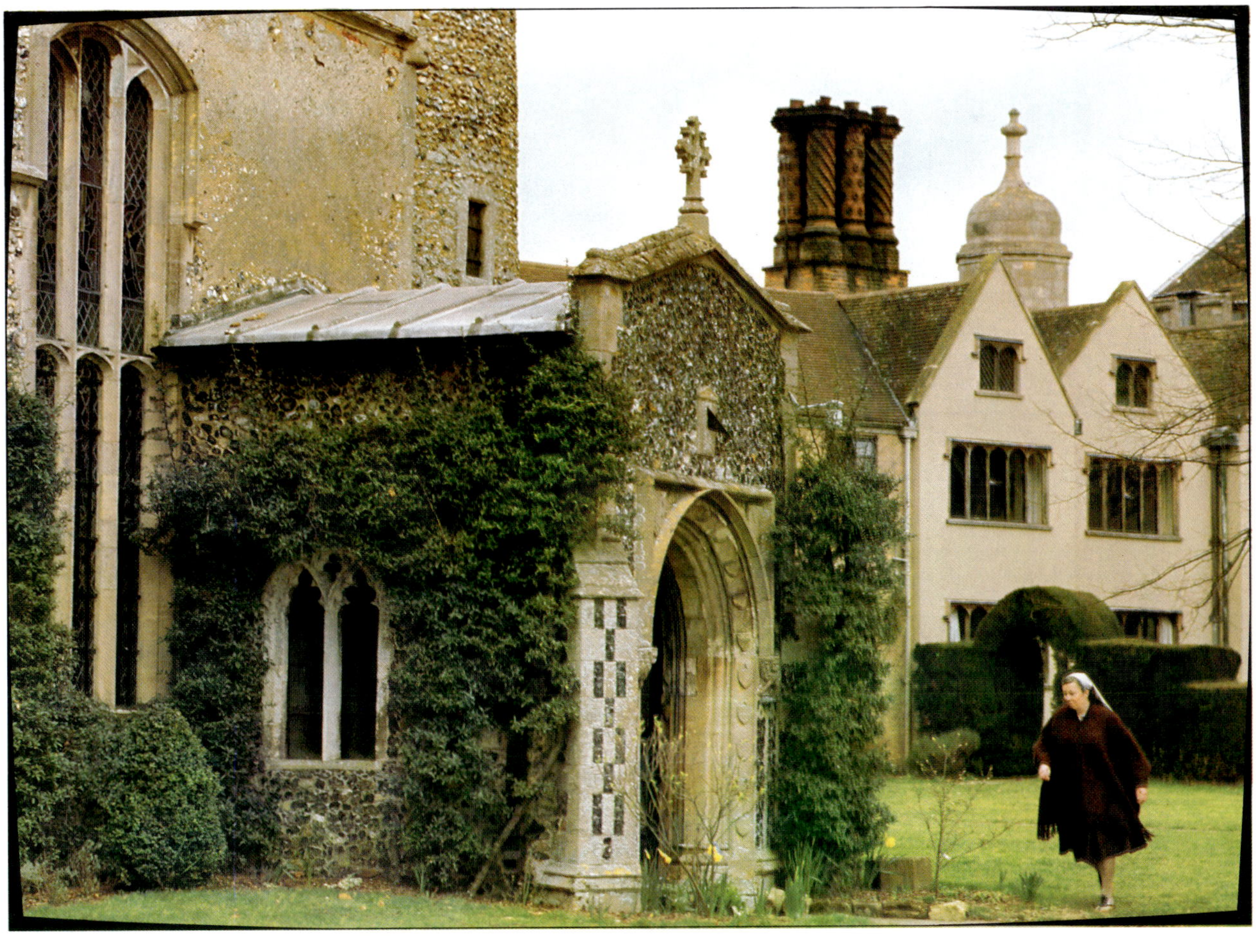

3: *A sudden cut to the alternative closing sequence – the sisters at evening prayer – would have disturbed the pace of the video. Had this sequence been used it would have been introduced by shots of the sisters arriving at the chapel. This would have been pertinent since it confirmed the sense of a community, while the exterior shot prepared the viewer for the interior that followed it.*

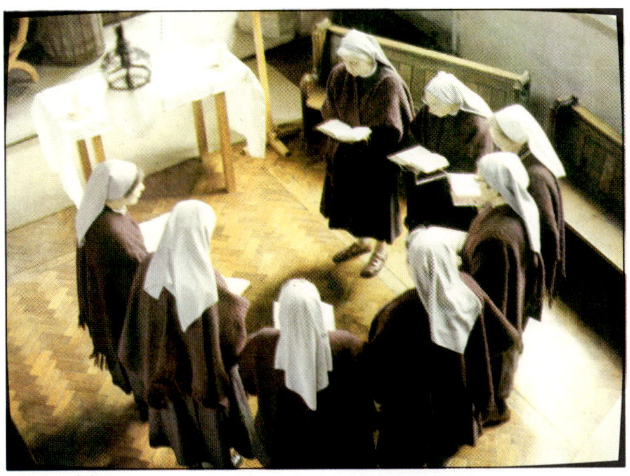

4-6: *The earlier sequence of the sisters at prayer was taken from quite close up and from shoulder height. For the concluding sequence a position above the sisters was used. This gives visual variety and implies a sense of distancing. The sequence first moves slowly into the nuns as the service begins. A slow zoom out leaves the sisters at worship, and a slow tilt allows the camera to rest on the stained glass window. The camera movements have to be slow and smooth to convey a sense of peace.*

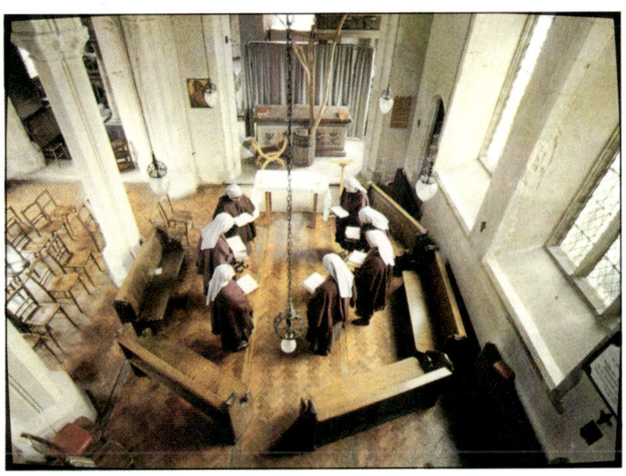

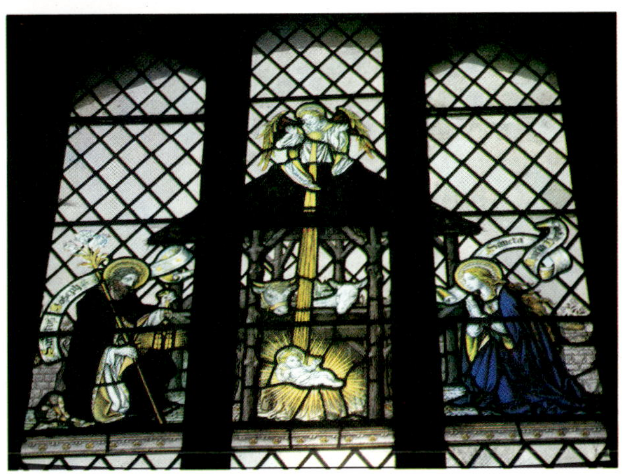

RESEARCH

What you don't know, you can't shoot. Consequently the more exhaustively you research your subject, the more ideas you'll have when creating the storyline, and the greater the chances of including interesting, unusual sequences to flesh out the main plot.

The materials on this spread were acquired for a weekend trip to Paris. In addition to suggesting subjects for filming, the postcards, streetplans and timetables can also be used to make an atmospheric introduction to the video.

Thinking visually

Once you have chosen your subject areas, you must decide how best to film them. When shooting a relatively unfamiliar scene, you could keep your techniques and innovative camera angles to a minimum. In other words, as director/camera operator you don't want your techniques to obstruct your audience's appreciation of the images. Viewers should be concentrating on the sequences and not how you are using the camera. But with a familiar landmark, why not show it from a striking, unusual angle, enabling people to see it as if for the first time?

You could also consider making visual contrasts. So, a sequence of the Louvre art gallery, with its famous classical outlines, might gain when followed by shots of the ultra-modernist Pompidou Centre. Or would the juxtaposition be too jarring for the gentle, romantic pace you want for the video? Do also keep an eye out for detail – interesting shop fronts, window displays, and colourful posters could well merit a close-up. In addition to such filming techniques there are other practicalities to note. There will be some areas or buildings where you cannot get permission to film. In others, filming will only be possible after you have obtained written approval. And in other instances, as when filming in a restaurant, it is only polite to first gain the manager's permission. And finally, do check on opening and closing times. If you get them wrong, and are filming while on holiday, there may not be time to return for a second shoot.

SOURCES OF INFORMATION

The nature of a project will, to a certain extent, determine which are the most appropriate sources of information. If, for instance, you are making a video of farm life, the most profitable research would be a visit to the farm enabling you to witness exactly what goes on. Discussion with the farmer and the workers would establish further points of interest that you might decide to shoot. However, for most other video projects you will probably need to consult the following sources.

Libraries. Besides being sources of general information, libraries often have materials of specifically local interest which might yield profitable approaches.

Tourist authorities. Tourist board brochures and guides are excellent for checking that you have not omitted any places of interest.

City authorities. Municipal authorities provide a similar service. Many have information offices which will readily inform you of local interests and problems.

Newspapers. The 'locals' are an excellent source of information, listing festivals, street markets and other attractions.

Specialist societies. Specialist and local societies are usually very willing to provide information. Many districts have societies which concentrate on local history. Other groups can help with research on specialist subjects, such as conservation issues, and the arts.

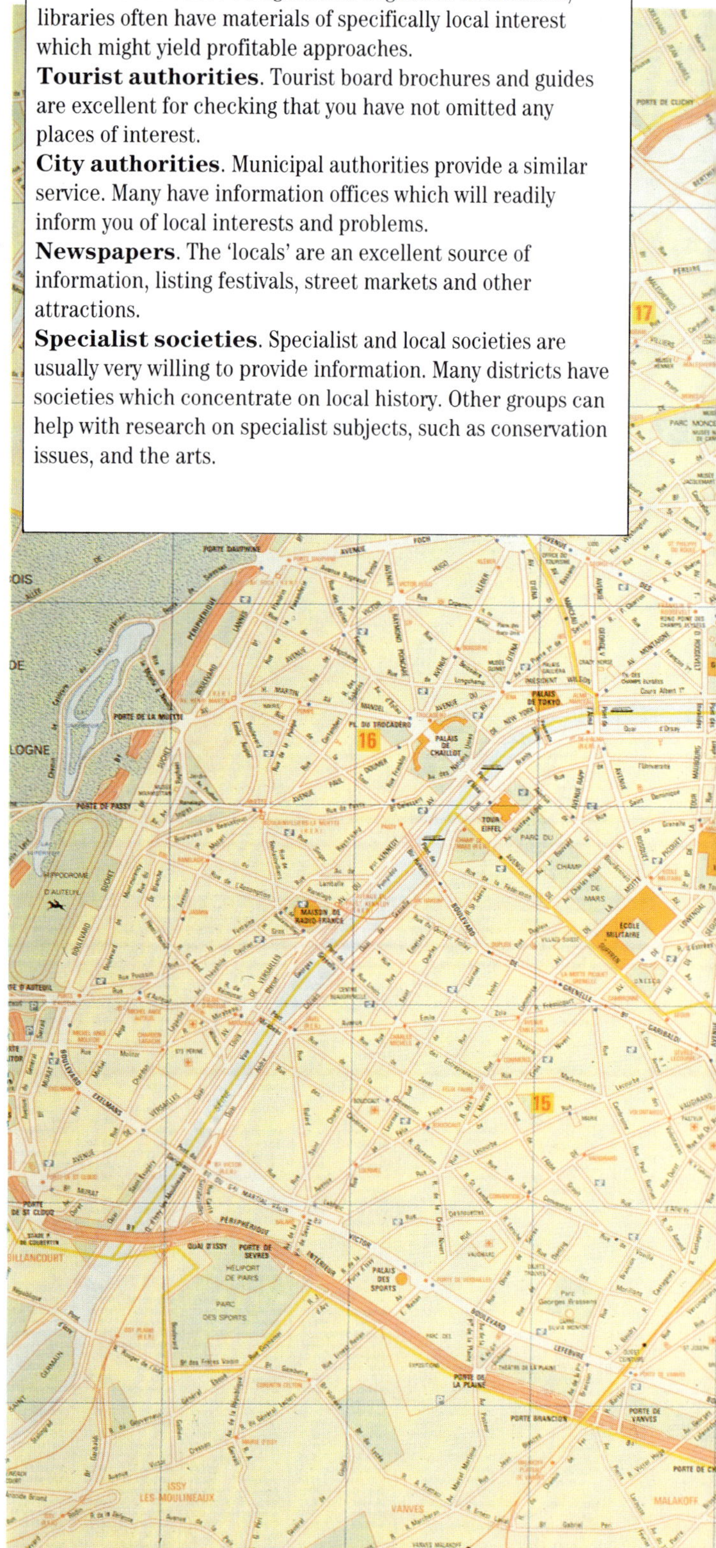

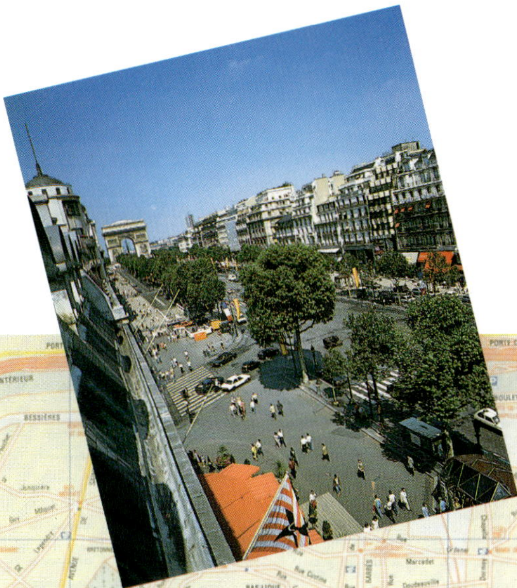

When researching an unfamiliar city use maps and guidebooks to pinpoint the sights. A still camera can give you a record of locations, from small shops to busy city streets.

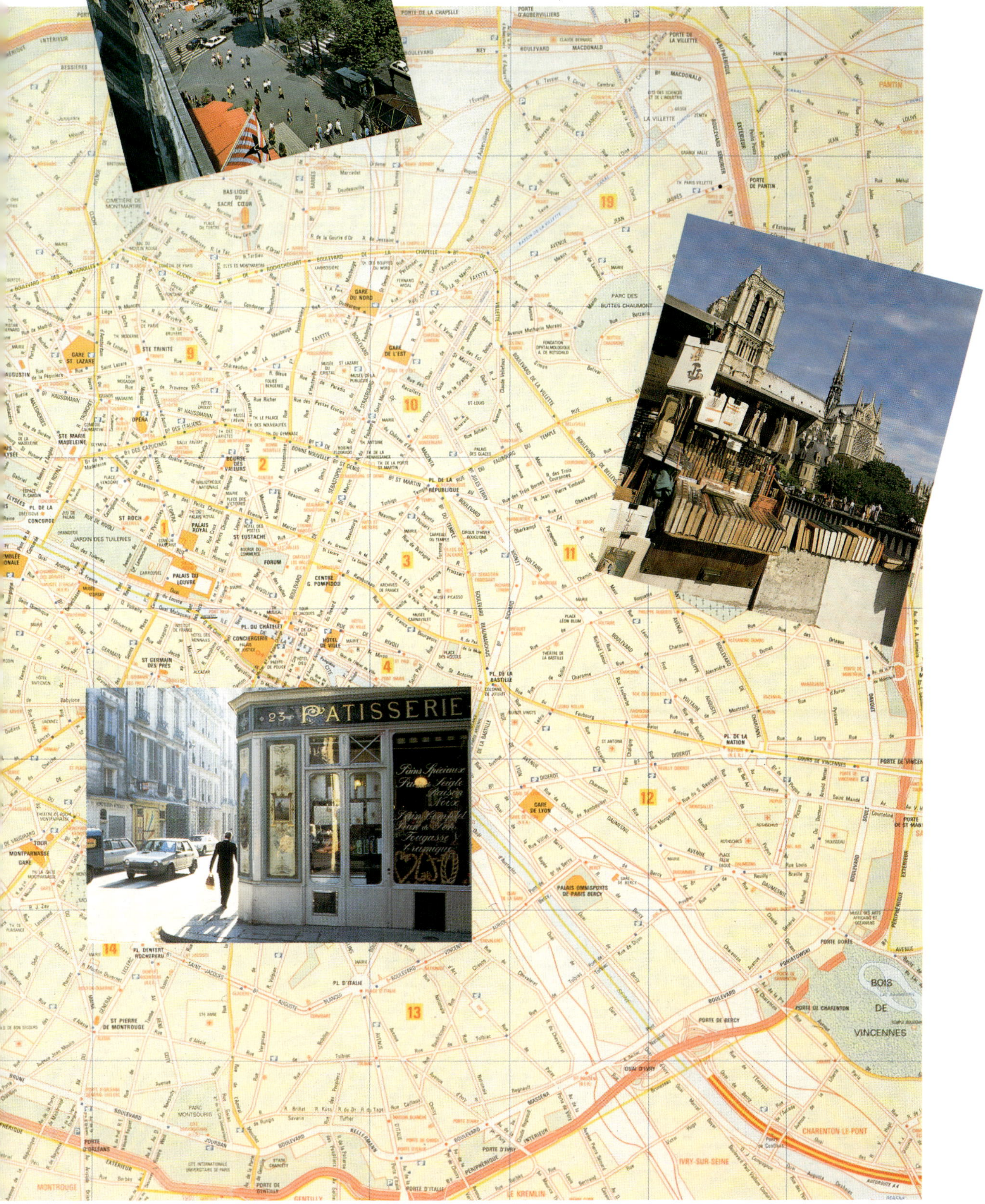

PROJECT NOTEBOOK

DOCUMENTARIES

Everyone and everything has a story, in fact, several stories, and each story has a beginning, a middle and an end. The purpose of making a documentary is to select which story you are going to tell, and then to decide how best to tell it. Stories unfold by setting up questions in the viewer's mind and then answering them. Where is this happening? – In this convent. Who is involved? – These are the main characters. As always, research time is never wasted.

■ Use your location. If it is an attractive old building, let the camera linger. If it is a busy scene like a bustling market, pick out details and individuals.

■ Establish the main characters early in the video. It is no good, for instance, to devote the first five minutes of tape to a character who never appears again. In many documentary situations, characters can form the narrative structure of the piece.

■ Remember the viewer, the end-user of your work. You might get carried away by a particular situation or conversation, but does the audience really want to watch twenty minutes of the cook explaining how to chop carrots?

■ All videos have an internal sense of pace and rhythm, so it's up to you to impose the pace you want and which suits the subject matter you're covering.

■ React to the moment. If something unexpected happens, shoot it. If it doesn't look good on review, you can always abandon it.

■ Before going on location, check your equipment thoroughly. To run out of battery power at a crucial moment is unforgivable – and frustrating.

■ Always get the appropriate permissions. If someone finds you shooting on their property without advance warning, they're entitled to be annoyed.

CREATING ATMOSPHERE

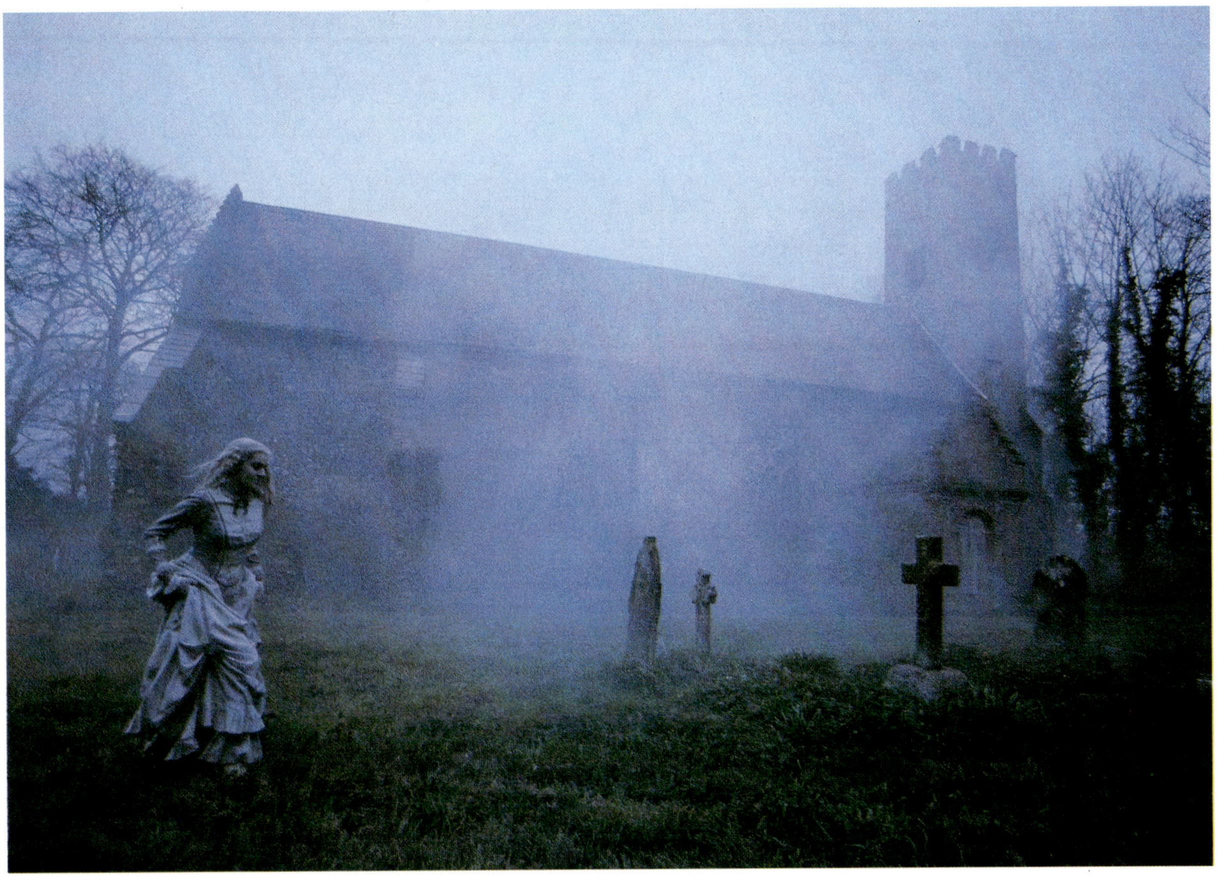

So far, the video projects examined in this book have been concerned with recording real events. In other words, they have been documentaries of one kind or another. But since cameras are just as useful for creating fictional work, it will not be long before the amateur video maker wants to try his or her hand at making a drama. This chapter therefore examines some of the techniques for this kind of filming. The two major projects used to illustrate these techniques are a short ghost story and a thriller set in a modern apartment.

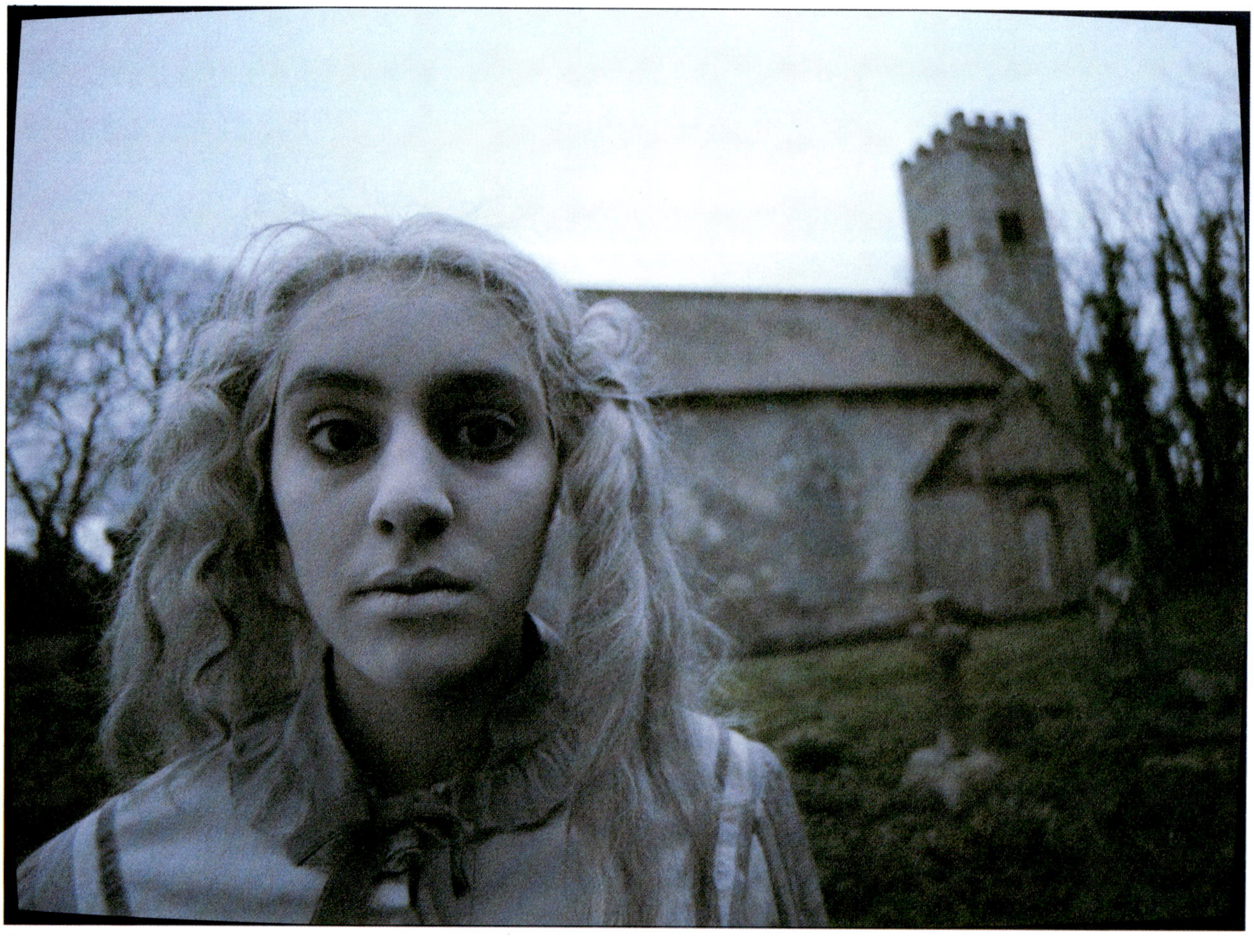

BASIC PROCEDURES

Since most television drama eats up large budgets and uses huge crews, you might not think that you have much chance of creating a decent fictional work with just a few friends and a camera. But in fact it's certainly possible to create some extremely slick, entertaining productions.

Your first requirement is a script. This need not be complex, but should contain an interesting, coherent narrative, continuously prompting the audience to ask itself what happens next (if inspiration fails, you can always adopt a plot line from a television programme). The story should contain elements of suspense, which resolve themselves at the denouement of the piece.

Imagine what a fairly basic plot will look like on screen. For instance, you could opt for a story with a surprise ending involving a woman being shown alone in her own home. Suddenly she hears an intruder. She is clearly agitated as the footsteps approach the door of her room. The suspense mounts. At this point you have several options. Either you can select an unpleasant ending, or alternatively you could reveal the intruder not to be a murderer but her husband, sneaking home to give her a surprise present.

Atmosphere is created in a number of ways. First, it depends upon location. There are a number of obvious backdrops which keep appearing in films, and for very good reasons. An old rambling house is a traditional setting for thrillers and instantly and effectively provides atmosphere, also signalling to the audience that they are in for a rough ride. A run-down inner city housing block is an equally good setting when creating a different sense of menace. Alternatively, use an 'ordinary' location, injecting it with the required atmosphere by the imaginative use of set design and props.

Lighting is also important, particularly when shooting interiors. A soft, warm light tends to create a mellow, peaceful atmosphere. Dim lighting with deep shadowy areas suggests menace and suspense. And between these two extremes, there are many other effects that can be achieved by lighting.

Finally, your camerawork and editing style are also vital means of conveying mood and atmosphere. Extreme, unusual camera angles are commonly used in thrillers. Furthermore, during editing, shots can be juxtaposed for extra effects, and the pace with which cuts are made from one scene to another will help propel the film to its climax.

1: *A scene from the ghost story project, which is set in a churchyard. The ghostly lady's make-up was achieved by using face whitener. The shot was taken deliberately underexposed to create an unworldy, misty atmosphere.*

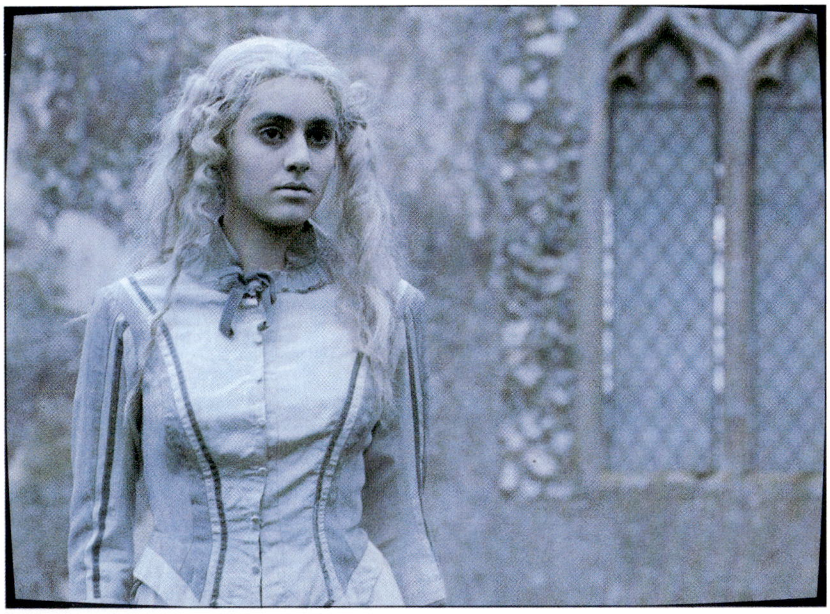

2: *Costumes are an excellent way of emphasizing a sense of period and are worth hiring for your video dramas. Alternatively, search amongst local sales for old clothes and outfits that can be adapted to your needs.*

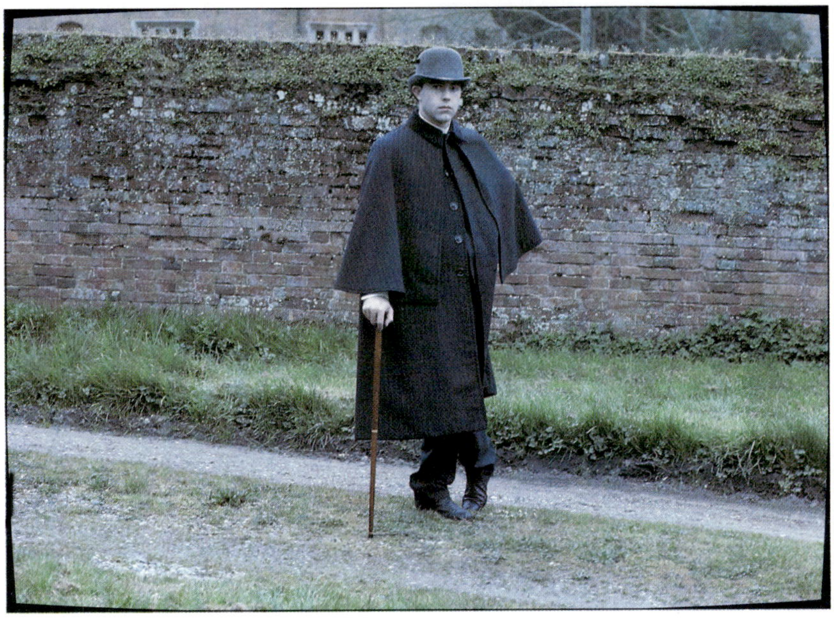

3: *When filming on location, scrutinize everything that appears in the frame. The last thing you want in a video set in the nineteenth century is the background appearance of a modern house! Surprisingly, such errors even occur in professional films. In this instance the wall has just shut out the intrusion of the twentieth century.*

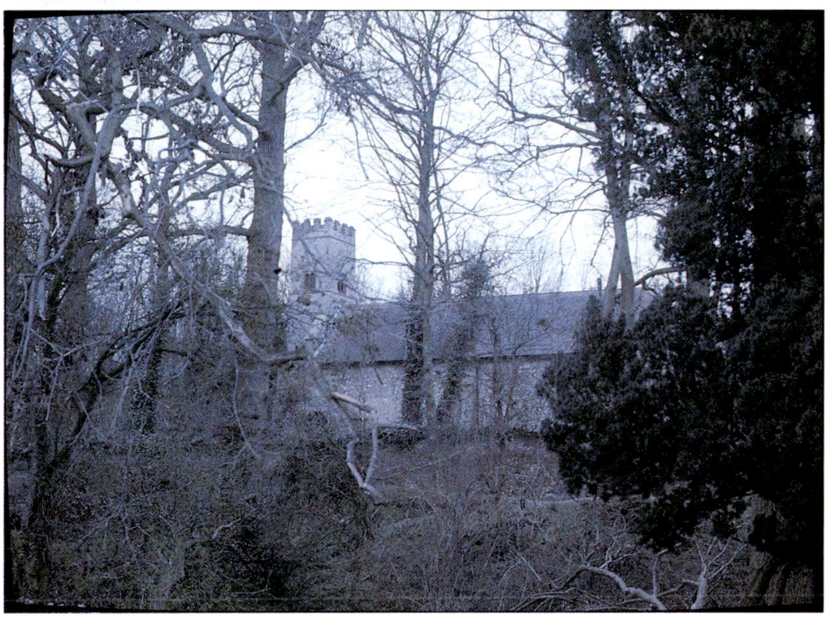

4: *Scout the location thoroughly, to discover which aspects most effectively convey the atmosphere you require. The churchyard seen through the tangled woods proved to be a highly effective shot.*

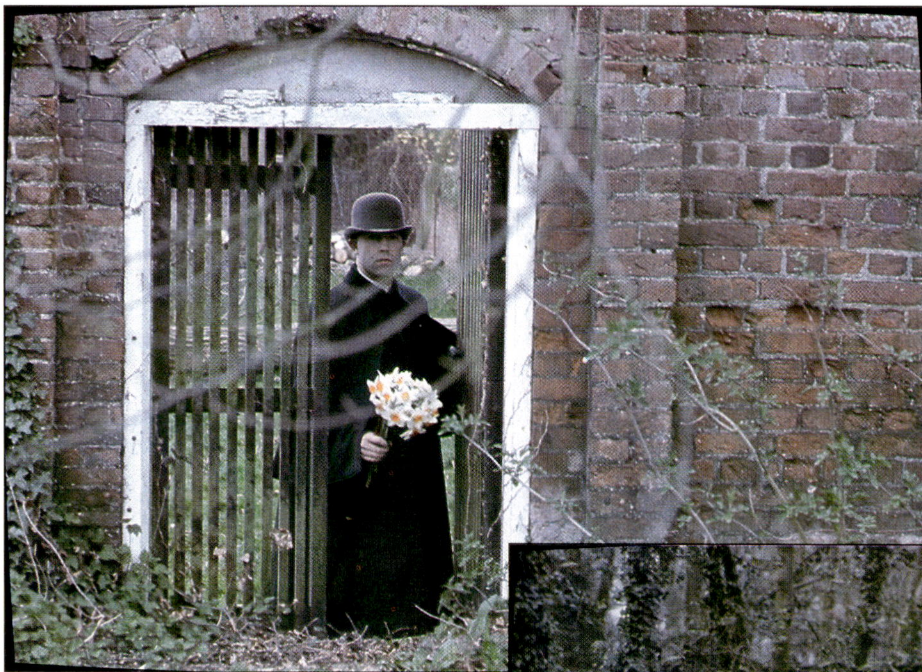

1: *The male character enters the churchyard carrying flowers. Framing the shot through foliage in the foreground cleverly increases the atmosphere and heightens our expectations.*

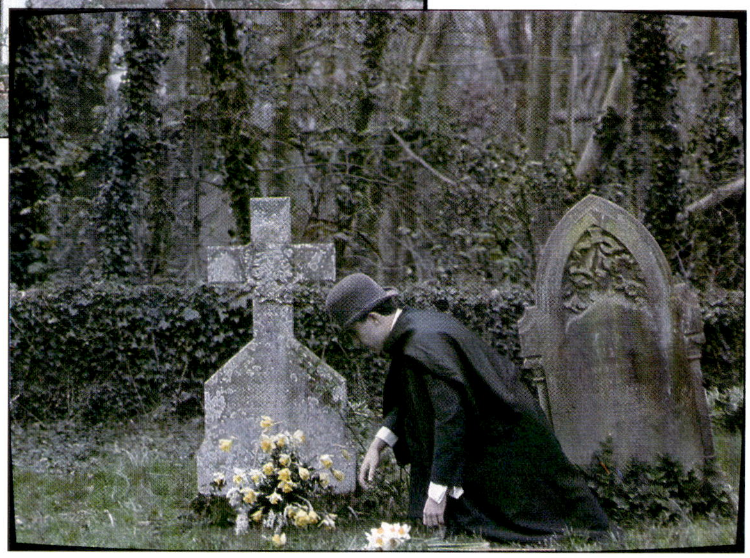

2: *The character at the graveside is first seen in a longer shot than that shown here. Then the camera moves in to hold the character in mid-shot. Note that the scene is slightly overexposed using the manual exposure settings.*

GHOST STORY 1

The plot outline for the ghost story is very simple. A man enters a churchyard and kneels at a graveside, perhaps that of his fiancée or wife. Perhaps it is the anniversary of her death. Suddenly, he catches sight of a figure in the distance. He recognizes it as his loved one. He pursues her across the churchyard and into the church, whereupon she approaches a stone figure and vanishes into it. While this plot is by no means Edgar Allan Poe, it doesn't mean that it won't succeed well, and it's a good vehicle for trying out some interesting techniques.

The first step is to translate the basic outline into a shooting script, which will describe each scene in detail, shot-by-shot. The opening image will establish the scene and set the atmosphere. It begins with the churchyard seen in long-shot through the trees. A slow pan follows, providing greater detail, building up the atmosphere and coming to rest on the churchyard gate. This leads to the entrance of the male character.

At this moment the audience instinctively asks: Who is he? and, Why is he there? The first question remains unanswered (you needn't clarify every point in a mystery), but as the camera shows him approaching the grave, the answer to the second is partly provided. A close-up of the gravestone inscription reveals that it is the grave of a young woman. The expression on the actor's face indicates that he is not merely paying his formal respects, but that there is a deeper sadness.

Up to this point, very little has actually happened. The atmosphere has been created by the location, the slow movements of the camera, and by the use of long-shots. Now, at last, the close-up on the gravestone and the actor reveal more specific information to the audience. And the video's pace increases when the actor sees the ghostly figure of the girl, first glimpsed fleetingly, as if it were a momentary hallucination. This sense of mystery is strengthened by the mist and the grey church.

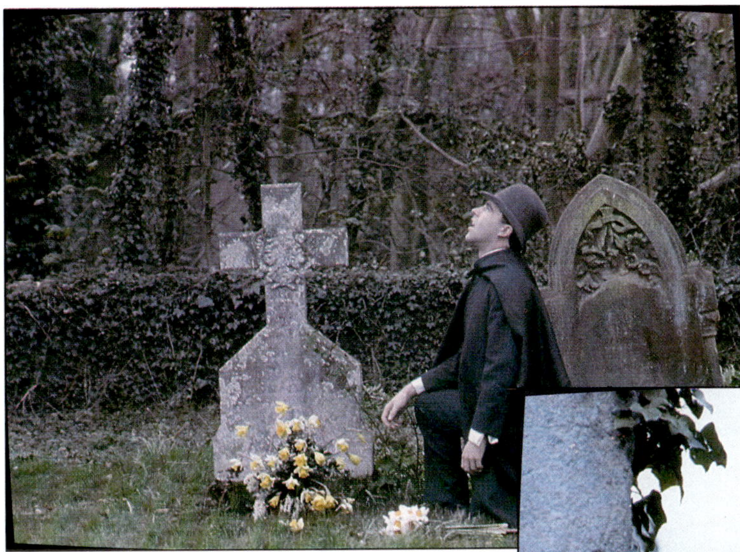

3: *The first reaction shot. The character sees something which shocks him. The audience's pulses are also quickened as they try to find out what it is.*

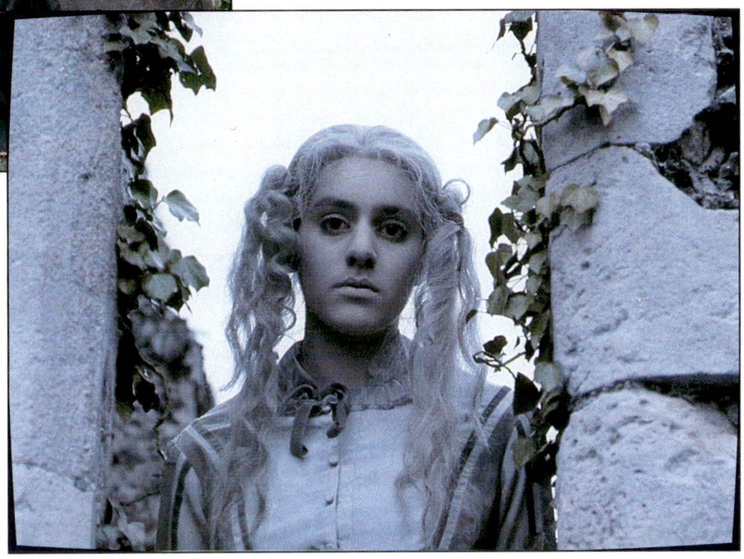

4: *The question is answered. The camera goes to a mid-shot of the ghostly figure framed in a gap between the pillars. This shot was cut during editing to make it appear on the screen only for a second or so, to add shock value and impact.*

5: *The end of the first sequence. The ghostly figure is seen about to turn and run. A smoke bomb provides the sudden 'mist'.*

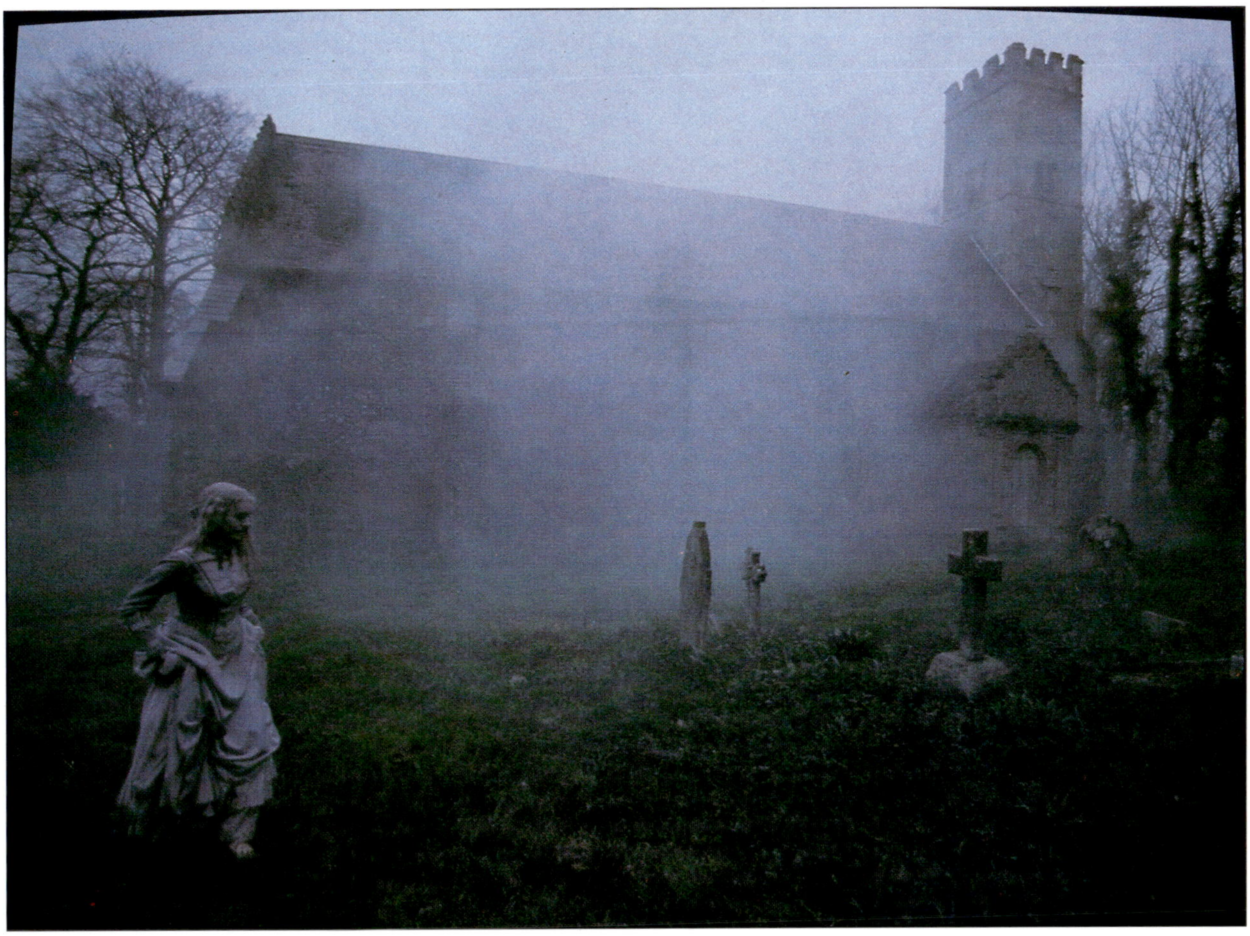

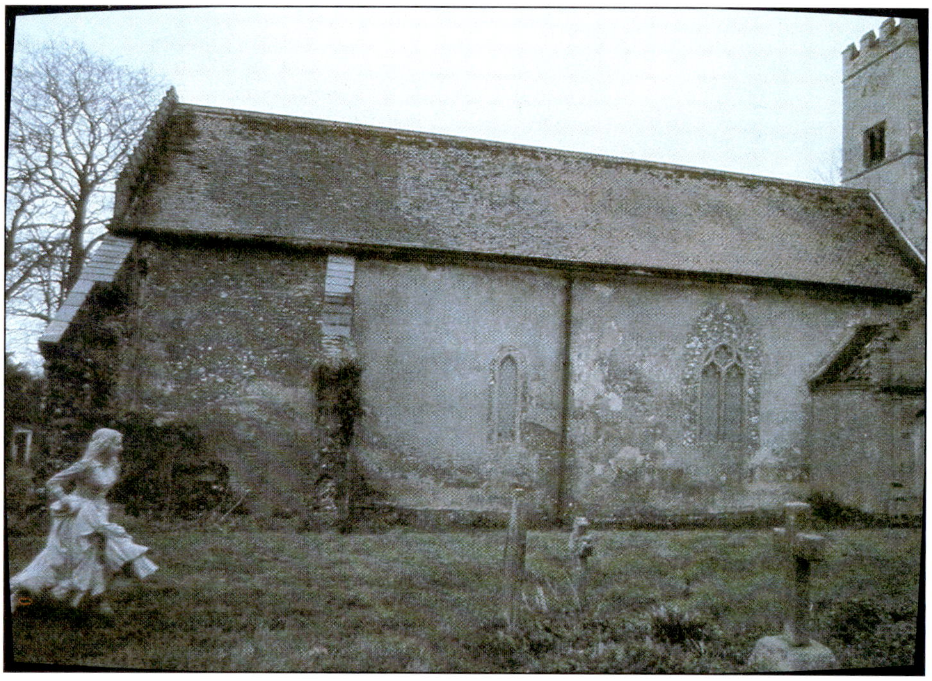

1: *The ghost figure moving in the churchyard is shown mainly in long-shot to retain a sense of distance and mystery. A big close-up would make her appear too obviously flesh and blood.*

GHOST STORY 2

2: *By cutting shots of the woman standing still with shots of the figure running during the editing stage, an extra supernatural effect is added: the ghost appears to be in two places at once.*

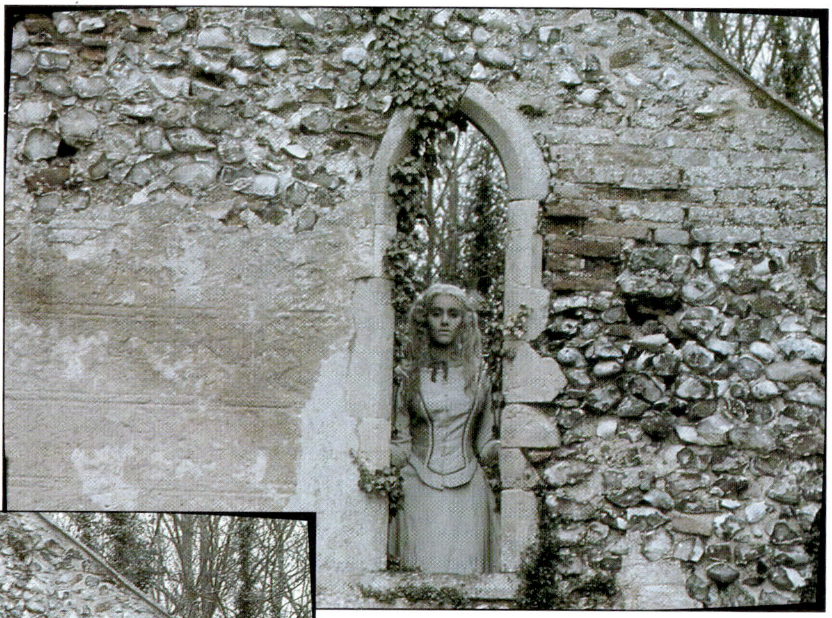

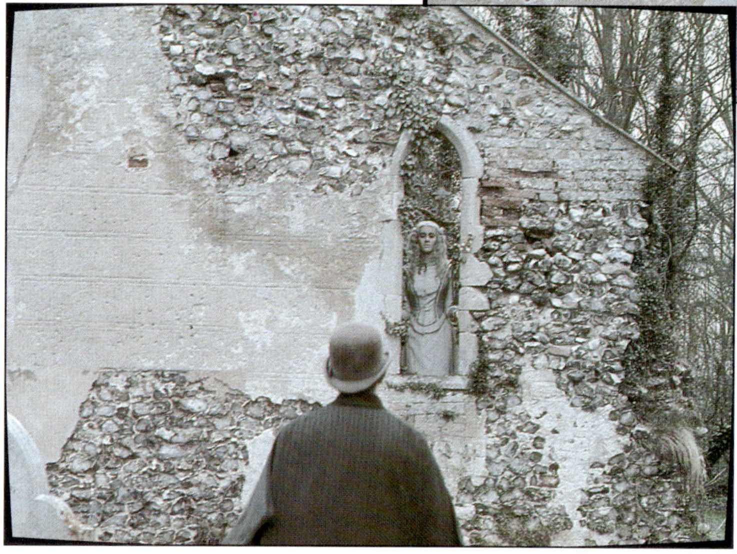

3: *For the first time the man and the woman appear in the same shot. With the man standing still and looking at the figure, so the pace of this sequence slows down. Now the audience has an opportunity to study each figure in more detail.*

The shots on this page are taken from what might be regarded as the key sequence of the short ghost story. Most of the action develops here, with your priority being to cover these events in such a way as to maintain the atmosphere of suspense created in the earlier sequences.

The great temptation with this sequence is to allow the action to develop too quickly. This would be a mistake, undermining the mood achieved by the earlier coverage, and unreal. For ghosts do not, on the whole, run vigorously like athletes, but glide and reappear mysteriously. Consequently, coverage of the ghostly figure moving through the churchyard was in two basic styles: long-shots of the figure moving around the tombstones, and close-ups of her face when she turns to face the male character. These different shots can be cut together during the editing stage to provide an extra degree of pace, if required.

The first part of this scene keeps the two characters separate. Now, as the climax of the action approaches, they appear in the same frame together for the first time, the woman seen from over the man's shoulder. As the camera goes into close-up on the woman, this becomes a point-of-view shot, seen from the man's perspective. The close-up is held for longer than that in the previous sequence. Next, the camera crabs round the action to give a reaction shot of the man. This shot is held until he speaks to the ghostly figure, whereupon she runs away. In order to convey an immediate change of pace, and a new section of action, the camera suddenly cuts to the woman in close-up, and then follows the chase across the graveyard in long-shot.

The next scene cuts to the interior of the church, to show the entrance of the woman. For the time being it is important to maintain the pace established in the preceding shots. An immediate, drastic slowing of the action would appear unnatural and obtrusive, prompting the audience to wonder why she had rushed towards the church, now to enter it at a snail's pace.

The change of location makes the audience ask why she is now in the church. What will she (and we) find there? You can gradually use this expectation to resume a slower pace. A pan shot around the inside of the building (perhaps taken from a low angle to add a sense of strangeness) will achieve this, as well as providing an establishing shot of the new location.

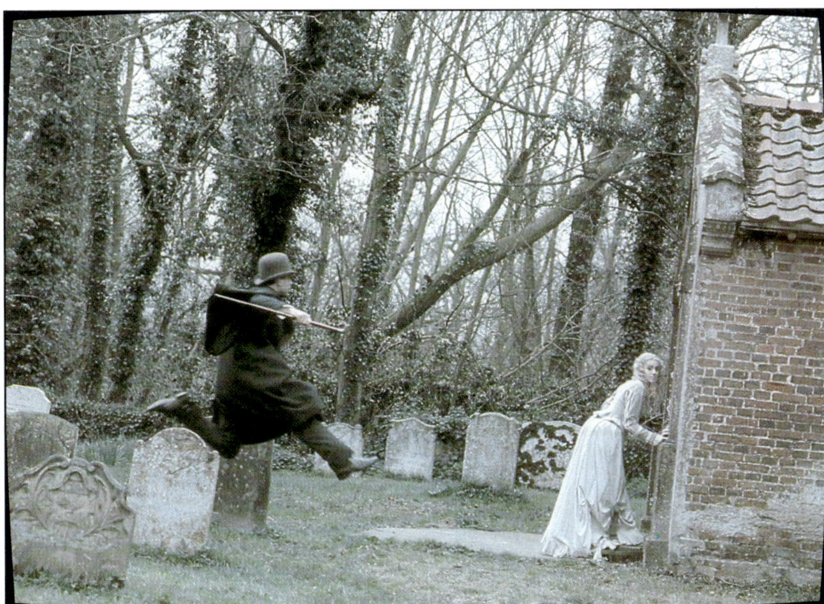

4: *Following the pause, the chase begins again. Try to make the action happen as suddenly as possible, to enhance the change of pace on the screen.*

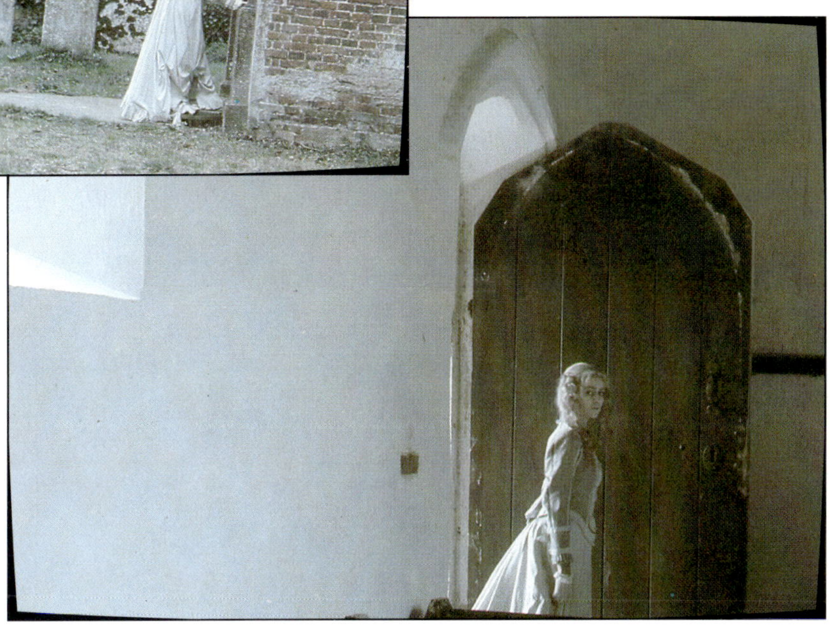

5: *This section of the video ends with a new location: inside the church. Remember that the actress should be seen to enter at roughly the same speed that she approached the building to preserve continuity of pace between the two scenes.*

The climax, or denouement of the story, needs careful treatment if it is to create the required impact on the audience. The ending of the ghost story is mysterious, not violent, so it is atmosphere that needs to be built up during the final sequences, not pace.

Following a slow pan around the interior of the church, the camera shows first the woman approaching a particular monument in one of the recesses. The next shot shows the man entering the church to pause by the door and watch her. The camera then follows the direction of his gaze. The shot should then be held, so that the audience is placed in the man's position, observing the actions of the ghost. Now she slowly turns to face the camera.

At this point the story requires the ghost to 'disappear' and merge into the monument. The shot is achieved by gradually losing focus on the woman, framed in a mid-shot. A second shot, taken from the

GHOST STORY 3

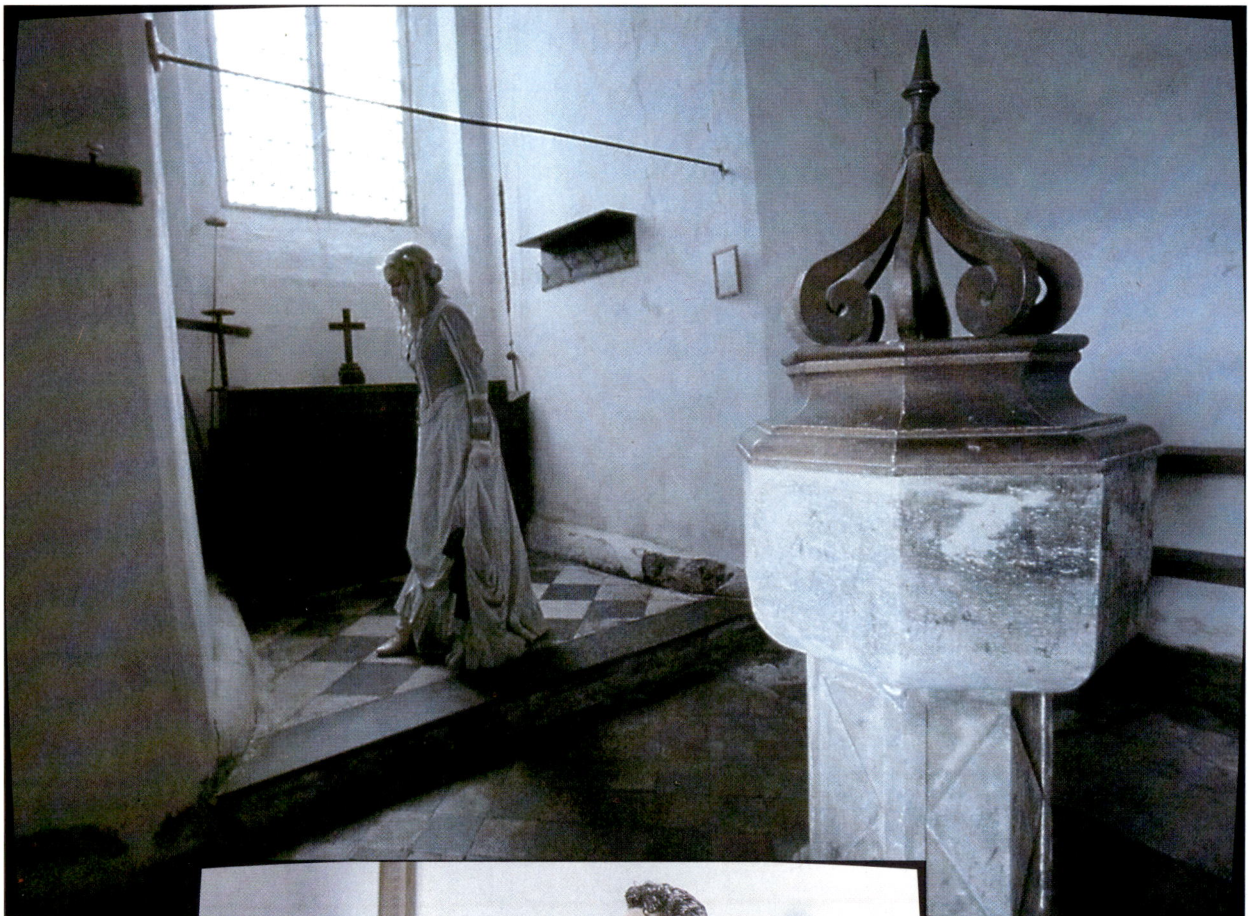

1: *The woman approaches the monument in the recess. Framing the shot with the font in the foreground gives the impression that the man is overlooking the scene.*

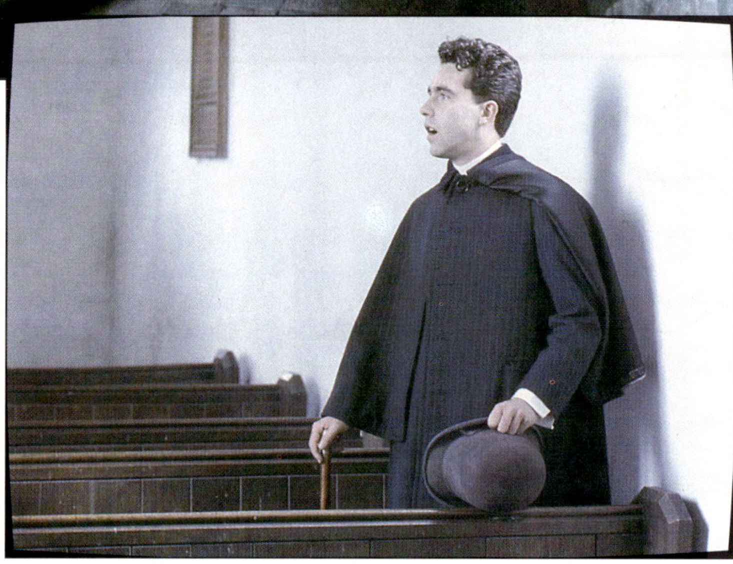

2: *The man, having entered the church, stands to one side and observes the scene. His position allows further coverage of the woman to be seen from his point of view.*

identical camera position, but with the woman absent, was then filmed, gradually bringing the monument into focus. This is now followed by shots of the man approaching the monument. A final close-up reveals that the statue bears a strong resemblance to the ghost, and an inscription which mirrors that shown earlier on the gravestone. The closing shots are of the man standing in front of the monument, receding into a long-shot, followed by an exterior of the church with the door open, again gradually receding into a long-shot which mirrors the opening of the video.

When preparing to shoot even such a basic project as this, allocate more time than you think you will need. With outdoor locations there is always the possibility of the weather preventing any shooting at all, and with this project bright sunshine would have made it more difficult to achieve a supernatural atmosphere. Each shot will have to be rehearsed a number of times and, quite probably repeated for the camera, before you get it just as you had visualized. Remember also that actors and helpers may not share your enthusiasm, so don't work them too hard. Plan for adequate breaks for meals and drinks during the course of the day. A contented crew is much more likely to work overtime than one that's been harrassed throughout a long day.

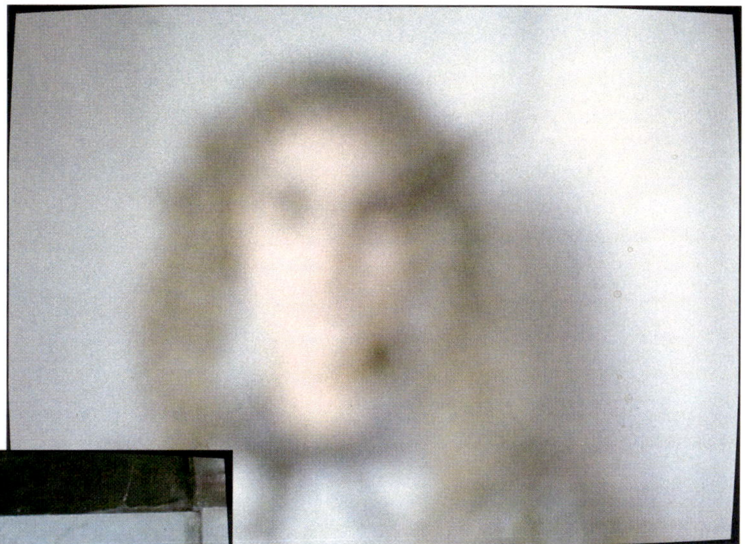

3: *This shot shows the woman going out of focus before she disappears. A more pronounced effect could be gained using filters and gels, or by placing a very thin gauze in front of the lens.*

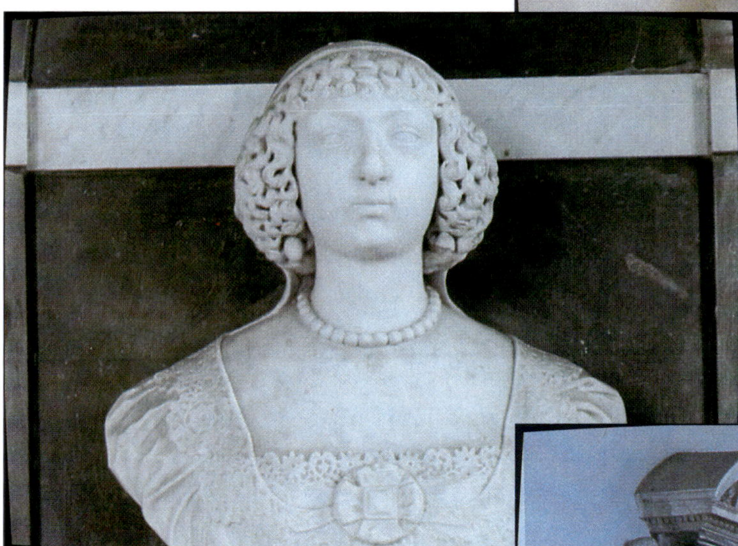

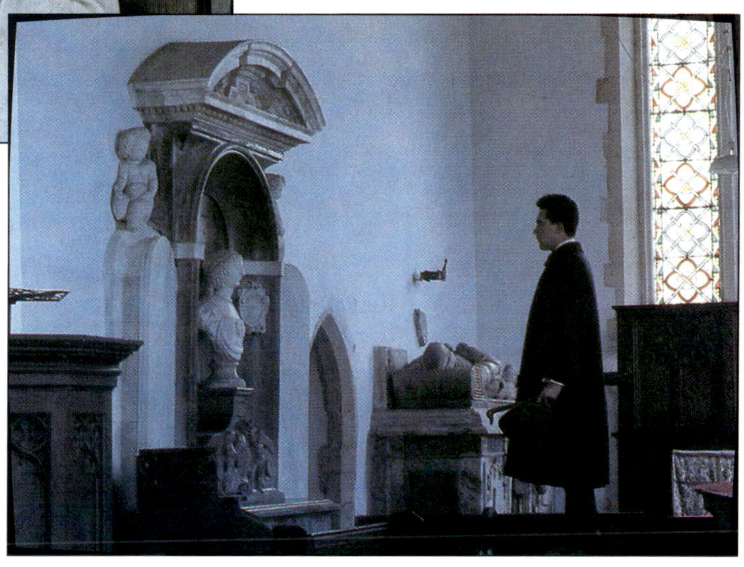

4-5: *The final interior shots show the man standing in front of the monument, absorbed by it. As the camera crabs round behind him it shows the audience what he has been studying. He realizes that the ghost was the statue come to life.*

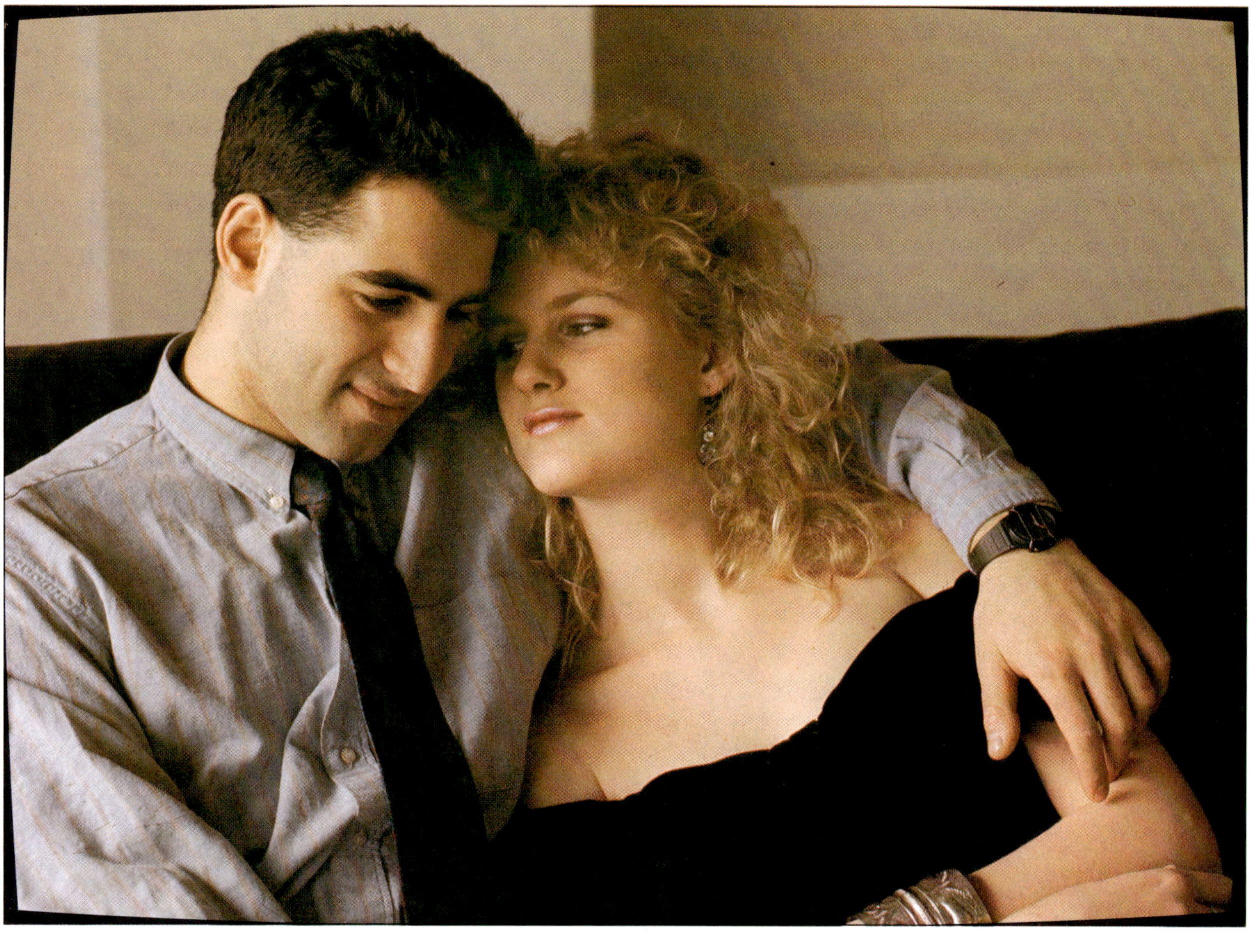

LIGHTING INTERIORS

On outdoor locations, you have minimum control over the lighting conditions. But recording indoors is a different matter. However, while you can quite easily use most cameras inside a building, the resulting images often have a flat, amateurish look to them. In order to achieve the polished images seen on television, you must therefore use supplementary lighting.

In the following project we reveal how to tackle a thriller shot inside a small appartment. The lighting arrangement was introduced first to create a 'natural' look and, second, to complement the tense atmosphere of the plot.

Since 'natural' lighting in video is anything but natural, the sense of flatness has to be overcome by directing lights at the characters, so 'lifting' them from their background. The problem is that when this is achieved with a single light only, large areas of contrast are produced. The light effectively acts as a 'spot'. If a second light is added, the situation is improved, but again there will be large areas of deep shadow. A third light is therefore required to 'lift' the subject from its background and create even lighting.

This system is known as three-point lighting. The first light is called the key light, and is placed at a slight angle in front of the subject. The second light is known as the fill. It is positioned to the other side of the subject, usually at a slightly greater angle, and relieves the shadowy areas created by the key. The third light is the backlight, positioned behind the subject, casting a slight rimming effect which helps to lift the subject from the background. On set, each light can be arranged so that it performs two functions – one character's key light acts as another's fill, and vice versa.

The positioning of lights on a set is a matter of trial and error. There are no absolute rules. The lighting must be even across the entire area where the action takes place and, of course, it must be hidden from the camera during any particular shot. This means planning camera and lighting positions in advance, and/or hiding the lights on set (lights can be hidden behind any opaque surface on set, such as a lace curtained window or a picture frame). You may also need to use reflectors (for example, large sheets of white card or pieces of white expanded polystyrene) to bounce the light to the place where you need it. Reflectors can be useful if your budget is limited and you do not have enough lights.

1: *Three-point lighting is used in this shot, in which both characters are fully lit and lifted from the background. The resultant shadowy areas appear entirely natural.*
2: *In this shot, the effect of the key light is most prominent. The fill is less powerful, so there is greater shadow on the right side of the girl's face. The effect is to concentrate the viewer's attention on the girl's face.*

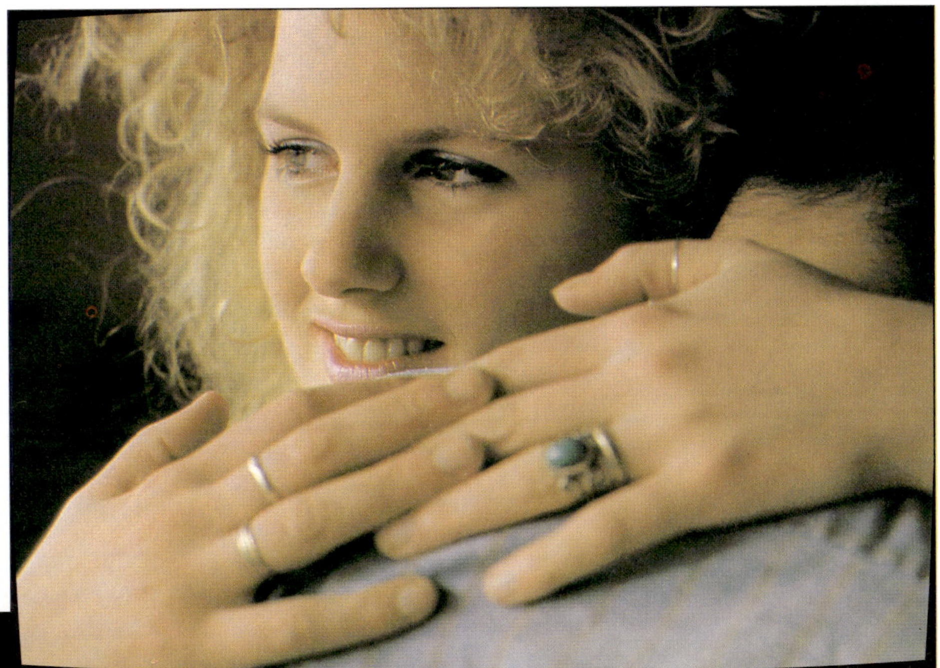

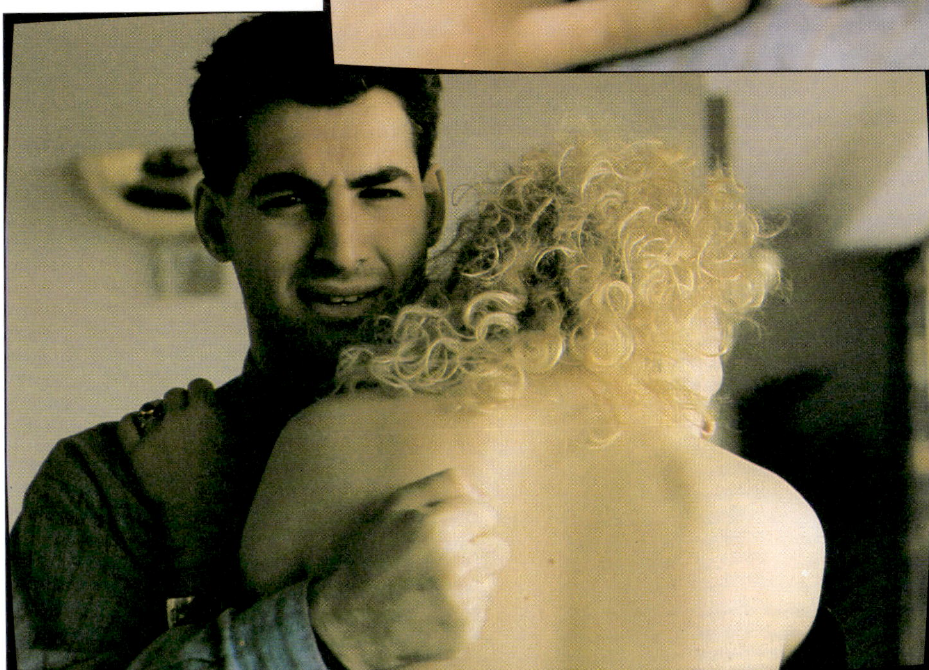

3: *With no additional lighting, this shot would appear flat on the screen. The highlights on the girl's hair give the shot added visual intensity.*

4: *Remember that the lighting effect will vary with the position of the camera. If you shoot from an unusual angle, check the lighting conditions, both directly and through the camera's viewfinder.*

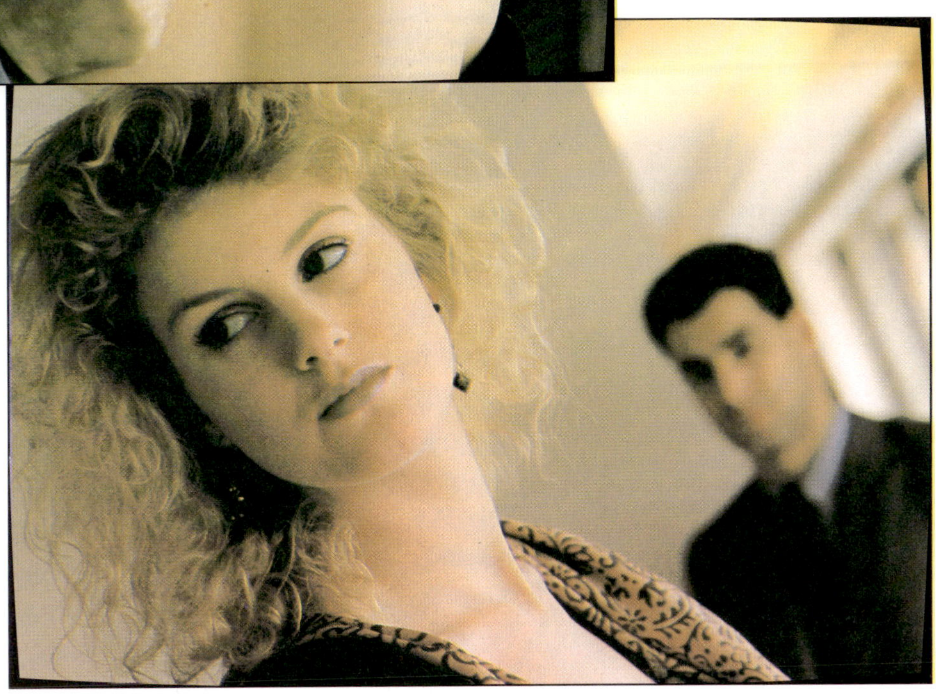

In a thriller the obvious intention is to keep the audience on the edge of their seats, whether or not that audience is in a packed cinema or in your own front room. In other words, the audience should constantly be aware that something unpleasant is likely to occur. To achieve this expectancy, the plot should develop shot by shot, building up to a climax. Timing is therefore more important in this than in any other type of video.

Although the tension should be inherent in the script, it is the video-maker's responsibility to exploit this to the full. One of the most useful devices for achieving this is the point-of-view shot, which places the audience in the position of one of the screen characters. So, in this video project, when the audience sees the door handle turning ominously, they see it from the point of view of the heroine who, in the last shot, is looking anxiously towards the door. Thus the previous shot establishes the meaning of the subsequent one – without the look of anxiety in the actress's eyes, the door handle would convey no sinister meaning, it would be simply another feature of the room.

The opposite of the point-of-view shot is one in which the audience is presented with information which it knows the characters in the drama don't share. This could be achieved by juxtaposing two completely different shots running simultaneously. A typical example would involve showing a woman relaxing by herself in her home. Her behaviour shows that she is unaware of any threat. A second shot shows male feet stealthily climbing a staircase. By cutting between these two shots, the audience assumes the two actions are related – they sense what is about to happen, while the woman remains ignorant, and they await the awful moment when she will share their knowledge.

Often, such sequences must be drawn out beyond a natural time scale to be fully effective. Although in real life it only takes a couple of seconds to mount a staircase, an audience will accept a much longer time span as tension is built up. Additional tension can be created by shooting from an unusual angle. An obliquely-framed shot automatically suggests the unusual or the bizarre, but it loses its effectiveness if used too often.

BUILDING TENSION

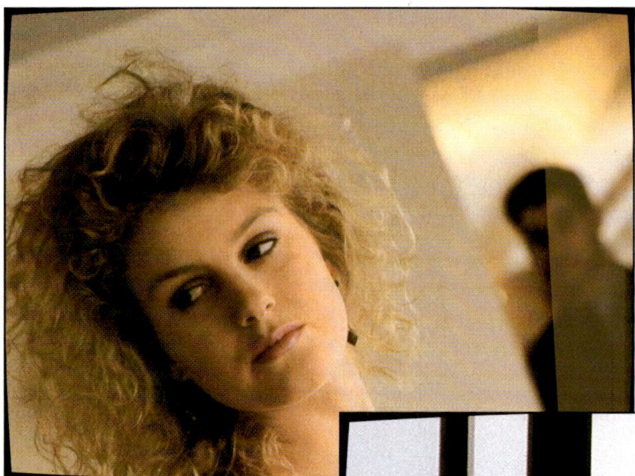

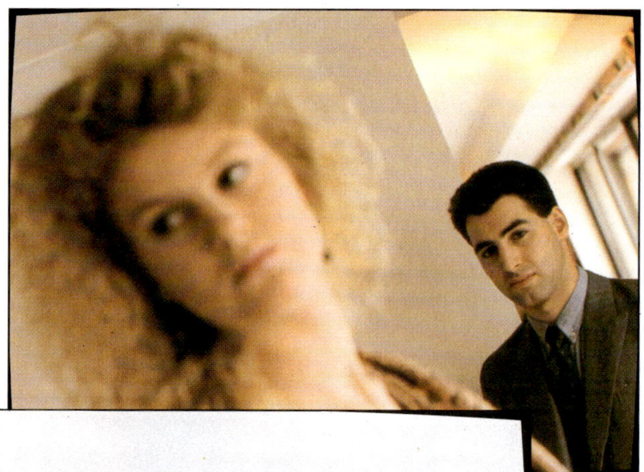

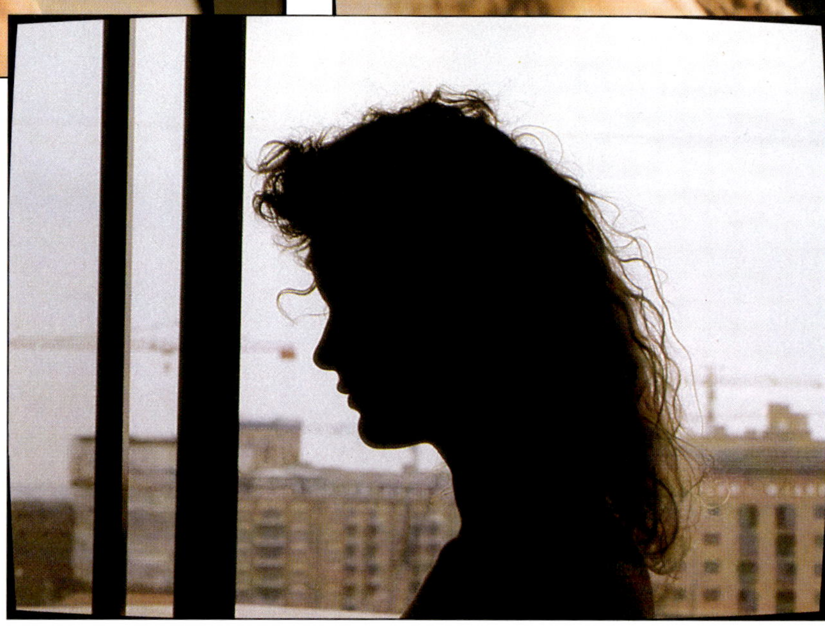

1-2: *Changing focus from the girl to the approaching man is a good way of building tension in this scene. The unusual camera angle also increases the sense of menace.*

3: *A cut to this silhouette gives a sense of the girl's isolation and vulnerability – and also her unawareness of the threat.*

4: *Shooting tense or violent scenes in close-up concentrates the viewers's mind on the essentials – the facial expressions and the close physical contact between the two people.*

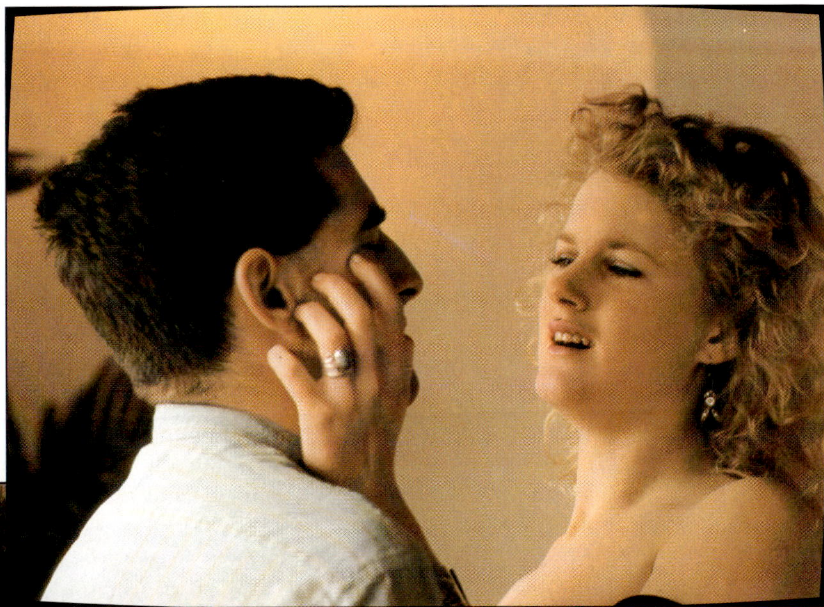

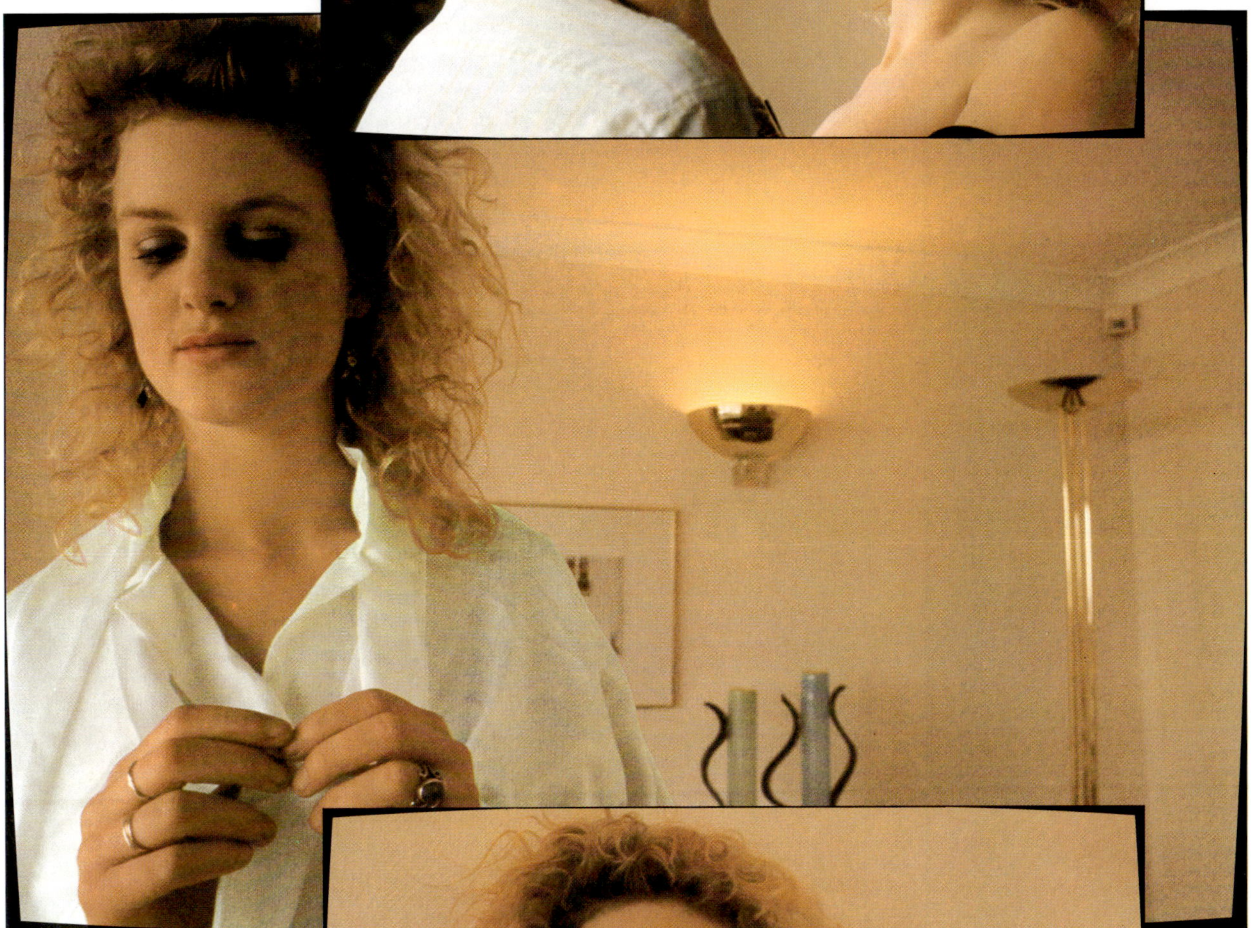

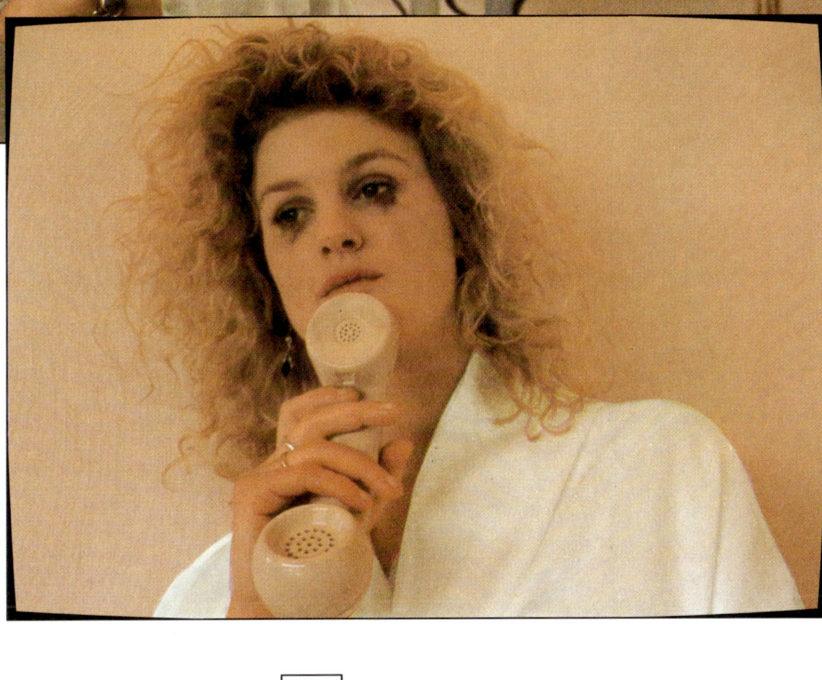

5-6: *When the telephone rings, the action slows down. The girl's reluctant steps towards the phone and the deliberate way in which she picks it up and holds it increase the audience's sense of expectation.*

Narrative comes first and foremost in creating suspense, and it evolves according to the way in which one shot relates to another – that is, according to how they are edited.

The audience will begin watching the thriller video knowing nothing. So before suspense can be created they must be supplied with a basic amount of information. What is the setting? Who are the main characters? What is their relationship? Is it satisfactory? Is there any underlying tension?

As the drama unfolds, so the audience is fed with increasing amounts of information that further define the story. If this flow of information comes too slowly, the audience will become bored. Too fast, and the audience will not be able to assimilate everything they are being told. Each scene should therefore either provide information or pose a question, prompting the audience to consider various aspects of the plot. What will she do now that the man has left her after a blazing row? Why is she going towards the bathroom?

Gradually, in turn, each answer leads to new questions. Will the man return to the flat in time to call an ambulance and save the girl following her overdose? And if he does, how will her suicide attempt affect their future relationship? While the timing of these questions and answers is the main function of plotting, which is the writer's primary concern, making these questions work on the screen is the central task of the editor, who cuts from scene to scene.

This question-and-answer process should lead up to an inevitable climax in which, in conventional stories, all the conflicting elements in the drama are resolved. You may, however, prefer a more realistic conclusion, in which there is no obvious solution. But if you chose this ending, remember that your audience may well feel cheated. After all, it is in the very nature of suspense to lead the audience to expect an ending that is conclusive. What is good for one form of video, such as a documentary, is not necessarily good for a thriller.

EDITING TO INCREASE SUSPENSE

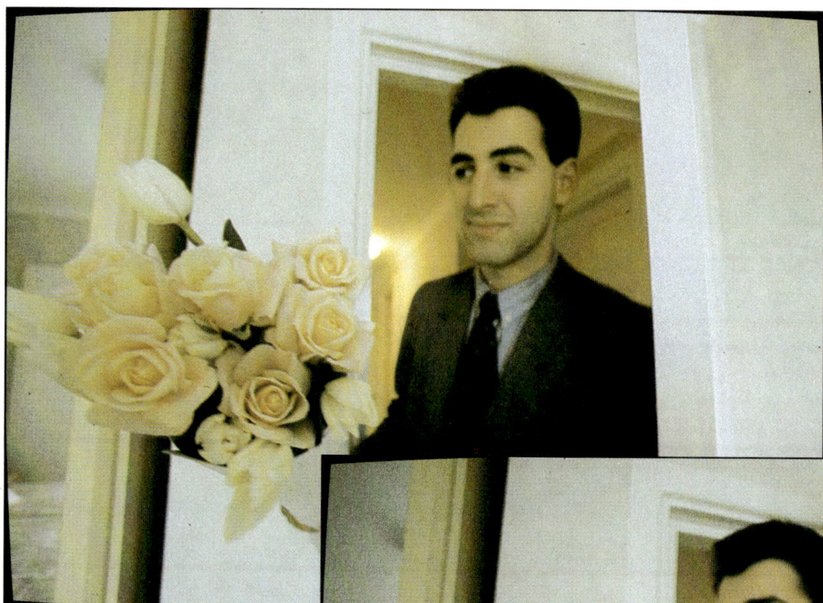

1: *The audience knows what the man doesn't – his girlfriend has taken an overdose of sleeping tablets. Shots of the man approaching the flat with a conciliatory bunch of flowers create a sense of anticipation in the audience: what will he do when he discovers the girl unconscious?*

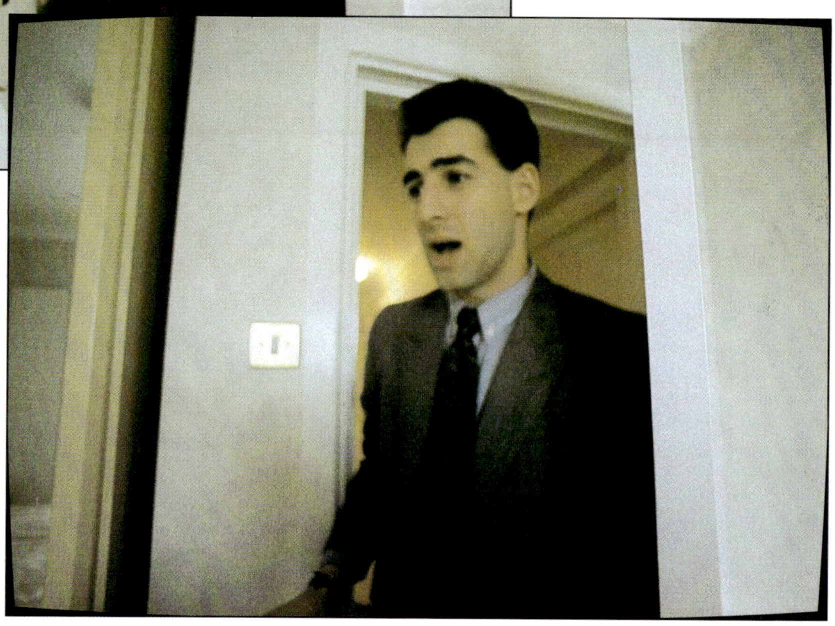

2: *The actor's reaction supplies the answer. The shot tells the audience that he realizes that something is wrong and sets up a second question: what will he do next?*

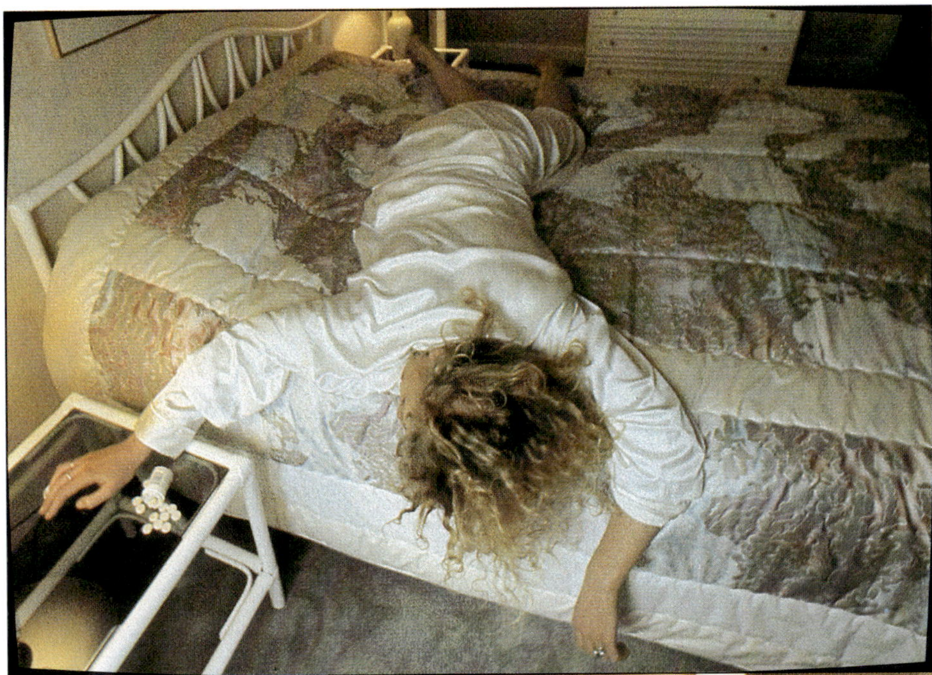

3: *Rapid intercutting between what the man sees and the overall scene heightens tension in this section of the video. The first shot shows the girl on the bed – the sight that confronts the man when he enters the room. We may glimpse the pills on the table before the cut to the next shot.*

4: *The fast cut to the shot of the two figures together shows that the man is moving quickly. Fast action like this keeps up the tempo and the tension.*

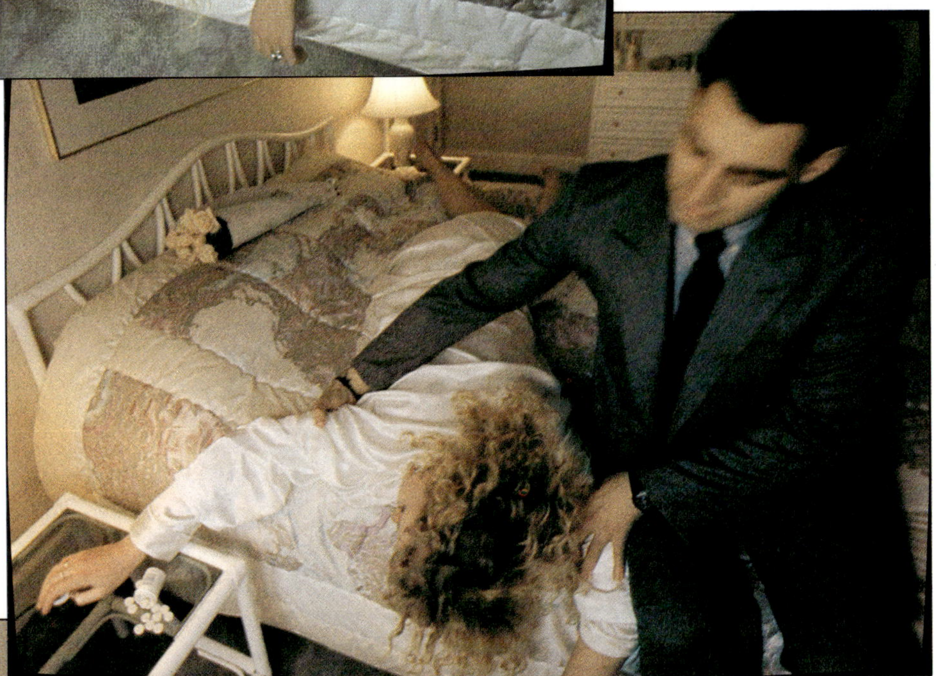

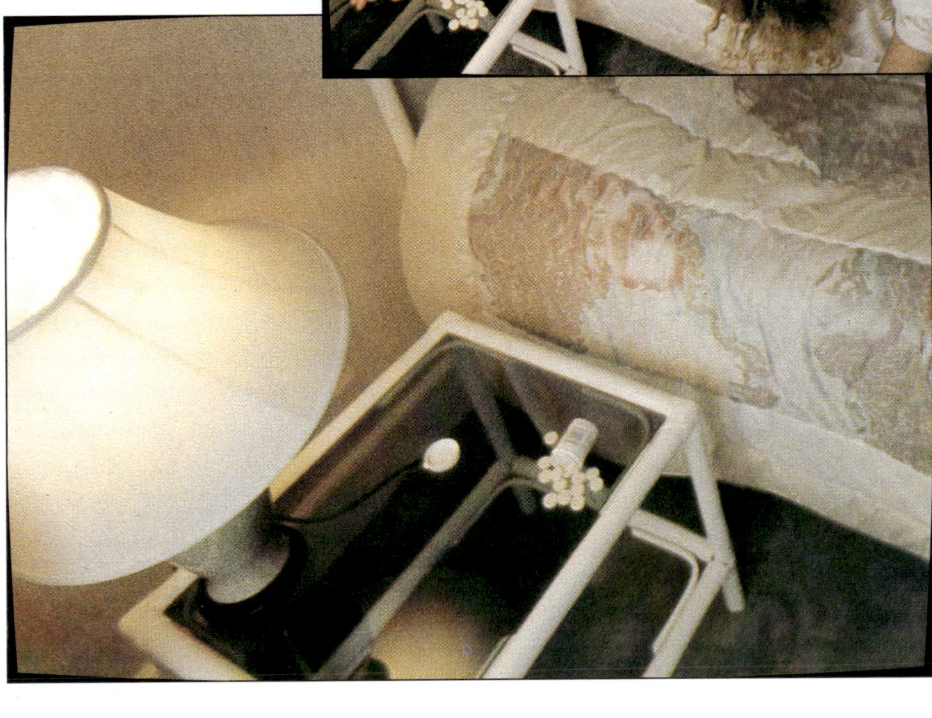

5: *Another quick cut to the pills on the table confirms our fears. As the camera dwells on this shot, we wonder whether the girl is alive or not – this time, suspense is increased by the lack of action.*

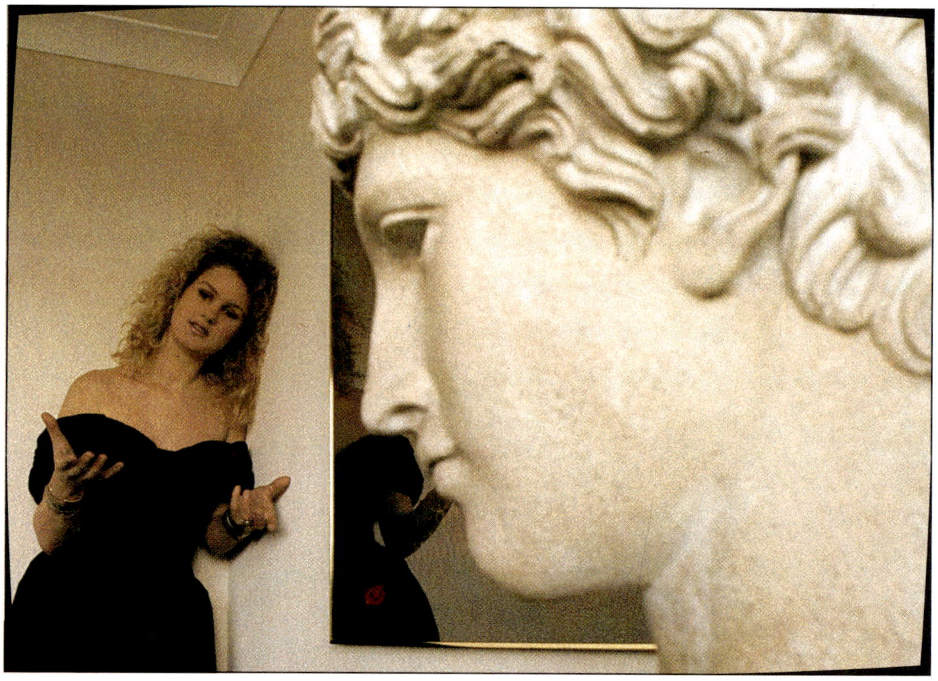

1: *This is a good example of a telling juxtaposition. The girl is tense, but the repose of the classical sculpture seems to make her even tenser by contrast. This is part of a sequence in which the girl moves towards the mirror and the camera crabs slightly to reveal her reflection – another way of underlining the strength of her mood.*

ADDITIONAL COVERAGE

When you are filming the tense action of this type of story, it is all too tempting to dwell on the characters themselves – they are, after all, the main subject and you are producing a film about their relationship. But a video that consisted solely of mid-shots of the characters would soon get boring. As you go along, look out for telling details and small pieces of action that allow you to use your technique to make some sort of comment about what is going on – details of their home that might tell us something about their past, or close-ups at tense points in the drama. You may end up with some isolated shots that you do not actually use, but experimenting will usually provide something that is worth keeping. Even if you are concentrating on isolated shots, bear in mind the potential for intercutting later. For example, a shot of something that reminds us of a character's happy past will be given an extra ironic twist when cut into a sequence about his unhappy present life. Above all, be observant, and do not be afraid to shoot too much material.

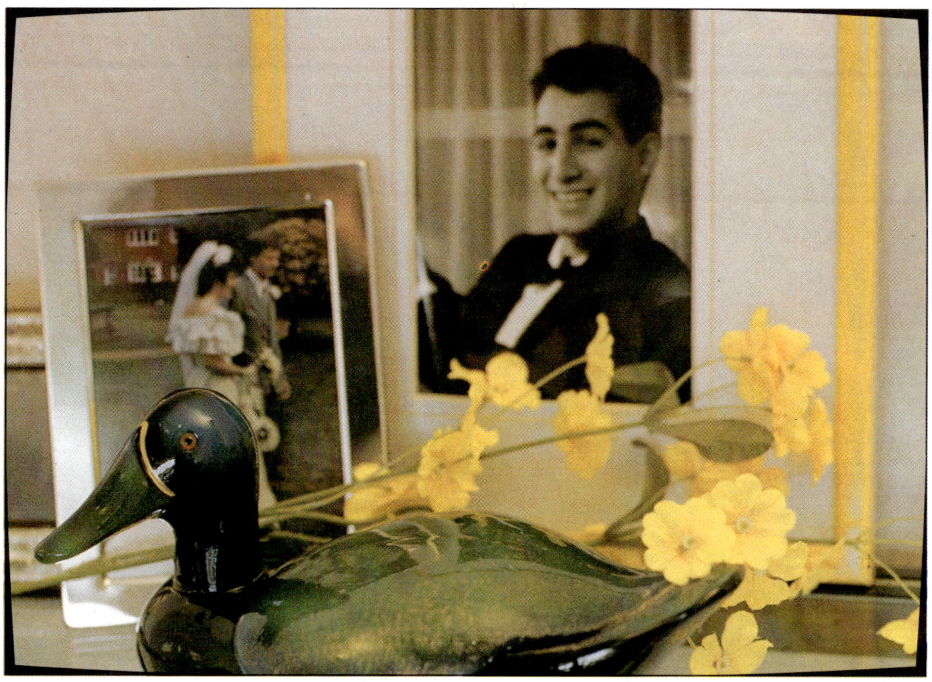

2: *Images from the past can have a powerful effect. Here, relaxed photographs create an ironic backdrop to the turbulent life that makes up the subject of most of the video.*

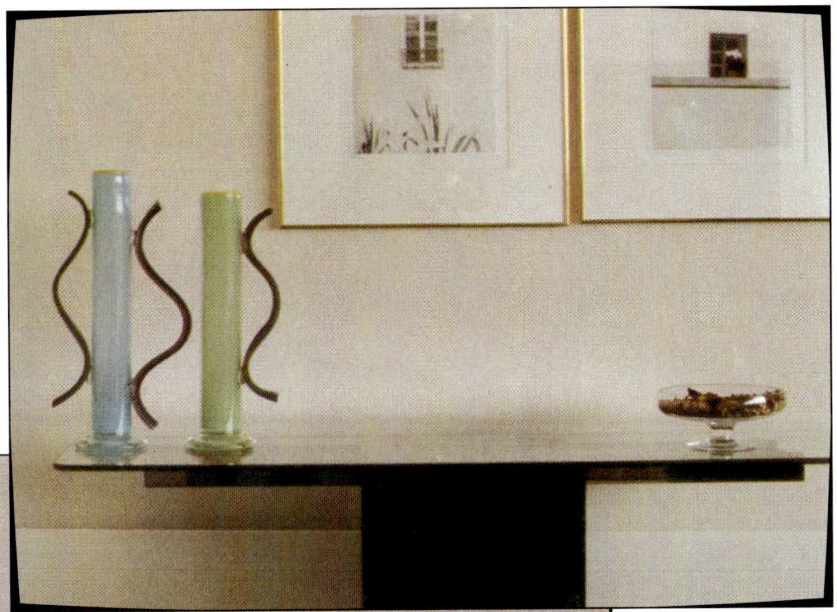

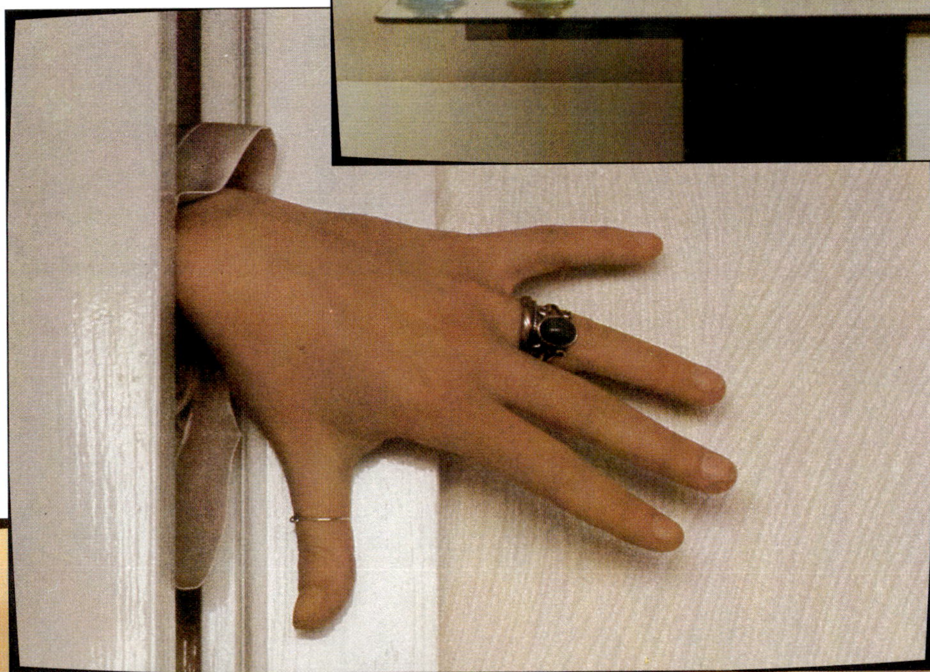

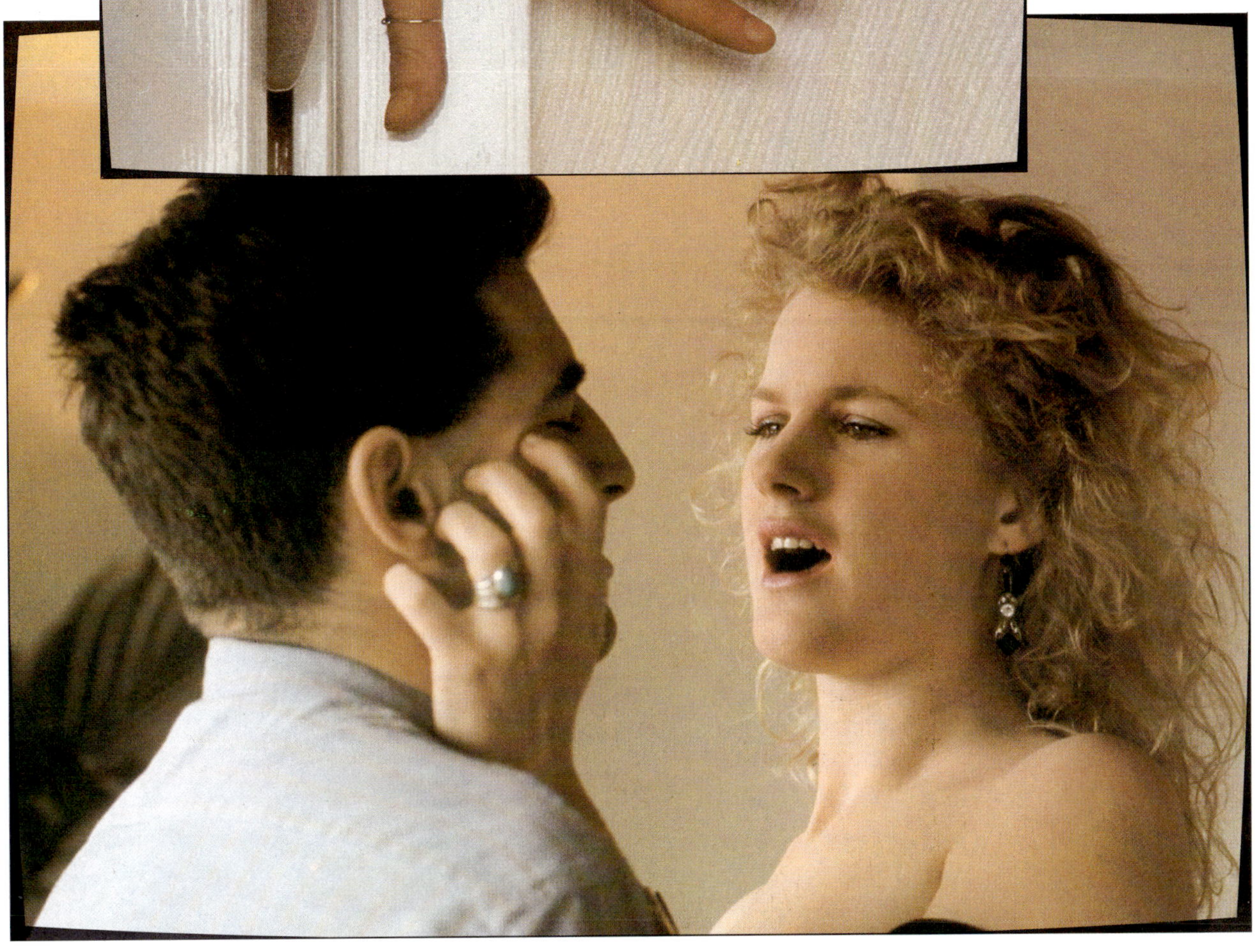

3-5: *In this sequence details provide tension and ambiguity right up to the last second. The quiet apartment, the approaching hand, and then the two figures – but it is a moment before we can decide whether the outcome will be a fight or a passionate embrace.*

The art of viewing lies in maintaining the illusion that the image on the screen is a part of reality. Any mistake you make in continuity (the consistency of details from one scene to the next) will be picked up by the audience, and the illusion will be destroyed. Continuity is most obviously lost when aspects of the actors' costumes change unaccountably between shots, or a prop is moved between scenes for no apparent reason. The only guarantee of maintaining continuity is meticulous attention to detail. If, in a previous shot, an actress is shown wearing shoes, she must not be shown barefooted in the following shot. An ashtray that was overflowing at the beginning shouldn't be pristine later on. In general, try to avoid situations that might give rise to continuity problems – if there is no reason for your characters to smoke, don't have them smoking. No matter how small the detail, the audience *will* notice. To ensure that props are not touched, declare the shooting area a total no-go area when shooting is not in progress.

In professional video someone is usually delegated to check for elements of continuity. You will probably have to do the job yourself. A good practice, particularly if there has been a long break in shooting, is to review the preceding shot before setting up the new one. Attention to continuity will at least ensure that you consider composition too.

CONTINUITY

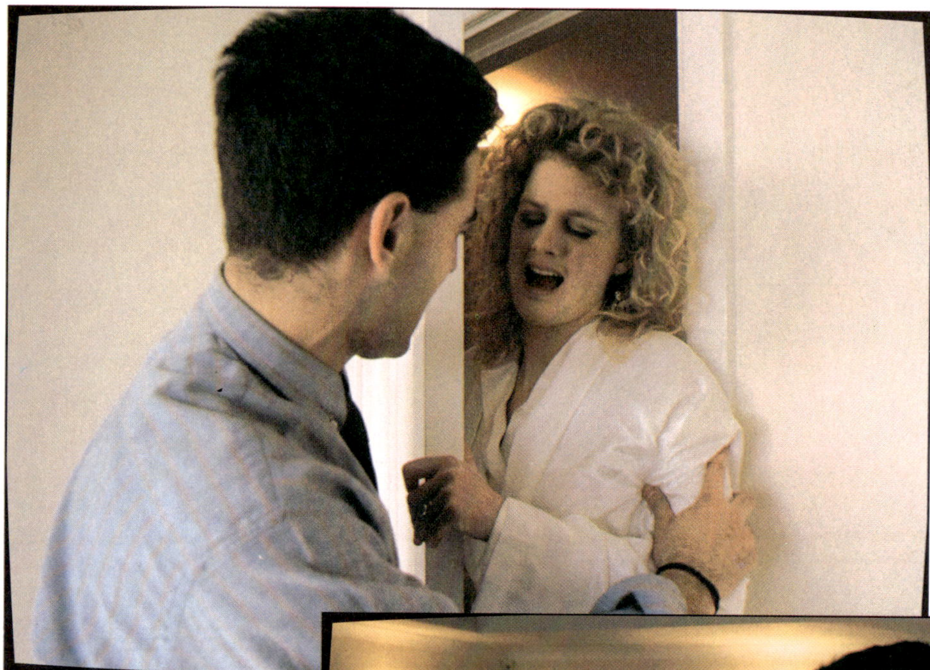

1: *As well as the girl's mood, we notice minor details such as the fact she is still wearing her dressing gown when the man arrives.*

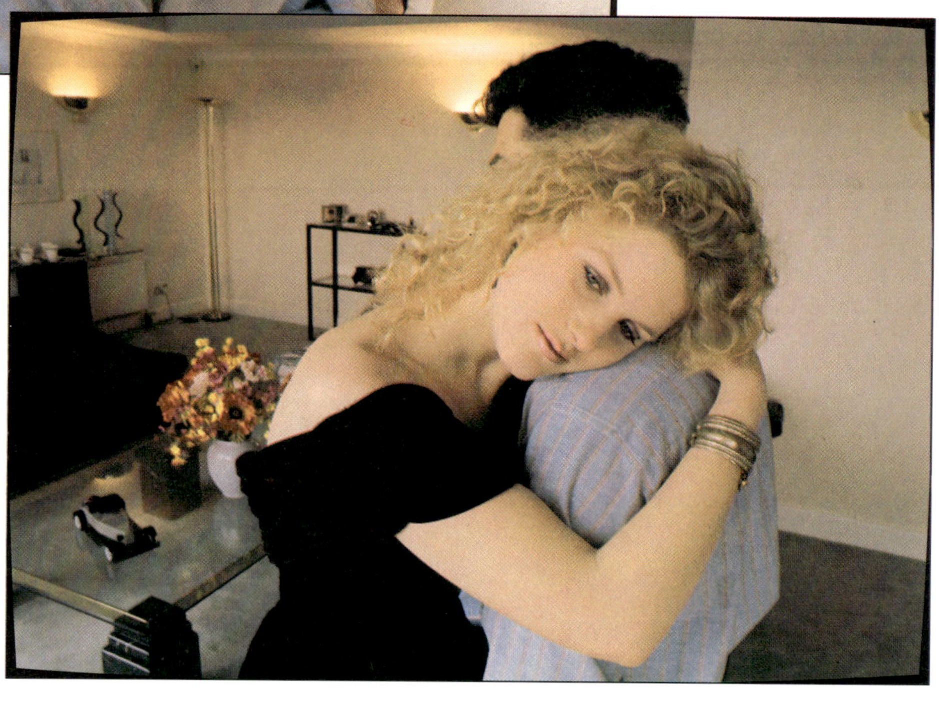

2: *A cut to the reconciliation scene, with the girl fully dressed, signals to the audience that some time has passed since the last shot.*

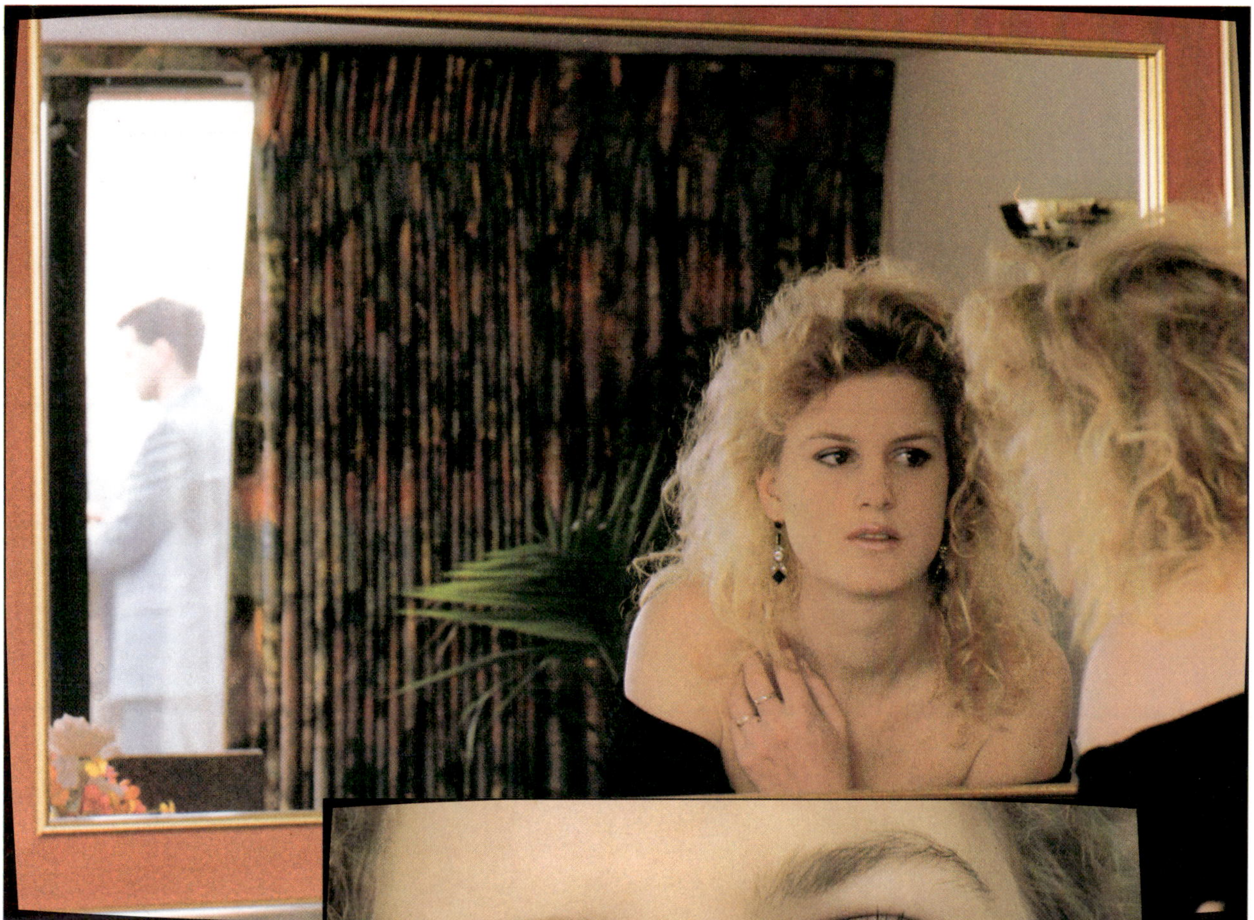

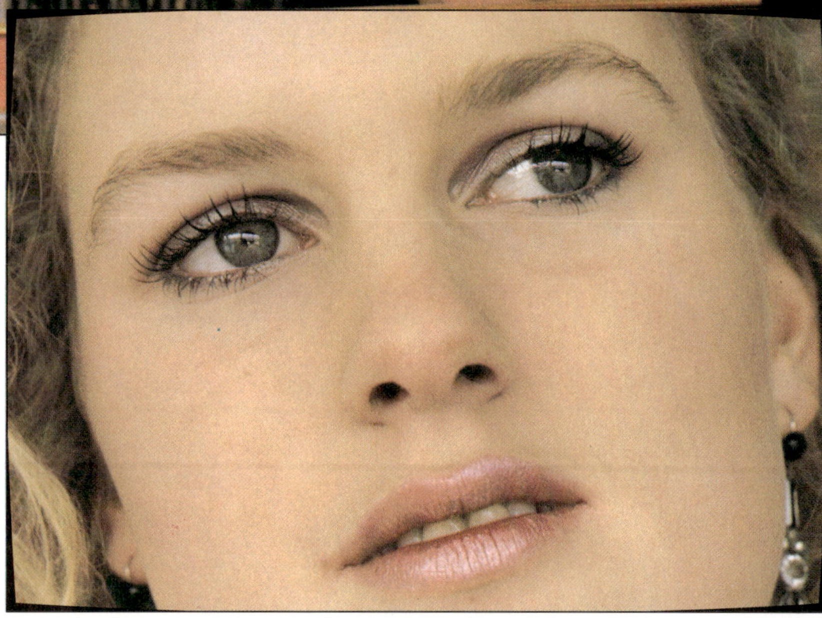

3.4: *A brief glimpse of the man leaving shows him wearing a jacket now. Even this tiny error of continuity before the cut to extreme close-up will attract the audience's attention.*

5-6: *Intercutting between shots of the girl wearing two different outfits will also confuse the viewer.*

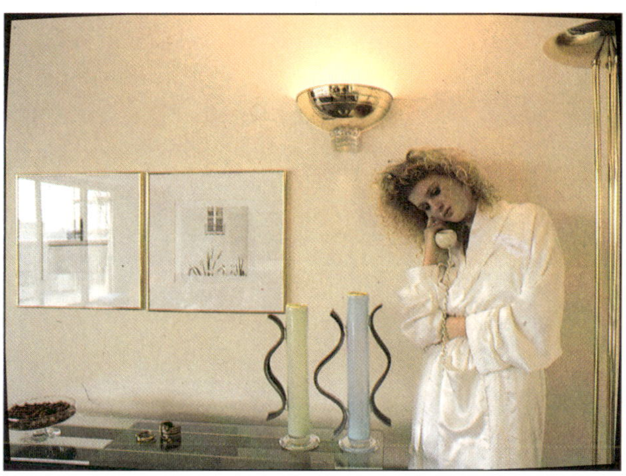

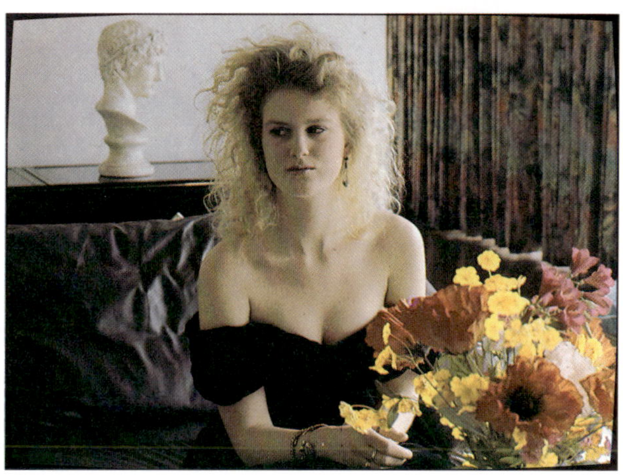

PROJECT NOTEBOOK

DRAMA

Drama is the glamorous end of video making – everyone wants to be Stephen Spielberg. But even with limited resources and a budget that consists of little more than the change in your pocket you can create an interesting, absorbing product. The first requirement is a script that works: it must be ingenious enough to have inherent interest, but it must also be conceived within the limitations to which you are working. The video-maker's job is to translate the words on the page into images on the screen in the most effective way.

■ Finding a good location is half the battle – it is easier to be spooky in an old churchyard that it is in a supermarket.

■ In drama, particularly suspense drama, it is essential that as soon as the audience has been given the answer to one narrative question, another is posed.

■ Pacing the plot is everything.

■ Obscure and unusual camera angles *do* add a disturbing sense to the image on the screen, but, used too often, they simply antagonize the audience and lose their effect. Be selective about their use.

■ The audience must believe that what they are watching is real. Simple continuity errors destroy the conspiracy between you and the audience.

■ Select camera angles and movements before you begin to shoot. Let the action happen in front of the lens, don't chase it.

■ An imaginative use of simple props and set decorations can add greatly to the effectiveness of the video.

SHOOTING ACTION

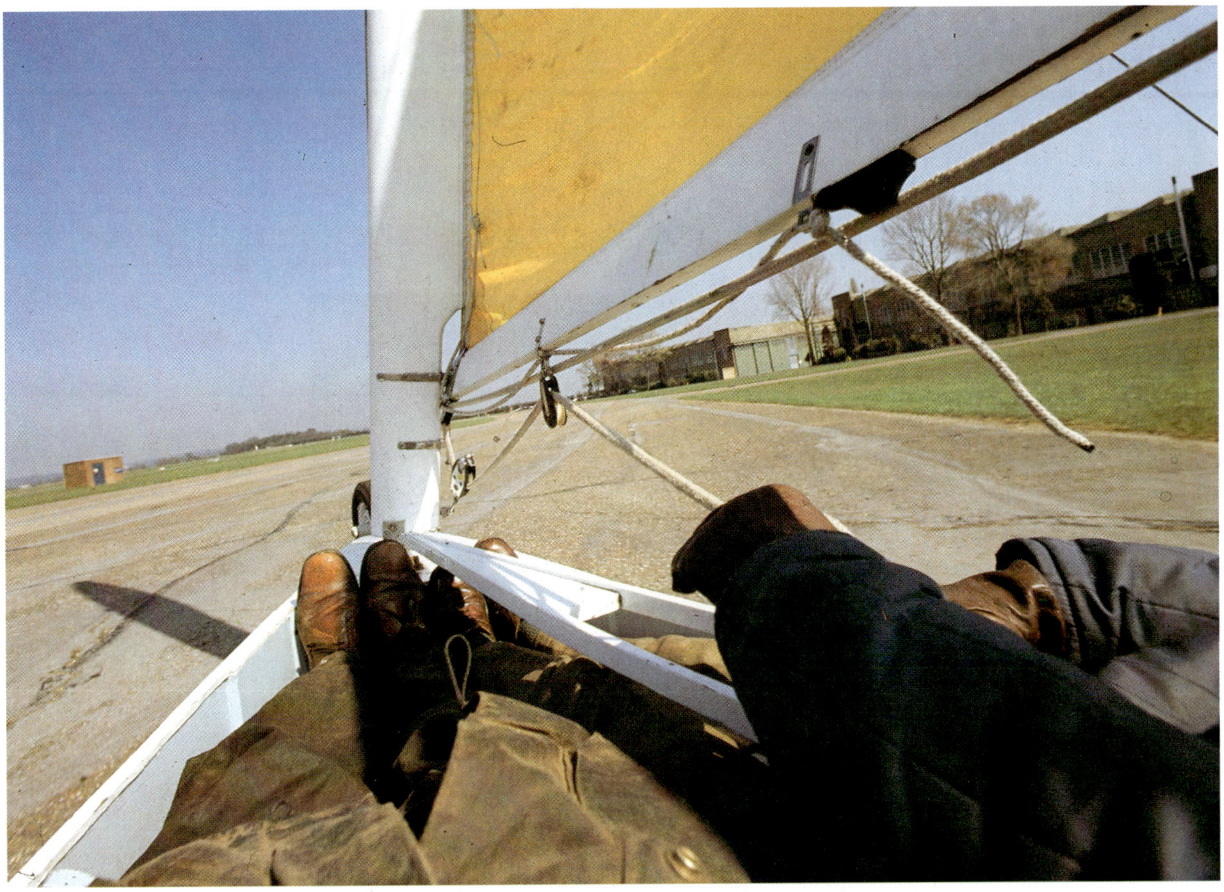

Video recordings of sports events demand particular techniques because the action being captured often happens at high speed, or at a distance. In addition, each kind of sport demands its own individual approach. Baseball, for instance, can be shot from one or two static camera positions, whereas golf demands far greater mobility for full coverage.

This chapter examines these various considerations, taking in camera positions and shooting techniques for field and track sports. It also provides invaluable suggestions for extending and applying these techniques to other kinds of video work, and looks at the preparations you should make before going on an 'action' shoot.

In sports where the action is channelled once only along a set course, you must ensure that you get the right shot first time. If you fail, there's no second chance. You must therefore put a great deal of effort into visualizing the event in the preceding days, so that there is no chance whatsoever of your being unprepared. You should also try to envisage how the action may not go according to plan, so that you are ready to tackle the unexpected. The last thing you want is to be incorrectly positioned at a highly dramatic moment.

This video of white-water canoeing reveals ways of ensuring that you overcome any problems that might prevent you from filming one-chance action, and also how to tackle many extra considerations.

Practical considerations

The first problem was deciding where best to film from because the river banks were covered in thick undergrowth. Eventually, after much thought, four fixed points were chosen: the start; a bridge over a straight section of river; a bend near the road; and the finishing point, 1 mile (1.6km) downstream. Although the canoeists moved fast, test runs revealed that manual focusing gave a better result than the autofocus because it was too easily confused by other foreground objects, including heavy spray hanging in the air.

ONE-CHANCE ACTION

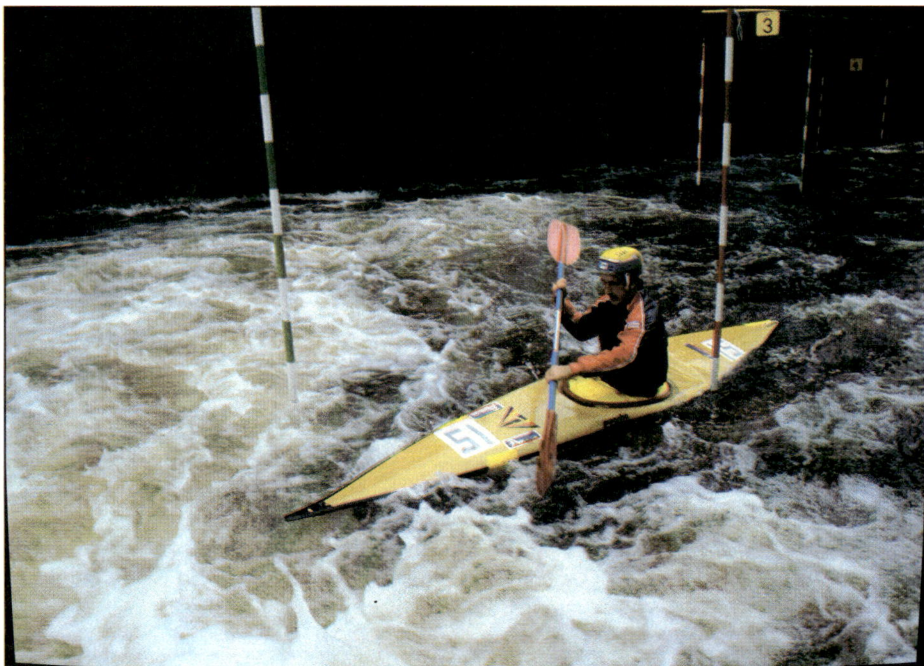

1-2: *High-speed slaloming between upright poles in turbulent water is one of the main skills of this sport. The most advantageous camera position for capturing this particular moment was by a river bend. As the conoeists hold their position while manoeuvring between the poles, it's possible to obtain good close-up shots using the zoom.*

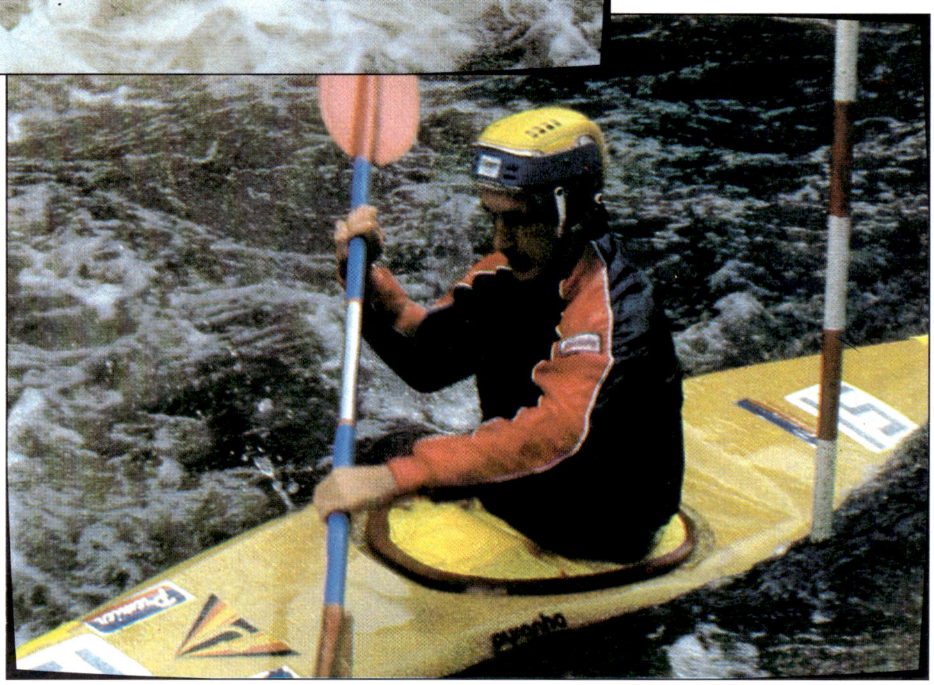

Checklist

☐ Study the map for good vantage points for shooting.

☐ Check that access to these positions is readily available.

☐ Establish the significant points of action in the event.

☐ Time how long it takes to get from one location to another.

☐ Make sure you have spare batteries and tapes.

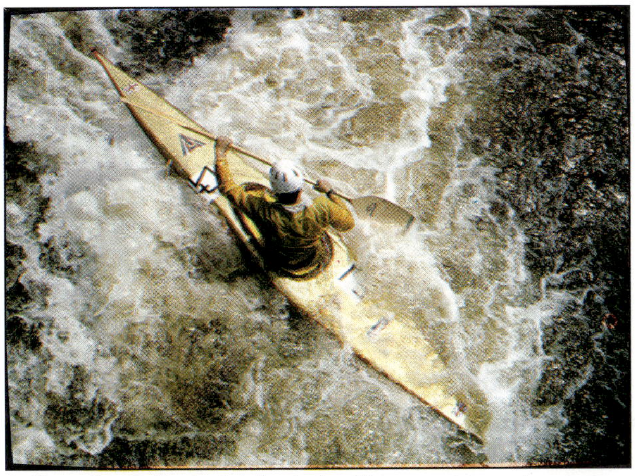

3: *For a dramatic start, take shots of the canoeists racing away from you.*

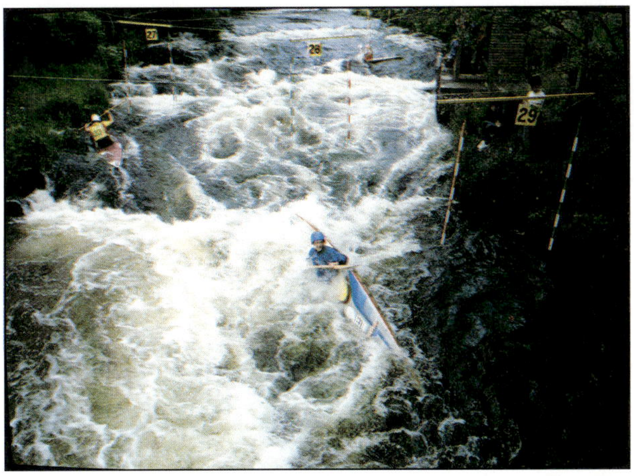

4: *The following sequences, shot from the road bridge, begin with the canoeists approaching the camera 'head on'. The shot begins at the telephoto end of the zoom lens and is 'held' as the canoeists approach. As they move between areas of deep shade and the brighter parts of the river, the autoexposure takes a few seconds to adjust to the new lighting conditions.*

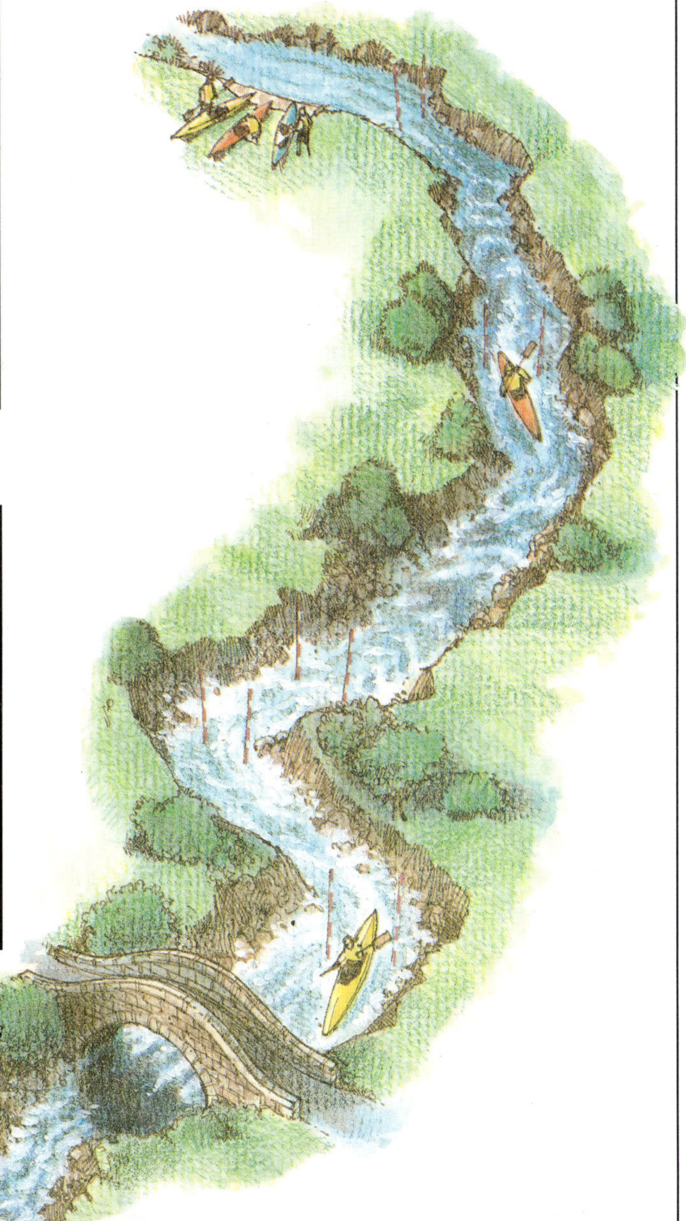

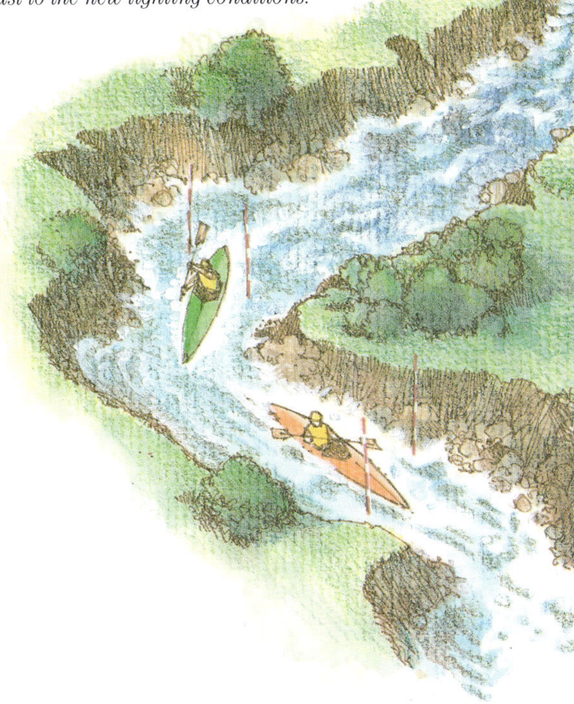

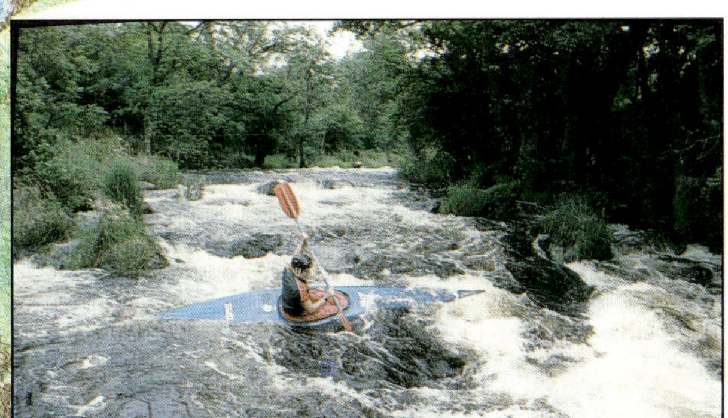

5: *Filming the end of any sporting event is vital. Here the camera position enables you to film the canoeists approaching the 'line', before panning to show each contestant crossing the finish. Since the pan should be quick, reflecting the speed of the event, you should be close to the action for a relatively small camera movement.*

1: *American football is one of the most thrilling and colourful of sports. This shot was taken from the sidelines, about one-third of the way down the pitch. From this angle, you get a sense of immediacy, but much of the pattern of play may be obscured by the players.*

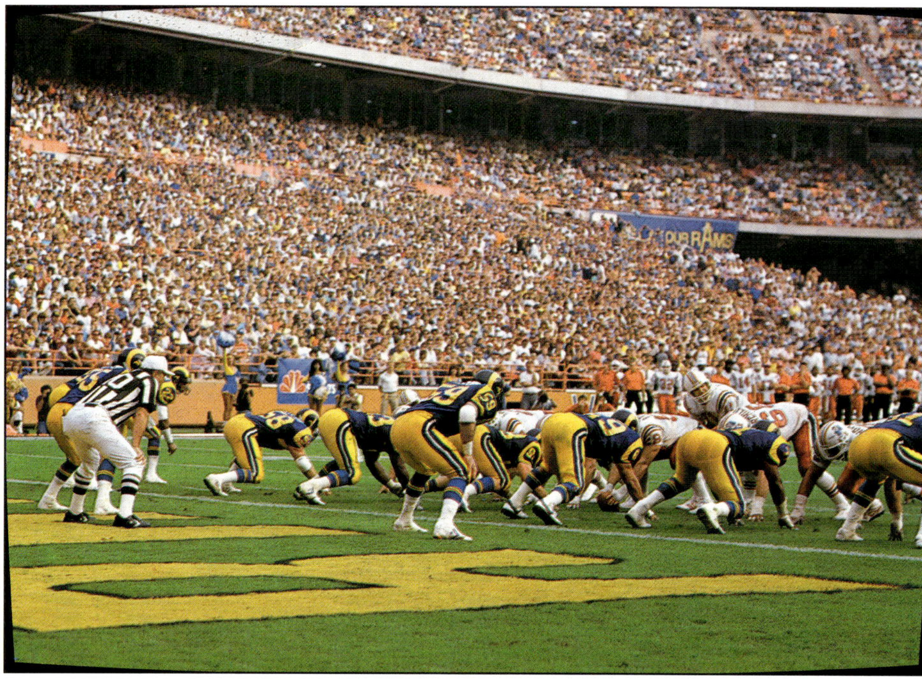

PITCH AND COURT COVERAGE

Sports events such as tennis, American football and basketball, which take place on a court or field, present different problems to the video-maker. Such games are distinguished by there being opposing players or teams in which the *direction* of play is important, so creating problems to the video-maker of 'crossing the line'. Fortunately, though, the action occurs in a fixed arena, so the camera positions can avoid this problem.

There are two basic camera positions (where you will need to use a tripod) for covering such events: side-on to the play, and behind it. These positions will provide full coverage of what is happening. If you use more than two positions the viewer is liable to lose a coherent sense of space and direction.

However, if you are only going to record snatches of play, you can adopt extra camera positions, so enabling you to show, for example, 10 minutes recorded from the centre of the right-hand touch-line, followed by another sequence from behind the goal-line. But remember that if you move from the right side of the court to the left, you will effectively change the direction of play on screen. Such a change of shot would confuse the viewer hopelessly, particularly since in field and court sports players often change sides periodically through the game.

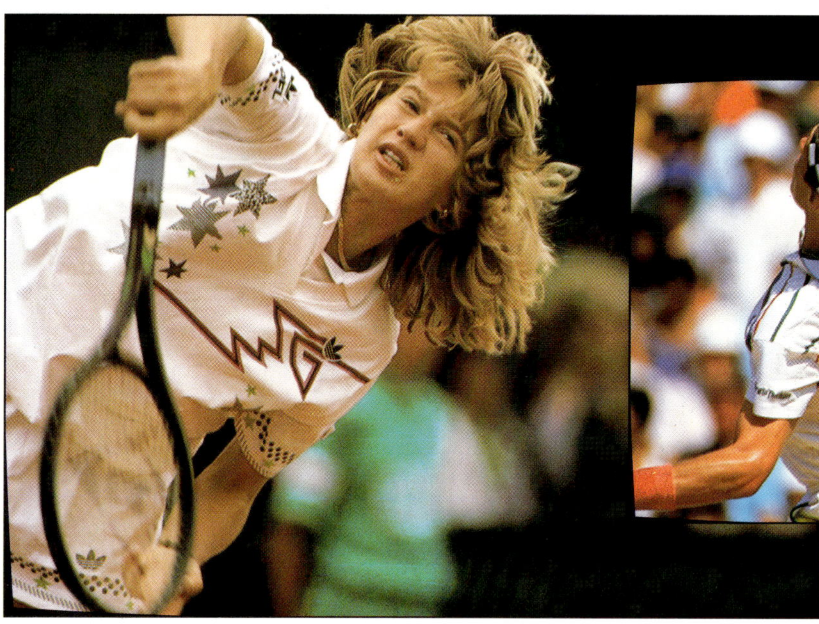

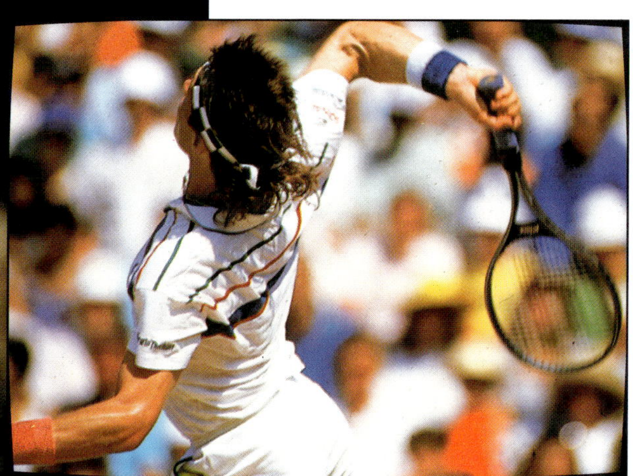

2-3: *The tennis court is on a smaller scale than a football pitch, and so you will be more able to get close-ups of the players.*

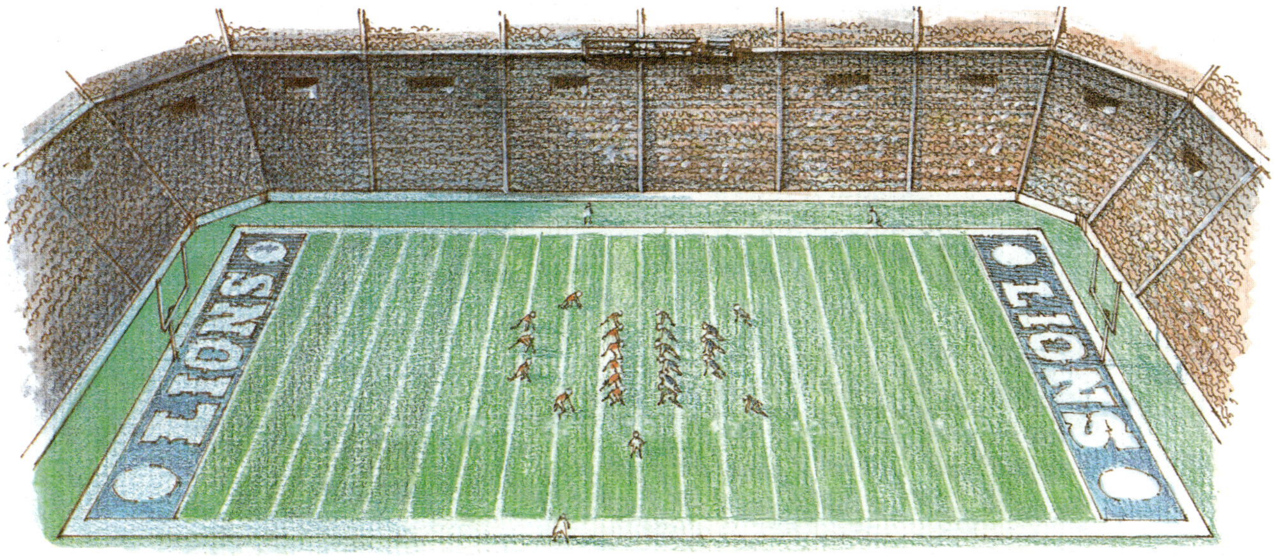

Camera position 3, *allows you to get good shots of action along the sidelines and in the deep zone.*

Camera position 1, *on the half-way line, allows good overall coverage and is ideally placed for the kick-off and for general, wide-angle shots showing mid-field play.*

Camera position 2, *behind the goal, will give good coverage of goal shots and attacking play in the mid-field. Don't forget to turn and record the spectators' excitement.*

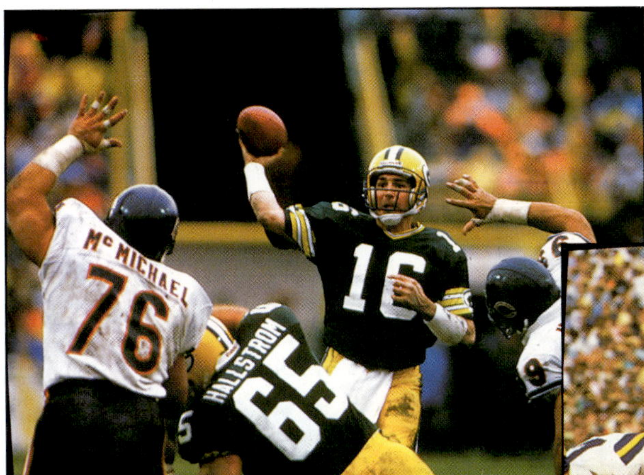

4: *A head-on shot of the quarterback about to make a play. The shot was taken from position 2, using the telephoto end of the zoom – notice the compressed background.*

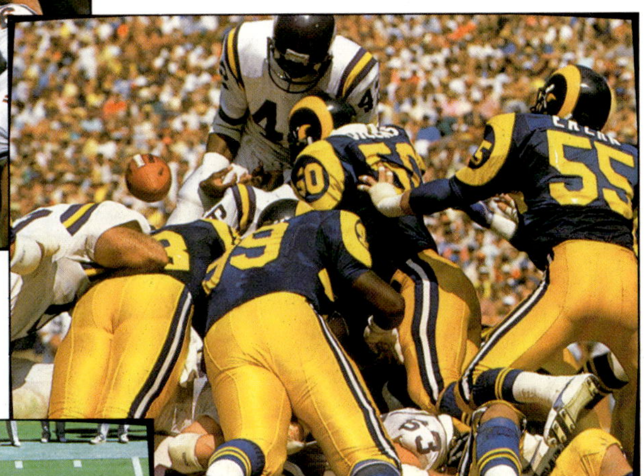

5: *A zoom-in shot taken from position 3 when the action was on the same side of the pitch as the camera.*

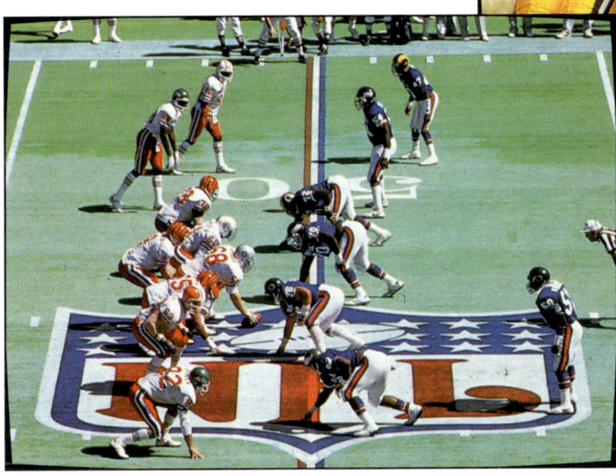

6: *This shot was taken from the half-way line, but from a raised position in the stand. This gives a better overall view of the game than a similar shot taken from pitch level.*

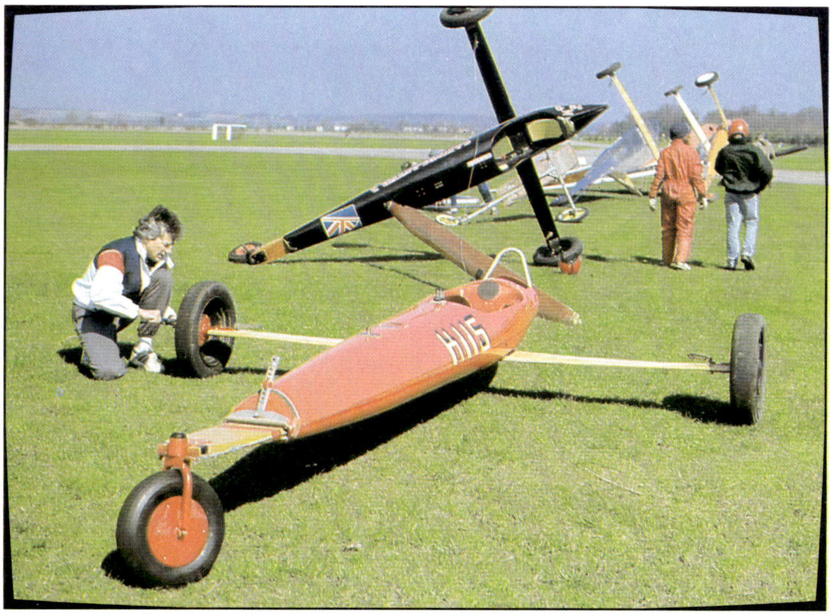

1-2: *The opening sequence shows the land-yachts and the competitors preparing their vehicles for the race. This gives the opportunity for some dramatic shots of the land-yachts outlined against the sky.*

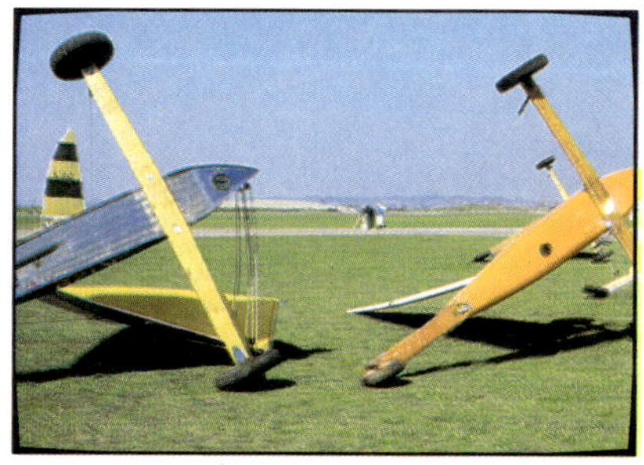

SETTING THE SCENE

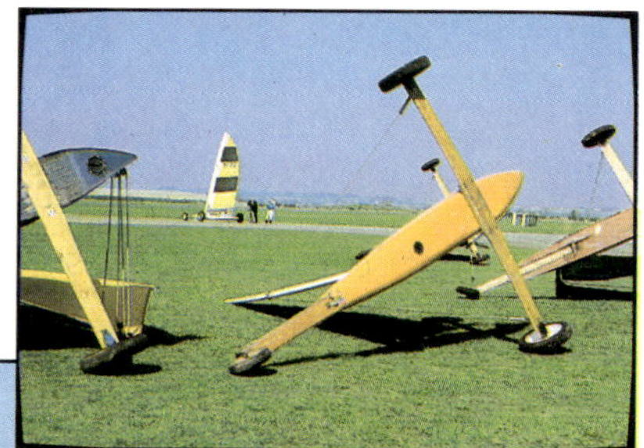

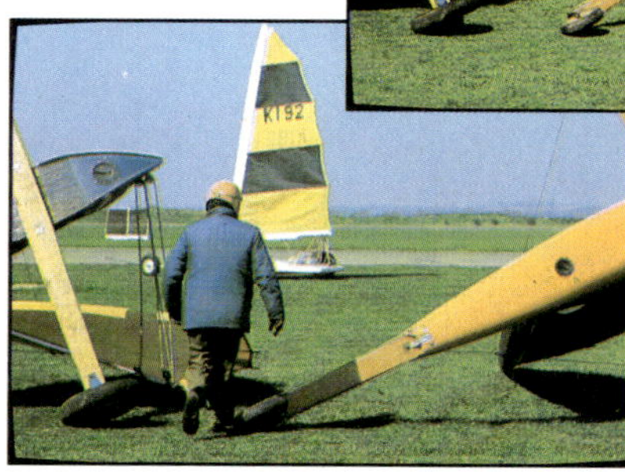

3-4: *This is succeeded by shots of the vehicles moving out on to the track for practice runs.*

Checklist

- ☐ Establish who are the competitors, and ask them to talk about their sport.
- ☐ Film the full range of preparations (including checking the yacht and examining the course) before the event begins.
- ☐ Decide on which aspects of the sport you wish to concentrate, and plan your camera positions accordingly.

With unfamiliar sports and activities, it is important to introduce the audience to the nature of the event so that they are not totally lost. A video of people engaged in an apparently pointless activity is not going to hold their interest for too long!

The coverage on this spread is taken from a video of a land-yachting meeeting. The film begins with an interesting section on land-yachts being constructed by the competitors. The early part of the meeting and film therefore features the assembly of and final checks to these vehicles. Shots of the competitors talking and exchanging jokes as they fine tune their machines contribute to a lively opening sequence.

These sequences are also useful for introducing the principles of the sport. The sound commentary allows the competitors to explain that they race against each other and the clock, increasing speed by skilfully tacking with the wind in the same way as do nautical yachtsmen. The event takes place on the runways of a small airfield, where the prevailing wind conditions enable competitors to reach top speeds in excess of 40mph.

Another bonus of this early coverage is that it provides an opportunity to feature selected competitors. This gives the sequence a focus, and provides subsequent sequences of the race with extra dramatic impact as viewers follow the competitors' progress. But while setting the scene is a vital part of the film, do not dwell on it for too long. After all, the video you are making is one of a land-yachting *race*, not a documentary about the lives and thoughts of land-yachting devotees.

Since the coverage should be paced to give a sense of the build-up to the race, it's a good idea to interview some of the contestants, asking them how they rate their chances? how nervous they feel? who they think are their main rivals? and so on.

The more you can inject a sense of the anxieties and hopes of the participants, the more the audience will watch the video in these terms, waiting to see whether their aspirations are fulfilled, or their fears confirmed. In other words, the race should be converted into a human drama. Without this element, you are dependent on an exciting race with a close finish which may not necessarily happen.

This sequence could conclude with shots of competitors putting on their crash helmets and climbing into their yachts to indicate that the race is about to begin.

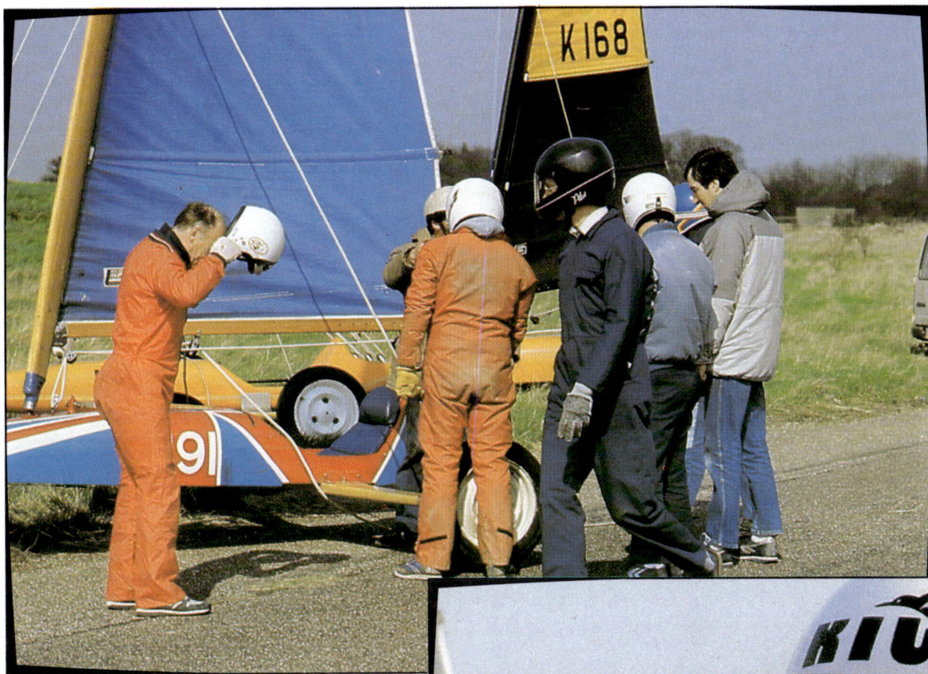

5: *A second short sequence shows the land-yachtsmen grouping by the starting line. Their light bantering as they get ready for the race reinforces the sense of camaraderie and friendly rivalry.*

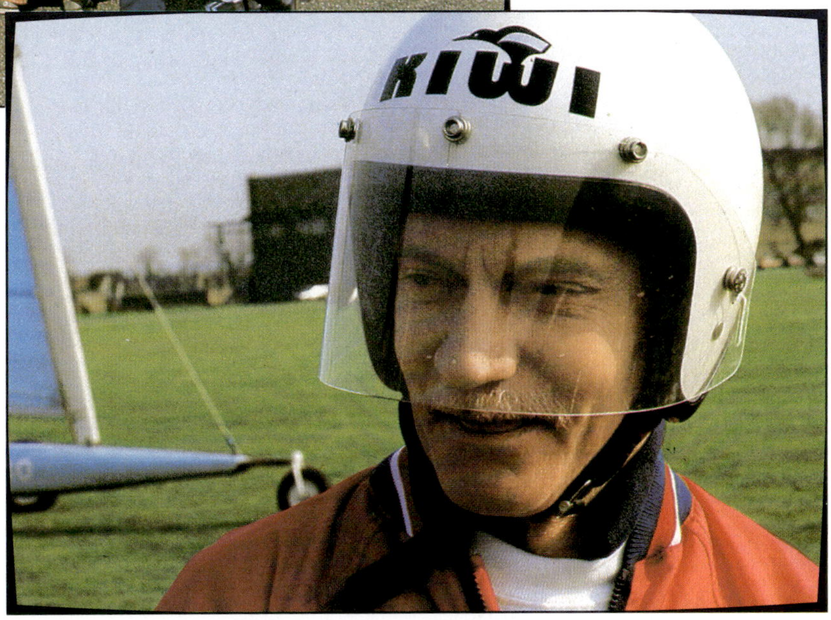

6: *The camera moved in to isolate and identify individuals and their yachts, so that the viewer can follow their progress during the race. If you don't manage to include the winner at this stage, it will be necessary to try to get this shot after the race.*

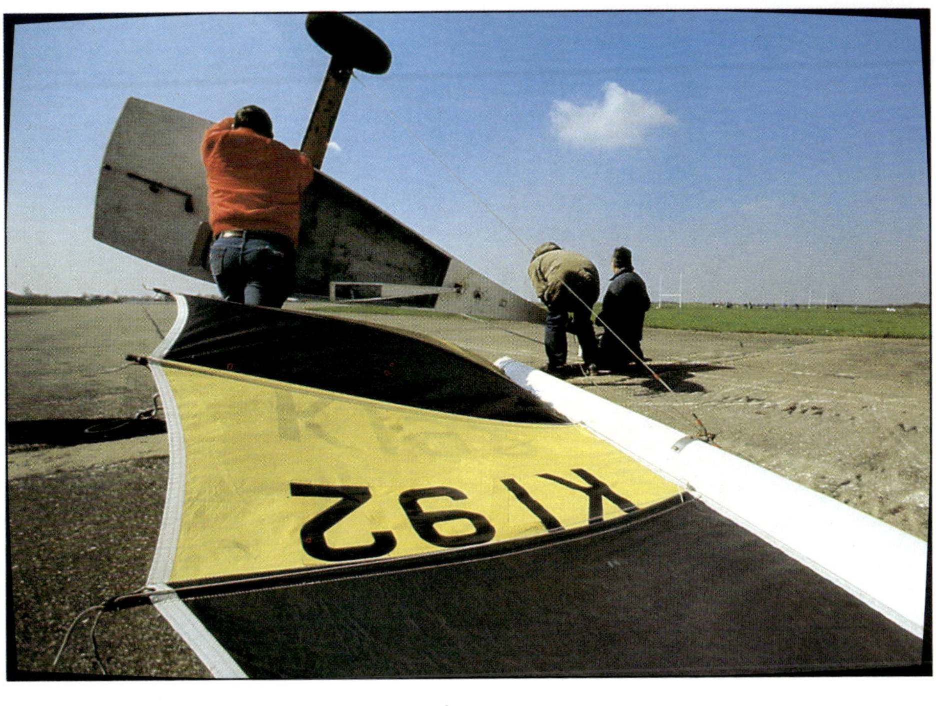

7: *When the race itself is in progress, you will have little time to think about unusual or interesting camera angles and shots. The comparatively calm moments as the competitors prepare themselves is the time when such shots are best attempted. This shot along the plane of the yacht's sail adds both visual variety and gives a good impression of scale.*

Many games have important set pieces within the course of play – for example, the service in tennis, the line-up in American football and the pitch in baseball. Since these set pieces are often the most dramatic moments of the game, a sports video should feature them, particularly if the video is only going to contain highlights.

Because the play is temporarily held up at this point, the video-maker will have extra time in which to set up the shot. This can often give you a great opportunity to get close-ups of the key players which will vary the visual pace of the video, and give a sense of individual competition.

Depending on your position, the camera may have to pan quickly to capture an exciting moment following on from a set piece, for which a smooth tripod action will be invaluable. This is particularly useful in such games as ice hockey and soccer where you need to follow fast action. As an alternative, follow the set piece using the zoom lens. But as when making any video, try to minimize sweeping camera movements as much as possible – a side-on tennis video shot which goes back and forth between the two players would soon instil a feeling approaching seasickness in the viewer. Keeping the camera still has one particular advantage – it helps give an authentic feeling that the viewer is a 'live' spectator.

SET PIECES

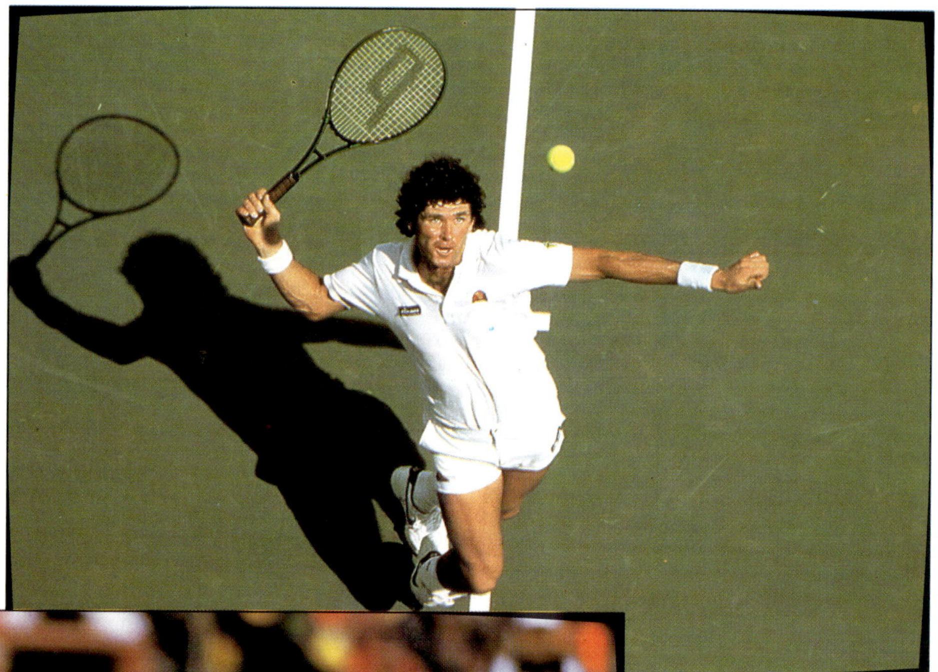

1: *In tennis, the basic set piece in the action is the serve. The player takes up position on the base line, so framing is relatively simple. This shot was taken from a high angle, slightly in front of the base line.*

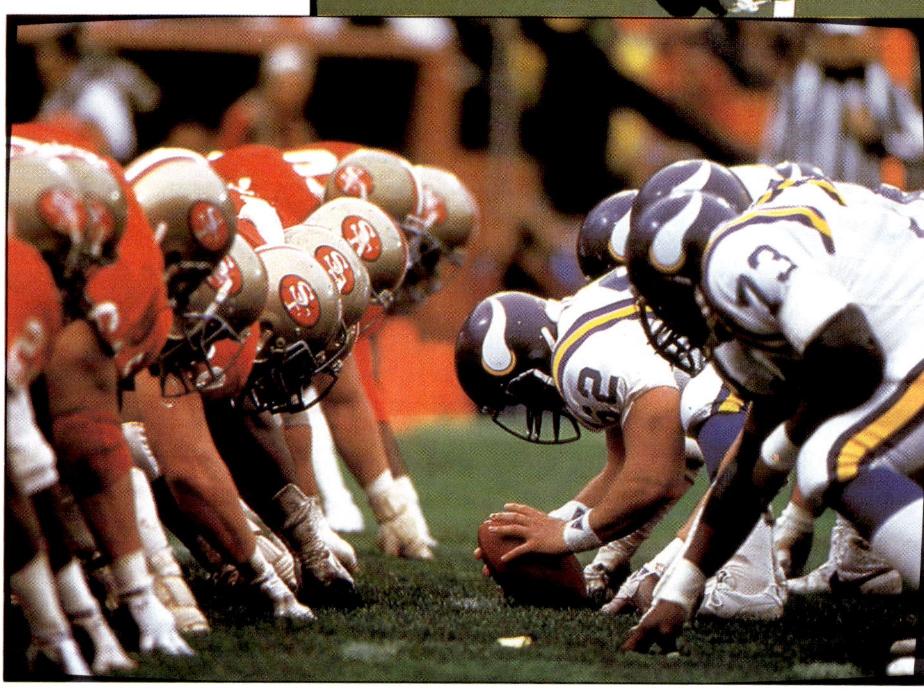

2: *American football is almost all set-piece play. At the beginning of each play, the opposing forwards line up against each other. This shot was taken from the sidelines, using the zoom, to catch the big crunch when the ball is played.*

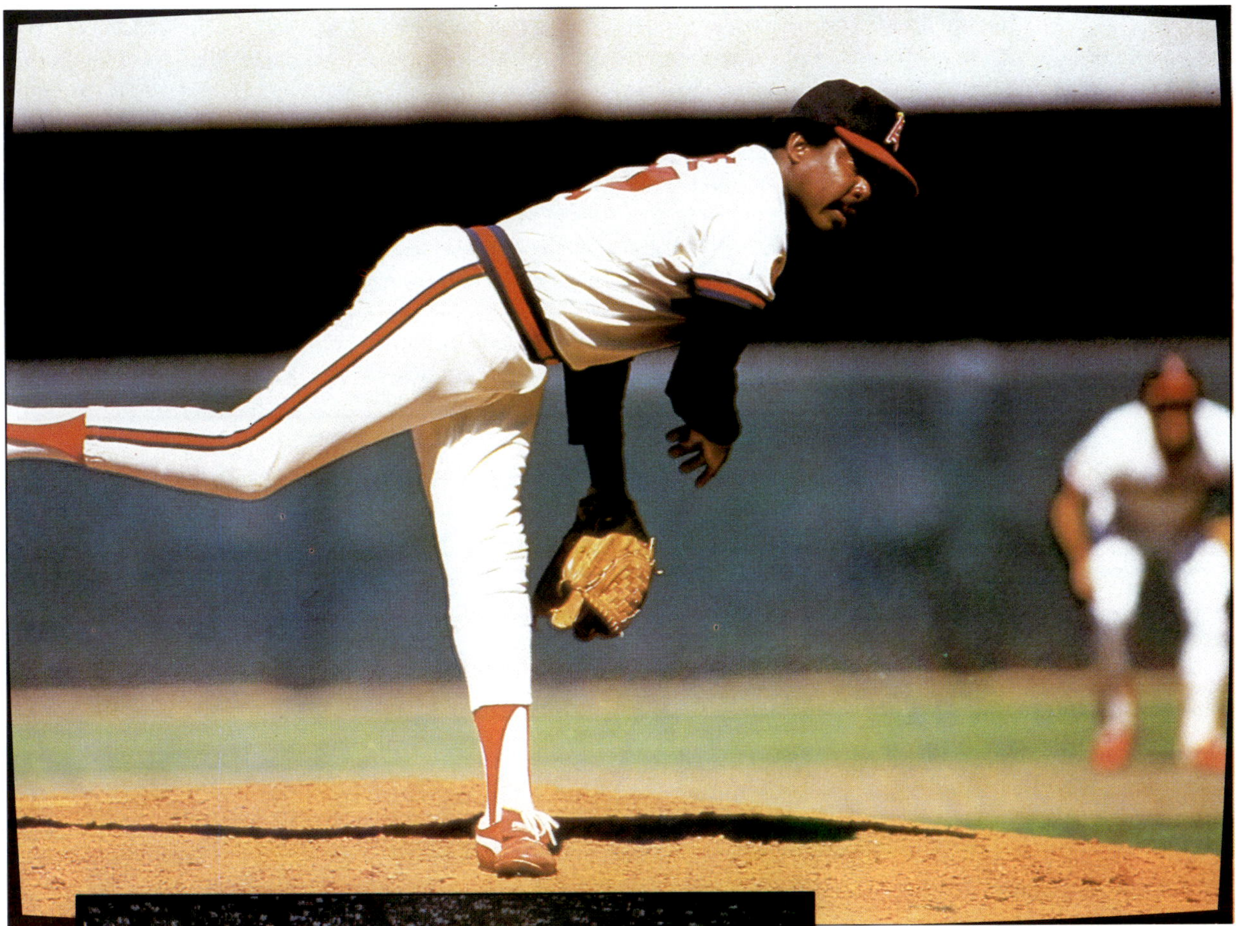

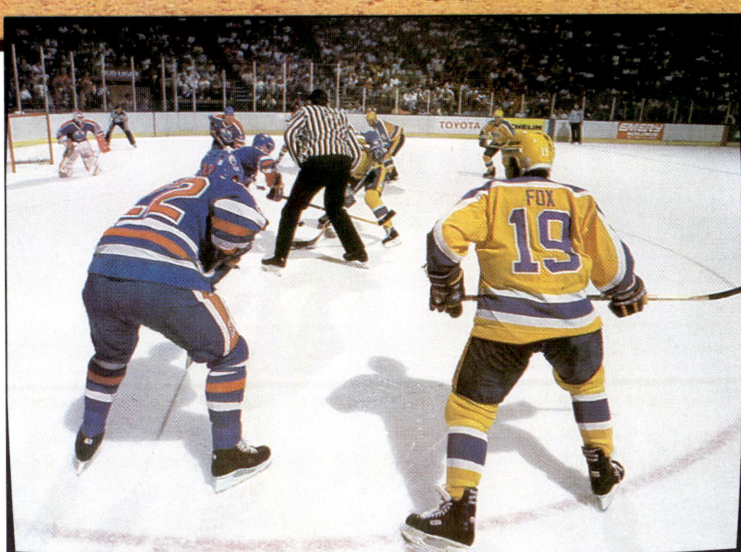

3: *Baseball is a comparatively stationary game, and hence provides good opportunities for set piece coverage. The pitcher throws from a fixed position, so it is easy to frame this action. Similarly, you could concentrate on the batsman, who also remain still while waiting for the delivery.*

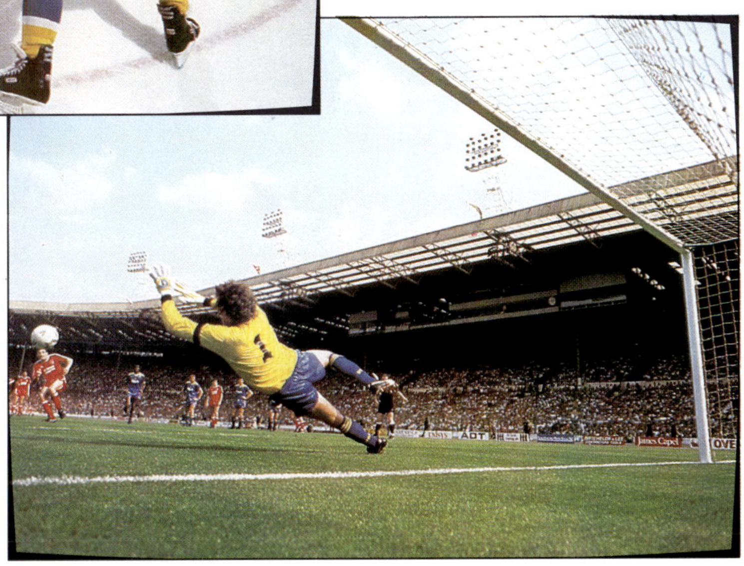

4, 5: *Ice hockey and soccer are more fluid games, so coverage must be more free-ranging. However, both contain penalty hits or kicks, and these can be treated as set pieces. These shots are perhaps best taken from behind the goal, facing the direction of the action.*

Returning to the land-yachting video, you can see that the action takes place on a track, as it does in athletic track events and in motor sport. In this case, the track is a long oval with sharp corners. Having set the scene with informal coverage of the pre-race activities, it is now necessary to decide from which parts of the track the shots of the race should be taken.

Obviously there have to be shots of the start and finish, and of the most spectacular aspects of the race. These include the land-yachts cornering at speed, and keeling over so dramatically that only two wheels hold the ground, a crash being prevented by the drivers' fine sense of balance.

The course is just 1 mile (1.6 km) long. With this kind of coverage it is important to keep a sense of direction on the screen – any apparent reversal of direction of the land-yachts caused by switching from different camera positions would ruin the coverage. When the cameras are moved, great care must therefore be taken to switch from the outside of the track on the outward circuit to the inside of the track on the opposite side.

The track layout with camera positions and some of the types of shots that can be achieved are shown here. It is actually worth drawing a sketch or map of the track to work out your camera positions in advance of the day of the shoot itself.

TRACK AND CIRCUIT ACTION

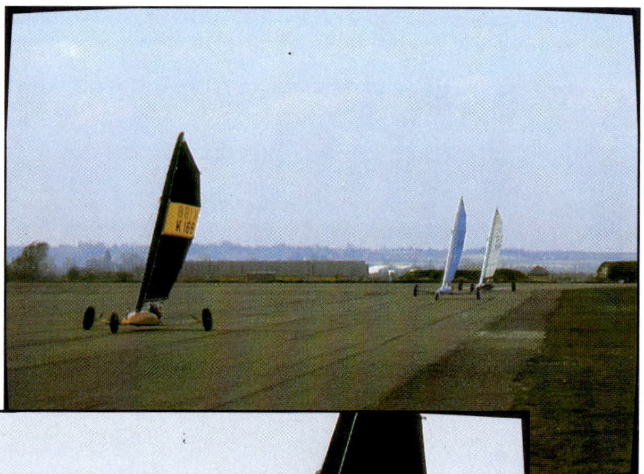

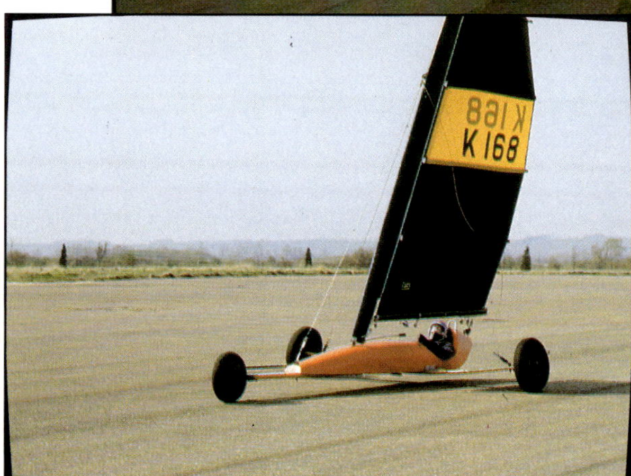

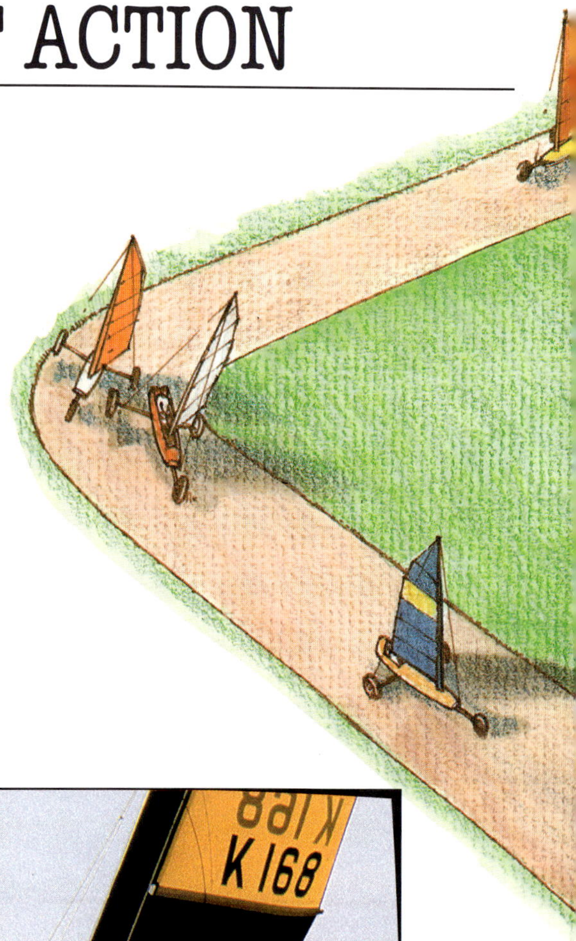

1-2: *The position at the top corner of the track provides good, almost head-on coverage of the yachts gathering speed down the straight.*

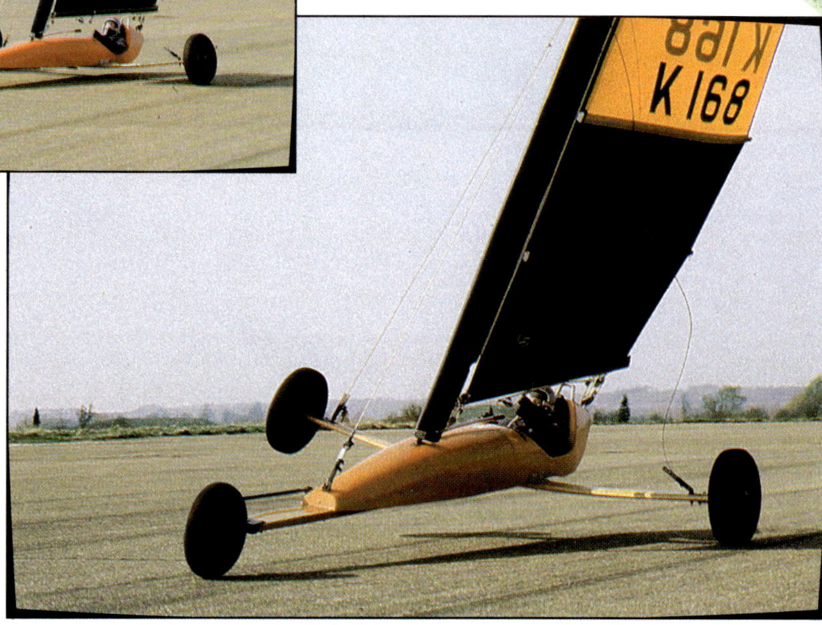

3: *A position close to the first bend produces exciting shots of the yachts doing 'wheelies'. Although the vehicles appear to be on the point of going out of control, there are no major upsets.*

5: *By taking up a filming position at the far end of the circuit, you will obtain excellent film of the land-yachts racing down the home straight.*

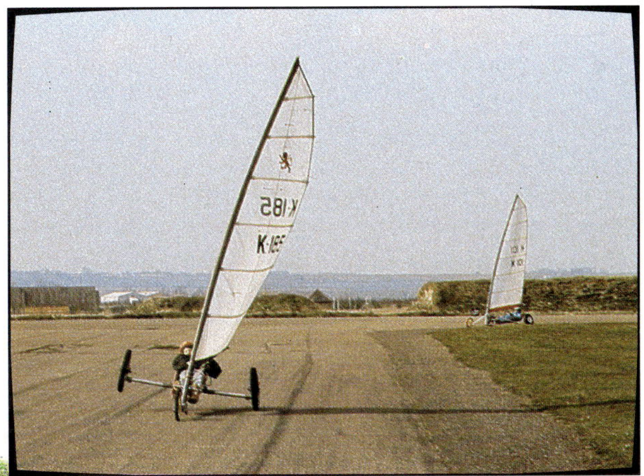

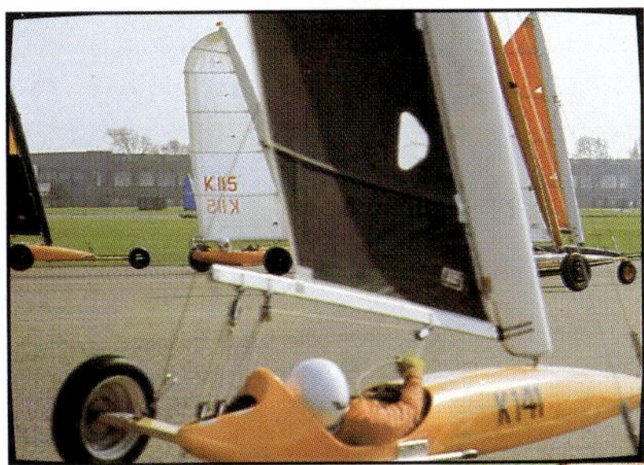

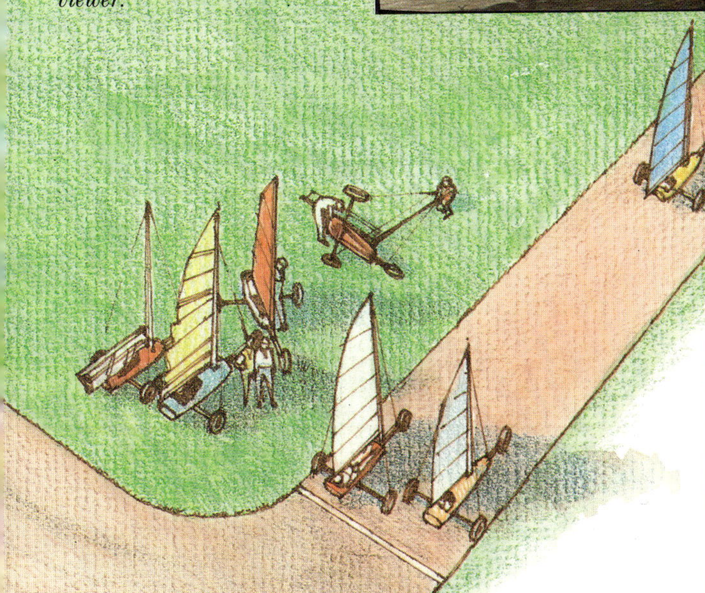

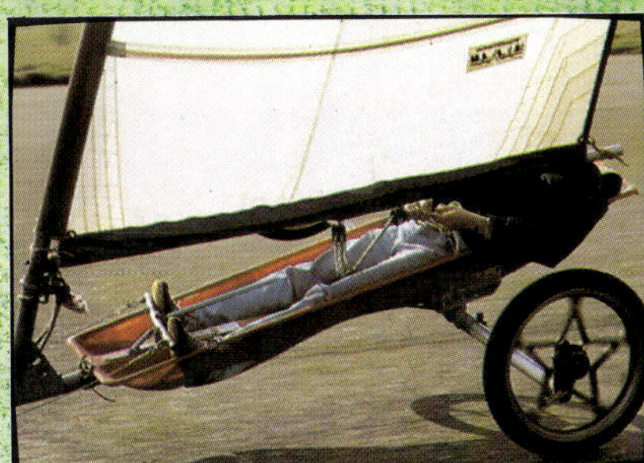

4 and 6: *For variety of coverage consider taking good close-up, square-on action shots. They will also convey a real sense of speed to the viewer.*

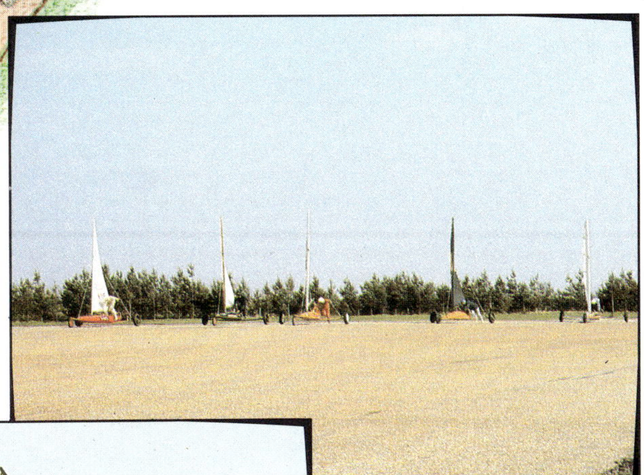

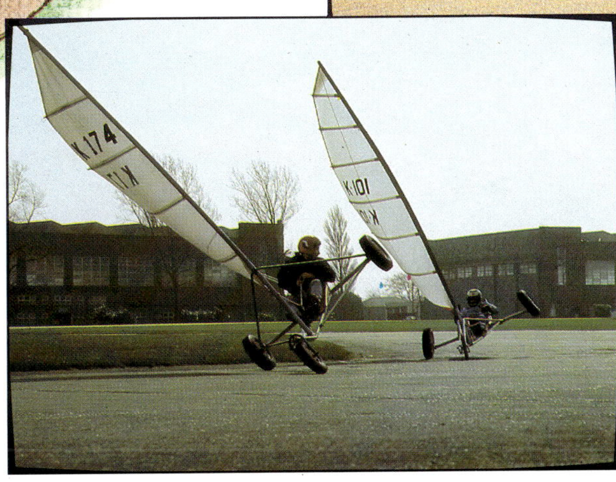

7: *A good, almost head-on shot for the start of the race, when the yachts are tacking backwards and forwards. Crisscrossing in this way enables the yachts to take full advantage of the prevailing wind. This particular shot will be held until the yachts are so near that they are almost in close-up.*

8: *The following shot, taken one lap later, can be filmed in one of two ways. The method used here allows the yacht to approach the bend and then move around it out of camera as the other competitors approach. The alternative is to track a particular yacht around the bend, letting the others move into view.*

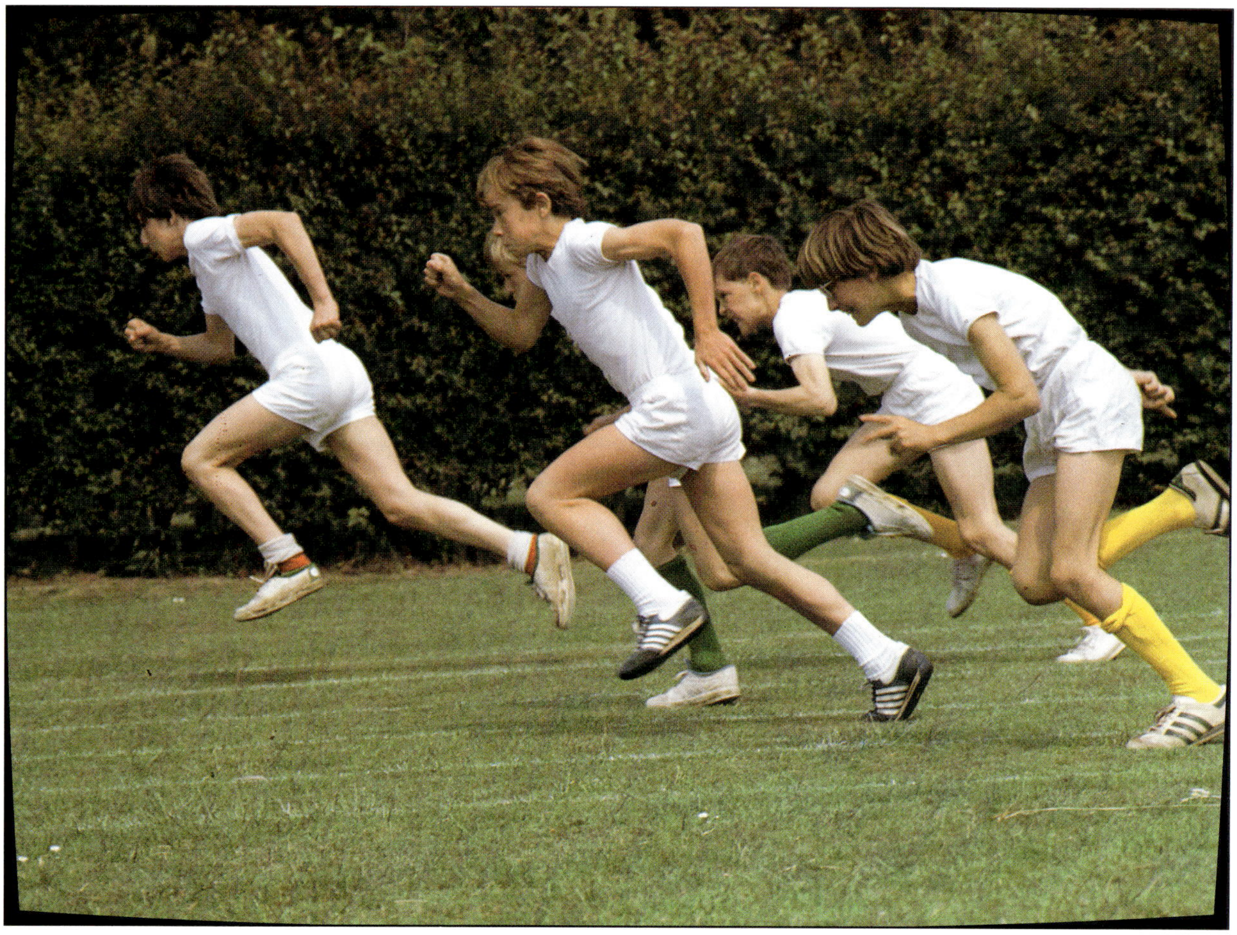

DAY OF ACTION

Sports and action coverage, no matter what the subject, has one common element: movement, and usually movement at speed. Perhaps the most popular situation in which to begin exploring the techniques of action coverage is at a school sports day. The subjects will usually be friends and family, so the video will have a guaranteed audience to watch it.

Athletics will comprise track and field events. In track events, the action takes place over a large area, so you will need to select camera positions which provide you with the best view of what is going on. This is dealt with in a later part of the chapter. Field events, such as throwing the javelin, or the high jump, take place in a limited area. This means it is relatively easy to select a camera position from which you can get good coverage of individual performances. Remember, to convey the full atmosphere of the day, you should also get shots away from the action: parents greeting their children after a race, the presentation of the prizes, and the picnic in the school grounds afterwards.

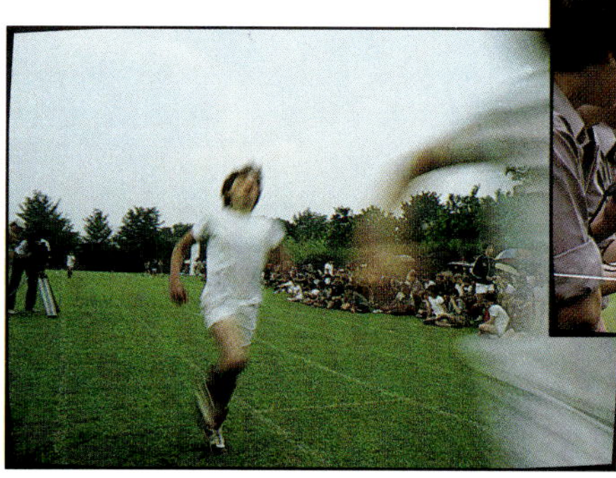

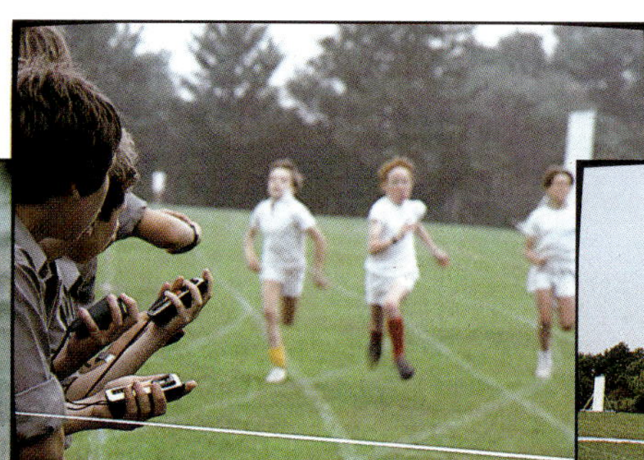

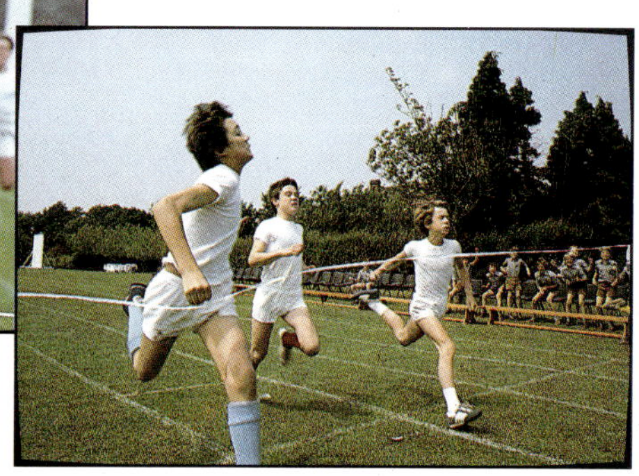

2-4: *Head-on to the action gives the viewer a better sense of the speed at which the race is taking place.*

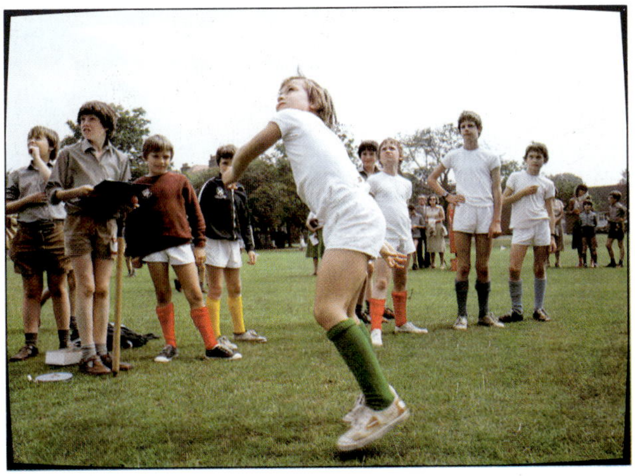

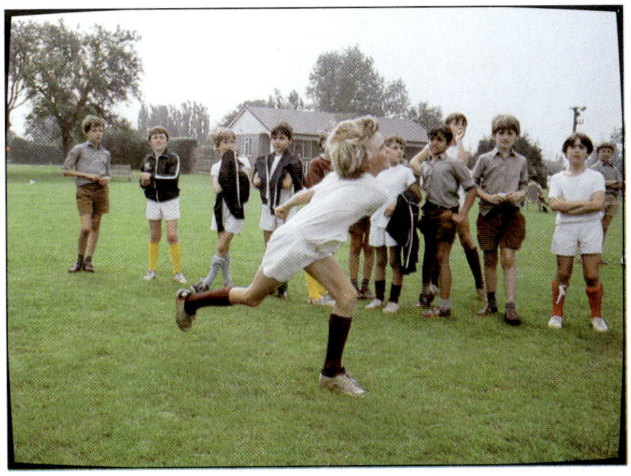

1: *Side-on views of track events tell the viewer the most important thing they wish to know: who's in the lead. You can choose to concentrate on the battle for the lead, or perhaps concentrate on an individual athlete.*

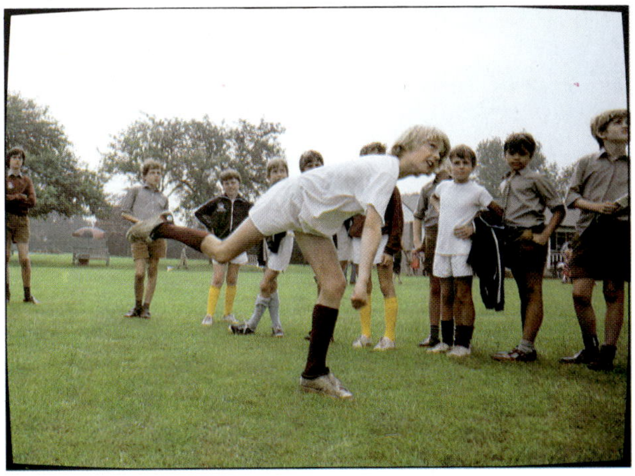

5-7: *Field events present fewer problems. You can record the throw or jump from a fixed position. With practice, it is possible to follow the flight of the javelin through the air.*

8: *The glittering prizes. Coverage of the presentation of prizes allows you both to record the overall scene and obtain close-ups of individual competitions.*

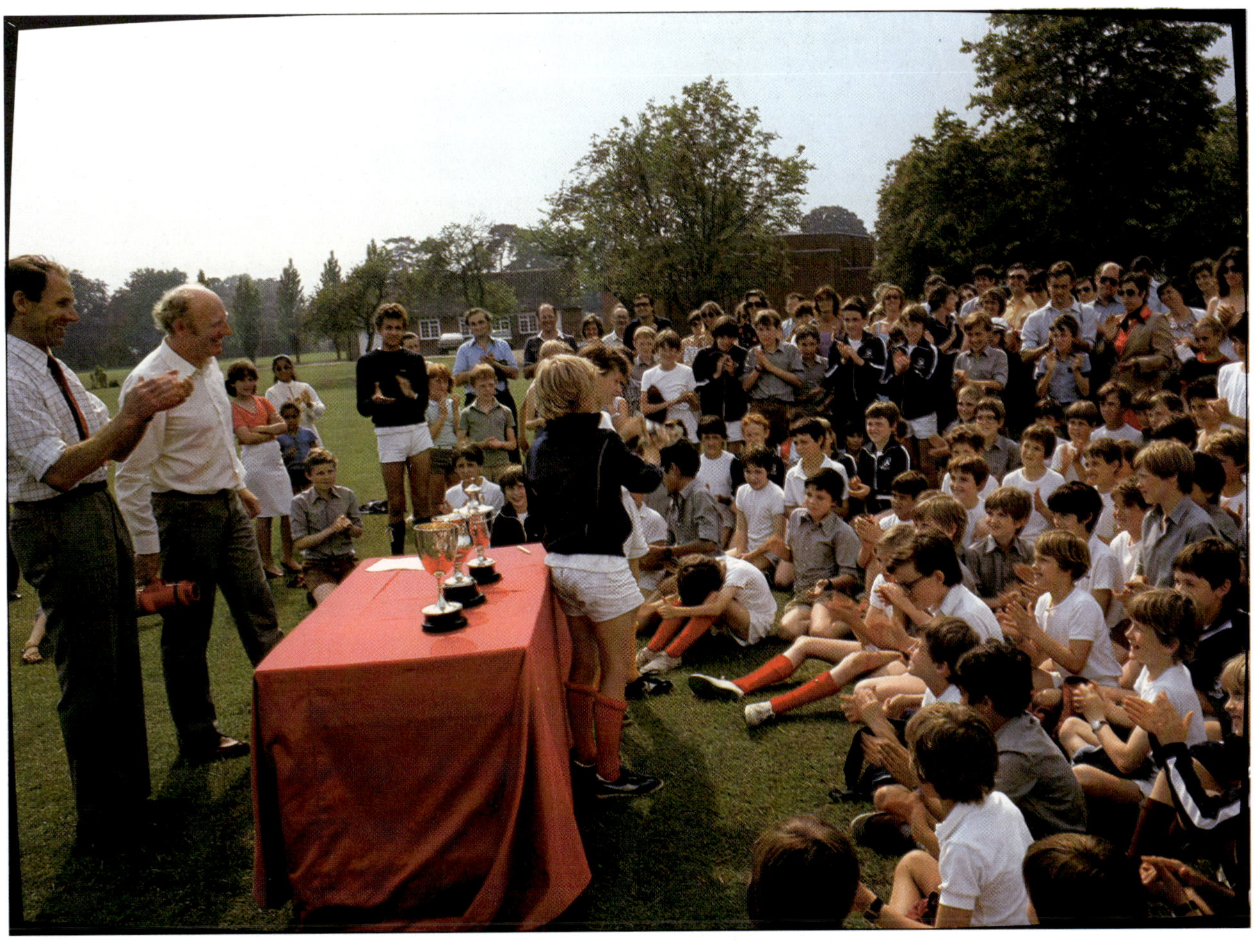

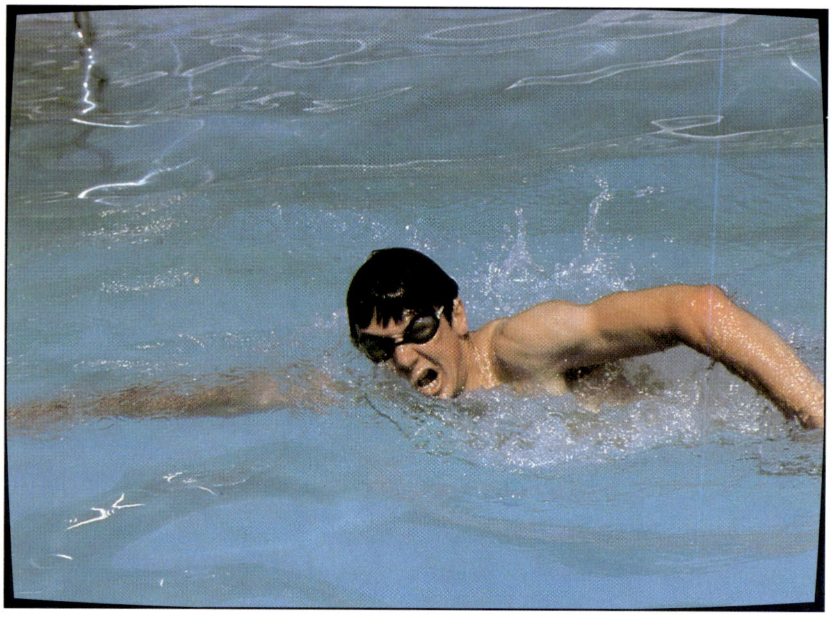

1: *In swimming, it is relatively easy to track an individual's performance, and to frame the shots in mid-shot to allow later analysis of performance. In particularly bright conditions, you need to use a polarizing filter to cut down glare from the water. Remember that indoor swimming pools cause problems with the acoustics, so that the soundtrack may well be too distorted to listen to – dub in a commentary later.*

DIFFERENT APPROACHES

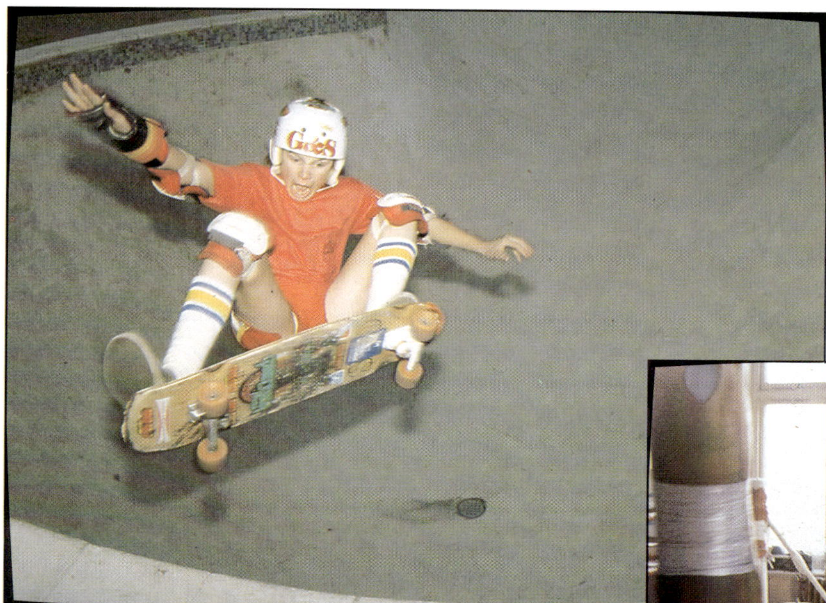

2-3: *Skateboarding and boxing are two sports which have little in common. Speed and balance characterize the former. In the latter, video is a useful tool in analysing training performance.*

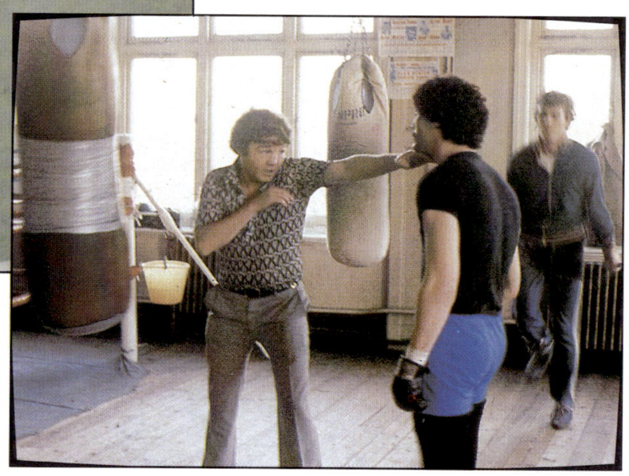

There is, of course, no limit to the types of action event you can cover. Analyse the event in terms of whether it is a team game, or an individual sport, whether it is engaged in a large or small area, and in terms of the equipment and resources you have at your disposal to obtain coverage.

The shots shown on these pages are taken from a number of sources. The coverage of the sumo wrestling, a traditional Japanese sport surrounded by complicated ritual and ceremony, was more in the area of documentary footage. For most viewers, the rules of the sport are secondary to the spectacle of the giant wrestlers, and their preparations are as fascinating as the actual wrestling bout itself.

Such considerations are really an anticipation of audience interest. If your tape is going to be watched by sports professionals, or by avid followers of the game you are covering, then they will tend to appreciate colourful asides from the action rather less. Analysis of the game becomes your prime aim. A less specialized audience will be more interested in the overall atmosphere, and the background to what's going on – use interviews of players to help convey the principles of the game being played.

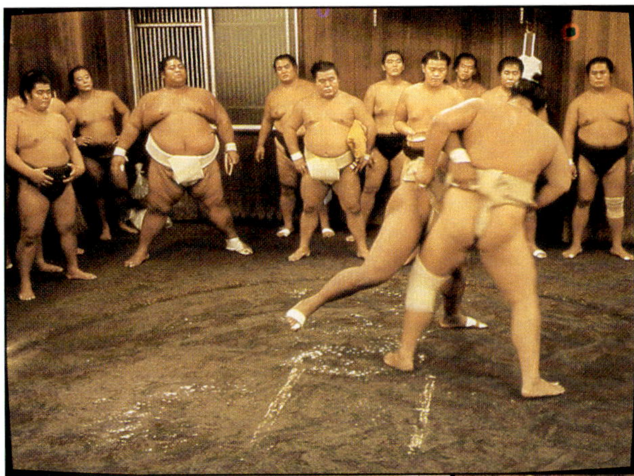

4-5: *This sumo wrestling was shot on a trip to Japan. The wrestling itself takes place in a small ring, and each bout is fast and furious, usually over in seconds. Shoot in long shot.*

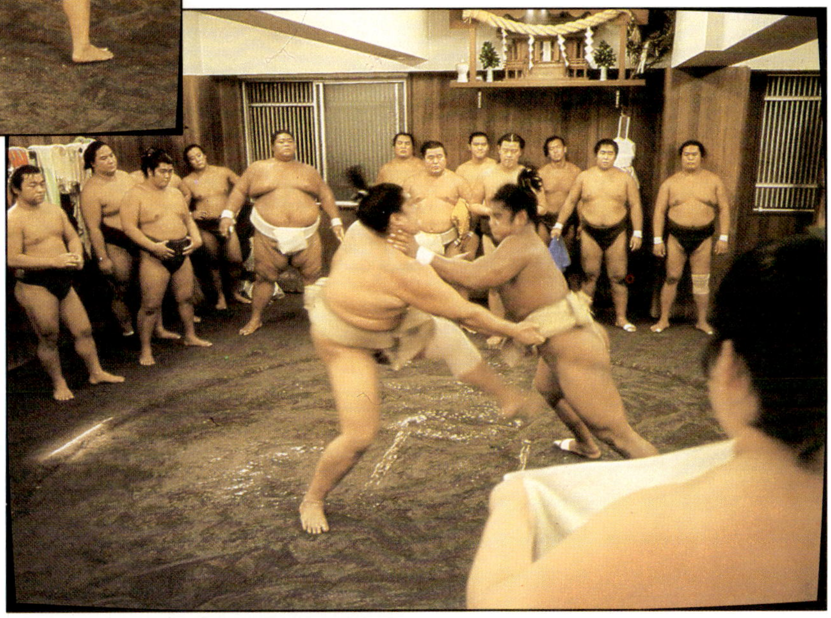

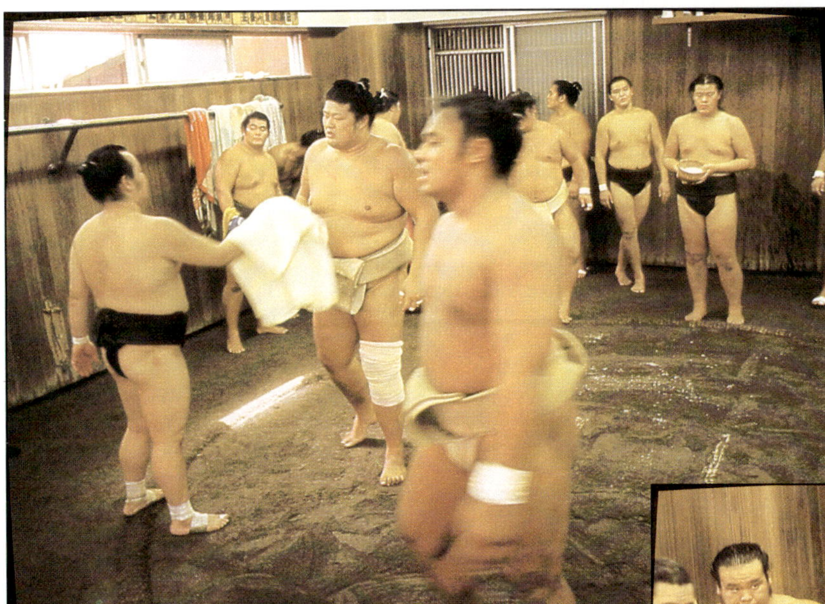

6-7: *For most non-Japanese, sumo wrestling remains a somewhat bizarre spectacle. The coverage was not particularly selective, since almost all of what was going on in the training hall was full of fascination.*

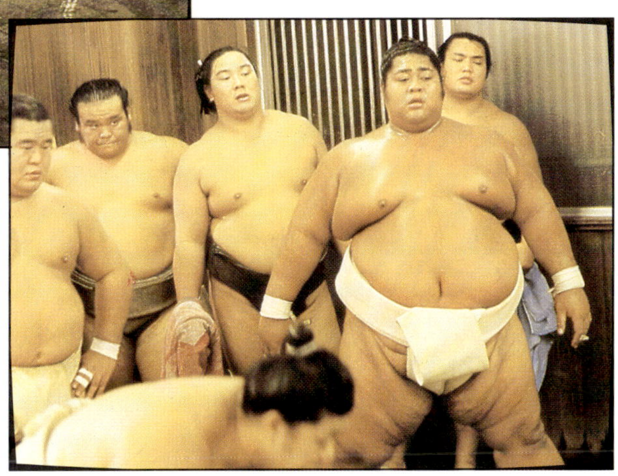

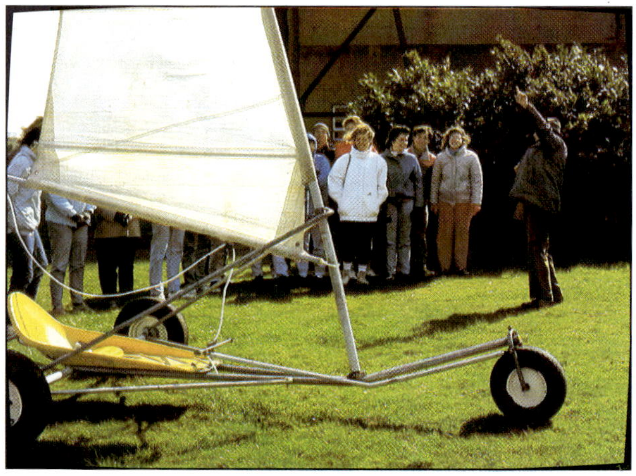

1: *This shot shows the trainer in action with a group of potential land-yachters. This kind of coverage can be useful to show to other beginners to give a general grounding in the sport.*

VIDEO TRAINING

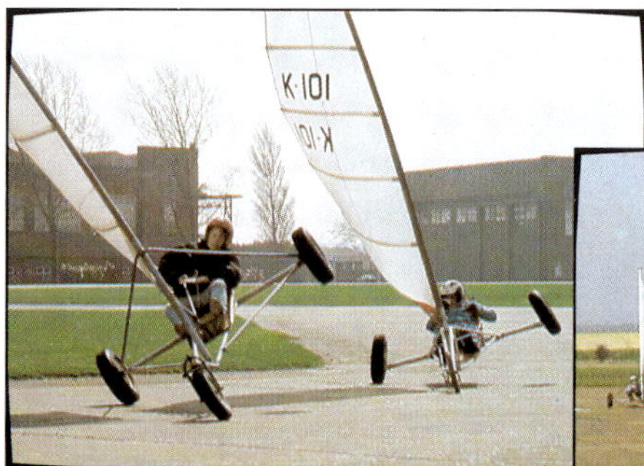

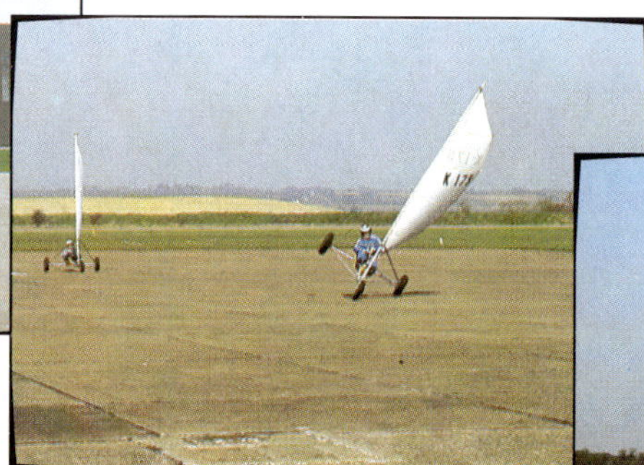
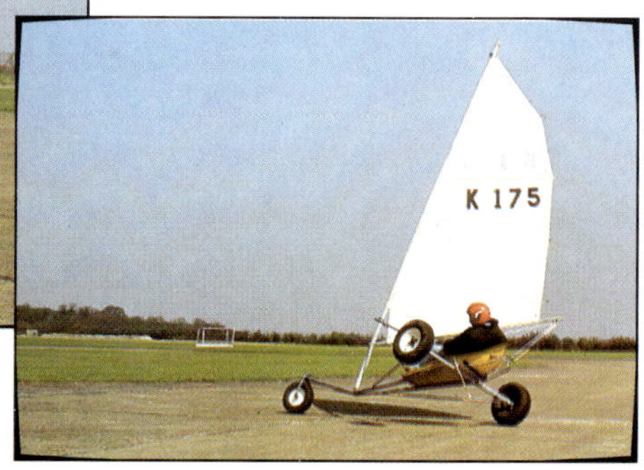

2-4: *By strategic placing of the camera, it is possible to study technique at key moments. In land-yachting, these include cornering and the final straight to the finishing line.*

One of the major reasons for making a video of a sports event is to use it as a coaching aid. Individual performances can be reviewed and analyzed in detail, using the slow motion and freeze-frame functions of the VCR. Professional players make great use of such video recordings to study their own and their opponents' games. You could supplement such a home-made video with those made by professional coaches, which cover everything from archery to *aikido*.

5: *Shooting into the sky for this pole vault has its own special problems. This camera must be very carefully positioned in order to get maximum coverage while avoiding sun glare.*

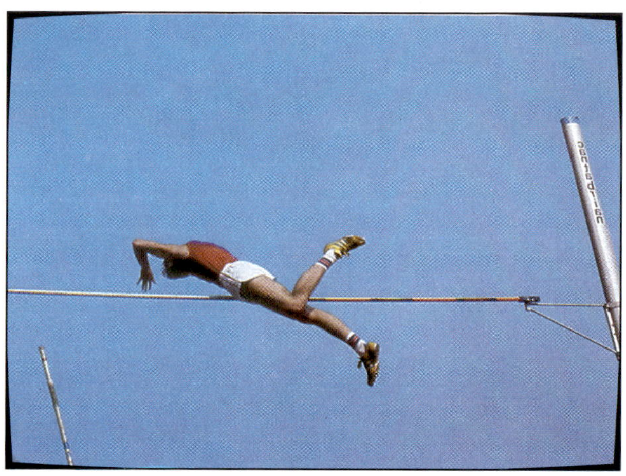

Making a coaching video

If you are going to make a coaching video, how should you approach the task? In many cases, individuals are concerned about a particular aspect of their game. They will tell you, for example, that their backswing, when driving a golf ball, is creating terrible problems.

If you are unfamiliar with the techniques of the game in question, you may have to ask for a quick run down on the most important aspects. When you know exactly on which area of his or her game the player wants to concentrate, shoot it over and over again. Take long-shots, highlighting the player's posture and balance. Then shoot close-ups of particular parts of the body: the feet to record

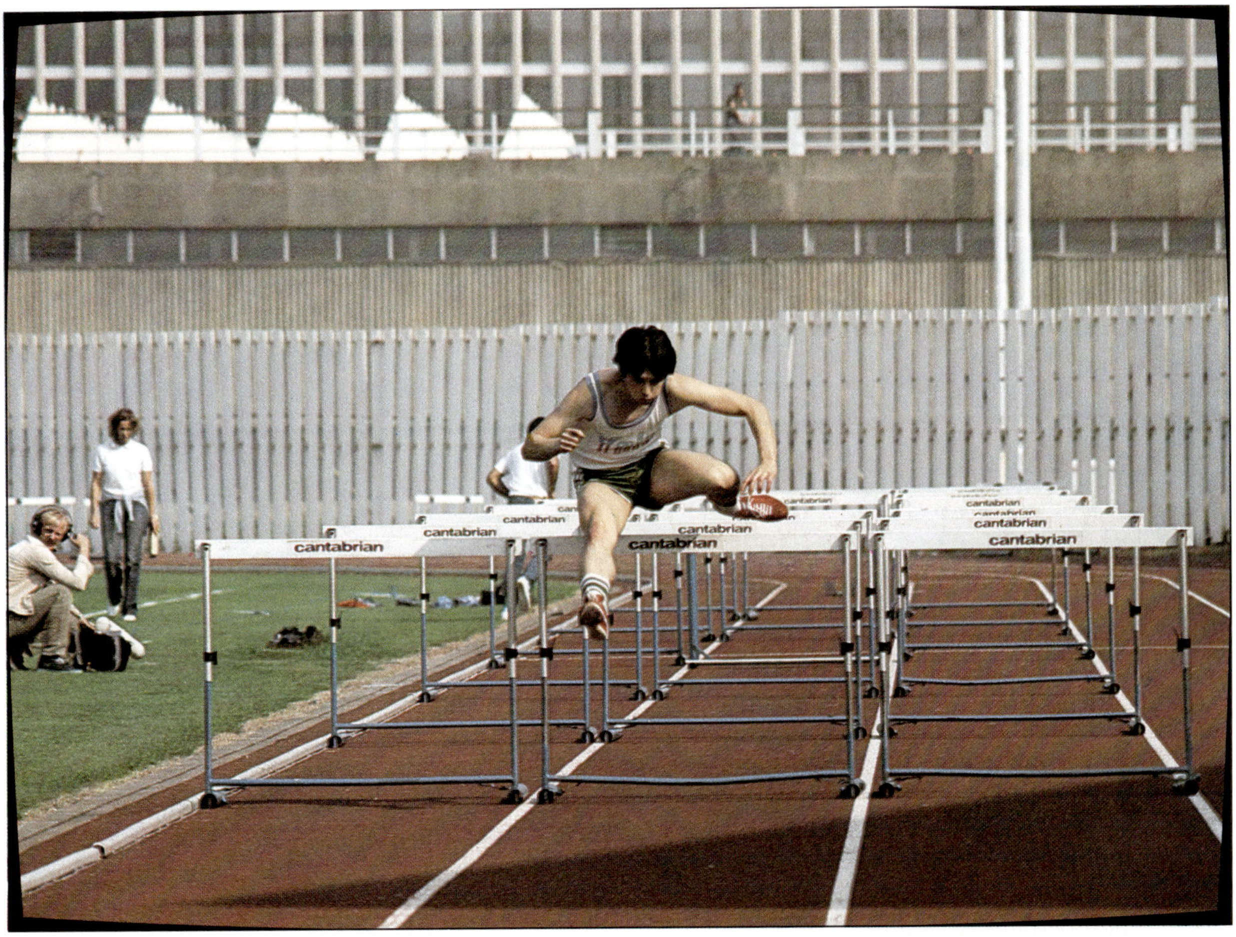

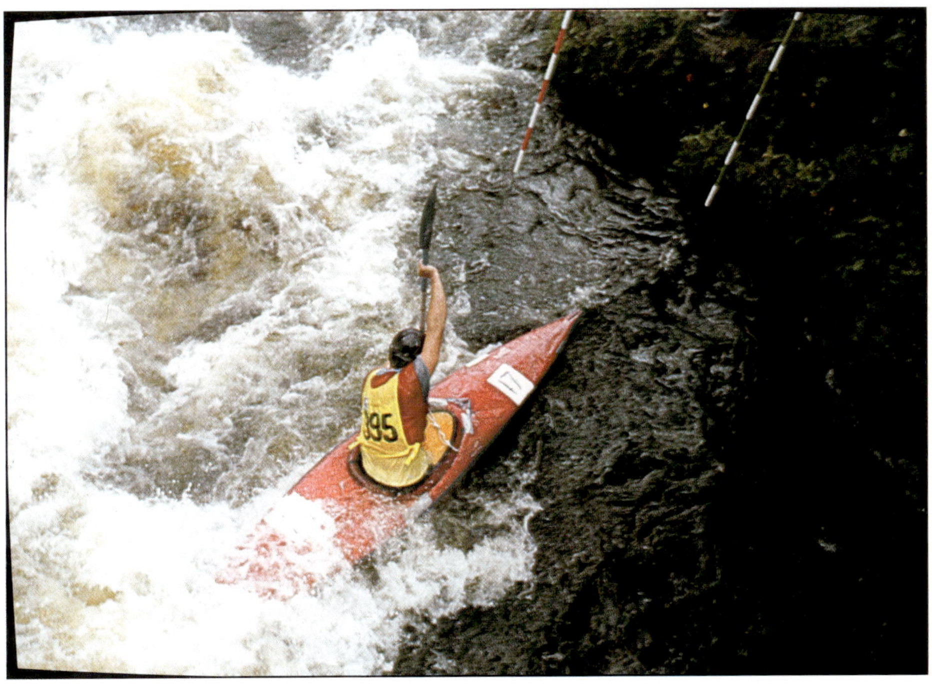

6: *If you wish to record your own performance, you will have to set up the camera in advance and place markers to indicate the positions you should take up while practising. In this case, this simply means head on to the hurdler.*

7: *A strategic moment in canoeing technique involves this manoeuvre through the poles beside the bank.*

stance, and the hands to show grip. Next, record the player from different angles: head-on, from side-on, and from behind, giving the same coverage as before. If the player is trying out alternative techniques, record these too. And finally, to ensure that you can study the tape without any distractions, use a tripod to avoid camera shake.

Such coverage is fine if the player is more or less stationary, as in golf or pool, but an athlete may want to study his or her performance over ¼mile (½km). In this case you could set up camera positions around the circuit as described in Track and Circuit Action. Or place the camera at the far end of the track, but only during practice sessions.

PROJECT NOTEBOOK

SPORTS

Sports coverage is a specialized area of video, requiring special skills and quick reaction times. Since you have only one chance to capture the action, there's no room for mistakes – you can hardly ask them to run the Olympic 100 metres again, just because you forgot to remove the lens cap! So you should immerse yourself in the sport that you are going to cover, in order that you will be able to anticipate how the action is likely to develop.

■ Selecting the best camera positions before the action begins is the single most effective way of ensuring that you get full, informative coverage.

■ Remember that in many games, switching camera positions from one side of the action to the other is going to confuse the audience. By crossing the line, you apparently reverse the direction of play.

■ Close-ups are effective, but you should always leave the audience with a clear sense of the play as a whole.

■ Sport doesn't happen in a vacuum. Set the scene beforehand: cover the competitors preparing for the event, the spectators arriving – all the razzmatazz.

■ Video comes into its own as a training tool. Co-operate with the player to analyse his or her game in full, then replay the results, using freeze-frame to pick out details.

■ The accidental and the unexpected happen every day in sport. Such coverage always has audience interest and is worth duplicating for a compilation tape.

■ The spectators are an intrinsic part of any sports event, creating the unique atmosphere. Remember to get some shots of spectators' behaviour, perhaps during breaks in the play.

ADDITIONAL RESOURCES

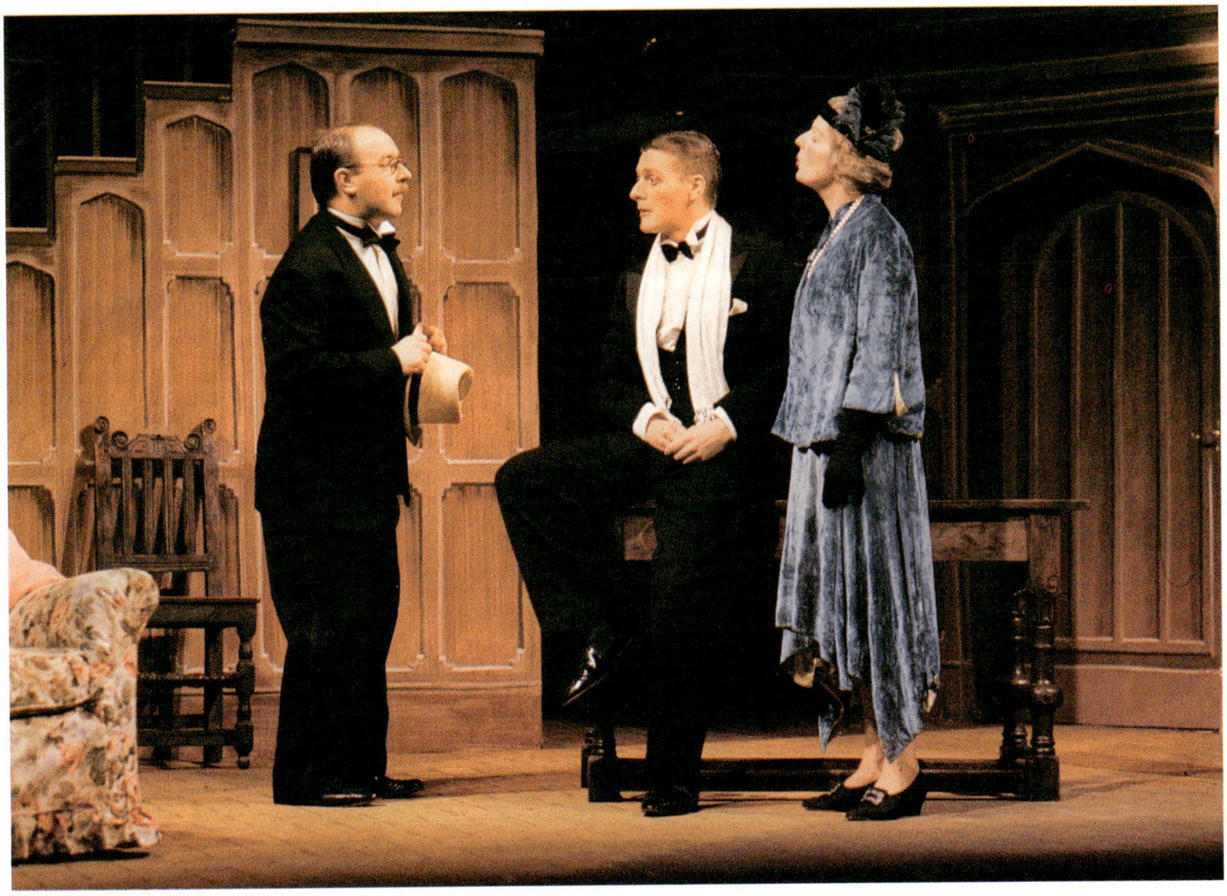

As you master the camcorder, so the number of subjects you can successfully film greatly increases. One particularly exciting and challenging project is the progress of an amateur theatrical production from its earliest days on. This not only provides an entertaining record of a lively, evolving group activity, but also enables you to acquire a wide range of important skills (including directing two or more cameras and working with a team). The latter is a highly worthwhile experience because there will be few occasions when you can work surrounded by and controlling lighting and make-up people, props buyers, script editors, producers, and so on. The theatre project is therefore also an excellent, albeit very gentle, introduction to the professional world of movie makers – George Lucas, Stephen Spielberg and all.

By acquiring a second camera and operator you more than double your possibilities for making a video with excellent coverage, and a varied range of camera angles. You will be able to record the action from two different camera positions simultaneously, or have one camera roving while the other takes the basic shots. So, at the editing stage, your options are greatly increased. However, with two cameras at your disposal, you must also think about your approach much more carefully.

Your first criterion is to establish a clear, agreed objective amongst all those working on the video. Is the film to be a recording of the theatre group at work, featuring behind-the-scenes activities and rehearsals, so becoming a semi-documentary? Or is your prime aim to lead up to and highlight the actual performance?

Assuming that you have selected the second option, let's clarify your shooting options. The best time for filming close-up shots of facial reactions and gestures is during the rehearsal. This really won't be possible 'on the night' when a camera on stage will disrupt the play and certainly obstruct the audience's view. During the public performances, the cameras must be unobtrusive.

Your second objective is to set up the cameras in two different positions before recording one performance in its entirety. These two tapes will provide most of the material that you will require for the final edited recording.

Choosing the camera positions depends, to a large extent, on the layout of the theatre. For example, if there is a balcony, make the most of its effective camera angle which will provide an excellent alternative to one right in front of the action. It can also be used for those moments when a personal drama subsides, and we see the characters in a wider perspective. Or, commence the action from high up, revealing the set and the characters, before closing in as the tension increases.

Another camera position well worth considering is the side of the stage. But do check during rehearsals that props, stage lights, and actors waiting to enter do not obstruct the viewpoint.

USING TWO CAMERAS

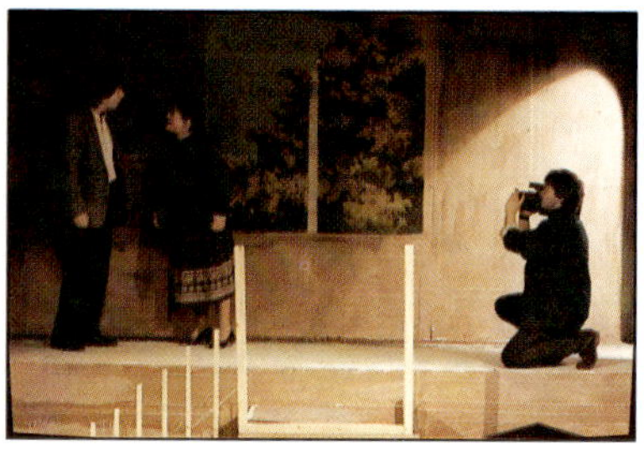

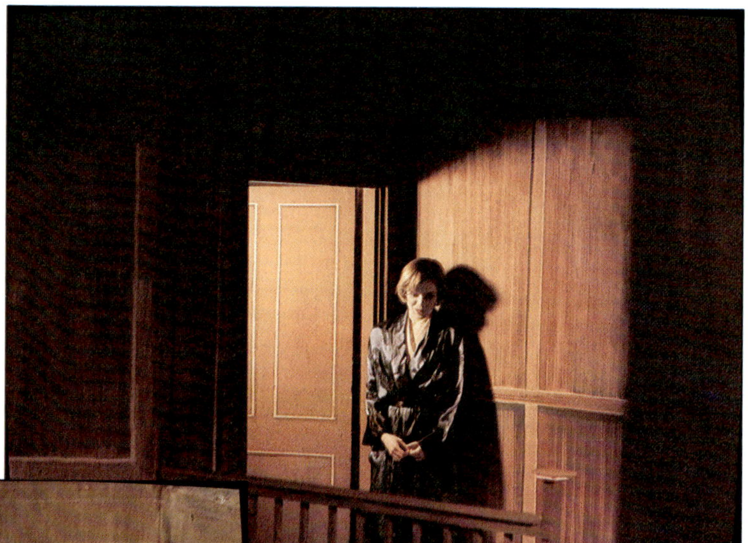

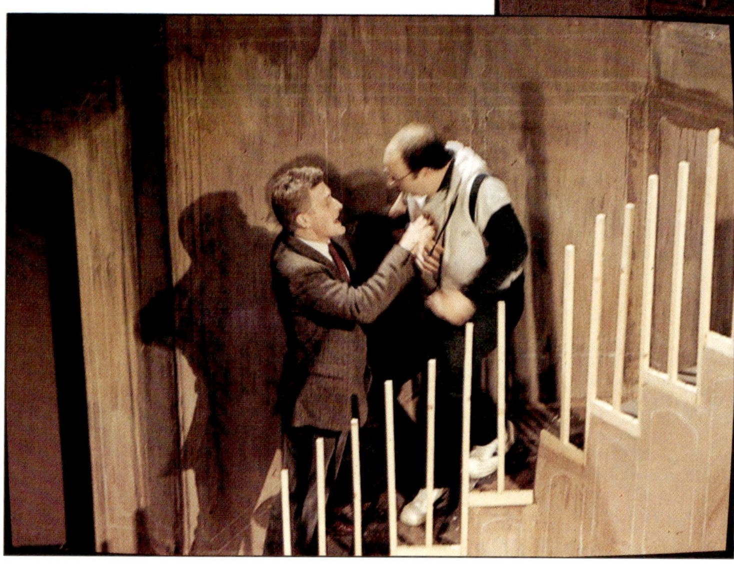

1-3: *During dress rehearsals, you will be able to get a camera on stage to record close-ups of actors' expressions, to be cut in at the editing stage.*

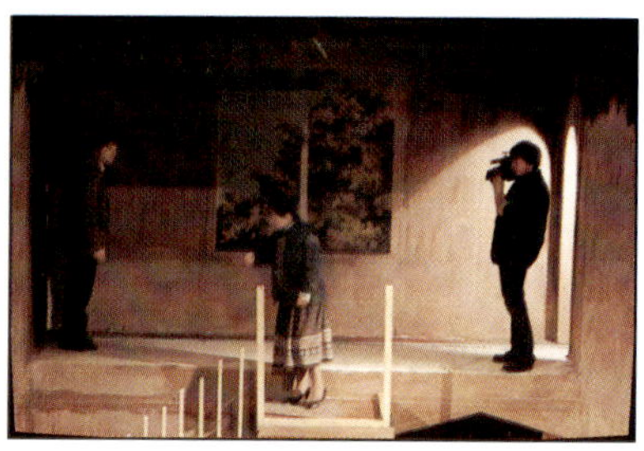

4: *It is important that the shots taken on stage should not be from too many different angles, as seen here, otherwise you will have problems matching the various cuts. Therefore choose a position that allows greatest coverage with least movement.*

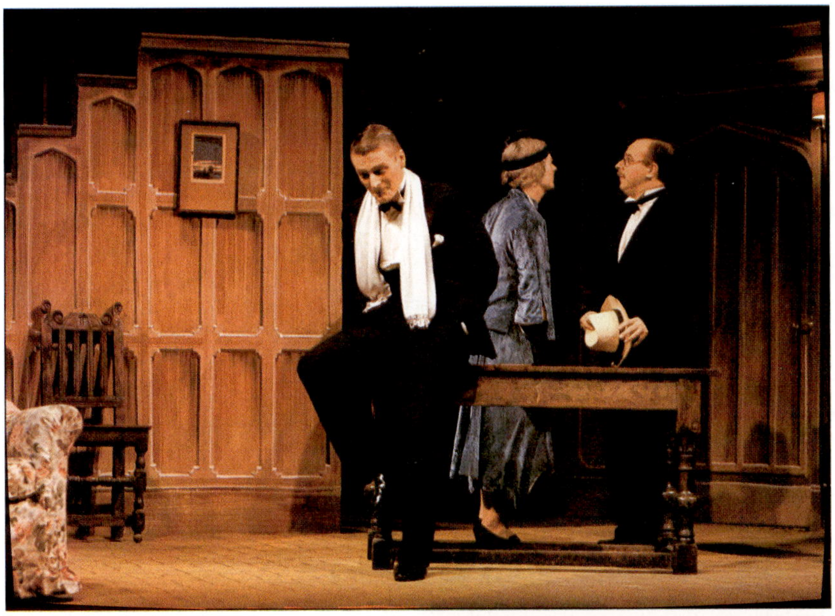

5: *This shot is taken with the camera placed to the front and just to the right of centre stage (do check that such a position provides a wide enough angle of view). Being close to the action in this way is important for establishing a sense of intimacy, but if you are forced to move the camera too much to follow the action, you will end up sacrificing intimacy for irritating distraction for the actors. In this particular play –* Rookery Nook, *a knock-about farce by Ben Travers – there is a great deal of fast action on stage and so the cameraman would have to be very knowledgeable about the actors' moves to avoid getting in their way.*

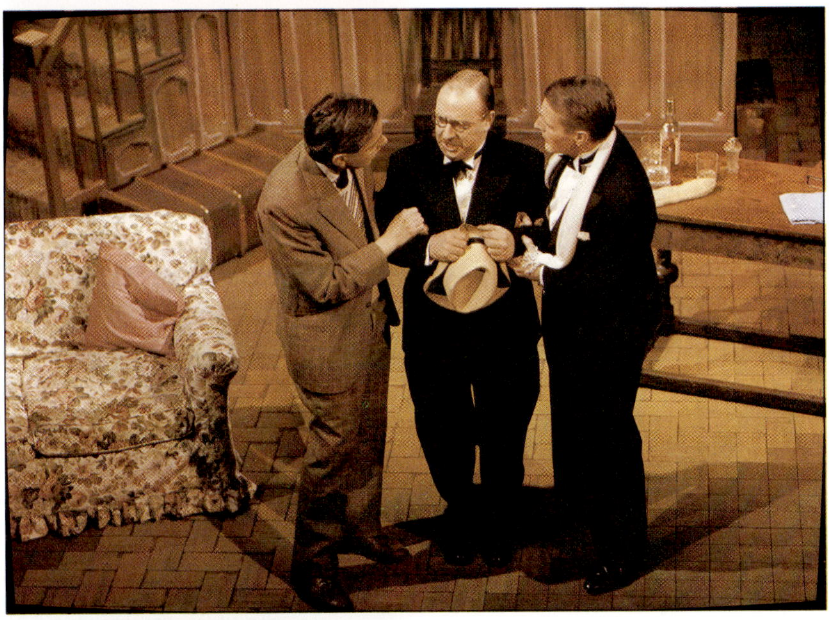

6: *This shot from high up is part of a trial sequence taken from the balcony during dress rehearsals. From here you can use the zoom to close in on the players during significant dramatic moments. Mark such points in your script so that you are well prepared for them as the play unfolds. On the whole, shots taken from such a high angle look particularly theatrical. This is not necessarily a bad thing, but it could create problems when you change shots to other camera positions.*

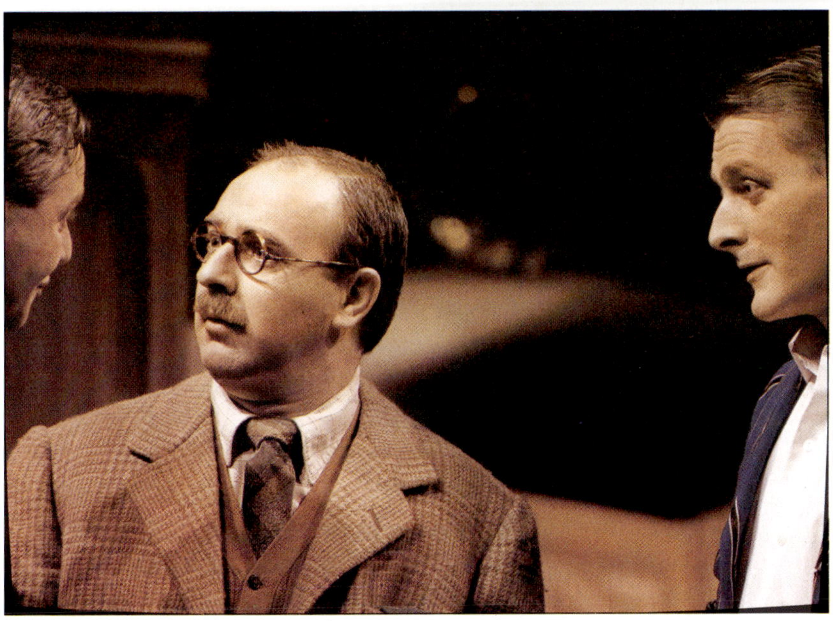

7: *Close-ups should be treated with care, and certainly practised at rehearsal. You will need to know exactly what positions the actors will take up and be aware of the course the dialogue takes, so that you can plan shots of character's reactions. Again, remember to keep moves to a mimimum, so letting the action develop in front of the camera and tell its own story. Another point to bear in mind is that some of the actors – those with malleable comic faces, in this instance – are going to make more interesting subjects than others for close-ups. The actor in the centre of this trio was perfect – playing the stool pigeon, he had a marvellously expressive face.*

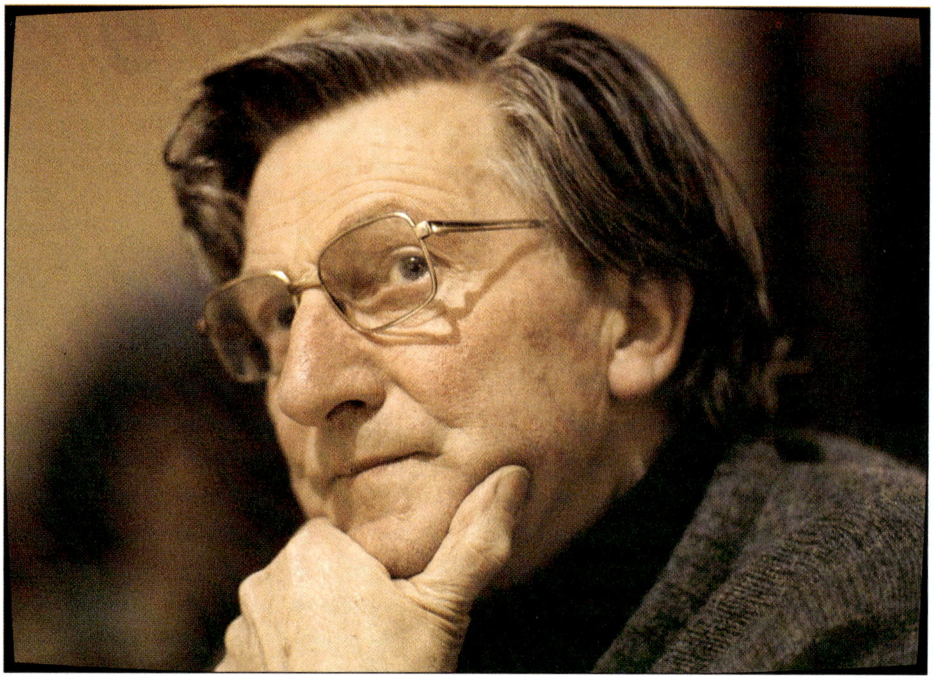

1: *The director is the linchpin of any production, providing creative stimulus as well as practical support to the cast and to the video crew.*

THE DIRECTOR

A video production with a team of helpers, no matter how small, needs someone in control, someone to provide direction and to allow specialist members of the crew to pursue their own tasks. In other words, someone needs to be the director.

In some Hollywood legends the director is a tyrannical, creative monster. But try imitating that severe style with friends and you'll soon be the only person on the project! The ideal director therefore combines an overall creative vision of the project with fastidious attention to detail, and tact, humour and diplomacy when managing the crew. The director must also be efficient and organized, but sufficiently flexible to change plans when the unexpected happens (as it inevitably does in unscripted events).

Long before shooting starts, there should be discussions about the aims of the project and a precise allocation of the duties of each team member. The director must not approach these sessions as a general discussion, but guide the

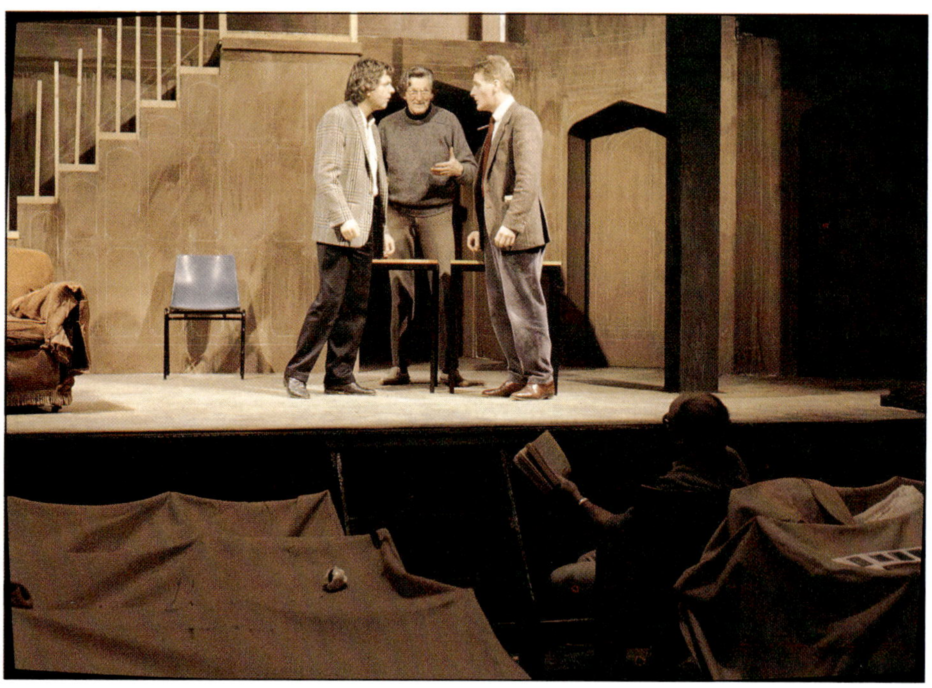

2: *Besides being a master of video techniques, the director must also know how to get the cast to adapt their acting techniques for the camera. This is, in fact, a highly specialized craft. The most important elements on which to concentrate include conveying emotions through small gestures, such as a sudden, darting eye movement, or a raised eyebrow. In a large theatre such gestures could go unnoticed, but provided the camera operator is instructed to home in on them your home video audience will appreciate their significance.*

In addition, the director must bear in mind other practicalities, such as the actors taking up suitable positions.

meetings having come prepared with a flexible story board, shooting scripts and video examples of the type of work he or she is trying to achieve.

It is virtually impossible to give a definitive list of the duties of a director on an amateur video project. But two of the most important involve obtaining good, wide coverage of the event, and selecting specific shots. The camera operators must therefore be given specific briefs that leave nothing to chance. And the director should not be shy of checking his proposed shots through the viewfinder or through video monitors.

One of the most important abilities any director should have is a talent for dealing with people. This means first of all assessing what everyone's strong and weak points are. You will then be able to make best use of the crew, cast, and any other helpers you may have at your disposal. Give them tasks that they can perform well and you will not only get the best results possible – everyone will get a certain amount of satisfaction from the project.

You will also have to learn, if it does not come naturally, how to criticize without being too negative. If you are too critical, you will only alienate your cast – and since they are probably only volunteers anyway, this is pointless. So it is usually best to find something in a performance to praise, and allow the actor to build on this, rather than being destructively critical of the parts of a performance you do not like. The same thing applies to the crew. You will find that you will have to become something of an expert in every area – sound, lighting, stage management and acting – in order to be able to instruct your cast and crew and to keep an overall eye on standards. The more you know, the more you will command respect. But don't impose your own knowledge for its own sake – each member of the team will have some suggestion to make and you should try to benefit from these rather than dismissing them in favour of your own.

Directing for the screen

If you are dealing with actors who are used to performing 'live' you will probably have to remind them that theatrical gestures often look exaggerated in front of the camera. This is especially true if you are working in close-up, where often a simple raising of the eyebrow or a slight shrugging of the shoulders is enough to convey the sort of strong emotion that might require a much more emphatic movement in the theatre.

Another difference between theatre and video is that the director should always check the scene as it looks through the camera. You can do this by looking through the viewfinder, of course, but it is better to use video monitors connected to the cameras. The monitors provide a better check on composition than is available through the viewfinder; they also allow you to assess colour balance. It is much the best thing to make these checks as you work – constant repetition of the same sequence will bore the cast and waste a great deal of time.

Once the director has total control of the shooting side of the video, instructing the camera operators and checking proposed shots, he must ensure, with the aid of the lighting technicians, that the lighting conveys the required atmosphere. And finally, in addition to being in control of the technical side of the project, the director must just as importantly inspire the cast to perform for the camera, not an audience.

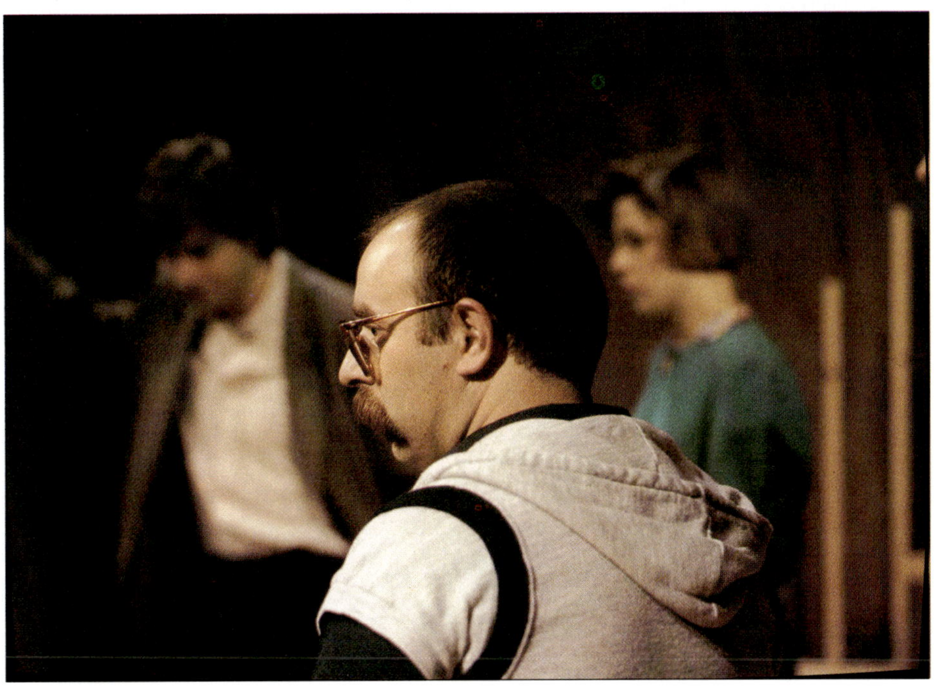

3: *Always survey the on-stage area from all possible angles. While the bulk of your coverage will probably be taken from a conventional point of view, it might be useful to obtain additional, more unusual footage in subsequent performances which you can incorporate into the tape at the editing stage.*

The size of your crew will depend upon the project at hand and the resources at your disposal. For most people, these resources will be minimal, so what is the minimum crew to aim for in a reasonably ambitous video project?

First, there must be someone to operate each camera. While it may be possible for the director to take control of one camera, this will restrict his or her other duties. You will also need someone to control and monitor sound – a vital job, since a poor soundtrack will render all the other work a waste of time. In addition to these tasks, you will require a general electrician/floor manager. This person will be responsible for everything outside the specialized tasks of the rest of the crew – checking electrical connections, passing messages and offering back-up whenever needed. That makes a total of five – any fewer and even the most basic multi camera shoot will be running short.

Of course, there are an additional number of particular skills that are extremely useful if available. A set-designer-cum-art-director can help style the whole production. This contribution can be limited to choosing costumes and designing the set, or expand into creating storyboards in collaboration with the writer and/or director and choosing locations for outdoor work.

Lighting is another specialist responsibility. If you are working in a fully staffed theatre, there will be lighting staff on hand to achieve the effects required by the video director. Make sure the crew are able to carry out your requirements. But without this support you will need your own electrician/lighting controller. This means that you will have to set up the lighting for each individual scene before it is acted, recording the stops for each lighting change.

THE CREW

Below: *A storyboard is a useful visual aid for the director, even though he or she will be familiar with the play from watching it during rehearsal.*

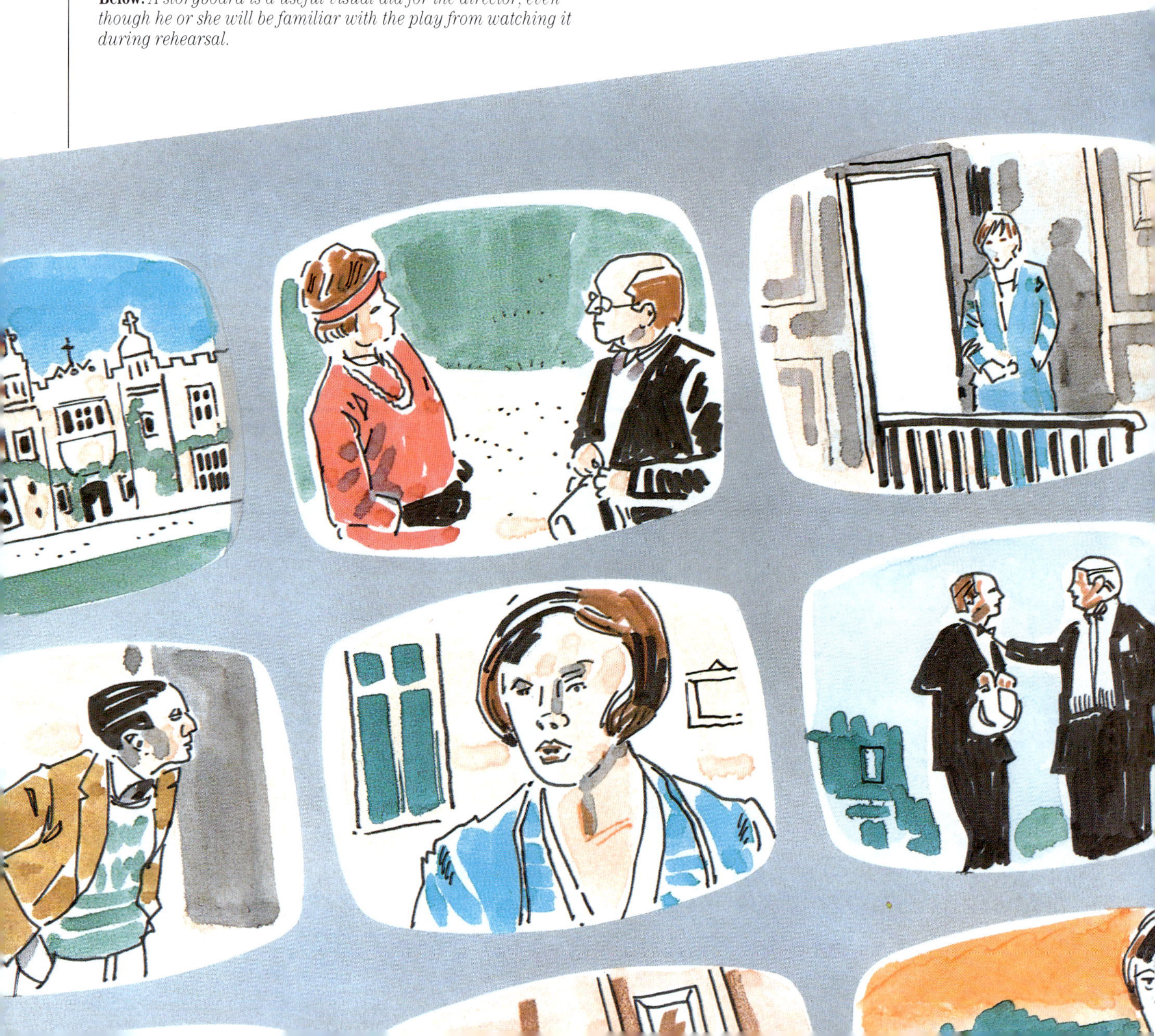

■ **The sound engineer** positions the microphones and monitors the quality of recording throughout each take, and also gives the cue for sound effects.

■ **The lighting supervisor** arranges the lights as required by the director, operating them from the lighting gallery in a theatre.

■ **Camera operator 1** will need to be fully briefed on the shots required (unless the director is filling this role).

■ **Camera operator 2.** This camera can either be in a fixed position, or 'rove' to capture the action from different angles.

■ **The director** – although he/she is nominally the head of the crew, the best results will be obtained where everyone contributes to the project.

■ **The technician/ manager** co-ordinates all aspects of the production, as well as filling any gaps whenever required.

■ **The cast** are initially the responsibility of the theatre director, unless he is the same person as the video director. If not, the latter may be allowed to modify the cast's positions and gestures during special shots taken during the rehearsals.

■ **Below:** Each member of the crew should have a copy of the shooting script, marked where they must perform their specific tasks. For camera operators these will principally be indications of change of shot: the introduction of close-ups, or a slow pan, for example. Camera cues are usually written on the left-hand margin of the page beside the appropriate section of dialogue. The sound operator will have cues where sound effects must be introduced, and which will have been rehearsed during rehearsals.

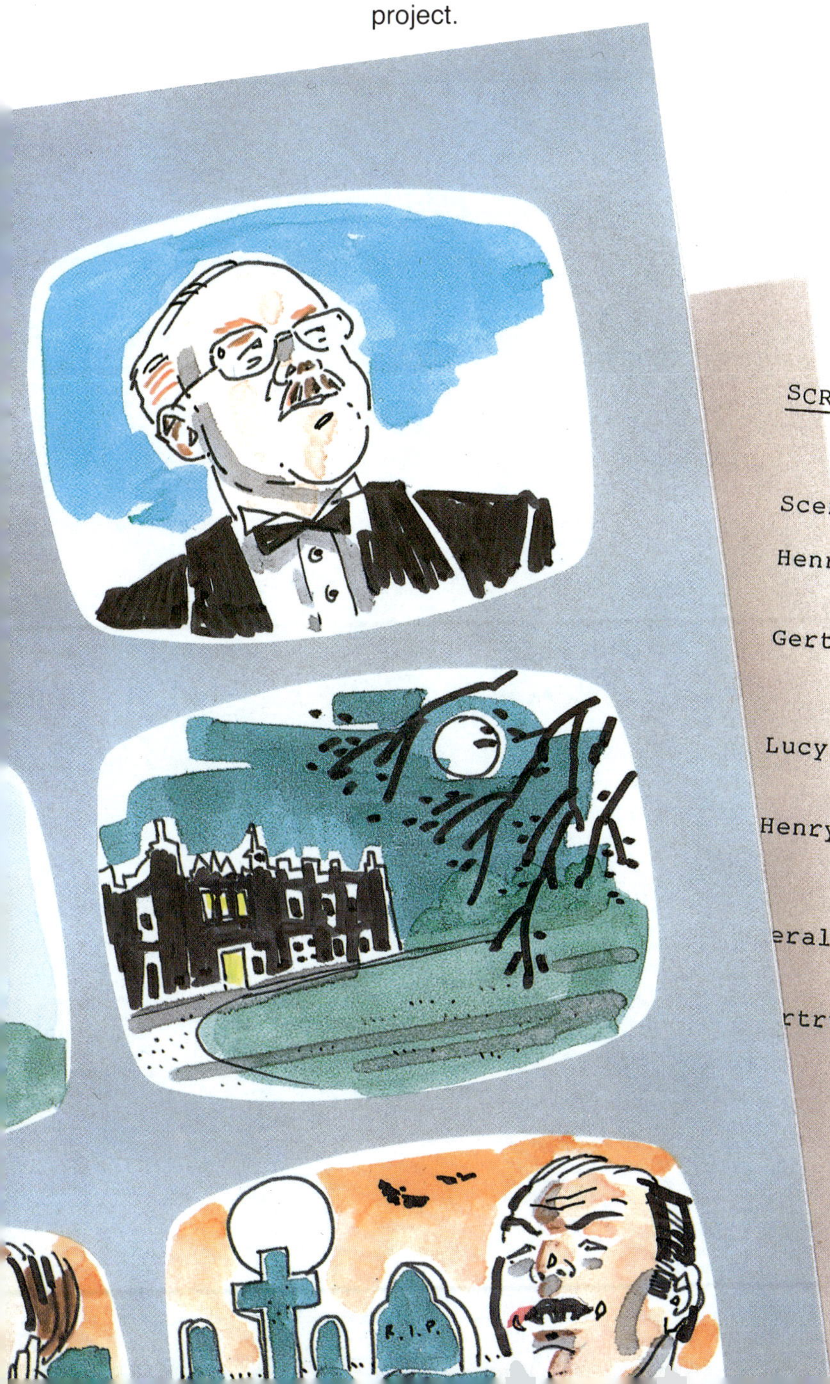

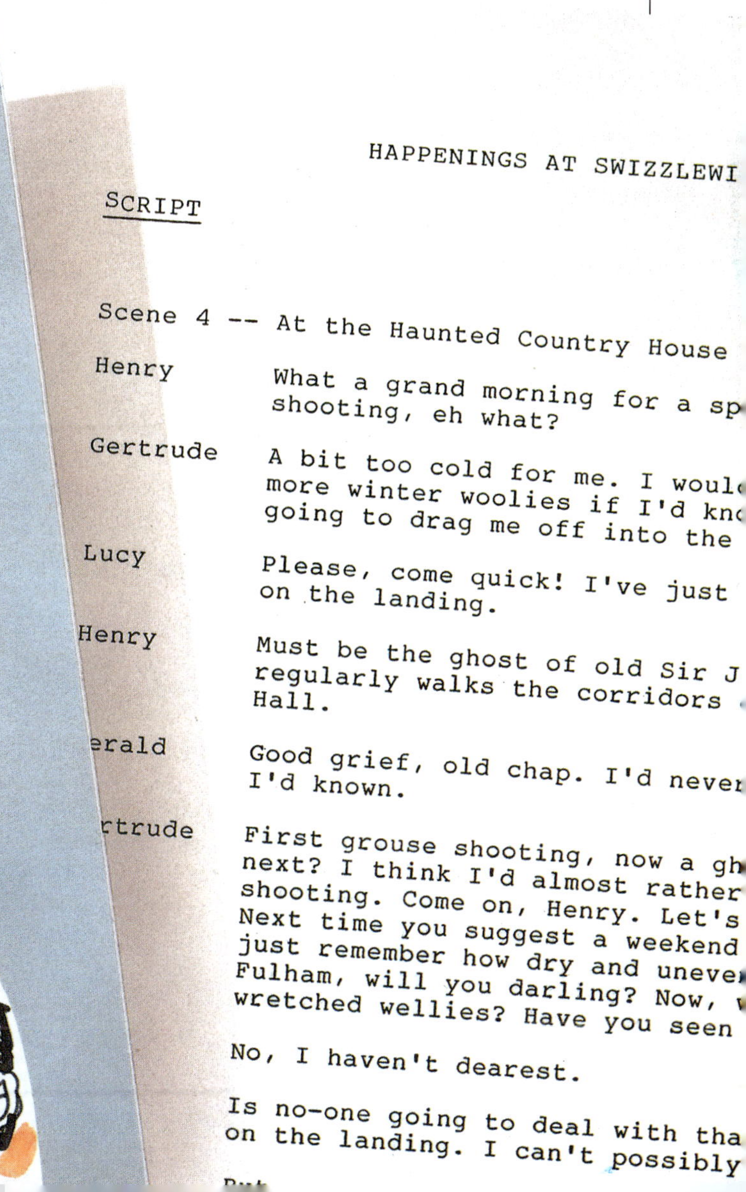
HAPPENINGS AT SWIZZLEWI

SCRIPT

Scene 4 -- At the Haunted Country House

Henry What a grand morning for a sp shooting, eh what?

Gertrude A bit too cold for me. I woul more winter woolies if I'd kn going to drag me off into the

Lucy Please, come quick! I've just on the landing.

Henry Must be the ghost of old Sir J regularly walks the corridors Hall.

erald Good grief, old chap. I'd neve I'd known.

rtrude First grouse shooting, now a gh next? I think I'd almost rather shooting. Come on, Henry. Let's Next time you suggest a weekend just remember how dry and uneve Fulham, will you darling? Now, wretched wellies? Have you seen

No, I haven't dearest.

Is no-one going to deal with tha on the landing. I can't possibly

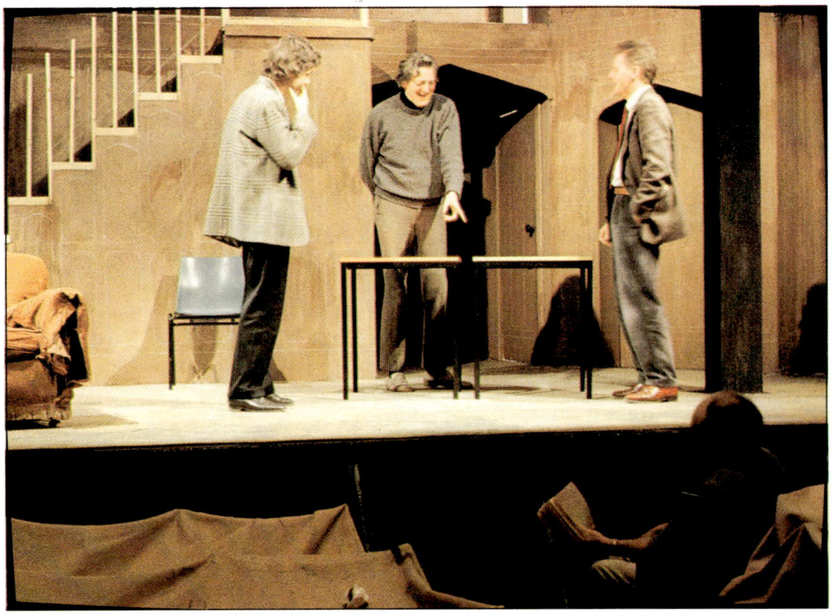

1: *If the video director is also the play's director, he must acquire a wide range of skills. Directing actors involves encouraging them to explore their parts for themselves, and helping to shape their performances and isolate those aspects which are most successful. The director must also be sensitive to the relationships between characters on stage, and their movements and body language. However, it is all too easy to get carried away with this aspect of direction, leaving the technical aspects of the production to other members of the team.*

USING REHEARSALS

Right: *Rough sketches of the actors' positions in each scene are useful for planning the shots you wish to get. In performance, the actors will have their positions marked on stage.*

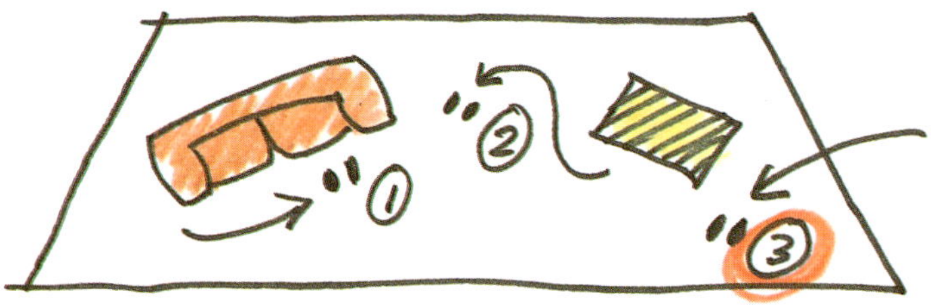

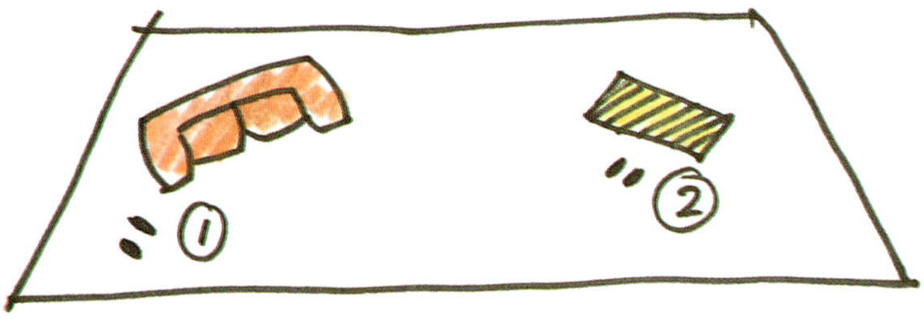

Make as much use of rehearsal time as you can, since there will never seem to be enough of it. The first rehearsal will be a complete read-through of the text which should be attended by the entire video crew – director, and camera, sound and lighting operators. This will enable you and your team to begin visualizing the production, the best possible ways of filming it, and how each member can contribute.

Later, at the early rehearsals, the actors will begin to develop their characters and establish their stage movements. As director, you must now consider the piece in video terms, always having to work round the theatrical production. Remember that even if you are also the play's director, you can not alter matters too much or the cast will be unsure whether they are acting for the audience or the lens. However, when filming at the dress rehearsal, for instance, you can take certain liberties. The most appropriate involves breaking down the drama into convenient 'takes' (which is standard practice in films). Each scene is rehearsed, after which the sound and lighting are set up. Then the scene is repeated and recorded. If anything goes wrong, or the video director is unhappy with the performance, retakes are possible. Quite often, scenes are shot out of the order in which they appear in the play when all the relevant characters are already assembled, and the appropriate scenery is in place. But while professional actors and actresses may be used to this way of working, amateurs will almost certainly find it hard to adapt. Using the take method of working, there is no need to arrange moves in advance. But if a continuous performance is to be recorded, you must have first thought carefully about each scene, determining the best positions for your cameras. And while doing so, ensure that characters will not be obscuring each other.

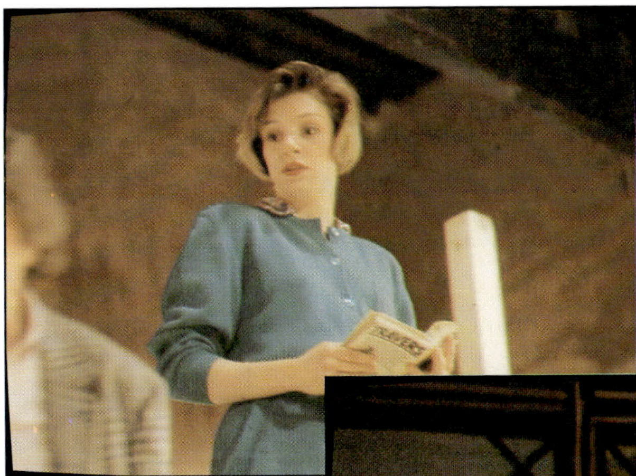

2: *During the early rehearsals, the actors will be in their everyday dress. If you are going to use the subsequent dress rehearsal (3) to get close-up shots for inserts in the final tape, you can use this early period to plan your camera positions. And this means knowing exactly what camera positions you will be using for the full performances, since an insert shot won't work if it is taken from an opposing angle to that used for the major sections of the tape.*

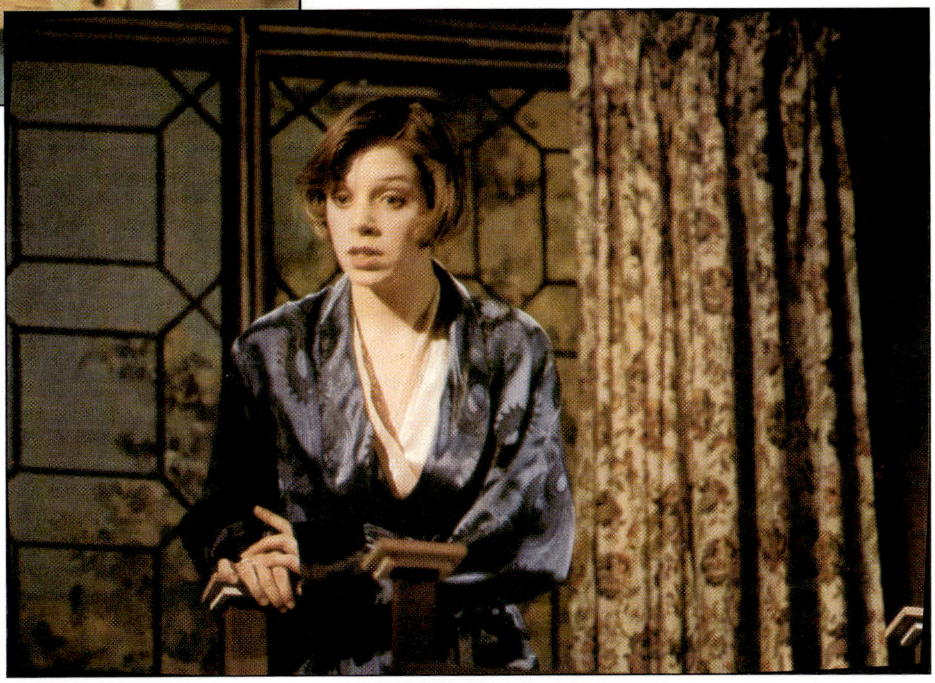

4: *Another vital consideration is the appearance of groups on stage. While you don't want the actors to have their backs to the camera, you don't want too many head-on shots either. Since the video camera will be recording from the position of the live audience, it is important to adjust the actors' positions for the performance. Such problems should be spotted during the rehearsals.*

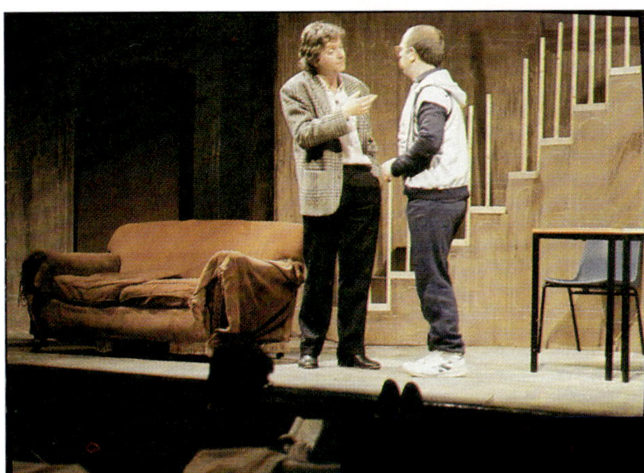

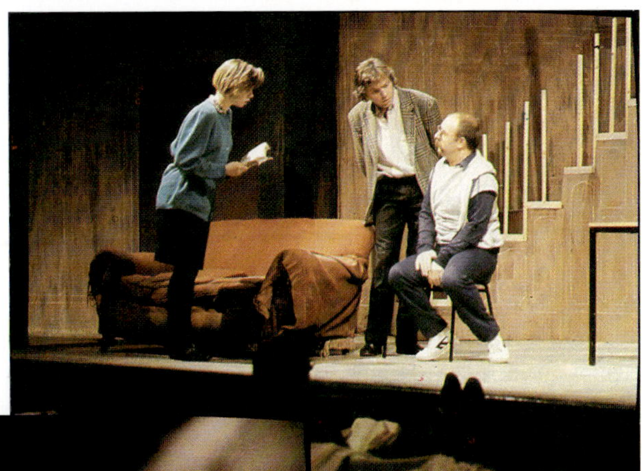

5: *In a theatre, the lighting priority is for the stage effect, for what the audience will see. During rehearsals, check that from the camera positions you have chosen, no member of the cast accidentally falls into an area of deep shadow. If so, the remedy may be moving one of the props or modifying the scene to suit your needs.*

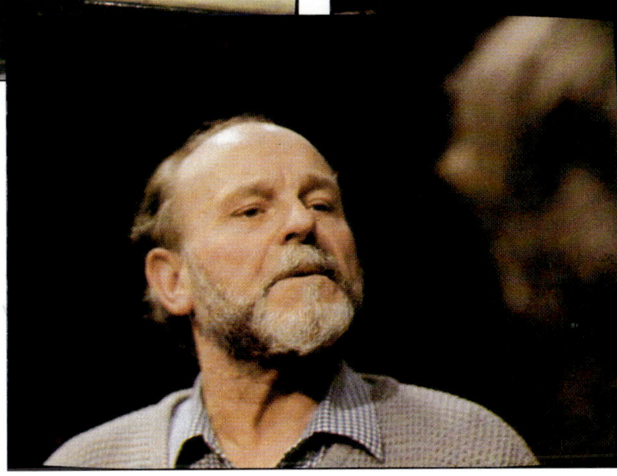

6: *The use of close-ups in recording this performance should be treated with care. A close-up will work well if one of the actors is delivering a monologue alone on stage. But with other characters present, a close-up of one person alone will prevent you from showing the reactions of others, an equally important part of the performance.*

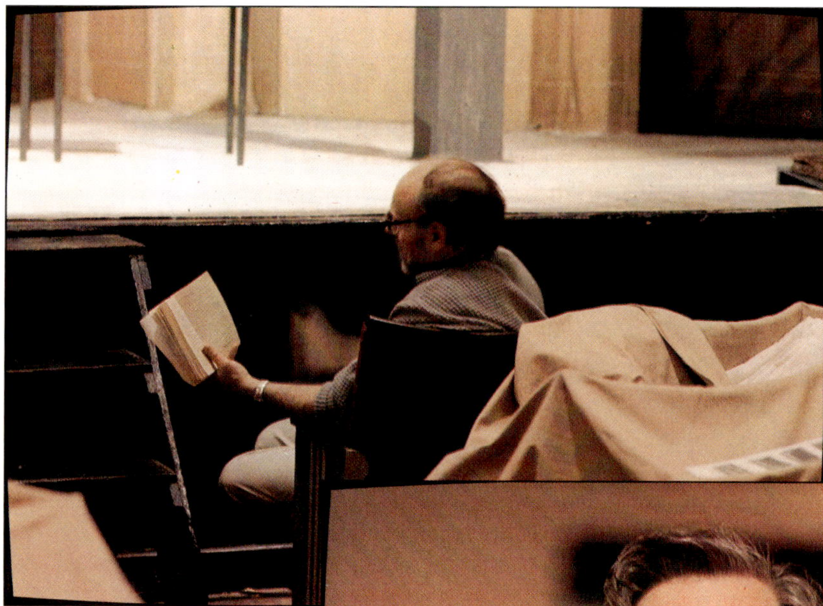

1-2: *When filming a rehearsal, look around the theatre and capture any action in front of the stage. Shots of figures like the solitary actor learning his lines or the director concentrating on the play may seem static, but they can provide interludes that will enable you to vary the pace of the video.*

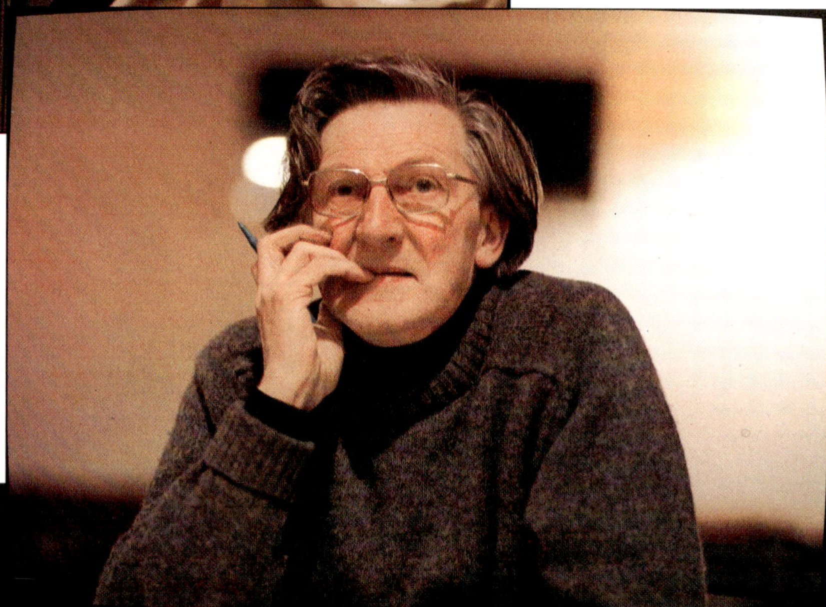

3: *Mid-shots and close-ups of actors discussing their lines and listening to the director are vital in rehearsal coverage. They show the relationship between the director and the cast, and provide insights into how the production is put together.*

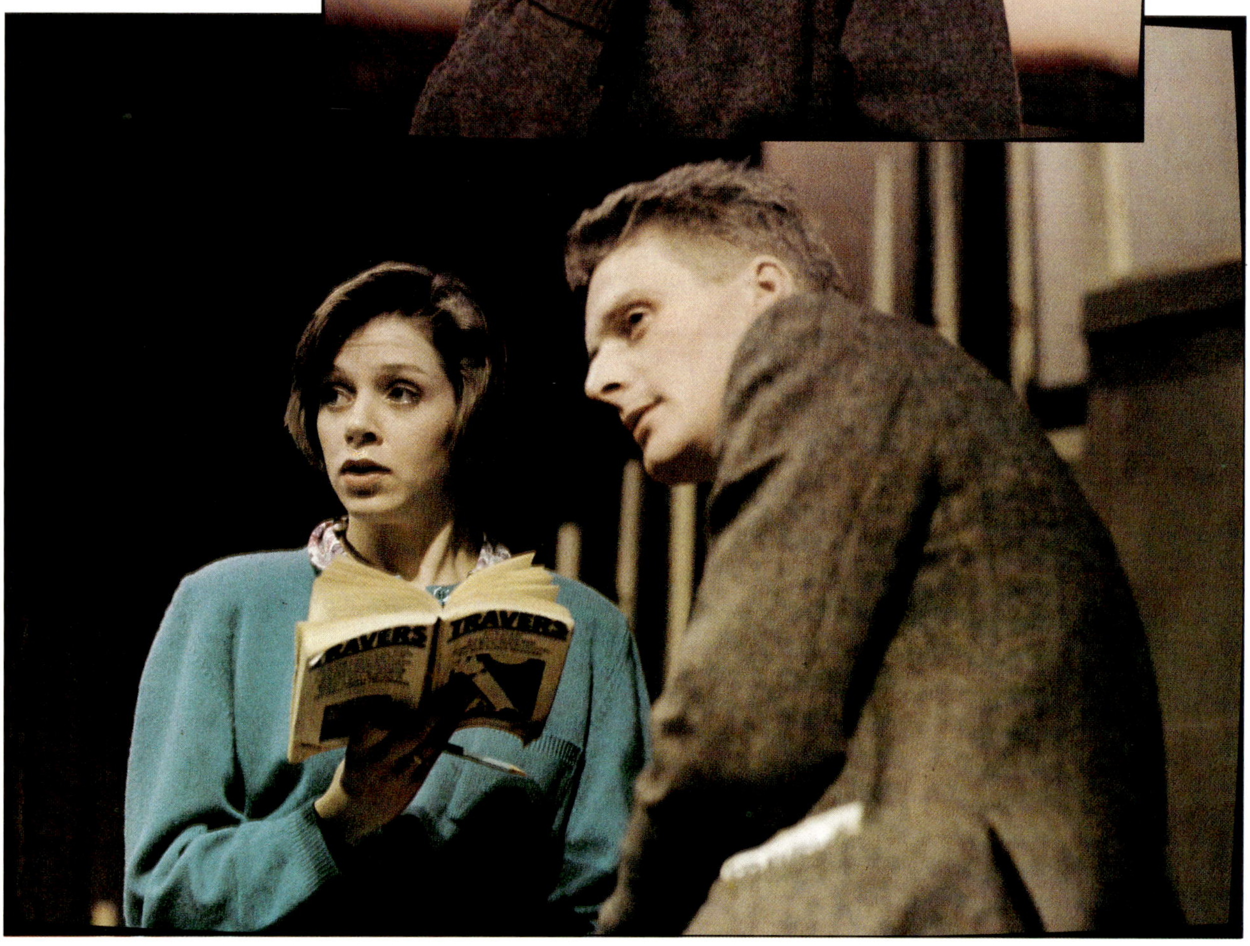

4-6: *This shot of the scene-painter at work was one of a sequence showing the backdrop – different parts still at different stages of completion. In the lighting gallery there is a wealth of interesting action to cover. But conditions are likely to be cramped, so you will have to take your position carefully – don't get in anyone's way!*

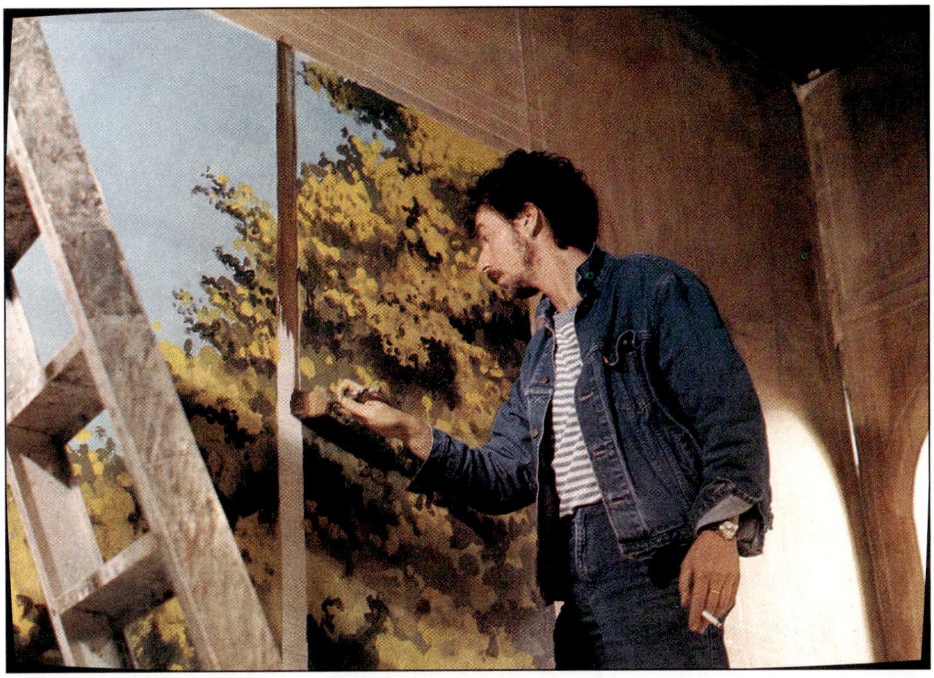

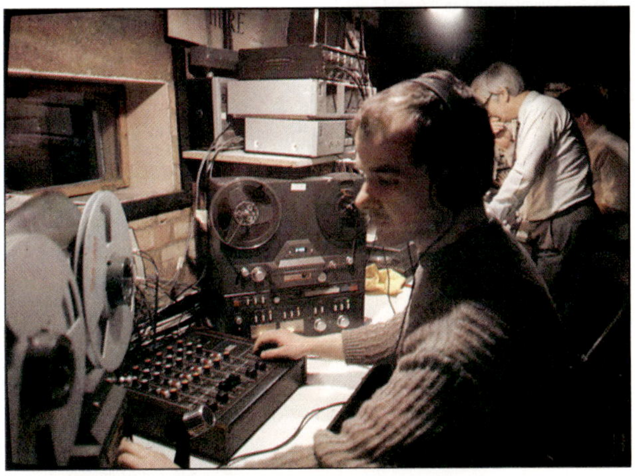

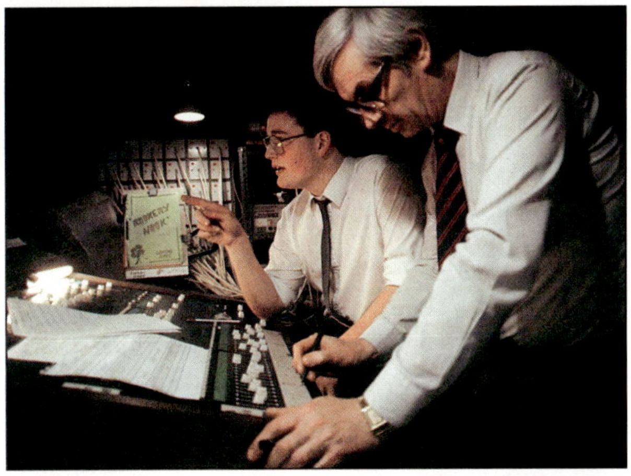

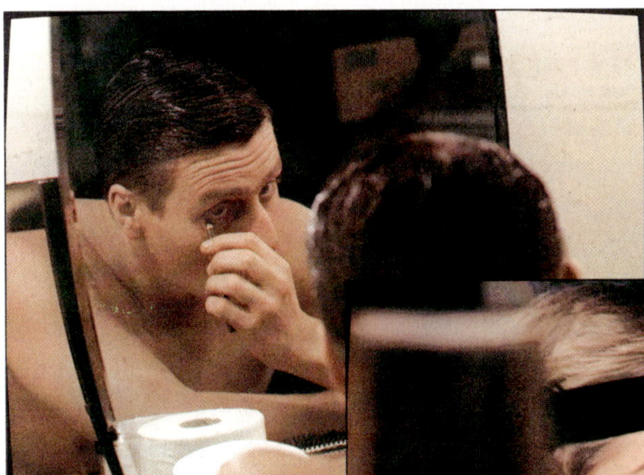

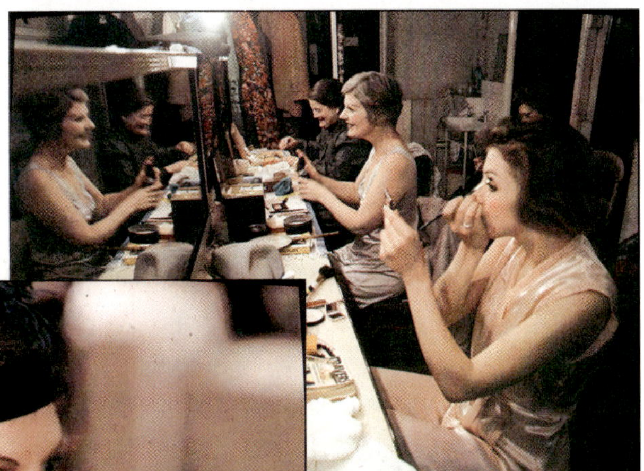

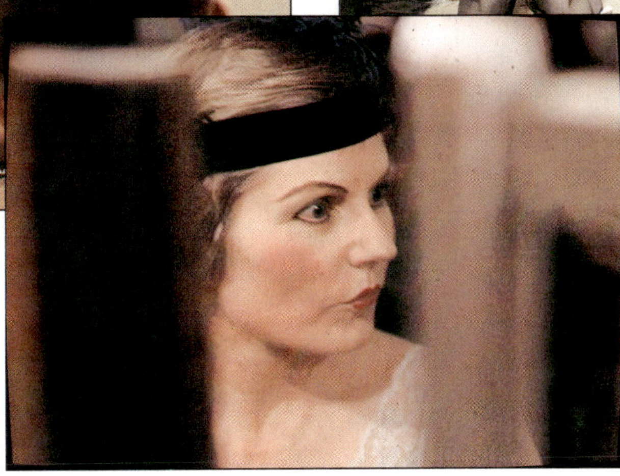

7-9: *As the actors make up for the dress rehearsal you should be on the alert to capture telling close-ups and long-shots as they exchange nervous jokes.*

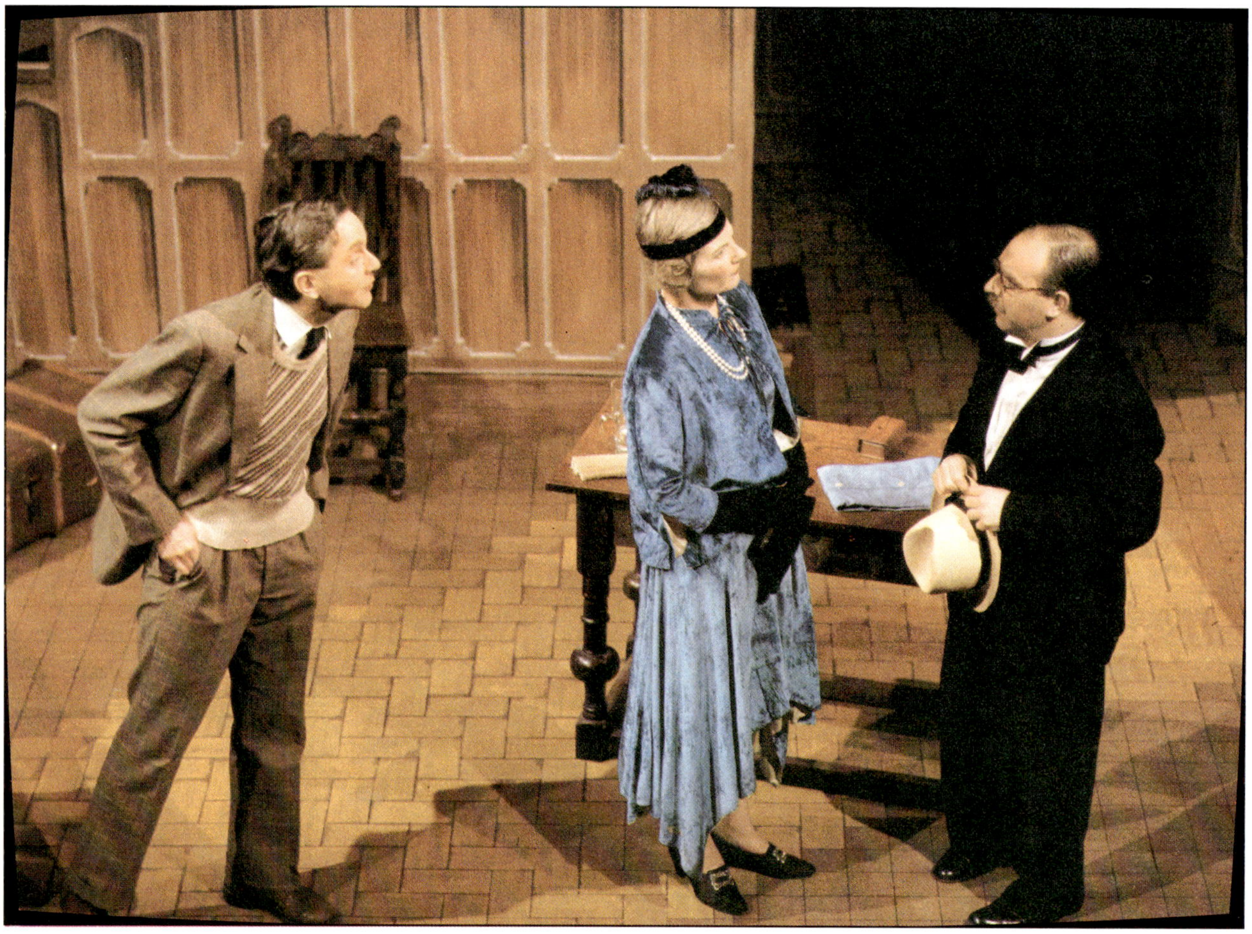

IN PRODUCTION

'It'll be all right on the night' could just as well be the optimistic battle cry of the video director about to shoot the real performance. You've thought of everything during rehearsals, so it should now, hopefully, be just a matter of letting the cameras 'roll'.

However, it is wiser to take a pessimistic view and plan for the worst. Before filming go through every conceivable check. Ensure that the equipment is in perfect working order and that the electrical connections are sound. Give the cables a good, though not too enthusiastic, tug to ensure that they are firm in their housings. If you are using batteries to power the camcorders, make sure that they are fully charged and that you have spares ready to hand. Double-check the camera positions and the tripod mountings. And finally, before the production begins, carry out a 15-minute test recording, reviewing it on a monitor to check that the camera is working properly. (Don't use this test tape for the actual recording, since although you can record over the test, quality might be impaired.)

For the first performance, the sound operator will have to double-check sound levels because the accoustics in a full theatre are very different from those in an empty one. You should also record the expectant hum of the audience in the moments before the curtain opens. This serves as a good introduction, builds tension and, as the noise subsides, signals that the action is about to begin.

When the action does begin, the director should keep in touch with the camera operators. This does not mean hovering behind their backs all the time. They will have their camera moves marked on their scripts and will have rehearsed their shots. The director's purpose is simply to reassure or to help out in emergencies.

After the performance is over, the temptation is immediately to review the material you have shot. But don't. The end of a performance is a time for releasing the tensions that have built up over the past few days or weeks. In any event you will be too close to the material to look at it objectively. Pack the equipment and wait until the next morning before evaluating what you have shot. If you can bear to wait for longer then do so. After two or three days you will approach the piece far more objectively, seeing the film as your intended audience might, instead of watching the version fixed in your imagination.

1: *During the first performance, one camera was positioned in the balcony to the left of the stage. This view is very theatrical, which is no bad thing in this context. Since the camera has a wide angle of view, slow pans to follow the action were possible, and do not appear too obtrusive to the viewer.*

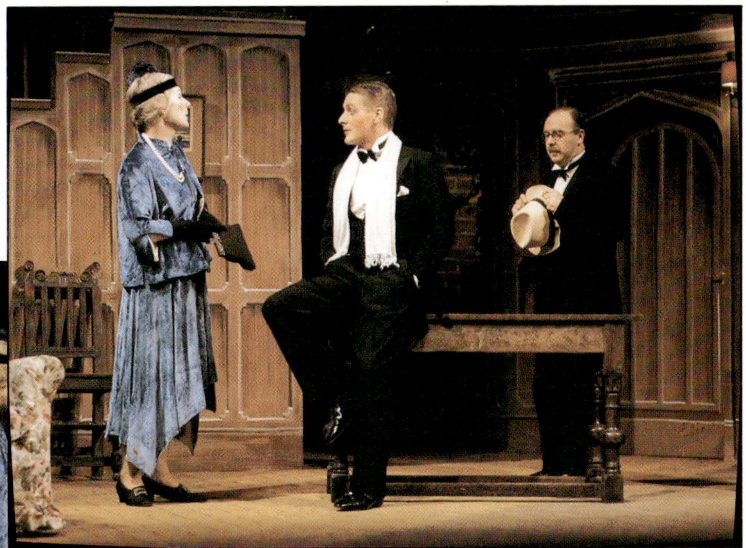

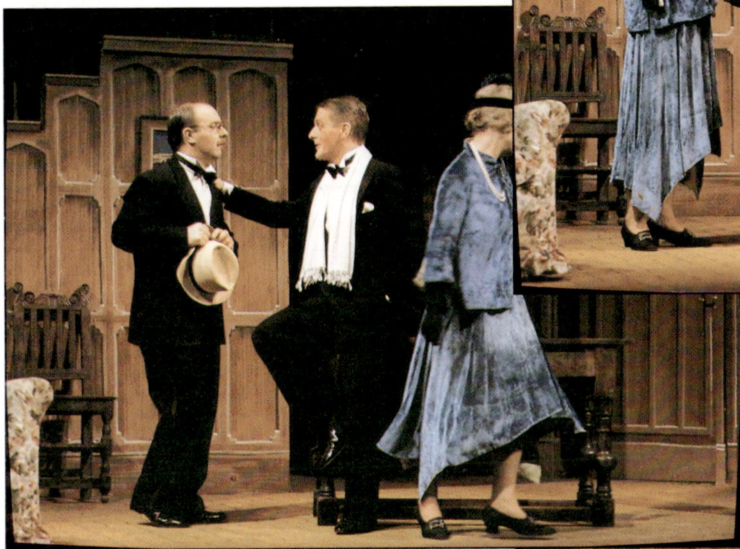

2-3: *Keep the main characters in the centre and do not move the camera too much. Do not worry if the shot is temporarily unbalanced.*

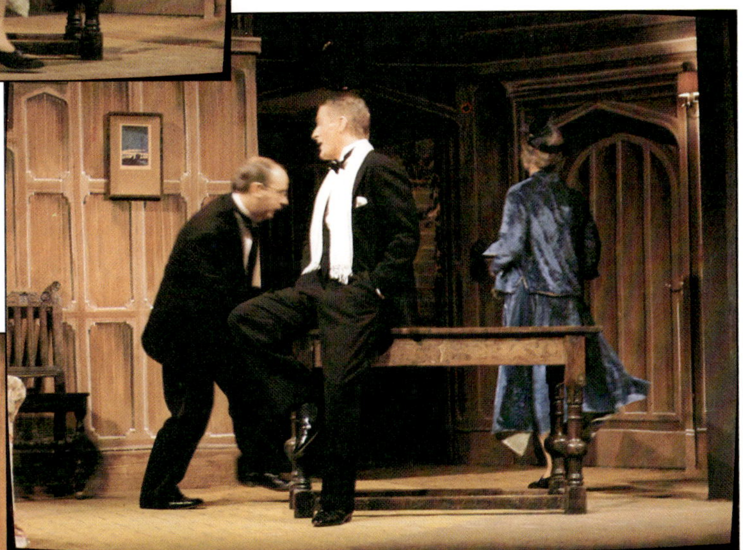

4: *Only small movements of the camera are necessary to highlight the character who is speaking. By placing him in the centre of the shot, the audience will instinctively direct their attention to him, rather than to others in the shot.*

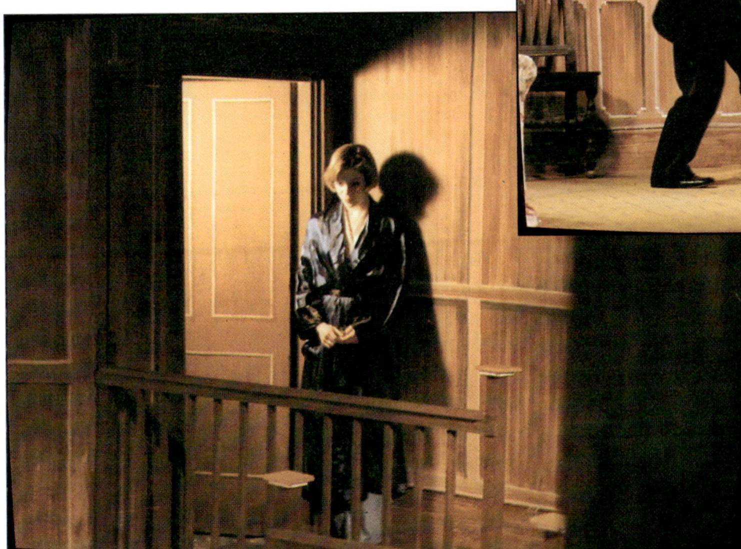

5-6: *Track the actress unobtrusively as she comes down the stairs, pulling out to end with both characters in long-shot.*

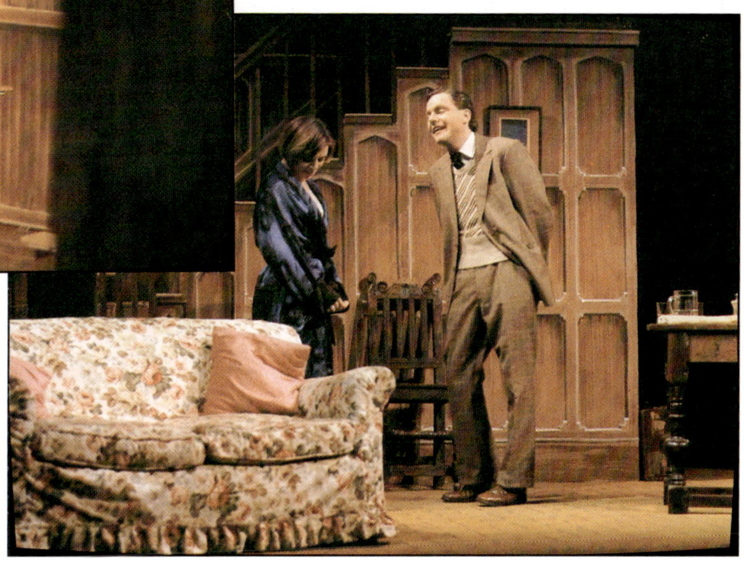

DRAMA CHECKLIST

Title ....

Company ....

Venue ....

REHEARSAL COVERAGE

PRELIMINARY REHEARSAL

Dates	Times	Details of coverage

TECHNICAL REHEARSAL

Date	Time	Detail of coverage

DRESS REHEARSAL

Date	Time	Detail of coverage

PRODUCTION RUN

Dates	Times	Details of coverage

OTHER SUBJECTS FOR COVERAGE

BACKGROUND TO PRODUCTION

Date	Time	Details of coverage

SOUND, MUSIC AND LIGHTING

Date	Time	Details of coverage

MAKE-UP AND COSTUMES

Date	Time	Details of coverage

MISCELLANEOUS

Date	Time	Details of coverage

VENUE DATA

POWER SUPPLY ....
LIGHTING REQUIREMENTS ....
SOUND REQUIREMENTS ....

TELEPHONE NUMBERS

VENUE ....
DIRECTOR ....

EQUIPMENT REQUIRED

- ☐ CAMCORDER AND ACCESSORIES
- ☐ LIGHTS
- ☐ BATTERIES
- ☐ TAPES

PEOPLE

DIRECTOR ....
STAGE MANAGER ....
LIGHTING ....
SOUND ....
DESIGNER ....
CAST ....
FRONT OF HOUSE ....
VENUE ADMINISTRATOR ....

A video of a theatrical production can be much more than a simple record of the actors on the stage with a few rehearsal sequences added for extra interest. The whole story of how the play is put together and the relationships between the different people involved can make a fascinating story in their own right. To achieve this type of coverage you will, of course, need the full cooperation of all the people involved – you will be filming them off-stage as much as on-stage – and you will have to be discreet. One of the most rewarding areas will be recording the activity backstage. Although you may not be welcome backstage during the run of the production, you will probably be able to film at the dress rehearsal – in fact your presence may help to release tension and dispel nerves.

Before you begin, decide what your approach is going to be – is it the characters of the actors that most interest you, or the mechanics of the production itself. The shots on this page come from sequences showing the actors applying their make-up. Video is an ideal medium with which to explore this area – the gradual transformation of the actor's face can be shown much better than in still photography. But there are pitfalls. Beware of poor or uneven lighting – the light is likely to be good around the mirrors, but poor elsewhere, so you may have trouble judging the exposure in longshots.

A STORY WITHIN A STORY

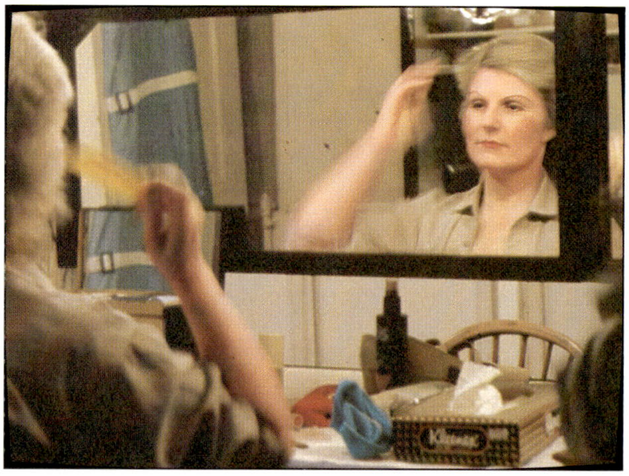

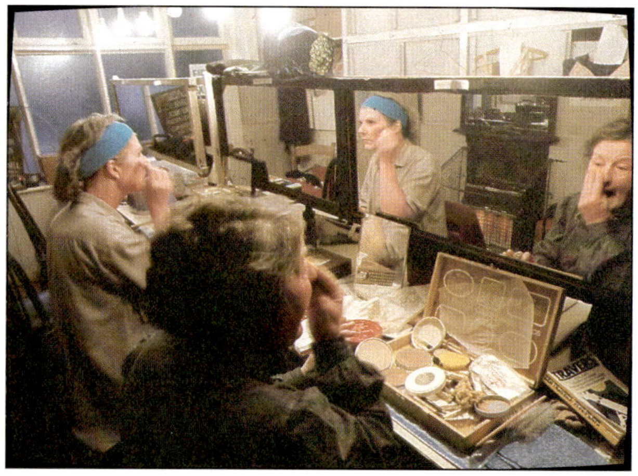

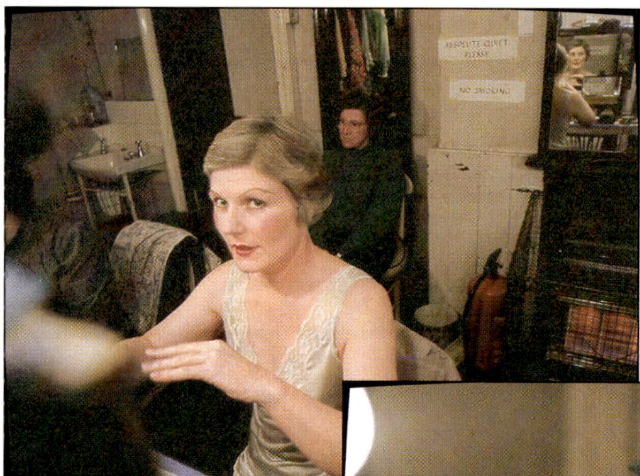

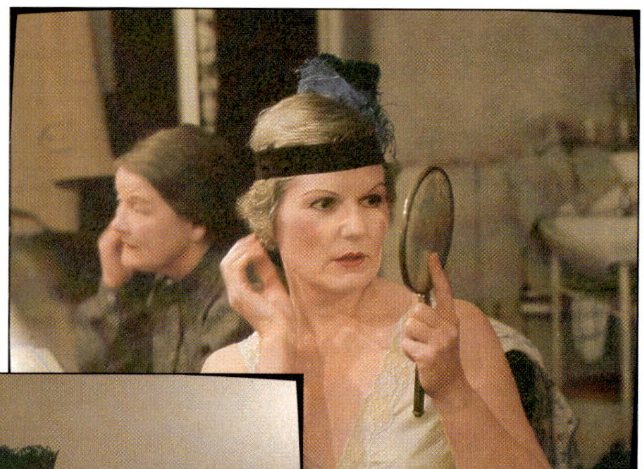

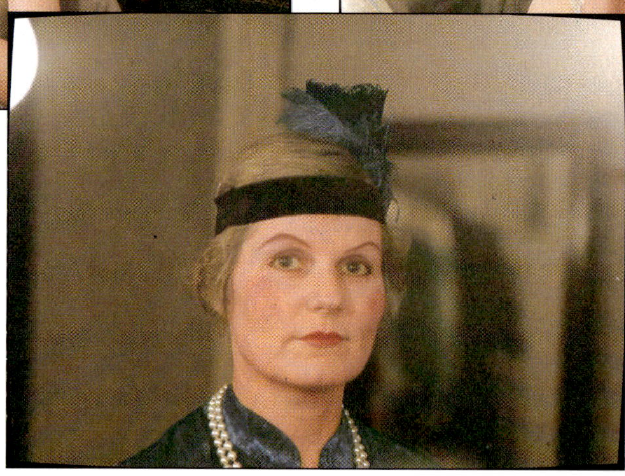

1-4: *The actor making up is a fascinating subject, but it is usually necessary to inject some movement into the sequence by using different camera positions. It will also help if the subject's concentration is broken occasionally, as in the shot above, in which she pauses momentarily to glance at the camera.*

5: *The transformation is complete. This head-on shot shows us the finished effect as the actress leaves the dressing room.*

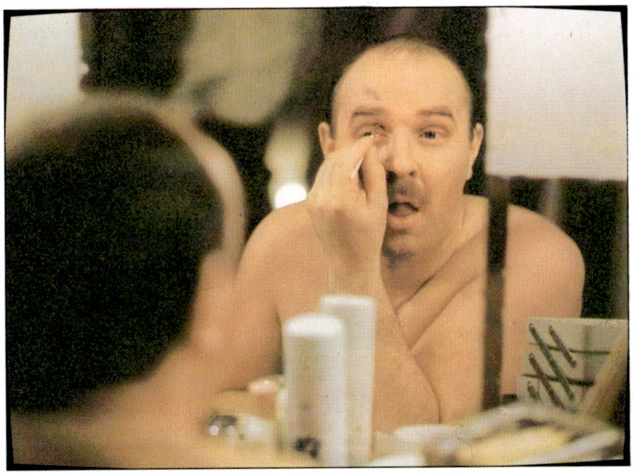

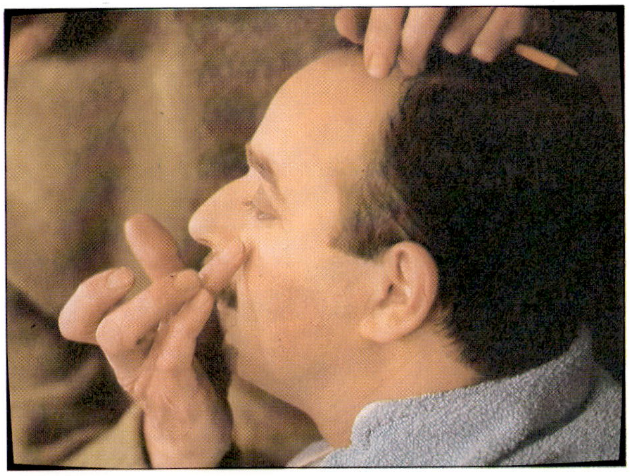

6-8: *Close-ups can be an ideal way of showing the viewer exactly what is going on. Again, the subject is static, so it helps if the camera position changes. More apparent movement can be obtained by changing the focus from the subject to his mirror image.*

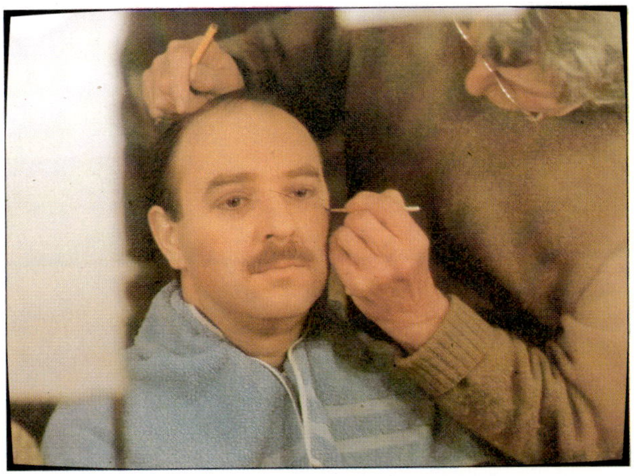

9: *Longer shots relieve the intensity of the close-ups – and give an impression of the atmosphere and clutter of the dressing room.*

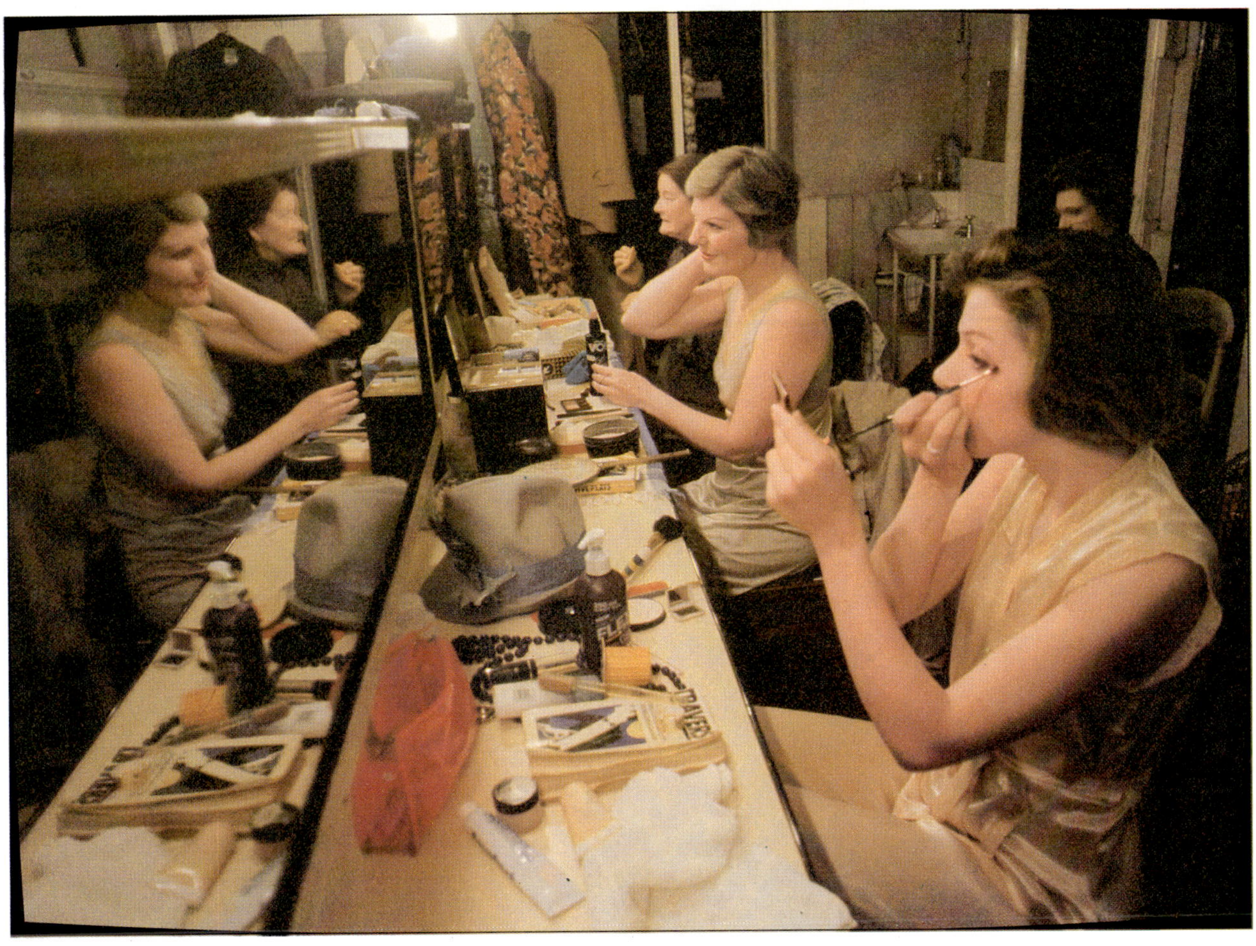

SOUND AND LIGHTING PLAN

LIGHTING

PRODUCTION ....

DATE ....

POSITION ON GRID	BAR ONE	BAR TWO	BAR THREE	STANDS
LANTERN NUMBER				
CIRCUIT				
TYPE NUMBER				
COLOUR				
SETTING/FOCUS				

CUE	PAGE NUMBER	WORD CUE	DESCRIPTION	TIME				

Photocopy these sample sound and lighting forms and make a record of the theatrical effects that are being produced. This will give you an indication of the adjustments that you will have to make to the video sound and lighting to reproduce the same effects.

SOUND

PRODUCTION ....

DATE ....

CUE	PAGE NUMBER	EFFECT	TAPE	VOLUME	SPEAKERS

PROJECT NOTEBOOK

THEATRE

The possibilities for effective coverage expand with additional equipment and extra crew. But so do your responsibilities. You are, after all, using the time and talents of a number of people to achieve your results. Acting the 'director' in the tough, Hollywood mould is going get you nowhere. The right approach combines co-operation, consultation and courtesy. You should master the art of delegation, too. If you entrust someone with the sound, let them get on with it. Your job is to plan and co-ordinate the coverage and to decide exactly which shots you want.

■ Take an overall view of the project, but don't forget to think about the details too.

■ Choose a method of working, explain it to your team, and then stick to it. If you suddenly decide to change your mind, explain to everyone exactly why you have done so.

■ Don't replicate material unnecessarily. This sounds obvious, but it is easy, when, say, taking a second shoot, to leave a camera in the same position as it was in the first – from which you already have perfect coverage. The new material that you get from a new position might not be of any use, but, on the other hand, it just might be.

■ When working with a limited team, make sure that each person is capable of carrying out the roles you have allocated. Remember, no-one can check for continuity lapses and at the same time monitor sound levels. Give them compatible roles.

■ Think of the others. *You* might be ready and eager to go for the twenty-second take of a scene. The actors might appreciate a lunch break.

■ Make clear at the outset what rewards your helpers will get – an end-of-shoot meal, perhaps, or an invitation to a party for the first showing of the tape – everyone works better with some treat in store, no matter how small.

EDITING TECHNIQUES

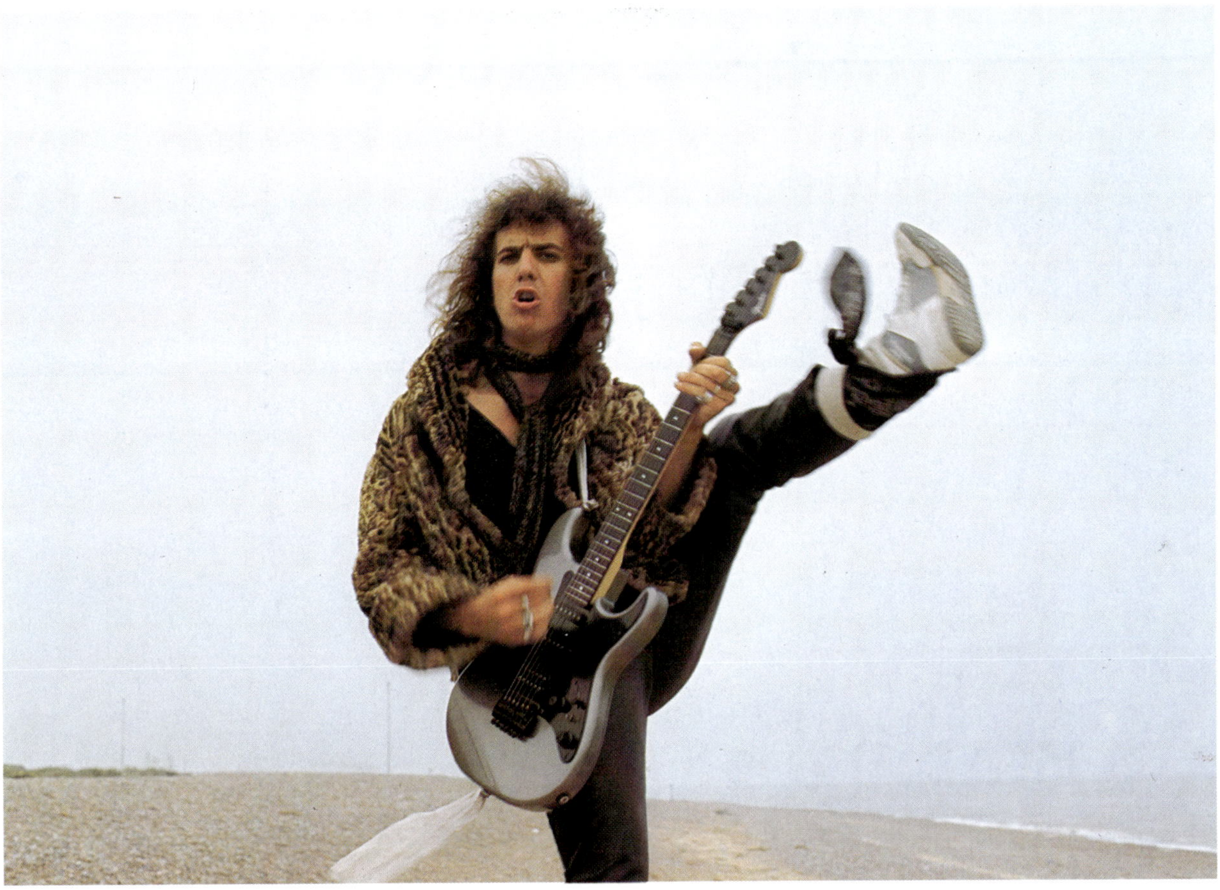

The question of editing has been touched upon at various stages in this book. This chapter looks at editing and other post-production options in detail. It examines editing procedures and the different styles of editing that can be used to shape your coverage into a polished, finished tape. Many of these techniques can be achieved at home, but to achieve stable, professional looking tapes may require the use of more professional studio equipment. Sophisticated electronic special effects, familiar to everyone through the explosion of pop videos, may be expensive, but the chapter also offers alternatives available to the amateur.

Rock videos borrow from all other video disciplines, using elements of drama, fantasy, documentary and action coverage. The intention is to produce a tape which conveys an 'image' of the band and matches their kind of music.

Before editing, however, you have to make several basic decisions. For example, will you be using a studio tape for the soundtrack (as is likely), so making redundant sound recordings on location? (The only exception to this circumstance would be when recording a live performance, for which professional sound engineers would be essential.) Also, when scripting the video (which will probably be done with the band) you will have to decide what is, and what is not possible in terms of video technique and the resources available.

Once such matters have been tackled, you must then consider your coverage in detail. If you can shoot with two or more cameras so much the better. If not, ask the band to perform a number of times to get shots from as many different angles as possible. A pre-shoot location check will be necessary to ensure that you have unusual backgrounds and camera positions.

In a rock video, the editing conventions that would apply, for instance, to a drama, are far less important. For example, you can jump from one shot to another, changing camera angles and frame sizes between cuts in a way that would be incoherent in conventional work. In fact, the main danger is that your coverage will be too static and that there will not be enough variety of material with which to edit. Don't be afraid to try the seemingly preposterous in such a situation – you can always discard it when editing. Remember that your musicians will probably prefer an original approach in their video.

SHOOTING TO EDIT

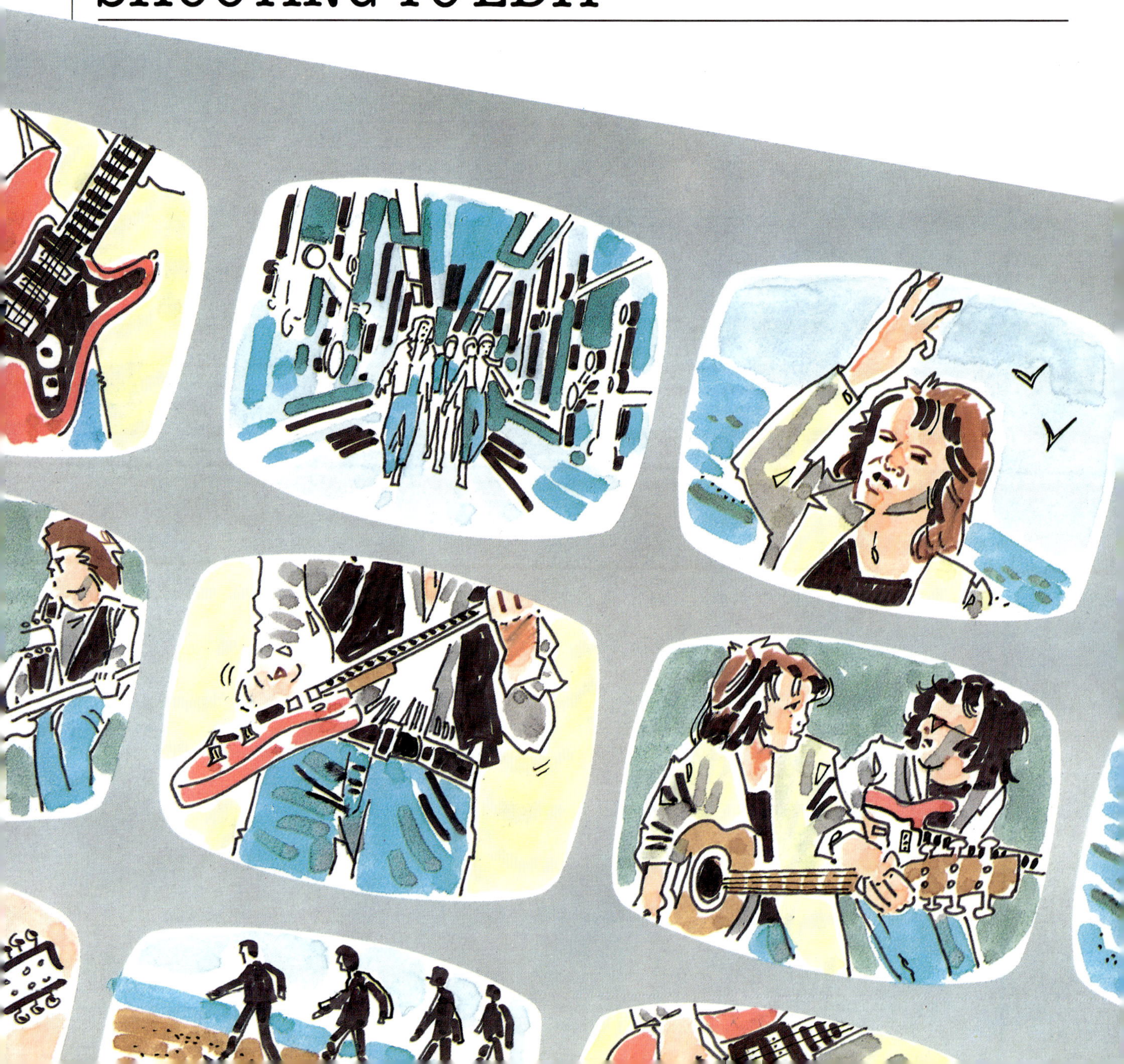

Using locations

A rock video allows you to be bold with locations. In recent years particular styles have been established by professional producers. The two styles that stand out are the exotic tropical beach and the backstreet city scene. Factory interiors, run-down and derelict sites, docklands and underground car parks are other alternatives.

When drawing up rough storyboard ideas for the rock video, keep the band's music in mind. A heavy metal group are not going to be too keen on a rural setting. Listen to the lyrics of the song to discover if there are any references you can illustrate visually, or which can become the basis of your narrative. And finally ensure that your video ideas match the image which the members have of themselves.

Below: *When you plan a rock video don't get so carried away by the images that you forget the music itself. Keep listening to a tape of the song and refer to the score.*

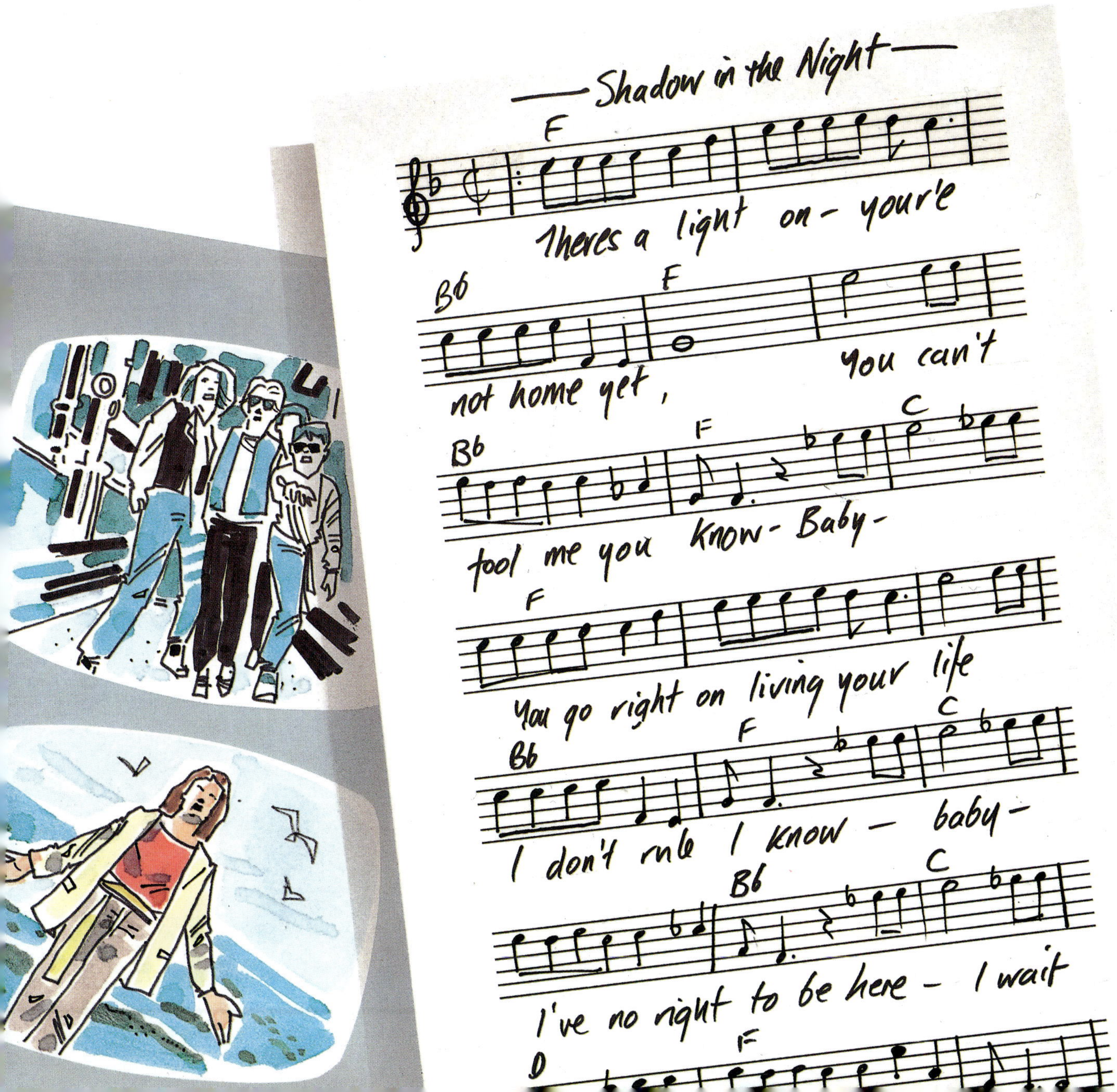

Editing is at the heart of the video-making process. At the most basic level, its purpose is to eliminate poor shots and other mistakes, ensuring that your audience sees a slick, polished video. But in most cases, the value of editing is far greater than this.

Extensive editing means imparting a sense of pace and rhythm to a tape. In the case of a rock video this is a particularly important consideration. The images must match the soundtrack for pace and

The shots on this page show some of the raw material available for use when editing a rock tape. The coverage shows the group playing inside the hall of a power generating plant, which though initially it may seem an unlikely setting it is in fact highly appropriate. Being an unexpected backdrop it provokes interest. And there is also a deliberate, implied link between the potentially explosive nature of energy and the group's music.

THE POWER OF EDITING

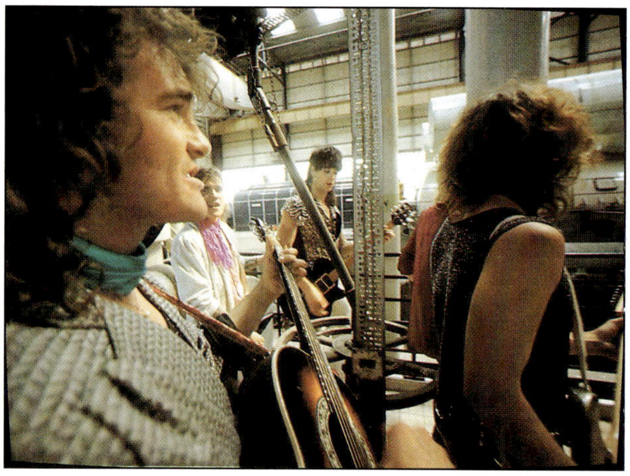

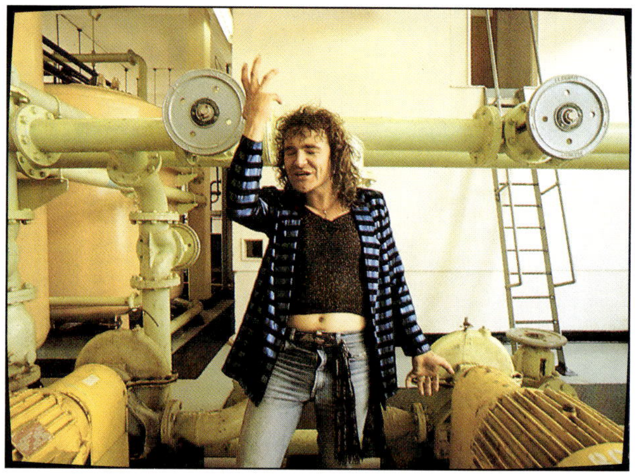

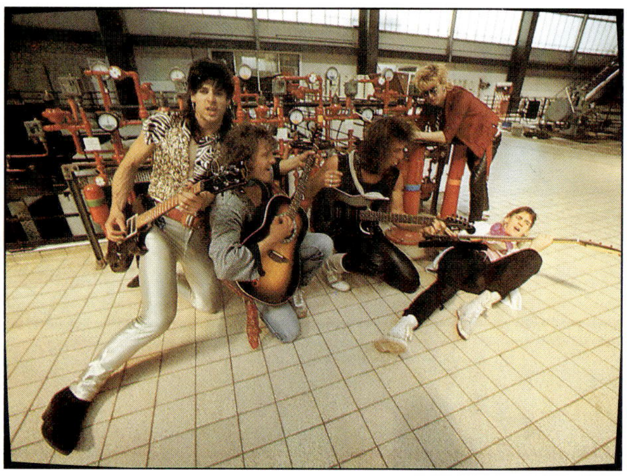

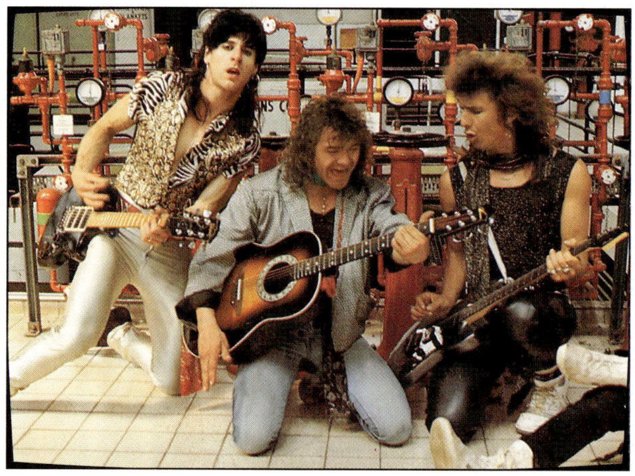

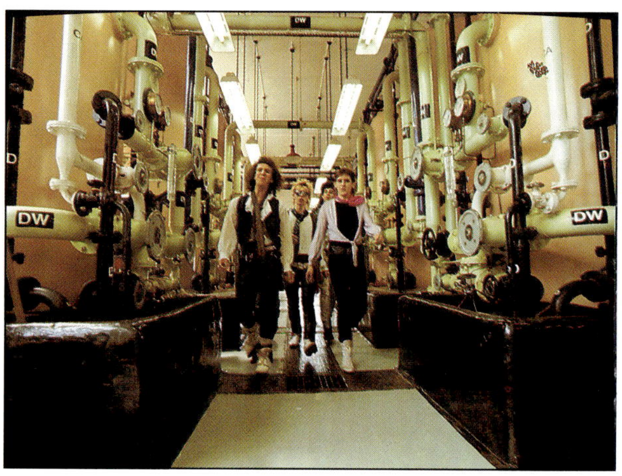

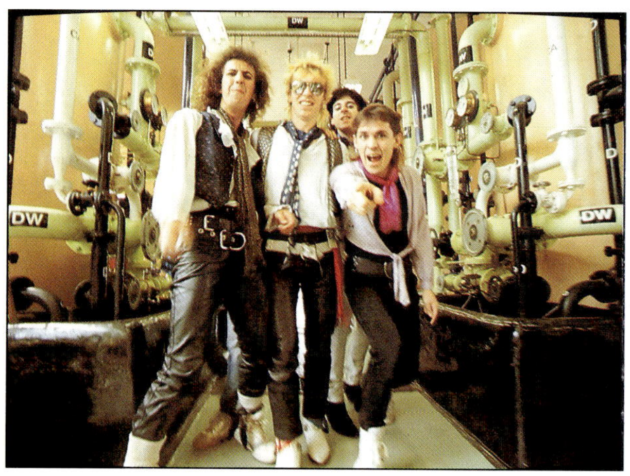

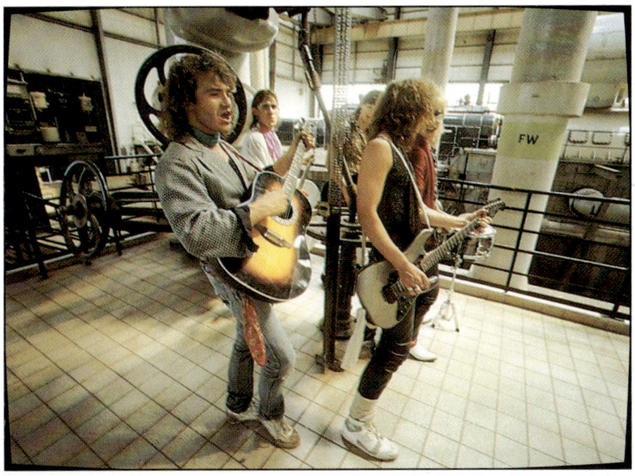
FW
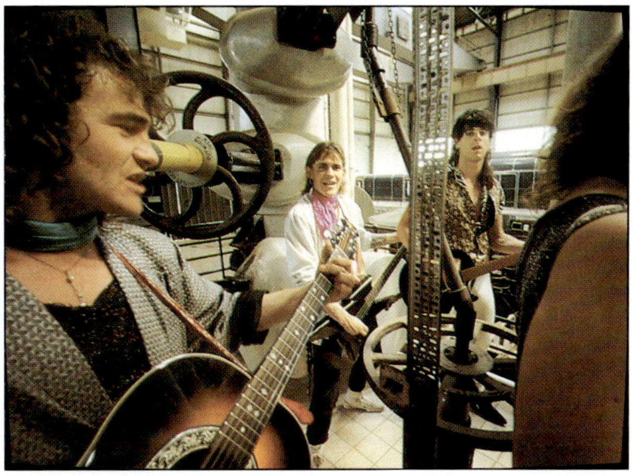
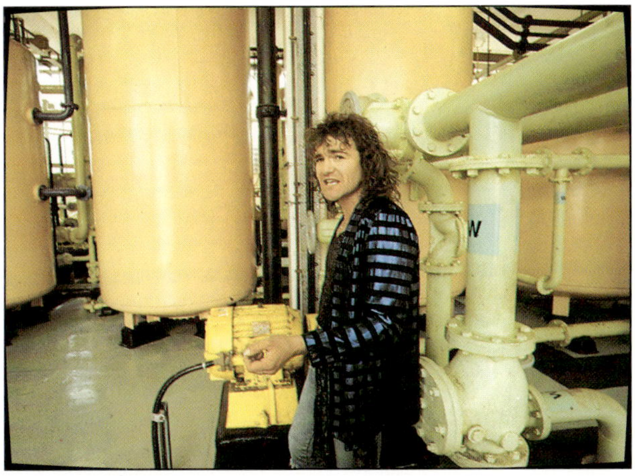
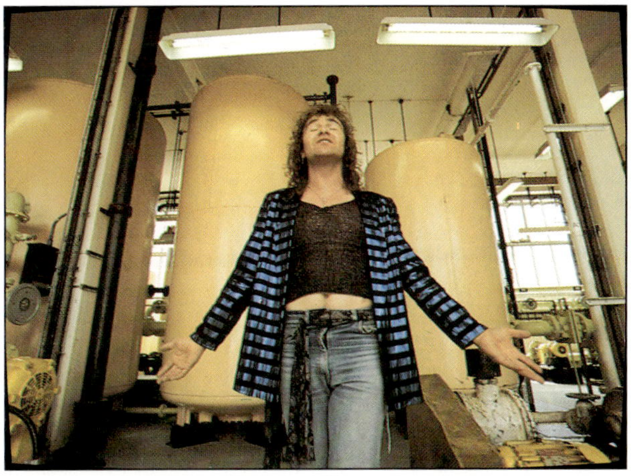
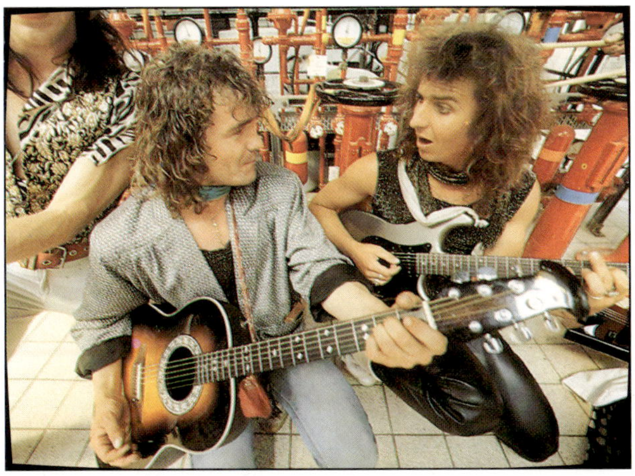
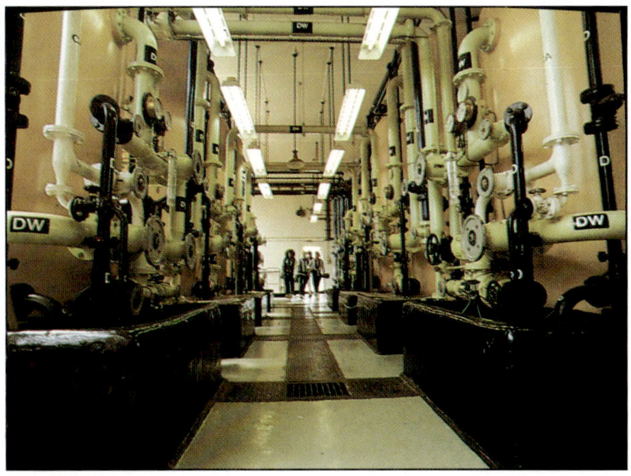
DW
DW
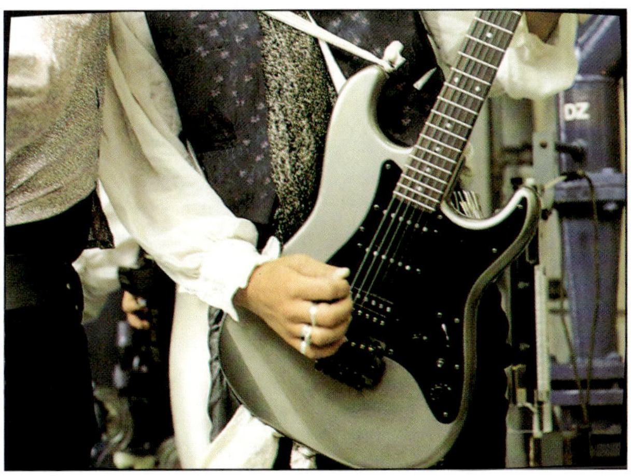
DZ
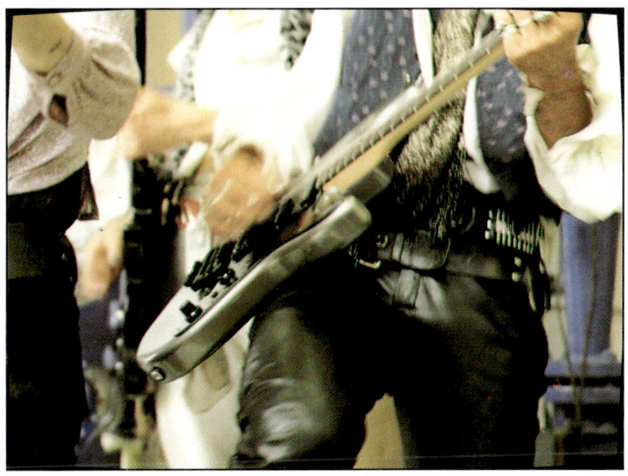

excitement. In professional rock videos, therefore, cuts between shots tend to be rapid and obtrusive, with the video director drawing his audience's attention to his techniques. With quieter, more melodic soundtracks, the reverse is the case – cuts should be unobtrusive and serve only to allow the story to unfold clearly.

Editing can also have a profound effect on the meaning conveyed by the images. Consider, for example, a sequence showing a group of youths walking down a street and another showing a senior citizen out shopping. By rapidly cutting between each one, you could easily create a sense of menace, implying that the youths were about to attack the senior citizen. If instead the two sequences are shown consecutively, there is no menace, just street scenes. The power of editing to manipulate how a viewer interprets visual information should never be underestimated.

On the other hand, there need not necessarily be a sense of menace when using these two elements, so much as a sense of identity. By clever intercutting you could suggest that one day these youths will resemble the senior citizen – or that the senior citizen would like to relive his own youth. You could make any one of these suggestions using the same basic material just by editing it differently. But in a rock video these techniques will have to reflect the words of the song – then their effect will be even more powerful.

Another possibility is to make the images reflect the music in a more abstract way, responding to the changes in rhythm, pitch and dynamics rather like disco lights. In this case it would matter less what the actual subject matter of the video was. It would be much more important to make the edits so that they synchronise exactly with the music. This sort of technique could produce a rather relentless result if

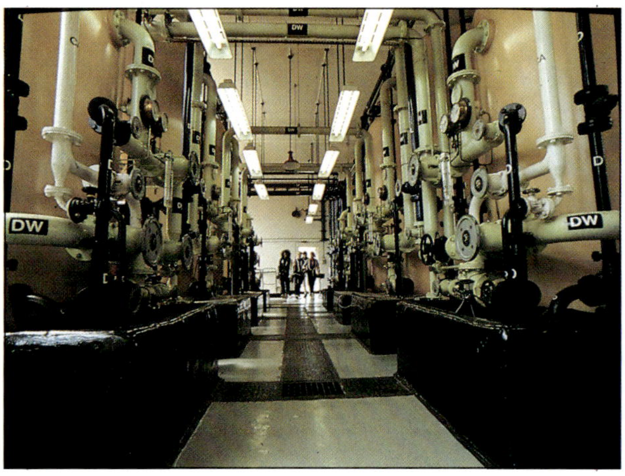

1: *Sequence showing the band approaching the camera along one of the long interior corridors. Could use as a repeated cut on the beat of the song. Make sure band recognizable when they are at far end of corridor.*

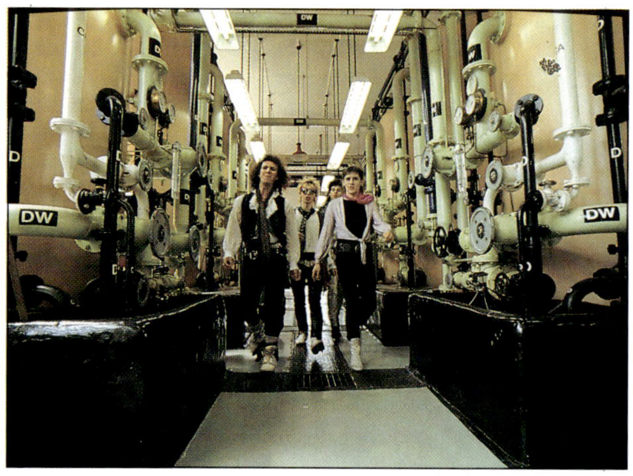

2: *Check this sequence for any interference caused by the fluorescent lighting. Colour correction filter seems to have worked. Watch out for distortion of verticals caused by camera angle.*

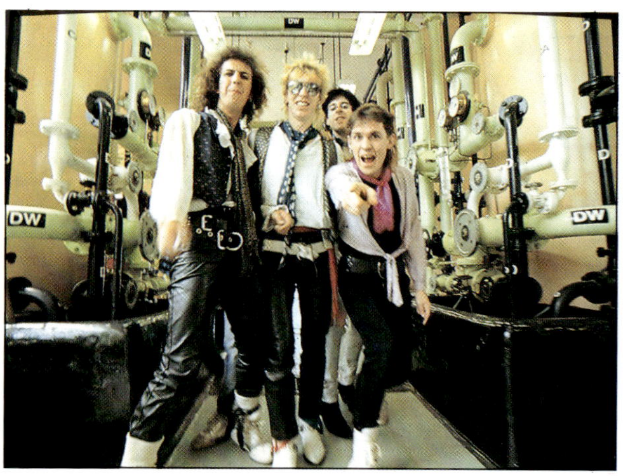

3: *This end-of-sequence shot looks a bit too posed. Like shot 1, it could be used as a repeated cut, but only for very short bursts – probably better to stick to earlier shots from the sequence.*

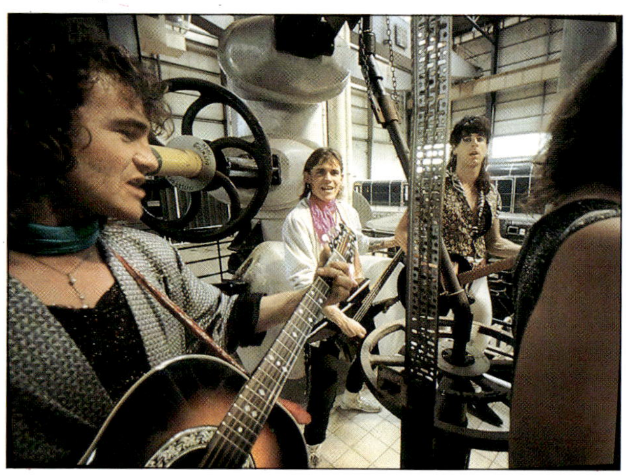

4: *Don't like the framing in this – it seems confused and no one is really prominent. Movement is too horizontal across frame – no diagonals. Not exactly no good, but would prefer to drop it.*

used all the way through a video. But employed in a short, dynamic sequence it can be very effective, forcibly drawing the viewer's attention to the patterns in the music.

At the end of the day, the way you edit a rock video should depend on the effect that the musicians want, and there are as many ways of editing as there are of making music. Listen as much as you can to the track you are making the video for and some influence is bound to rub off. Finally, remember that, although the musicians will probably demand to have the final choice, you can make as many different suggestions to them as you like. They will not necessarily know about every effect that you can create in video, and there is a world of difference between a romantic, Hollywood-inspired approach and a staccato, post-modernist one. You should be aware of as many different alternatives in editing methods and approaches as possible.

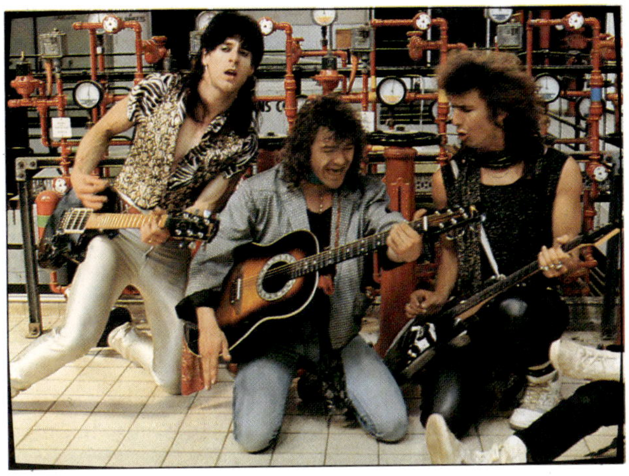

5: *OK, but a bit contrived. The main problem really is that these shots are a bit too friendly – they don't convey the hi-tech, hard-edged atmosphere we are looking for. Suggest that we cut them out.*

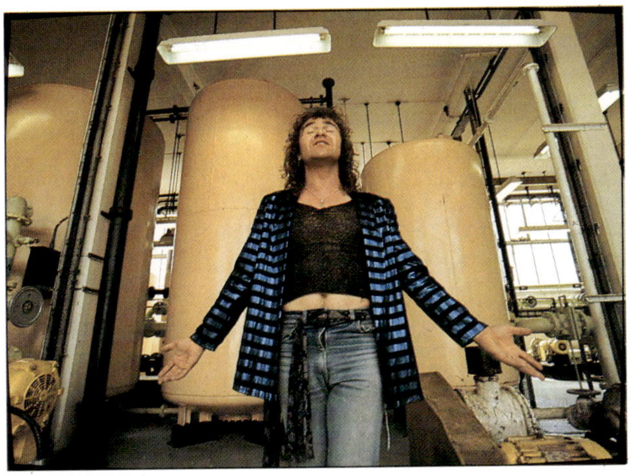

6: *No. This is the place to bring in the cut. I like the low camera angle which both emphasizes the size of the building and gives a good frame for the singer. Background not too confusing but still hi-tech enough.*

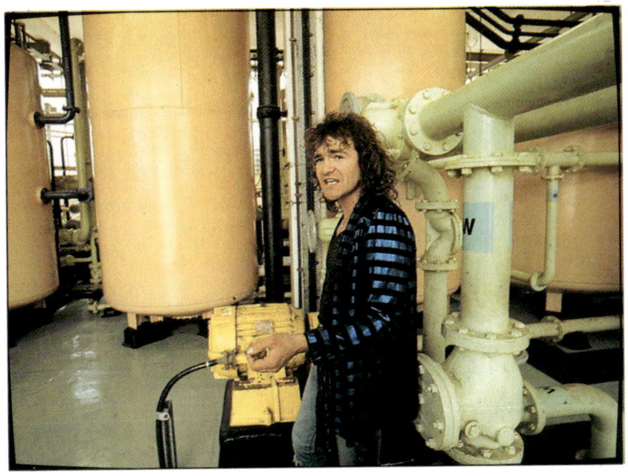

7: *Again, this has the background we are looking for, and continues nicely where the crab-shot left off. Definitely use this footage.*

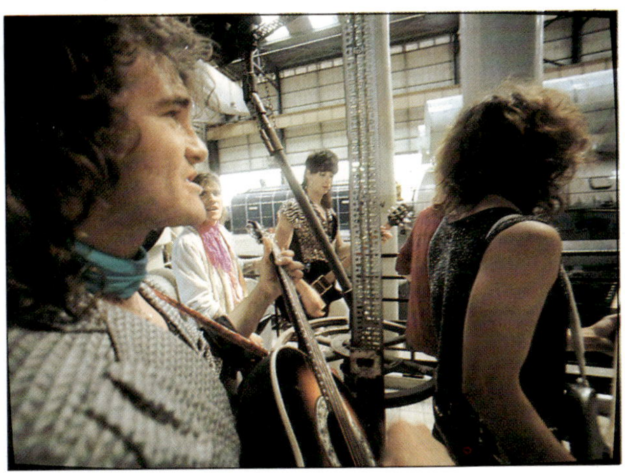

8: *Good, strong performance coverage. Watch out that the two performers at back are not obscured for too long as camera crabs round. Can use provided that we also keep wide-angle shot showing all of band.*

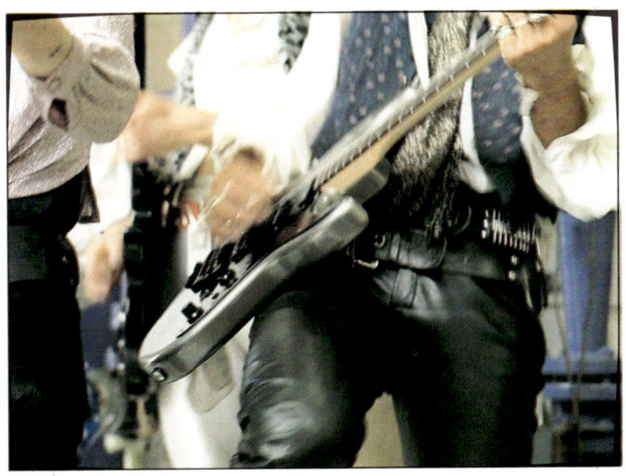

9: *Zoom in from shot of whole band. Good close-up to cut in during guitar riff.*

THE MEDIUM

As we have emphasized throughout this book, video is an electronic medium, not photographic. The video image consists of lines of information recorded on magnetic tape. Editing video means copying those elements of information you require on to a new tape in the order that you require them. In theory, this sounds like a simple procedure, but in practice it raises problems which can only be totally overcome by means of sophisticated electronic equipment. However, there is much that can be achieved by simpler equipment or manual means.

The first difficulty is caused by the fact that the lines of video information are recorded diagonally on the video tape. Imagine that a new signal is introduced. It would, more likely than not, start somewhere in the middle of one of the slanting lines with the new picture beginning to be scanned somewhere between the top and bottom of the screen. This causes a slight blip, but provided that the record-VCR has the feature known as 'automatic backspace' (or 'fine edit'), the transition is normally invisible on screen. Although simple edits can be carried out by manual control of the 'source' and 'record' VCRs, it is much easier and quicker to use an automatic edit controller. This will make the location of the edit-points easier to find. For really accurate edits, the 'backspace time' on the 'record' VCR (an interval of 1-2 seconds during which it 'finds' and 'locks onto' the end of the previous shot before it begins to record) has to be offset by setting the 'source' tape 'early' by the same amount. This can be done either automatically, or manually on the newer VCRs which feature forward/reverse 'jog' controls.

Edit-points are set by holding the machines on 'pause', but the time spent waiting on pause should be minimized as this wears the tape and can affect the stability of the edit.

A third consideration is that copying from tape can only be accomplished a number of times before the quality of the image degenerates. Usually, tapes will not stand more than two generations of copying – one copy of a copy. You can overcome this to some extent by editing with a copy tape and then going back to the original for the final copy.

How video works

It helps an understanding of the editing process to know something about what happens inside the camcorder – how light is turned into electronic signals that are recorded on tape. The camcorder's lens works in the same way as the lens in a still camera – it is essentially a piece of equipment for gathering rays of light coming from the subject. But here the resemblence to a conventional camera ends. On early video cameras the light was gathered into a pick-up tube which worked rather like an old-fashioned radio valve. This system was slow to warm up, heavy, delicate, and used a lot of power. Modern camcorders replace the tube with charge-coupled devices (CCDs), which are light-sensitive cells connected to circuitry that generates an electrical charge that varies according to the amount of light present. The CCDs are grouped in three to deal with the three main colours (red, blue and green) of which light is made up. They are lightweight, need only low power, and work as soon as you switch on. These advantages mean that most modern camcorders use CCDs.

There is some variation in the way in which the video information is actually recorded on the tape. On tape for use in regular home video, the information concerning the image is recorded in diagonal lines across the magnetic coating of the tape. The audio information, on early models, was recorded in a band running along one edge of the tape. On more recent hi-fi audio models, it is recorded in diagonal lines along with the video, and so is not separately dubbable. The latest equipment has pulse-code modulated (PCM) audio, which can be dubbed.

Professional tape formats like U-matic follow the same principles as versions designed for the home market. Greater image quality is achieved because the tape is larger and can therefore carry more information. In addition to a control track, professional tape may also have a time code, essential for accurate professional editing.

Right: *The diagram shows the degeneration of the video image as successive copies of a tape are made. The degeneration is more likely to occur in a heavily-edited tape, since this will have more inherent electronic instability.*

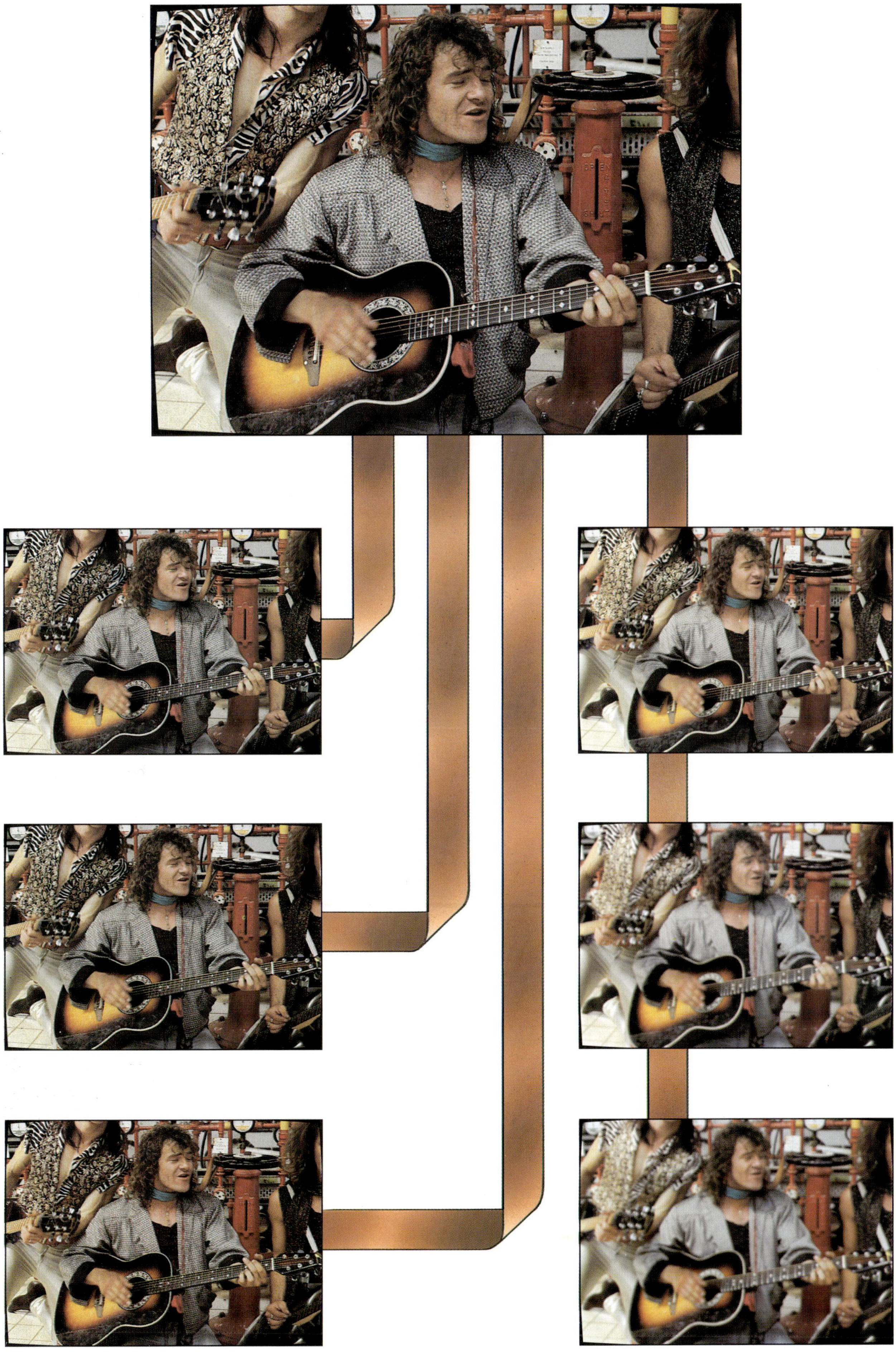

In professional video, the budget may allocate as much money for the post-production stage as for the actual shoot. The complex computer-based editing equipment found in professional editing suites is very expensive indeed. Hire rates can be calculated in terms of thousands of pounds per hour. However, there are opportunities for the amateur to use such equipment. Many video clubs and societies have contacts with independent companies who are keen to encourage new talent. And local colleges or arts clubs may also have basic professional facilities. Polite persistance can win through – it never does any harm to ask.

If you do obtain access to such facilities, precisely what equipment might you use, and what advantages will such equipment bring? Knowing this in advance will enable you to be more ambitious when planning your own project.

The most sophisticated editing suites resemble the mission control rooms for space shuttle flights. The computer power available is not much less. Here, images can be manipulated at will to create a huge range of special effects. And there is still the basic editing equipment to perform the fundamental editing process of arranging cuts in the required sequences.

The editing suite consists of a panel of in-built monitors and a huge array of controls. Many of these controls have solely technical functions, regulating the transport and playback of the tape on source and edit decks. Others control the audio signal, allowing levels to be adjusted. Those which control the image alone allow varying degrees of adjustment – colour tone, brightness and contrast, for example, or speed, so that fast or slow motion sequences can be introduced. There may also be the option of fade-out or fade-in and wipes and dissolves between shots. In most studios there will be a technician who will be thoroughly skilled in using the facility and who will work according to your instructions, so you should not worry overmuch about precise technicalities.

PROFESSIONAL EQUIPMENT

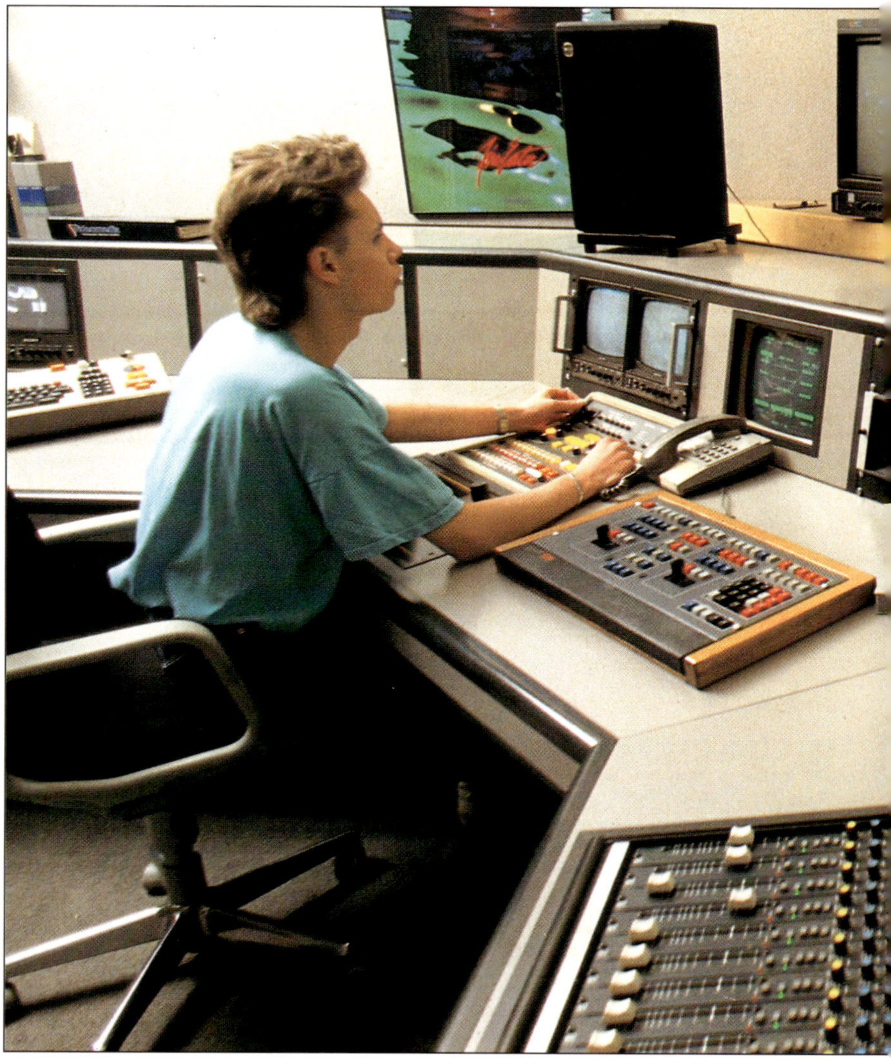

Right: *A modern, computer-controlled editing suite provides the full facilities for mixing video and audio material. A professional editor will operate the suite and help you obtain the effects you require.*

If you do get into an editing suite remember that time is money, big money. You should therefore arrive well prepared knowing exactly what you want to achieve. This is not the time to be indecisive, wondering, perhaps, whether another idea would be more appropriate.

Take along your clearly labelled master material (the original tapes) and an editing script with each cut marked and timed. It should also indicate on which of the master tapes the material is located, and exactly where it is on that tape. Before getting down to work, you will be able to go over material with the studio editor.

Once the editing begins, the editor will inform you of any problems that occur. Perhaps a required cut that you wish to make is not possible at the exact point indicated because you neglected to allow enough editing margin on the shot. (When shooting, remember to set the camera rolling five seconds before action begins.) After each cut, the editor will replay it to check that you have the footage you want and that the edit is stable.

While making the edit, the editor will be continuously checking audio and video levels and looking for signs of instability in the image. He may point out small glitches that had escaped you when you reviewed the material. Also, he will be available to answer any questions you might have.

A vital piece of equipment in the suite is the editing controller. This is linked up to two video recording decks, the 'source' deck and the 'record' deck, and ensures that they perform in synchronization. It will then switch the 'source' deck to play and the 'record' deck to record, so that they are 'in sync'. For example, it ensures that the roll-back on both decks is identical. It will then switch the source deck to play and the edit deck to record so allowing the edit to be made at the precise point required. The edit can then be reviewed on the monitors attached to the two decks.

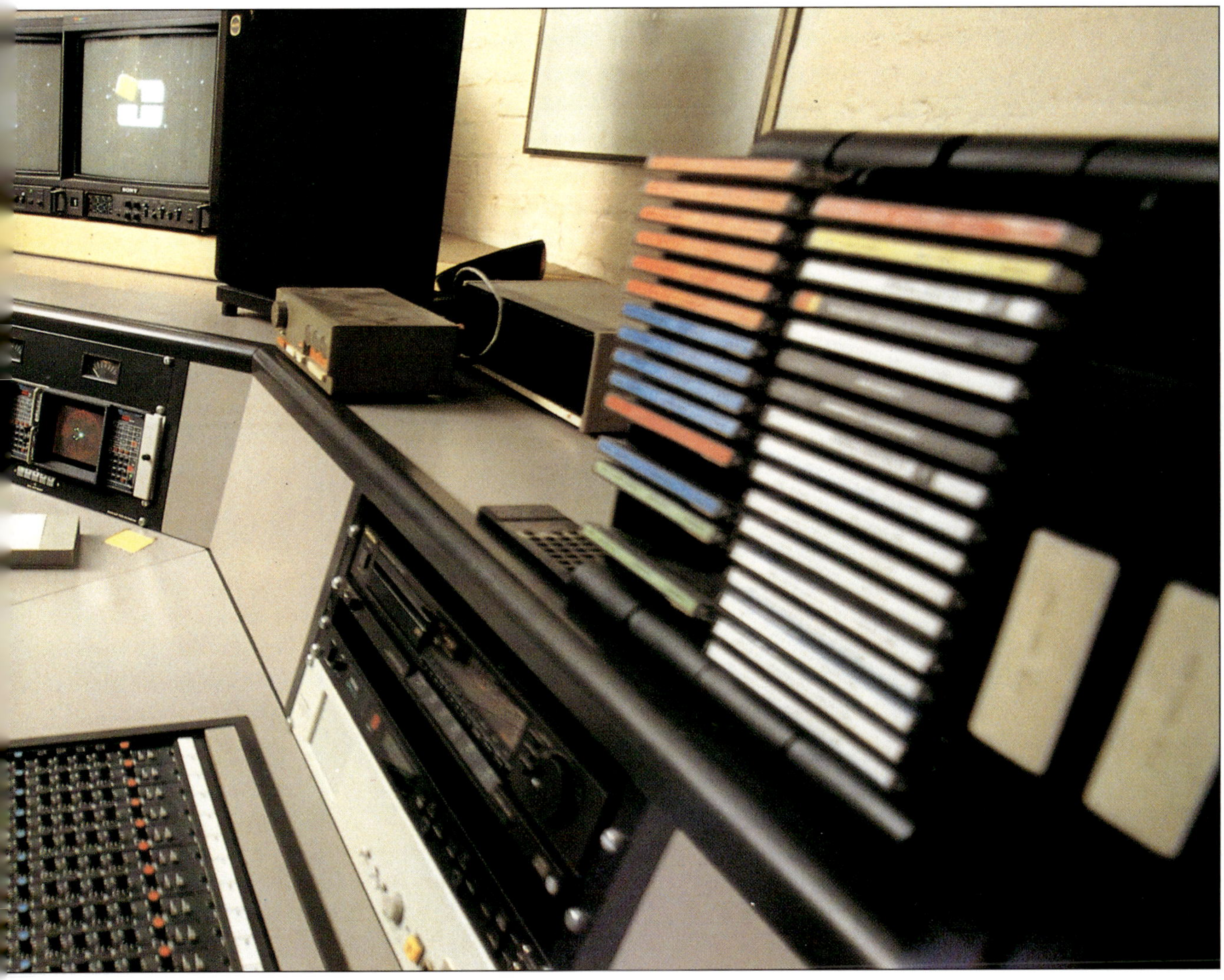

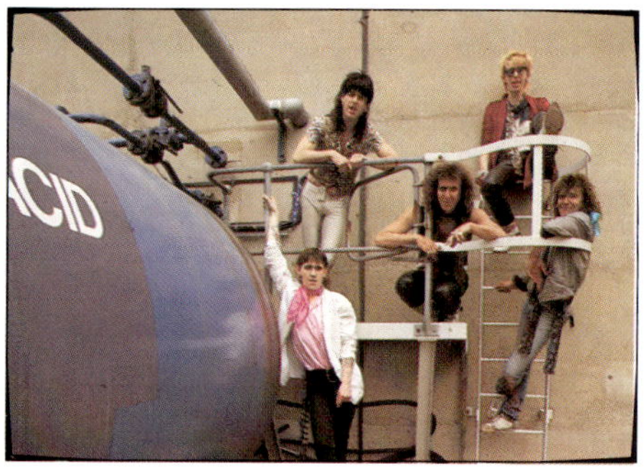

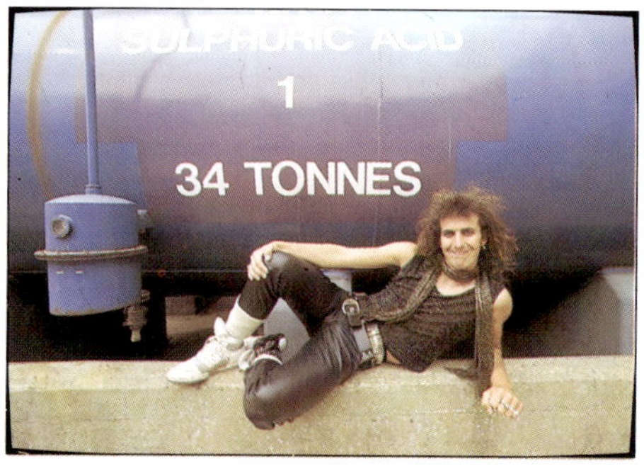

1-2: *A review of sequences taken by a tank of sulphuric acid was painstakingly logged, even though on first sight the material did not look too promising. The trouble was that the sequences were taken early on in the shoot when the band appeared too static. Why not incorporate the shots of the lead singer lying down as a flash insert?*

3-4: *The band performed a number of times in different locations, both inside and outside the power station. Material that seems superficially similiar should be clearly described on the log sheet, so that you can quickly find the shot that you want. Also, note who is in shot for each sequence.*

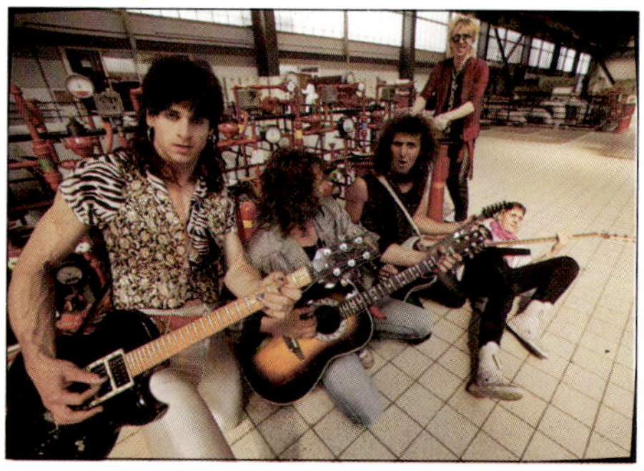
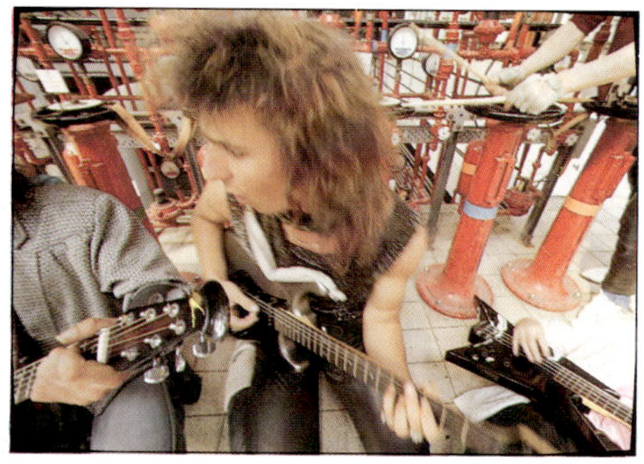

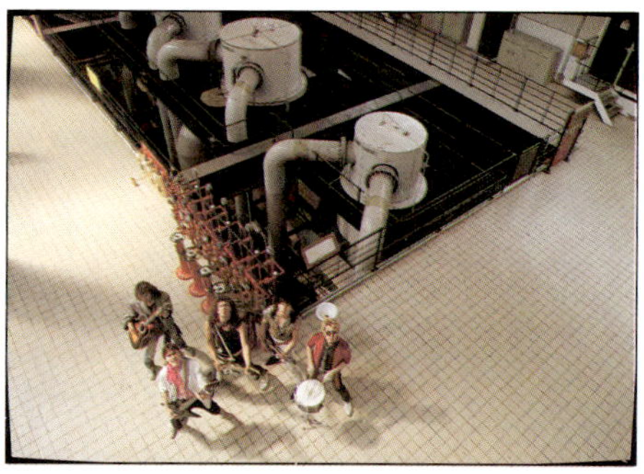
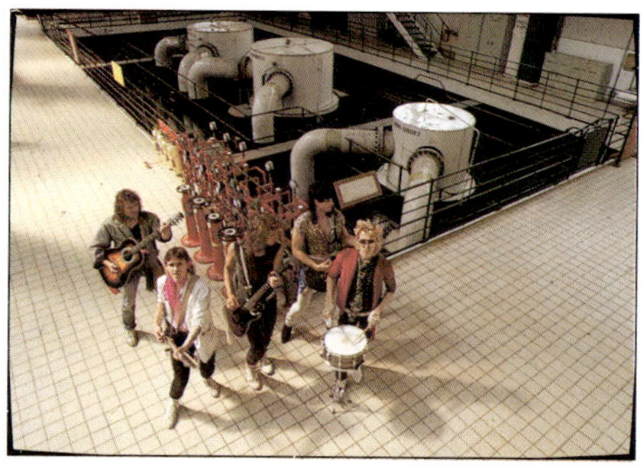

5-6: *Some of the coverage was tried from unusual angles. This bird's eye sequence taken from a gantry high above the group gave a good sense of the location used. Since it is easy to ignore background in the heat of the moment, it is always worth taking a few shots in which it is prominent for use when editing, if it seems appropriate.*

ANALYSING THE COVERAGE

At the end of the shoot you will have a number of tapes containing different areas of coverage. These tapes are your masters, the ones from which you will eventually create the final high-quality edit.

The first step is to take copies of these tapes – known by many professionals as 'dubs' – to work with during the rough editing stage. At this point it is best to dub all of the material on the master tapes, even if you are sure that some of it is unuseable – you may find you do want to use it, after all.

The next step is to review all the coverage and write down the scenes on a logging sheet. Each should be given a brief description, plus the counter number and its time into the tape (taken with a stop watch). Also, indicate if some of the shots are poor, or don't work in any way. This log sheet will be the basis from which you will develop a full editing script.

Logging is a laborious process, but repays the effort. Review the dubs a number of times, so that you are absolutely familiar with your material (always remember to reset the tape counter on the machine to zero each time you replay the tapes). And when stopping the tape to enter a description on the log sheet, put the machine into a full stop, since the pause mode can damage both the tapes and the machine's video heads.

With the rock video, the music acts as the lead to the script. Naturally, you will want to follow the music in terms of pace and also tie the visuals in to the soundtrack so that the guitar solo music shows the lead guitarist and not the drummer! A brief timed breakdown of the soundtrack is therefore useful for matching with the times of sequences recorded in the logged dubs.

The task now is to select sequences and images that will match the pace of the soundtrack and also offer visual variety and excitement. From the log sheet you will probably be able to select these in rough outline and begin the first rough cut of the final tape. It doesn't matter if at this stage the images are not in synchronization with the sound – the fine tuning can come later.

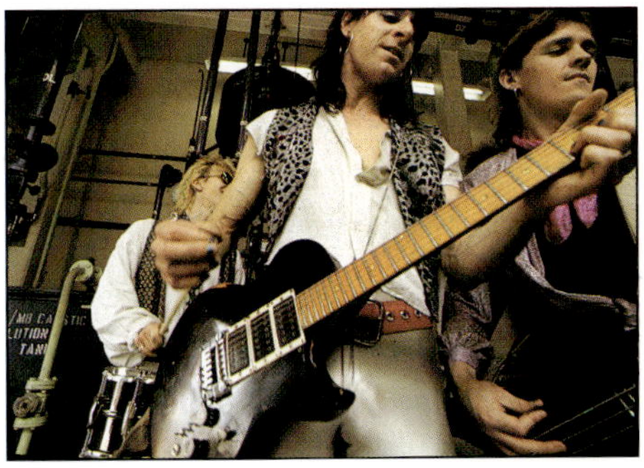

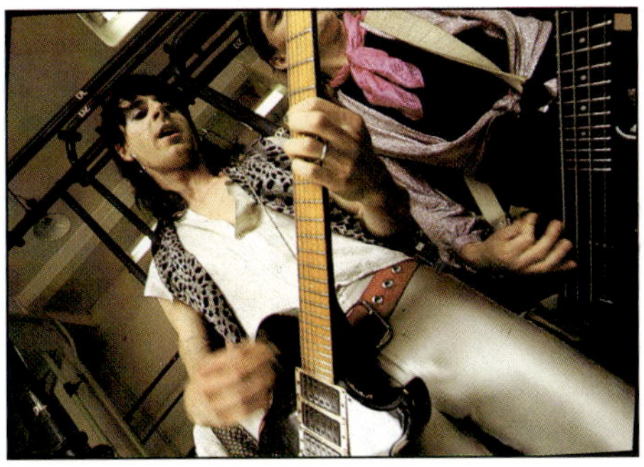

7-8: *While a rock video allows for a freer structure than most other kinds of work, it should have a basic outline – either a storyline or the band in performance – to which you can return. Here, the band performs a highly theatrical act, with much coverage taken in close-up to highlight individual performances.*

9: *Since the power station was located close to the coast, beach scenes were also taken for variety. Although the weather was gray and overcast, the situation was salvaged by using special effects filters, so making the shots deliberately unnaturalistic. In fact, the coverage obtained using the filters was an improvement on the original idea. However, shots of the group against the real gray background were also taken for possible inclusion in the tape at the editing stage.*

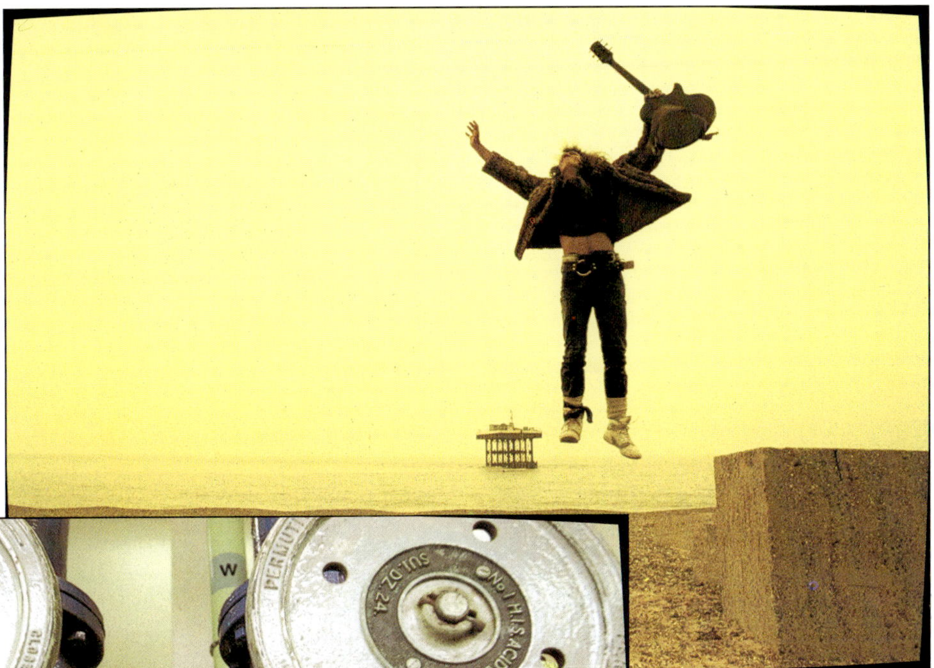

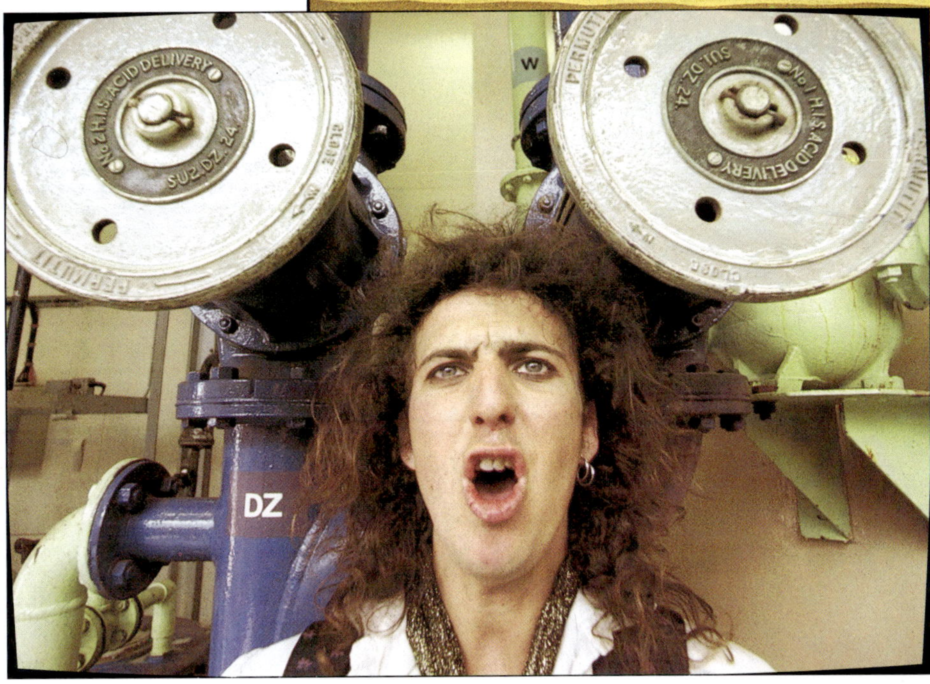

10: *When examining the material you have obtained, you often discover shots that you didn't realize you'd taken. This composition of the singer's head framed by two large valve-ends is a case in point. At the time the shot was just another close-up of an individual band member in a different location. It was only afterwards that it became obvious that a striking image had been filmed that had to be included.*

11-12: *Two-colour filters of different strengths provided simple special effects.*

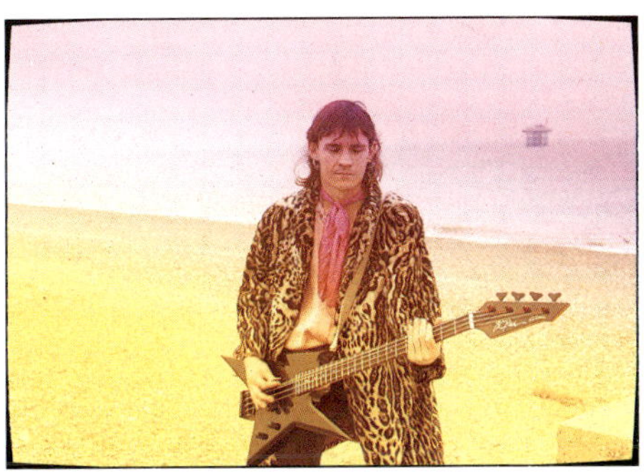

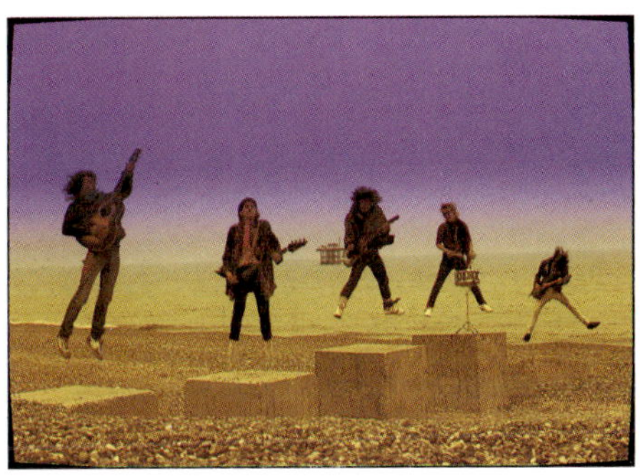

When you begin editing a piece of work, you must have a clear idea of your intentions. With the rock video, these are obvious: to create an exciting blend of sound and image that successfully conveys the group's music and personality. But in other areas of video the intentions may be more complex. In a documentary, for example, you may wish to edit your material in such a way that a particular argument is strengthened. In a drama, your first priority will be to ensure that the narrative is clearly presented and that cuts from one scene to another do not confuse the viewer, but you may also decide to emphasize the dramatic or the comic in your coverage.

For the rock video, the choices were narrowed down. The material consisted of the band in a series of different locations. There were also shots of individual band members, some taken using the special effects filter. Finally, there was a great deal of material showing the band performing, taken from a range of angles and using a range of different shots, from extreme long-shot to extreme close-up. The editing problem, once the unsatisfactory shots had been weeded out, involved assembling this material to create a fast-moving video tape. In fact, once the major sequences had been chosen, the creation of the actual edit was largely a matter of trial and error, using the dub tapes.

EDITING CONSIDERATIONS

1-3: *When reviewing the material in the log sheet, it was decided to place sequences of the group on the beach, and those filmed using colour filters, one after the other for a dramatic effect. The effect was further heightened by beginning the sequence using the filtered shot, cutting briefly to the natural scene and then resuming with the filtered material. When making the cut, it is important to achieve a similarity between the two shots, in terms of camera position and camera angle.*

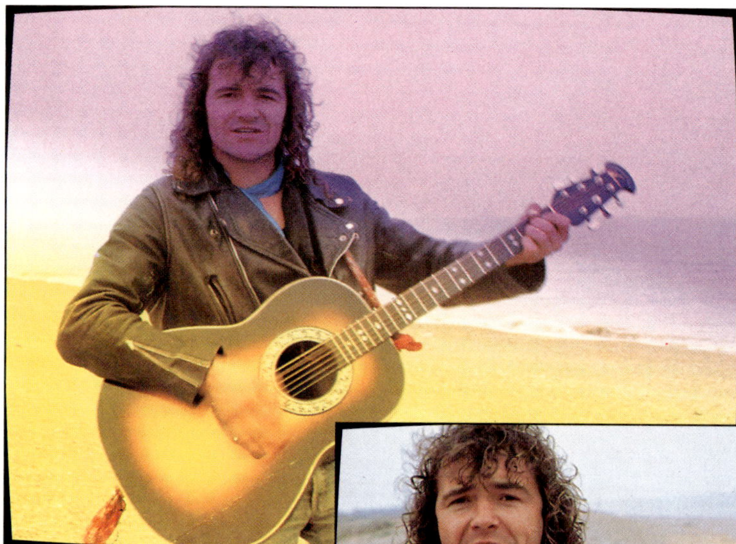

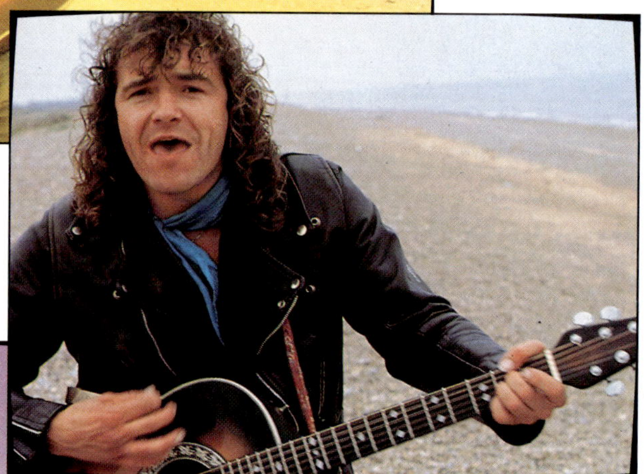

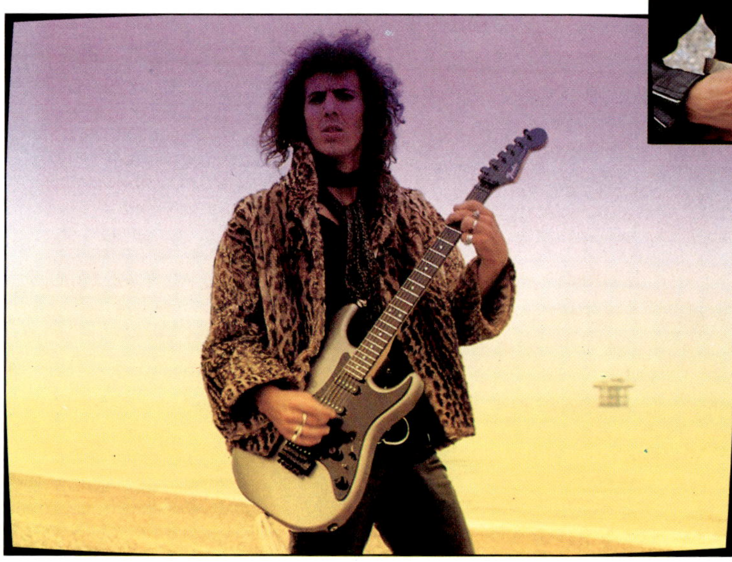

Notice the position of the horizon in the two filter shots. **above.** *When using half filters, the effect is diminished if the coloured areas 'float' too much on the screen. This is particularly important when making cuts – a sudden jump in coloured areas will appear obtrusive on the screen.*

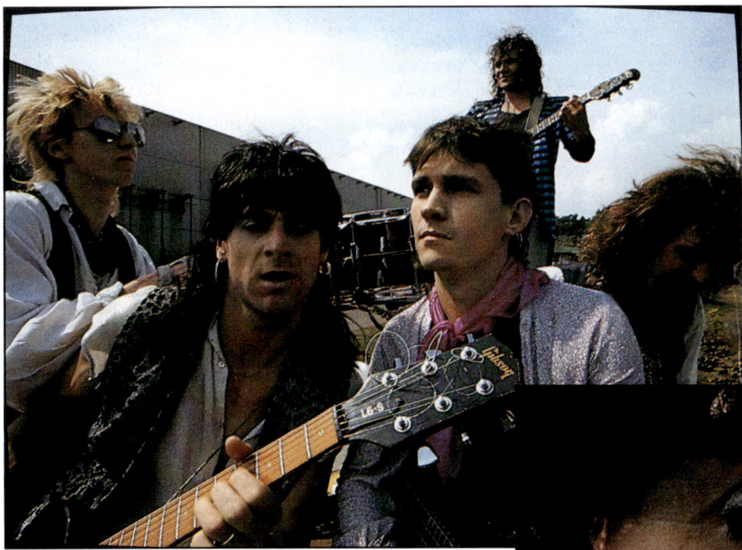

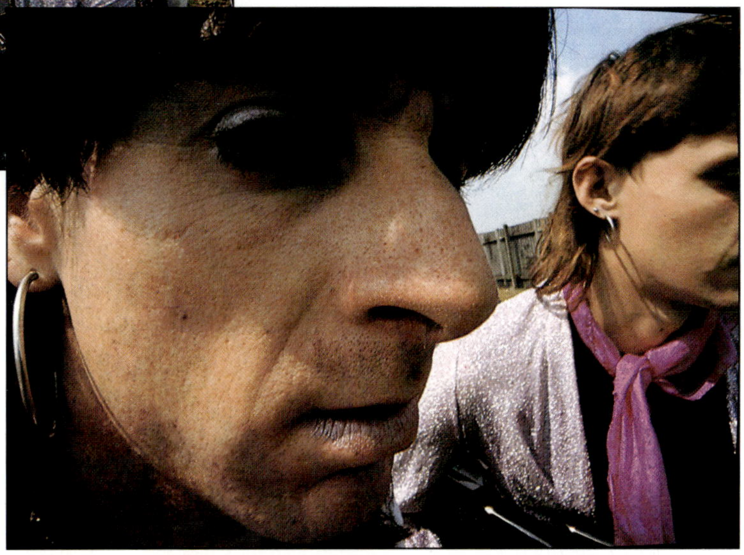

4-5: *Don't rely totally on rapid changes of shot to give pace and rhythm to the edited tape. Some of the coverage should have included moving camera shots which can be used in short sequences. These shots come from a circling pan and zoom taken on one of the outdoor locations on the shoot.*

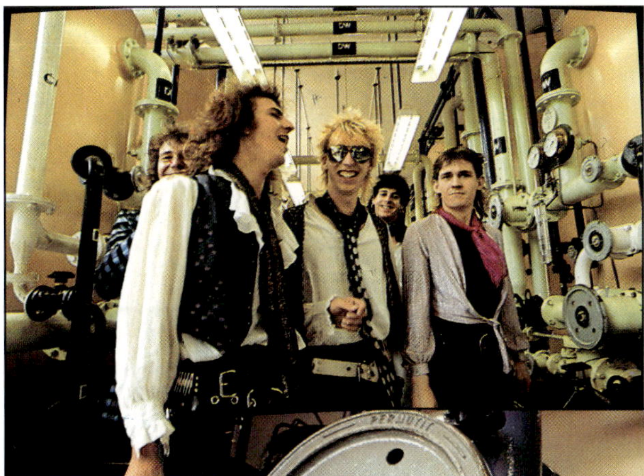

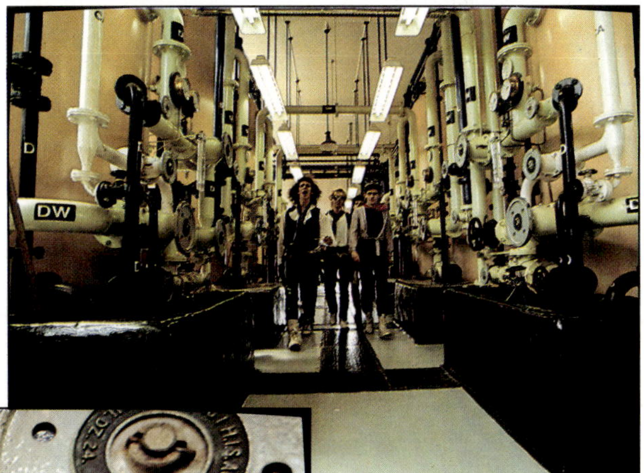

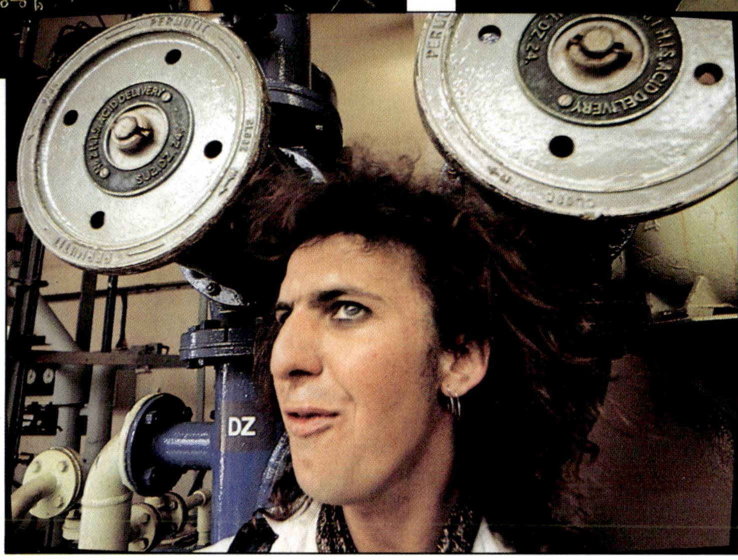

6-8: *Scenes taken in the interior of the power station. In the two shots* **above** *the band walks along one of the aisles of heavy machinery towards and then past the camera. The close-up on the* **left** *is one of several similar shots that were used as rapid cuts throughout the course of the tape.*

The soundtrack is critical in a rock video. Usually, sound will be recorded separately in a studio, to be dubbed onto the audio track of the video tape at the editing stage. The process is simple: connect the sound input to the audio-in socket in the edit deck. You will not need to adjust levels since this will have been done in the studio.

Suppose, however, that you intend to make a video about the group: its history and the views of its members as well as their music. This means that you will have to deal with three types of sound in the edit: studio recording, location sound, and a voice-over or commentary. Each of these sound sources will have a different level and quality.

Editing the soundtrack means establishing a uniformity, for a sudden drop or rise in sound levels sounds bad. Assuming that you are using a basic arrangement of source and edit decks and an editing controller, you will be able to adjust sound in a limited way.

The first necessity is to rehearse the edit and listen to the sound on headphones, while watching the levels on the volume unit meter on the edit deck. Rely on what the VU meter tells you rather than on the evidence of your ears. You adjust the level using the volume control on the edit deck, not the source deck. Play back to the beginning of the cut, and then make the edit, adjusting the levels to those established in the rehearsal. Review the edit, and make a note of the levels shown on the VU meter (they will always be slightly different to those you rehearsed). The levels on this edit are those to match on each succeeding cut, and this will be the case no matter what the sound source.

EDITING SOUND

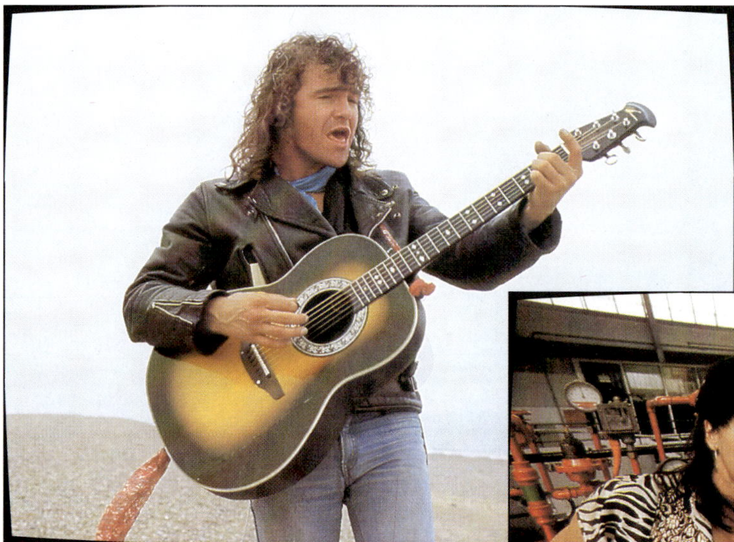

1-3: *If you are going to record sound on location, you will have few major problems using relatively sophisticated equipment. Note however that the sound environments of these three locations differ greatly. Yet with the use of a graphic equalizer, the three sound signals can be modified so that they could be used in the final edit.*

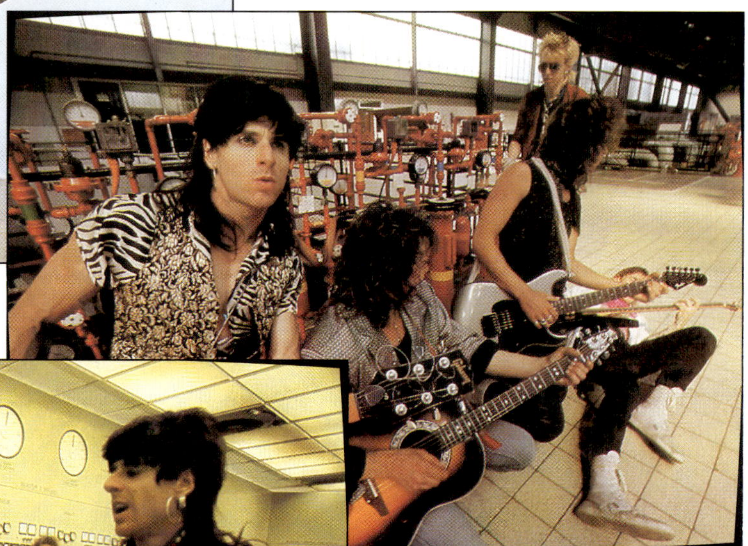

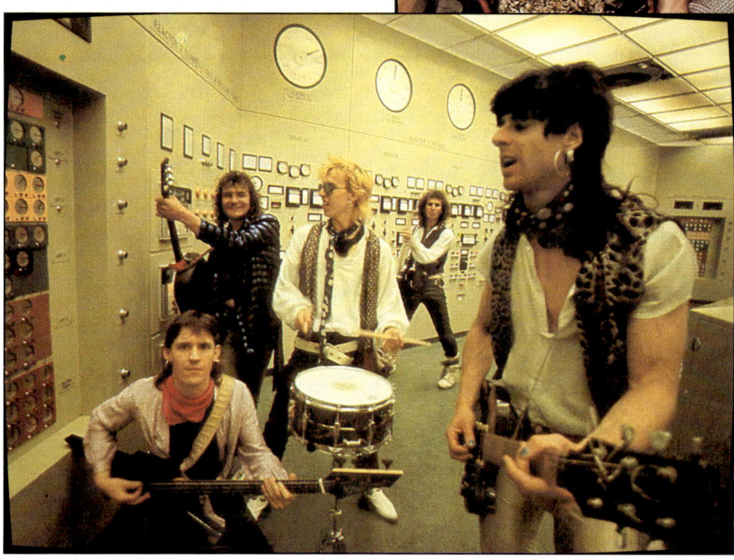

You will probably lay the soundtrack down on the first rough edit. Remember that once you do that any sound on the original audio track will be lost. Check for obvious discrepancies: for example, don't have extended close-ups of one particular instrument when another is dominating the soundtrack.

The level of control you will have over your soundtrack depends very much on the kind of equipment you are using. Fortunately, the march of miniaturization has extended even into audio equipment, bringing increased sophistication and lower prices. Quite sophisticated multi-track recording units, synthesizers and sequencers are now available for a few hundred pounds which allow considerable adjustment of the sound signal, offering, for example, reverb, repeat and echo effects. With this equipment, you can edit the soundtrack independently before dubbing it onto the video tape. In fact, unless you have access to studio equipment, this is probably the best route to take. Most musicians will either have such facilitiies or know someone who has.

On a straightforward dub to video, the procedure is relatively simple. Sound can be heard through headphones or through the output of a monitor if a microphone input is not being used. When working with multiple sound sources, remember that deterioration also occurs with audio tape, so use dub sound for rough cut stages, preserving the original material as masters.

You will find more information about sound editing, including instructions for a simple sound-edit using a multi-track tape recorder, in the section on Basic Sound Editing (pp. 56-7).

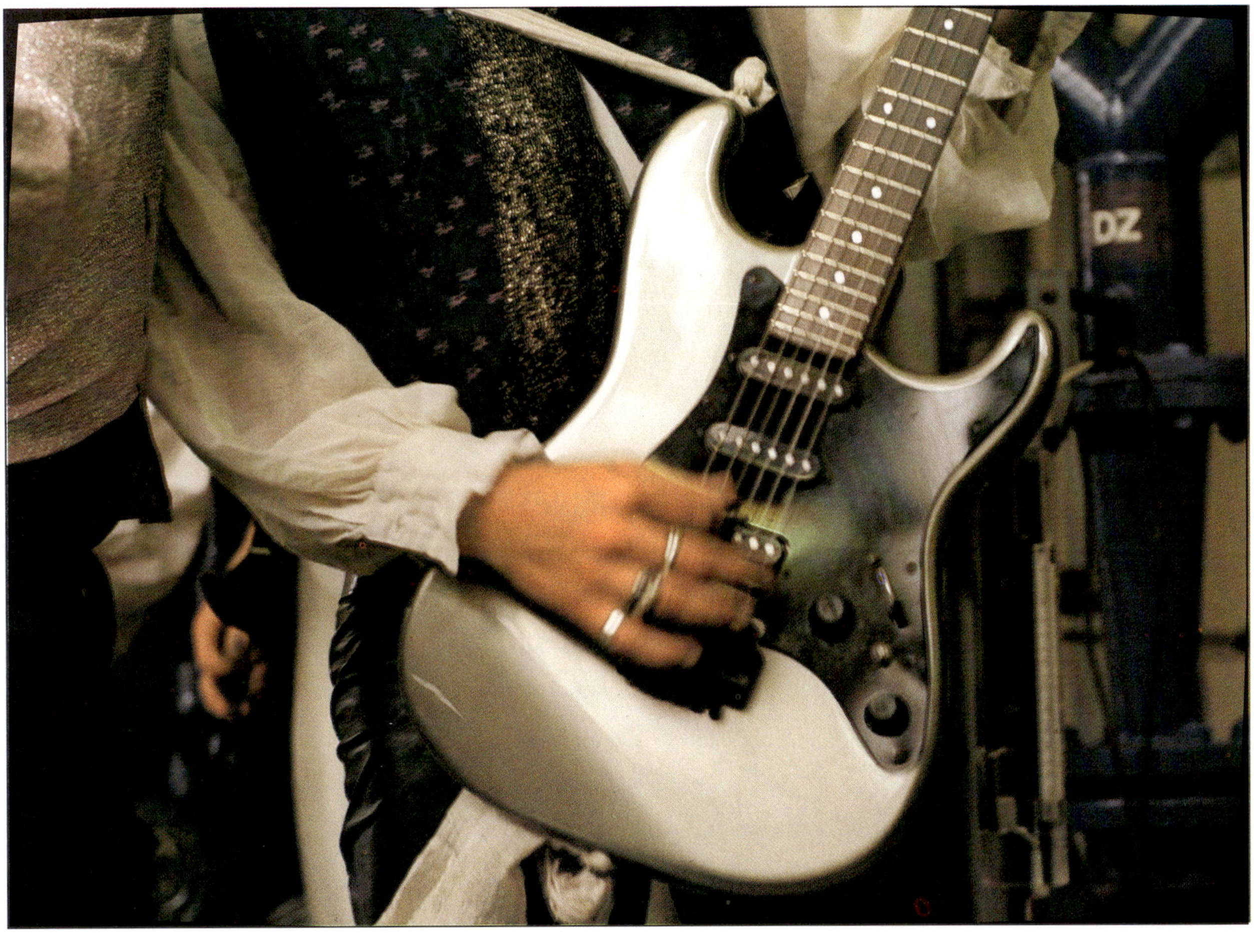

4: *On the final video, pictures and sound will be synchronized, and the modified sound will suit the environment at each point.*

The sport of ballooning is not only physically challenging but also visually exciting. We wanted to reflect this by making a 'musical' video, and we began by going for colourful close-ups of the preparation of the balloon for its flight. One of the shots pulls in gradually from out-of-focus, revealing a mysterious pattern of yellow and red – it is a balloon envelope before inflation. At the editing stage, we decided to begin the video with this shot, and then to go on as planned to show the process of getting the balloon airborne. Although the shots were covered with good location sound recorded in synchronization with the pictures (the roar of the gas burner and the voices of the crew) we needed something extra to heighten the feeling of mystery and adventure, so music was used as a major element of the sound track. We aimed to weave it into the video at appropriate points, which had the additional advantage of strengthening the continuity of the piece – there was no spoken commentary to play this role. Atmospheric music that would reflect both the sense of expectation before take-off and the soaring of the balloon as it made its way across the sky.

The sound track was built up on a separate multitrack tape recorder that was electronically sync-locked to the video pictures. This was a specially adapted machine with mixing facilities, which allowed us to build up the sound track in stages before laying it back on to the video tape. When the shots had been assemble-edited on to a copy video tape, the location sound was transferred on to one track of the sound tape. The mood music was then dubbed at the right points on a parallel track, and additional spot effects were either dubbed into the spaces on the second track or recorded on to a third track. The roar of the gas burner, for example, was not quite strong enough on the original location video sound track, and so was reinforced with a spot effect that had been recorded on a cassette machine. The premixed effects track and the music tracks were recorded at full level to maximize sound quality and, when completed, they were then dubbed on to the video tape via a sound mixer. During this process, the levels were adjusted to fade the music in and out of the natural sound. It is possible to do this redubbing operation in stages, but it is best to do it as a single nonstop process if possible. You will find this hard at first, but with practice you will be able to keep up with the flow.

MUSIC ON VIDEO

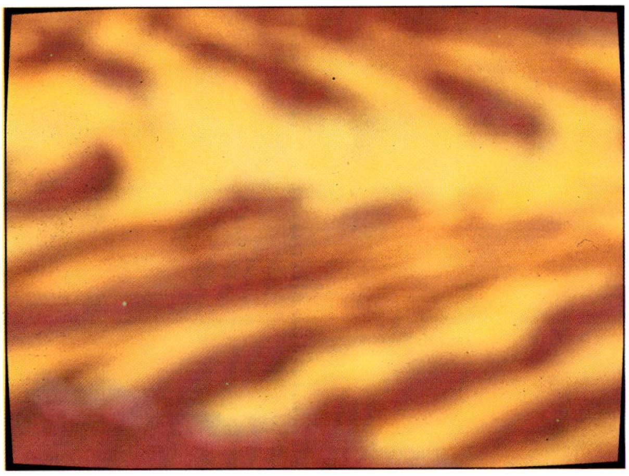

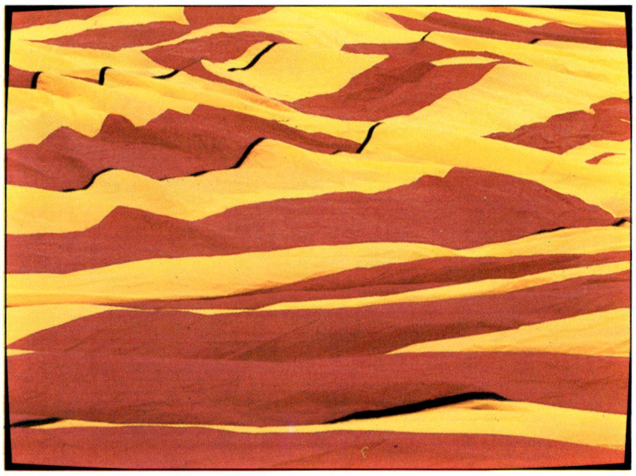

1: *The video begins with the puzzling image of red and yellow stripes. The camera slowly pans over these and the focus is pulled so that the true nature of the subject is gradually revealed. Music on the sound track sets the mood.*

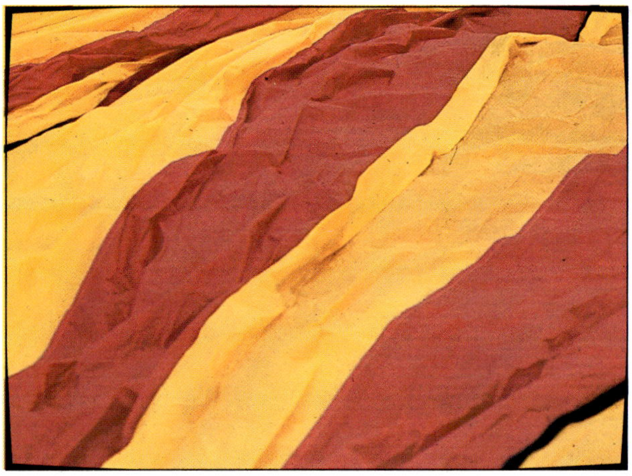

2-3: *The rippling of the fabric as the envelope starts to inflate is complemented by slow camera pans and the music rippling along on the sound track. As the inflation continues, the horizontal stripes turn to verticals and the music shifts up in mood to match this.*

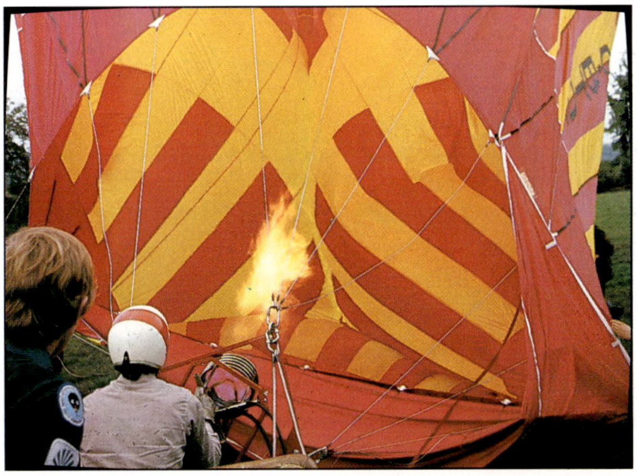

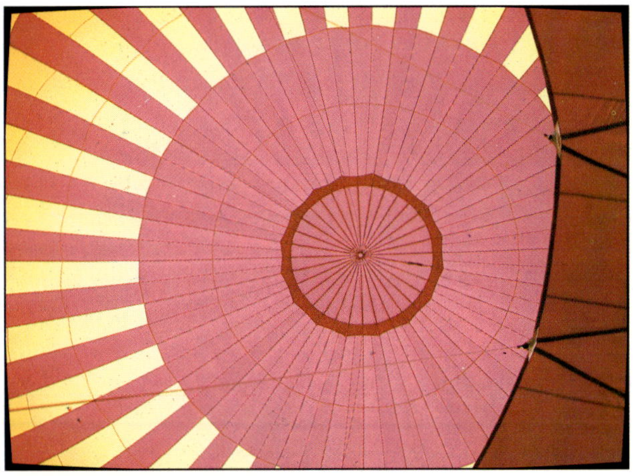

4: *A human element is introduced, helping us to see what is happening more clearly. Location sound is faded in, but the music is still the dominant element on the sound track.*

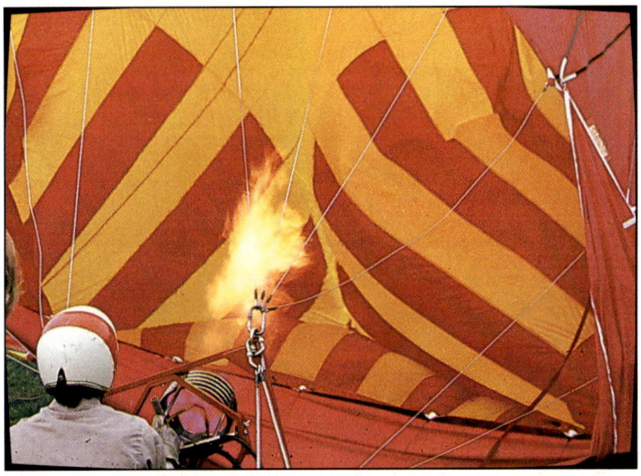

5-6: *A cut to a close-up of the balloon interior seen from its underside heightens the drama, and the taut fabric now makes a bold pattern. On the sound track the noise of the burner increases, and the music drops back further in level. At the cut to shot 6, a closer view of the crew and burner, the location sound takes over completely.*

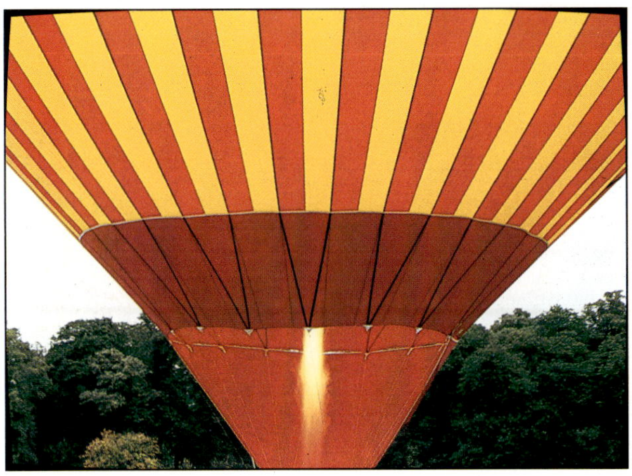

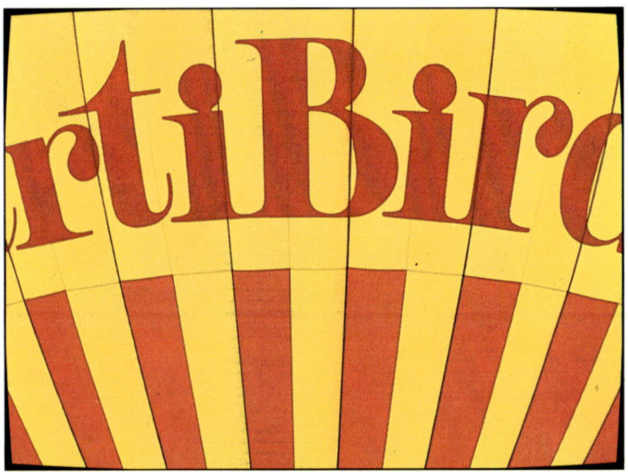

7-8: *These two shots give us our first views of the balloon exterior. We can still hear the noise of the burner, but the other sounds at the location become increasingly audible. The music is faded out completely.*

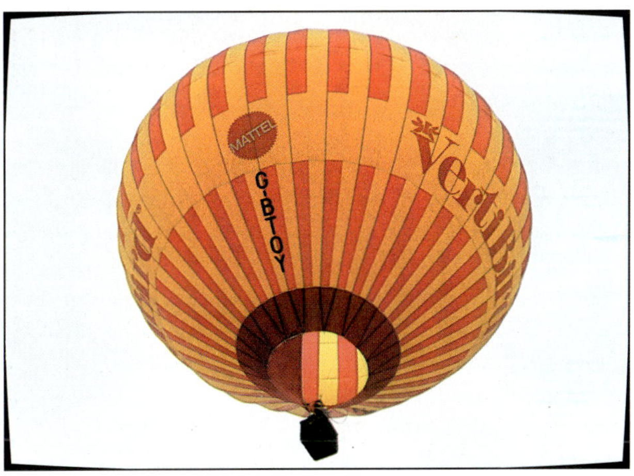

9: *With take-off, a completely different mood takes over. First there is the feeling of triumph at the liftoff, then an atmosphere of peace takes over as the balloon travels farther away from the ground. The music returns and gradually swells to dominate the sound track, with the voices of the spectators on the ground barely audible.*

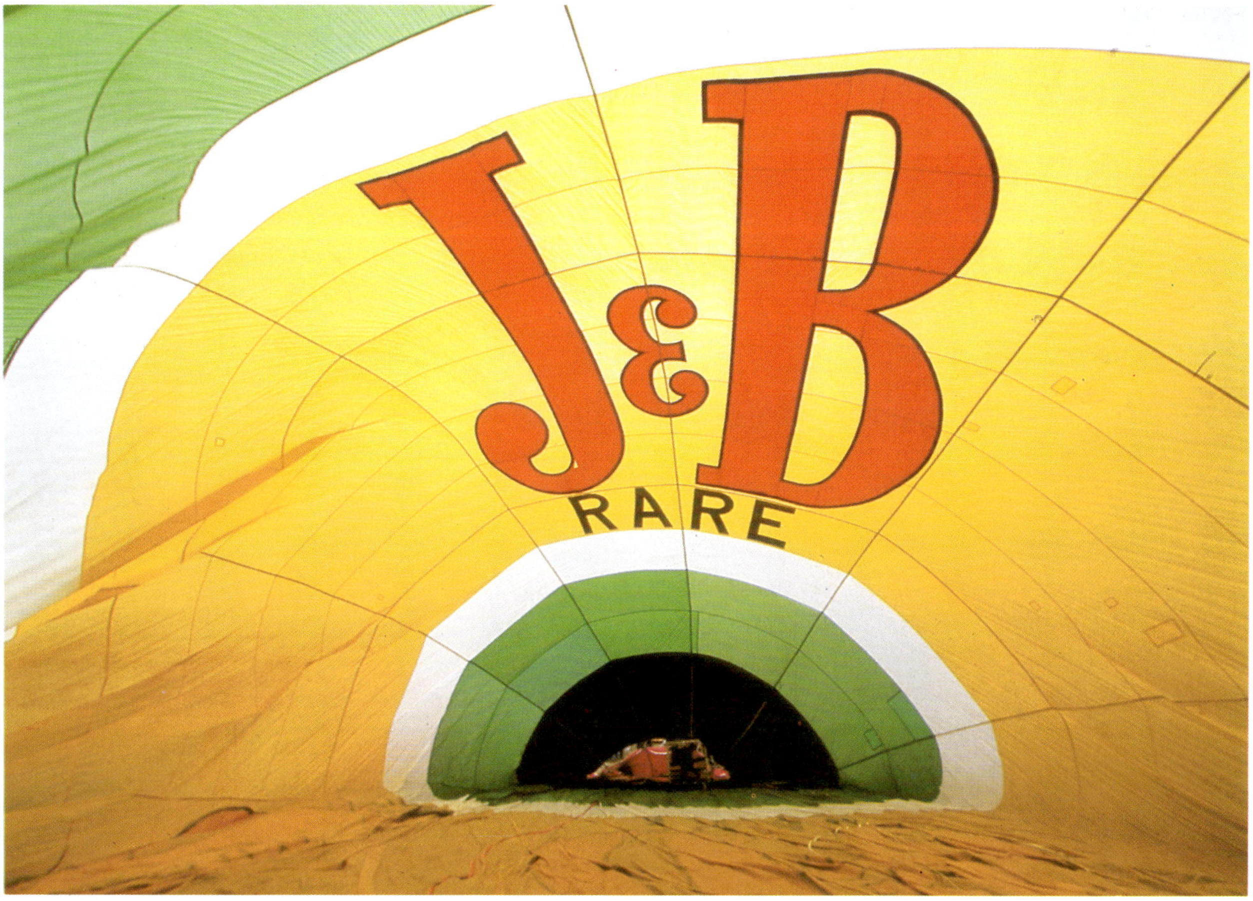

VOICE-OVER

At the ballooning event described on the previous two pages, a second production team were also present to shoot material for a video with a very different approach. Their intention was to make a straight documentary which would be shown mainly to enthusiasts of the sport; there was also the possibility that the video might be used commercially by one or more of the balloon sponsors. The team had the services of a keen balloonist who advised them about which aspects of the sport to cover, so that the video was technically complete and authoritative – a must when there is a potential audience of experts and enthusiasts. This consultant also helped with the scripting of the commentary at a later stage in the production.

So, instead of the dominant music on the first video, the sound track was limited mainly to the sound of the commentator, with some background sound. The latter was mostly made up of long-running sound effects which were recorded on to separate sound tapes at the event; this allowed the team to avoid intrusive cuts in the sound when making picture edits later, and to use the sound background to bridge over the edits within groups of shots. But there were a few shots – mainly action close-ups – in which the original location sync-sound was retained. In contrast to the previous video, music had a minor role – but it was used to set the all-important mood at the beginning and to end the video.

The same basic techniques were used as for the 'musical' video, with the addition of commentary recording facilities. The sequence illustrated is a final one, showing the balloons taking to the air. The video was first edited and the original sync location sound was lifted and transferred on to a sync-locked multi-track sound tape. The separately recorded non-sync background sound was then premixed on to another track of the tape. The shots were timed, the commentary scripted to match, and the voice-over was recorded on to a parallel track of the sound tape. To ensure that the commentary was covering the right points at the right time in the video, a playback of the pictures was used to provide the start-cues for each section of the voice-over. The combined voice-over and background tracks were finally played back on to the video tape via a mixer to produce the finished mixed sound track.

1-3: *These are the opening shots of a sequence showing the take-off of a group of balloons. To satisfy both the enthusiasts and the sponsors, the commentary includes a blend of technical and topical information – including references to the people, the balloons, and who provided the money. The commentary is supplemented by background sound.*

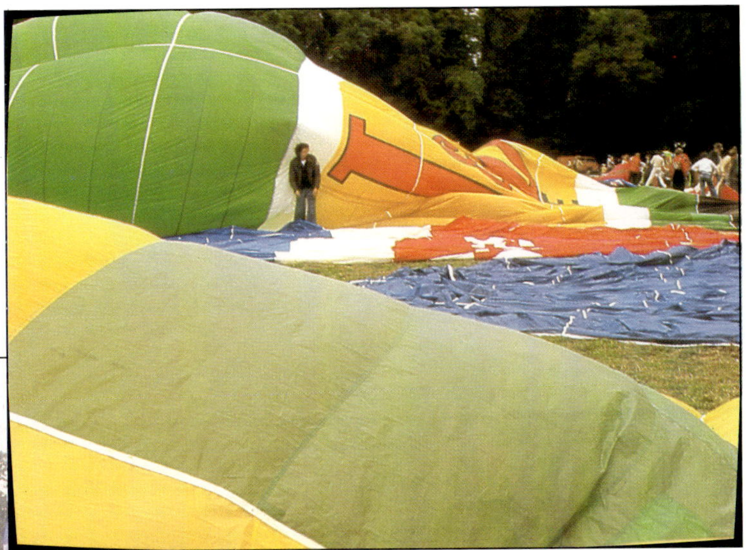

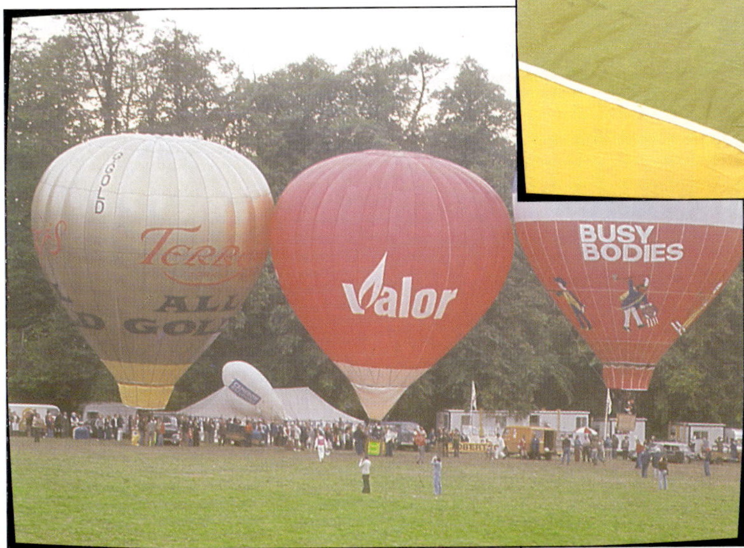

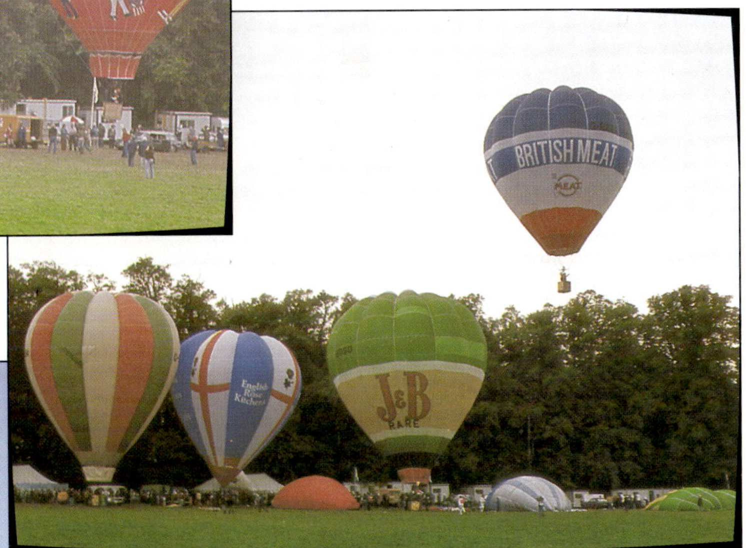

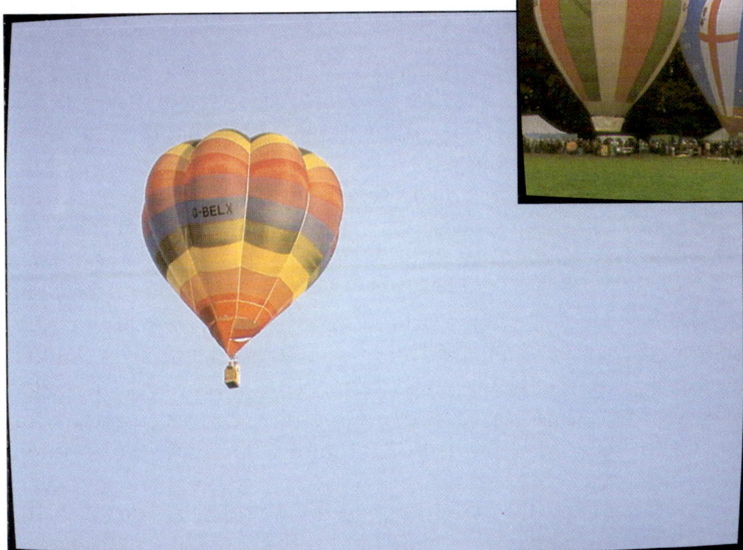

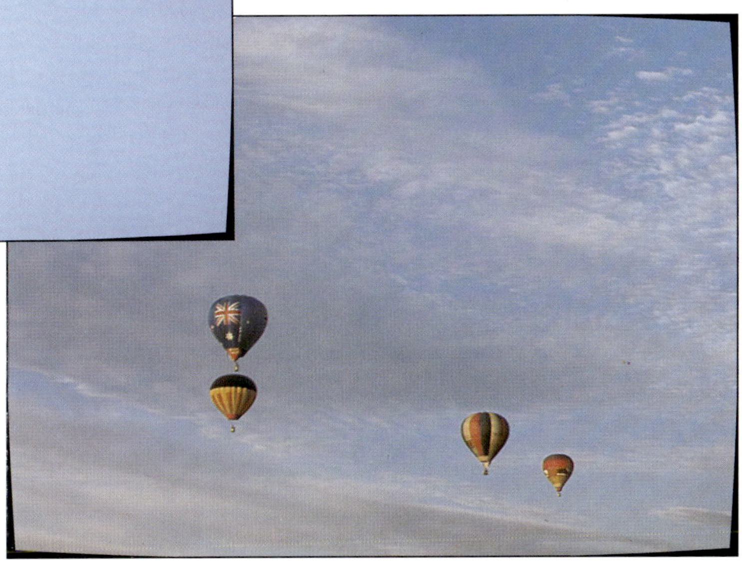

4-6: *As the balloons are ready to take off, their sponsors' names are clear. Further shots of individual balloons follow, intercut with wide-shots of the balloon-filled sky. The background sound broadens too, with more ambient sounds and fewer clear details on the sound track.*

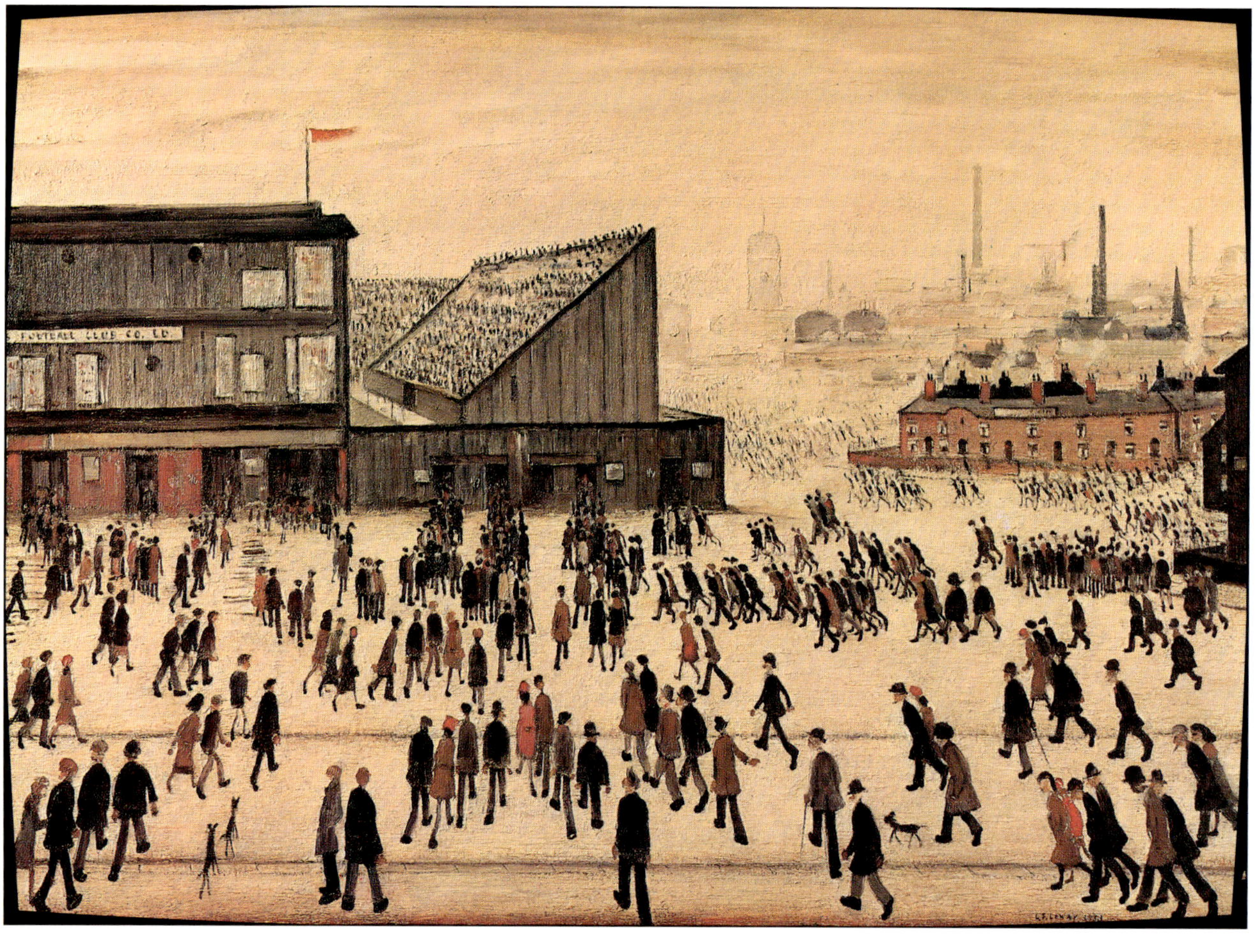

ROSTRUM CAMERA TECHNIQUES

Television arts programmes have made us familiar with the close-up of a work of art, in which the camera travels across the canvas picking out particular details. The success of such shots depends upon the quality of close-up available on your lens, the stability of the camera, and your analysis of the details you wish to show.

To check how close you can go with your lens while maintaining acceptable picture quality, take a few sample shots and review them on a full-size monitor or screen (the quality of the image in the camcorder's viewfinder is not really good enough for this purpose). Be strict with yourself – it is tempting to try to get that little bit closer in: don't.

The camera should be mounted on a tripod or rostrum. A good tripod head, which allows smooth movement yet will also hold the camera in a fixed position, is essential. Plan out the way you intend to shoot the image in advance. Your analysis should not be too 'bitty', with the camera jumping from one area of the subject to another. Remember that the viewer needs to be able to relate the position of each close-up detail to the whole image at all times during the sequence, so move in a steady, continuous motion and return to the full frame at the end.

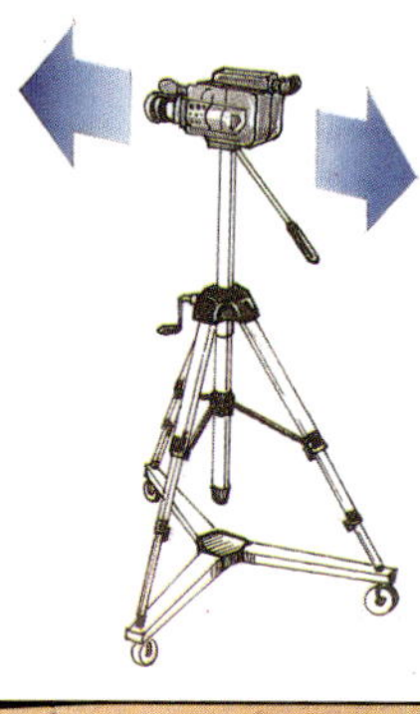

Above and below: *Use the zoom to pull back from a fixed camcorder position or to give the effect of moving in close.*

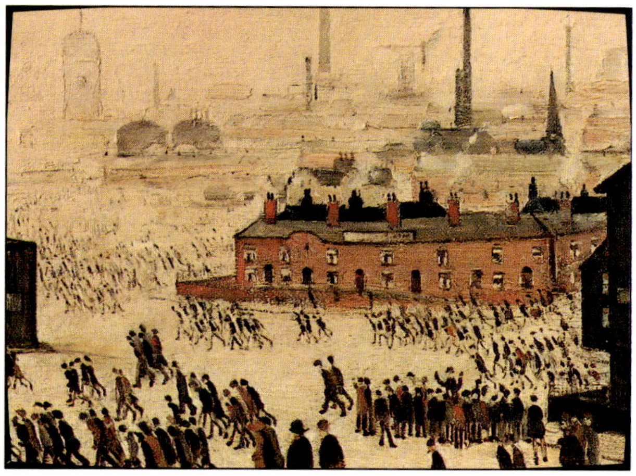

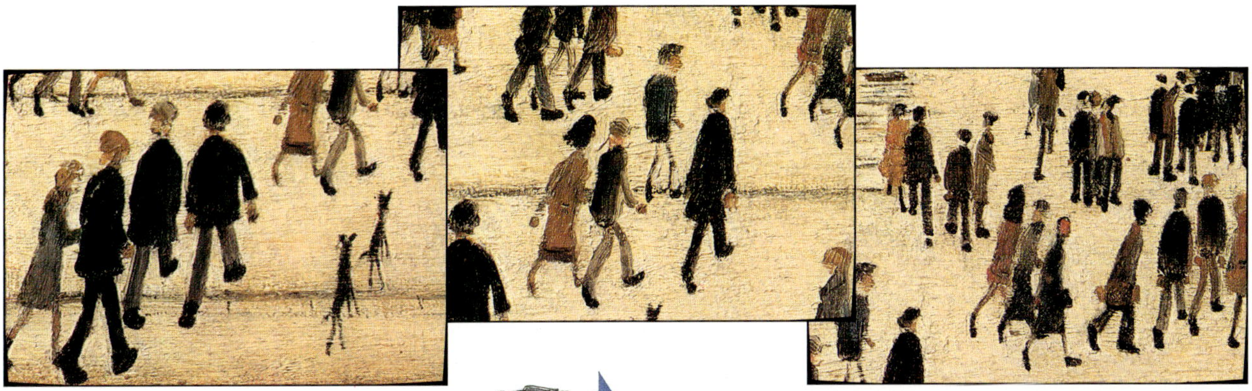

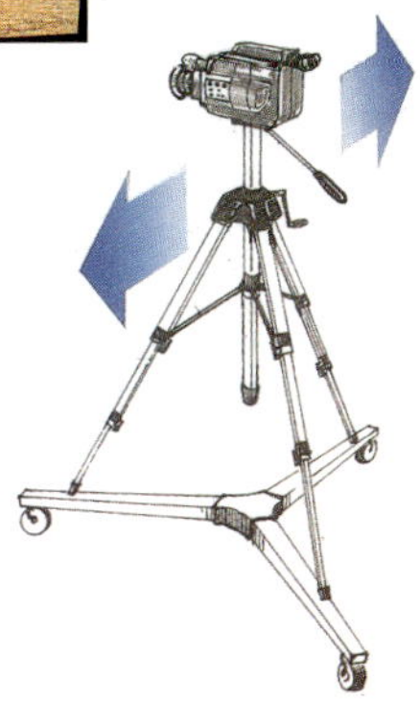

1-3: *Moving the camera slowly across the surface of a painting can actually give the viewer a feeling that the people in the image are themselves in motion. But you should not continue such close-up sequences for too long or the viewer will forget how they relate to the painting as a whole.*

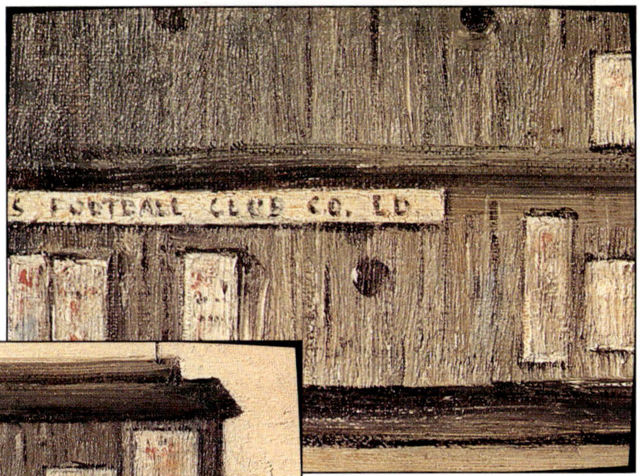

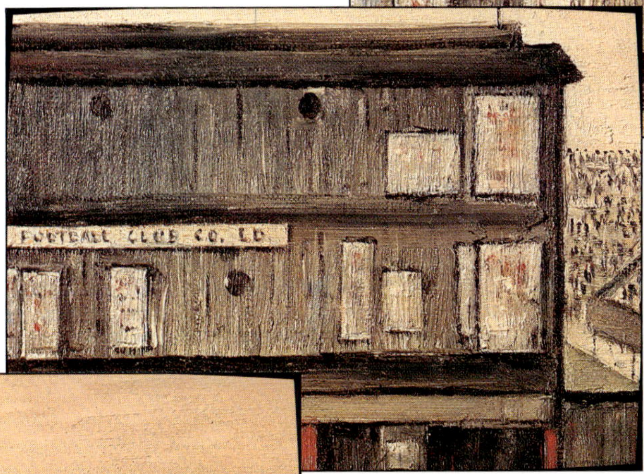

4-5: *Close-ups can give a good idea of the texture of the paint on the canvas.*

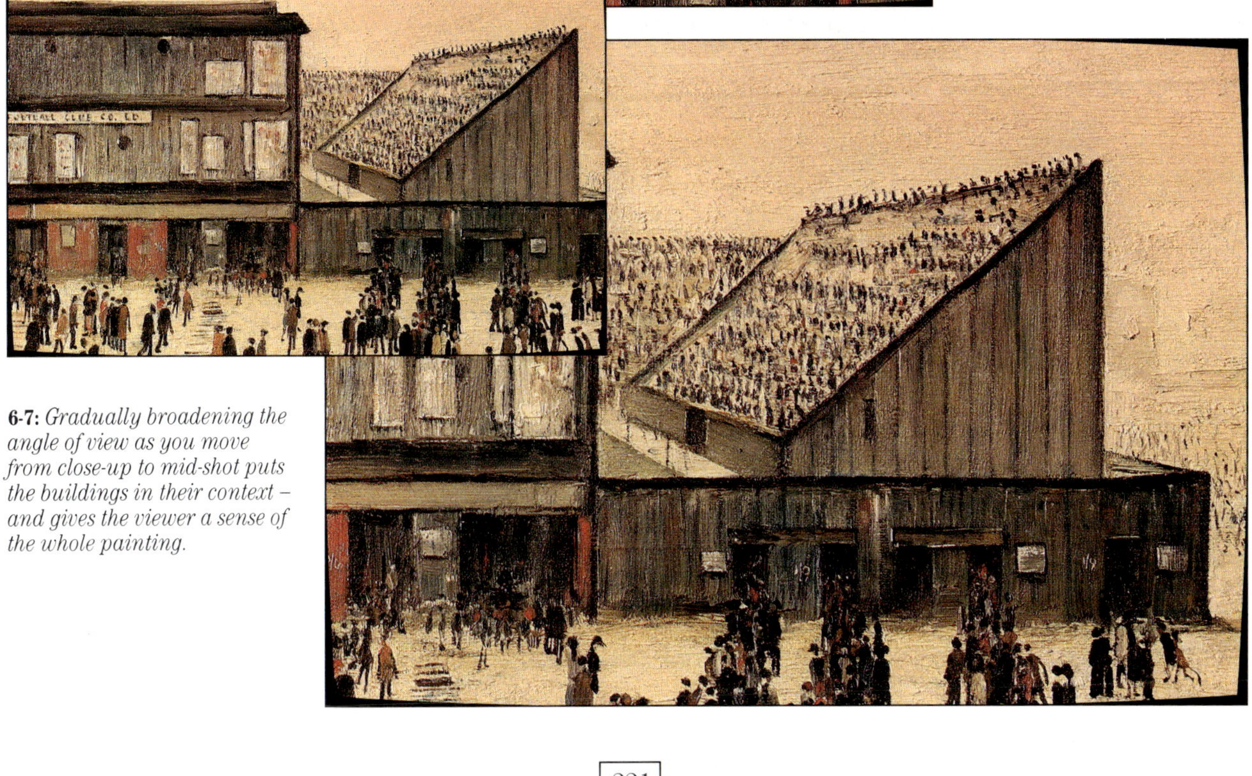

6-7: *Gradually broadening the angle of view as you move from close-up to mid-shot puts the buildings in their context – and gives the viewer a sense of the whole painting.*

The amazing range of special effects that characterizes so many professional rock videos is achieved only at enormous cost. But it is nonetheless interesting to see how they are achieved.

Like everything else in video work, special effects must be planned in the early stages of a project. The simplest effects are achieved in-camera, using filters, gels and mattes, or by using special lighting techniques. One effect commonly used in all forms of video work, from news broadcasts to science fiction series, is known as colour separation overlay, or, more often, chromakey, the trade name for the technique. Chromakey relies on electronically removing one particular colour value from the shot – traditionally blue – and then filling in the available space with another scene. For example, actors in a science-fiction film might perform on an all-blue background. But when the blue is removed it can be substituted with a fantasy background: suddenly the actors are on the surface of an alien planet! (Of course, care must be taken that no part of the actors' costumes contains blue, since that will also disappear when the background is wiped.)

Picture-in-picture effects are also commonly used. This is the electronic addition of two shots, or parts of two shots. It is commonly used to include the talking head of a foreign correspondent in the top corner of the screen, while the action fills the rest of the area.

Superimposition, wipes and dissolves are carried out using a special effects generator or a mixing board. The equipment receives signals from two or more sources. To achieve a dissolve, one signal is gradually reduced as the other is strengthened. If the two signals are held midway, then a superimposition is achieved. With a wipe, one image gradually pushes another from the screen.

In recent years, the increasing computerization of editing equipment has meant that the image can now be manipulated in many other ways. Since the video signal is electronic, it can be analyzed down to its smallest components: those which dictate every aspect of the image on the screen. Once the signal has been analyzed, the electronics in a computerized edit suite can alter it in any number of ways. The image can appear to be torn in two, crumpled up, or repeated hundreds of times. Colour values can be changed and graphic images can be superimposed on real action.

SPECIAL EFFECTS

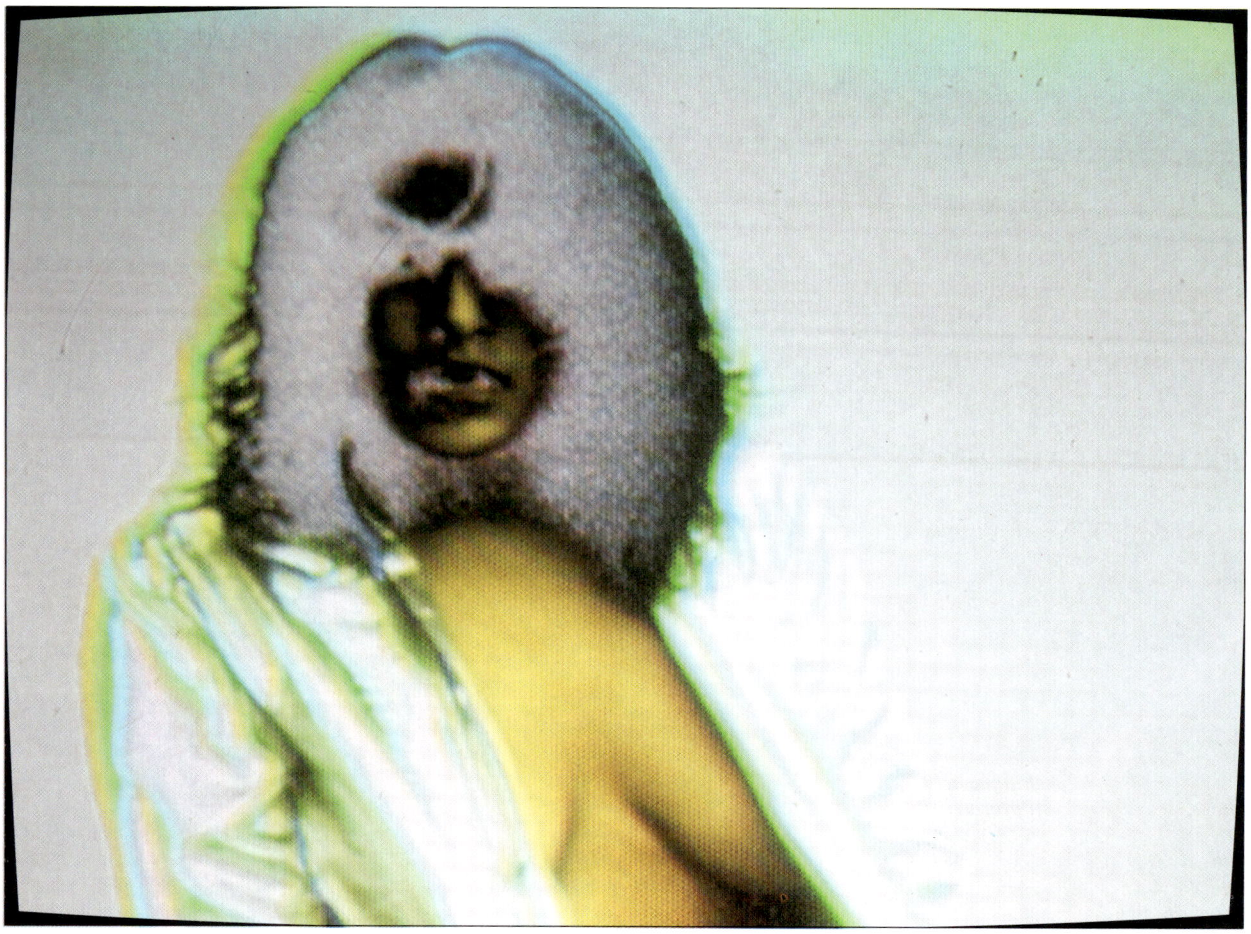

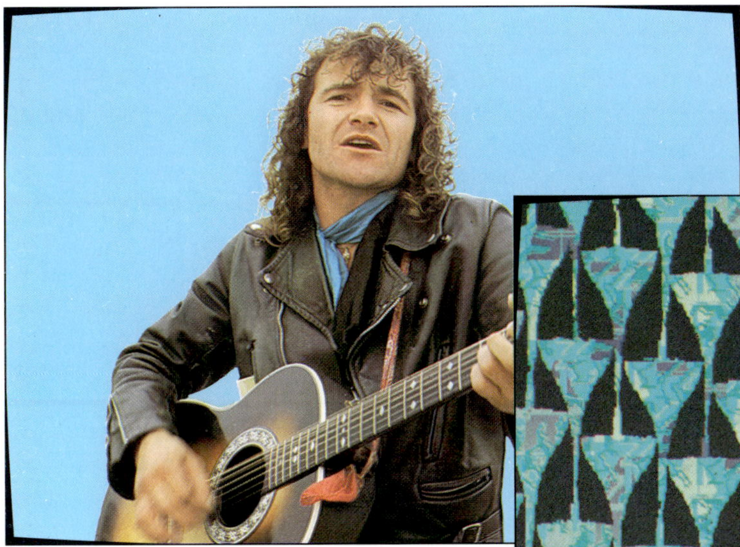

2: If colour separation overlay is to be used, it must be taken into account during the original shoot: it's not a technique which can be used at the post-production stage only. This shot illustrates the blue background which is later electronically removed, and a new background substituted.

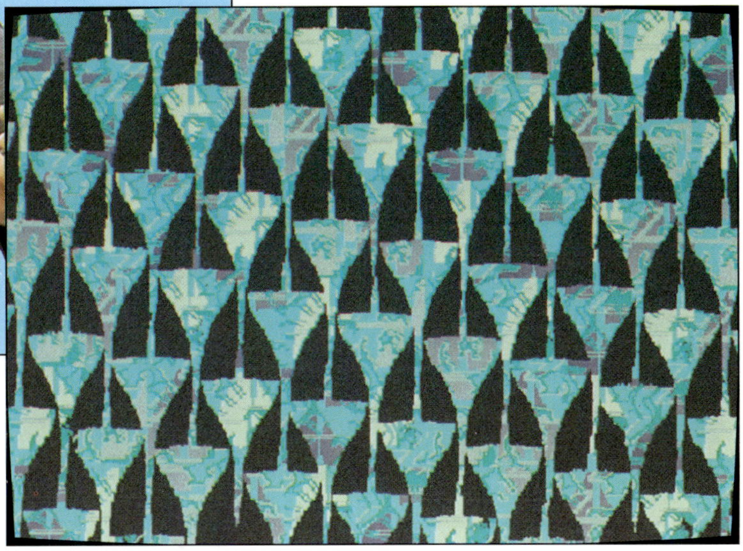

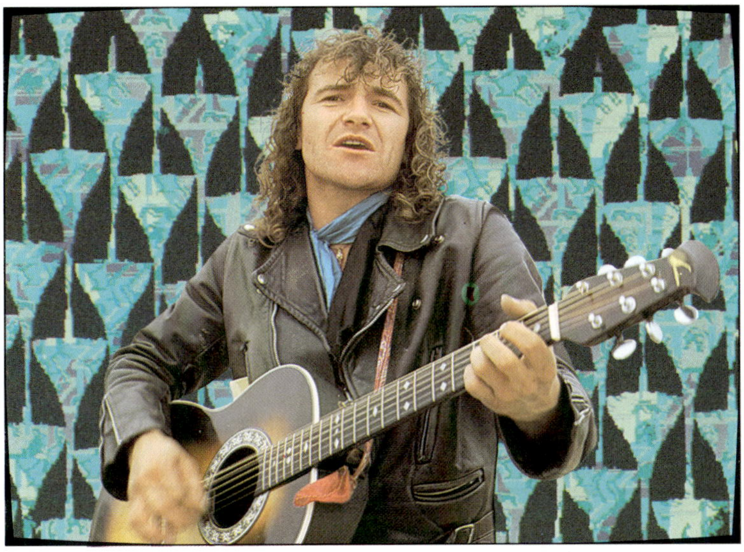

3: The new background is cued in electronically behind the performer. The problem with the basic colour separation overlay technique is that depth in the shot tends to get lost. This can be minimized by using CSO in the foreground, and by electronic 'tweaking' of the final edit.

4: A simple special effect involves using a video negative, or reverse video. Some video cameras allow this option when shooting. At the post-production stage, the effect can usually be readily obtainable with most editing controllers. The technique simply reverses the colour value of the signal, creating, in effect, the equivalent of a negative in conventional photography.

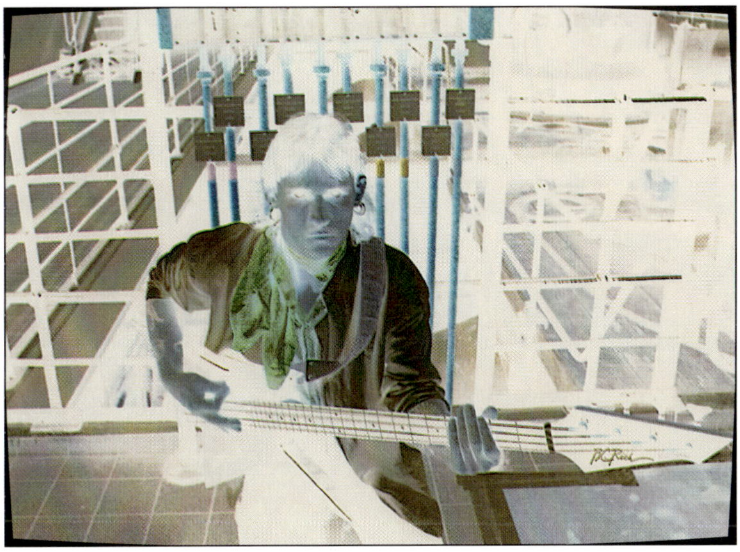

1: Solarization is a technique achieved in photography by special processing of the film. The same effect can be achieved electronically with a video during the editing stage if reasonably sophisticated special effects equipment is available in the editing suite.

Below: *A good computer, with enough memory to run a sophisticated graphics program, can be linked to a camcorder and VCR.*

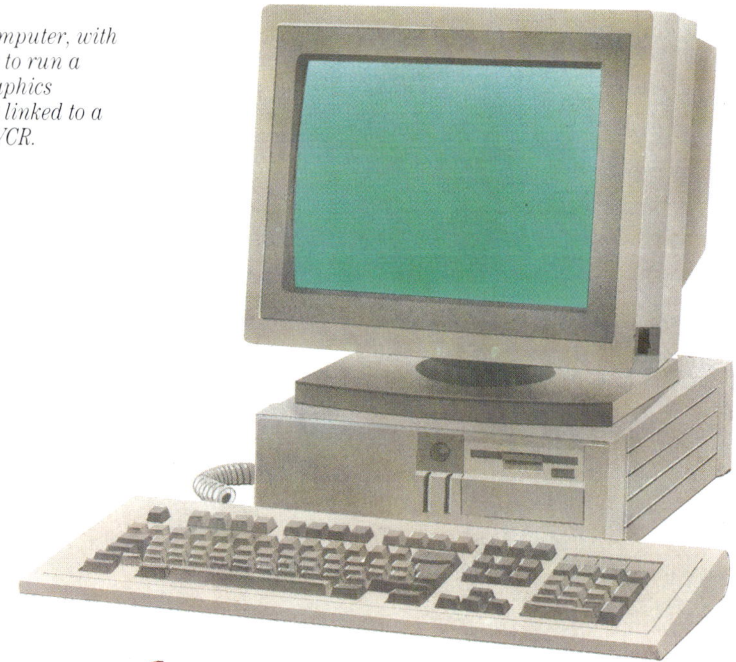

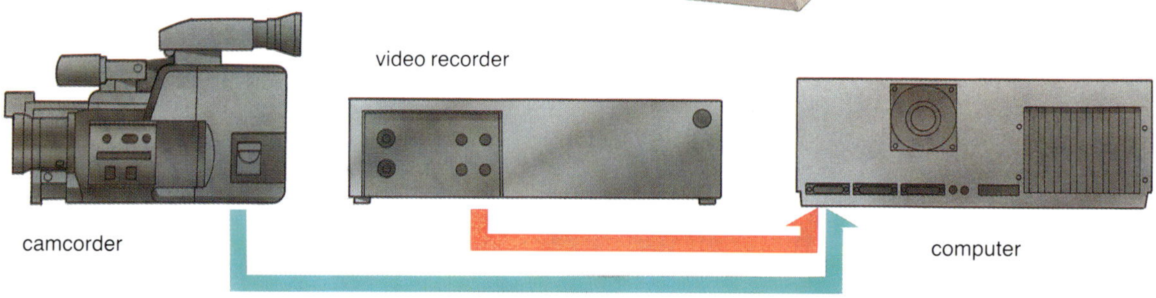

COMPUTER GRAPHICS

The term computer graphics applies to images that are generated entirely inside a computer. Some computers have a graphics capability, others can be programmed to provide a graphics output. The sophistication of the available graphics is dependent entirely on the processing power of the computer. Of course, any images that the computer displays on screen can also be recorded on video tape.

Reasonable animated graphics can be obtained with simple home computers. Graphics-generating programs can be bought, but you can obviously obtain more wide ranging results if you write your own programs. The animated scenes you can obtain are only short, but they could be incorporated with other material in an experimental video. If you decide to try this, remember to treat the tape as a master, and put at least 10 seconds lead time before each graphics sequence to edit easily.

Dedicated graphics computers allow a much greater array of effects to be achieved, and do not require programming skills to operate. These computers can be expensive, although some, such as the Amiga, are now being aimed at the lower end of the market, selling for a few thousand pounds. With many graphics computers, outlines can be drawn either on a pad or directly on the monitor screen. Colour is filled in by defining colour areas and keying in the correct values on a keyboard. The image can be manipulated in a variety of ways: parts of the image can be squeezed or stretched, it can be rotated through 360 degrees on any given plane, and separate images can be synthesized to form a new whole. These images can either be static on the screen or form part of an animated sequence. With the electronics industry developing at its present rate, it will not be long before such technology is available to a wider a market.

One of the most flexible graphics computes available on the market today is the Commodore Amiga 2000. This is in effect a miniature special effects studio. It can generate excellent graphics, or video images can be fed in and manipulated when an image digitalizer is added to the package. In fact, with the Amiga, you can mix your own video images with stills, and computer graphics. There is also an optional stereo sound processing system. This will allow you to manipulate the soundtrack with the same flexibility as you have with the images. In all, it is an exciting machine.

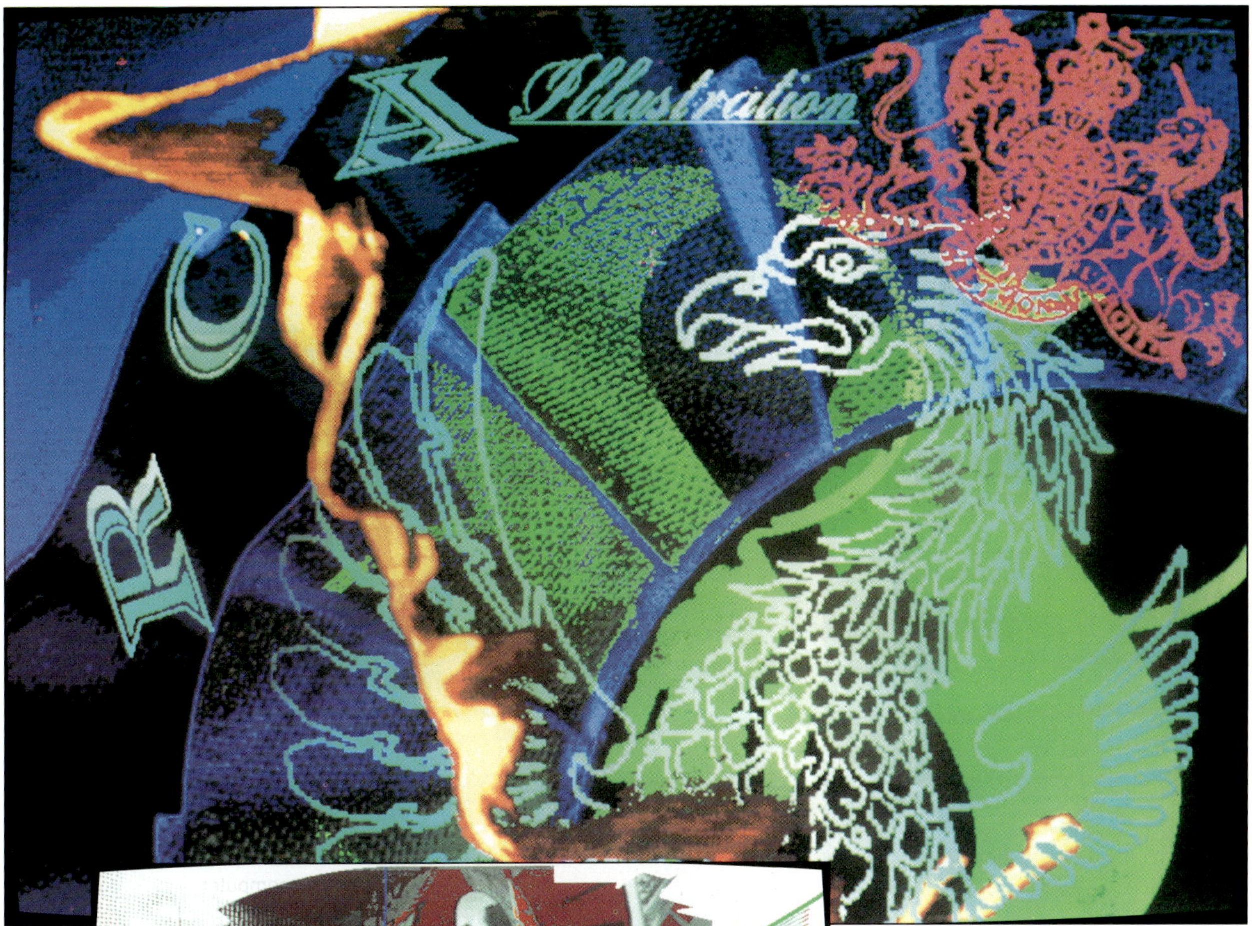

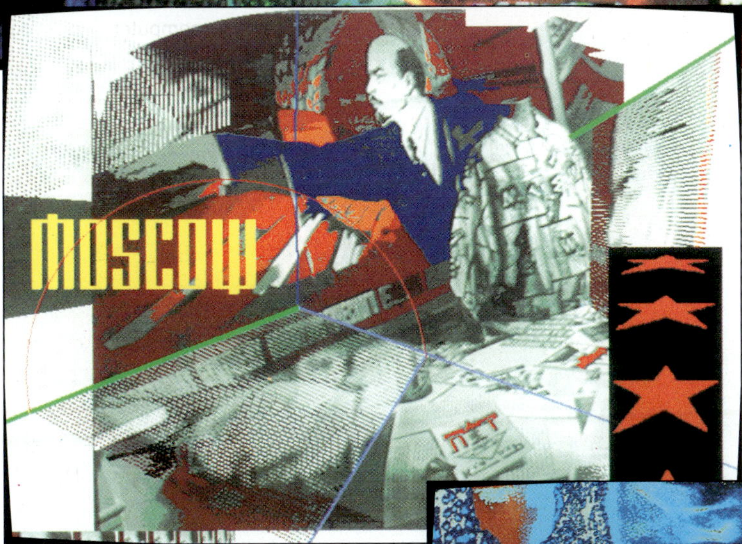

1-2: *These images were created by an artist using a powerful computer graphics facility. They were achieved by building up the image stage by stage over a series of operations. Such sophistication is available only on very specialized, highly expensive computer graphics systems.*

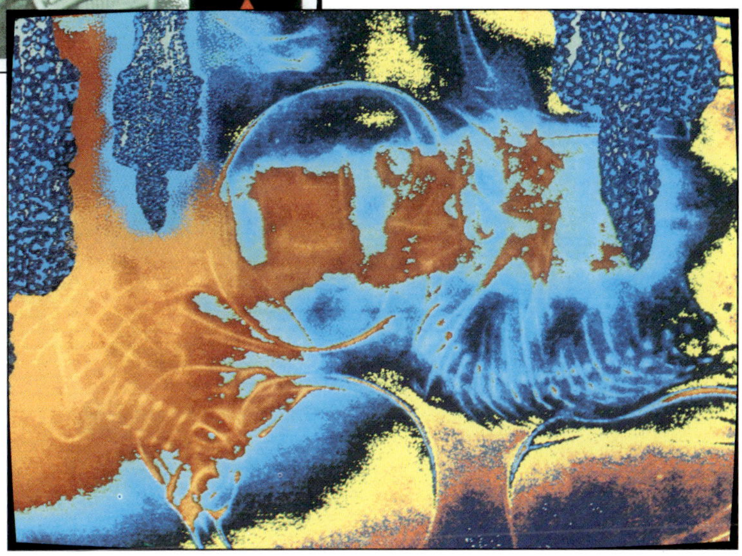

3: *In this image a solarization effect is prominent. The high resolution achieved is indicative of considerable computing power – less sophisticated systems do not permit work in such detail.*

PROJECT NOTEBOOK

ROCK VIDEO

As pointed out in the Introduction, editing considerations are vital to video. You must shoot your material with editing in mind. This means always checking how you covered the scene the last time you shot before you go for another take. It's not just continuity errors that can cause problems – if you cross the line between two takes you are going to have major headaches when trying to edit the material. For the editing process itself, nothing is more valuable than complete familiarity with the material – exactly what you've got and where it is on the tapes. That's why it is so important to log the tapes before you try to do anything else, no matter what kind of editing set-up you've got at your disposal.

■ Editing is a process of elimination and juxtaposition – eliminating material that is no good or simply redundant, and juxtaposing sequences so that the story unfolds.

■ Editing serves to hone the story you want to tell. You can't do that until you yourself are sure exactly what that story is.

■ Remember that the soundtrack is just as important as the images. Listen to it with the same attention to detail as you pay to your visual coverage. In a well-edited tape, sound and image have a matching rhythm.

■ Edit to the prospective audience. In an educational tape for children, the information should be given in smaller doses, and more slowly, than in a tape covering a similar subject for adults.

■ The way a piece is edited can radically affect the meaning it conveys on the screen. Watch out that the way you juxtapose images and sequences does not convey meanings that you never intended.

■ High-technology editing suites are expensive. Be persuasive and persistent – after all, everyone has to start somewhere.

■ Finally, whatever its level of sophistication, the technology is there to serve you, to make your life easier, or to enable you to achieve better results. Use it, don't be intimidated by it.

APPENDICES

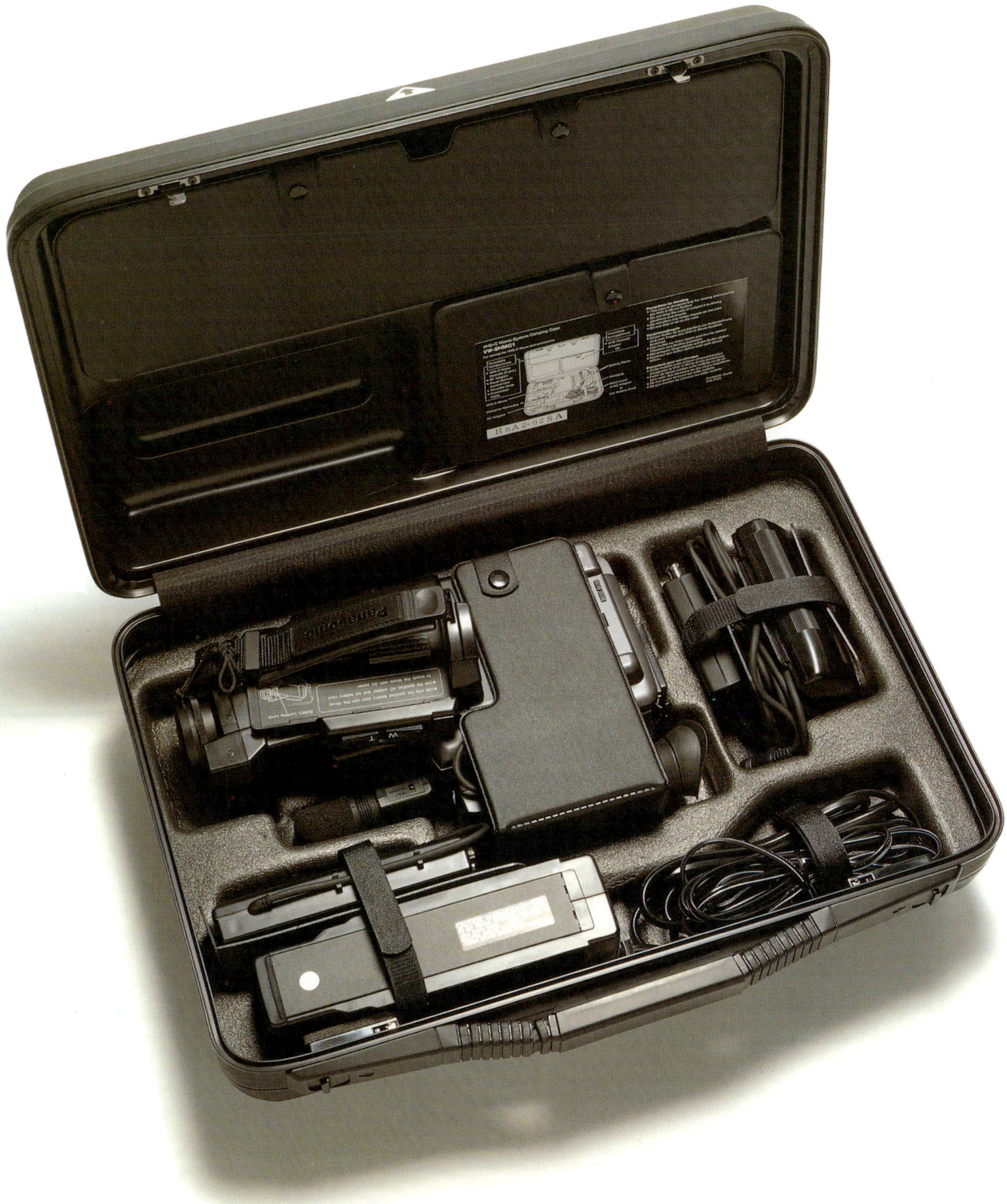

TECHNICAL INFORMATION

The invention of the camcorder has meant that video has extended its reach from the recording of television programmes and the home viewing of movies, to becoming a popular creative medium in its own right. And it is a medium which is available to everyone, not merely as yet another leisure interest but as a means of communication and self-expression. Although the equipment is expensive compared with that used in still photography, its cost in real terms at the 'budget' end of the market, and in value for money at the 'quality' end, is coming down as the demand grows and competition amongst manufacturers becomes keener.

The rapidly growing interest in creative video is a world wide phenomenon, which theoretically enables people who are separated by distance to keep in touch with each other through the exchange of video tapes. The main drawback is that there are invisible electronic barriers which prevent the free interchange of recordings between machines, and from country to country.

One type of barrier has already been mentioned, the existence of a number of different formats, which are incompatible with each other. Video 8 cassettes, for instance, will not replay on VHS machines unless the recording is first copied onto a VHS-format tape, and although video users often wish that there was a single universal world-format to encourage the exchange of tapes, technical developments and commercial pressures have so far contrived to make this impossible. A current example of this situation involves VHS which, despite its near victory against its old rival Betamax, is now having to contend with the up-and-coming mini-format 8mm video, with the possibility of an even smaller mini-format 4mm video not far below the horizon. Similarly, super VHS – the new improved (and compatible) version of standard VHS – will no doubt have to compete in due course with a resurrected Betamax in the guise of ED-Beta (Extended Definition) or its future equivalent.

Format, then, is one barrier to universal tape-to-tape compatibility. The differences in the television 'line standards' between each country is another problem. Suppose you have shot a family video and wish to send it to your relatives in Australia. Will they be able to play it? The answer as to whether this is possible, even if their video machine is of the same format as the one you use, depends on whether your country's television line standards are the same as theirs.

In order to enable you to understand this fully, it is necessary to realise that there are three colour TV systems world wide: PAL, NTSC and SECAM. PAL is the colour system which is used in the UK, much of Europe, and in other countries including Australia. It operates to a picture-standard of 625 lines (from the top to the bottom of the screen), and a 'scanning frequency' of 25 'frames' (pictures) per second. In America, Canada and other countries (including Japan) the NTSC system is used – this has a standard of 525 lines and a frequency of 30 frames per second. SECAM operates to yet another set of standards and is used in France, the USSR, and elsewhere.

Since television sets and video recorders will work only on the broadcast system for which they were designed, it follows that recordings made in the UK can be played back in Australia but not in Canada, while the reverse is true for American recordings. In the following panel you will find a list of countries and their television line-standards to help you sort out what can be played where. You will also see from the standards list that there are variants on the PAL system which are denoted by letter. Because of these slight differences you could not, for example, take your *camcorder* from the UK and plug it into an Ausralian television set, although the *tapes* it produces will play on an Australian VCR.

However, it's quite likely that you will be able to get a colour picture without sound off your tape, so you could at least check on the colour balance of your recordings. Some machines now have a 'compatibility switch' to make it suitable for more than one kind of standard, or for colour checking you could take with you one of the newer camcorders which have colour viewfinders or miniature colour screens built into their sides.

While we are discussing the practicalities of travelling with a camcorder, one important factor to bear in mind is whether electrical power supplies will enable you to recharge your camcorder batteries. If you are staying within your own country, you will probably never be too far away from a mains power socket. The problem arises mainly when you are abroad because you may then encounter not only different kinds of electric sockets, but also different voltages and frequencies. Solution one is to use a battery charger of the type which can be powered from the battery of an automobile. If you are filming when standing by your car, you can then plug the camcorder into the car battery by means of a special adaptor lead – but take care to check that the polarity of the current is correct for your equipment.

Future developments

One of the notable facts about videos is the rapidity with which model changes and other improvements appear. The quality of both video pictures and sound has developed at an amazing pace, with equipment becoming ever more sophisticated in the features offered. While this is very good news for video enthusiasts, it does mean that the rate of obsolence is high, so we take a gamble each time we buy a new camcorder or VCR: a model even better than the one in the shop window may be just around the corner. So to try and prevent you from being stuck with an obsolescent model, let's dust off the crystal ball to see if some predictions can be made about the future of video.

Two trends are discernible from the latest wave of new models and from what is known about current developments. One is a move down-market towards cheaper, simpler and lighter camcorders. Pocket-size record-only models for video 'snapshotters' are appearing in increasing numbers, and there's even a rock-bottom specification camcorder for children to use. It is hard to visualise where the lower limit to camcorder miniaturization might be, such is the power of the microchip to condense size and increase achievement.

Not only are the electronics getting more compact, but so are the tape cassettes. The 8mm tapes are much less bulky than their VHS and Beta predecessors, and if 4mm video becomes a commercial reality, still more shrinkage in the size of the cassettes and the camcorders will be possible. CCD imagers – the gadgets which convert light to electrical currents in video cameras – are also likely to continue being reduced in size as ways are found to cram more light-sensing pixels onto their already tiny surfaces. This will make it possible to reduce further the bulk of lens and imager units.

'Smaller, cheaper' is therefore one trend, while at the other end of the scale the move is towards very much higher picture quality and ever more technical complexity. The introduction of S-VHS, first in Japan and the United States, and now in the UK and Europe, has been a gigantic leap forward, as it takes the hitherto 'domestic standard' VHS format right into the professional field of video-making because third-generation copies of edited masters can be produced from it. S-VHS is even capable of developing a recorded picture which is superior in definition to broadcast television as received on present-day television sets. This is due to a number of factors which include the use of special 'metal' tapes, and the way in which the signal is fed to the screen as separate 'brightness' and 'colour' signals instead of the normal 'composite' television signal. Metallic tapes have been in use for 8mm video for some time now, of course, and a 'super' 8mm format called 'Hi-band' has lately been announced to keep 8mm in the quality race. ED-Beta – a third super-format – is already in the offing. The advent of the super-formats has produced a problem with the quality of the television screens which the manufacturers are now seeking to overcome. The main bar to progress is the definition limitations imposed by the PAL/NTSC/SECAM television systems, although changes are afoot which will eventually replace these with new and better standards.

The key to High Definition Television (HDTV) lies in the doubling of the scanning lines which make up the television picture, a change that will give a dramatic improvement in the ability of the screen to resolve picture detail. The PAL system, for instance, would then increase from a standard of 625 interlaced lines to one of 1250 lines. It is claimed that such a system, when fed with super-format pictures, would produce screen images with a definition comparable to 35mm film.

Another advantage of HDTV ('HD-MAC', 'HDS-NA', 'MUSE', or whatever HD system is eventually adopted – and different countries may adopt different standards), is that a much bigger picture can be produced without an unacceptable decline in definition. Conventional television screens, in fact, are already increasing in size, and 35-inch monsters are appearing in the shops. Some of these have the special 'S-connectors' which are needed to feed super-format video signals for optimum results. Great efforts are being made to eliminate annoying 'cross colour', 'picture noise', and other forms of disturbance. New forms of digital circuitry are being developed and used to this end, and also to provide 'picture-in-picture' effects. 'Non-interlaced scanning' is also being tried as a means of improving the definition.

While conventional sets are already delivering magnificent pictures together with stereo sound (or even surround-sound), they do have their limits. Imagine, though, what it will be like when we are watching, and *making*, videos on wide-screen! Really *big* screens will be possible when high-definition television arrives and projection-television at last comes out of the cold and into its own. You will then have a real home cinema!

Paradoxically, colour screens are also getting *smaller* thanks to liquid crystal display (LCD) technology. Micro-miniature 'Walkman' colour video television will soon be widely available, probably being as commonplace as personal stereos. The use of small LCD colour screens as camcorder viewfinders has been noted earlier, and it seems probable that this type of imaging system will eventually supplant conventional cathode-ray tubes on bigger sets and make the flat wall-screen television receiver a practical possibility.

Mention of digital technology brings us to a new area of development which is having a major impact on video recording and on what we see on our screens. Fully digital audio recording and playback has been with us for quite a time now, but its application to video is still limited to use as 'frame stores' for freeze frames, strobe, picture-in-picture

TELEVISION SYSTEMS

Afghanistan	**P**
Albania	**S**
Algeria	**P**
Andorra	**P**
Argentina	**P**
Australia	**P**
Austria	**P**
Bahamas	**N**
Bahrein	**P**
Barbados	**N**
Belgium	**P**
Bermuda	**N**
Bolivia	**N**
Brazil	**P**
Bulgaria	**S**
Burma	**N**
Canada	**N**
Chile	**N**
China	**P**
Cyprus	**S**
Czechoslovakia	**S**
Denmark	**P**
Ecuador	**N**
Egypt	**S**
El Salvador	**N**
Ethiopia	**P**
Fiji	**P**
Finland	**P**
France	**S**
Germany, East	**S**
Germany, West	**P**
Ghana	**P**
Gibraltar	**P**
Greece	**S**
Greenland	**N**
Guam	**N**
Guyana, French	**S**
Haiti	**N**
Hawaii	**N**
Honduras	**N**
Hong Kong	**P**
Hungary	**S**
Iceland	**P**
India	**P**
Indonesia	**P**
Iran	**S**
Iraq	**S**
Ireland	**P**
Israel	**P**
Italy	**P**
Japan	**N**
Jordan	**P**
Kenya	**P**
Korea, North	**S**

Korea, South	**N**
Kuwait	**P**
Lebanon	**S**
Liberia	**P**
Libya	**S**
Luxembourg	**P/S**
Malta	**P**
Mexico	**N**
Monaco	**S**
Morocco	**S**
Netherlands	**P**
New Zealand	**P**
Nicaragua	**N**
Nigeria	**P**
Norway	**P**
Oman	**P**
Pakistan	**P**
Panama	**N**
Paraguay	**P**
Peru	**N**
Poland	**S**
Portugal	**P**
Puerto Rico	**P**
Romania	**S**
Saudi Arabia	**S**
Senegal	**S**
Singapore	**P**

KEY	
P	PAL countries
N	NTSC countries
S	SECAM countries

South Africa	**P**
Soviet Union	**S**
Spain	**P**
Sri Lanka	**P**
Sweden	**P**
Switzerland	**P**
Syria	**S**
Tahiti	**S**
Taiwan	**N**
Tanzania	**P**
Thailand	**P**
Togo	**S**
Trinidad	**N**
Tunisia	**S**
Turkey	**P**
Uganda	**P**
USA	**N**
Venezuela	**N**
Vietnam	**N**
Yugoslavia	**P**
Zaire	**S**
Zambia	**P**
Zimbabwe	**P**

and other special effects. The ultimate aim, though, is to carry out the whole video recording and playback process digitally, because such recordings are very resistant to degradation of the signal as it is being copied onto other tapes. Theoretically, the thousandth-generation copy would be indistinguishable from the original recording! Although audio has found it relatively easy to adopt the digital system, it has so far not been possible to introduce it to the video mass market because of the enormous amount of signal information which needs to be stored and handled in order to deal with a colour television picture. So its use on domestic video machines and amateur camcorders is some way off, although professional digital video machines for 1 inch tape already exist.

As and when digital video recordings become available to the consumer, their freedom from quality loss at copying will become a major piracy problem if they continue to be distributed in the form of magnetic recordings on tape. No doubt electronic measures to prevent unauthorized copying of tapes will continue to be developed, but it seems that for every new anti-piracy recording system there is always an electronic countermeasure which can be applied.

From this point of view, compact discs would seem to have the advantage over magnetic tape, Laser-video CD systems are aleady commercial and are growing in popularity due to their excellent reproduction. They take the form of 'compact discs', but unlike audio CDs they handle their signals in analogue, not digital, form at this stage in their development. And as they are not home-recordable, copying onto other CDs is not possible. However, the recordable CD is already being talked about as a future possibility, and the fully digital camcorder which uses some form of disc instead of magnetic tape may one day become reality.

Stretching the imagination still further, what about a no-moving-parts solid-state video recording system? It's theoretically possible to dream up a super-chip with the capacity to store a video recording, just as data is stored in memory chips in a computer. As we've seen earlier, chips are used to hold picture information for the special effects that are now offered with the new televisions and recorders. However, they are only able to store individual frames, and even to achieve this limited amount of storage they need solid-state memories with multi-megabyte capacities – to put it into computer terminology. When you consider that television pictures are scanned at a rate of 25 per second in the UK, and 30 in the USA, and that there are 3,600 seconds in every hour, it is easy to see that colossal memory capacity is required to cope with the average two-hour film. So it seems that for the time being the day of the solid-state video recorder is some way off, at least as far as the general public is concerned.

However, who would have thought at the beginning of the present century that devices receiving and processing 11 million pieces of signal information a second would stand in virtually every living room in the land? And that's what a colour television does – so the solid-state recorder is perhaps not so impossible, after all. In fact there is already one such recorder available – it has a playing time of just over one minute, weighs over 100lb (45kg), runs red-hot, and is very expensive. Needless to say, it is used only for specialised professional editing and effects work.

Computer technology is beginning to integrate with video in a major way in two areas: video editing, and in what are referred to as 'desktop' systems. Desktop enables you to create complex screen images without using a camera, and these can range from simple character-generated titles to the most fantastic changing-colour image patterns. Naturally, the scope of what you can achieve depends on the degree of sophistication of your computer hardware and software; the professionals, who have the best of everything, are now able to produce graphics which look completely 'real', and they combine these with live action to create a seamless fusion of fantasy with reality.

As we have seen in Chapter 8, computer graphics technology is filtering down in a simpler form to amateur levels. There are lots of programmes and special computer-to-video interface connections available to enable you to experiment in this new and exciting field. Computer-aided editing is another progressive facility which is beginning to appear in scaled-down versions on the amateur market. At least one edit controller with memory circuitry has been around for some years in what has up to now been a somewhat neglected area in terms of equipment availability. Two new models are on the way, however, one of these being a budget version of the original model, while the other will have an increased specification offering more 'professional' facilities at a relatively modest price.

No doubt other edit controllers will soon appear, and hopefully one day it will be possible to produce results which hitherto have only been achievable in commercial editing suites. The advent of the super-formats will reinforce this trend, as there will be a growing army of low-budget video producers attracted into the business by the cheapness of the super-formats compared with U-format, and these will generate a demand for better budget-priced editing facilities. Standardization of the tape-control signal functions and socket interconnections by the VCR manufacturers will help – if it becomes more widespread to promote the use of edit controllers on domestic equipment. The appearance of 'synchro-edit' sockets on many machines is certainly a welcome pointer in this direction. Synchro-edit is simply a way of simultaneously releasing the 'source' and 'record' machines from 'pause' when starting the copying of a new shot during an assemble editing session. It's a handy means of controlling the two machines with one button. Apart from the 'synchro' socket, the machines can be quite ordinary domestic VCRs provided that the 'record' machine has 'fine edit' and preferably 'insert' as well. However, video editing does involve a lot of back-and-forth searching of the tapes to find the edit-points, which not only increases the rate of wear and tear on the tape transport mechanisms but is also rather fiddly and time-consuming. The newer machines (fitted with 'jog' dials) make the searching easier by enabling you to play in forward and reverse at any speed from slo-mo to fast.

Eventually, though, it is expected that low-budget professional-type editing VCRs will be available; these will be built to more rugged standards, and will make the task of finding and holding edit-points to one-frame accuracy much easier than it is on present-day equipment. The edit controllers of the future will no doubt incorporate not only better facilities for producing 'wipes', 'dissolves' and so on, but also include comprehensive picture enhancement and audio mixing controls. The latter facilities are now available in add-on form.

Strangely, the facility to mix audio onto the original soundtrack without losing synchronization is still one of those things which eludes the amateur market, in the sense that true sound-on-sound mixing is not featured on domestic video machines. As you may have already found out for yourself, 'audio dub' erases the original sound recording while the new sound is being dubbed in, and if you wish to mix the two you have either to do it while copying the original pictures and sound onto another tape, or alternatively you have to dub the sound onto a separate sound-tape using an audio recorder which has sound-on-sound mixing; when the mix has been completed, the sound is re-recorded back onto the video tape.

The problem is how to do this without the sound going out of synchronization with the pictures, and although there are one or two relatively low-priced 'video-sync' systems available which will enable this 'lifting off' and 'laying back' of sound to be done accurately, they have to be operated 'blind'. In other words, the sound mixing has to be done to cues because the operator is not able to see the pictures at the same time. One day, our video and audio editing will be integrated to bring it all together into one user-friendly unit.

How would you like to make videos in 3D? It's been tried before, of course, but until now the results on the screen have not been very watchable. There's a new system being developed, though, which is said to be a great improvement and it probably won't be long before the first stereoscopic video recorders arrive. To begin with, they will be expensive and intended for professional use, but the chances are that scaled-down amateur versions will then follow. The system, which is already in prototype, works on the basis of displaying 'left eye' and 'right eye' pictures alternately. To see these in 3D you have to wear special spectacles. These incorporate liquid crystals whose function is to alternatively blot out the 'left' and 'right' images in synchronization with the screen display. The old problem of flicker is avoided by reproducing each picture twice, so doubling the flicker-frequency to one which is invisible to the eye.

As we have shown in this section, video technology is reaching out into all kinds of areas which are of interest to the home movie maker. The pace of development is ever-increasing, and video products have reached levels of complexity and quality which would hardly have been thinkable just a few years ago.

Ironically, the commercial quest for 'something new' to sell next year's model has, in some cases, led to a reduction in the availability of basic facilities in order to make way for some more marketable feature. The omission of audio dub because of the way in which hi-fi FM sound is recorded on 8 mm video is one example of this trend.

Happily, the growth of video as a creative activity, and the merging of the amateur and 'budget' professional markets due to the introduction of the super-formats, is now producing its own commercial pressures, and the video manufacturers are already responding to this as they plan their future product ranges and draw up the machine specifications.

We live in an exciting video age, and the sky really does seem to be the limit for what the technicians can dream up to help us record pictures that move and speak. A/V units to handle high-wattage sound are the latest arrivals. Perhaps budget vision-mixers – to enable us to work a number of video cameras as happens in a television studio – will be the next things to hit the video headlines.

It's important, though, not to let the flashing lights on our video machines dazzle us into believing that high technology is the be-all and end-all of video making. It's nice to have clear crisp pictures with vibrant colour and rich sound. It will be great if one day we can record our epics onto a microchip the size of a fingernail, and lose ourselves in a fantasy world of 3D and psychedelic imagery. But as we've seen, it still depends on human creativity and imagination to make a good video – and it always will!

Glossary

A

Aperture
The opening in a camera iris which controls the amount of light passing through the lens.

Aperture ring
Used to control the aperture.

Assembly editing
A method of editing (electronically in video) in which shots are arranged in sequence, one after the other.

Audio In
The port on a video recorder which receives an audio signal.

Audio mixer
A device which allows several audio signals to be laid down on a single track. Audio levels and quality can be adjusted in the process.

Automatic gain control (AGC)
Circuits within a camcorder which automatically adjust the incoming video and audio signals to determined levels.

Available light
The prevailing light in any scene – sunlight or domestic lighting in interiors.

B

Background
The furthermost plane in any shot, behind the main subject of the shot.

Backlight
A light source positioned behind the subject of a shot.

Barn Doors
Metal flaps that are attached in front of a lamp, which can be adjusted to illuminate a scene selectively.

Betamax
A video format developed in the 1970s by the Sony company, eventually eclipsed by the VHS format and no longer in production.

Boom
A pole which is more or less parallel with the floor, used to mount microphones above characters in a scene.

Bounced light
A light source reflected off surrounding walls or ceiling before it falls upon the subject.

Burn
The damage caused in tube cameras when exposed to a very bright light source.

Bus
Term used by engineers to describe a complete audio or video channel.

C

Camcorder
A video camera and recorder housed in one portable unit.

Cardioid
Term which describes the heart-shaped pick-up zone of some microphones.

Character generator
A microprocessor which generates written characters on a TV screen.

Charge-coupled device
A photoconductive semi-conductor chip which is responsive to light of different wavelengths. It generates the electronic video signal in many video cameras and camcorders.

Chromakey
Term often used for colour separation overlay. In fact, a trade name.

Close down
To close the aperture down and thus reduce the amount of light passing through the lens.

C mount
A standard thread on the lens barrel on many video cameras, allowing the use of additional lenses.

Colour balance
The ratio between the three primary colours in any given image.

Colour separation overlay
An electronic system by which two images can be combined, so that the first scene appears to have the second as background.

Contrast ratio
The range of brightness between the lightest and darkest areas in any scene.

Control track
The track of signal pulses along the length of a video tape which acts to control the speed of replay.

Cookie
Slang term for a cucaloris, a device placed in front of a lamp to give a broken shadow effect to a scene.

Coverage
The shots required to convey fully the subject being recorded. Also, the shots required to allow continuity to be maintained.

Crab
A camera movement sideways across the action being recorded.

Crash edit
Editing by switching from playback to record on a deck connected to another deck. Such an edit results in a momentary picture break-up.

Crash zoom
Switching rapidly from wide angle to telephoto settings on the zoom lens, or vice versa.

Crosslighting
A lighting arrangement using key and fill lights of equal luminance.

Crossing the line
Moving the camera from one side of the action to the other. This can disrupt the audience's understanding of the spatial relationships displayed on the screen.

CU (Close-up)
Shot taken at short range from the camera. With people, a shot framed at head and shoulders.

Cut
An instantaneous change from one shot to another.

Cutaway
A shot within a sequence that is not central to the main action, but which adds additional information for the audience to absorb.

D

Denouement
The climax, or ending of a story.

Depth of field
The range of distances in which objects in a scene are in acceptably sharp focus. Depth of field varies with aperture size and focal length.

Dissolve
To change from one shot to another by gradually fading out the first and fading in the second.

Dolly
A camera mount on wheels which allows a smooth tracking action.

Draft
An early version of a script.

E

Editing controller
A device which enables the operator to adjust the signal between source and edit decks during the editing process.

Edit deck
The deck on which the edited tape is created.

Edit script
A document identifying the points at which cuts should be made on the tapes to be edited.

Electromagnetic spectrum
The entire range of electromagnetic radiation, both visible and invisible.

Electronic viewfinder
A small cathode ray tube which displays the image seen by the camera electronically, rather than optically.

Establishing shot
A shot which provides the audience with basic information: where the action is taking place, and who are the main characters. Also called an establisher.

Eyeline
The direction of gaze of a person shown in a scene.

F

Fill light
The light used in a three-point lighting arrangement to lift the shadows caused by the key light.

Filters
Semi-opaque glass or plastic devices used to modify the quality of the light received by the camera. Some filters remove glare, others add distinctive colours to a scene.

Flags
Used in lighting to block part of the light from a lamp.

Flat lighting
Lighting in which the subject is not readily lifted from the background.

Floods
Lights which produce a wide, evenly dispersed spread of illumination over a scene.

Focal length
In a camcorder, the distance from the centre of the lens to the CCD, when the lens is focused at infinity.

Focus
To adjust the lens so that the image is sharply delineated.

Follow focus
To adjust the focus, while shooting, so that a moving subject is always kept sharp.

Follow space
The area behind a subject when moving across the screen.

Foreground
The area in the shot in front of the main subject of the shot.

Frame
The area in which the image is presented: the TV screen. Also used to describe the act of placing subjects in shot in an aesthetically pleasing way.

G

Gel
Gelatin, often used as a filter on lights or windows.

Gun mike
A highly directional microphone.

H

Headroom
The screen space above a subject's head.

High angle
A shot taken from a position in which the camera looks down on the subject.

I

Insert editing
An editing method in which video material is electronically inserted into an existing recording.

Iris
The diaphragm in the lens, which regulates the intensity of the light entering the camera.

J K

Jump cut
A cut which indicates to the audience that an appreciable passage of time has taken place.

Key light
The major component in a three-point lighting arrangement, illuminating the subject from the front.

L

Lag
Faint smears on the television screen sometimes left by light sources in shot as the camera moves across them, particularly when overall light levels are low.

Lavalier
A small microphone, often worn around the neck.

Lead space
The area in front of a person moving in a shot.

Level
The overall strength of an audio or video signal.

Logging
The act of listing the contents of a video tape prior to editing.

Long shot
A shot which contains, at its closest, a complete human figure.

Low angle
A shot in which the camera is positioned below the subject.

Lux
A unit measuring light intensity in a scene.

M

Macro lens
A close-up lens capable of high magnification.

Master
The final version of a tape.

Master shot
A shot covering the major element of the action being conveyed.

Matte
A mask which cuts out part of the frame in order to achieve a special effect. Can be electronic or physical.

Matte box
A device attached to the end of the camera lens, to hold mattes.

Mid shot
A shot containing the human figure framed just above waist level.

Monitor
A TV connected directly to a video camera or VCR, to allow the video output to be checked.

N

Narrative
The unfolding of a story that takes place through changes in the plot.

Nickel-cadmium
A common type of rechargeable battery used in camcorders.

Noise
Unwanted electronic disturbance to the video signal.

NTSC
Acronym of the National Television Systems Committee. The television system employed in the USA and Japan.

O

On Camera
In a position in front of the camera so as to be visible in a shot.

Open up
To increase the aperture and thus allow more light into the camera.

Out of shot
Not seen by the camera.

P Q

Paintbox
A computer system which can generate complex graphics and images.

PAL
Acronym for Phase Alternation Line, the television system used in most of Europe (but not France).

Pan
A horizontal movement of the camera on its mount, taking in new areas of a scene.

Photoflood
The basic type of light, commonly called a flood. It illuminates a wide area.

Pick-up tube
In older cameras, a part of the camera which converts light into the electronic video signal. The CCD does the same thing in more recent models.

Pixel
The smallest unit on a TV screen which helps to build up the complete image.

Playback deck
When editing, the deck which plays the original tape to be edited. Also called the source deck.

Point of view
A shot in which the camera takes up a character's position in order to reveal what he or she sees to the audience.

Props
The objects apparent in a shot.

Pull focus
A technique in which focus moves from one plane to another as the shot progresses. This technique is also known as throw-focus.

Quartz-lighting
High intensity lighting which uses quartz halogen bulbs.

R

Rehearse and record
A production technique in studios in which segments of a programme are rehearsed and then recorded before proceding to the next part of the show.

Research
The gathering of information and visual materials before beginning a production.

Rig in
To set up lights, sound equipment and cameras before shooting begins.

Rim light
The halo effect caused by back-lighting on a subject. Can be more or less pronounced according to the light's intensity.

Rough cut
The early stages of the editing process from which the final edit emerges.

S

Saturation
The intensity of colour in an image.

Scoop
A large flood light.

Scrim
Gauze placed in front of a light source to diffuse the light falling on a scene.

Script
A detailed description of the production to be recorded, including camera angles and shot descriptions.

SECAM
Acronym for Sequential Couleur à Mémoire, the television system in use in France and the USSR.

Sequence
A discrete part of a narrative, usually with its own recognizable beginning and end.

Shoot
To operate the camera.

Shot
The material recorded by the camera in a single operation. Also the image seen by the camera.

Source deck
The deck used to replay original material when editing.

Special effects
Illusions created either during shooting or added electronically during the editing stage.

Special effects generator (SEG)
A unit which allows the electronic manipulation of the video signal during editing in order to create a range of special effects.

Spots
Lights which produce an intense, concentrated beam of light.

Still
A single photographic image.

Storyboard
A detailed drawing of the sequence of shots to be taken during coverage of a particular event or story.

Switching
To switch from one electronic source to another.

T

Talent
Professional term for performers.

Target
The area of the CCD on which the in coming light falls.

Telecine
A system for transferring film or slide material on to videotape. This usually involves projecting the film on to a specially designed screen and recording the result with a video camera.

Telephoto
A lens of long focal length which gives an enlarged image of a distant scene. Also the longest focal length available on a zoom lens.

Three-point lighting
The standard lighting system used in artificially lit scenes. It consists of backlight, key light and fill light.

Three-shot
A shot in which three people are shown within the frame.

Throw focus
The same as pull focus.

Tilt
A vertical movement, up or down, of the camera on its mount.

Time code
A frame-by-frame time reference recorded on the spare track of a videotape.

Track
A movement of the camera parallel to the action.

Treatment
A brief outline of a proposed story or programme.

Tripod
An adjustable three-legged camera mount with a head allowing pan and tilt movements of the camera.

Two-shot
A shot in which two people are seen within the frame.

U V

U-Matic
A semi-professional ¾″ videotape format marketed by Sony. Offers higher quality than domestic formats.

VCR
A video cassette recorder.

VHS
Video Home System, the dominant domestic videotape format, marketed by JVC.

VHS-C
Compact version of VHS, which can be played back on a VHS machine using an adaptor.

Videotape
A plastic-based material with a metallic coating on which the video signal is recorded as a series of magnetic stripes.

Viewfinder
An optical or electronic device allowing the image seen by the camera to be monitored.

Voice-over
A commentary heard by the audience without the speaker being in shot. Often used in documentary work.

VU meter
Volume Unit meter, a device which measures and displays the relative loudness of an audio signal. Used to help balance sound levels during recording.

W

Wavelength
The distance from one point in a given wave to a corresponding point on the next cycle. Light of differing wavelengths is perceived by the eye and brain to be of different colour.

Whip pan
A rapid pan movement of the camera so as to create a deliberately blurred image.

White balance
The system for determining true colour values on a video camera.

Wide-angle
A lens with a short focal length which gives a large angle of view. Also the shortest focal length available on the zoom lens.

Wind gag
Acoustic foam placed around a microphone to reduce wind noise on outdoor locations.

Wipe
A special effect in which one image gradually replaces another on screen.

Z

Zoom lens
A lens of continuously variable focal length, and therefore variable angle of view.

INDEX

AND

ACKNOWLEDGMENTS

INDEX

T

U

V

W

Z

ACKNOWLEDGMENTS

The Publishers would like to thank the following organizations for their kind co-operation in supplying video equipment for photography:

Panasonic Consumer Electronics UK
300-318 Bath Road, Slough, Berks SL1 6JB
and
Keith Johnson & Pelling Ltd
93 Drummond Street, London NW1 2HJ
and 11 Great Marlborough Street, London W1A 3AF

The map on page 149 is reproduced with the permission of Michelin from their *Motoring Atlas of France.*

Illustrations by:
Mei Lim, Jim Robins, Chris Forsey, Bob Reed, Tony Hannaford

Editors:
Philip Wilkinson, John Stace

Additional Photography:
Equipment: Andrew Hayward
People & Places: Sally and Richard Greenhill

Additional Design:
Sue Rawkins, Ron Samuels

All photography is by John Hedgecoe except on the following pages and as indicated: 10-11, ET Archive; 12-13, BBC Hulton Picture Library; 20-1, 24-5, 45 (top) Octopus Books Limited; 45 (right) and 149 (bottom), Tony Stone Worldwide; 48-49, 52-53, Templar Publishing Limited; 118 Wisniewski/ZEFA; 120 (top and bottom), Claude Nuridsany and Marie Perenou/Science Photo Library; 121 (top, middle and bottom), Dr Jeremy Burgess/Science Photo Library; 122-3, 149 (top and middle), ZEFA; 218-9, John Cole/Impact Photos.